A
HISTORY OF THE BRITISH ARMY

A History of
The British Army

BY

THE HON. J. W. FORTESCUE

SECOND PART—TO THE CLOSE OF THE SEVEN YEARS' WAR
TO THE SECOND PEACE OF PARIS

VOL. III
1763–1793

The Naval & Military Press Ltd

Published by
The Naval & Military Press Ltd
Unit 10, Ridgewood Industrial Park,
Uckfield, East Sussex,
TN22 5QE England
Tel: +44 (0) 1825 749494
Fax: +44 (0) 1825 765701

www.naval-military-press.com

© The Naval & Military Press Ltd 2004

CONTENTS

BOOK XI

CHAPTER I

	PAGE
The new British Empire	1
Ties that bound the Colonies to the Mother Country: the Tie of Sentiment	4
The Tie of Interest	6
The Tie of Commercial Legislation; Trade and Navigation Acts	8
State of Parties in England	9
England's Position in Europe	10
Peace Establishment of the Army for 1764	10
Neglect of the Question of Imperial Defence	11
Insurrection of Indians in America; Pontiac	11
Inadequacy of the British Garrison	12
Outbreak of the Insurrection	13
Attack on Detroit	14
Fall of the remaining British Posts	14
Amherst's Difficulties in raising a Force to quell the Rising	15
Colonel Bouquet advances upon Fort Pitt	15
Action of Bushy Run	16
Hostility of the Six Nations in the North	19
Siege of Detroit raised	19
Continued Apathy of the Americans	20

	PAGE
Bradstreet's March to Detroit	20
Bouquet's Advance to the Muskingum	21
Final Subjugation of the Indians by British Troops	22

CHAPTER II

Political Changes in England; George Grenville succeeds Bute	24
He determines to enforce the Acts of Trade and impose Stamp Duties on the American Colonies for Support of the British Garrison	24
The Institution of this Garrison a reasonable Measure	25
Grenville consults the American Colonies as to a voluntary Contribution from them towards Imperial Defence	26
Negotiations fail; the Stamp Act passed	26
Organised Agitation and Riot in Massachusetts	27
Rockingham's Ministry replaces that of Grenville	28
Pitt's reckless Encouragement of the Agitation	28
Repeal of the Stamp Act	29
Fall of Rockingham's Ministry; Pitt, created Earl of Chatham, forms an Administration	29
His Failure to form an Alliance of the Northern Powers of Europe	29
His Incapacity to deal with the American Difficulty	29
Agitation and Hostility of the Americans against British Troops	31
Inconsistency and Insincerity of this Agitation	31
Charles Townsend carries a Measure to levy Duties in the American Colonies	33
Renewal of the Agitation; two Regiments sent to Boston	33
Traditions of Rebellion in Boston	34
The Troops placed at the Mercy of the Mob of Boston	35
Patience of the Troops exhausted; the "Boston Massacre"	38
Resignation of Chatham and Grafton; Lord North becomes Chief Minister	39
He repeals all the Duties except that on Tea	39
Weak State of the Army	40

CONTENTS

	PAGE
The Pay of the Men insufficient	41
National Danger owing to the Difficulty of Recruiting	41
The Carib War in St. Vincent	41
Improvement of the Situation in America	43
Trouble revived by the Acts of Trade and Navigation	44
Agitation renewed in Massachusetts; the Committees of Correspondence	45
The landing of Tea in American Ports prevented	45
Coercive Measures against Massachusetts	46
The Quebec Act	47
Meeting of the American Congress at Philadelphia	47
Failure of Coercion at Boston owing to the Insufficiency of the Force	47
Rapid Advance of the Revolution in New England	48

CHAPTER III

Affairs in India; Shah Alum's Invasions of Bengal	49
Caillaud marches against him	51
Defeat of Ramnarain before Patna	51
Investment of Patna by Shah Alum	52
Battle of Seerpore	53
Manœuvres of Shah Alum; he again marches on Patna	55
Siege of Patna	56
Relief of Patna by Captain Knox	57
Battle of Beerpore	58
Close of the Campaign	61
Rise of Meer Cossim	61
Dethronement of Meer Jaffier in his Favour	62
Defeat of Shah Alum at Suan	62
Peace concluded with him	63

CHAPTER IV

Meer Cossim forced into Hostility by the Council at Calcutta	65
The British surprise Patna	65

	PAGE
Recapture of the City by Meer Cossim's Troops	66
The British Garrison compelled to surrender	67
The Calcutta Council restores Meer Jaffier	67
Major Adams marches against Meer Cossim	68
Lieutenant Glenn defeats one of Meer Cossim's Detachments	69
Advance of Adams ; Action near Cutwa	70
Adams occupies Moorshedabad	71
Meer Cossim retires to Sooty	72
Battle of Sooty	73
Meer Cossim retires to Oondwa Nullah	74
His Position described	75
Adams opens Trenches before it	75
Surprise and Capture of Oondwa Nullah	76
Adams resumes his Advance	79
Siege of Patna	80
Storm and Capture of Patna	81
Adams pursues the Enemy to the Karamnasar	82
Death of Adams ; Summary of his Achievements	83

CHAPTER V

Shah Alum and Shujah Dowlah form an Alliance with Meer Cossim	84
Mutiny in the British Force	85
Major Carnac assumes Command of it	88
His Sloth and Incapacity	88
He is forced back to Patna	89, 90
The Allies attack him there and are repulsed	90-92
Shuja Dowlah retreats to Buxar	92
Major Munro assumes Command of the British	92
Fresh Outbreak of Mutiny	92
Munro's stern Measures	93
The British advance upon Buxar	94
The Passage of the Sone	95
Shuja Dowlah offers Battle	95
Battle of Buxar	96-102

CONTENTS

	PAGE
Pursuit of Shuja Dowlah	102-104
Shuja Dowlah surrenders	104
General Pacification under the Direction of Clive	105
His Reforms in Bengal	105
Mutiny of the Officers and its Suppression	106, 107
Death of Clive	108

CHAPTER VI

Madras; State of Things at the Peace of 1763	109
Schemes of Mohammed Ali	110
Rise of Hyder Ali in Mysore	111
Foolish Policy of the Council of Madras	112
A British Force takes the Field under Colonel Joseph Smith	113
Imbecile Plans of the Madras Council	113
Action at Changama	116
Second Action near Trinomalee	117
Faulty Disposition of the British Cantonments	119
Hyder's Raids upon the British Posts	119-121
Bombay Forces capture Mangalore, but are driven from it	121
Plan of the Madras Council for a new Campaign	122
Foolish Dispositions of Colonel Wood	123
Supreme Imbecility of the Madras Council	123
Smith invades Mysore from the North-East	124
His masterly Dispositions for crushing Hyder Ali	125
Failure of the Plan owing to the Incapacity of Wood	126
Hyder's Overtures for Peace rejected	126
Narrow Escape of Wood's Force from destruction	127
Smith recalled to Madras	129
Hyder outmanœuvres Wood at Baugloor	129
Second narrow Escape of Wood	129, 130
Hyder invades the Carnatic	130
Madras sues Hyder for Peace	131
Conclusion of a Treaty with Hyder	131
Summary of the Campaign	131, 132

CHAPTER VII

	PAGE
Mohammed Ali's Intrigues with Politicians in England	134
The Mahrattas invade Mysore	135
Madras breaks its Engagements with Hyder Ali	135
Final Alienation of Hyder Ali	137
Troubles raised by the Mahrattas in Bengal	137
Origin of the Rohilla War	138
Battle of Babul Nullah	139
Bombay; Aggressive Policy of the Council	141
Dispute as to the Succession to the Title of Peishwa	142
Bombay embraces the Side of Ragobah	142
Capture of Salsette by the British	143
Beginning of the First Mahratta War	143
Action of Arass	144
Advantageous Peace concluded by Bombay	146
It is cancelled by the Council at Calcutta and a new Treaty made	146
Follies of the Indian Councils	147

CHAPTER VIII

The American Colonies; Helplessness of English Statesmen in Face of the Crisis	148
The Expedition to seize American Stores at Concord	149
The Affair of Lexington; Disastrous Retreat of the British	150, 151
The Colonists take the Offensive; Capture of Ticonderoga	153
Weakness of the British in that Province	153
Reinforcements reach Boston from England; Howe, Clinton, Burgoyne	154
The American Army surrounds Boston	155
The Americans seize Breed's Hill	155
Action of Bunker's Hill	156
Heavy Losses of the British	159
Indirect Results of the Action	160

CONTENTS

	PAGE
Washington chosen Commander-in-Chief of the Americans	161
Gates, Lee, Montgomery, Benedict Arnold	161
Montgomery and Arnold invade Canada	162
Evacuation of Montreal	162
Repulse of the Americans from Quebec	164
Folly of the Invasion of Canada	164

CHAPTER IX

Difficulties of Reconquest of America by Land	166
False Basis on which the British Operations were planned	168
Indecision of the English Ministers	169
Armed Weakness of Britain	170
Hire of Foreign Troops	170
Absurdity of the Outcry against England on this Account	171
Obstruction of the Opposition in Parliament; Charles Fox	172
Preparations and Plans in England	173
Howe's Preference for a sounder Plan	174
Germaine assumes Direction of the War	174
His singular Unfitness for the Duty	174
Difficulties of Howe and of Washington at Boston	175
Blindness of the American Congress	176
Washington takes the Offensive	177
Howe evacuates Boston and withdraws to Halifax	177
Tardy Arrival of the British Reinforcements	178
Carleton takes the Offensive in Canada	178
The Americans driven out of the Province	179
Carleton closes the Campaign without taking Ticonderoga	180
British Expedition against Charleston	180
It is repulsed with heavy Loss	181
Concentration of Howe's Army at Staten Island	181
Washington's Dispositions for Defence of New York	182
Howe opens the Campaign; Action of Brooklyn	183
Washington is allowed to escape	186
False Dispositions of the Americans	187
Howe captures New York	187

His subsequent Inactivity 188
He resumes the Offensive 188
Action at White Plains 189
Retreat of Washington 190
Attack and Capture of Fort Washington . . . 191-193
Pursuit of the Americans to the Delaware 194
British Occupation of Rhode Island 195

CHAPTER X

Preparations for next Campaign 196
Unfriendliness of Europe to England 197
Efforts to improve the American Army 197
Washington's Raid upon Howe's Frontier Posts . . . 199
He outmanœuvres Cornwallis 200
The Americans recover New Jersey 202
Revival of American Hopes 203
Germaine's Plans for Campaign of 1777 204
Burgoyne submits a Scheme for an Advance from Canada . 205
Disastrous Confusion of Germaine's Orders 207
Petty Operations of Howe during Winter Quarters . . 209
He opens the Campaign in New Jersey 210
Embarkation of his Army for the Chesapeake . . . 211
He advances upon Philadelphia 212
Battle of Brandywine 213
"No-flint" Grey . . . . : . 217
Occupation of Philadelphia 217
Action of Germantown 218
Opening of the Navigation of the Delaware . . . 221
Howe resigns his Command 222

CHAPTER XI

Burgoyne's Preparations in Canada 223
He turns the American Position at Ticonderoga . . . 224

CONTENTS

xiii

	PAGE
Pursuit of the Americans; Action at Huberton	225
Continued Retreat of the Americans	226
Difficulties of Burgoyne's Situation	226
His attempt on Bennington	227
Its disastrous Failure	228
St. Leger's Advance upon the Mohawk	229
He is repulsed from Fort Stanwix	230
Critical Situation of Burgoyne	231
Action of Bemis Heights	231
The Americans fall upon his Communications	234
Clinton's Diversion on the Hudson	234
Burgoyne's second Attack on the American Position	237
He is compelled to retreat to Saratoga	238
Capitulation of Burgoyne	239
Shameful Behaviour of Congress to the Prisoners	239
Summary of the Campaign	240

CHAPTER XII

Effects of the Disaster of Saratoga	243
Exultation of the Opposition in Parliament	244
Patriotic Spirit throughout the Country	245
Futile Endeavours of the Opposition to counteract it	246
Alliance of France with the revolted Colonies	247
Disunion of the Opposition on the American Question	247
Death of Chatham	248
Revision of former Plans against America	249
Continued Infatuation of Germaine	250
Washington at Valley Forge	251
Inaction and Apathy of Howe	252
He resigns the Command to Clinton	253
Clinton evacuates Philadelphia and retreats to New York	253
Action of Freehold	254
Arrival of the French Fleet under d'Estaing off the American Coast	255
Its unsuccessful Attempt upon Rhode Island	256

	PAGE
Washington's Difficulties with French Officers	257
D'Estaing sails for the West Indies	258

CHAPTER XIII

Influence of the American Rebellion on the West Indies	259
Disloyalty in several Quarters	260
Dutch and French Assistance to American Privateers	260
Strategic Distribution of the Islands	261
Bouillé seizes Dominica	263
Grant and Barrington seize St. Lucia	264
Crushing Repulse of D'Estaing's Troops at Vigie	265
Masterly Skill of the British Commanders	266
General Grant decides to hold St. Lucia at all Risks	266
D'Estaing captures St. Vincent and Grenada	266, 267
Naval Action off Grenada	268
Grant's true Insight into the Situation in the West Indies	268

CHAPTER XIV

British Expedition to Georgia	270
Colonel Campbell's Action outside Savannah	271
Capture of Savannah	272
General Prevost joins him from Florida	272
Recovery of Georgia by the British	273
Causes of the savage Character of the War in the South	273
The Americans threaten the British Posts in Georgia	275
Defeat of one of their Columns by Mark Prevost	275
Augustine Prevost invades South Carolina	275
He retreats from before Charleston	276
And falls back slowly to Savannah	277
D'Estaing's Fleet arrives off Savannah	277
Siege of Savannah by the French and Americans	278
Their Assault of the Town repulsed	279, 280
Impotence of Clinton at New York	280

CONTENTS xv
PAGE

Continued Mismanagement of Germaine 280
Petty Operations about New York 281, 282
Expedition from Boston against the Loyalist Settlement at
    Penobscot 282
Ensign John Moore 283
Destruction of the American Fleet and Army at Penobscot . 284
Continued Weakness of Clinton's Force 285
Corresponding Weakness of the Americans 285

CHAPTER XV

Spread of factious Quarrels in the Navy 287
Rise of voluntary Associations for Defence in Scotland and
    Ireland 288
Declaration of War by Spain 289
Plymouth at the Mercy of the Allied Fleets . . . 289
New Levies raised in 1779 290
Rise of a Territorial System 291
Mutinous Behaviour of the Duke of Richmond . . . 291
Disaffection in Scotland 292
Increasing Animosity of the Opposition in Parliament . . 293
The Volunteers in Ireland 294
The Irish Parliament refuses to recognise the English Mutiny
    Act 295
The Gordon Riots 296
Change in the Military Situation owing to the Spanish
    Declaration of War 297
Incapacity of Germaine to grasp it 298
Gibraltar 298
Minorca 299
The Windward Sphere in the West Indies 300
The Leeward Sphere 301
Pensacola 301
Honduras ; Storm of Omoa 302
Projected Expedition to Nicaragua 304

CHAPTER XVI

	PAGE
Germaine's Zeal for the Conquest of Carolina	305
Fallacy and Danger of the Project	306, 307
Clinton sails for Charleston	307
Investment of Charleston	308
Siege and Capture of Charleston	309, 310
Reduction of the Province committed to Cornwallis	310
Extraordinary March of Tarleton	310-312
Diversity of Races in South Carolina	312
Revival of the Loyalists after the Capture of Charleston	313
Dispositions of Cornwallis	314
Opening of Guerilla Warfare by Sumter	315
Advance of Gates into South Carolina	316
Defeat of his Force by Cornwallis at Camden	317-319
Surprise of Sumter by Tarleton	320
Treachery of the Militia formed by Cornwallis	321
Advance of Cornwallis towards North Carolina	322
Destruction of Ferguson's Column at King's Mountain	323
Cornwallis retreats and abandons the Advance	324

CHAPTER XVII

Miserable State of Washington's Army	325
Arrival of a French Squadron and Troops	326
Blockade of the French Squadron in Narragansett Bay	326
Distraction of the Americans	327
Benedict Arnold	328
His treacherous Overtures to Clinton	329
Arrival of Rodney with half of his Squadron at New York	329
Arnold's Treachery revealed by the Capture of Major André	329
Execution of André	330
Clinton detaches a Predatory Force to the Chesapeake	331
He allows it to join Cornwallis	332
Benedict Arnold's Plan for ending the War	333

CONTENTS

	PAGE
Superiority at Sea the Key of the Situation	333
Windward Sphere of the West Indies	333
Arrival of Reinforcements at Barbados under General Vaughan	335
His Operations cramped by the false Dispositions of Germaine	335
Failure of a French Attack on St. Lucia	336
Indecisive Action between Rodney and de Guichen	336
Failure of the Windward Campaign owing to Mismanagement in England	337
Rodney sails to New York	337
The Hurricane of 1780 in the Windward Islands	338
Leeward Sphere; Operations in Nicaragua	338
Capture of Fort St. Juan	339
Futility and disastrous Close of the whole Enterprise	339, 340
Capture of Mobile by the Spaniards	341
Frightful Mortality of Troops in West Indies	341

CHAPTER XVIII

The Armed Neutrality	343
England declares War against Holland	344
Siege of Gibraltar	345
The Fortress revictualled by Admiral Darby	345
Repulse of the French Attack on Jersey	346
Capture of St. Eustatius by Rodney and Vaughan	347
The true Reason for the Attacks on Rodney after the Capture	348
Capture of Demerara and Essequibo	349
De Grasse sails against Tobago	349
Surrender of Tobago; Close of Campaign to Windward	350
Leeward Sphere; Treachery of Jamaica Planters	351
Siege and Capture of Pensacola by the Spaniards	351, 352
America; Clinton detaches a Force under Arnold to Virginia	352
Its narrow Escape from being cut off	353
Despair of Washington	354

b

CHAPTER XIX

	PAGE
Carolina; American Successes in Guerilla Warfare	356, 357
Greene succeeds Gates in Command of the Americans	358
Alteration of Cornwallis's Bearing towards Clinton	358
He resolves to prosecute the Invasion of North Carolina	359
Destruction of Tarleton's Column at Cowpens	360-363
Cornwallis still persists in his Advance	364
His unsuccessful Pursuit of Greene	365-367
Greene offers Battle at Guildford Court-house	367
Battle of Guildford	368-374
Cornwallis retires to Wilmington	375

CHAPTER XX

Clinton's Ignorance of Cornwallis's Designs	376
Further Confusion caused by Germaine's Orders	377
Cornwallis marches for Virginia	378
Greene turns upon South Carolina	378
Skilful Capture of Fort Watson by the Americans	379
Rawdon defeats Greene at Hobkirk's Hill	380, 381
Retreat of Rawdon; Capture of several English Posts	381
The Americans besiege Ninety-six	381, 382
Rawdon relieves Ninety-six and withdraws the Garrison	383
Rawdon resigns his Command owing to Ill-health	383
Colonel Stuart succeeds him	383
Greene attacks Stuart at Eutaw Springs	384
Both Armies retire after the Action	386
Cornwallis joins Forces with General Phillips in Virginia	387
His unsuccessful Pursuit of Lafayette	388
Clinton orders him to send back troops to New York	388
Washington summons de Grasse from the West Indies	388
Discontent of Cornwallis	389
Contradictory Orders of Clinton	389, 390
Germaine responsible for the Confusion	390

CONTENTS

	PAGE
Cornwallis fortifies Gloucester and Yorktown	391
Washington and de Rochambeau concentrate at White Plains	391
Clinton's Anxiety to strike at Rhode Island	391
Washington advances southward	392
Hood's Squadron arrives in the Chesapeake and sails for New York	392
De Grasse arrives in the Chesapeake	392
Indecisive Naval Action; the British Fleet retires to New York	392
Cornwallis remains inactive at Yorktown	393
Siege of Yorktown by the French and Americans	394
Capitulation of Cornwallis; the American War practically ended	395
Cornwallis's Share in the Reponsibility for the Disaster	395, 396
Clinton's Share	397
Germaine's Share	397
The American Revolution on the eve of Collapse at the Time	398
Comparison of the Advantages gained by both Sides in the War	399
Causes of the Inferiority of the American Troops	400, 401
The Part played by the American Militia	401
Washington's Claims to Military Fame	402
Greene's Qualities as a Commander	403
Benedict Arnold's inborn Military Genius	404
The British Commanders	404

CHAPTER XXI

Fall of Lord North's Administration; Lord Rockingham succeeds him as Prime Minister	406
The new Government recalls Rodney	406
Capture of St. Eustatius by the French	407
The West Indies; the French attack St. Kitts	407
The Island is lost through the Treachery of the Planters	408
Fall of Nevis and Montserrat; Recapture of Demerara and Essequibo	409

	PAGE
The whole Situation changed by Rodney's Victory of The Saints	409
The Mediterranean ; Siege of Minorca	409
Fall of Minorca	411
Siege of Gibraltar	412
Eliott's Sortie	412
Active Preparations of the French and Spaniards	413
The French Floating Batteries	414
Eliott's Methods of Discipline	414
The grand Attack on Gibraltar	415
Its utter Failure	416
Relief of Gibraltar by Lord Howe's Fleet	417
Close of the Siege	418
Eliott	418

CHAPTER XXII

India ; the Situation in 1775	421
Bengal ; Warren Hastings and his Colleagues	422
Madras ; Lord Pigot and his Colleagues	422
Bombay; French Intrigues with the Mahrattas	423
Renewal of the Mahratta War	424
Colonel Egerton's Campaign	425
Convention of Worgaom	427
The Convention annulled ; Colonel Goddard's Operations	427
Captain Popham's Operations ; Surprise of Gwalior	429
Siege and Bapture of Bassein ; Peace sought with the Mahrattas	430
Madras ; War with the French	430
Capture of Pondicherry and Mahé	431
Hyder Ali declares Mahé to be under his Protection	431
Hyder Ali's Army	432
He invades the Carnatic	432
Disposition of the British Forces	433
Lieutenant Flint occupies Wandewash	433
General Munro's Plan of Campaign	434

	PAGE
Hyder Ali's Movements	434
Colonel Baillie moves upon Conjeveram	435
Munro reinforces Baillie	436
Hyder's Plans	437
Tippoo Sahib attacks Baillie's Detachment	437
Destruction of Baillie's Detachment	439, 440
Retreat of Munro	441
His Blunders	441, 442

CHAPTER XXIII

Further Operations of Goddard against the Mahrattas	443
Colonel Camac's Campaign in Malwa	444
Peace with the Mahrattas	445
Sir Eyre Coote arrives at Madras as Commander-in-Chief	446
His first Operations	447
Narrow Escape of his Force at Cuddalore	448
His Failure to take Chillumbrum	449
Battle of Porto Novo	450
Relief of Wandewash	455
Battle of Pollilore	456
Coote resigns Command, but recalls his Resignation	458
Battle of Sholinghur	458
Relief of Vellore	461
War with the Dutch; Capture of Negapatam	463
Capture of Trincomalee	464

CHAPTER XXIV

Hyder Ali retires to the Malabar Coast	465
Siege and Defence of Tellicherry	465
Disaster to the British on the Coleroon	466
Naval Operations	466
First two Engagements between Hughes and Suffren	467
The French recapture Cuddalore	467

	PAGE
Interference of Lord Macartney with Coote	468
Action of Arnee	469
Third Engagement between Hughes and Suffren	469
Suffren recaptures Trincomalee; his fourth Engagement with Hughes	470
Operations in Tanjore and on the Malabar Coast	470, 471
Death of Hyder Ali	472
General Stuart succeeds to the Command during Coote's Illness	472
Lord Macartney's further Interference with the Operations	473
Death of Coote	474
Stuart advances to Cuddalore	474
Battle of Cuddalore	475
Fifth Action between Hughes and Suffren	476
Deliverance of the British by the Peace with France	477

CHAPTER XXV

Campaign of General Matthews on the Malabar Coast	479
His Advance on Bednore	480, 481
Edmund Burke's Libel on his Army	482
Capture of Mangalore	483
Tippoo surrounds and captures Matthews's Force at Bednore	483
Major Campbell's defence of Mangalore	483-485
Lord Macartney's Diversion to North of Madras	485
Colonel Fullarton's Campaign to the South-East of Mysore	486
His tactical Reforms	487
His advance to Palghautcherry	487
His Preparations to invade Mysore	488
He is delayed by the Council of Madras	488
Surrender of Mangalore	489
Peace with Tippoo Sahib signed	489
Services of Warren Hastings	490
Sir Eyre Coote	490

CHAPTER XXVI

	PAGE
England; Lord Rockingham's Administration	493
Quarrel between Fox and Shelburne	494
Death of Lord Rockingham and Resignation of Fox	495
The Negotiations for Peace	496
America the only Gainer by the Treaty	496
The American Loyalists	497
Shelburne driven from Office by the Coalition between Fox and North	498
Shelburne's Folly in dealing with the Reduction of the Military Establishment	499
Still greater Folly of the Coalition Government	500
Fox's East India Bill	501
The Coalition Government wrecked by the King	501
William Pitt forms an Administration	501, 502
The Need for Military Reform	502
Pitt's Foreign Policy; Holland	503, 504
The Eastern Question	504
British Quarrel with Spain over Nootka Sound	506
Diplomatic Defeat of Pitt by the Empress Catherine	507
Pitt advocates Fortification of the Dockyards	508
His Resolution defeated by the Opposition	509
Similiar Opposition to Fortification of the West Indies	510
The Report of the Special Commissioners on the Office of the Paymaster-General	510
Reforms instituted in consequence	514
Inadequacy of the Soldier's Pay	515
Dearth of Recruits and Increase of Desertion in consequence	516
Pitt resorts to the hiring of Hessian Mercenaries	517
Frightful Increase of Desertion	518
Alarming State of the Army in 1790	519
The Soldier starved by excessive Stoppages	520
Insufficient Concessions made for his Relief	521
Pitt's Military Economies a Blot on his Financial Administration	523

HISTORY OF THE ARMY

	PAGE
Neglect of the Militia	523
Decay of Discipline from want of a Commander-in-Chief	524
Dangerous Indiscipline among the Troops in Ireland	525
Mental Malady of King George III.	526
Danger to the Army removed by his Recovery	527
Reforms in the Army; Luttrell's Scheme for short Service	528
The Infantry; Tactical Lessons of the American War	528
Tendency to carry their Teaching too far	530
David Dundas and his System of Drill	531-533
Improvements in Clothing for Troops in India	533-534
Alterations in Armament and Equipment	535
The Cavalry; Increase of the Light Dragoons	537
Defects of the Cavalry	538
The Life Guards formed into Regiments	539
The Artillery; Institution of Horse Artillery	539
The Engineers; Improvement in their Condition	539
The Ordnance; National Powder-Mills established	540
New Corps formed for Colonial Garrisons	540

CHAPTER XXVII

India; Pitt's East India Bill	542
Insane Character of its Restrictions on the Governor-General	542
Lord Cornwallis appointed Governor-General	542
The Attacks on Warren Hastings	543
Lord Hood's Defence of him in the Commons	543
Impeachment and Trial of Warren Hastings	544-546
Advantages given to Tippoo Sahib by Pitt's East India Act	546
Intrigues of the French in India	547
The East India Declaratory Act	547
Reforms of Cornwallis	547, 548
He rejects the Overtures of Nizam Ali and the Mahrattas	548
Designs of Tippoo Sahib against Travancore	548
Cornwallis thwarted by the Madras Council	550
He forms an Alliance with Nizam Ali and the Mahrattas against Tippoo	551

CONTENTS

	PAGE
Opening of the Campaign by General Medows in the South-East	551
His slow Progress	552
Brilliant Service by Colonel Floyd	553
Dangerous Dispersion of Medows's Force	554
Tippoo attacks Floyd at Sattiamungalum	554
Retreat of Floyd	555, 556
His Junction with Medows	557
Tippoo's Raid upon Medows's Communications	558
Tippoo's rapid March to Arnee	558
He retires towards Trichinopoly	559
His further Attacks on British Posts	560
His Negotiations with the French	560
Successes of Hartley and Abercromby in Malabar	561

CHAPTER XXVIII

Cornwallis takes Personal Command of the Army in Madras	562
His Plan of Campaign	562, 563
His Advance upon Bangalore	564
Serious Mishap to his Cavalry before Bangalore	565
Siege of Bangalore	567
Storm and Capture of the Town	567, 568
Storm and Capture of the Fort	569
Preparations for Advance on Seringapatam	570
Advance of Abercromby from the side of Malabar	571
Cornwallis's Difficulties of Transport	571
His March upon Seringapatam	572
Tippoo offers Battle	573
Cornwallis attacks him without Success	574, 575
Retreat of Cornwallis	576
He secures his Lines of Communication	577
Tippoo detaches a Force against Coimbatore	577
Defence of the Place by Lieutenant Chalmers	577, 578
Siege and Storm of Nundy Droog	579, 580

	PAGE
Siege and Storm of Savan Droog	580-582
Storm of Ootra Droog	582

CHAPTER XXIX

Junction of the Nizam's and Mahratta Forces with Cornwallis	584
The Army encamps before Seringapatam	586
Cornwallis's Dispositions for Attack	587, 588
Storm of Seringapatam	588-597
Siege of the Fort of Seringapatam	597
Tippoo driven to a humiliating Peace	597
The Difficulties of the Campaign	598
Cornwallis	599
Tippoo's Allies in the British Parliament	600

INDEX 603

MAPS AND PLANS

PLATE I. BUSHY RUN AND BOUQUET'S CAMPAIGN OF 1764.

PLATE II. PLANS FOR NORTHERN SPHERE OF OPERATIONS IN AMERICA.
(1) Bunker's Hill, 1775. (2) Boston, 1775. (3) Operations about New York, 1776. (4) Brandywine, 1777. (5) Germantown, 1777. (6), (7) Bemis Heights (two Plans), 1777.

PLATE III. MAPS FOR THE AMERICAN CAMPAIGN OF 1777.
(1) Course of the Hudson River southward to Albany. (2) Course of the same from Albany to New York. (3) New York to Philadelphia.

PLATE IV. PLANS FOR THE SOUTHERN SPHERE OF OPERATIONS IN AMERICA.
(1) Savannah, 1779. (2) Charlestown, 1780. (3) Camden, 1780. (4) Cowpens, 1781. (5) Guildford, 1781. (6) Hobkirk's Hill, 1781. (7) Yorktown, 1781. (8) Eutaw Springs, 1781.

GENERAL MAPS OF NORTH AMERICA

PLATE V. *Northern Sphere of Operations*—QUEBEC to PHILADELPHIA.

PLATE VI. *Central and Southern Spheres of Operations*—PHILADELPHIA to SAVANNAH.

PLATE VII. *Extreme Southern Sphere and West Indies*—SAVANNAH to NICARAGUA, and WEST INDIAN ISLANDS.
(*With enlarged Plans of* NICARAGUA *and* ST. LUCIA.)

MEDITERRANEAN SPHERE OF OPERATIONS

PLATE VIII. GIBRALTAR, MINORCA.

EAST INDIAN SPHERE OF OPERATIONS

PLATE IX. PLANS OF ACTIONS FOUGHT IN INDIA.

North-Eastern Sphere—(1) Sooty, 1763. (2) Oondwa Nullah, 1763. (3) Patna, 1763. (4) Buxar, 1764. (5) Babul Nullah, 1774.

Southern Sphere—(6) Pollilore (Baillie's action), 1780. (7) Porto Novo, 1781. (8) Pollilore (Coote's action), 1781. (9) Sholinghur, 1781. (10) Cuddalore, 1783.

PLATE X. ACTIONS FOUGHT IN THE SOUTHERN SPHERE (*continued*).
(1) Seringapatam, 1791–92. (2) Bangalore, 1791.

GENERAL MAPS OF INDIA

PLATE XI. INDIA—North-East.

PLATE XII. INDIA—North-West.

PLATE XIII. INDIA—Southern.

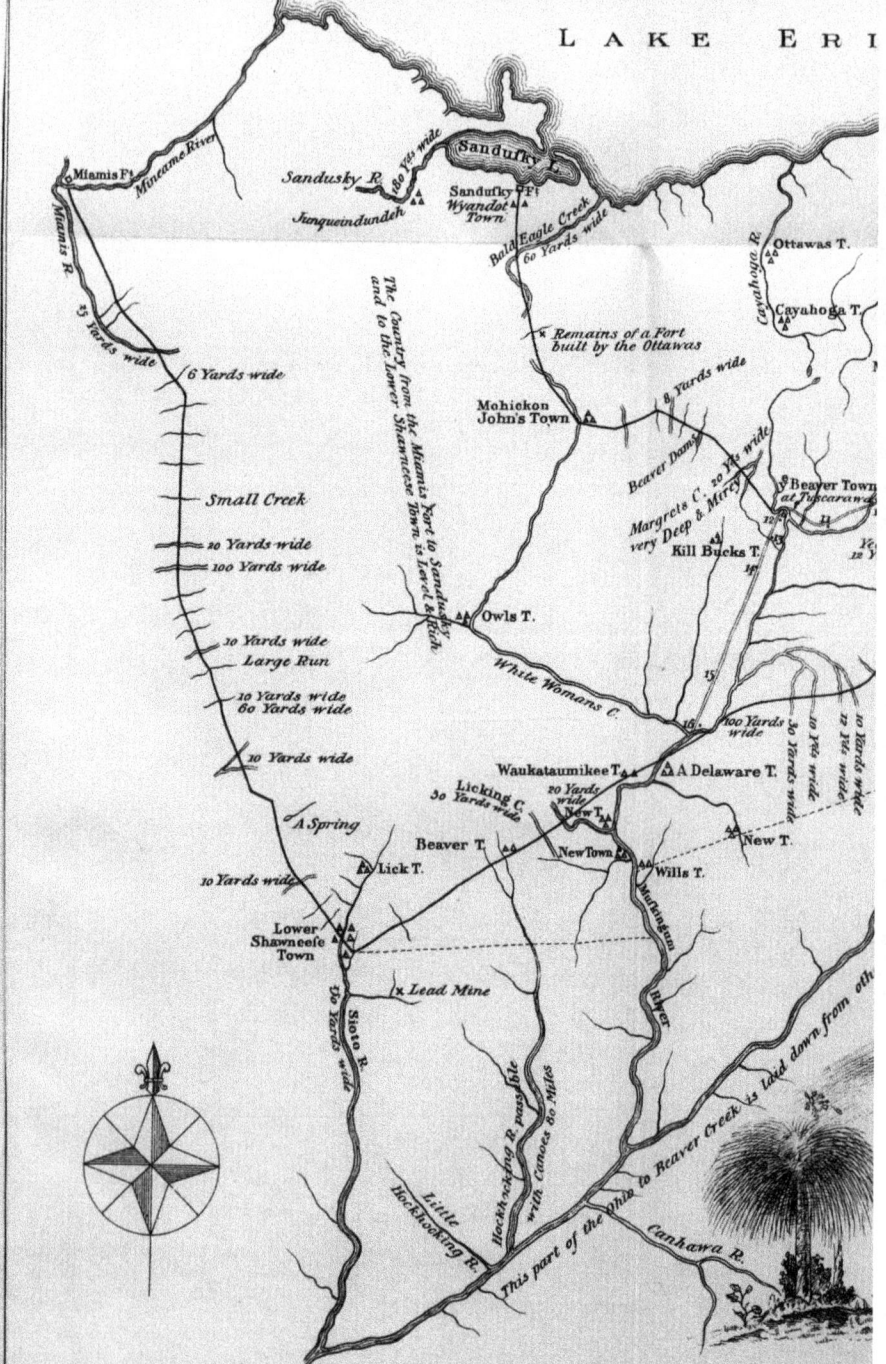

History of the Army, Vol. III.

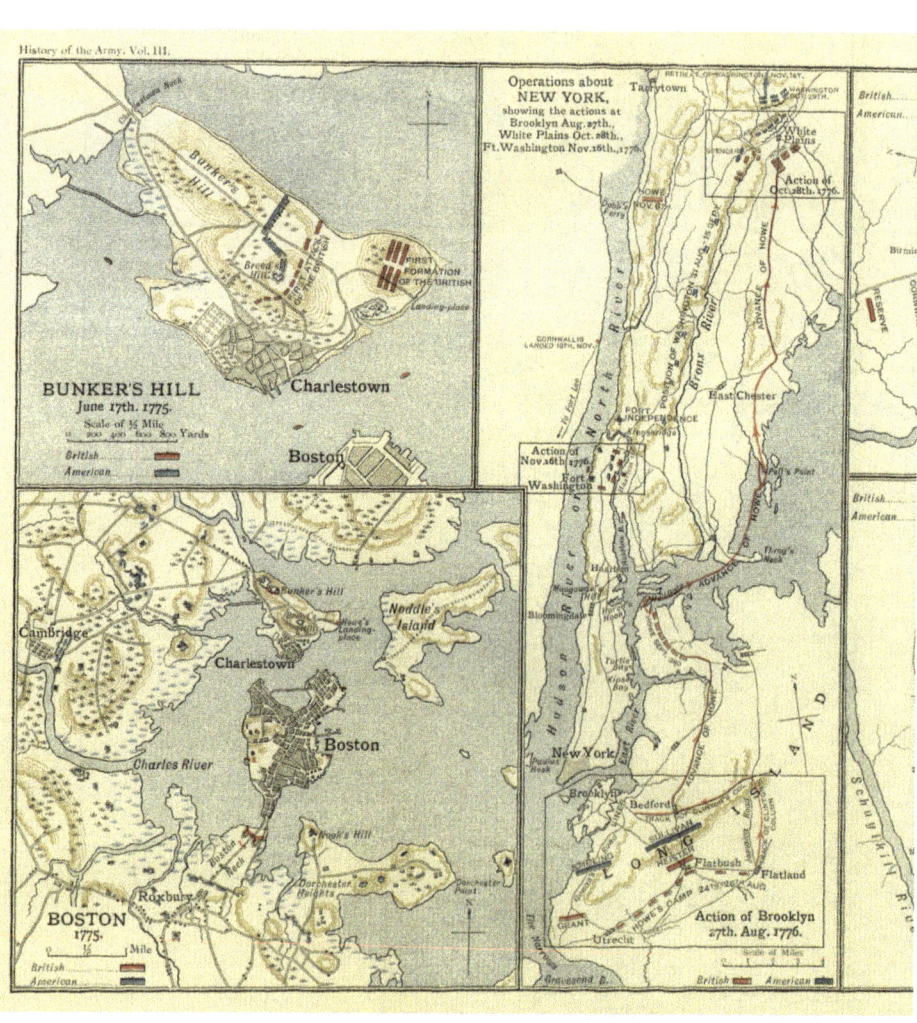

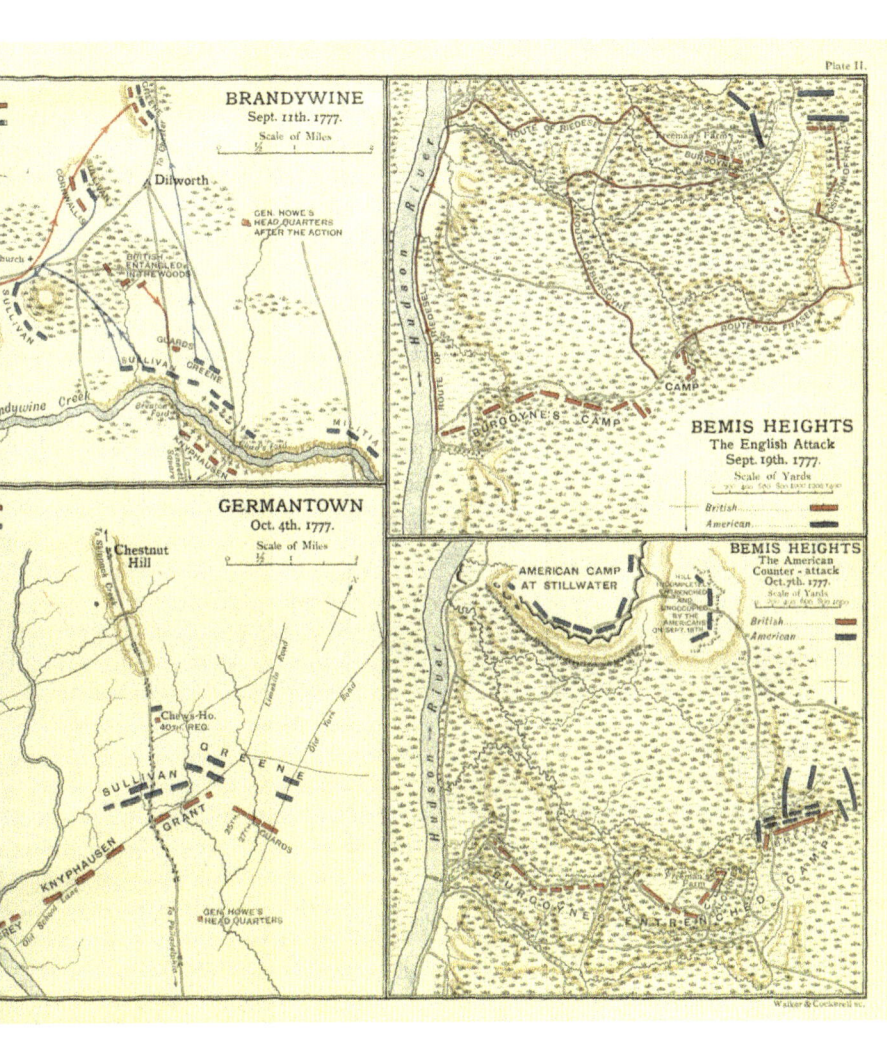

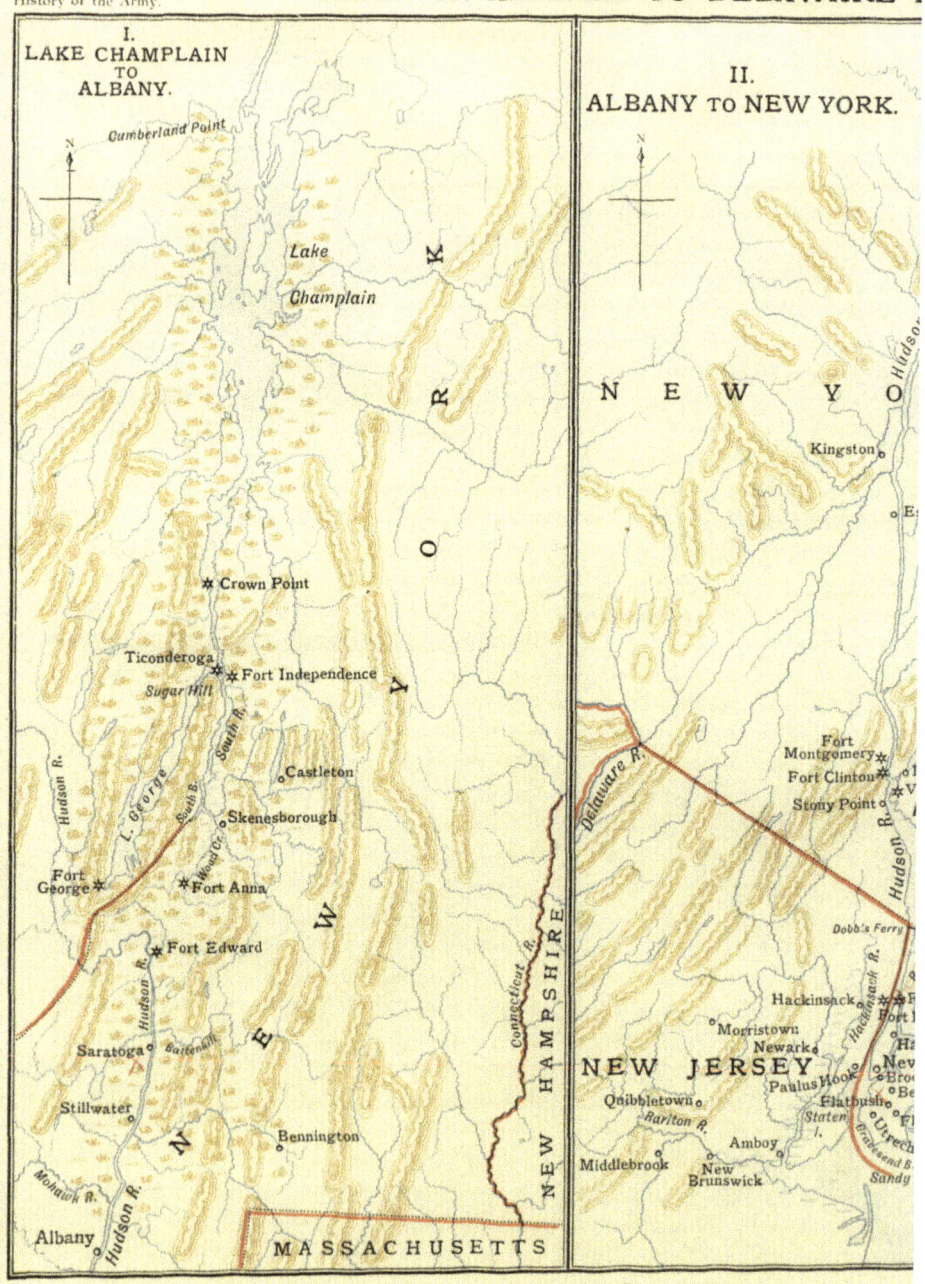

(New York, New Jersey, Pennsylvania.)

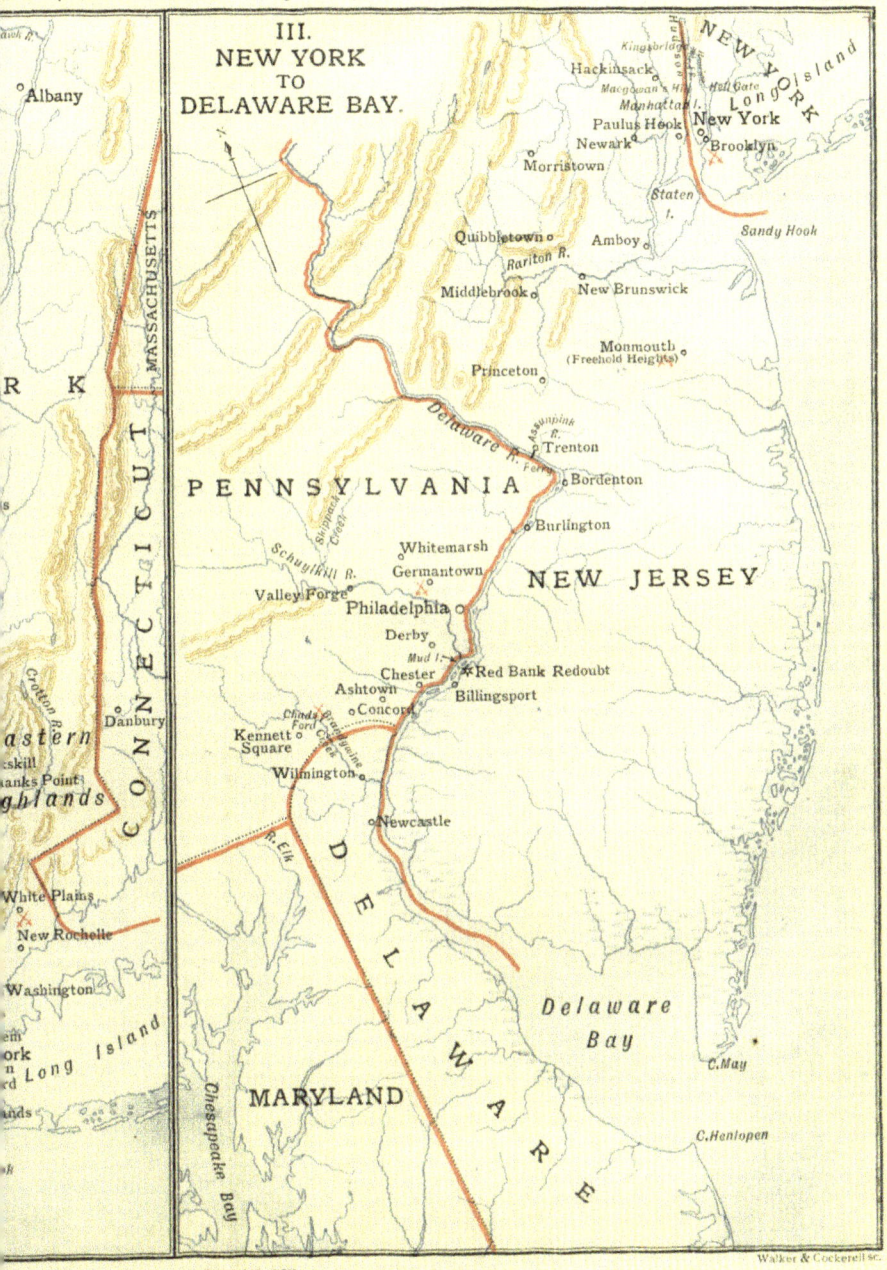

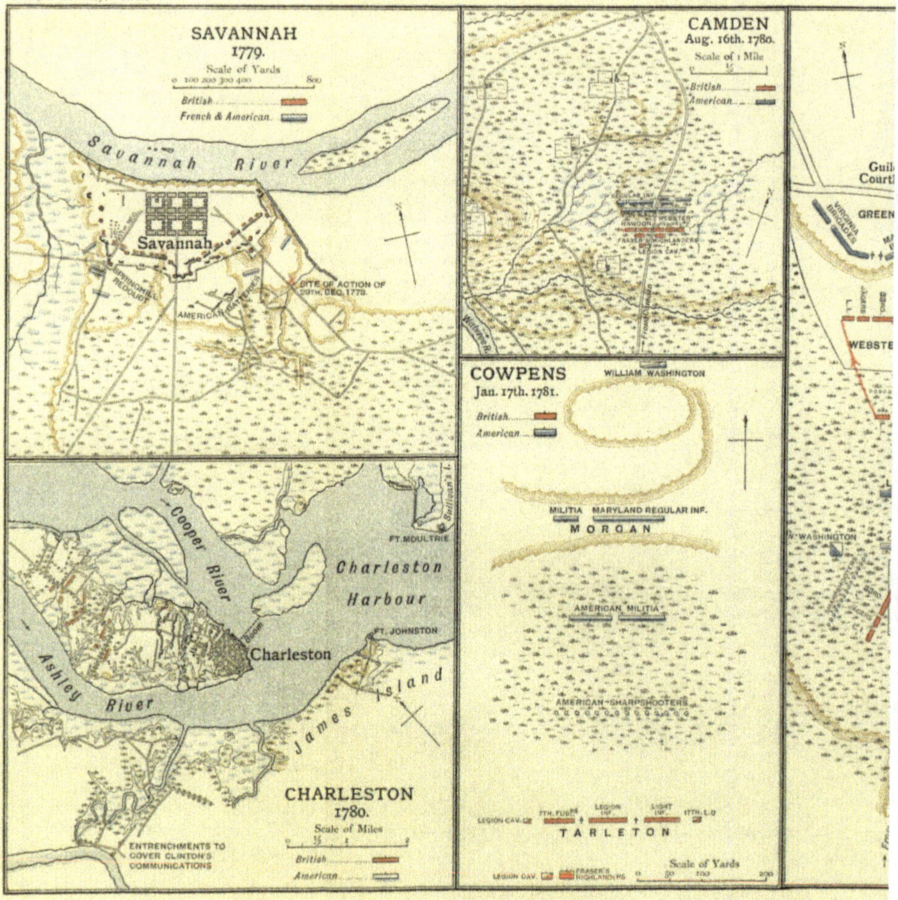
SAVANNAH
1779.
Scale of Yards
British
French & American
Savannah River
Savannah
SPRINGHILL REDOUBT
AMERICAN BATTERIES
SITE OF ACTION OF 29TH. DEC. 1778.
CAMDEN
Aug. 16th. 1780.
Scale of 1 Mile
British
American
COWPENS
Jan. 17th. 1781.
British
American
WILLIAM WASHINGTON
MILITIA
MARYLAND REGULAR INF.
MORGAN
AMERICAN MILITIA
AMERICAN SHARPSHOOTERS
LEGION CAV.
TARLETON
FRASER'S HIGHLANDERS
Scale of Yards
Cooper River
FT. MOULTRIE
Charleston Harbour
FT. JOHNSTON
Charleston
Ashley River
James Island
CHARLESTON
1780.
Scale of Miles
British
American
ENTRENCHMENTS TO COVER CLINTON'S COMMUNICATIONS

Plate IV.

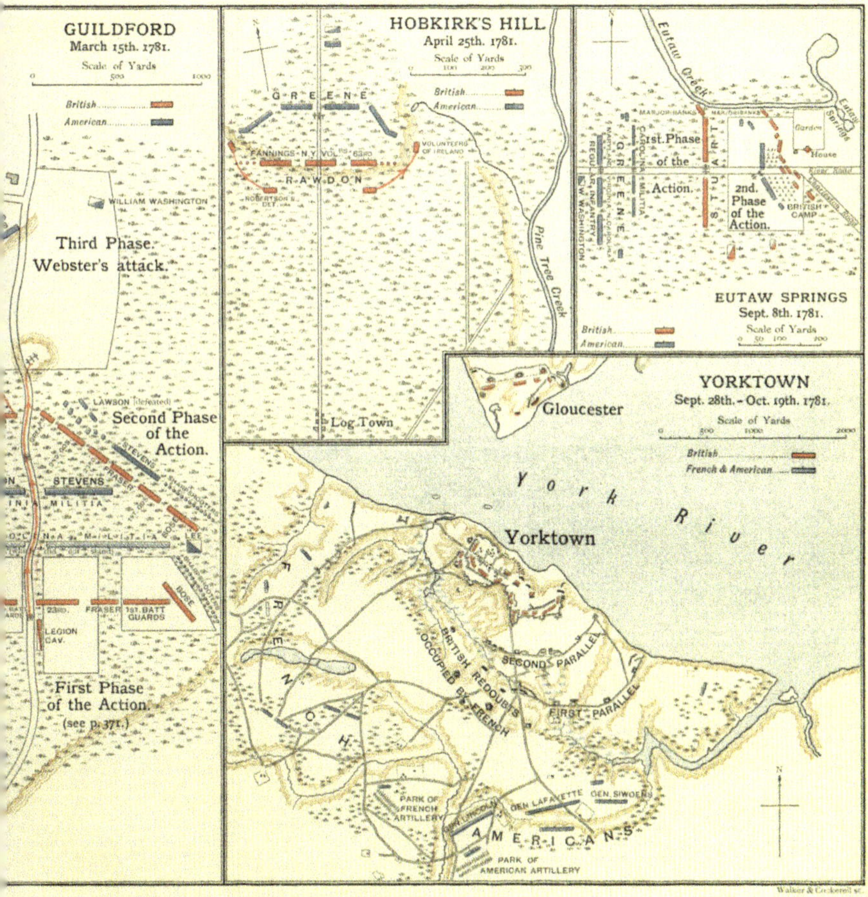

GUILDFORD
March 15th. 1781.

Third Phase.
Webster's attack.

Second Phase
of the
Action.

First Phase
of the Action.
(see p. 371.)

HOBKIRK'S HILL
April 25th. 1781.

Log Town

EUTAW SPRINGS
Sept. 8th. 1781.

1st Phase
of the
Action.

2nd.
Phase
of the
Action.

Gloucester

YORKTOWN
Sept. 28th. – Oct. 19th. 1781.

Yorktown

Walker & Cockerell sc.

Lake Superior

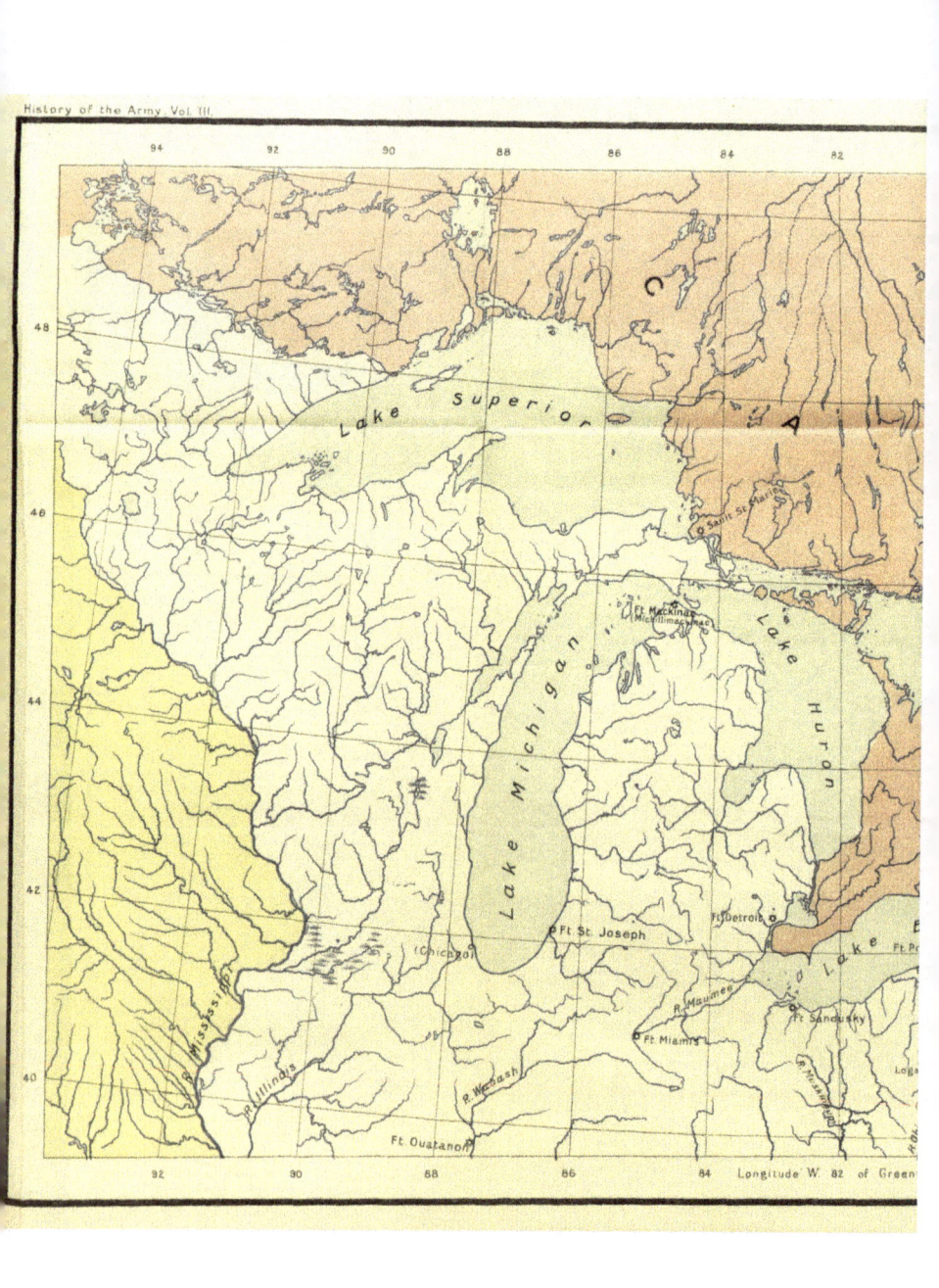

Sault St. Marie

Ft. Mackinac
Michillimackinac

Lake Michigan

Lake Huron

(Chicago)

Ft. St. Joseph

Ft. Detroit

R. Maumee

Ft. Sandusky

Ft. Miami

R. Wabash

Ft. Ouatanon

Mississippi R.

R. Illinois

Longitude W. 82 of Greenwich

AMERICA,
SECTION I.
Northern Sphere, QUEBEC TO PHILADELPHIA

Natural Scale, 1 : 5,500,000.
Scale of Miles.

British
United States
Spanish

Ft. de Chartres
Ft. François

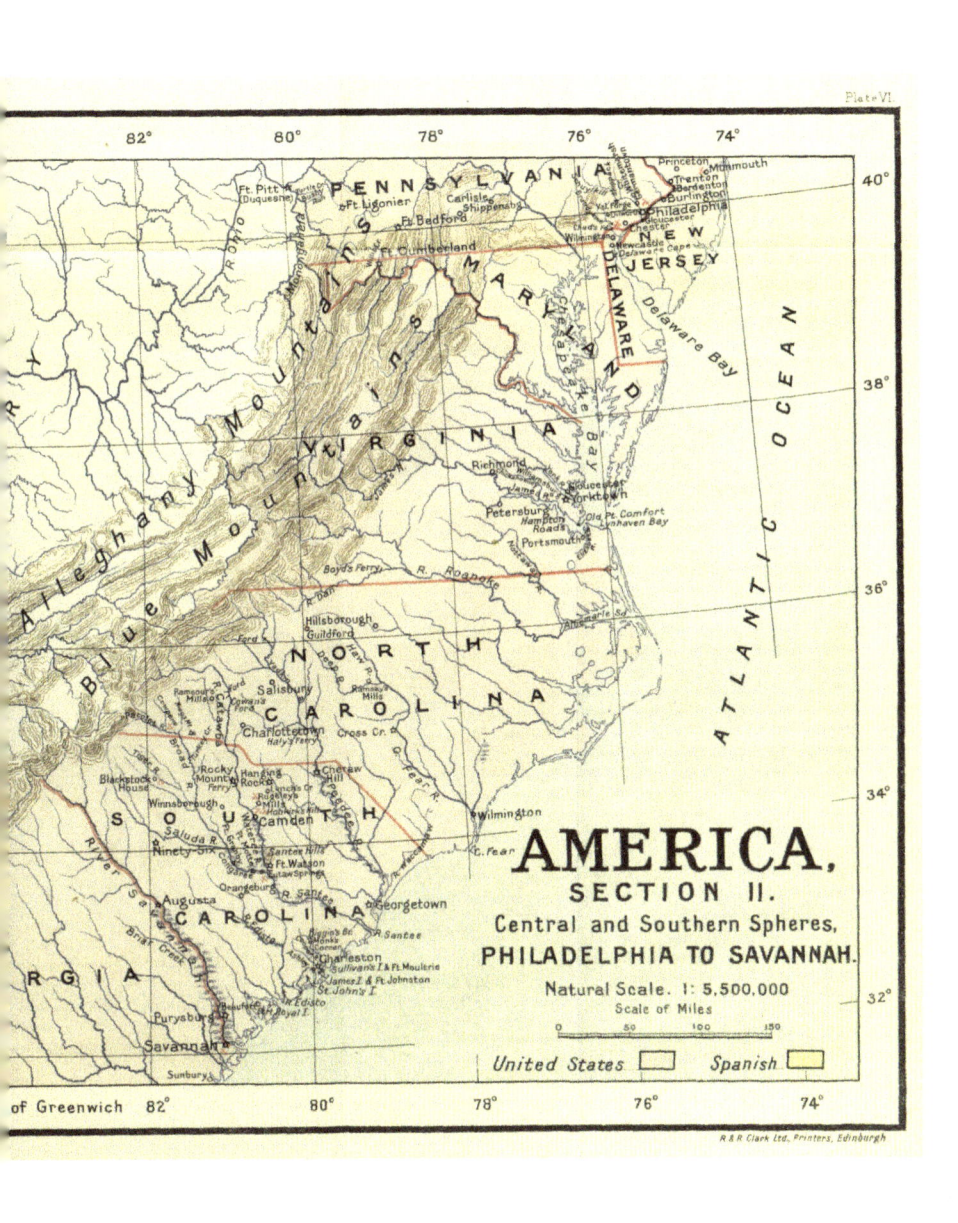

AMERICA,
SECTION II.
Central and Southern Spheres,
PHILADELPHIA TO SAVANNAH.
Natural Scale. 1: 5,500,000
Scale of Miles

United States   Spanish

AMERICA
1776.
SECTION III.
Extreme Southern Sphere & West Indies.

Natural Scale 1:11,000,000.
One half scale of Sections I and II.
Scale of Miles.

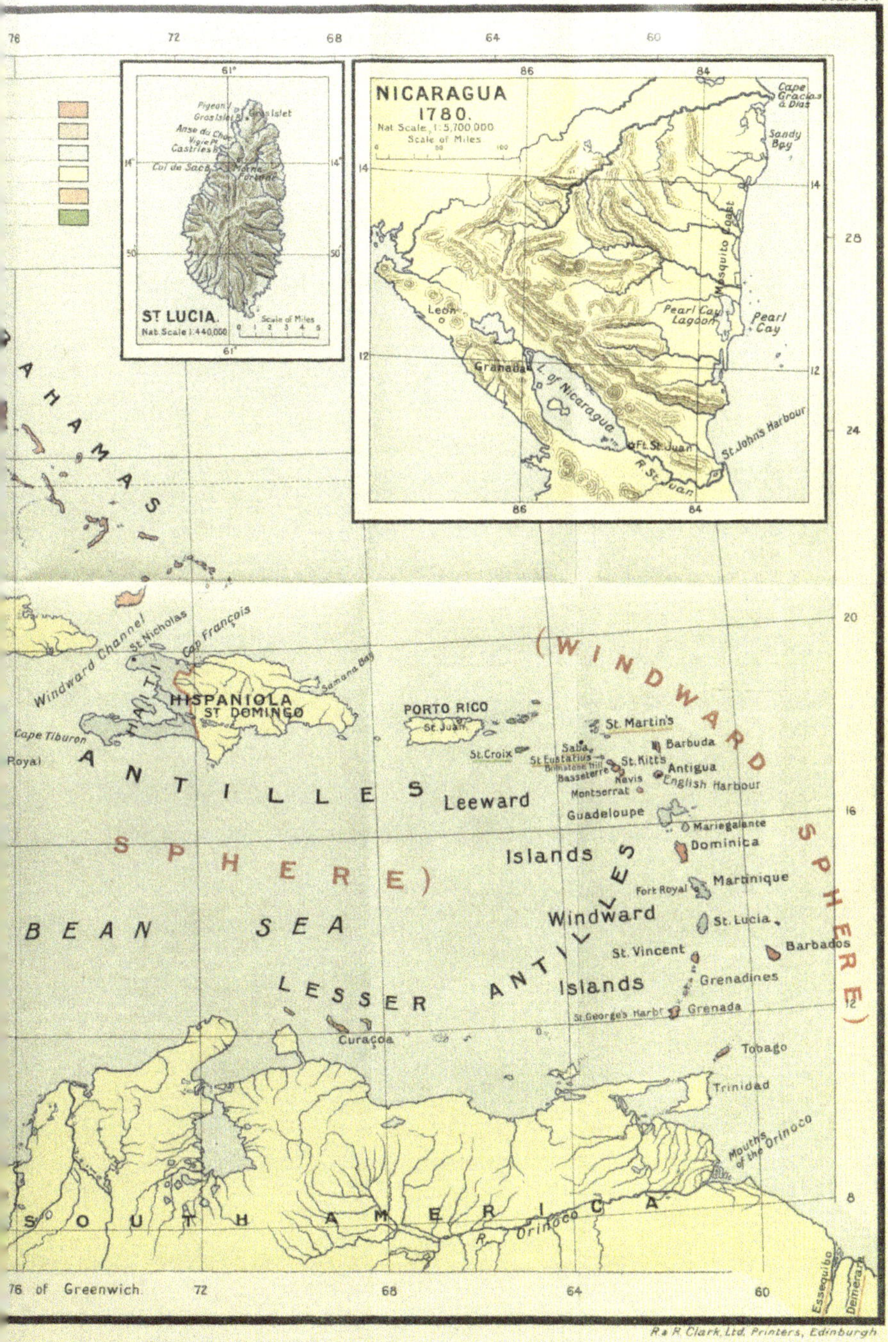

R & R Clark, Ltd, Printers, Edinburgh

History of the Army, Vol. III. Plate VIII.

GIBRALTAR
1779-83.

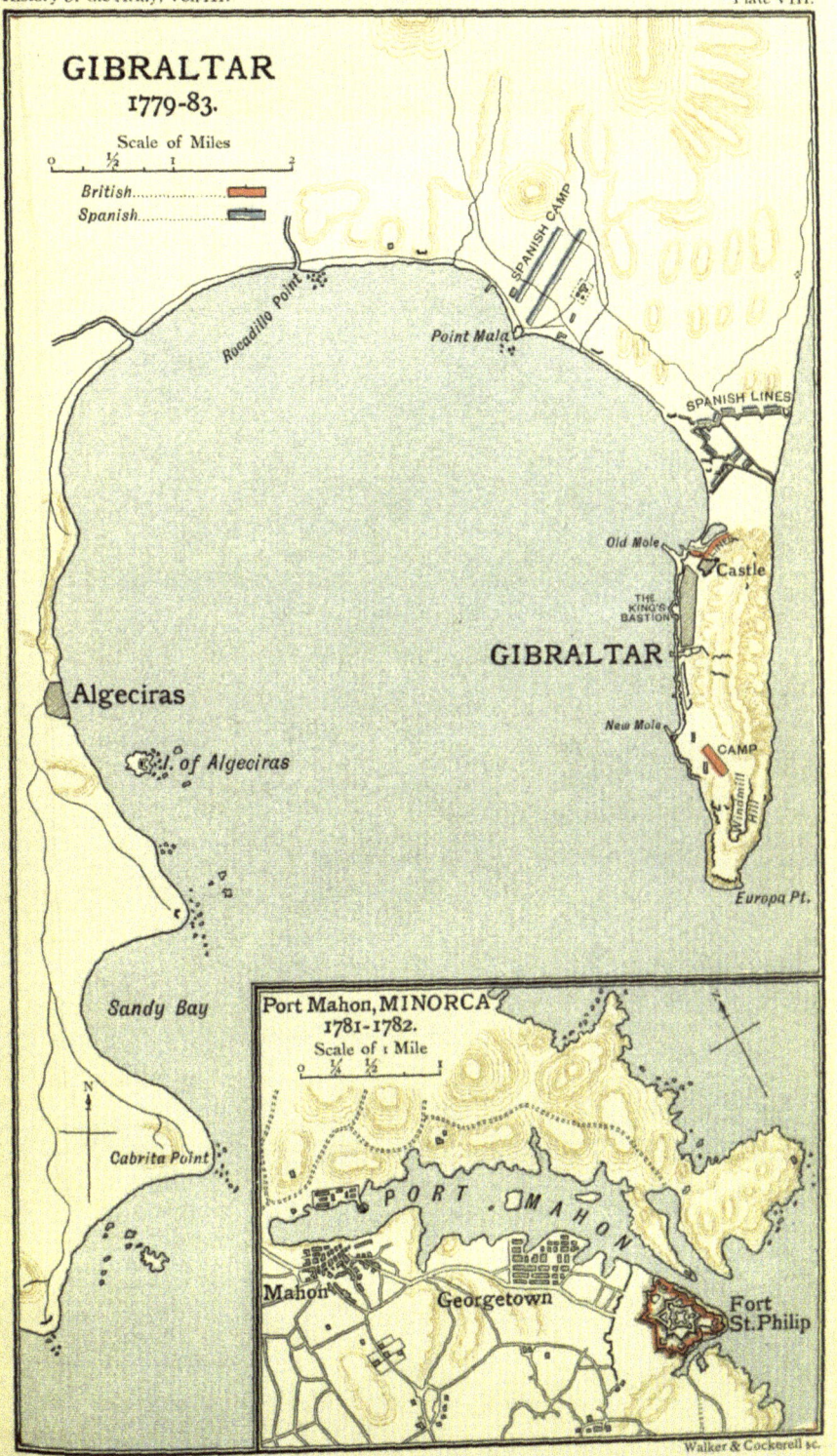

Scale of Miles

British
Spanish

Rocadillo Point
Point Mala
SPANISH CAMP
SPANISH LINES
Old Mole
Castle
THE KING'S BASTION
GIBRALTAR
New Mole
CAMP
Windmill Hill
Europa Pt.

Algeciras
I. of Algeciras
Sandy Bay
Cabrita Point

Port Mahon, MINORCA
1781-1782.
Scale of 1 Mile

PORT MAHON
Mahon
Georgetown
Fort St. Philip

Walker & Cockerell sc.

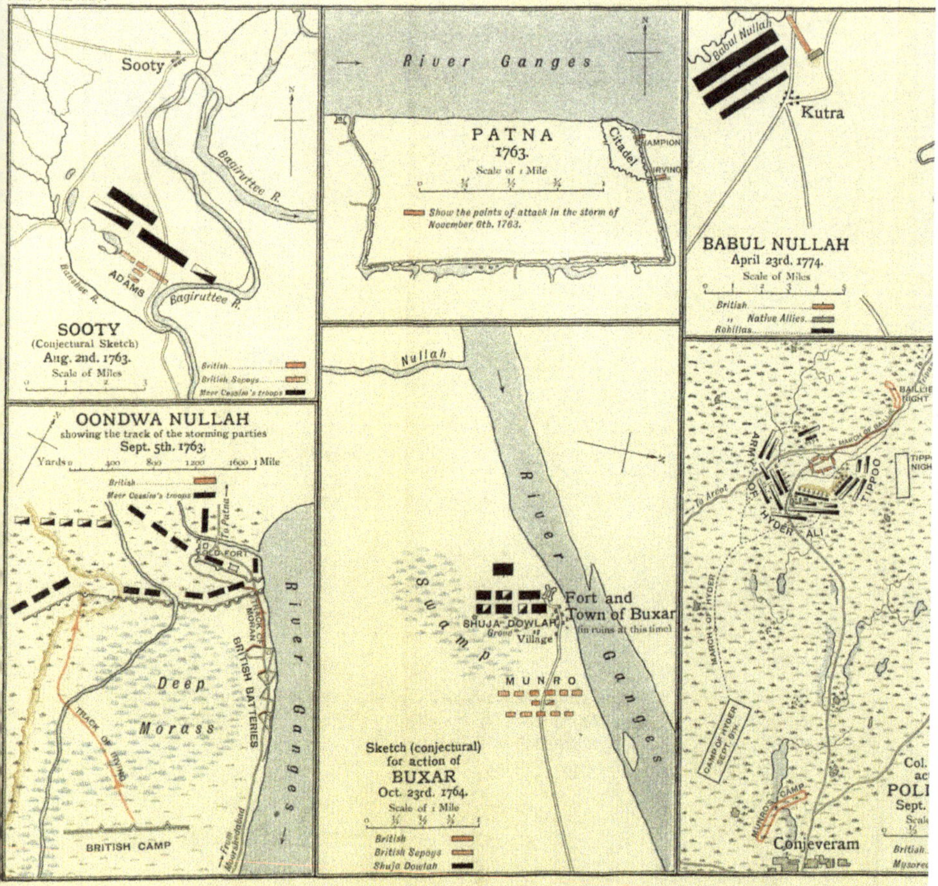
Sooty
Bagiruttee R.
ADAMS
Banshee R.
SOOTY
(Conjectural Sketch)
Aug. 2nd. 1763.
Scale of Miles
British
British Sepoys
Meer Cassim's troops
River Ganges
PATNA
1763.
Scale of 1 Mile
Citadel
CHAMPION
IRVING
Show the points of attack in the storm of November 6th. 1763.
Babul Nullah
Kutra
BABUL NULLAH
April 23rd. 1774.
Scale of Miles
British
Native Allies
Rohillas
OONDWA NULLAH
showing the track of the storming parties
Sept. 5th. 1763.
Yards 0 400 800 1200 1600 1 Mile
British
Meer Cassim's troops
To Patna
OLD FORT
TRACK OF MORAN
BRITISH BATTERIES
Deep
Morass
TRACK OF IRVING
BRITISH CAMP
From Moorshedabad
River Ganges
Nullah
River Ganges
Swamp
Fort and
Town of Buxar
(in ruins at this time)
SHUJA DOWLAH
Grove
Village
MUNRO
Sketch (conjectural)
for action of
BUXAR
Oct. 23rd. 1764.
Scale of 1 Mile
British
British Sepoys
Shuja Dowlah
BAILLIE
ARMY OF HYDER ALI
TIPPOO
To Arcot
MARCH OF HYDER
CAMP OF HYDER SEPT. 9TH.
MUNRO'S CAMP
Conjeveram
Col.
POLI
Sept.
British
Mysorea

Plate IX

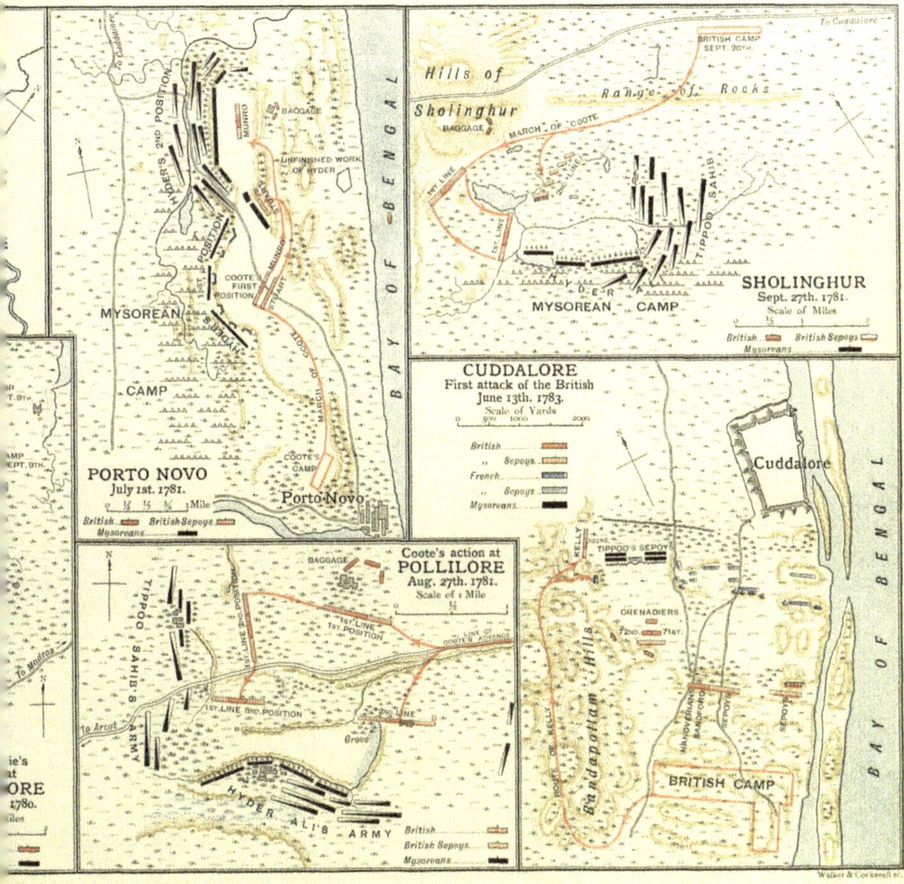

Walker & Cockerell sc.

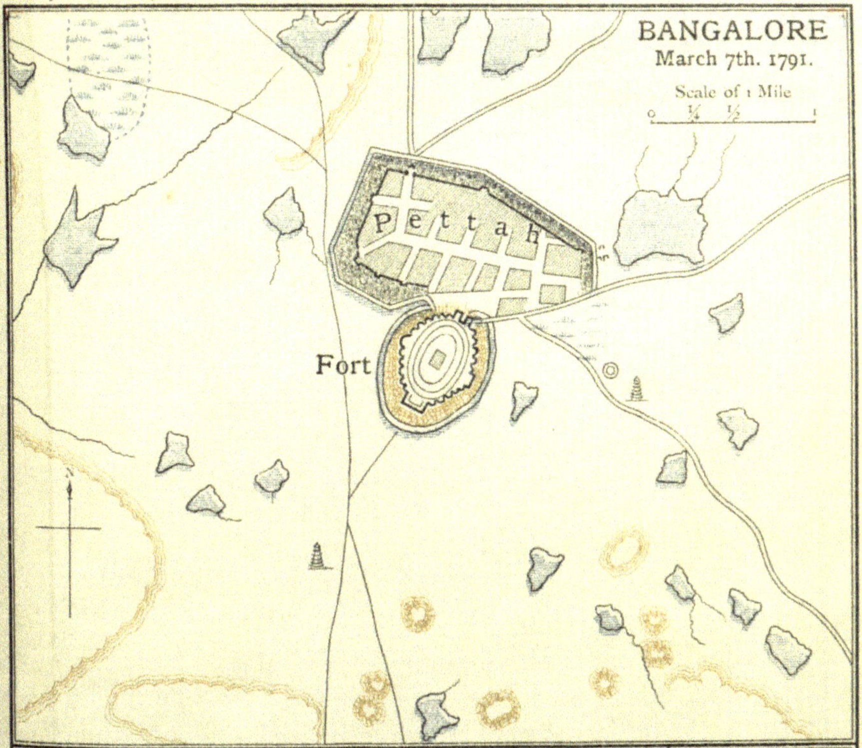

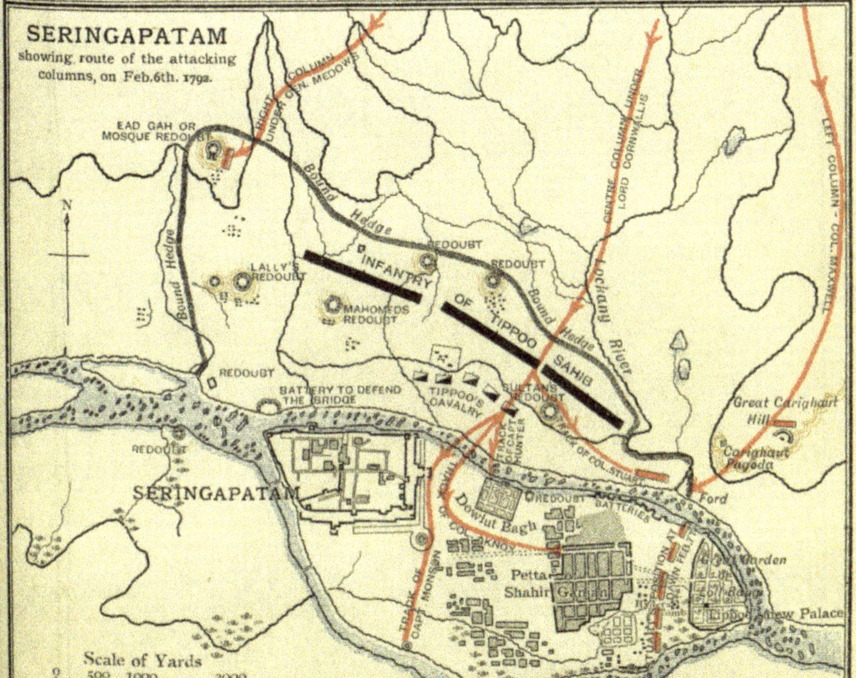

Walker & Cockerell sc.

82°
84°
86°
88°
28°
24°
22°
20°
18°
Himalaya Mo
Lucknow
Cawnpore
Fyzabad
R. Gogre
Bettiah
The Doab
R. Ganges
Coral
Calpee
O U D E
Goomtee
Jaunpore
R. Jumna
Allahabad
Banda
Benares
Sultanpore
Chunar
R. Ganges
Manjee
Chuprah
Hadjipore
Patna
Purneah
Monghyr
Behar
Sasseram
Rotas
Gya
Maunpore
Moulda
Rajmahal
Sooty
Gheria
Moorshedabad
Cossimbazar
Daoodpore
Plassey
Cutwa
R. Adjee
Dummooda
Mungulkote
Burdwan
Hooghly
Chandernagore
Chinsura
R. Dummooda
Calc
Budge Bu
Mayapur
Fulta
Balasore
Mout
R. Mahanuddy
Cuttack
BAY
Chilka Lake
I
(No
Natura
Cicacole
Vizagapatam
Cossimcotah
R. Godavery
Condore
Peddapore
Rajahmundry
Mouths of the Godavery
Madapollam
Narsapore
Masulipatam
Mouths of the Kistna
0
50
Names and approximate Boun
British Possessions prior to 175
States under British protecti
Mahratta States

Plate XI

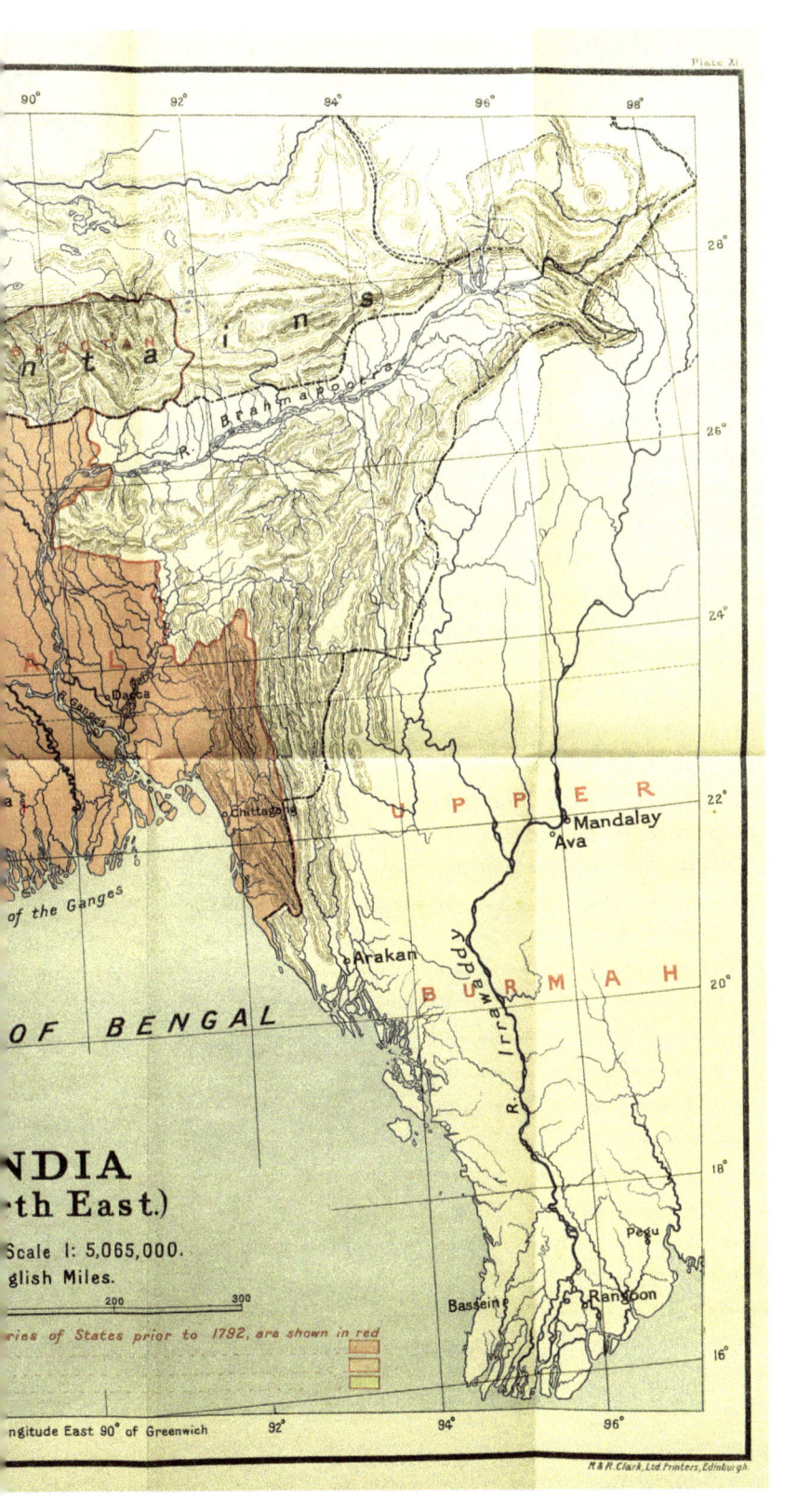

INDIA
(North East.)

Scale 1: 5,065,000.
English Miles.
200   300

...ries of States prior to 1792, are shown in red

Longitude East 90° of Greenwich

R. & R. Clark, Ltd. Printers, Edinburgh.

INDIA (North-West)

Natural Scale, 1 : 5,065,000.

English Miles

Names and approximate Boundaries of States prior to 1792, are shown in red.
British Possessions prior to 1792
States under British protection
Mahratta States
Rajput States
Sikh States

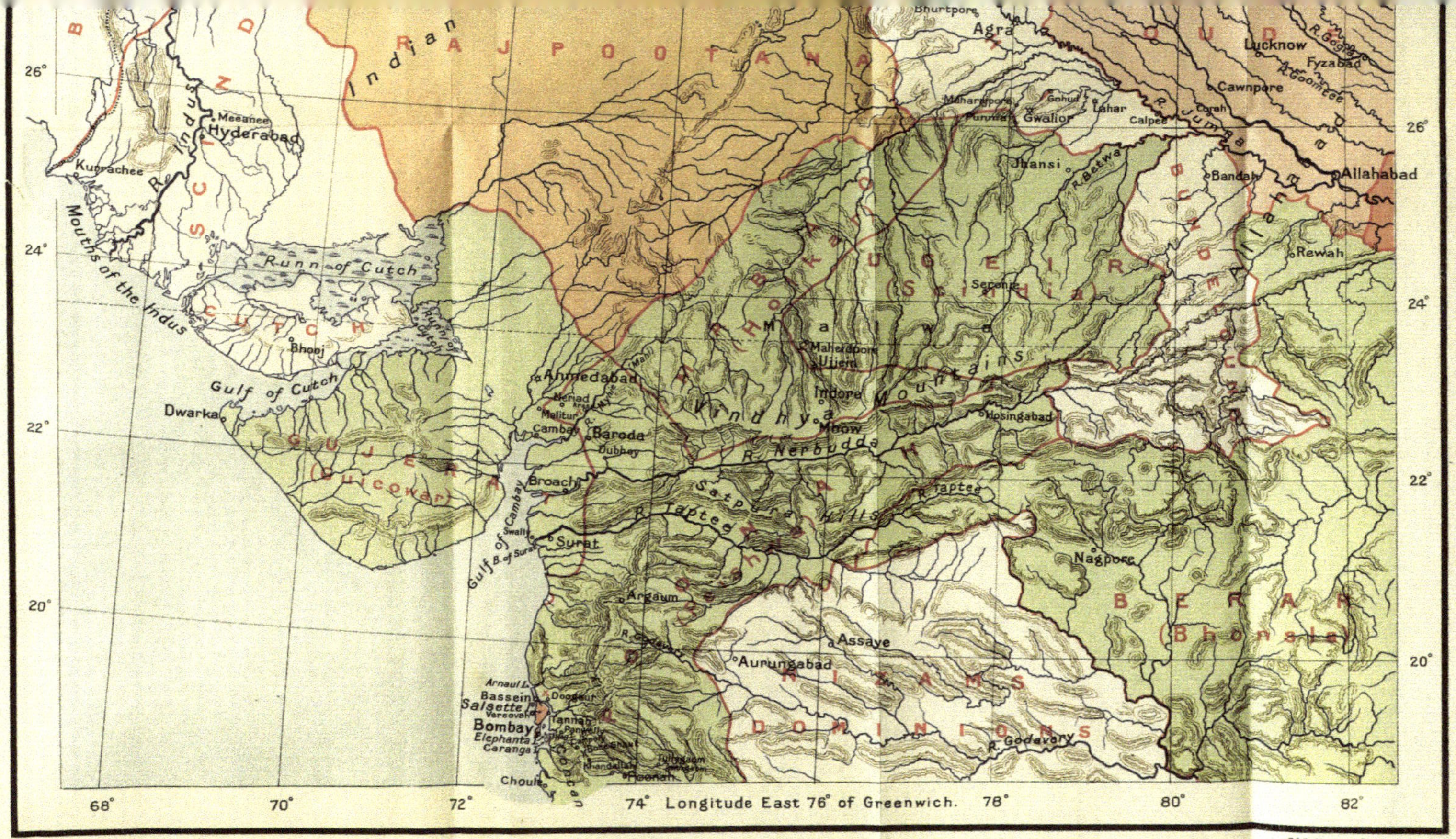

R.&R. Clark Ltd, Printers, Edinburgh.

Gulf of Cutch
Runn of Cutch
Bhooj
Dwarka
Ahmedabad
Neriad
Cambay
Baroda
Dubhoy
Baroach (Broach)
Surat
Gulf of Cambay
B. of Surat
Swally
(Guicowar)
Malwa
Ujjein
Indore
Mhow
Vindhya Mountains
Hosingabad
R. Nerbudda
Satpura Hills
R. Taptee
Nagpore
Berar
(Bhonsla)
Bundelcund
Argaum
Ajunteh
Assaye
Aurungabad
R. Godavery
Nizam's Dominions
Arnaul I.
Bassein
Deogaur
Verasovah
Salsette I.
Tannah
Bombay
Panwelly
Campoly
Bore Ghaut
Elephanta I.
Caranga I.
Khandallah
Tullygaom
Wurgaom
Choule
Poonah
Concan
Western Ghauts
R. Kistna
Satara
Beejapore
Hyderabad
Condore
Peddapore
Rajahmundry
Ellore
Madapollam
Narsipore
Masulipatam
Guntoor
Petapolee
Ongola
Mouths of the Kistna
Mths of the Godavery
Belgaum
Darwar
Copule
R. Toombuddra
Anjediva I.
Goa
Curwar
70°
72°
74°
76°
78°
80°
82°
22°
20°
18°
16°

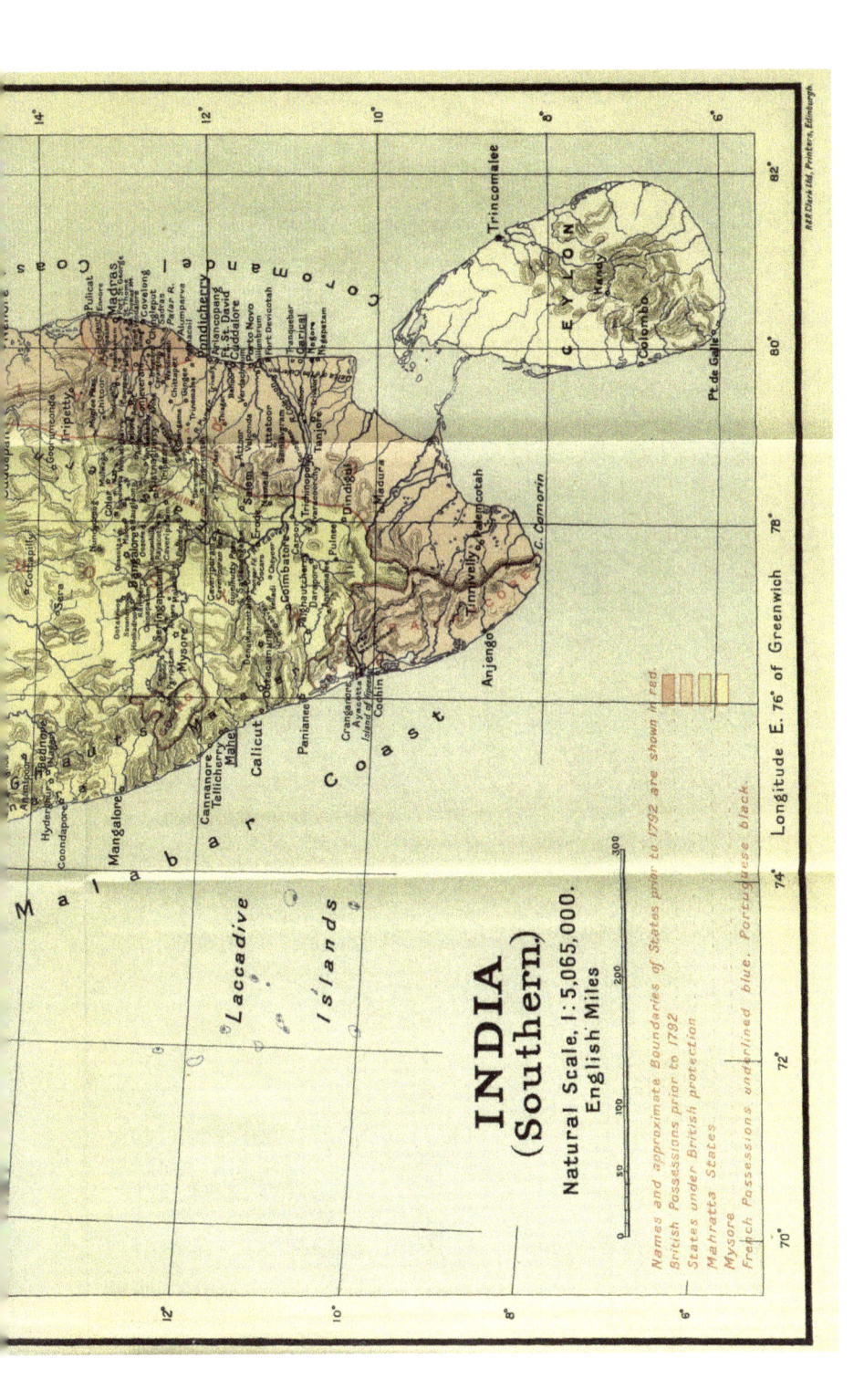

INDIA (Southern).

Natural Scale, 1:5,065,000.
English Miles

Names and approximate Boundaries of States prior to 1792 are shown in red.
British Possessions prior to 1792
States under British protection
Mahratta States
Mysore
French Possessions underlined blue. Portuguese black.

Longitude E. 76° of Greenwich

BOOK XI

CHAPTER I

An empire had been won: there remained the task of 1763. providing for its administration and for its defence. The gain in mere territory was in itself stupendous; and though much of it might be but thinly populated, yet new territory necessarily implied new subjects. Apart from India, where, as shall be told in its place, the work of conquest had not been bounded by the expulsion of the French, the Spaniard required to be conciliated anew in Minorca; while in the West Indies, and still more in Canada and Florida, there were not only French and Spanish Colonists that must be absorbed, but large tribes of Indians, formerly dependent upon them, who must be summoned suddenly to cancel ancient treaties and friendships, and, though themselves unconquered, to transfer their amity to the nation that had vanquished their former allies.

Nor was this all. In the West Indies and North America alike the newly acquired possessions lay alongside of clusters of British communities, which, though in the Caribbean Sea divided by but a few leagues of salt water and on the continent actually contiguous with each other, were riven asunder by passionate local and commercial jealousy. There was not one of these communities, not even the tiniest of the Antilles, but possessed its little legislature on the English model, and consequently not one but enjoyed facilities for excessive indulgence of local feeling, local faction, and local folly, to the obstruction of all broad measures of Imperial policy. Never yet had it been possible to

1763. combine the whole of the American provinces for common defence, even when the enemy was assailing their frontiers; never yet had the Leeward Islands suffered from a foreign foe, but Barbados had rejoiced over the weakening of a commercial rival. Thus the unification of the Old Empire, at any rate for purposes of defence, called as urgently for accomplishment as the incorporation of the New.

Such unity as the Empire had hitherto enjoyed was due to three principal causes: common attachment to the Crown as representing the Mother Country, common recourse to the Mother Country for protection, and common submission, which was rather nominal than real, to a commercial code imposed by the Mother Country. Thus there was one tie of sentiment, a second of interest, and a third which was entirely artificial and which might prove, if highly tested, to be opposed alike to interest and sentiment.

As to the first of these ties it is difficult, from the nature of the case, to speak with any precision; but there can be no doubt that there was in the Colonies at large a strong traditional attachment to the Crown, and, at the close of the Seven Years' War, a genuine pride in the prowess of the British arms and in the extension of the British dominions. Had King George the Second lived for another ten years, it is likely that the loyal affection of the British beyond sea would have centred itself about his person. As matters stood, it fastened itself with unerring instinct upon the great though now discarded minister, William Pitt; that is to say, upon the head of a party and not upon the head of the State. But it must never be forgotten that the large measure of self-government vouchsafed to one and all of the Colonies from their foundation could not but foster continually a spirit of independence; and this spirit had displayed itself at critical times in the most unexpected quarters. In a former chapter I have spoken of the early assumption of independent sovereignty by the New England provinces, and in 1763, particular by Massachusetts; but it is less generally known that at the Revolution of 1688 such tiny communities as the Island of Nevis and the Bermudas had also attempted to put on the airs and graces of independent republics.[1] It must also be borne in mind that the chief delight of every Colonial Assembly lay in thwarting, in season or out of season, the representative of the Crown in the person of the Governor.

In truth, the sentiment that is strongest in the Colonist of Anglo-Saxon race is that of attachment to the land wherein he has made his home. This may still be found flourishing exuberantly in such unpromising soil as the tropical islet, where the white man's offspring is pale, sickly, and listless, and the black man's progeny alone can thrive and increase; much more must it abound in vast continents or great islands, where the white man can see his children and his children's children growing up in health and vigour, spreading further and further over forest and plain, past mountain and river, insatiable till they reach the Briton's true boundary, the sea. As a rule very little romance is to be found in the settler of a new country, and such as there is reaches not to the little group of islands, called the British, in Western Europe, not to the noble minsters which recall the birth of their civilisation, nor to the ancient cities which were the cradles of their freedom. The heart of the Colonist goes out to the natural grandeur of his own possessions, to the great forests which would hide whole English counties, to the huge trees which dwarf the British oak to insignificance, to the broad rivers which humble historic Thames to a rivulet, to the snow-capped mountains which bring low such paltry heights as Snowdon. To the European romance is of the past; to the Colonist it is of the present and future. The citizen of the old world looks down on the pioneer of the new as

[1] *Cal. S. P. Col.*, 1689-1692, Governor Codrington's letters, and the Bermuda papers.

1763. provincial; and the officers of Braddock and Amherst in America had carried this spirit of condescension to a height which provoked just and natural resentment. But be the Mother Country never so perfectly maternal, loyal sentiment is and must be powerless against local attachment in a Colony.

Strengthening the doubtful bond of sentiment there was the tie of interest. In a former chapter [1] I have sketched the early arrangements, hardly to be dignified by the name of organisation, which existed for Colonial and Imperial defence, and have traced the course of events which tended to throw the burden of that defence more and more upon the Mother Country. In the days of the Protectorate and of the Protestant Revolution even the West Indies had been able to furnish levies of white men not only for their own protection but also for attack upon the French and Spanish Islands; but this old order had speedily passed away, and there had not yet arisen the new system of forming permanent regiments of negroes. So for two full generations the brunt of the fighting ashore in the Caribbean Archipelago had fallen upon British troops, while the dominant factor had been, as it still is, the British Fleet. In North America, New England had long striven to dispense with British protection, and, as has been told, had early taken the offensive unaided against the French in Canada; but she had been obliged to invoke the help of the Mother Country; and the final expulsion of the French had been achieved only by uniting to the colonial forces the full strength, both in Europe and America, of the British Army and the British Fleet.

For the aid thus granted and for the success thus gained, Massachusetts, the chief of the New England States, had thanked the King in effusive terms, adding, doubtless with sincerity at the moment, that the people would show their gratitude by every possible testimony of loyalty and of duty. But gratitude is one thing and

[1] Book vii. ch. ii.

interest is another. Moreover, the Americans had 1763. taken a full share in the peril of the fighting and in the glory of the conquest—a fact which was full of significance, for young communities, like young hounds, must be blooded before they can take their place in the pack of nations. The deliverance of the American provinces from their dangerous neighbour in Canada—a neighbour whose presence had haunted New England night and day for a century—freed them, as they supposed, from all internal peril. For protection from external foes they relied on the British Fleet; and since the French had now no naval station on the North American coast, it was evident that any hostile operations of France against the continent must be beset by almost insuperable difficulties. Quebec, the most inviting point for a French attack, was held by a British garrison; and at New York also there was a small body of regular troops, paid by Great Britain, as a nucleus for defence. Spain, it is true, held New Orleans and Havana, but no Anglo-Saxon treated Spain seriously as a naval power; and, with the whole breadth of the Atlantic Ocean between them and any probable enemy, the Americans were not far wrong in considering themselves invulnerable. Thus the tie of interest, though as strong as ever in the West Indies, was seriously weakened in North America.

Finally, there was the artificial tie of commercial legislation. By the Acts of Trade and Navigation the trade of the British Empire was restricted to vessels built in British dominions and manned, in very large proportion, by British subjects, which was fair enough; but, besides this, certain enumerated articles of commerce were forbidden to pass between foreign countries and British Colonies except by way of England, while rigorous legislation prohibited all manufactures in the Colonies which could possibly compete with those of England. On the other hand, Englishmen were equally interdicted from the purchase of any tobacco except that grown in British Colonies; while bounties on

1763. certain colonial products and the favouring of others to the prejudice of foreign powers, went very far towards balancing the scale of advantage and disadvantage between Mother Country and Colonies. Such regulations, selfish though they might be, were the rule in those days, and must not be too hardly judged ; but it is to be noted that they were purely commercial, and contained no suggestion whatever of a fund for Imperial defence.[1]

It need hardly be said that these restrictions on trade were absolutely impossible of enforcement. Many of them were winked at with the connivance of the authorities, and the whole of them were from the first evaded by a gigantic and scarcely concealed system of smuggling. In Great Britain the chief duty of troops in time of peace was the protection of revenue officers and reinforcement of the preventive service ; and a sufficiently dangerous duty it frequently proved to be. The Isle of Man was described by Burke as a citadel of smuggling, and, when it was annexed to the Crown in 1762, it was found necessary to overawe it immediately by a squadron of light dragoons. On the immense Atlantic coast-line of America and in the West Indian Islands, where there was practically no preventive service, smuggling had flourished virtually unchecked for more than a century ; and probably it was as well that this should have been so, for the Colonies would otherwise have been in a state of chronic rebellion. In many of the provinces and islands there was hardly a man, from the Governor downwards, who was not more or less interested in this illicit traffic ; for it is the supreme danger of smuggling on a large scale that it involves the whole population, consciously or unconsciously, in violation

---

[1] In Barbados and the Leeward Islands, the local Assemblies had indeed granted a duty on exports in perpetuity so far back as in the reign of Charles the Second, on condition that the proceeds should be devoted to local defence ; but this formed no part of the commercial code.

of the law.[1] It may justly be pleaded that laws to 1763. impose artificial restraints on trade are an evil; but from violation of a bad law to general contempt of all law is but a very short step, especially where, as was the case in the Colonies, the executive is dangerously weak.

Thus, then, stood the relations between the Mother Country and the American Colonies at the close of the Seven Years' War. The tie of sentiment was strengthened for the moment by gratitude and pride, but the tie of interest was weakened by the expulsion of the French from Canada and by the oversetting of what was called the balance of power in America. There remained the tie of commercial legislation; and it is significant that as early as in 1761, after the fall of Montreal but before the conclusion of peace, James Otis, a lawyer of Boston, had lifted himself into prominence by a violent attack upon the entire commercial code. Herein it is true that he was guided at first by private animosity alone, but the proceeding was ominous; for the close of a great war, as the Peace of Ryswick had shown, is always a dangerous period, when politicians and agitators, who have been long thrust to the wall by generals and admirals, return again to their places with louder voices and enhanced importance.

For Britain itself, of course, the same critical moment had come. At a time when the high problem of Imperial defence seemed likely to prove insoluble, except as part of the still higher problem of Imperial union, the country was torn by factions innumerable. Bute, albeit the most unpopular man in England, remained in office until April 1763; but as though there was not enough against him as an individual, the bitterest reproach levelled at him was that he was a Scotsman; and hence there arose a rage against the

---

[1] Thus Governor Nicholson of Maryland, in 1695, described some of the leading inhabitants as "honest men, except in the matter of illegal trade."

1763. sister kingdom which was as mischievous as it was unworthy. On the other side, the once powerful Whig party was split up into four or more sections, owing to the petty jealousies of the leading Whig families; while Pitt, the only commanding figure among a host of pygmies, stood moody and implacable aloof. At a time when all public men should have been working together to secure the vast possessions acquired during the war, and to lighten the burden of debt which was one of its inevitable bequests, they were squabbling, intriguing, and caballing for their own supposed interests, forgetful of their country and of the Empire which was committed to their care. Abroad, England had not a friend in Europe. France and Spain, humiliated by defeat and loss of territory, awaited only the moment for taking their revenge. Frederick the Great, unmindful of the help that he had received, and remembering only that of which he had been disappointed, lay like some surly old dog, licking his wounds and growling as he thought how he had received them. No more unpromising time could have been conceived for the inception of a task that demanded the highest constructive statesmanship.

As must needs be at the close of every war, Bute's first duty was the reduction of the Army to peace-establishment, which was effected by disbanding or dooming to disbandment all Infantry of the Line junior to the Seventieth Foot, and all Cavalry junior to the Eighteenth Light Dragoons.[1] The establishment for Great Britain was fixed at seventeen thousand five hundred men, including nearly three thousand invalids; that for the Colonies at ten thousand men; and that for Minorca and Gibraltar at rather more than four thousand men; which, with eighteen hundred artillery, and the invariable twelve thousand men on the Irish establishment, made up a total of rather more than forty-five

---

[1] This regiment was disbanded in 1821, but its honours have been transferred to the present Eighteenth Hussars, which was raised in 1858.

thousand men in all. It was a paltry handful of troops 1763. to guard so vast an Empire, with its many important naval stations ; and the King's speech explained that the reorganised Militia was counted upon to secure the safety of Great Britain.[1] Yet it was less the weakness than the undue strength of the Army which met with reprobation from men of repute for wisdom. Edmund Burke wrote in 1774 of the "huge increase of the military establishment" at the peace, and could see no more in twenty new regiments than twenty fresh colonels capable of holding seats in the House of Commons. The comment is typical of the spirit in which the question of defence was approached. It is an undoubted and lamentable fact that colonelcies of regiments were freely given as rewards for political service ; but it is not difficult to show that Burke's contention was on the face of it childish. The foreign garrisons included Minorca, Gibraltar, Bermuda, the Bahamas, St. Vincent, Dominica, Tobago, Grenada and the Grenadines, Jamaica, New York, Halifax, Quebec, Mobile and Pensacola, besides a chain of posts extending for some three thousand miles from the St. Lawrence in the north to the lower Mississippi in the south of America. The whole of the West Indies were subject always to the danger of an insurrection either of negro slaves or of savage natives ; while the entire western frontier of North America lay exposed to attack by Indians. Yet the huge force allotted for the protection of these possessions did not exceed fifteen thousand men.

Within a month of the voting of the new establishment, a sudden movement in America threw startling light on the vexed question of Colonial defence. It will be remembered that after the fall of Montreal in 1760, Major Rogers, the famous ranger, had been sent with a few troops to enforce the capitulation of the French posts on the great lakes and at the back of Canada. During his progress he was met by an Ottawa

[1] *C.J.* 19th April 1763.

1763. chief named Pontiac, who asked him what he did there, but, being answered that the French had surrendered the entire country to the English, seemed to acquiesce in the new state of affairs. None the less the whole of the Indian tribes were galled to the quick by the thought that the territory, which they claimed as their own, should have been transferred by one white nation to another, without a word of consultation with them. French traders and French adventurers who had penetrated into these remote regions, where they lived a half-savage life among the native tribes, lost no opportunity of inflaming the resentment of the Indians against the British; while the British on their side took small pains to conciliate their new subjects. Finally Pontiac, who went near to be a man of genius, planned a great confederation of all the Indian tribes, to attack the whole of the British posts simultaneously and to drive the hated intruders, as his ignorant followers hoped, into the sea. His emissaries flew far and wide to the various chiefs, northward to the head of Lakes Michigan and Huron, southward to the very mouth of the Mississippi; and by the spring of 1763 the weapon of offence was forged and Pontiac ready to strike.

On the British side the chances of parrying such a blow were slender indeed. Amherst's force had been reduced to a mere skeleton by the costly expeditions to Martinique and to Havana; thousands of men had died and as many thousands had been rendered unserviceable by sickness. The consequence was that the posts for security of the Indian territory were held with ridiculous weakness, though there was hardly one of them within distance to support another. Beginning at Niagara and following the southern shore of Lake Erie, there came in succession Forts Presquile, Le Bœuf, and Sandusky; while Fort Detroit guarded the passage to Lake Huron, and Michillimackinac, now called by the shorter name of Mackinaw, the strait between Huron and Michigan, with a small outpost, Sault St. Marie, a few miles to northward. In the south-east corner of Lake Michigan stood Fort St. Joseph, a connecting link with Ouatanon on the Wabash, while Fort Miamis on the Maumee preserved communication between Ouatanon and Lake Erie. Finally, there was the chain of posts on the line from Pennsylvania to the Ohio, Forts Cumberland, Bedford, Ligonier, and Pitt, all of them familiar to us since the days of Braddock, with Fort Venango northward of Fort Pitt, to secure the passage to Presquile and Niagara.

1763.

The garrisons of these stations were formed almost entirely by the Sixtieth or Royal American Regiment, a corps which was still composed in great measure of foreigners, both officers and men. A dreary life these detachments led in the wilderness, hundreds of miles from any civilised settlement, ill-fed, ill-provided, ill-cared-for—in a word, forgotten. " We have no kint of flesh nor vension nor fish," wrote one poor German from Presquile, in quaint mis-spelled English, "and that we could suffer with patience ; but the porck is so bad that neither officers nor men can eat it . . . and self lief [I myself have lived] more than seventeen weeks upon flour and peace-soup, and have eat no kint of meat but a little bear at Christmas." "My garrison," wrote an English officer from Ligonier, "consists of Rodgers, unfit for any kind of fatigue, Davis, improper to be entrusted on any duty, Shillem, quite a little boy, my servant, an inactive simple creature . . . and one more. Two stout fellows would beat the whole five of them."[1] Lonely and friendless, the officers took to themselves Indian girls for companions, a practice which, whatever judgment be passed on it, was destined to prove the salvation of the British.

On the 7th of May 1763, Pontiac and sixty other chiefs entered Fort Detroit, the strongest of all the posts, ostensibly for friendly conference with the commandant, Captain Gladwyn, but every man with a

May 7.

[1] Ensign Schlösser to Bouquet, 24th January 1762 ; Blane to Bouquet, 5th May 1762. *Add. MS.*, 21648.

1763. weapon under his blanket ready for a treacherous attack. Gladwyn, warned by his Indian girl, was on his guard and able to frustrate the whole plot, but foolishly let the chiefs go instead of keeping them as hostages; and
May 10. three days later the fort was beset on every side by some six hundred Indians. Gladwyn, though he had provisions for but three weeks, held out stoutly, and by the help of a friendly French settler contrived to replenish his stores. He had but six score of regular soldiers, besides some forty traders and half-breeds, who were by no means implicitly to be trusted; but he thrust arms into the hands of all, and stood vigorously at bay. Meanwhile, from all quarters came tidings of
May 16. disaster. On the 16th of May Sandusky fell, and the entire garrison was killed or taken; on the 25th the like fate befell Fort St. Joseph; and on the 28th a relieving force of one hundred men, with stores and ammunition from Niagara, was cut to pieces within a day's march of Detroit. The fall of Fort Miamis, of Presquile, Le Bœuf, Venango, Ouatanon, and Mackinaw, followed hard upon these in the last days of May and the first days of June, some few, but very few, of the men escaping. Sault St. Marie and another outlying post were evacuated; and by the middle of June there was not a British soldier in the region of the Lakes except at Detroit. Hideous though were the scenes of massacre and torture, it is impossible not to admire, from a military standpoint, the masterly swiftness and precision of Pontiac's stroke.

On the route from Pennsylvania to the Ohio, however, Forts Pitt, Ligonier, and Bedford repelled the Indian attacks; while Gladwyn, though the number of his besiegers had been augmented fivefold by the fall of the neighbouring posts, had received a reinforcement of some sixty men, with stores and ammunition, and more than held his own. A second reinforcement of some men of the Fifty-fifth and of Gorham's Rangers, under Major Rogers, also found its way to him
July 29. at the end of July; and, though he narrowly escaped

disaster by attempting a sortie, he had, with a force of three hundred men, little to fear. The first violence of the storm had spent itself, and the British had gained a little breathing-time. Amherst, at first incredulous of the extent of the mischief, and unduly contemptuous of his enemy, had already set himself to arrange for the despatch of a relieving force; but despite the urgency of the danger, he was cruelly hampered by want of men. Though the posts between Pennsylvania and the Ohio still held out, the whole of the country between them was laid waste; while the forts themselves were crowded with refugees, who waited only for rumour to revive fresh panic in them before they fled away in wild terror to eastward. Fort Ligonier was held by but twelve soldiers, yet not one of the flying settlers would remain to stand by them. Amherst early decided that his relieving column must move along the line of these forts, and with excellent judgment decided to place Colonel Bouquet in command; but in the dearth of regular troops he was fain to apply to Pennsylvania for local levies. It is hardly credible, but it is a fact, that even in the face of the deadly peril upon its borders the province refused to provide a man.

None the less, by the end of June Bouquet had with great difficulty assembled five hundred regular troops at Carlisle, designing to move from thence, by Forbes's route of 1758, upon Fort Pitt. His force consisted mainly of detachments of the Forty-second, Sixtieth, and Montgomery's Highlanders, strengthened by drafts from other corps; but, even so, many of Montgomery's were so much enfeebled by the West Indian campaign as to be quite unfit for duty, and no fewer than sixty, being unable to march, were carried in waggons to reinforce the posts on the way. Early orders had been given for the preparation of a convoy of provisions at Carlisle, but such was the terror inspired by the Indian invasion that nothing had been done. Eighteen days therefore were lost before Bouquet, having with much difficulty collected transport and supplies, began his

1763.   march southward by Shippensburg upon Fort Bedford.
July 25. Arrived there, he halted for three days, and had the good fortune during his stay to engage thirty backwoodsmen to accompany him; for though, ever since his coming to Carlisle, he had been besieged by refugees with terrible stories of massacre and destruction, not a man of them could be persuaded to join him. Thence pursuing his way by the rough track hewn by Forbes
Aug. 2. through the forest, he on the 2nd of August reached Fort Ligonier, fifty leagues from his starting-point; and leaving there his oxen and waggons, continued his
Aug. 4. march on the 4th with three hundred and fifty pack-horses and a few driven cattle only. On that night he encamped but a few miles from Fort Ligonier, intending to start early next morning, push on as far as a stream called Bushy Run, rest there till night, and pass through the dangerous defile of Turtle Creek, which lay a short distance beyond it, under cover of darkness.
Aug. 5. Early on the morning of the 5th, the troops moved off accordingly, over steep and broken ground shrouded everywhere by dense forest, and at one o'clock, after a tramp of seventeen miles, were approaching the appointed halting-place, when a sharp fire in the van told that the advanced guard was engaged. Two companies were at once sent forward, which, charging through the forest, speedily cleared the ground with the bayonet; but this was hardly accomplished before renewed firing showed that the Indians, true to their usual tactics, had developed a simultaneous attack on both flanks and in rear. Bouquet thereupon recalled his men to protect his pack-horses, and formed the whole of his troops in a ring around them. The Indians attacked with great gallantry, charging again and again with wild yells up to the line, only to be driven back by steady and telling volleys. But the counter-attack of the bayonet was of little avail against so active an enemy in the forest; and the savages, skipping nimbly from tree to tree, kept themselves under cover, constantly changing the point of assault and pouring in always a destructive fire. For

seven long hours the fight raged fiercely, until at night- 1763.
fall the Indian fire at last slackened, and the weary Aug. 5.
soldiers enjoyed a little respite from the eternal rain of
bullets. It was but a respite, for there was little rest for
them that night. To move in the presence of such an
enemy was impossible, so, though not a drop of water
was within reach, the troops bivouacked where they
stood, lying down in order of battle. Numerous outposts were pushed into the forest to guard against
a night-attack; and in the centre of the bivouac a
wall of flour-bags was thrown up as shelter for the
wounded. In truth Bouquet's heart misgave him lest
his force should share the fate of Braddock's. His
losses had been severe, several officers and some sixty
men having fallen killed or wounded; and he could
feel no confidence in the issue of a combat on the
morrow with his men worn out by fatigue, fighting,
and thirst.

Throughout the night occasional whoops told of the Aug. 6.
presence of the enemy, and at the first glimmer of dawn
the Indian attack was renewed, with the same deadly
fire from unseen marksmen and the same furious rushes
at point after point. The British still fought on bravely,
but with renewed exertion and the increasing heat of the
sun their thirst became intolerable. From time to time
a mob of pack-horses, maddened by wounds, would
break away from their place by the wall of flour-bags,
crash through the fighting line, and scour away into the
forest, while their drivers hid themselves in abject terror
without an effort to control them. At ten o'clock the
British, though thinned by heavy losses, still kept the
ring unbroken, but began to waver from sheer exhaustion. Encouraged by these signs of weakness, the Indians
attacked with fresh confidence; and as a last desperate
resource Bouquet withdrew two companies into the
interior of the bivouac, extending the files of the troops
on each flank across the gap, as though to cover the
retreat. The Indians, now assured of victory, pressed
furiously into the space thus weakened, and seemed to

1763.
Aug. 6.
be on the point of carrying all before them, when they were staggered by a destructive volley full upon their flank. Bouquet, taking advantage of a fold in the ground, had sent the two withdrawn companies to fetch a compass through the forest; and these now opened their counter-attack. The Indians, though heavily punished, with great bravery wheeled to return the fire, but would not stand to await the bayonets that came charging upon them through the trees. They turned and fled in wild confusion; but Bouquet had not done with them yet. Two more companies had advanced by his order before the ring, and now lay in ambush ready for the fugitives. As the Indians passed them, these poured in a volley as destructive as that of their comrades, and the four companies uniting drove the savages through the forest without rest or respite, killing several and dispersing the rest. The Indians on the other side of the ring, seeing the rout of their fellows, did not await attack, but fled likewise; and in a short time the British stood alone upon the ground, every sign of a living Indian having vanished.

Around the ring lay the corpses of some sixty dead warriors, but Bouquet's loss was little less severe, amounting to eight officers and ninety-six men, or fully a fourth of his force, killed and wounded in the two days' fighting. The action was one of the fiercest ever fought with Indians; and had any man of less experience in such warfare than Bouquet been in command, its issue might well have been disastrous. Nothing but perfect confidence in him, added to the dread of being roasted alive, could have kept the exhausted troops to their work; while the final stratagem whereby success was won reflects equal credit on the resource of the commander and the perfect steadiness of the men. Long though the combat has been forgotten in England, the history of the Army can show few finer performances on its own scale than this victory of a handful of English, Highlanders, and Germans under the leadership of a Swiss colonel. The result of the action was

CH. I   HISTORY OF THE ARMY   19

immediate, for the column reached Fort Pitt with little 1763. further opposition or loss on the 10th. There Bouquet Aug. 10. left another officer in command and returned eastward for the further work that lay before him. A reinforcement of three hundred provincial rangers would have enabled him to finish the campaign there and then; but the Americans, who had not been ashamed to save themselves while British soldiers, too weak to stand on their legs, encountered their enemies, very consistently declined to furnish a man.

So far the depredations of the Indians had been confined to the remoter British posts and to the western borders of Virginia, Maryland, and Pennsylvania. The Iroquois, or Six Nations, who lay between Lake Ontario and New York, had for the most part been kept firm to the British alliance by the influence of Sir William Johnson, and only a single tribe, the Senecas, had thrown in their lot with Pontiac. These Senecas, however, with other insurgent tribes, wrought no little havoc on the western border of New York, and actually suc- Sept. ceeded in surprising a convoy near Fort Niagara, and in destroying seventy out of eighty men of the escort. This in the existing scarcity of troops was a serious matter. Detroit was still blockaded; and affairs were not improved when a force of six hundred regular soldiers, assembled with infinite difficulty at Niagara for its relief, was caught by a storm on Lake Erie and compelled to return with the loss of all stores and ammunition and of seventy men drowned. It was not until the end of October that Pontiac and his warriors broke up from before Detroit, and then not for military reasons, but in ostensible deference to orders from the French. The chief, however, withdrew only with full though secret intention to return.

Meanwhile Amherst, having again appealed to the provinces to call up levies for their defence, resigned his command and embarked for England, leaving the final suppression of the rising to his successor, General Gage. The Colonies returned no very willing response to his

1763. summons. Massachusetts and Connecticut made their assistance conditional on a renewal of the war with the Western Indians; Rhode Island, always churlish, sent no answer whatever; New Hampshire was profuse in excuses; and only New York and New Jersey promised to furnish one thousand men between them, stipulating, however, that two-thirds of them should remain on their own frontiers.[1] Virginia had already sent a force to protect her outlying settlements; but Pennsylvania refused to vote her contingent of one thousand men, and even denounced an expedition, conducted voluntarily by some of her citizens against the Indians, as seditious and murderous. Nothing less than the march of a body of Pennsylvanian border-men, fully armed and equipped, upon Philadelphia, was necessary to awe the Quaker Assembly[2] into taking care for the defence of its own people. But by that time the season was too far spent for further operations, and it was plain that the complete subjugation of the Indians would require another campaign.

It was accordingly decided that, as soon as the spring of 1764 should permit, two separate columns should march, one under Bouquet from Fort Pitt into the settlements of the Delawares and Shawanoes, who were the soul of the insurrection, in the valley of the Ohio, and the other under Colonel Bradstreet from Albany, to quell the tribes about Detroit. Bradstreet, the hero of Fort Frontenac in 1758, was the first to move, with a force made up partly of regulars and partly of pro-
1764. vincial levies;[3] but in spite of the fair promises of the previous year the entire provincial contingent did not exceed one thousand men, and those of very poor quality. The service, promising little honour or

[1] Gage to Halifax, 10th March, 12th May 1764.
[2] The study of our early colonial history is a severe trial to any man who desires to hold the sect of Quakers in respect.
[3] New York troops, 500; New Jersey and Connecticut, 500; H.M. 17th and Gage's Light Infantry, and Royal Artillery with ten guns. Gage to Halifax, 12th May 1764.

advantage, was naturally unpopular; and notwithstanding professions of zeal to encounter internal enemies, the provinces took little pains to encourage men to enlist. There is little worth narrating of the expedition itself, for Bradstreet, though he duly relieved Detroit and reoccupied Sandusky and Mackinaw, disobeyed his orders to punish the offending tribes, and contented himself with accepting vain promises and concluding fallacious treaties with his enemy. By November he had returned to Niagara, having accomplished nothing, but added rather to the difficulties of Bouquet's column.

1764.

Bouquet meanwhile had undergone the common fate of British commanders who relied on provincial levies. Virginia and Maryland flatly refused to send him a man; and a contingent of one thousand men, which had at last been wrung from Pennsylvania, was not ready to move until July, by which time the season for navigation of the Ohio was past. However, on the 5th of August he reached Carlisle with his provincials and a detachment of the Forty-second and Sixtieth, for the most part veterans of Bushy Run. Within five days two hundred of the Pennsylvanians had deserted, and Bouquet was obliged to beg for Virginians to fill their place; but none the less he continued his march, reaching Fort Pitt on the 17th of September with no further loss than that of another hundred Pennsylvanian deserters. Here he picked up a welcome reinforcement of Virginian backwoodsmen, and marching again at the beginning of October entered a wilderness never before trodden by an army. Advancing with every precaution, he made his way steadily south-westward for one hundred miles into the heart of the Delaware and Shawanoe settlements on the river Muskingum. The moral effect of his invasion and a little well-timed severity accomplished the object of the campaign without the firing of a shot, and Bouquet returned to Carlisle with a difficult task well done. From that time, although there was still to be a little trouble before the posts on the Illinois could

Aug. 5.

Sept. 17.

1764. be occupied, the power of the Indian conspiracy was broken.

I have dwelt, it may seem, with undue fulness upon certain details of these campaigns, but not without a purpose. It is no more than the truth to say that the brunt of this most dangerous and trying warfare had fallen wholly upon the King's troops. It was they who held Detroit; it was on them, in their miserable ruined forts, that the refugees of Pennsylvania had rallied for a time; it was they who fought and won the action of Bushy Run, saving the province from horrors untold; it was they who formed the backbone of the force that marched to the Muskingum; finally, by a strange irony, it was they whom the panic-stricken burghers of Philadelphia had summoned (though they could not be spared) for defence against the righteous indignation of their own people. It might have been supposed that the harried provinces of Virginia and Maryland would have felt gratitude to Bouquet for their deliverance; but it was not so. Virginia refused to pay the volunteers that had accompanied him to the Muskingum, and tried hard to fasten the cost upon the Colonel himself. He was only relieved, after endless annoyance and vexation, by the Assembly of Pennsylvania, which made tardy amends for past shortcomings by taking the burden upon itself. The gallant man did not long survive this last campaign, for within three years he died at Pensacola, having first received promotion to the rank of Brigadier for his services; and it can only be said that the end of his career was not untimely. The only conclusion that could be drawn from the attitude of the Colonies towards him was that they would take no burden upon themselves which they could lay upon the British soldier— that in fact they would even allow sick Highlanders to be dragged out of hospital to the front to defend able-bodied Americans. Such a spirit was not encouraging for a happy solution of the problem of Imperial defence.

AUTHORITIES.—Despatches of Amherst and Gage, *America and* 1764. *West Indies*, 120, 121 (Record Office). The best account of Bouquet's campaigns is contained in a thin quarto volume, *Historical Account of the Expedition against the Ohio Indians* (Philadelphia, 1766), which is of some rarity and great interest. Parkman has told the whole story, somewhat diffusely, in his *Conspiracy of Pontiac*. Curious particulars may be gleaned also from the *Bouquet Papers* (Brit. Museum).

CHAPTER II

1763.
April.
While Bouquet's operations were going forward in the backwoods of America, the Ministry in England was beginning to attack the question of Imperial defence in earnest. Bute, on his resignation, had been succeeded as First Lord of the Treasury by George Grenville, an able, upright, and resolute man, but straitened by a mind of that academic type which is of all least fitted for the government of men. Overtures were made to Pitt to join the Ministry, but without success; and Grenville, who was esteemed a master of finance, was left, unchecked by a statesman's tact, to prosecute his own designs. Careful scrutiny of the working of the Acts of Trade and Navigation quickly revealed to Grenville the fact that they had been systematically violated in America, and that the revenue derived from the custom-houses in the thirteen provinces was not only trifling in itself, but insufficient to pay as much as one-third of the cost of collection. He resolved that this failing should be remedied forthwith; and accordingly, not only were stringent measures devised for enforcing the Acts, but by statute of 1764 new duties were imposed in addition to those already existing. The severity of the new enactment was, however, tempered by the grant of additional bounties and by removal of some of the earlier restrictions, while the terms of the Act expressly reserved the revenue raised under its provisions to defray the cost of protecting the Colonies. In the same session Grenville carried a resolution in favour of the imposition, by Act of the

British Parliament, of certain stamp-duties in the 1764. Colonies, as a further contribution to the cost of colonial defence. These measures all formed part of a scheme for quartering ten thousand British troops permanently in America, who should be paid, in whole or in part, by the Colonies themselves.

That such a garrison was by no means in excess of the requirements of the long Atlantic coast-line and the equally extensive western boundary of the Mississippi can, I think, be contested by no reasonable man. Even if the French had been removed, the Spaniards still held New Orleans and Louisiana, with nominal sovereignty over the whole of the territory west of the Mississippi; while recent experience had shown that the Americans could not be trusted to defend themselves even against Indians. Again, whatever the power of the British Navy for protection, a fleet requires naval bases, and naval bases require garrisons. Nor was the demand upon the Colonists excessive, for the American Colonies had gained more than any other portion of the Empire from the great defeat of France. It is true that in America they had furnished forces exceeding the Imperial troops in number for the expulsion of the French; but in urging this point they conveniently ignored the fact that the sixty thousand men, all paid by England, under Ferdinand of Brunswick, and the British fleets in the Channel and the Mediterranean, had quite as much to do with the conquest of Canada as the squadrons of Holmes and Saunders and the armies commanded by Amherst and Wolfe.

At the first conclusion of peace it is probable that thoughtful Americans foresaw some such scheme; and it is certain that at the beginning of 1764 Benjamin Franklin, the strongest intellect to be found at that time in the whole Anglo-Saxon race, looked upon the quartering of British troops in America as reasonable, and welcomed the prospect for its promise of security not only against foreign invasion but against intestine disorder.[1]

[1] Franklin, *Works*, iv. 89-90.

1764. It is more than probable that Grenville also saw an advantage in the presence of disciplined men to enforce the law in a new country, where the people, from long habits and traditions of self-dependence, were extremely impatient of any restraint; but it is beyond question that nothing was further from his thoughts than injustice to the Colonies. Far from hurrying the Stamp Act forward, he candidly told the agents of the various provinces that he was not wedded to any particular form of tax, that he wanted no more than a contribution to the defence of the Empire, and that he would be quite willing to accept any method of raising it that the Americans might prefer. It is even said that he appealed to the Americans privately through their friends in London, to bear their share of the burden and to save him from resorting to legislation, but was met by a most uncompromising refusal.[1] Be that as it may, in February 1765 he expressed to the agents his willingness to accept a voluntary contribution voted by the Colonial Assemblies, putting only the pertinent question whether the provinces were likely to agree on the proportion that should be paid by each. The agents were silent, for it was written in the history of the Colonies, beyond all denial, that it was hardly possible for any two of them, much less for thirteen, to agree on the simplest and least controversial of measures. The Stamp Act was accordingly introduced and passed almost without comment. It provided for the raising of £100,000 annually, or rather less than a shilling a head on the white population of the North American Colonies, with an express stipulation that every penny of it should be spent in America for defraying the cost of its defence.

Such a measure presents at first sight no visible appearance of oppression; but the year's warning before its final enactment had given time for the manufacture of an agitation, which the strict enforcement of the Acts of Trade made the Colonists only

[1] Speech of Lord Temple, *Parl. Hist.* xix. 846.

too ready to welcome. The profits of smuggling had 1764. been grievously curtailed ; ships had been seized, condemned, and forfeited ; and angry merchants were asking with indignant sarcasm whether, under the new regulations, there were any form of trade which was not reckoned smuggling. The King's ships had been actively employed on the preventive service, and, once welcomed as symbols of British protection, had come to be loathed as engines of tyranny. Loud and bitter 1764-1765. were the complaints of arbitrary and violent proceedings on the part of the King's officers, and of their ignorance of the law, which, in all probability, they knew inconveniently well. In all this there was nothing new, for every attempt from the very beginning to enforce the Acts of Trade had been met with the same outcry, and indeed with something more than outcry. There were probably old men still living in Baltimore and in Boston, who could recall how a Governor of Maryland had shot a revenue-officer dead with his own hand in cold blood, and how a Governor of Massachusetts had brutally assaulted a Captain of the Royal Navy, when the unfortunate officer was still disabled by a wound received in action against the French. The mob of Boston had long ago learned to meet any unpopular measure with lawless violence, and their congregational ministers to search the Scriptures for their encouragement. The trade of Boston was already on the wane, and the town was full of able and ambitious lawyers, panting for a wider sphere of activity and influence, who had carefully laid their train for a violent explosion at the favourable moment. The Stamp Act set the match to this train ; and the populace of Boston rose, wrecked the house of the Commissioner of Customs, attacked and rifled the Custom-house, sacked and burned that of the Chief Justice, who had dared to proclaim his resolution to uphold the law, and released some few of their number, who had been arrested, from the gaol. To stay the riot was impossible, for the only force at the disposal of the

1764-1765. executive was the militia, and the whole of the militia were already employed as rioters. In New York also there were violence and intimidation; and though the rest of the Colonies expressed their feelings by legitimate resolution or remonstrance, there was everywhere a simultaneous manifestation of resentment. The news of the tumult in Boston was received in England with profound dismay. The Colonies, hitherto submissive to the authority of the British Parliament, had rejected it with contumely, and that on so vital a matter as contribution to Imperial defence. To excuse the inconsistency of their long acquiescence in the Acts of Trade with their present attitude towards the Stamp Act, the opponents of that Act drew distinctions between external taxation for regulation of commerce and internal taxation for purposes of revenue. This subtle definition was embraced to the end by Pitt, accepted for a time by Franklin, and maintained or controverted through a wilderness of pamphlets; but it was rejected from the first by Burke, and was soon discarded by the majority of sensible men as meaningless and futile. Nevertheless the Colonists carried their point. Grenville's Ministry 1765. had fallen in July 1765; and after vain endeavours to persuade Pitt to form a government, a weak administration had been brought together under Lord Rockingham. Pitt, in the Commons, warmly espoused the contention of the Colonies, pleading their cause with an intemperance of rhetoric which strengthened the hands of the agitators beyond all estimation. "I rejoice," he said, "that America has resisted. Three millions of people so dead to all the feelings of liberty as voluntarily to submit to be slaves, would have been fit instruments to make slaves of the rest." Wherein the Acts of Trade, to which the Americans had submitted for a century, and to which he himself was indissolubly wedded, were less enslaving than the Stamp Act, he did not pause to explain; but Pitt was guided by passion rather than reason. Had he used his vast influence towards a remodelling of the entire 1765. commercial code, to which course he was bound by the logic of such an utterance as that quoted above, he might have done much to heal the breach between the Mother Country and the Colonies. By acting as he did he contributed more than any man to the widening of it. However, the Stamp Act was repealed, and the wounded pride of England was salved by a Declaratory Act, whereby the authority of Parliament over the Colonies was upheld without any reservation whatever.

Shortly afterwards Rockingham's Ministry, after 1766. useless efforts to secure the adhesion of Pitt, fell from July. power; and Pitt at last consented to place himself at the head of affairs, though at the same time greatly impairing his influence by accepting a peerage as Earl of Chatham. Always on his guard against the possibility of an attack by France and Spain, he attempted, as one of his first measures, to form an alliance of the Northern powers of Europe; but Frederick the Great, the most important power of all, refused to accede to it, and the negotiations ended in absolute failure. Meanwhile the problem of Imperial defence still clamoured for solution, and Chatham had not the remotest idea how to deal with it. Convinced even to bigotry that the commercial prosperity of England depended on the Acts of Trade, he would gladly have seen things revert to their former condition of 1763. But this was now impossible; and, in view of the agitation begun by Otis against the Acts of Trade in 1761, and of the losses caused to the Colonies by the Indian insurrection, it would have been impossible, even if the Stamp Act had never been passed. The movement against the commercial code in America had never ceased. Otis quite logically said that if Parliament had a right to impose the Acts of Trade on the Colonies, it had an equal right to expect obedience to the Stamp Act; wherefore if the latter enactment were unconstitutional, so also were the others; and

1766. he boldly told the merchants of Boston that they were fools to submit to any Imperial restrictions on their trade whatever.[1] The situation was one of extreme difficulty, which was increased by the factious and intemperate language of the Opposition in Parliament, and above all by the resistance, violent beyond all proportion to the provocation, of the Colonists. To do nothing, which was the policy of Chatham and Burke, was no remedy. The Colonists had enjoyed Free Trade under the guise of smuggling for over a century, and had no intention of parting with it. Nothing less than entire recasting of the commercial code would have satisfied them; but there were only two wise men—Burke and Governor Pownall—who would have welcomed such a reform, while Chatham would have raved against it with his dying breath.

Apart from this deadlock on the commercial question, there were troubles of another kind even more intimately connected with the question of Imperial defence. The Americans cherished all the prejudice of their race against a standing Army; and it was made a principal grievance by the agitators that the money to be extorted from them by Act of the British Parliament was to be expended on the maintenance of a permanent force. Such a force, they urged, could be needed only for the abridgment of their liberties; and therewith the story of Pontiac's invasion was conveniently laid aside, and a stream of trash about chains and slavery, hirelings of oppression, brutal instruments of tyranny, and so forth, flowed inexhaustibly from the tongues of orators and the pens of pamphleteers. Even before the Stamp Act there had been refusals to recognise the validity of the Mutiny Act in the Colonies, except in respect of such clauses as contained specific mention of British dominions beyond sea; and when the Act was amended to meet this difficulty, the Assembly of New York persistently evaded the whole of its provisions. Concurrently the

[1] Governor Bernard to Secretary of State, 18th August 1766.

practices of seducing soldiers from the service,[1] of 1766. harbouring deserters, and of buying their arms and clothing, were unchecked by the American magistrates; while if an officer arrested a deserter, the man was claimed from him as an indented servant, and he himself was prosecuted and fined. Officers were even prosecuted and imprisoned for occupying the quarters allotted to them; while magistrates made captious difficulties over granting sites for military storehouses, and were even suspected, in one case, of inciting a mob to destroy a storehouse and to pillage its contents. Georgia followed New York in raising persistent obstacles against the working of the Mutiny Act; and the obstruction rose to such a height that, in 1767, Parliament passed an Act prohibiting all legislation of any kind in the province of New York until provision should have been made for the King's troops. This sharp measure quickly brought the colony to reason; and it is noteworthy that on this occasion Chatham condemned New York's protest against the Mutiny Act as "improper, absurd, excessive in pretension and grossly fallacious in reasoning," uttering not a word about chains and slavery.[2]

Notwithstanding the animosity displayed against the troops in America at this time, they were anything but idle; for the provincial governments were by no means too proud to utilise their services when it suited their purpose. In 1766, when the outcry against the Mutiny Act was at its loudest, there were riots at Albany and elsewhere in New York over a dispute as to the ownership of certain lands. The British troops

---

[1] Even at a time of deadly peril both for America and England, when William III. with great difficulty sent a few hundred men to New York in response to the wailing of the Colonies, the first thing that the Colonists did was to seduce them to desertion, to gain the advantage of their labour. *Cal. S. P. Colonial.* New York, 1694.

[2] Gage to Halifax, 23rd January, 21st December 1765; 22nd February, 11th November, 23rd December 1766; 17th April 1767. *Chatham Correspondence*, iii. 188.

1767. were at once called out, and, having received the fire of the rioters, dispersed them with a single volley and drove them away in flight to the border of Massachusetts, where, amusingly enough, an armed force under a sheriff of that State was waiting to protect the rioters and to fight the British troops if they should cross the frontier.[1] The secret of this mysterious action lay of course in the passionate jealousy of rival provinces; and indeed in the heat of their wrangles over their boundaries, the Colonies took no account of the constitutional principle for which they professed such zeal in their controversy with England. Even in 1770, when that controversy had become inflamed to violent heat, the government at Philadelphia made no scruple of asking for British troops to secure some land that was in dispute between Pennsylvania and Connecticut; a request which was answered by the biting retort that when the courts of law had determined which party was in the right, then, but not till then, the General would, if invited by the civil power, send troops to enforce their decision.[2] Again, endless trouble was made by the back-settlers of Virginia and Pennsylvania, who, despite the terrible warning written in the blood of hundreds during Pontiac's

1767-1768. invasion, returned almost immediately to their evil practices of encroachment and outrage on Indian territory. The officer at Fort Ligonier was compelled to remove a number of these lawless ruffians from the Monongahela River lest they should provoke a fresh onslaught of Indians; but they only returned in larger numbers, the provincial governments being afraid to cope with them. Finally, when the Pennsylvanian government sent a commissioner to conciliate the Indians, the settlers threatened to shoot him, and the General was entreated to provide him with a military escort.[3] In truth, so contemptibly weak and cowardly

[1] Gage to Secretary of State, 26th August 1766.
[2] *Ibid.* 24th April 1770.
[3] *Ibid.* 13th June, 10th October 1767; 21st January 1768.

was the executive in all the provinces, that the people 1767.
could do, and very often did, very much what was
right in their own eyes; and England was hated as
the protectress of native races and as the upholder
of law and order.

The most trying time of all for the unfortunate
British soldier was now close at hand. Soon after taking
office Chatham fell so ill of suppressed gout that he
became unfit to transact any business whatever, and can
hardly be said to have been of sound mind. Though
he remained in name at the head of the Government, the
supreme direction of public affairs passed into the hands
of the Chancellor of the Exchequer, Charles Townshend,
a man of great cleverness, great eloquence, and no
principles. Townshend approached the American question exactly in the spirit that might have been expected
from a spoiled darling of the House of Commons. Seizing hold of the American acknowledgment of England's
right to impose external taxation, he levied duties on
tea and on certain other articles which had hitherto
been free, and assigned the proceeds of these new duties,
estimated at £40,000 annually, not to the defence of
the Colonies, but to the formation of a civil list for
payment of the Governor and of the judges in each
province. Thus the strong foundation of Imperial defence, on which England so far had based her claims, was
abandoned; and everything was sacrificed for the passing gain of a petty controversial triumph. Townshend
died a few months later, but, young though he was, he Sept.
had already lived for a year too long. His foolish
trifling with a great problem set all America seething
once more; and since Massachusetts was rightly
held to be the centre of discontent, General Gage
was ordered, in June 1768, to send to Boston a force 1768.
sufficient to assist magistrates and revenue-officers in
enforcing the law generally, and in particular the Acts
of Trade.

Accordingly, on the 30th of September, Colonel Dalrymple with the Fourteenth and Twenty-ninth Foot and

1768. one company of Artillery with five guns arrived at Boston from Halifax. He was met by a prompt refusal of the local authorities to provide quarters, on the ground that there were barracks on an island in the harbour which must first be filled before quarters could be granted. The plea was strictly legal, and Gage, who was himself on the spot, bowed to the inevitable and quartered the men at the King's expense. Such a beginning promised no easy duty to the troops in carrying out their instructions. Since the passing of the Stamp Act there had been practically no government in Boston but that of the populace. The machinery of municipal administration permitted the assembling of mobs under the name of town-meetings, whenever the agitators might require them; and by dint of wrecking houses, tarring and feathering unsympathetic persons, and the like methods, the revolutionists had intimidated the party of law and order into silence. Yet so admirably was the agitation conducted, so cunningly were its measures chosen to preserve apparent compliance with the letter of the law, and so skilfully were the manifestoes of its leaders drawn up to represent the revolutionists as injured innocents and the party of order as traitors in league with the oppressor, that even shrewd men, unacquainted with the methods of Boston, might well have been misled by them. For there was, I repeat, nothing new in these methods; one and all of them had been in practice almost from the foundation of the city. The state-papers and remonstrances, many of them very ably drafted, with their pretence of humility and submission, their grave and ceremonious insolence, and their frequent shameless perversion of facts; the ready connivance of the magistrates with the violence of the rabble, and their equally ready abuse of legal forms for the perversion of justice and the persecution of persons obnoxious to them; the unblushing partiality of juries, and the inflammatory discourses of congregational ministers—all these things by long tradition came quite naturally to the people of Boston. The student passing from the records, say, of 1683 or 1689 to those of 1775, might 1768. well think that he had turned the page, not of three-quarters of a century, but of a single week. Nor is this matter for surprise, since the settlers of Massachusetts had left England originally as an irreconcilable faction, deeply imbued with the doctrines of republicanism and independence. They had enjoyed something hardly distinguishable from independence during the great Civil War; they had spared no effort of lying and subterfuge—the natural weapons of the weaker party—to retain it after the Restoration. They had made a bold stroke for it by force in 1689; and I have little doubt that, if Sir William Phips had succeeded in taking Quebec, they would have dictated their own terms to King William. Now, with the French expelled from Canada, they had raised the old issue once more, and the British Government had resolved, as in 1684, to meet it by force.

Without entering into any discussion as to the right or expediency of resorting to coercion at Boston, it is certain that, if troops were to be employed at all, they should have been employed in sufficient strength and with sufficient powers. Two weak battalions, together barely numbering eight hundred men, were not an adequate force; and even though these were augmented in January 1769, by the arrival of the Sixty-fourth and 1769. Sixty-fifth, yet they still remained powerless to act until called in by the civil power. To invoke their aid was more than any magistrate's life was worth; yet the Government in England, though perfectly aware of the fact, gave no instructions to the General to proclaim martial law. The result was that the troops were laid absolutely at the mercy of the mob of Boston. In July the Sixty-fourth and Sixty-fifth were removed from the town, and Major-general Mackay wrote to Gage words of significant warning. "Whatever troops are left in the town," he said, "must be ruined in a year. They will be seduced to desert, or driven to desertion by the oppression of the magistrates. A soldier was lately

1769. confined to gaol for some petty theft, tried by the justices, condemned to pay damages to the amount of (I think) seventy pounds, and for not paying has been indented as a slave and sold for a term of years."[1] The reader may be incredulous, but it is an incontrovertible fact that the practice of selling white men into servitude, though condemned by one of the earliest Governors of Massachusetts more than a century before, was still in full usage in this land of liberty.

This was but one of many outrages against the troops. The soldiers were daily accosted by such endearing names as "lobster scoundrel," "red herring," and "bloody back," this last term alluding of course to the results, soon to be experienced by American soldiers under Washington, of a flogging at the halberts. The troops, having strict orders never to strike an inhabitant, whatever the provocation, endured these insults with a forbearance which speaks volumes for their discipline; but this did not save them from most violent and barbarous assaults. Such was the brutality of the worst ruffians of Boston that they would attack a sick man when hardly able to hobble out of hospital; and when reviling the soldiers they always encouraged each other by the words, which were unfortunately too true, "They dare not fire." Once at least the populace tried to break into the guard-room, attacked the relief on its way thither with sticks and stones, and only desisted, though then with precipitation, on the firing of a shot into the air. But the magistrates behaved even worse than the mob. On one occasion a constable came round to the barracks and arrested a soldier who was not named in his warrant; but when his officers appeared on his behalf in court, they were indicted for riot and rescue, and fined. Officers and men were frequently arrested upon frivolous charges and required either to find heavy bail, which when produced was generally refused for no reason whatever, or to go to gaol; then, when the case came up for trial, the prosecution disappeared and

[1] Enclosure in Gage to Secretary of State, 2nd July 1769.

the accused was instantly acquitted.¹ In one such case 1769. the accuser offered a private two hundred dollars to bear false witness against his officer. Again, one justice openly threatened an officer from the bench with the vengeance of the populace, while another encouraged the rabble in court to hail an officer as a " bloody-back rascal." It was small wonder that under such oppression soldiers should have deserted, especially as the mob was always ready to rescue them if arrested ; and it is significant that temptations of another kind were also made to seduce men from their colours, one of the garrison confessing that he had received an offer of fifty pounds a year to go into the country and teach the people their drill. But violence and persecution were the usual measure meted out to the soldier ; and matters reached at length such a pitch that on the application of two privates to General Mackay for redress after a murderous assault upon them, the General was fain to give them half a guinea apiece, and advise them to abandon the prosecution of their assailants, since, however good their cause, there was no redress for soldiers in Boston.²

Such a state of things, notwithstanding the extra- 1770. ordinary forbearance of the troops, could not continue for ever. On the 4th of March 1770, there was an angry altercation between a few soldiers and some rope-walkers, the latter as usual giving the provocation ; and

¹ This again was an old and common trick in Boston. The most notable instance is that of Sir Edmund Andros, the Governor, who was imprisoned by the revolutionists in 1689 and accused of a number of terrible crimes by the Revolutionary Government. A certain number of false affidavits were collected in support of them ; but when the case came before the Privy Council, the accusers, of whom one was a minister of the Gospel, dared not sign the charges, whereupon the case, in the default of prosecutors, was dismissed.

² Gage to Secretary of State, 4th December 1769 ; 12th November 1770. I have been careful to give these details, since Mr. Fiske, generally an impartial writer, has written that " any manifestation of brute force in the course of a political dispute was exceedingly disgusting and shocking " to the Americans. *American Revolution*, i. 71.

1770.
March 5.
on the following day there was a general rising against the troops, who were attacked in the streets with sticks and snowballs. An officer passing by at once ordered the men back to barracks, and the mob then turned upon a sentry before the Custom House, raised a cry of "Kill him," and began to pelt him. Captain Preston hurried down with a sergeant and twelve men to rescue the sentry, and was at once attacked and pelted, the rabble pressing close to the party with ironical shouts of "Fire, fire!" while Preston in advance of his men entreated the assailants to go quietly home. At length one of the soldiers, receiving a violent blow on the arm, either voluntarily or involuntarily fired his musket, though with no effect; and the mob, thinking that the soldiers were loaded with powder only, grew bolder and more violent, till at last, either in desperation or in bewilderment at the eternal cry of "Fire!" all round them, seven of the men did fire without orders, killing four men outright and wounding seven more, two of them mortally. Thus at length the rabble of Boston received a lesson which it needed sorely.

The blame for the bloodshed rests wholly with the magistrates of Boston; and, considering the shameful treatment of the troops during eighteen long months, the populace escaped with very light punishment. Yet still, from sheer weakness of authority, the troops were kept under the heel of the mob. Preston and his party were at once committed to gaol; and Samuel Adams, the leading spirit of the revolutionary party, by threat of a general insurrection actually awed Lieutenant-Governor Hutchinson into withdrawing both battalions to the barracks at Castle William, on an island in the harbour. Had there been, as there ought to have been, five thousand troops in Boston, Hutchinson could have defied Adams; and indeed the populace would never have dared to provoke them. Now, however, the mischief was done. The affray was at once dubbed the Boston Massacre, and sensational reports of it, full of falsehoods, were at once sent to England to regale the friends of the insurgents at home and the British public at large.[1] However, the magistrates and the mob were so plainly in the wrong that two of the revolutionary leaders came forward to defend Preston and his men, of whom all but two were acquitted, and those two but lightly punished. It should be added that thenceforward this trial was always paraded as a specimen of the impartiality of American justice.

Meanwhile, affairs in England were going from bad to worse. Chatham had resigned owing to ill-health in 1768, and the Duke of Grafton, who had been really premier during the greater part of Chatham's reign, resigned also in 1770. No power on earth could induce the hostile sections of the Whig party to work together; and Grafton was the third Prime Minister who had resigned in seven years. It may have been blameworthy, but it is not surprising that, with a set of drivers whose only care was to elbow each other from the box-seat, the King should have taken the reins of Government into his own hands. Lord North succeeded Grafton as chief minister, and almost immediately initiated a new policy of conciliation by removing all the new American import-duties except that upon tea, and pledging the Government to raise no further revenue from America. The reservation of the duty on tea, though no grievance, was the height of folly, for, while gathering practically no money into the Treasury, it afforded to the revolutionary party a pretext for continuing its agitation. Moreover, the whole question of Imperial defence, which was the real point at issue, was still left studiously in the background. Nevertheless, the new policy was not wholly without good effect. For a short time there was a lull in the agitation; and the old commercial relations between the Mother Country and the Colonies, which had been interrupted by voluntary associations of the Americans against the

[1] A good specimen is in the *London Evening Post*, 21st April 1770.

import of English goods, were in great measure resumed. Throughout the years of which I have so far treated, the Army had suffered little apparent change. Ligonier remained as Commander-in-Chief until 1767, though in 1763 he was shamefully ousted from the post of Master of the Ordnance for political ends, in order to make room for Lord Granby, who in due time succeeded him also as Commander-in-Chief. Mr. Welbore Ellis continued as Secretary of War until 1765, when he made way for Lord Barrington, who had enjoyed long experience of the office. The numerical establishment remained practically unaltered on paper from the strength assigned to it in 1763; though in 1769 an important reform was effected by permanently raising the Irish Establishment from twelve thousand to rather over fifteen thousand men, which enabled regiments in Great Britain and in Ireland to be maintained at the same strength. Yet there were troubles and difficulties in the military administration which threatened to become serious. In the first place, there had been reversion to the evil system of employing military penalties to punish officers for political indiscipline. Thus in 1764 Generals Conway and A'Court were deprived of their regiments and Colonel Barré of all his military appointments, because they voted against the Ministers on some matter concerning the arrest of the notorious John Wilkes. In the second place, recruits were so scarce that, although the King rightly judged the Army to be of dangerous weakness and worked his hardest to keep it up at any rate to its attenuated establishment, it was found impossible to fill the ranks with effective men. So great was the cost of obtaining recruits, that officers were loth to part with old soldiers, however inefficient, so long as they could crawl. Strict orders were issued to remedy this evil, but with so little effect that two years later no fewer than eighty men were peremptorily discharged from a single weak battalion on the day after inspection, as unfit for further service.[1] The dearth of recruits was due not to any 1763-1770. new distaste for the service, but to a raising of the general standard of comfort and luxury in all callings except that of the soldier. In a word, the pay of the private soldier was too small; but it was hopeless in the prevailing temper of the House of Commons to expect that it should be increased.

Several causes conspired to make the paucity of recruits of dangerous consequence. French officers had been at work in England all through 1767 and 1768, surveying the southern coast and taking note of the country and of the best military positions inland; and there were even traces of a joint design of France and Spain to surprise and burn the dockyards at Portsmouth and Plymouth.[2] Again, sickness made heavy drains upon the West Indian garrisons, while Pensacola, Mobile, and the posts on the Illinois promised to be as unhealthy as any West Indian island.[3] Finally, in 1770, a Spanish attack upon the British settlements in the Falkland Islands threatened to bring about immediate war. An augmentation of twelve thousand men was at once ordered for the Army; but such was the difficulty of raising even a fraction of them, that, although it was undesirable to enlist Protestants in Ireland and illegal to enlist Papists, recruiting parties were sent into Leinster, Munster, and Connaught to gather in whatever material they might.[4]

The difference with Spain was composed without 1771. war; but already there was another cloud on the horizon. In the newly annexed Island of St. Vincent there was a fierce race of men known as the Black Caribs, bred of the Yellow Caribs, indigenous to the

[1] General Harvey to Secretary at War, 8th December 1767, 19th April 1769.
[2] Mahon, *History of England*, v. 247, 248.
[3] The garrison of Pensacola within six weeks after landing had lost 3 officers, 95 men, and 45 women and children. At Fort Chartres but 19 men out of four companies were fit for duty. Gage to Secretary of State, 3rd February 1769.
[4] *Cal. H.O. Papers*, 11th January 1771.

1771. Archipelago, and of negro slaves who had escaped, or, as tradition goes, had been wrecked on the coast and had taken refuge in the forest. They were not numerous, little exceeding fifteen hundred souls in all; but they were by nature warlike and ferocious, and were secretly encouraged to insubordination by Jesuit missionaries and French agents. They claimed two-thirds of the best and richest land in the island—whether rightly or wrongly I cannot pretend to decide—and were consequently a great obstacle to settlement. After much restlessness they at last, in 1771, took advantage of the transfer of a part of the garrison to Dominica to capture a surveying party, together with its escort of forty men. Attempts were made to conciliate them, to which their only response was an appeal to the French in Martinique and St. Lucia for arms and ammunition, which were covertly though abundantly supplied. In view of the urgent representations of the Governor, the Ministry decided
1772. in April 1772 that the Caribs must be suppressed by force of arms; and orders were sent to General Gage to detach two battalions from America to join those already in the West Indies and others to be embarked from England, for the service. The operations were begun in October; but it would serve no purpose to trace the movements of several tiny columns through the forest of St. Vincent. Suffice it to say that the Caribs, using every artifice of savage warfare, made a brave and stubborn resistance; that the difficulties and suffering of the troops were very great and the impediments to the transport of supplies almost insuperable; but that on the 27th of February 1773 the Caribs were finally forced to submission. Two thousand five hundred men, including six whole battalions and parts of two more,[1] besides artillery and marines, were employed on this petty but troublesome expedition, at the close of which one hundred and fifty men had

[1] The regiments employed were the 6th, 14th, 31st, 32nd, 50th, 68th, six companies of 2/60th, detachments of 70th.

been killed and wounded, over one hundred more were 1772. dead of sickness, and close upon four hundred men in hospital, from which doubtless the majority were carried to their graves.[1]

Throughout 1771 and the earlier months of 1772 the reports of the Commander-in-Chief in America were decidedly encouraging. The alarm of war with Spain seems to have revived the old feelings of loyalty. All the provincial Governors, even those of Rhode Island and Connecticut who were elected by the people, gave assurance of all possible help to the King's recruiting parties; while three regiments, which actually began to enrol recruits, met with such success that Gage felt no doubt of raising the whole of his battalions to their full strength, if occasion should require it. The disputes with the Assemblies of New York and New Jersey as to the quartering of troops also came to an end; and on the removal of a battalion from New Jersey in the ordinary routine of service, many of the people protested with unexpected warmth that their capital ought never to be left without a regiment in garrison.[2] In North Carolina, indeed, there was a rising of some bands of lawless settlers on the western border; but this being no more than a defiance of all constituted authority, such as is common among remote settlers in a new country, was of no Imperial significance, and the insurrection was crushed by the provincial militia in a fierce pitched battle, without the aid of Imperial troops. The whole situation was in fact improved; and it is, I think, probable that a great opportunity was lost, at the close of the dispute with Spain, for removing the tea-duty as a graceful concession to the loyal spirit shown in America, and inviting the colonial agents to a general conference on the subject of Imperial defence.

---

[1] The documents treating of the expedition will be found in the Record Office. *Board of Trade, Grenada,* 1, 3, 5. *America and West Indies,* 8.

[2] Gage to Secretary of State, 2nd April, 6th November 1771; 2nd January, 5th February 1772.

1772. But in 1772 the old mischief sprang up afresh from the enforcement of the Acts of Trade, which, it cannot be too often repeated, were the true root of all the troubles in America. Rhode Island had long been notorious for smuggling, every man from the Governor downwards having an interest in the traffic; and as far back as in 1763 one of the batteries had actually fired upon a King's ship which was in pursuit of a smuggling craft.[1] The King's ship *Gaspee*, commanded by one Lieutenant Duddington, had been particularly active, and, according to American accounts, wantonly predatory in suppressing this illicit trade; and on one June. night in June she had the misfortune to run aground while in chase of an American ship. On the following night she was attacked by eight boats full of armed men, captured after a smart fight in which Duddington was severely wounded, and burned to the water's edge. All efforts to obtain redress were fruitless; the outrage remained unpunished; and yet another triumph was won by the party of violence.

A few months later the agitation in Massachusetts found fresh fuel in a Royal Order that the judges in the province should henceforward be paid by the Crown and should hold office during the Royal pleasure. This measure was doubtless due to the shameful denial of justice to the troops while quartered in Boston, and was designed to secure the legal rights of the loyal as well as of the disloyal in Massachusetts. Obviously, however, it lay open to a different interpretation, while from its purpose it could not but be obnoxious to the revolutionary party; and Samuel Adams was speedily at work. He now made a masterly addition to the existing machinery of rebellion by the institution of committees of correspondence, in order to guide not only every town within the province, but the whole of the provinces together, towards united action. This was in fact the first step towards American Union;

[1] Admiral Montague to the Admiralty, 18th April 1772; Governor Bernard to Secretary of State, 14th December 1764.

and it is a tribute to Adams's genius for organisation 1772. that these committees of correspondence soon found imitation in Europe. The efficiency of the arrangement was soon tested. Vast stores of tea belonging to the East India Company lay at this time unsold in its warehouses, and, since the Company was in extreme financial difficulty, it obtained permission to export 1773. this tea directly to the Colonies. As fate ordained it, Boston was the first port to be entered by the tea-ships. A gang of forty or fifty men, disguised as Indians, under the immediate direction of Samuel Adams, boarded these ships on the 16th of December, and threw the whole of the tea overboard. The magistrates as usual took not the least notice, the troops remained unsummoned at Castle William, and the heroic action [1] (for such appears to be the American view of it) went forward without the slightest risk of interruption. The other Colonies quickly followed this example, and from Boston to Charleston the landing of the tea was prevented by force.

The news of this outbreak was received with not 1774. unnatural indignation in England. On the 7th of March 1774, a Royal Message brought the whole matter before Parliament, which proceeded in due course to pass a series of coercive measures directed against Massachusetts. By these the port of Boston was closed, until peace should be restored and the East India Company indemnified for the destruction of its property. Further, the government of the province was altered so as to confer much additional power on the Crown, though with abridgment of no privilege of the Lower House beyond that of electing the Council. Lastly, power was given to the Governor to transfer to England the trial of any magistrate, revenue-officer, or soldier indicted on a capital charge in Massachusetts, if in the interests of justice he should deem it necessary. Gage, who was in England on leave, was appointed Governor of the

[1] Fiske, i. 90.

1774. province, and empowered by a new Act to quarter soldiers on the inhabitants. It is noteworthy, as a sign of the intense irritation aroused in England by the violent behaviour of Boston, that the Act for closing the port was approved even by such warm partisans of America as General Conway and Colonel Barré. Burke, however, took a different line, reviewing the whole dispute in his celebrated speech on American taxation, a discourse full of profound wisdom in itself, but offering no suggestion except a return to the relations with the Colonies that existed in 1763. For all practical purposes he might as profitably have urged a return to the relations that existed at the time of the flood.

There was yet another Act of this session which, though eminently statesmanlike, provoked greater controversy than any of the preceding, namely, the Quebec Act for fixing the boundaries and regulating the government of Canada. The Ministry, looking to the religion, the traditions, the prejudices, and the expressed wishes of the majority of the Canadians, very wisely determined for the present to abstain from the introduction of representative institutions, trial by jury, or any popular system whatever. The Act also enlarged the boundaries of Canada so as to include outlying districts, not regularly settled, but inhabited chiefly by Frenchmen and controlled by the commanders of military posts ; and finally, it to all intent established the Roman Catholic religion, which was that of more than ninety-nine in every hundred of the population. This last provision woke all the bigotry dormant in the British character. Insular prejudice stood aghast at the thought of a people which could prefer to submit its causes to a skilled judge rather than to twelve unskilled men, who, as experience had repeatedly shown, were not always to be trusted for either honesty, integrity, or moral courage. Orators, pamphleteers, and scribblers raved with voice and pen against the measure, and no one raved more loudly and less intelligently than 1774. Chatham.

The Colonies, having early information of all that was going forward, made their own preparations accordingly. A circular was issued from Boston to the various provinces to concert united action; and at the suggestion of the revolutionary party at New York, a Congress, to which every colony except Georgia sent delegates, assembled at Philadelphia on the 5th of September 1774. It was a curious body, and, to judge by its first action, not a very straightforward one. After drawing up a declaration of rights, Congress issued addresses to the people of Great Britain, of the Colonies, and of Canada. Of these the two first contained, among other matters, a violent attack on the Quebec Act as designed to overthrow the liberty of the Colonies by the pressure of a vast influx of Catholics; while the third artfully insinuated to the Canadians that this same Quebec Act was a danger and a snare to them, and that their only hope of salvation lay in joining with the English Colonies. These productions, though on the face of the matter not admirable even as specimens of lying, are remarkable as indications of the early hunger of the Americans after Canada.

In Massachusetts the coercive Acts proved a complete failure, from the absence of sufficient means to enforce them. The whole working of the new Government was defeated by intimidation of every official appointed by the Crown, and by the setting up of a rival government, which was omnipotent everywhere except under the shadow of British bayonets. Gage found himself helpless, though he had four battalions in Boston, a force which might possibly have saved the situation in 1769, but was now far too small. The troops were encamped on a common just outside the town; and since the revolutionists were busier than ever in the encouragement of desertion, Gage placed a guard on Boston Neck, the

1774. narrow isthmus which connects the town with the mainland. This innocent action was promptly magnified by the agitators into a design to reduce Boston by famine, and went near to bring about a collision July. with the country-people. Matters grew rapidly worse and worse. Relentless intimidation of the loyalists continued; the insurgents began to collect ammunition and military stores, and the young men to assemble to learn their drill; so that at the beginning of the autumn Gage judged it prudent to remove the contents of outlying magazines to Castle William, and to fortify Boston Neck. It was indeed high time, for a provincial congress of Massachusetts had already resolved to raise twelve thousand men, and to invite Connecticut, Rhode Island, and New Hampshire to increase that number to twenty thousand. "If force is to be used at length," wrote Gage on the 30th of October, "it must be a considerable one; for to begin with small numbers will only encourage resistance and not terrify." A fortnight later he issued a proclamation warning the inhabitants against obedience to the revolutionary government; whereupon the populace in Rhode Island rose and seized forty cannon, which were mounted for the protection of Newport harbour. In New Hampshire likewise a small fort in Piscataqua harbour was taken and a large quantity of stores with it. Though no blood had yet been spilt, it was now plain that the quarrel could not be settled without war.

But before entering on the story of this conflict and of the terrible struggle which grew out of it, not with insurgent America only but with half of Europe, it is necessary to the comprehension of its full extent and magnitude to turn for a time to affairs in India.

CHAPTER III

OUR last dealings with India closed with the capture of Pondicherry by Colonel Eyre Coote in 1761, and with the disappearance of the Bourbon flag from the entire peninsula. By the peace of Paris, however, Pondicherry, Chandernagore, and Mahé were restored to France, though a special provision forbade her to erect forts or raise troops in Bengal; but the power of France in the East was none the less broken, though her resentment was naturally stronger than ever. The victory of Badara, it will be remembered, had also destroyed all hope of a Dutch Empire in India, so that the East India Company was delivered for the present from all menace of European rivalry. Its only danger was lest its own failings and vices should bring it into collision with native States, and lest native rulers, taught by their enemies, should introduce into their armies the discipline of Europe.

In Bengal so long as Clive remained at the helm all was well, though the outlook ahead was always threatening. It will be recollected[1] that at the close of 1758 Meer Jaffier, the puppet ruler of Bengal, 1758. Orissa, and Behar, had been compelled by imminent peril of invasion from the west to throw himself on Clive's protection. The invader was Shah Alum, eldest son of the Mogul Emperor, who, as heir to the throne of Delhi and as his father's viceroy, claimed the three provinces as his own. After an abortive siege of Patna, Shah Alum had been repelled almost

[1] Vol. ii. of this *History*, p. 441.

1758. by the mere terror of Clive's name; but he was only one of many enemies to whose aggression the Nabob of Bengal was always exposed. Besides the Emperor there was the Nabob of Oude, who might well cast a greedy eye upon his territory; and above all there were the Mahrattas, ever restlessly seeking to extend their empire, and not yet checked, as before many months they were to be checked, by the crushing defeat of Paniput. A quarrel might arise at any time, for the boundaries within the country were extremely vague; and any English provincial officer was ready to seize any territory that he could, if by chance there were troops at his disposal, in the hope of winning favour with the Company. Thus the situation was full of peril; and it was not long before the peace of
1759. Bengal was again disturbed. In December 1759 Shah Alum for the second time advanced upon Patna, no longer as viceroy but, through the death of his father, as titular Emperor, and therefore enabled to collect a far more formidable force. Clive, however, was not now to take the field against him. Immediately after the quarrel with the Dutch had been brought to an end, he had made up his mind to go home, his health having suffered seriously from the climate and from overwork. For his successor as Governor of Bengal he nominated Mr. Vansittart, and as Commander-in-Chief would fain have appointed Colonel Forde; but, being overruled in this choice by the Court of Directors, he obtained the selection of Major Caillaud, the officer who had so greatly distinguished himself under Stringer
Nov. 27. Lawrence in the South. Two days after Badara, Caillaud arrived with a draft of two hundred men from Madras, and by Clive's order marched with three hundred and fifty Europeans[1] and one thousand
1760. Sepoys for Moorshedabad. There Clive himself joined
Jan. 6. him ten days later, in order to commend him to the good offices of Meer Jaffier, and with considerable difficulty collected a body of the Nabob's native

[1] 300 men of the 101st Foot, 50 European artillery.

troops, under his worthless son Meerun, around 1760.
Caillaud's little nucleus of disciplined men. Finally,
on the 18th of January, Caillaud began his march Jan. 18.
on Patna with a total strength of fifteen thousand
men and twenty-five guns, and Clive returned to
Calcutta. Thence, after making over the government
to Mr. Holwell, pending Vansittart's arrival,
Clive sailed on the 25th of February for England.
With his withdrawal, to use the words of an observer
of the time, " it seemed as if the soul were departing
out of the body of Bengal."

Meanwhile, the Emperor Shah Alum, having Feb.
assembled a sufficient force, had appeared at the
beginning of February before Patna. The disciplined
garrison of the place was trifling, consisting of one
hundred regular European infantry and seventy European
artillery with two guns, three local companies of
all nationalities, and five companies of Sepoys, the whole
under command of Captain Cochrane; but to these
there were added native levies from all quarters, which
raised the total of troops to close on forty thousand
men. Rajah Ramnarain, the native Governor, who held
supreme command at Patna, had strict orders both
from Meer Jaffier and Caillaud to await the arrival of
the army from Moorshedabad, and on no account to
risk an action; but none the less, finding himself in
superior force to the Emperor, he moved out on the
9th of February and offered him battle. Cochrane, Feb. 9.
who had protested in vain against this imprudent step,
decided to keep his contingent in reserve and to take no
part in the action except to protect the Rajah against
injury or capture, which latter duty had been specially
enjoined upon him. After some skirmishing the Emperor's
cavalry charged impetuously down, broke
through Ramnarain's lines, and threw them into confusion.
Several of the Rajah's troops thereupon deserted
in whole bodies to the enemy, but the rest,
rallying on the reserve, for a time held their own. So
hardly were they pressed, however, that the Rajah sent

1760.
Feb. 9.
an urgent message for assistance to Cochrane, who promptly fought his way to him with four companies of Sepoys. For a time this little band stood firm, until, after repelling several attacks, Cochrane and three of his subalterns were killed, and his Sepoys giving way were cut to pieces. A sergeant of the Hundred-and-First with great difficulty rallied a small party of them and succeeded in escorting the Rajah to the Europeans in rear, who were only by great efforts holding their own against large bodies of Mahratta horsemen on both flanks. By this time, out of seven British officers six had been killed, and the command devolved upon the surgeon, Dr. Fullerton, who with great coolness and gallantry brought the remnant of the reserve into Patna, spiking one of the guns, which he had been compelled to abandon, with his own hand.

Fortunately the Emperor did not follow up his success, and Ramnarain, though severely wounded, spared no energy to strengthen the defence of Patna, at the same time entering into negotiation with Shah Alum in order to gain time for Caillaud to arrive. The city was invested, but the siege was not pressed, and on the 19th of February Caillaud and Meerun were
Feb. 20. reported to be no more than thirty miles distant. Shah Alum moved off next day to meet them, and by sunset the advanced parties of both armies were within sight of each other. Caillaud was urgent for attacking on the morrow, but Meerun, after consultation with his astrologers, pleaded for twenty-four hours' delay. On
Feb. 22. the morning of the 22nd, therefore, Caillaud, now reinforced by the small remnant of regular troops from Patna, continued his advance; but so dilatory were the movements of Meerun that, the morning being far spent, he resolved to encamp within three miles of the enemy, and to attack on the following day. While his tents were pitching, Caillaud rode forward to reconnoitre the enemy's position, and, finding all quiet in their camp, occupied two villages which lay a mile beyond his own camping-ground, posting a company of Sepoys in each,

CH. III   HISTORY OF THE ARMY   53

with the remainder of the battalion a little in rear. 1760.
Observing these dispositions, the enemy advanced some Feb. 22.
heavy guns, with cavalry and infantry in support; to
which Caillaud replied by moving the whole battalion
of Sepoys into the village and reinforcing them with a
company of Europeans and two guns. So matters
rested for an hour, when Caillaud perceived that the
enemy had struck their camp and were in full march
against him. Thereupon he formed his first line of
battle between the two villages, the Europeans occupying the centre, with three guns on either hand, and
on each flank of the guns a battalion of Sepoys, with a
single company in each village. The second line was
assigned to Meerun's troops, which were directed to take
station in the rear of the British with the cavalry extended to right and left; instead of which Meerun
massed the whole of them in a deep column to the
right rear of the British, showing a front of but two
hundred yards with the whole of his thirteen thousand
men.

Shah Alum was not slow to take the advantage
offered to him by such a disposition. Advancing with
his army in three divisions, he launched one of them
upon the left of Caillaud's line, as if to seize the village
of Seerpore, on which rested the British left flank.
Caillaud thereupon pushed his guns slightly forward
and raked this division with so hot a fire as speedily to
check the movement. But in truth this attack was but
a feint, though one party of horse did indeed sweep
round Caillaud's left to the rear of Seerpore, where, being
unable to resist the temptation to plunder the camp, it
passed at once out of action. The remainder wheeled
rapidly away to Caillaud's right, and together with the
two other divisions fell fiercely upon Meerun's unwieldy column, which showed little sign of resisting the
attack. Caillaud therefore moved the whole of his six
guns to the village on his right and opened a heavy
cannonade upon the flank of Meerun's assailants; but,
notwithstanding the cross-fire of the British battery and

1760.
Feb. 22.
of Meerun's artillery, the Mogul horse charged gallantly home, drove Meerun's gunners from their guns, and threatened to make havoc of his entire force. Worse than this, four of the British gun-carriages broke down in the rough heavy ground whereon they were posted, and for a time the guns were out of action. It was a critical moment, but Caillaud was equal to it. Taking personal command of the right-hand battalion of Sepoys, he led them straight upon the enemy's flank, poured in a volley at forty yards' range, and charged with the bayonet. The Emperor's troops recoiled in heavy, confused masses, and the Sepoys plied the steel among them with murderous effect. This counter-attack gave time to Meerun's cavalry to rally, when they charged with vigour and scattered the enemy in all directions. In half an hour Shah Alum's host had vanished from the field, and after four hours of anxious work, though with trifling loss to his own troops, Caillaud was able to mark his first victory in command of the Bengal army with the name of Seerpore.

Shah Alum fell back sixteen miles to Behar, and Caillaud was impatient to pursue his success and end the campaign; but Meerun, who, though he had showed abject cowardice in the field, had been slightly wounded by an arrow, thought it necessary to withdraw to Patna, where his army encamped about the city while he enjoyed himself within. At last, on the 29th, he joined Caillaud for the march on Behar, but moving in his usual
March 2. dilatory style did not reach it until the 2nd of March, when it was discovered that Shah Alum had made two forced marches towards Bengal, and having thus got well in the British rear was hastening to occupy certain districts which had promised him support. Even Meerun now realised the danger of the situation. He and Caillaud at once started off in hot pursuit, and in four days had nearly overtaken the enemy, whose way was barred by a swollen river. Had Caillaud been in supreme command, he would have lost no time in making a night attack, but Meerun as usual was

obstinately obstructive, and the Emperor escaped to 1760. the south-west, through a country of hill and jungle which was absolutely unknown to his pursuers, with the British in hot chase and Meerun following leisurely behind them. On the 4th of April Meer Jaffier, with a reinforcement of five hundred of the Hundred-and-First, as many Sepoys, and a few artillerymen with six light guns, joined the allied forces at Mungulkote on the Adjee, and Caillaud seized the opportunity to send two hundred Europeans under Captain Fischer to garrison Moorshedabad. He then pressed on after Shah Alum, only to discover, after another opportunity of attack lost through the perversity of Meerun, that this miserable ally was making secret overtures of friendship to the Emperor. Continuing the pursuit, nevertheless, he on the 7th April arrived over against Shah Alum's April 7. camp, which lay on the south bank of the Dummooda, and prepared to force the passage of the river; but the Emperor, without awaiting the attack, set fire to his tents and withdrew beyond touch of Caillaud's troops, when he suddenly doubled round and hastened back to northward. He had lost his chance of surprising Moorshedabad, but he might hope for better success at Patna.

Caillaud's situation was now embarrassing in the extreme, and not the less so for that the purport of the Emperor's clever movement was not discovered for some days. Meerun was known to be a traitor; and Shah Alum had been careful to leave a large body of Mahrattas behind him, which, in the unsettled state of the surrounding districts, absolutely forbade Caillaud to follow him with his entire force. Patna itself was held by but a handful of Sepoys; and worse than all, M. Law, with a corps of French adventurers, had come to terms with Shah Alum and was waiting before it for the arrival of the Mogul troops in order to carry the city before the British could send succour. Happily, Captain Knox with a small reinforcement had recently reached Burdwan, close at hand; and to him, with the

1760. honours of Masulipatam and Badara still thick upon
April him, Caillaud entrusted two hundred men of the Hundred-and-First, one battalion of Sepoys, and a detachment of artillery with two guns. Knox's orders were to march northward with all speed to Rajmahal, cross the Ganges there so as to avoid all risk of interception by the Emperor's troops, and thence to follow the left bank to Patna, recrossing the river so as to aid in the defence of the city. Caillaud himself after several days' halt fell back at the end of April to Moorshedabad.

Meanwhile, at Patna all was dismay. Ramnarain's troops were much dispirited by their recent defeat, and apart from them but three hundred Sepoys could be collected for defence of the city, so that Law, had he made the attempt, could easily have overpowered the garrison with his own force alone. Happily, though he encamped for a time before the walls, he moved down to join Shah Alum at Behar; and thus time was gained to make preparations for defence, which were pressed with great energy by Shitab Roy, a Hindoo officer of great ability and pre-eminent courage, and by Dr. Fullerton, who was the only English officer present. Shortly afterwards the siege was opened under the scientific direction of Law. The walls were speedily breached in several places, and an escalade, attempted five days after the opening of the trenches, was only with difficulty foiled by the bravery of Fullerton and Shitab
April 28. Roy. At dawn of the 28th of April a second attack was delivered, when the Emperor's flag was actually planted on the ramparts by one of his bravest officers; but Fullerton and his little band of Sepoys hurried to the spot, and after a desperate conflict hurled back the assailants with heavy loss. But the walls of the city now lay open in all directions, another assault might come at any moment, and the defenders, worn out by fatigue after their success, were reduced almost to despair; when, with the breaking of broad daylight, there appeared on the other side of the river a cloud of

dust creeping nearer and nearer until there emerged 1760.
from it first a gleam of firelocks and then a solid array of
red coats. It was Knox's detachment, which in thirteen
days' march under the Indian sun had traversed three
hundred miles, the passage of the Ganges included.
Boats were sent across to them, and before sunset the
whole force had entered the city, fatigued indeed by
long strain and many privations, but elated by the
success of their marvellous effort. One secret of their
spirit may be found in the fact that Knox had tramped
every yard of the way with them on his own feet.

But the indefatigable leader did not yet seek rest. At
nightfall he crept out with two of his officers towards
the enemy's position, mastered the several approaches
to it with its points of strength and weakness; and at April 29.
noon on the following day, while the Emperor's troops
were enjoying their siesta or preparing their midday
meal, fell suddenly upon them and drove them in panic
from their camp, capturing it at a stroke with the whole
of their guns, stores, and ammunition. The enemy then
fell back to Gya Maunpore, some sixty miles to southward, abandoning the prosecution of the siege. But this
relief of Patna was but momentary, for meanwhile a new
danger had arisen. The Nabob of Purneah, Kuddum
Hoosein, who owed allegiance to Meer Jaffier and only
in the previous month had solemnly avowed it, finding
himself released from supervision by British troops,
openly embraced the cause of Shah Alum, and set out
to join him with an army of sixteen thousand horse and
foot. Caillaud and Meerun at once marched in pursuit
of him along the southern bank of the Ganges, but
Kuddum Hoosein's force had gained too long a start
to be overtaken; and in this critical situation Caillaud
could do no more than send instructions to Knox to
hamper the march of this new enemy by all practicable
means, and if possible to prevent him from joining the
army of Shah Alum. By the 14th of June Kuddum June 14.
Hoosein had reached Hadjipore, on the north side of
the Ganges, over against Patna; and on the 15th Knox,

1760.
June 15.
to the amazement of that bewildered city, very calmly led his handful of troops across the river to oppose his passage. So desperate seemed the adventure that Ramnarian's troops shrank from it; and only Shitab Roy gathered together his own little band of two hundred men, chiefly cavalry, and, deaf to all dissuasion from Ramnarain's generals, resolved to throw in his lot with the English commander.

Knox's sole chance of success was to fall upon his enemy by surprise; wherefore, on hearing that Kuddum Hoosein was but ten miles distant from him, he marched off soon after the middle of that same
June 16. night to attack. But fortune sided against him. His guides mistook their way, and after several hours of fruitless wandering in the dark the troops returned weary and harassed to their camp. Hardly had they enjoyed an hour's rest, when Kuddum Hoosein's army appeared in sight, more numerous than had been either reported or supposed. But it was not for nothing that Stringer Lawrence had faced the swarms of Mahratta horse in the plain before Trichinopoly, and Knox was not for a moment dismayed. Leaving a single company of Sepoys to guard his camp, he boldly advanced, took up an advantageous position, and forming his troops in a hollow square awaited attack. He had but two hundred of the Hundred-and-First Foot and about six hundred Sepoys, which added to Shitab Roy's troopers made up a total of between one thousand and eleven hundred men, with five field-guns. Meanwhile the enemy drew nearer and nearer, six thousand horse and ten thousand foot, with thirty guns; and now their columns parted to right and left until they enclosed Knox's little band on every side. At about six o'clock the attack began, and for the next six hours charge after charge of cavalry was delivered against the ranks of the square, only to be shattered to pieces by deadly showers of grape and musketry, or turned back discomfited at the bayonet's point;

while Shitab Roy's squadrons hovered about, ever ready to give aid where the enemy pressed hardest. Once only, when the troops after long hours of fighting were ready to sink with fatigue, did the Sepoys give way; and then it seemed as if the whole of the devoted little band must be overwhelmed. But Knox led his own Grenadier Company of the Hundred-and-First to a fierce counter-attack which relieved the Sepoys, giving them time to rally and recover lost ground. At length, about noon, Kuddum Hoosein, wearied out by repeated failures, gave the order to retreat, leaving behind him four hundred dead upon the ground, three elephants, and eight guns. Knox instantly followed him, capturing and blowing up several ammunition-waggons; nor was it until dusk that he desisted from the pursuit and ordered the troops to bivouac for the night.

1760.
June 16.

Meanwhile the threatened city of Patna had suffered agonies of apprehension. Very early in the day a party of the enemy had overwhelmed Knox's camp-guard and plundered the camp; and a stream of panic-stricken fugitives had poured across the river with wild stories of disaster. But still for hour after hour the thunder of cannon continued, and the distant cloud of smoke grew denser, giving good hope that all might yet be well. At noon the cannonade ceased, and presently even the mutter of the musketry fell silent; and then came explosion after explosion, moving further and further from the field of battle, but none could tell that these signified the destruction of the enemy's tumbrils. Finally, after the closing of dusk, Knox and Shitab Roy, grimed with smoke and dust, came into the city alone, with not a man of their force at their back; and then men's hearts misgave them that the worst had come, and that these alone were left of the troops that had marched in such brave array out of the walls. It was long before the two leaders could persuade them that they were indeed victorious; but when at length the terrified townsfolk

1760. accepted the truth, they were more than ever assured of the invincibility of the British; and the fame thus gained was soon to stand the conquerors in good stead. Yet it was to Shitab Roy that Knox awarded the palm of valour on that day; and it is probable that but for the commemoration of the fact in one of the greatest of English essays, few Englishmen would ever have heard of the astonishing action which bears the name of the battle of Beerpore.[1]

But it was to obtain supplies and not to sing praises that Knox had returned to Patna. His losses had not been great, one European officer and sixteen men of the Hundred-and-First only having been killed, besides a larger number of Sepoys, and he was determined to give his enemy no rest; so returning forthwith to his army, he resumed the chase of Kuddum Hoosein, who was retiring north-westward upon Bettiah. On the

June 22. 22nd of June Caillaud and Meerun arrived at Patna, and, recalling Knox's detachment to garrison the city, took up the pursuit in his stead. Impeded by a large train of supplies, Kuddum Hoosein made but slow

June 25. progress, and on the 25th he was overtaken. Though he had occupied a strong position with twenty-two guns, Caillaud hesitated not for a moment in deploying for attack and marching straight upon him, when the enemy after a feeble resistance fled, leaving the whole of their artillery and baggage and a large quantity of stores behind them. Meerun, as usual, was dilatory in bringing his troops forward, and thus, not for the first time, the British commander was balked of striking a decisive blow through his dependence on native allies for cavalry.

[1] "On that memorable day on which the people of Patna saw from their walls the whole army of the Mogul scattered by the little band of Captain Knox, the voice of the British conquerors awarded the palm of gallantry to the brave Asiatic." Macaulay, *Warren Hastings.*

This is of course a rhetorical statement, for the people could not see more than a distant cloud of smoke, and the army was not the whole army of the Mogul. *Seir Mutaqherin*, ii. 118-113.

CH. III   HISTORY OF THE ARMY   61

None the less Caillaud continued the pursuit for 1760. another week, when a sudden accident brought the expedition abruptly to a close. On the 2nd of July July 2. Meerun was killed by lightning; and the death of their leader, miserable creature though he was, threatened to bring about instant dissolution of his forces. Happily Caillaud, by his influence with the officers and by promises to procure payment of the men's arrears, was able to keep them together for a time; but he considered active operations too hazardous under such unsatisfactory conditions, and retired to Patna, where he arrived on the 29th of July. The July 29. monsoon being at its height, he put his troops into cantonments, Shah Alum being then encamped about thirty miles to westward. The native troops, only for the moment pacified by Caillaud's promises, at once began to desert to the Emperor in large numbers, and from them the infection spread to the Sepoys. The pay even of the European troops was four months in arrear, and the whole outlook was so serious that Caillaud was not reluctant to hand his command over Sept. 10. to Knox and to obey a summons to attend the new Governor, Mr. Vansittart, at Calcutta.

At headquarters the results of Clive's departure had already betrayed themselves. The Government was in serious financial straits, the servants of the Company were given over to rapacity and corruption, and the whole of the dominions under the nominal rule of Meer Jaffier were filled with misery and discontent. The death of Meerun raised a question as to the succession to the throne, which was cleverly turned to account by Meer Cossim, son-in-law to Meer Jaffier and an extremely able man, who had been deputed by the Nabob to welcome Vansittart. On arriving at Calcutta, Meer Cossim quickly perceived that he could buy his own terms of the Council, and by expenditure of about £175,000 obtained a treaty whereby he was appointed Meer Jaffier's successor and deputy, with immediate powers so absolute as virtually

1760. to supersede those of his nominal master. Caillaud opposed this treaty and would be no party to it, but it is to be feared that Captain Yorke, who had behaved so gallantly at Masulipatam, was troubled by no such scruples. Meer Jaffier, naturally objecting to these arrangements, was surrounded by troops and carried to Calcutta, where provision was made for him to pass the remainder of his days in comfort and obscurity.

Meer Cossim for his part lost no time in forcing the favourites of Meer Jaffier to disgorge their ill-gotten gains and sending the money thus obtained to fill the empty treasury at Calcutta. No service could have been more welcome to the British; and Caillaud was presently despatched to Patna with a sum sufficient to discharge the arrears due to the British troops. The rest of the year was employed in small expeditions for the reduction of disturbed and disaffected districts to order, one incident in which led to very momentous consequences. It so happened that in the course of the operations a body of five-and-twenty thousand native troops was dispersed with heavy loss by a combined movement of two tiny parties of regular soldiers upon its front and rear simultaneously. To the British officers such a feat was too familiar to arouse unusual interest; far other was its effect on Meer Cossim, who was present, and who was so greatly impressed by the precision and order of the manœuvre that he resolved from that moment to form an army trained and disciplined by Europeans.

At the end of 1760 Caillaud returned to Madras, leaving to Major Carnac the task of finishing the war against Shah Alum, who had now fixed his headquarters at Behar, with detachments posted between the Sone and the Fulgo, for the purpose of levying contributions.

1761. Having with immense difficulty induced the remnant of Meerun's army to join him, Carnac marched upon
Jan. 15. Behar, and on the 15th of January engaged the Emperor's army at Suan, almost six miles to westward of that town. The action opened none too favourably

for the British, but a lucky shot from a field-gun 1761. wounded the elephant on which Shah Alum was riding, and the animal, maddened by pain and fright, rushed away with him from the field. The enforced flight of their leader spread panic and confusion among the Emperor's troops, and Carnac, seizing the moment to reform his line, soon swept them from the field. Law and about a dozen French officers alone stood firm with a handful of men, but surrendered and were dismissed on parole. Though the victory was by no means decisive, Shah Alum was greatly disheartened, and a fortnight later, finding himself much straitened Jan. 29. for supplies, he made overtures for a cessation of hostilities. After some parley this was granted, and on the 14th of February Shah Alum was escorted by British troops into Patna, where Meer Cossim was induced to meet him and was formally installed as Nabob of Bengal, Orissa, and Behar. The Emperor would gladly, if he could, have obtained a like escort of British to place him on the throne of the Moguls. It was true that his claim thereto had been recognised by the chief of the Afghan conquerors, who for the second time within twenty years had sacked Delhi, and only a few weeks before had overthrown the Mahrattas on the terrible field of Paniput; but he Jan. 7. knew too well that his right could only be established by force. For some time he lingered in the vain hope that British bayonets would encompass him on his entry into Delhi; and then, yielding to the invitations of several leading chiefs, he reluctantly turned his back upon the red-coats and marched westward to take his throne for himself. So Meer Cossim was left untroubled in his new dominions.

CHAPTER IV

1762. REMEMBERING what Meer Jaffier had been in the hands of the English, and determined to be no such puppet himself, Meer Cossim took care first to make himself master, and independent master, within his own domain. His earliest step was to remove all the greedy favourites of Meer Jaffier, his next to pay off the whole of his debts to the English, his third to form himself a regular army on the European model. By the end of 1762 he had, by strict and able administration, achieved the two first of these objects, and had done much towards the accomplishment of the third. He shifted his capital from Moorshedabad to Mongeer, as remoter from the sphere of English influence, and covered it with strong fortifications; and seeking out European adventurers from all quarters, entrusted the making of his army to them. Reinhard, an Alsatian, who was known as Sumroo, and Markar, an Armenian, were the most prominent of these foreigners, while useful tools were found also in two more Armenians, named Aratoon and Gurghis Khan. Within a year Meer Cossim had raised twenty-five thousand infantry and a regiment of excellent gunners, the latter almost to a man European, all equipped in every respect in the European fashion and fit for immediate service. He had further established a cannon-foundry, which could produce weapons as good as those from Woolwich itself. But apart from all military measures, he had a conscientious desire as a ruler to do his best for his subjects; and it was in this laudable work that he found himself embarrassed at every turn by the rascality and corruption of the East India Company's servants. I have no space here to tell the disgraceful story of those years : it must suffice that the English lost all sense of civilised feeling in their mad lust after riches, and developed a positive genius for exaction. The final cause of rupture between Meer Cossim and the English was the insistence of the latter on certain privileges of trade which they had most shamefully abused. Failing to obtain redress by pacific remonstrance, the Nabob took matters into his own hands by proclaiming all trade to be free and preparing to uphold his edict, if necessary, by force. The Council at Calcutta, long accustomed to bully without receiving a blow in return, was taken aback, and treated the Nabob's action as equivalent to a declaration of war.

1762.

1763.

As early as in the middle of April orders were issued to the British troops for the expected campaign ; but at the urgent representation of Vansittart and Warren Hastings the Council consented to send two of its members, Mr. Hay and Mr. Amyatt, to remonstrate with the Nabob. While negotiations were still going forward, however, it came to Meer Cossim's knowledge that Mr. Ellis, a member of Council and the Company's agent at Patna, was making preparations to seize that city. Naturally he protested against such treachery, but the Council refused to hear him ; and meanwhile, in the false belief that Hay and Amyatt had left Mongeer, and in the hope of anticipating the despatch of the Nabob's reinforcements from thence, Ellis thought fit to hasten his attack on Patna. Early in the morning of 25th June the British troops at the factory, some three hundred Europeans and twenty-five hundred Sepoys in all, scaled the walls of the sleeping city and possessed themselves almost unresisted of the whole of it, excepting the citadel, which was held by only a weak garrison. Instead, however, of overpowering this petty stronghold while panic was

June 25.

yet alive, most of the English officers returned to the factory to breakfast, while the troops, under no restraint, betook themselves to plunder. Never were carelessness and indiscipline more speedily punished. Markar with a brigade of Meer Cossim's regular infantry was already on march for Patna, and, on receiving news from fugitives of all that had gone forward, determined to attempt the recapture of the city. Within two hours of the British attack he was at the eastern gate, where there had been posted a detachment of British artillery with two guns. The British officer in command at once collected such troops as he could, and awaited the attack, which, however, was so skilfully conducted by Markar that the British detachment, after enduring for some time a destructive fire of rockets and musketry, was compelled to spike its guns and retire. The remainder of the men, dispersed as they were all over the city in search of plunder, were seized with panic and fled headlong to the factory, leaving the recovery of the town as easy a task to Markar as had been their own conquest. Markar at once invested the factory, which as was usual was fortified, and pressed the British so hard that on the 29th of June they crossed the Ganges and marched towards Chupra, hoping to gain the frontier of Oude, the Nabob of which province was on friendly terms with the Company. The rains, however, had now set in with great violence; the troops had no provisions and little ammunition; the whole population was against them; Markar's brigade was in hot chase of them from the south, while Sumroo's brigade, which was hastening to the relief of Patna from the west, crossed the Ganges near Arrah to cut off their retreat. Despite all difficulties the British fought their way to the village of Manjee, where they sighted Sumroo's brigade in their front. The situation was hopeless, yet it was only such as men like Clive, Forde, and Knox had turned to triumphant account. Above all things it called for vigorous attack upon Sumroo in front, since it was too late to double back against Markar in rear. But the troops were discouraged, weary, half starved, and drenched to the skin; and their commander, Captain Carstairs, was not the man to infuse new life into them. In an evil moment he decided to stand on the defensive, and took up a position in the usual formation, with his Europeans in the centre, two battalions of Sepoys to right and left of them, and a third battalion in reserve. The first attack of the enemy was gallantly repelled by the Sepoys on the right, who, having exhausted their ammunition, charged with the bayonet; and had this offensive movement been followed up, the day might have been saved. But the Europeans, exhausted by fatigue and disorganised by the disaffection of several Frenchmen in their ranks, could not or would not move. Reinforcements arrived to strengthen the enemy, and at length, after Carstairs with eight other officers and fifty European soldiers, besides a number of Sepoys, had fallen, the remainder of the British force laid down their arms. The survivors were sent prisoners to Patna, where most of the foreigners entered Meer Cossim's service. Many of the Sepoys also enlisted in his army, while the rest were stripped of their arms and equipments and released. In a word, one-fourth part of the British army of Bengal was annihilated.

1763. July 1.

This was a crushing disaster. Meer Cossim wrote at once to the Council at Calcutta repudiating certain concessions, which he had made in order to gain the sovereignty of the three provinces. The Council replied by declaring Meer Cossim to be deposed, and by restoring old Meer Jaffier—who undertook to grant the whole of the said concessions and even more—to his former position. But the real issue was to be decided by force; and to meet this issue Meer Cossim had forty thousand men, more than half of them well trained, with a well-stocked treasury and plenty of arms and ammunition; whereas on the British side the Govern-

1763. ment was demoralised, the treasury was empty, and the entire force at disposal for the field, after the calling in of every detachment, did not exceed five thousand men. Given equality of generalship, the result of the contest was hardly doubtful. On the one side stood Meer Cossim, whose military capacity was at best untried; on the other Major Thomas [1] Adams, who had lately succeeded to the command in Bengal, an officer of the school of Clive.

July. In spite of the orders issued for the march of troops in April, nothing was ready in Calcutta in July. The greatest difficulty was experienced in procuring transport and supplies; and Adams actually started on his campaign with but one thousand pounds in his military chest. The force first committed to him consisted of the remains of Coote's regiment,[2] four companies of the Hundred-and-First, a weak corps of French infantry under Lieutenant Martine,[3] which had taken service with the British after the fall of Pondicherry, one company of artillery with ten guns, and three weak battalions of Sepoys—making up a total strength of eight hundred and fifty Europeans and fifteen hundred Sepoys. In addition to these, about two hundred Europeans and one thousand Sepoys, together with two troops of Mogul horse and as many of British cavalry, were on their way to join Adams from the region of Burdwan; Moorshedabad being named by him as the place of junction. But before Adams could reach Moorshedabad, Meer Cossim had sent thither an overwhelming force which speedily captured the garrison of British Sepoys; which done, he pushed forward a respectable corps under Mohammed Taki Khan, one of his best generals, to Plassey, in order to hold Adams's

---

[1] Broome gives his name as John; and Colonel Malleson, always careless, of course follows him. But his real name was Thomas.
[2] The regiment which fought at Wandewash and was then numbered 84th.
[3] The founder of the Martinière College at Lucknow.

main army in check, and disposed three smaller corps on the western bank of the Bagiruttee to intercept the detachment from Burdwan. Owing to want of transport the advance of Adams was so slow that he did not reach Cutwa until the 16th of July, from whence he crossed the Bagiruttee to Agurdeep, about three miles south of Plassey, little knowing that on that very day the first action of the campaign was actually in progress a little to westward of Cutwa. A valuable convoy of supplies, including twenty thousand pounds in specie for the use of the army, was on its way to Agurdeep from Burdwan, under command of Lieutenant Glenn, when it was attacked near the Adjee river by one of Meer Cossim's outlying corps, composed of almost seventeen thousand irregular troops, chiefly cavalry, but fortunately without a single cannon. Glenn's escort numbered no more than from five to six hundred Sepoys, with a few sergeants of the Hundred-and-First and a detachment of Artillery with six guns ; but he promptly took up a position on some rising ground amid a network of ravines, posted his treasure and cattle in rear, and coolly awaited attack. The enemy, greedy for plunder, swept down upon him with great determination ; but the ground was too much broken to be favourable to cavalry, and the first attack was beaten off by the usual fire of grape and musketry. Maddened by loss and failure, the enemy redoubled their efforts, and delivered charge after charge with the greatest courage and resolution. Thrice the guns and treasure were captured and thrice they were recovered at the bayonet's point by the Sepoys with the British sergeants at their head ; till at last after four hours of heavy fighting the enemy drew off, heavily punished, leaving Glenn in possession of his convoy but with hardly a man of his few Europeans alive. After waiting a few hours, however, Glenn pushed on to Cutwa, where he had expected to join Adams; but finding the place occupied by a small force of the enemy, he attacked forthwith, took it without difficulty, and thus added a large quantity of

1763.

July 16.
July 17.

1763.
July 17.
July 19.

grain and a number of bullocks to the stores which he had brought with him for the army. So gallant a day's work was no ill opening for the campaign.

Having picked up Glenn's detachment, Adams on the 19th advanced with his whole force to encounter Mohammed Taki Khan, who had moved forward to a strong position almost opposite to Cutwa. The irregular troops, which had been so roughly handled by Glenn, sulkily held aloof from their leader on account of some petty quarrel, and remained in rear at too great a distance to take part in the fight; but Mohammed Taki Khan, without heeding them, exhorted his own troops to put an end by one victory to foreign rule in Bengal, and advanced gallantly to meet the British. He had some reason to hope for success, since his army included a chosen corps of *jezailchees*, chiefly Afghans, Rohillas, and Persians, who bore a very high character alike as soldiers and as marksmen. Details of the action are rather obscure; but it should seem that Mohammed Taki Khan stood at first on the defensive, and that Adams's advanced troops after suffering heavily from a deadly fire of *jezails* and rockets were driven back on the main body. Elated by this success, Mohammed Taki then took the offensive, and with great numerical superiority in his favour fought a very desperate fight, apparently alternating the fire of cannon and *jezails* with furious charges of cavalry. The British stood firmly as was their wont; the fire of their artillery and musketry was as deadly as usual, and the horsemen that passed through it unscathed could never break the wall of bayonets. But the fighting was very severe; the handful of British cavalry could avail nothing against the masses of the enemy, and at length Mohammed Taki, observing some unsteadiness in the ranks of the Sepoys, rode off to lead a final and decisive attack. At that moment his foot was grazed and his horse killed under him by a cannon-shot; but heedless of pain he mounted another horse, and placed himself at the head of a chosen corps of Afghan cavalry for a supreme effort against Adams's right flank. That flank rested on a 1763. watercourse wherein Adams, with excellent judgment, July 19. had disposed a single company of Sepoys *en potence*, concealing the men in the jungle upon the bank. To this point Mohammed Taki now led his Afghan squadrons with all the impetuosity of a dashing and intrepid cavalier. As he swept past the front of the British battalions he was struck by a bullet in the shoulder. He whirled the skirt of his garment over the wound in order to hide the blood, galloped on, followed by his men, into the nullah, and was ascending the opposite bank, when up rose the hidden Sepoys from their ambush and poured a volley full into their faces. A bullet flew into Mohammed Taki's brain, and he fell with a half-spoken curse on the colleagues who had failed him. The men at his back, startled by the fire and dismayed by the fall of their leader, took to flight; and the entire army gave way and fled, leaving the whole of their artillery and stores, besides an acceptable supply of cattle, behind them. Nor did they rally until they reached the detachments in rear, which, had they been in front, would have won the day for Meer Cossim.

The loss of the enemy was very heavy and that of the British considerable.[1] Adams halted on the field in sight of the hunting-lodge of Plassey, and gave Clive as the parole and Plassey as the countersign for the night. The three following days were spent in forming an hospital and a magazine at Cutwa, and in replenishing supplies; and on the 23rd the army resumed its march upon Moor- July 23. shedabad. The enemy had entrenched a position two miles south of the city, but made no attempt to hold it, retiring on their main defences at Sooty, some thirty-five miles to the north-west and on the western side of the Bagiruttee. Adams accordingly occupied Moorshedabad, into which Meer Jaffier was escorted with due ceremony on the 25th. The change of government was not July 25.

[1] No details of the casualties seem to exist. Two European officers were killed.

1763.
July 27.
unpopular; and on the 27th, Adams, having left a small garrison behind him, crossed the river accompanied by Meer Jaffier, with such followers as he had been able to collect.

So far Adams's campaign, conducted in the very hottest season of the year, had been difficult enough, though none but irregular troops had been opposed to him; but there now confronted him the more formidable task of beating Meer Cossim's disciplined regiments under scientific leaders. Reinforced at Moorshedabad to a strength of one thousand Europeans [1] and four thousand Sepoys, with Carnac as second in command and Knox as quartermaster-general, he continued his march up the right bank of the Bagiruttee, and at dawn

Aug. 2. on the 2nd of August came upon the enemy on the plains of Gheria, astride of the road to the north. Meer Cossim had already entrenched a strong position at Sooty, from which it would have been extremely difficult to dislodge him; and his advance to meet Adams in the open field can be explained only by confidence in the numbers and discipline of his troops. His force counted close upon forty thousand men. The regular brigades of Sumroo and Markar were in line in the centre, commanding the great road. On their right was a corps of some eight thousand cavalry and twelve thousand infantry, partly regular and partly irregular troops; and on their left stood a smaller body of irregular cavalry with its left flank resting on the Bagiruttee. The enemy's artillery numbered sixteen guns. Adams, having crossed the Banslee river, formed his troops across the angle between this stream on his left and the Bagiruttee on his right, so that both of his flanks were protected. His line was formed as usual with two European battalions in the centre and three Sepoy battalions on either flank of them; and of his ten guns, four were posted in pairs at each extremity of the line, and four more in the intervals between the

[1] Of the Europeans 150 were cavalry and 120 artillery with ten guns.

Europeans and the Sepoys. One battalion of Sepoys, two guns, and the cavalry were held in reserve. With his retreat barred by two rapid streams, Adams, if beaten, could not escape annihilation.

1763.
Aug. 2.

The action opened with a duel of artillery, during which both armies advanced slowly, Adams keeping his flanks close to the two rivers. Once arrived within range of musketry, the British by the steadiness of their fire soon shook the brigades of Markar and Sumroo; and Meer Cossim's general ordered a body of horse, by one account of no more than eighty men,[1] to relieve them by an attack on the British left. These gallant horsemen charged home, and falling upon the left flank battalion of Sepoys shivered it to fragments. Numbers of the men were cut to pieces, numbers pushed into the river and drowned, and the battalion was almost annihilated. Adams at once ordered up the reserve to its support, and so saved what remnant was left; but meanwhile a large body of the enemy's cavalry had poured through the gap. These now galloped up behind the British left centre, fell with great impetuosity upon the rear of Coote's regiment, and captured the two guns on its left flank, while at the same time a party of the enemy's rocket-men engaged the hapless regiment in front. It was a perilous moment, for Adams's left was shaken if not shattered, and his centre dangerously assailed both in front and rear, so that a determined attack upon his right could hardly have failed to break up his line of battle altogether. Fortunately the leader of the enemy's left division of cavalry made but a feeble advance; and Adams at once wheeled up the Hundred-and-First to clear the front, and the reserve battalion of Sepoys to relieve the rear of Coote's regiment, whereupon the gallant corps quickly recovered itself and recaptured its two lost guns. The leader of the hostile cavalry in rear of the British line being wounded, his men began to lose heart, and the leader of the mass of the enemy which was advancing

[1] *Seir Mutaqherin*, ii. 261, 262.

1763.
Aug. 2.

against Adams's centre hesitated and retired. Adams seized the moment to reform his line and charge with the bayonet ; whereupon the whole of Meer Cossim's host began to give way. The brigades of Markar and Sumroo had already begun their retreat, with perfect discipline but without resistance, as soon as the British centre had regained its order ;[1] and of the remainder of the army only the rocket-men strove to stem the British advance, and were heavily punished for their pains. The retreat soon became a flight ; and Adams, pressing on the heels of the fugitives, drove them beyond their entrenchments at Sooty before they could rally to defend them. The enemy's camp, with seventeen guns, vast quantities of stores, and one hundred and fifty boats laden with munitions of war, was captured, and Adams was left master of the field, after one of the hardest fights recorded in the history of India.

The losses of the enemy were very heavy, but those of the British, relatively, were heavier. Four British officers were killed, the gallant Glenn among them, and several wounded, of whom some were terribly mangled by the sabres of Meer Cossim's horse. Moreover, though the victory had been won, the enemy had not been crushed, hardly even cowed. Having cleared the entrenched position at Sooty, Adams returned to Gheria,

Aug. 4. and after a day's halt moved on the 4th a short distance beyond Sooty, directing his march towards the stronghold where Meer Cossim had decided to make his final stand. Meer Cossim himself remained at Mongeer, where he found vent for his rage and disappointment in the execution of several of his native prisoners ; but though he sent large reinforcements to his army, he lacked the physical courage to join it in person.

Aug. 11. A week's marching up the southern bank of the Ganges brought Adams to Palkipore, where he pitched his camp within less than four miles of the enemy's entrenchments at the famous pass of Oondwa Nullah. This position was one of extraordinary strength. About

[1] *Seir Mutaqherin*, ii. 263.

five miles to southward of Rajmahal the passage between the Rajmahal hills and the Ganges is straitened by a jutting spur to a gorge, which at its widest point exceeds not a mile, and at its narrowest hardly attains to thirteen hundred yards, in breadth. Across this gorge the enemy had drawn a formidable line of entrenchments, running from the Ganges on the east to a steep isolated hill, which was strongly fortified, on the west; and from this point the line was prolonged in a southerly direction to the ravines and precipices of the main range of hills. The ramparts were sixty feet thick and ten feet high, the parapet above them eighteen feet thick and seven feet high, the ditch before them sixty feet wide and twelve feet deep in water. Batteries were erected at proper intervals, mounting in all upwards of one hundred cannon. About half a mile in rear of these fortifications ran an old line of works and the rivulet called the Oondwa Nullah, the latter in itself a strong natural defence owing to the steepness of its banks. Across the Nullah was thrown a stone bridge, which was strongly guarded, and in the interval between the new and the old defences was encamped the whole army of forty thousand men, including the trained brigades of Sumroo, Markar, and Aratoon. But even thus the full strength of the position was not exhausted, for almost the entire front of the new entrenchments between the hills and the river was covered by a deep morass, reducing the narrow slip of sound ground, along which ran the road, to a breadth of no more than two hundred yards. Through this tremendous barrier it was now Adams's task to force his way, against odds of eight or nine to one.

The only possible access to the enemy's entrenchments lying along the road, Adams began to open his approaches in form along that line, probably with the advice of Knox, who was a skilled engineer, for Adams himself had never witnessed a siege in his life. His progress, however, was necessarily slow owing to the paucity of his numbers, while his force was perpetually

1763. harassed by parties of the enemy, which stole out of the entrenchments by the foot of the hills and forded the morass in the dark. Adams was therefore obliged to throw up entrenchments to cover the whole of his own front, though these troublesome raids gave him at least the information that the morass was fordable by some unknown passage. Thus it was almost a full month before three batteries, the nearest of them three hundred yards from the enemy's works, had been completed along the road, and armed with siege-guns that had Sept. 4. been brought up the river in boats. On the 4th of September these batteries opened fire, but the effect of the cannonade on the massive earthworks of the enemy was hardly perceptible, and only one very imperfect breach was made near the gateway by the river. In spite of all his pains and labour, success seemed to be as remote from Adams as ever.

On that very day, however, fortune came to his aid. An European soldier, who had deserted from the Company's service, came over from the enemy's camp and promised that, if pardon were granted to him, he would point out a ford whereby the British could pass the morass to attack the entrenchments on the hill. The man was fortunately recognised by some of the officers; and, since the existence of such a ford was indubitable, his offer was accepted. Adams lost no time in making his dispositions. The grenadiers of Coote's and of the Hundred-and-First, together with two battalions of Sepoys, were placed under command of Captain James Irving, with orders to move out three hours before dawn, ford the morass under the deserter's guidance, and fall upon the isolated hill on the enemy's right. The remainder of the army was at the same time to march quietly out of camp into the approaches, one division under Captain Moran to make a false attack on the breach by the river, and the reserve under Major Carnac to act as occasion might dictate. The flare of a torch was appointed to be the signal from Irving which should launch Moran's force into action; and Adams, having taken every precaution which human foresight could devise, sent forth his troops to their desperate adventure.

Punctually at the appointed time Irving's column, carrying scaling-ladders with it, moved off in all possible silence through the darkness, and headed by the deserter plunged straight into the swamp. The passage was harder than any had suspected. It is not easy to realise the trial of those thousand faithful men as they floundered, knee-deep, waist-deep, shoulder-deep, through that terrible half mile of morass, their pouches on their heads and their muskets held high in air; with no sound but the dull heavy splashing of their own advance, stilled or broken from time to time by hoarse whispers of warning or command, and with the haunting dread ever about them that their guide might be playing them false. At length the treacherous ground was passed; and with a last command to his men on no account to fire but to trust solely to the bayonet, Irving led his party forward to the edge of the entrenchments. All was quiet; for the enemy reckoned their position so strong as to need no watching, and the officers were more occupied with wine and dancing-girls than with military vigilance. No ditch had been dug before the rampart on the hills; so the attacking force silently planted their ladders and scaled it without trouble. Then Irving, perceiving that he was close to the isolated hill and that it was strongly stockaded, rightly judged it to be the key of the position, and resolved to carry it by surprise. Several of the enemy were found asleep under the parapet as the British advanced, but these were secured without noise by a hand pressed over their mouths and a bayonet thrust into their hearts; and the grenadiers were already swarming up the steep ascent to the stockade, when suddenly the alarm was given. It came too late. The grenadiers dashed forward with the Sepoys hard at their heels, the stockade was captured with a rush, and not a man of the enemy within it left alive. Then the darkness was broken by the flash of flint and steel, and a torch held high aloft leaped suddenly into flame, shedding wild light on huddled corpses and reddened bayonets and dripping, mud-stained, panting men.

Irving looked eagerly for the answering signal, which came forthwith, not in feeble flicker of torches, but in a jet of fire from every gun in the advanced battery, where eyes as anxious as his own were weary with watching. Moran's column instantly advanced under cover of the cannonade upon the breach by the gate. It was only with immense difficulty that the ditch was passed, and the breach, when gained, was found to be so narrow as to admit men only in single file; but the volleys of Irving's column could be heard approaching from the west, and the enemy were too much distracted to offer much resistance. The rampart was scaled, and the gate thrown open. The men swarmed in, driving all before them, and Moran's column joining with Irving's fell to work in earnest. It was still barely daylight, and the enemy, bewildered by the apparent presence of the British in every quarter simultaneously, turned and fled in confusion for the bridge over Oondwa Nullah. But the guard stationed by the bridge had instructions to shoot down all deserters or fugitives, in order to compel them to return to the fight, and this command was obeyed with disastrously good discipline. The passage was speedily blocked by a heap of corpses; and then there came such a scene of panic as has rarely been matched in the history of war. The few fighting men that attempted to make a stand in the old works were speedily overpowered by the British, and the rest fled wildly they knew not whither, some hurling themselves into the Ganges, where many were drowned, but the great mass plunging into the Oondwa Nullah, where the press and the steepness of the banks brought death to hundreds. Others skirted the hills, by which track only, though many perished amid the precipices and ravines, the bulk of those that escaped found safety. The British held their hands from slaughter, contenting themselves with 1763. the capture of prisoners, yet it is said that some thousands of the enemy lost their lives in the action and in the flight; while the tide of fugitives, unstemmed by the fortified town of Rajmahal, unchecked by two passes as formidable as that of Oondwa Nullah itself, flowed on and on till it broke at last on the walls of Mongeer, a hundred miles away, and brought to Meer Cossim the tidings that the decisive battle had been fought and lost.

Thus by good fortune, joined to matchless skill and daring, was wrought this marvellous feat of arms, a feat which has hardly its peer in our military history. From a position where men could have defied five times their own numbers, Adams had dislodged a host of eight times his strength, and not only dislodged, but routed, consumed, and demoralised it, with inconsiderable loss to himself. Of his Europeans, six officers and seventeen men were killed, nine officers and sixty-five men wounded, and of his Sepoys four hundred and forty were killed and wounded—no great price to pay for the destruction of an army and the capture of over one hundred cannon, large quantities of stores, and a vast number of horses and cattle. The blow drove Meer Cossim to the abject rage of despair. He wrote to Adams threatening to kill the British officers whom he held as prisoners, Sept. 9. unless he suspended his operations; to which Adams answered warning him at his peril to touch no hair of their heads. It was no idle monition, for the British commander had moved from Oondwa Nullah on the 6th, and after one day's halt at Rajmahal, had resumed his march upon Mongeer. Towards the end of September a strong advanced detachment arrived before the city and began to open trenches; and on the arrival of the main body on the 1st of October the batteries Oct. 1. opened fire. In twenty-four hours a practicable breach had been made, but there was no occasion for an assault. Meer Cossim had already fled to Patna, and the governor whom he had left behind him accepted a sum of money

1763. to surrender himself and two thousand trained infantry as prisoners of war.¹ Adams sent forward his siege-train, together with parties to repair the bridges broken down by Meer Cossim, and, having made his arrangements to convert Mongeer into an advanced base of operations, pushed on relentlessly upon Patna.

Maddened by the fall of Mongeer, Meer Cossim now fulfilled his threat against his British prisoners. The task was entrusted to the Alsatian Sumroo; and under the eyes of this ruffian from one hundred and fifty to two hundred British officers and men were massacred, fighting hard with bricks, stones, and bottles to the last man. Dr. Fullerton and four British sergeants, one of whom bore a charmed life,² alone escaped and rejoined the army of Adams. Meanwhile that officer steadfastly pursued his march; and Meer Cossim withdrew to a distance of twenty miles from Patna, with Sumroo's brigade and a party of horse, ready to escape to a last stronghold at Rotas, to which he had already sent his family and his treasure.

Oct. 28. On the 28th of October Adams encamped on the eastern side of Patna, so much reduced in health and strength by the cares of the campaign that he only with difficulty retained command. Patna was a fortified place of considerable strength, its northern face abutting on the river, while the three other sides were protected by thick ramparts and by a wide and deep ditch. At the north-eastern corner stood the citadel, an enclosure of rhomboidal form with thick walls of masonry, to which Meer Cossim had added on the eastern or external side an outer rampart of earth

¹ Such is the story of the *Seir Mutaqherin*, ii. 285.
² The name of this man was Speedy. He enlisted in the 32nd Foot at the beginning of the War of the Austrian Succession, fought at Dettingen, Fontenoy, and Lauffeldt, joined the Bengal European Regiment (101st) in 1748, was one of the few survivors of Kirkpatrick's detachment at Fulta in 1756, fought with Clive at Budge Budge, Calcutta, Cutwa, and Plassey, and with Forde at Condore, Masulipatam, and Badara. He left the service in 1767.

to the height of twenty feet. These walls were 1763. strengthened by flanking towers, wherein cannon were mounted, and the eastern face was further fortified by a broad ditch. By Knox's advice the attack was directed against the north-eastern angle of the citadel, near the river, and the work proceeded briskly, though after the 31st the garrison made so many determined sallies that it was necessary to reinforce the Sepoys in the trenches with European troops. By the 5th of Nov. 5. November two practicable breaches had been made, one in the north-east angle of the citadel and the other on the eastern face near the eastern gate; and on the same evening orders were issued for an assault on the morrow. The remains of Coote's regiment, one company of the Hundred-and-First, and five companies of Sepoys under Captain Champion, were told off to the breach at the angle, while that by the gate was assigned to Major Irving with two companies of the Hundred-and-First and as many of Sepoys. The rest of the force was held in reserve under Major Carnac.

An hour before daybreak the storming parties Nov. 6. moved forward, and Champion's reached the breach in the angle unperceived, and had begun the ascent before the alarm was given. The enemy opened a heavy fire of artillery from the flanking tower to southward of the breach, with trifling effect; but at the summit of the breach itself the garrison met the assailants gallantly and fought them desperately hand to hand. Meanwhile Irving, finding it impossible to cross the ditch to the other breach, brought his column to join that of Champion, when the two together quickly forced an entrance. Champion then turned to clear the ramparts to westward and again joined Irving, who, having captured the southern tower, had hurried to the eastern gate to admit the main body. But now it was found that the inside of the gate was guarded by a wall of masonry containing a courtyard of about forty yards square, which was accessible only by a wicket too narrow to admit two men abreast. This

1763.
Nov. 6. courtyard was strongly held, and Irving and Champion were almost immediately struck down by the fire from it, Irving receiving a mortal wound. Lieutenants Nicoll and Crow at once took their places, charged the wicket, and by sheer hard fighting cleared the courtyard. The gate was then opened and the main body rushed in, but the officer at its head was instantly disabled by a bullet, and the command reverted to Nicoll. He paused only to collect ammunition from the pouches of the fallen, and renewing the attack on the garrison, who had rallied in the south-east bastion, drove them from it at the point of the bayonet, and completed the capture of the city.

The loss of the assailants was heavy both in officers and men, but the enemy suffered far more severely, three hundred of their dead being found within the citadel alone. The assault had been in reality no more than the extinction of the flame which had been three parts quenched at Oondwa Nullah; but Adams did not look upon his work as finished so long as Meer Cossim kept even a semblance of a force in the field. The deposed Nabob had still thirty thousand men about him, including Sumroo's battalions, and had made preparations for a last stand at Rotas. No sooner therefore had Patna been placed in a state of defence, supplies been replenished, and the army been made ready to march, than Adams started again in pursuit. By the 19th of November he had reached Daoudnagar, half-way to Rotas, where he heard that Meer Cossim, abandoning all hope of further resistance, had sent for his treasure from Rotas and was about to throw himself on the protection of the Nabob of Oude. Instantly he sent off a detachment, which unfortunately arrived too late to seize the convoy of treasure, and crossing the Sone with his main body followed in the track of the fugitive as far as the

Dec. 5. Karamnasar, at which river, being the boundary of Oude, he abandoned the chase pending orders from Calcutta. He did not omit, however, to direct a survey of the road to the Karamnasar in the event of 1763. further operations.

But the gallant man had fought his last campaign. Worn out with the strain and hardships of the past five months, he handed over the command to Knox, Dec. 9. hoping to return to England for recovery of his health; but the weight of the burden had broken his strength before he could lay it down, and on the 16th of January 1764 he died at Calcutta. Few Englishmen know so much as his name; and yet he had wrought marvels such as can be matched by few generals. Starting at the height of the hot season with a handful of British veterans and little more than a handful of Sepoys, chiefly raw recruits, with deficient transport and with an empty treasury, he marched against the most powerful force in India, trained and partly commanded by European officers, well appointed, well equipped, and full of courage and spirit. He came up with it within one hundred miles of his base, and left his enemy no peace till he had forced him back step by step four hundred miles, and finally driven him from his country. In the course of these operations he supported himself always from his enemy's supplies, beat him in three pitched battles on the plain, forced him from one entrenched position of stupendous strength, and captured two fortified cities. Had Napoleon fulfilled his dreams and added such a campaign in India to his exploits in Europe, the whole world would still ring with it; yet the conquest of Meer Cossim by a simple English Major of Foot is forgotten. Nevertheless, be it remembered or forgotten, one of the great names in English military history is that of Thomas Adams.

CHAPTER V

1763-1764. Two days after Meer Cossim crossed the Karamnasar he had received from Shuja Dowlah, the Nabob of Oude, a letter promising him protection and support, in reliance whereon he went with his troops to await his host at Allahabad. The province of Oude had been held by Shuja Dowlah and by his predecessors nominally as a fief of the Empire; but since the death of the Emperor Alumgeer the Second in 1759 and the vacancy of the throne claimed but not occupied by Shah Alum, Shujah Dowlah had seen visions of adding Bengal and its two sister provinces to Oude and of setting up an independent sovereignty. With this view he had assembled an army at Lucknow to be ready to fight the winning side, whichever it might be, in the contest between Meer Cossim and the British. At Lucknow he was joined by Shah Alum, who, after an unsuccessful campaign for the recovery of his throne and of his capital of Delhi, now threw himself upon Shuja Dowlah as the "Protector of the Empire." Shuja Dowlah, knowing that he could use the titular rights of this wandering potentate for his own purposes, received him with respect; and beginning, in view of the results of Adams's campaign, to repent of his friendly assurances to Meer Cossim, he induced Shah Alum to join him in a message of congratulation to Meer Jaffier, who for his part was earnest in desiring the amity of Oude. Pledged to both parties and still hesitating as to his choice between them, Shuja Dowlah now repaired to Allahabad, where his mind was made up for him. On his approach 1763-1764. Meer Cossim drew out the whole of his troops to salute him; and the sight of this powerful force, perfectly equipped, trained, and disciplined, decided him and also Shah Alum to throw in their lot against the British. Money, however, was needed in addition to troops; but here Meer Cossim was ready with the treasure brought from Rotas. One difficulty alone remained. One of the principal Rajahs of Bundelcund, a vassal of Oude, had like his lord-paramount conceived high notions of independent sovereignty, and had actually invaded the dominions of Shuja Dowlah. Once more Meer Cossim stepped into the breach. His disciplined troops under European leaders quickly reduced the rebellious Rajah to submission; and after this the alliance was speedily concluded. Finally, in March 1764, the united armies of the three parties 1764. marched to Benares and prepared to cross the river.

Meanwhile the British had fallen upon evil days. Adams, as has been told, had delivered his command to Knox; but Knox also, broken down by many campaigns, was soon obliged to relinquish it, and, following his great leader to Calcutta, died there like him of overwork. It is pitiful to see how quickly this Indian warfare devoured its own heroes, alike those of made reputation, like Adams and Knox, and the most promising of their successors, such as Glenn and Irving. In the absence of Major Carnac the command devolved temporarily upon Captain Jennings of the Artillery, who soon found himself face to face with the most terrible of all military dangers. During the long halt of the army at the river Durgowtee on the borders of Oude, some effort was made to fill the depleted ranks of the European battalions. The order for the disbandment of Coote's regiment, consequent on the Peace of Paris, had arrived; but this corps was already reduced to a scanty remnant, of which nearly every officer and man gladly transferred themselves to the Hundred-and-First. This, however, was only

1764. a transfer, not a reinforcement; and the only European recruits to be obtained were foreigners, chiefly Dutch and French, who preferred service with the British to confinement as prisoners. The result was that in the spring of 1764 the Hundred-and-First was made up in the proportion of two-thirds alien to one-third British. With these foreigners their compatriots in Meer Cossim's army were in constant communication, while emissaries from that astute man himself never ceased to tamper alike with aliens, British, and Sepoys, in the hope of seducing them from their allegiance.

In such circumstances every nerve should have been strained to keep the troops in good humour, whereas the Council in Calcutta did its utmost to provoke their discontent. At the outset of the campaign it had been agreed that the troops should abstain from plunder, and that at its close a large sum should be paid to them in lieu of prize-money. The army had faithfully observed its side of the contract; but after nearly two months' halt on the Durgowtee not a penny of the promised reward had yet been distributed. The Council at Calcutta was, in fact, so busy enriching itself that it could spare not a rupee for the troops.

Jan. 30. On the 30th of January the Hundred-and-First when on parade refused to obey the word of command, and answered Jennings' rebuke by stating their grievance and their resolution to do no further duty until it should be redressed. Jennings by remonstrances and a promise to second their claims contrived to quiet them for the time, and sent away on detached duty the companies which appeared to be most disaffected; but he did not fail to write to Calcutta begging earnestly for the means to satisfy the army. On the

Feb. 11. 11th of February, however, the Hundred-and-First paraded without orders with their arms and ammunition, posting three field-guns, which they had seized, on their flanks, and two small bodies of native and of European cavalry on the flanks of the guns, according to the usual order of battle. The officers at once went to them, and Jennings, seizing the ringleader, 1764. an Englishman, by the collar, attempted to drag him to the guard-room; but the mutineers quickly rescued their comrade, and, announcing that they would march on Calcutta to obtain their rights by force, strode off in perfect order, followed by several of the Sepoys.

Meer Jaffier on learning of their approach to his territory offered them ten thousand pounds to return to their duty, but in vain. Jennings and his officers, however, followed them and succeeded in recovering one hundred men and the field-guns; and presently the whole movement was checked by Lieutenant Claude Martine, who discovered from a French soldier that the Frenchmen were at the bottom of all the trouble, and that their design was not to march on Calcutta, but to Allahabad, there to enter the service of Meer Cossim. The British soldiers, on discovering how they had been duped, at once returned to their officers; the Germans, who always worked well with the British, joined them; many of the Sepoys were also reclaimed; and ultimately fewer than two hundred Europeans, French almost to a man, and one hundred Sepoys joined Meer Cossim at Allahabad. Having received meanwhile ten thousand pounds from Meer Jaffier, Jennings at once paid an instalment of prize-money, but made the mistake of awarding to the Sepoys but a sixth part of the share given to the Europeans. Thereupon the Sepoys mutinied, to the immense indignation of the now contented Europeans, and a conflict between the two was only averted by the extraordinary prudence and firmness of Jennings. Two battalions of Sepoys did indeed march away from the camp, but were quickly recalled by the trebling of the share of prize-money first offered to them, after which they returned loyally to their duty. Jennings rightly judging that the reaction of a long halt after an extraordinarily arduous campaign had done much to create insubordination and discontent, marched the army to Sasseram, and thence to Harrigunge on the

1764. Sone, where on the 6th of March he was relieved of his command by Major Carnac.

The new commander was, unfortunately, a very unworthy successor to Adams and Knox. He found the force in excellent spirit despite recent troubles, and only anxious to wipe off its disgrace by speedy action. The army was also of considerable strength, for strong drafts for the Hundred-and-First, two companies of Marines, and as many of the Hundred-and-Third regiment from Bombay were within a few days' march, which, added to seven complete battalions of Sepoys, made up a total of nearly seven thousand regular troops, irrespective of the twelve thousand native levies of Meer Jaffier, which, though of no great fighting value, were serviceable for guards and escorts. In a word, there was plenty of good material for an active commander, though there was indeed some difficulty in the matter of supplies. Yet to the amazement of the army Carnac gave no order to march, and added indignation
March 7. to that amazement by withdrawing himself from the camp of his own troops to take up his quarters with Meer Jaffier on the other bank of the Sone. On the same day he issued instructions that all reports should be sent in to his second in command, "who, when there is anything extraordinary, will report to the Commander-in-Chief." By a strange irony something extraordinary was actually going forward during those very hours; for the forces of the Allies were in the act of passing the Ganges on a bridge of boats at Benares, some eighty miles away. One half of them only had accomplished the crossing when the bridge was swept away, giving the British an opportunity to march swiftly and overwhelm the isolated division upon the southern bank. But Carnac never moved. With inactivity the old spirit of insubordination showed itself anew among the troops, and there was considerable trouble both with Europeans and Sepoys, until at length
March 12. after six days of delay Carnac struck his camp, and moving north-westward arrived on the 17th of March

at Buxar. Here he halted, collected supplies, and 1764. solemnly entrenched himself, with intent to stand on the defensive.

The Council at Calcutta was corrupt and not unfrequently foolish also, but it had learned by this time that the offensive is the only way against Asiatics, and it lost no time in ordering Carnac to act accordingly. Carnac therefore on the 22nd gave directions for March 22. throwing a bridge across the Karamnasar; but still the army remained inactive, with occasional recrudescence of insubordination, until the 4th of April, when Carnac, after taking the advice of a council of war, began his retreat to Dinapore. Arriving at his destination on the 13th, he was joined by a welcome reinforcement of the April 13. Hundred-and-Third, and on the 18th advanced again upon Daoudnagar, with the design of opposing the enemy's passage of the Sone. The idea was excellent, the only objection being that the enemy had already crossed the Sone before he started to prevent them, and were able to bring the fact home to him in a very unpleasant fashion. Annoyed by the bitter comments of the troops on his habit of placing his headquarters near Meer Jaffier's in the rear, Carnac during this march pitched his tent far in advance, with the result that on the 20th, while playing whist with his staff, he narrowly April 20. escaped capture by a party of the enemy's horse. Thus actually for the first time he learned that the forces of the Allies had passed the river, and this although, unlike Adams, he was well provided with money for the purchase of information. This remarkable commander next laid a scheme for drawing the enemy into an ambuscade; but when the British cavalry had succeeded by admirable skill in enticing them into the chosen ground, it was discovered that Carnac had changed his mind and withdrawn the ambuscading force. While he was thus halting and hesitating, Shuja Dowlah detached two divisions to make a wide circuit round the British army and cut it off from Patna; and this bold design was only frustrated by the accident that one of his

1764. columns ran against a British convoy, of which the escort made so skilful and stubborn a resistance that the hostile division retreated, not daring to press the attack against
April 23. a force of unknown strength. After this Carnac gave the order to retreat, and on the 25th the army, weary, harassed, and discontented, arrived at Patna.

Here a strong defensive position had been entrenched outside the walls of the city, whereof the eastern side and the greater part of the southern side were allotted to Meer Jaffier's troops. The Europeans were concentrated at the south-western angle, which was the weakest point, and the remainder of Carnac's troops was extended along the western front to the Ganges. The united armies numbered about nineteen thousand
April 26. men. On the following day appeared the army of the Allies, estimated at five and thirty thousand men, and for a week both parties remained inactive, until on the 2nd of May a report that British reinforcements were approaching determined Shuja Dowlah to make an attack. His plan, not ill conceived, was to concentrate his main assault and the best of his troops against the Europeans, and if possible to overwhelm them, while his irregulars should hold the levies of Meer Jaffier in check. Accordingly he entrusted the eastern and southern fronts of the British lines to Shah Alum, and himself took post with a chosen body of troops, supported by three thousand Rohilla horse, on the southern front, nearly opposite to the south-western angle. More of his own troops and a body of five thousand naked fanatics prolonged the line to his left. At the angle where the British line was bent to follow the western front of the city, Sumroo was stationed with his regular brigades, while other of Meer Cossim's troops were extended along the western front to the Ganges, Meer Cossim himself standing in rear with a reserve.

May 3. The action began with a heavy cannonade from both sides, under cover of which Shuja Dowlah led his troops forward and maintained a heavy fire of musketry from the shelter of some buildings. Sumroo's brigades

also advanced against the Europeans, but finding no
protection in the ground were heavily punished by both
musketry and artillery, and driven back in disorder to
a ravine some eight hundred yards away. Some of the
guns of the fort were at once turned upon this ravine,
but the shot, flying high, fell into the masses of Meer
Cossim's reserve, causing great unsteadiness and disorder. Further to the British right the enemy was
little more successful, though Meer Cossim's cavalry
charged gallantly enough up to the British position.
Shuja Dowlah now pushed forward the whole of his
division, and brought up his artillery nearer to the
entrenchments, but after two hours of hard fighting was
forced to retire with heavy loss. He sent urgent
messages to Meer Cossim to bring him reinforcements,
but physical courage was no quality of Meer Cossim,
who moved not himself nor sent forward a man. Shuja
Dowlah then let loose his five thousand fanatics against
the Europeans; and the poor creatures, naked and
smeared with ashes, their long hair streaming wildly
behind them, rushed forward sword in hand with yells
and screams. The British held their fire until they
came within close range, and then gave them a volley
and a shower of grapeshot which brought hundreds to
the ground and sent the rest shrieking away. They were
hardly gone when the Rohilla horse charged impetuously
up to the same point, but were likewise shattered to
pieces. Finally, at about three o'clock, Shuja Dowlah
rallied his whole force for a last attack upon the
British line, when, owing to the exhaustion of the
European troops, his infantry actually broke into
the entrenchments at one point and carried off three
drummers of the Hundred-and-First. The men, stung
by the sight, at once dashed forward to rescue them,
and sweeping the enemy out of the lines returned
triumphant with their drummers safe. Elsewhere the
whole of the attack failed, and a last desperate charge of
cavalry was likewise beaten back. The enemy then
retreated, and the British officers at once moved out of

*1764.
May 3.*

1764. their entrenchments to pursue. One party had already captured two guns, and bade fair to inflict still greater loss, when all were recalled by Carnac's order to the lines; and thus Shuja Dowlah and his allies were allowed to escape, defeated indeed, but without material injury. The losses in the action were never exactly stated, but appear to have been heavy only on the enemy's side. The two armies remained inertly face to face until on May 30. the 30th Shuja Dowlah began his retreat to Buxar. Even then Carnac made little effort to follow him; and indeed energy was hardly to be expected from a commander who had kept the largest British force that had ever been assembled in India cooped up behind entrenchments in face of a native enemy. In vain the Council of Calcutta strove by letter after letter to infuse a little activity into this insufferable man. Happily, on the 28th of June he gave up the command, having been dismissed, though for conduct unconnected with the campaign, from the Company's service. But we shall meet with him again, as we part with him at present, in disgrace.

His successor was Major Hector Munro of Morris's regiment, lately employed in Bombay, who was on the point of embarking for England when his services were requested by the Council at Calcutta. He brought with him the remains of his own and of Morgan's regiments,[1] and on his arrival at Patna on the 14th of August set himself forthwith to restore discipline by issuing a code of regulations, and by constant practice of a new system of manœuvre. The Europeans bore the tightening of the reins without a sign of restiveness; not so the Sepoys, in whom the spirit of insubordination, owing chiefly to dearth of European officers, had never been really broken. After sundry small outbreaks the senior battalion of Native Infantry, then quartered at Manjee, paraded without orders, imprisoned its officers, though only for a very short time, and vowed that it

[1] These, until disbanded, had been numbered 89th and 90th.

would serve no longer. Another battalion was sent at once to overawe it, when the mutineers surrendered on the spot. Twenty-four of the ringleaders were forthwith tried and sentenced to be blown from guns, and a general parade was ordered for execution of the sentence. The first four of the culprits were actually about to meet their fate, when four grenadiers of the battalion stepped forward and asked that, as grenadiers and therefore entitled to the post of honour in the field, they might take their place. Their request was granted, and they were tied up and blown away. The whole parade shuddered at the sight; the Europeans were all of them actually in tears; and the officers of the Sepoy battalions hurried forward to warn Munro that their men would not allow the execution to proceed. Munro, humanest but firmest of men, ordered the Europeans to load with ball and the gunners with grape, and drew up the infantry in two lines on either side of the mutineers. Then, ordering the officers back to their posts with the Sepoy battalions, he gave those battalions the word, "Ground arms." Every Sepoy instinctively obeyed. "Quick march." The Sepoys marched forward, and the Europeans filed down in their rear, so as to cut them off from their grounded arms. The Sepoys were then halted and reformed, and the provost-marshal was directed to proceed with his duty. Sixteen more of the doomed men were then blown from the guns, four being reserved for the same fate in another place, as a warning to another mutinous battalion. Then the army was ready again for its work, and Munro could say, like Lord St. Vincent on a similar occasion, " Discipline is preserved."

1764. Sept.

Munro now bent all his energy to preparation for an advance against the enemy at Buxar. The troops that he selected for the campaign were eight companies of the Hundred-and-First, two of the Hundred-and-Third, two of Marines, some two hundred men of the King's regiments who had not volunteered for service with the Company, two companies of artillery, and one troop of

1764. cavalry—in all about one thousand Europeans, with eight battalions of Sepoys and one thousand Mogul cavalry. Of this force the Marines and two Sepoy battalions, then stationed at Chupra, were placed under command of Major Champion, with orders to cross the Ganges and join the main army on the 10th of October at Kalverghat on the Sone. Both main body
Oct. 6. and detachment marched on the 6th of October; and the campaign was begun.

Meanwhile the Allies had begun to lose concord in the entrenched camp at Buxar. Shah Alum felt that he was little more than a state-prisoner, and longed to come to terms with the British. Still worse was the case of the unfortunate Meer Cossim. Shuja Dowlah had never forgiven him his inaction at the battle of Patna, and was determined to be quit of him as soon as the unhappy man's supply of money should be exhausted. In due time the last rupee was expended, and then Shuja Dowlah turned upon him with a demand for a monthly contribution which he had promised towards the expenses of the war. A period of studied insult and persecution followed, at the close of which Meer Cossim discovered that Sumroo, Markar, and the rest of his mercenaries, together with their brigades, had all of them been bought over by Shuja Dowlah, and that, with the exception of a single faithful attendant, he had not a friend in the world. On the 22nd of October, before he could meet with the English again, he was turned out of the camp with every mark of degradation; and it may be well to dismiss the poor unlucky man forthwith from this history, by adding that he died in 1777 in the last stage of poverty. Meanwhile his troops had passed into the service of an abler commander than himself.

Oct. 10. Early on the morning of the 10th of October, Munro, true to his appointment, reached Kalverghat, where he found the enemy drawn up on the opposite bank of the Sone, with breastworks and batteries constructed to oppose his passage at the ford. Almost

CH. V HISTORY OF THE ARMY 95

simultaneously there was heard from the northward the 1764.
preconcerted signal which announced the arrival of
Champion, who punctual to a minute was moving up
the western bank of the river full upon the enemy's
flank, though for the present hidden from them by
dense fog. When the fog lifted, the enemy at first
changed front to meet Champion, but presently retired
to Arrah, leaving the ford, thus skilfully won, to
Munro. The passage of the river occupied two days,
and a further day's halt was made for the distribution
of the united army into three divisions under Majors
Champion, Pemble, and Stibbert. On the 13th the Oct. 13.
advance was resumed by way of Arrah, beyond which,
at the Bonass Nullah—not yet a memorable name—the
cavalry of the advanced guard was lured into an ambuscade and very severely punished. Throughout the
march the troops were exercised in the rapid formation
of a new order of battle, designed to meet the enemy's
superiority in cavalry. On the 22nd of October they Oct. 22.
came in sight of the enemy's entrenched position at
Buxar, and on reaching the plain at about nine o'clock
in the morning found them drawn up in line of battle
in advance of their trenches, and about three miles
away. For an hour the two armies watched each other,
exchanging only a few desultory shots; after which
Shuja Dowlah withdrew within his entrenchments, and
Munro likewise retired to his camp, having first occupied a village and a grove about one thousand yards to
his front.

The heavy baggage was then packed away into
boats, and a council of war was held, at which it was
resolved to give the troops rest on the following day
and to attack on the 24th. The general plan of
the attack was agreed upon, and early in the morning
of the 23rd Major Champion went out with a small Oct. 23.
detachment to choose sites for the construction of
batteries, when to his astonishment he perceived the
whole army of Shuja Dowlah moving out from its
entrenchments, evidently to offer battle in the plain.

1764.
Oct. 23.

The alarm was at once given, the advanced detachments were recalled, and the British were quickly formed in Munro's chosen order of battle, of two lines with the reserve midway between them. In the centre of the first line stood two composite battalions of Europeans, the one made up of Marines and fragments of the King's regiments, the other of four companies of the Hundred-and-First and Hundred-and-Third, with two battalions of Sepoys on either flank. Twenty guns, in pairs or threes, were posted in the intervals between battalions and on the flanks of the first line. Fifty yards in rear of it stood the reserve, made up of the grenadier-companies of the Hundred-and-First and a body of cavalry. Fifty yards behind the reserve came the second line, formed like the first of four companies of the Hundred-and-First in the centre, with two Sepoy battalions on either hand; the guns, eight in number, being distributed in pairs on each flank of the Europeans and at the extremities of the line. The intent of this formation was that, in case of an attack of cavalry on either flank, the first and second lines should each wheel half a battalion at right angles into the space between them, while the reserve should step into the gap and complete the formation of three sides of a square; and it was this manœuvre which Munro had practised so sedulously during his march. The baggage-guard consisted of four companies of Sepoys and the Mogul cavalry. Munro's force numbered altogether close upon one thousand Europeans of all ranks, five thousand three hundred Sepoys, and a little over nine hundred Mogul horse, making rather more than seven thousand men all told, of whom six thousand were ranked in the order of battle.

The ground before Munro was awkward and afforded a formidable position for his enemy. In front of his left wing was an extensive swamp, beyond which, about a thousand yards from his line, stood a village. About the same distance before his right wing was a large grove, between which and the village aforesaid the ground was clear; while to the right of the grove and beyond the extreme right of his line was a second village. Both villages and the grove had been occupied by the enemy and made powerful advanced posts to their line. Shuja Dowlah's force, numbering from forty to fifty thousand men, necessarily covered a far greater front than Munro's, and was disposed with no little skill. Its left rested on the Ganges, where the ruined town and fort of Buxar were held by a number of native infantry. Next to these was a chosen body of horse, known as the Sheikhzadas, which carried the line as far as the grove. This, the left wing of the army, was under the personal command of Shuja Dowlah. Next to them, forming the centre, stood the eight trained battalions of Sumroo, with eight guns worked by European gunners in their intervals, and a powerful battery of heavy ordnance on each flank; and in second line behind these were from six to seven thousand horse and foot. The right wing, commanded by the Rajah of Benares, included a considerable force of Rohillas, mounted and unmounted, besides a splendid corps of five thousand Afghan cavalry, known as the Douranee horse. In rear of all was a reserve, chiefly mounted, of Shuja Dowlah's own troops.

1764.
Oct. 23.

In this order Shuja Dowlah moved slowly forward, his heavy guns opening a heavy but ineffective cannonade on the British, who being outranged could make no reply. Munro therefore gave the word to advance, but was almost immediately obliged to incline his whole line to the right, so as to bring his left clear of the swamp. This movement took time, during which the enemy's right wing kept closing inward upon Munro's flank, maintaining always a heavy fire of artillery upon it with no great result, while the British field-guns gradually coming into action played with great effect on the dense masses before them.

1764.
Oct. 23.

The British left being at last clear of the morass, orders were given to resume the advance, when a large body of the Douranee horse came galloping down upon Munro's left flank, and made a daring rush to break in between the two lines. With the precision of machinery the left half-battalions wheeled inwards, the reserve infantry stepped in between them, and the interval between the lines was closed by a solid wall of men—Europeans in the centre, Sepoys and guns on the flanks—which met the charge with so furious a fire of grape and musketry as strewed the ground with crippled men and horses and sent the survivors flying back. Some of them, however, galloped round the morass and, picking up a reinforcement of Rohillas, fell upon the baggage-guard in rear. The Mogul horse at once fled, and the infantry, unable to resist so powerful an attack, abandoned the baggage and retired to the main body, accomplishing its retreat with success though not without loss, through the admirable skill and coolness of the officer in command. Flushed with their small success, the Douranees and Rohillas made an impetuous charge upon the rear of Munro's second line, which coolly faced about and met them with a fire that beat them off with heavy loss. None the less, they rallied and delivered a second charge so fierce and resolute that they sabred several men as they stood in their ranks; but those ranks were never broken, the bayonet was as busy and as deadly as the sabre, and the daring horsemen a second time drew off, leaving a frightful proportion of dead and wounded behind them.

Meanwhile the first line also was hotly engaged, Sumroo's brigades keeping up a heavy fire of musketry and artillery, while the cavalry swooped down from time to time upon all parts of the line. Moreover, Shuja Dowlah with great readiness had moved a battery of heavy guns to the village on the British right, which searched their lines with oblique fire, and wrought great havoc. Seeing that his right wing showed signs of unsteadiness, Munro ordered the right flank battalion of his first line to advance and storm the battery; but whether from misapprehension or misconduct, the officer in command hesitated to obey. It was no time for hesitation. Munro there and then placed Lieutenant Nicoll in charge of the battalion, who led it first rather wide to the right, and then suddenly wheeling rushed upon the battery in flank and carried it with the bayonet. Munro at once sent the right flank battalion of the second line to his support; while Nicoll prepared next to carry the grove, which lay to his left and was held by a large force of cavalry and infantry with several guns. In due time Nicoll moved forward in excellent order, but being met by a steady fire and attacked in both flanks by cavalry, was forced to retire, not without severe loss.

Munro instantly realised that if the fight was to be won, the grove must be carried at any cost, and ordered Champion with all that was left of the right wing, namely, the mixed battalion of King's troops and two battalions of Sepoys, to Nicoll's assistance. Champion, after recalling the battalion from the village on the right, advanced with these troops in line and with the artillery in support, having given the order that not a shot must be fired, but that the grove must be carried with the bayonet. As the line moved on, Nicoll's battalion rallied and took its place on the right flank, and presently the whole body charging forward dashed headlong into the grove. The enemy's infantry shrank from the shock, and a volley completed their discomfiture. They quickly abandoned the grove, leaving twenty-seven guns in Champion's hands.

Thus forced from this stronghold by a flanking attack, the retreating troops were driven across the front of Sumroo's brigade, where they rallied and reformed, compelling Sumroo to take ground further to his right and form his battalions on a new alignment

1764.
Oct. 23.

with them. The evolution was an awkward one to be executed at a critical stage in a great battle; and its awkwardness was increased by the undisciplined action of one of Shuja Dowlah's officers. The leader of the reserve in rear of Sumroo's brigade, hearing the volley fired by Champion's men in the grove, rushed to the conclusion that it was the work of his own side, that the British had been driven back, and that the moment was come for him to assail Munro's left. Forcing his way, therefore, along the outskirts of the marsh with six thousand horse and foot, he fell upon the British left front and flank, masking the fire of Sumroo's battalions but at the same time delivering no effective attack, since the morass compelled his troops to straggle up in detail instead of in compact order. The British Sepoys made short work of such an attempt. Their array, says a native chronicler, looked like a wall vomiting fire and flame,[1] and charge after charge of the enemy was swept away by the storm of shot. At length the leader fell with a bullet through his brain, and the whole of his followers turned and fled in disorder. Sumroo, who seems always to have considered an orderly retreat to be the first of all military duties, thereupon faced his battalions about and led them, with their artillery, very decorously from the field.

The supreme moment was come. Munro galloped along the front of his line, and, hat in hand, called for three cheers and a general advance. The whole army then broke into columns, the left of the first line following the retreating right of the enemy, the right turning away towards the entrenchments. Munro followed with the second line. The right column of British on entering Buxar found the garrison ignorant of what was passing and the whole of their cavalry dismounted. The latter rushed to

[1] *Seir Mutaqherin.* It is curious that he should have fallen upon the same simile as is employed by a French writer to describe the British array at Fontenoy.

their horses under a heavy fire from the Sepoys, 1764.
mounted and galloped off; and the infantry, which Oct. 23.
so far had stood firm, fled likewise at the first volley.
In the centre Shah Dowlah by great exertion had
rallied a considerable body of men, but the rush of
the fugitives from the entrenchments speedily set
them running, and the explosion of a few ammunition-
waggons, blown up by the Nabob's own order, increased the panic. The Douranee horse, breaking
from all restraint, fell upon the camp and baggage
of their allies and began to plunder, cutting down all
who opposed them. But the worst was yet to come.
In rear of the position was a stream, on that day little
more than a bed of mud, across which Shuja Dowlah
had thrown a bridge of boats. Having traversed this
with his bodyguard, his treasure, and with Sumroo's
brigades, he ordered the bridge to be broken down,
thus saving himself, but leaving the remainder of
his host to a terrible fate. For as the British troops
drew nearer, there was a general rush for the bridge,
the confusion being increased by some of the Sepoys
in whom lust of slaughter had got the better of
discipline, and who kept up a constant fire. And
then came a scene such as has rarely been matched
in all the dreadful annals of war. Elephants, camels,
oxen, horses, men and women, poured down in a
seething mass to the nullah, screaming, bellowing,
trumpeting, shrieking, in all the agony of panic. The
bridge was gone, and the bed of the river was a
quagmire; but from sheer weight the fugitives kept
forcing each other down and on until, it is said, there
arose at last a causeway three hundred yards long of
corpses densely packed and trodden together, over
which the rearmost made their escape.

So in horror and destruction unspeakable ended
the famous battle of Buxar, an action memorable not
less for the discipline and endurance of the troops
than for the cool and rapid judgment of the commander; for the enemies opposed to them were brave

1764. and resolute, and the general at their head distinguished no less for skill than for courage. The losses of the British were not slight. Of the Europeans two officers and thirty-seven men were killed, nine officers and fifty-five men wounded, while of the Sepoys two hundred and fifty men were killed, four hundred and thirty-five wounded, and eighty-five missing, making a total of eight hundred and forty-seven casualties in all. Of the enemy upwards of two thousand dead and a still larger number of wounded were left on the field; while the victims that perished in the nullah were reckoned also to have been thousands. The trophies were one hundred and sixty-seven guns, about one-third of which were mounted in the entrenchments, together with plunder which gave twelve thousand pounds of prize-money to the troops. The blow was crushing, and decided conclusively the fate of the campaign.

The army remained at Buxar for the next three days, burying the dead and succouring the wounded, who suffered greatly from dearth of medical officers. A detachment was indeed sent forward under Major Sir Robert Fletcher, to pursue Shuja Dowlah, but was recalled on the intelligence that he had safely passed the Ganges. Meanwhile the Emperor Shah Alum wrote congratulations to Munro on his success, and insisted on following the British camp and enjoying its protection. On the 27th the army advanced on Benares, always in the strictest order, for Munro was merciless in enforcing his prohibition of plunder; on the 7th of November he encamped before the city, and on the following day accepted its surrender on payment of a ransom of forty thousand pounds, which was added to the prize-money of the troops. Here reinforcements of two companies of Europeans and two battalions of Sepoys arrived to strengthen Munro; and hither came also emissaries from Shuja Dowlah, who, utterly crushed by his defeat at Buxar, was anxious to make his peace. Munro, however, would listen to no

Oct. 27.

Nov. 8.

overtures unless Sumroo and Meer Cossim should first be delivered to him. In vain Shuja Dowlah offered large sums for the troops, for the expenses of the war, for the Major himself. Munro of Novar was made of different stuff from the Council of Calcutta; and the unhappy Nabob was fain to collect his scattered and discouraged forces and to conclude an alliance with the Mahrattas for another campaign.

Munro therefore moved twenty miles up the river to Sultanpore and detached fifteen hundred men to the opposite bank for the reduction of Chunar, a fortress of great natural strength, situated on a rock which marks the final abutment of the Rajmahal hills upon the Ganges. The attack on Chunar, however, was repulsed with heavy loss, for the notable reason that the commanding officer violated the established rule that Europeans should always take the lead and Sepoys form the support in the storm of a fortified position. Disquieting reports as to Shuja Dowlah's movements now reached Munro, and on the 5th of December he fell back once more on Benares. There a month later, broken down like his predecessors in health, he resigned his command. He had found his army slack, discontented, and mutinous; he left it reformed, disciplined, reorganised, and inspirited by one of the greatest of British victories in India.

On his departure the command of the field-force was assumed by Sir Robert Fletcher; for Major Carnac, who had been reinstated and was already in Calcutta, showed his usual dilatoriness in making his way to the front. Fletcher waited for a few days at Benares, in the hope that Shuja Dowlah might attack him; but the Nabob had lost his taste for pitched battles after Buxar, and fell back on the wiser course of harassing the British perpetually with his cavalry and trying to intercept their supplies. Fletcher thereupon wisely resumed the offensive, left a strong garrison to hold Benares, and with some nine hundred Europeans, eight battalions of Sepoys, and a strong party of Mogul

1765.
Jan. 18.

horse marched north-westward against the enemy, arriving before their camp on the 18th. Heavy rain was falling at the time, and the enemy's cavalry, rightly judging that not one in fifty of the British muskets could be fired owing to the damp, advanced boldly to the attack.[1] The firing of a couple of cannon-shot, however, caused them to retire in haste, and therewith their entire host turned and fled, leaving several guns in Fletcher's hands. Fletcher continued the pursuit as far as Jaunpore and thence swung south-westward upon Allahabad, at the same time despatching orders to Benares for a second attempt upon Chunar. Both fortresses capitulated after a trifling resistance, Chunar on the 8th, Allahabad on the 11th; and the country of Shuja Dowlah, overawed by these successes, offered little more resistance to the British.

Feb. 8, 11.

On the 13th of February Carnac arrived to take command, and concentrated the whole army at Allahabad, from whence he presently shifted his headquarters to Fyzabad, while small columns threaded the conquered territory to collect the revenues. There was no force to dispute the British supremacy, but the Mahrattas made constant incursions between the Jumna and the Ganges, even to the walls of Allahabad; and at the end of April the advance of Shuja Dowlah in considerable strength, as was supposed, called the British army into the Doab. However, neither the Rohillas, whom Shuja Dowlah had courted, nor Sumroo, who for the second time was about to sell himself and his troops to new masters—the Jats—were with him. Two small actions at Korah and Kalpee sent the Mahrattas flying back towards Gwalior, and Shuja Dowlah, deserted and alone, delivered himself up into the hands of the British.

April.

May 2, 21.

May 26.

Fortunate it was that during these same weeks Clive, now a peer of Ireland, had returned to Calcutta, for there was work which required an honest and able administrator. Shah Alum, the titular Emperor, Shuja

May 3.

---

[1] Caraccioli, ii. 467.

Dowlah, Nabob of Oude, and Bulwant Sing, Rajah of 1765. Benares, were all suppliants to the British and waiting to know their fate, while old Meer Jaffier, after many vicissitudes of fortune, was dead. Clive decided to turn former enemies into friends, reinstated one and all of the fallen potentates, stipulating only for British garrisons to be kept in Allahabad, Chunar, Benares, and Lucknow, and received for the Company the practical though not ostensible sovereignty of Bengal, Orissa, and Behar. An alliance was concluded between these three provinces, the Nabob of Oude, and the East India Company; and Clive decided in his own mind that the frontier of Oude should thenceforth be the permanent boundary of the British.

Even before this Clive had taken in hand those reforms of the corrupt administration of Bengal which are by many judged to be his highest title to fame. From the civil service he turned to the reorganisation of the Army, increasing the European regiment to three battalions and the artillery to four companies, and distributing the entire force into three brigades. Each brigade consisted of one European and three Sepoy battalions, one company of Artillery, and one squadron of Native horse under a European officer, so that, to all intent, each brigade constituted a small army ready to take the field, while the fourth company of artillery remained for the garrison of Calcutta. His next action was less popular and led to very serious consequences. From the moment of taking the field for active service, officers had always been entitled to a special allowance, known as *batta*. This allowance had in Bengal been doubled by Meer Jaffier to mark his gratitude after Plassey; but double *batta* was unknown in the other presidencies, and when the Company took over the entire control of Bengal and of the two sister provinces, it directed that double *batta* should be abolished. Clive issued an order accordingly for discontinuing it after the 1st of January 1766, thereby rousing great resentment among the officers, who had

1766. already suffered loss through the rules recently promulgated by Clive for the purification of the public service at large. Discontented in themselves and egged on by civilians who had lost even more than they from Clive's crusade against corruption, they conspired to send in their commissions simultaneously on a given day. The plan is said to have emanated from Sir Robert Fletcher, who alone of the field-officers took any share in the plot; and it was the more disgraceful since the Mahrattas were even then threatening a fresh invasion of the Doab.

So well was the secret kept that until the end of April Clive received no warning of what was going forward. His actions, however, were prompt enough to make up for lost time. Writing at once to Bombay and Madras to beg that all officers who could possibly be spared might be sent to Bengal at once, he set forth to meet the mutinous officers in person. He was met May 1. by the resignation, on the 1st of May, of the commissions of all captains and subalterns in the First and Third Brigades, and a few days later by the news that sixty thousand Mahrattas were already at Kalpee, and others moving down the Jumna upon Korah. Clive hesitated not a moment. The Second Brigade, being actually in the field against the Mahrattas, could, he felt, be trusted; so he hastened to confront the First Brigade, wherein, owing to Fletcher's countenance, the mutiny had advanced further than elsewhere. The European soldiers, who had learned the lesson of insubordination from their officers, were overawed by a couple of Sepoy battalions, and on Clive's arrival were easily recalled by a few words from him to discipline. The officers who had resigned he sent down at once to Calcutta, threatening to use force in case of disobedience. In the Second Brigade, which though in the field was as disaffected as the rest, the commanding officer put the whole of his officers, excepting four, under arrest, and, calling to his aid a battalion of Sepoys, gave them to understand that on the slightest sign of disturbance they should one and all be shot. Thereupon the officers submitted and returned to duty, six of the ringleaders only being reserved for trial by court-martial. The Third Brigade, which was the least violent of the three, yielded without need of compulsion. The repentance became general, and petitions poured in for restoration of the resigned commissions, which, however, Clive was careful not to grant until the offenders had passed through several months of suspense. Fletcher and a few more of the leading malcontents were cashiered, though only to be reinstated later as a personal affront to Clive. Of those that were pardoned there were few who did not atone later for their fault by faithful and unselfish service.

1766.

Thus was suppressed this extraordinary and most perilous conspiracy, wherein it is abundantly evident that civilians were the moving spirits. The mutiny was in fact simply the expression of the revolt of all branches of the Indian service against Clive's summary ending of the reign of robbery and corruption ; and the officers were made a catspaw, simply because a general strike of civilians would have been merely laughable. Never was Clive threatened with danger more formidable ; never did he face danger with grander strength and resolution.

This, and the gift of seventy thousand pounds as a pension-fund for retired officers, were Clive's last services to the Army in India. Early in the following year he embarked for England, much broken in health, and returned to his native land to be persecuted by the attacks of worthless men, such as Fletcher, whom he had rightly disgraced, and of jealous detractors and petty seekers of prominence in Parliament. The House of Commons, as he very justly complained, examined him as if he had been a sheep-stealer. Even so it had examined Marlborough ; in the same spirit it was before long to visit its petty malignity upon Warren Hastings ; and it must be noted that no man was more virulent against Clive in the Commons than

1767. Jan. 29.

1767. Colonel John Burgoyne, who himself was to learn to his cost how miserable a tribunal is the Lower House for the trial of military men. Fatigued as he was by a life of constant anxiety and overwork, distressed by agonising disease, and consumed above all by indignation, Clive stood up valiantly against his enemies at home; but the strain was too great, his malady increased, and at last he hastened his deliverance from the
1774. bondage of pain with his own hand. With all his
Nov. faults he was the greatest Englishman since Marlborough, and not unworthy to be ranked near the great duke for his genius as a soldier and a statesman. It is good to think that he wore the red coat, and that his work was to make not speeches but empires. Few men have wrought such transcendent service for the greatness of England.

AUTHORITIES.—*Official Despatches;* Broome, *History of the Bengal Army;* Innes, *History of the Bengal European Regiment; Seir Mutaqherin;* Caraccioli's and Malcolm's *Lives* of Clive. Colonel Malleson's *Decisive Battles of India,* like all his works, must be used only with vigilance and circumspection.

CHAPTER VI

THE last mutterings of war had hardly died out in
Bengal before they were renewed in Madras. In that
region, indeed, the Peace of Paris had left matters on 1763.
no very satisfactory footing. The French, it is true,
had renounced all pretension to their acquisitions on
the coast of Coromandel, and both France and England
had agreed to mutual restitution of conquests. But
whereas a special clause forbade the French to erect
fortifications or to keep troops in Bengal, the specifica-
tion of that particular province seemed tacitly to permit
them to do so elsewhere; and with the French flag
still flying at Pondicherry it was not likely that such an
opening would be neglected. The arrangements of the
treaty as regards the native states were also singularly
careless. Mohammed Ali, always the favoured candi-
date of the British, was declared to be lawful Nabob of
the Carnatic, and Salabut Jung to be lawful Viceroy of
the Deccan. But in the first place Salabut Jung had
been deposed, and was very shortly to be murdered, by
his younger brother Nizam Ali, who had already sat on
the throne of the Deccan for eighteen months; and in
the second, it was not for European powers but for the
Mogul Empire, nominally at any rate, to decide who
should or should not be sovereigns or deputy-sovereigns
within its dominions.

This nominal right had usually been observed by
the governments of the three Presidencies, which as a
rule preferred always to simulate dependence on native
sovereigns. They held the reins and they drove the

coach, but nothing could induce them to take the coachman's seat. In Bengal, indeed, as has been told, Clive obtained for the East India Company in 1765 practically the independent sovereignty of Bengal, Orissa, and Behar ; and at the same time, with his usual foresight, he procured for the Madras Presidency a similar tenure of the Northern Circars, which had been won by the genius of Forde. But the Madras Government went out of its way to make a fresh treaty with Nizam Ali, whereby it agreed to hold the Northern Circars as tributary to the very authority from which those territories had formerly been wrested, and in prejudice of which Clive had obtained independent rule over them for the Company. Not unnaturally Mohammed Ali resented this submission of the British to Nizam Ali; for he felt that if this pageant of a Viceroy could grant away the Northern Circars to them, he might do the like in favour of some other party with Arcot. Moreover, always full of ambitious schemes, Mohammed Ali was already aiming at the sovereignty of the Deccan and of Southern India for himself.

It was of course impossible for him to compass this end unaided ; but should he obtain allies, it was equally impossible for Nizam Ali to resist him. In every contest in India for many generations the Mahrattas had borne a principal part, with a policy which was uniformly the same, namely, to league themselves with one or other of the combatants, plunder him as far as possible while the alliance lasted, and secure the prize at issue for themselves. Lately the Mahrattas, in trying their mettle against the Afghan conquerors of Delhi, had received at Paniput a defeat which, in depth of disaster, has hardly its parallel in history. Still, the Mahrattas remained a factor which, even after Paniput, could not be ignored by any ambitious potentate in the peninsula ; and it was soon to be seen how the industry of a succession of great leaders, culminating in the genius of the greatest of all, could raise them, within a

1761.
Jan. 7.

generation of Paniput, to greater heights than ever. But meanwhile there had arisen in the south a new power, so weighty that it might well bear down any scale wherein it should be thrown—the power of Mysore under the rule of Hyder Ali.

A very slight sketch must suffice to trace the past career of this man, who was to prove so formidable an enemy to England. A Mohammedan and the son of a humble officer of native infantry, who had perished in one of the innumerable quarrels between native states, Hyder passed without any education through a boyhood of misery and an adolescence of violent excess, in the direction now of pleasure, now of industry and abstinence, till in 1749 he joined the army of Mysore in the field as a volunteer and found that his true calling was that of a soldier. He rose rapidly, fighting with success against all manner of enemies; contrived by intrigue and by good service to make himself necessary to the ruler of Mysore; and in due time, with the perfidy of his kind, turned against him, seized the virtual sovereignty for himself, and entered forthwith upon a career of conquest. First he subdued Baramahal, the narrow strip of land between the first and second ranges of the Eastern Ghauts, which separate Mysore from the Carnatic. He then wrenched Sera, to the northward, from the Mahrattas, and extended his boundary almost to the Kistnah; and from thence he turned upon Bednore in the Western Ghauts, the capture of which gave him vast wealth and enabled him to close his operations with the virtual conquest of Malabar. It must further be noted that during a visit to Pondicherry in 1751-52 he had imbibed a warm and constant admiration for the French, and that by the help of one who had long lived in that capital he had reorganised his army more or less on the European model. Once only had he come into contact with British troops, when aiding Lally for a time in 1760, and then he had utterly defeated one of Coote's detachments. For the rest, his success had been not unchequered by defeat, and had been won at least

1766.

1766. as much by perfidy and intrigue as by military capacity; but whether for negotiations in the closet or for operations in the field, the man possessed boundless energy, a seeing eye, and a bold heart.

Such was the new power now to be reckoned with in India. Clive, a true statesman, saw in it a useful counterpoise to the Mahrattas, and thought that good policy dictated a friendly attitude towards it so long as it should be kept within reasonable bounds; but in the Council of Madras there was little statesmanship, only infirmity of purpose, enfeebled still further by corruption. The remainder of the parties interested were all at cross-purposes. Mohammed Ali wished to depose both Hyder Ali and Nizam Ali, and to take Southern India for himself. Nizam Ali, much incensed by Hyder's conquests in the region of Sera, was negotiating with the Mahrattas with a view to a joint attack with them upon him; while simultaneously he was concluding a treaty with the British in reference to the Northern
Nov. 12. Circars, whereby he secured the assistance of an indefinite force of British troops "to settle the affairs of his Government in everything that is right and proper." With his usual duplicity Nizam Ali was intriguing either to turn the British against Hyder, or to set Hyder against the British and Mohammed Ali, or to accomplish both of these objects in succession.

Had it not been that, as coming events were shortly to prove, the Madras Government possessed an illimitable capacity for foolishness, it would be almost incredible that it should have allowed itself to be duped into so ridiculous a position. So, however, the matter stood; and the right and proper settlement of Nizam Ali's affairs was construed to mean a joint attack with him upon Hyder Ali. To meet the Nizam, the British, and the Mahrattas simultaneously, was beyond Hyder's power; so he hastened to detach the Mahrattas from the alliance by judicious restoration of territory, at the same time suggesting to Nizam Ali that it would profit him better to join with him in retaliation upon

CH. VI   HISTORY OF THE ARMY   113

Mohammed Ali and the British. Such was the state of 1767.
affairs when, early in 1767, a force of eight hundred of
the Hundred-and-Second Regiment with five battalions
of Sepoys marched to the Kistnah under Colonel Joseph
Smith,[1] an officer already well known to us, there to
unite with Nizam Ali for an advance upon Bangalore.
  Smith soon[2] became suspicious as to the trickery March.
which was going forward on all sides, and wrote his
forebodings to the Council at Madras ; but that deplorable body refused to attend. It had, as a matter
of fact, taken upon itself the virtual direction of the
operations and the supply of the army in the field ; the
latter most difficult duty being fulfilled by the simple
expedient of accepting the promises of Mohammed Ali,
a man of tried untrustworthiness, that all would be
well. On entering Mysorean territory on the 3rd of May.
May, and observing that Nizam Ali treated it as a
friendly country, Smith repeated his former warnings,
and begged the Council to prepare to meet a joint
invasion of the Carnatic by Hyder Ali and Nizam Ali.
The Council replied by making all movements of troops
against such invasion dependent on the consent of a
civil commissioner. A few days later Smith, having
open proof of Nizam Ali's hostile designs, withdrew
his force towards his own frontier, whereupon the Council
insisted that three battalions, with their six battalion-
guns, should be left as a guard of honour with this
open enemy. It was only by exhibition of unusual
chivalry on Nizam Ali's part that this detachment was
allowed to withdraw unmolested just before he turned
his arms without concealment against Smith.
  Meanwhile the Council of Madras, with the delight-
ful confidence of irresponsible strategists designing a
campaign with imperfect maps of an unexplored country,
had sent up a second column of three thousand infantry,
one-sixth of them Europeans, to endeavour to take

  [1] He had just become Commander-in-Chief, Stringer Lawrence
having resigned in 1766, and Caillaud early in 1767.
  [2] Letter of 9th March.

VOL. III   I

1767. Baramahal and extend the British frontier to the inward range of hills. With the Mahrattas advancing against Hyder from the north-east, Nizam Ali and Smith from the north, and this third column from the east, they reckoned to keep him fully employed; but since the Mahrattas had long since gone home with Hyder's money in their pockets, and Nizam Ali had already turned from friend to foe, the combination was naturally a failure. Moreover, from sheer ignorance of the country the Council had prescribed to this second column an impossible task. The force did indeed master Tripatore, Vaniambaddy, Caveripatam, and other "village-bulwarks" of little strength or importance; but the true strongholds, perched on the summits of lofty isolated mountains of granite, and from their inaccessibility called by the name of *Droogs*, were
June 3. beyond its strength. An attempt to surprise one of them, Kistnagerry, by night, was foiled with heavy loss to the assailants, the entire storming party being overwhelmed by masses of rock rolled down by the defenders from the summit. The investment of Kistnagerry was therefore turned into a blockade, which occupied the whole strength of the column.

Meanwhile Smith was directed to assume command of the whole of the troops on the frontier; but no magazines were formed to supply them, and, only three days before Hyder and Nizam Ali took the offensive, the Council actually ordered Smith to hand over to the enemy provisions of which his own army was in the greatest need. To befool him still more, the Council had informed Smith that there was but one ingress through the Ghauts into the tableland of Mysore, whereupon the General had fortified himself behind the pass of Singarapettah, in the firm belief that he had thereby closed the only possible outlet. He was rudely
Aug. undeceived. On the 25th of August the cattle belonging to his army was driven away by the enemy, and his native cavalry going out to rescue it was met by a far superior force, which had come down by a pass farther

to southward. The result was that one-third of Smith's 1767. mounted troops, already none too numerous, were cut to pieces, and his transport-bullocks captured. Meanwhile Hyder descended upon the British post at Caveripatam, and in spite of a desperate resistance overpowered it within forty-eight hours. Smith thereupon Aug. 28. fell back through the pass of Singarapettah to unite with another corps under Colonel Wood, which was on its way to Trinomalee to join him. His situation was indeed anxious in the extreme. His force at most numbered under six thousand infantry and eight hundred cavalry, with sixteen guns, while opposed to him was an army of forty-two thousand infantry, twenty-eight thousand cavalry, and over a hundred guns; and there was always the danger lest Hyder, with his vast superiority in cavalry, should interpose a force between Smith and Wood and prevent the junction.

Fortunately Hyder had been somewhat intimidated by the fact that his best troops had been twice repulsed by three companies of Sepoys at Caveripatam, though he speedily followed up Smith's army and harassed its flanks and rear continually with his cavalry and rockets. On the 2nd of September Smith reached Changama, and on the following day he kept his camp standing Sept. 3. until noon, in the hope of deluding the enemy with the idea that he had no intention of moving. Then suddenly he struck tents and continued his march; but Hyder was not so easily deceived. Smith's line of retreat lay across a river, on the further side of which the ground on his left was impracticable, while that on his right was covered with jungle and commanded by a range of low hills; and before the British could cross the river, Hyder was able to fill the jungle with native infantry and rocket-men, and to occupy the hills with his cavalry. Smith at once drove off this cavalry with his Sepoys, who held the hills gallantly against several attacks of Hyder's trained infantry, and with some difficulty clearing the jungle pursued his way; but the fighting was sharp and did not end until nightfall, when

1767.
Sept. 3. the enemy retired, having suffered very heavy loss, and left two guns behind them. Smith, however, dared not wait. Hyder's cavalry had attacked his baggage and carried off the whole of his rice; so that from sheer want of food he was obliged to continue his retreat with but two halts of less than two hours each, and only
Sept. 4. reached Trinomalee after twenty-seven hours of marching, without the least refreshment for man or beast.[1]

Then the arrangements made by the Madras Council for the commissariat were seen in their full beauty. The supplies promised by Mohammed Ali were not to be found at Trinomalee; and it was only with great difficulty that Smith was able to collect provisions for a few days from the neighbouring villages. The arrival
Sept. 8. of Wood on the 8th, though it raised his force to fourteen hundred Europeans, nine thousand Sepoys, and twenty-four guns, was therefore a source of new anxiety rather than of strength. Fortunately Hyder and Nizam Ali were too much occupied with mutual recrimination over the repulse at Changama to press operations with any vigour, so that when Smith returned
Sept. 14. on the 14th to Trinomalee, where he had left his sick, wounded, and stores, he found that the enemy had not yet got their guns into position against it, and was able
Sept. 15. to drive them off. Next day he moved forward with every intention to attack, but found the enemy too strongly posted to permit the attempt, and on the 16th he was obliged again to disperse his troops for the collection of stores. It was no fault of the Madras Council that the army was not cut off in detail.

In the circumstances Smith was for retiring and cantoning his troops at Vellore, Arcot, and Chittapett; but the Council insisted that he should keep the field, for Hyder's cavalry had overrun the country to the very gates of Madras. By infinite industry Smith contrived again to collect supplies, and at noon of the
Sept. 26. 26th moved out from Trinomalee against the enemy's

[1] I follow the dates given by Wilks, Smith being inaccurate as to the different days.

position. This was at first sight formidable enough. 1767. The approach to it lay over a morass, which though Sept. 26. not impassable was difficult, and was not recognisable as treacherous ground except after close examination. Beyond it, on Smith's left front, stood a line of redoubts, with the guns mounted and ready, for it was Hyder's hope that Smith would entangle his army in the morass; and he had accordingly massed his cannon and the best of his troops on Smith's left front and flank, in order to make an overwhelming attack as soon as the British should arrive within range of the redoubts. At first Smith acted just as Hyder could have wished, pushing forward his attack from his left; but quickly realising the nature of the ground, he withdrew it. Then rightly judging that a hill beyond the right of his own line must form the limit of the morass and the left of the enemy's position, he formed his right into columns in order to make the circuit of the hill and turn Hyder's left flank. The direction of these columns was to north-eastward, and the hostile commanders no sooner saw them moving than they concluded that Smith, being in straits for supplies, was in full march for Arcot. Accordingly they set the whole of their troops in motion to fall upon his flank and rear; and thus it came about that, while the British were circling round the hill from the eastward, the enemy was doing likewise from the opposite direction, neither party being aware of the other's movements until the advanced troops of both suddenly came into collision while skirting the northern extremity of the hill.

Then discipline told. The enemy made a hurried attempt to occupy the hill, but were promptly driven off by a battalion of British Sepoys, who thus secured a support for Smith's left flank during the first formation of his line. Some two or three rocks in the plain were likewise seized by the enemy, but from these too Hyder's infantry, though the best in his service and far superior in numbers, was dislodged after a sharp struggle by three battalions of Sepoys. Covered by

1767.
Sept. 26.
these advanced posts, the British deployed with great steadiness, while the enemy likewise formed on a commanding eminence before them, drawing up huge masses of cavalry, with trained infantry in the intervals between them, in the first line, and posting dense columns of native infantry and rocket-men in rear of their guns. Hyder's vast body of horsemen then moved forward in the shape of a crescent as if to envelop Smith's whole line, but delivered only a few futile attacks on both flanks, which were easily repulsed by the fire of the British artillery. The British line advanced cautiously from position to position, covered by the fire of its light cannon, to which Hyder, who had left most of his guns in the redoubts to his right, could make no adequate reply; and at last the British gunners turned twenty guns on to the deep columns of cavalry that confronted them, and riddled them through and through. For a time Hyder's horsemen endured the trial, but seeing the bayonets approach closer and closer they turned and fled. Nizam Ali made with all haste for Singarapettah, but Hyder, keeping his infantry and guns together, covered his retreat very coolly and skilfully until he had withdrawn the greater number of his cannon within the protection of his fortified lines. The British followed him up until nightfall, when they lay on their arms within a mile of Hyder's redoubts, having captured already nine guns, and awaiting only the order to advance and capture more.

At midnight Smith ordered a renewal of the attack; but if there was a department in which Hyder's skill shone bright it was that of intelligence; and the guide who offered to conduct the attacking columns being in Hyder's pay took care not to lead them
Sept. 27. aright. With the dawn, however, the British advanced in earnest, and despite all the efforts of Hyder, who still covered the retreat, captured forty-one heavy guns more, besides fourteen others which were found abandoned in a wood. Without cavalry and without supplies Smith could do no more, so fell back to

Trinomalee. Even while he was still pressing the pursuit, some of the Mysorean horse, under command of Hyder's son Tippoo Sahib, were plundering St. Thomé and the country villas of the Madras councillors; but Tippoo quickly withdrew on learning the issue of the action at Trinomalee, and Smith might justly claim that he had repelled the invasion of the Carnatic. His own loss did not excess forty-eight Europeans and sixty-seven Sepoys killed and wounded, whereas that of the enemy was reckoned at four thousand men, to say nothing of the capture of sixty-four guns and of a vast quantity of stores. Details of the action are meagre; but it is plain that Hyder was completely outmanœuvred and outfought, and that Smith handled his troops with a coolness and skill that deserve commemoration. Properly supplied with transport and with cavalry he would certainly have pushed his advantages much further; and that the victory was not one of the great victories of India was due not to any failing in Smith, but to the imbecility, and worse, of the Council of Madras.

With this engagement active operations came for the time to an end. Hyder and Nizam Ali retired into Baramahal, while Smith, counting on their inaction during the rainy months of October, November, and December, distributed his own troops into cantonments at Vellore, Conjeveram, Wandewash, and Trichinopoly. Such a disposition could not but be faulty, since the three first of these stations, though within easy distance of each other, were one hundred and fifty miles from Trichinopoly. Moreover the useless and indefensible posts of Vaniambaddy and Tripatore, together with Amboor, were still held by small British garrisons, offering positive temptation to an enemy to devour them piecemeal. In fact, the entire distribution of the troops was so vicious and unmilitary that only the Madras Council can be held responsible for it. Hyder quickly took advantage of the opportunity to recapture Tripatore and Vaniambaddy, after which he laid siege

1767. to Amboor. Here however he was checked, for the fort, situated at the summit of a mountain of smooth granite, was of considerable strength, and was resolutely defended by a brave officer and a sufficient garrison against not only the assaults but also the intrigues and bribes of Hyder. Meanwhile Wood's division was ordered from Trichinopoly to Trinomalee, while Smith, having concentrated at Vellore, advanced as quickly as possible to the relief of Amboor, which he duly accom-
Dec. 6. plished on the twenty-sixth day of the siege. Hyder then retired slowly southward, abandoning the recaptured posts, to a strong position which he had prepared at Caveripatam, and which Smith, even after the junction of Wood's division, could not venture to attack. Being moreover still hampered by the persistence of the Madras Council in trusting to Mohammed Ali for supplies, the General found the greatest difficulty in keeping his army in the field at all.

At this moment, however, events in more distant quarters came opportunely to relieve him. News of a revolt in Malabar caused Hyder to send his baggage and heavy guns to westward; while a series of operations in the Northern Circars, vigorously executed by a detachment of troops from Bengal, made Nizam Ali tremble for the safety of Hyderabad. Nizam Ali had already made overtures to Smith, which were rejected,
1768. and he now withdrew his army within the Ghauts and turned to the Council of Madras, with whom he con-
Feb. cluded a new treaty, under which the Presidency, while still admitting itself nominally to be his tributary and dependent, declared its intention, with his concurrence, of conquering and retaining the territory of Hyder Ali.
1767. Meanwhile Hyder was carefully veiling the withdrawal of his heavy equipment until it should be time for him to follow it with his main army; but being loth to quit the British without some real stroke of mischief, he directed in person an attack of six thousand men upon one of Smith's convoys in the pass of Singarapettah. The result went near to bring his career to an abrupt

end. Smith, always watchful and provident, divined 1767. Hyder's purpose and quietly reinforced the escort of the convoy. Hyder attacked with more than usual Dec. 29. boldness and resolution, but was driven back with heavy loss, owing to the skilful dispositions of Major Fitzgerald, the officer in command. Hyder's horse was shot under him, his turban was pierced by a bullet, and he was fain to retire, not a little discomfited, with increased awe and respect for Joseph Smith. On the following day he withdrew his whole army within the Ghauts, to the infinite relief of Smith, whose army, having gone already for two days without rations, was obliged to disperse immediately to find supplies.

Unfortunately, Hyder's failure was too soon to be 1768. redeemed by new success. The rebellion in Malabar had been encouraged by a British expedition from Bombay, which duly captured Hyder's little fleet and reduced Mangalore and several minor fortresses on the Malabar coast with little difficulty. But the garrisons of these captured posts absorbed the entire strength of the force, dispersed the troops in small parties over a line of one hundred miles in length, and left none for active operations in the field. The consequence may easily be guessed. Early in May, Hyder suddenly May. appeared in overwhelming force before Mangalore; and the garrison, though fifteen hundred strong, after a short resistance made a disgraceful retreat by sea, abandoning to Hyder over two hundred and fifty sick and wounded, and every field-gun of the artillery. The remainder of the posts were recovered by Hyder with little difficulty, and within six weeks he was free to reascend the Western Ghauts and to return, restoring order as he marched, to his operations against the British in the east.

Before withdrawing to Malabar, Hyder had assiduously circulated a report that he was about to move northward against a hostile body of Mahrattas, and that his plan of campaign against the British was to starve them out of his own territory and to follow

1768. them with fire and sword into their own. The difficulties of supply within Mysore were stated to be excessive; and Smith, knowing by bitter experience that with the peculiar commissariat of the Madras Council he could not move fifty miles from the British frontier without risk of starvation, was for occupying the fertile strip of land which extends for some two hundred miles between the first and second ranges of hills, from Vaniambaddy on the north to Dindigul and Palghaut in the south-east and south-west. The Council on the other hand favoured a concentrated effort against Bangalore, to be followed, if successful, by an advance upon Seringapatam. This latter was so evidently the sounder plan that it cannot be questioned that Smith, with an efficient administration at his back, would himself have preferred it. In the circumstances, however, he supported his own design, and ultimately it was decided that the plan of campaign for 1768 should be a compromise between the two extremes of concentration and dispersion. To Smith, with a division of about nine thousand men, was assigned the duty of invading Mysore; and to Colonel Wood, with another division of about five thousand men, the task of reducing the posts in Baramahal.[1]

Feb. 12. Wood was the first to move, receiving the surrender of Tingricottah, which lies about one hundred miles west of Pondicherry, on the 12th of February. From thence he moved north-westward to Darampoory, and thence southward, capturing without difficulty in succession a dozen or more posts,[2] ending finally with Dindigul, which surrendered on the 4th of August. The security of these conquests could, in Wood's opinion, be assured by occupying the passes which

[1] *Smith's force*—2 battalions of Europeans, foreign legion, 8 battalions of Sepoys; say 1500 Europeans, 7500 Sepoys.
 Wood's force—1 battalion of Europeans, 4½ battalions of Sepoys; say 600 Europeans, 4440 Sepoys.
[2] Salem, Attoor, Namcul, Errode, Satimungalum, Denaikancottah, passes of Gujelhutty and Caveriporam, Coimbatore, Palghaut, Darapore, Avaracoorchy.

connected them with Mysore; and since he had made 1768.
up his mind that those passes did not exceed three,
namely, Gujelhutty, Caveriporam, and a third intermediate
between them, he occupied these accordingly.
Apprised of his error a fortnight later by the appearance,
through another pass, of a party of the enemy's horse,
he went round to the opposite opinion, and declared it
impossible to prevent Hyder's troops from descending
by secret passages. Nevertheless, far from concentrating
his men, he only dispersed them rather
more widely than before, distributing thirty-four
companies of Sepoys into no fewer than thirty-eight
stations, large and small, and this in face of the warning
given by the fall of similar posts in the previous
year.

Smith's operations, of which the ultimate objective
was Bangalore, opened with an advance upon Caveripatam,
which was at once evacuated by the enemy. Feb. 23.
From thence he was called northward to quicken
the negotiations, already mentioned, of Nizam Ali's
emissary at Madras, and then set down to the blockade
of Kistnagerry, which fortress, though of no special
value as commanding any line of communications, was
esteemed by the sapient Council at Madras to be
essential to invasion of Mysore. After two months
thus wasted Kistnagerry surrendered; and then the May 3.
Council proceeded to outdo itself in imbecility. Jealous
or mistrustful of Smith, it appointed two of its members
to be field-deputies, after the Dutch manner, to assist
him in the conduct of operations. The object of this
measure becomes clearer when it is explained that one
of these individuals held the contract for victualling
the European troops and furnishing the army with
transport, a venture wherein every member of the
Council, the Governor only excepted, possessed an
interest. Further, this same gentleman was appointed
Commissary-general, so that as member of Council
he was the General's superior, as field-deputy his
colleague, and as Commissary-general his subordinate;

1768. and, in the words of the indignant chronicler,[1] to the end that no source of distraction, inefficiency, and encumbrance might be wanting, the Nabob, Mohammed Ali, accompanied the deputies to assume the fiscal management of the conquered territory. Finally, the deputies carried in their train as general military adviser a Frenchman calling himself the Chevalier de St. Lubin, who was certainly an impostor and probably a spy. Such was the staff of rogues and vagabonds provided to assist one of the ablest of living commanders in the operations of war, a gang perhaps even stranger than that which had encumbered Marlborough.

After the waste of three precious months, during which Hyder was fully employed hundreds of miles away, an advanced detachment under Colonel Donald Campbell was at length pushed three miles northward to Vencatigerry, in order to open that pass, with two others on either side of it, into Mysore. The duty was well and punctually performed. Vencatigerry and the strong and important post of Mulwagal, a little to
June 16, 23. northward of it, were captured with little trouble; and on the 28th of June Campbell received the surrender of Colar, whither Mohammed Ali and the field-deputies with the Commander-in-Chief in their train were slowly moving up the Boodicota pass. On the 3rd of July the whole army, turning southward, moved by Baugloor upon Oosoor, which fell after
July 11. three days' siege; and there the force was detained for three weeks, owing partly to want of supplies, partly to the illness, at first ceremonial but afterwards genuine,
Aug. 4. of Mohammed Ali. Eventually on the 4th of August it reached Ooscotta, some five-and-twenty miles farther to northward, where it was joined by about five thousand Mahrattas under Morari Rao.

Unfortunately, that very same day had seen the entrance of Hyder Ali's advanced guard into Bangalore, and it was not long before he made his presence felt. Within a few days his parties were harassing the

[1] Wilks, ii. 68.

skirts of the British camp, and on the 22nd of August 1768.
he made a bold attempt on that of Morari Rao, which Aug. 22.
however was beaten back, partly through the extraordinary coolness of the Mahratta, but chiefly through
the accident that a wounded elephant broke its tether
and plunged into Hyder's squadrons, wielding a fragment of its chain in its trunk like a flail. Foiled in
this essay, Hyder busied himself with completing the
defences of Bangalore, and on the 2nd of September Sept. 2.
marched off in the hope of intercepting Colonel Wood's
corps, which had been summoned from Baramahal to
join the main army. Mercifully, on that same day
Mohammed Ali's illness increased so far that it became
necessary to send him and the field-deputies to Colar;
but Smith could not rid himself of these useless burdens
without detaching two hundred Europeans and several
battalions of Sepoys for their protection, while he himself covered their retreat by an advance on Maloor.

Smith's situation was far from comfortable. He
had no information as to Hyder's movements, and
knew only that Wood was to be expected at Boodicota
on the 5th. On that very day, therefore, he threw Sept. 5.
his baggage into Maloor and began his march southeastward to join hands with this reinforcement. This
movement was entirely unexpected by Hyder, who had
counted upon his remaining at Maloor. Hyder himself
had laid his plans with his usual astuteness. Wood's
road to Boodicota trended for some miles in a northwesterly direction until, on reaching a comparatively
open spot where another defile joined it from the
north-east, it turned away at an obtuse angle to westward. It was by this three-cross-way, at the angle
where the road from the north-east came in, that
Hyder designed to lie in wait for Wood, hoping to
open fire from chosen positions upon his right flank,
and in the subsequent confusion to overwhelm him.
All three of the columns in motion, Smith's, Hyder's,
and Wood's, were hidden from each other by hills;
but Smith, sending scouts to the top of the hills,

1768.
Sept. 5.
ascertained the movements both of Hyder and of Wood, and hastened to occupy the three-cross-way before either of them could reach it, at the same time sending word to Wood of his intentions. He was just making his dispositions to catch Hyder in his own trap, when, to his immense disgust, all was spoiled by a *feu de joie* with which Wood had thought fit to honour the receipt of his message. Hyder at once took the alarm and retired; and, though the British started without delay in pursuit of him, the only result was the loss of two British guns, which the carelessness of Wood had left without an escort.

The miscarriage of Smith's very ingenious plans through the folly of his subordinate was a piece of cruel ill-fortune to him. He had started on a campaign so much hampered by the Madras Council that it seemed impossible for him to snatch success from it; and yet by sheer sagacity he had divined his enemy's schemes, and had improvised on the spur of the moment a counterstroke so unexpected that it could hardly have failed to ensure him a great victory. He vented his chagrin upon Wood in such terms as provoked that officer to resign his command; but the great opportunity was gone for ever. None the less he pursued Hyder, who had retreated northward, whither he had been called by the defection of his brother Meer Sahib. Hyder's prospects, indeed, at this moment appeared so doubtful that he offered Baramahal and an indemnity of one hundred thousand pounds to the British as the price of peace; which overture the Madras Council, in its wisdom, thought fit to reject. All military operations were, however, suspended during the negotiations, which lasted almost to the end of September; by which time Hyder had found means to reconcile Meer Sahib, and so to free himself for further work in the field.

Then a very few days sufficed to change the whole face of the war. The field-deputies, with an imbecility becoming their office, had taken upon themselves to withdraw the regular garrison stationed by Smith in the fort of Mulwagal, and to substitute for it a single company of Mohammed Ali's infantry. Hyder speedily found means to bribe the native officer in command, and to take possession of this most important post on the line of Smith's communications. Thereupon Wood, who being a favourite with the deputies had been restored to his command, made an attempt to recover it; but though he recaptured the lower fort, he was beaten back from the summit with some loss. On the following day Hyder pushed forward a few light troops to tempt Wood into a second advance; and Wood, falling at once into the trap, sent two companies and a single gun in pursuit, which after following the decoy for a couple of miles found themselves in the presence of Hyder's whole army. Wood at once summoned two more companies and another gun to rescue his advanced party, fought his way to them, and then forming the four companies in a hollow square abandoned his guns, and with great difficulty fought his way back to his main body, under overwhelming pressure from Hyder. Meanwhile the main body itself had deployed hurriedly and irregularly for action. The ground before them was strewn with huge boulders, amid which the Sepoys distributed themselves as best they could, while the Europeans were held in reserve about three hundred yards to the rear. Covered by these obstacles the Sepoys fought hard, but were steadily pressed back from position to position by superior numbers, while Hyder kept the reserve fully occupied by a turning movement upon its flank and rear. Thus threatened and punished on every side, the Sepoys began to lose heart, and the destruction of the entire force seemed to be inevitable.

Then, as so often happens, the coolness and resource of a single officer saved all. Captain Brooke, who had been wounded in Wood's attack upon Mulwagal, had been left near that fortress with four companies of Sepoys and two guns to guard the baggage and the hospital. Perceiving that Wood was in difficulties, he

1768.
Oct. 4.

collected his little garrison, with every sick and wounded man who could crawl, and manned his guns with wounded gunners. Then fetching a wide compass he climbed to the top of a hill, from which he opened a heavy fire of grape upon Hyder's left flank, while his men with one mind and one mouth shouted " Huzza! huzza! Smith, Smith!" The cry of Smith was murmured through the masses of the enemy and echoed with exultation by the English. The troops, recovering order and confidence, renewed their efforts, while the enemy fell back in every direction, excepting in that where the daring Brooke had taken his stand. Wood seized the moment to reform his Sepoys in a new position to right and left of the Europeans; and though Hyder, on discovering the trick, made a succession of furious attacks, he was repulsed at all points and at nightfall withdrew, leaving Wood almost destitute of ammunition but with his division still undestroyed. The fight had cost the British over two hundred and thirty killed and wounded, besides two guns, while Hyder's loss was estimated at a thousand men.

Oct. 7.

Three days later Smith arrived with his division from Colar, and Hyder promptly disappeared; but Wood's escape had been a narrow one, and his actions had proved his unfitness for command.

Oct. 14.

On the 14th of October the British marched in pursuit of Hyder in two divisions, vainly trying to entrap him or to force him to a general action. Hyder easily kept ahead of them with his main body, and harassed their flanks continually with his light troops. Smith was much troubled by deficiency in every branch of supplies, which no remonstrance could induce the Madras Council to make good; he was also much weakened by the detachment of a very large force to protect Mohammed Ali and the deputies at Colar; and after the experience of Mulwagal he had grave misgivings as to the prudence of separating his force into two columns. Still the name of Smith was potent against Hyder, who attempted little until the

CH. VI   HISTORY OF THE ARMY   129

Council, apparently with the object of giving Wood 1768.
a chance to distinguish himself, crowned all previous follies by the recall of Smith to Madras. To Nov. 14.
Madras accordingly he went, and the deputies and
Mohammed Ali with him, leaving Wood to command
in his stead.

No sooner had he left the field, escorted, as was
inevitable, by the greater part of his division, than
news arrived that Hyder had laid siege to Oosoor. On
the 16th of November, therefore, Wood marched to Nov. 16.
its relief with about five thousand men, including two
weak European battalions, and sixteen guns. On the
17th he reached Baugloor, where he left all his
baggage and encumbrances, and on the same night
moved off with the idea of overthrowing Hyder's
besieging army by a nocturnal surprise. Since, however, Oosoor was ten miles distant, and Wood did not
march until ten o'clock at night, it is hardly surprising
that he did not reach his destination until after daylight
on the 18th; and meanwhile Hyder, slipping round Nov. 18.
his rear to Baugloor, fell upon Wood's baggage-guard
and, amid a scene of panic and confusion which cost
the lives of two thousand camp-followers, carried off
two heavy guns and a vast quantity of baggage and
stores. Wood could only deposit such munitions as
were left to him in Oosoor and retire towards Colar;
but on the 22nd, while he was encamped at Arlier, an Nov. 22.
intermediate post on the way, his outposts were suddenly
driven in by Hyder's light troops, and presently twelve
heavy cannon opened fire from a distant eminence
beyond the range of the British guns. Wood, instead
of advancing to storm this battery, wasted ammunition in
attempting to return the fire, whereby he lost over two
hundred officers and men killed and wounded for no
advantage whatever. At ten o'clock of the same night
Wood resumed his retreat on Colar, harassed by
continual attacks on his right flank and rear, until at Nov. 23.
length, after a pursuit of some miles, Hyder fairly got
ahead of his column, and thus gaining time to bring

VOL. III   K

1768. his main body into action attacked with the greatest fury. Ammunition began to fail, and the British Sepoys to lose heart. A second time it seemed certain that Wood's entire force must be destroyed, and a second time it was saved by a subordinate officer, who was in command at Vencatigerry. This officer, Major Fitzgerald, on learning of the mishap of Baugloor, collected every man and every grain of rice that he could, and made a forced march on the 22nd and 23rd to join Wood. Hyder, mistaking Fitzgerald's force for Smith's division, hastily withdrew; and, thanks to the mere terror of Smith's name, Wood arrived in safety at Colar, having nearly lost his army and completely forfeited its confidence. The Colonel was indeed so despondent that Fitzgerald wrote privately to Smith, entreating him to resume command and to avert the total ruin of the Company's interests in Madras.

The Madras Council now recalled Wood under arrest; but it was too late. Hyder, relieved from any apprehension as to Baugloor, promptly sent a strong detachment down to Baramahal, and prepared to follow it in person with all speed. Then the full measure of Wood's incapacity was realised. Within the six weeks from the middle of November to the end of December the whole of his multitudinous posts fell one after another into Hyder's hands. Some of the garrisons made a brave resistance, one at least a disgraceful surrender; two, under the conduct of able officers, were brought off in safety; three only, namely Colar, Vencatigerry, and Kistnagerry, held their own. Colonel Dec. 10. Lang, who had succeeded Wood in command, detached five thousand men under Major Fitzgerald to follow Hyder, but too late to save the posts; and Hyder advanced into the Carnatic ravaging and burning, while Fitzgerald, obliged always to watch over the safety of Trichinopoly, and as usual ill furnished with transport and supplies, found it impossible to overtake him. The miserable Council of Madras, lately so haughty

in rejecting Hyder's offer of advantageous terms, 1768.
was fain to swallow its pride and make overtures for
peace.

Hyder received these advances with commendable 1769.
moderation, which was not lessened by the fact that
Smith had resumed command of the army and had
concentrated such scanty numbers of troops as he could Feb. 11.
collect at Chittapett. The negotiations were broken
off on the 6th of March; but though the Governor
and Council still kept a corps under their own orders,
Smith with the main body manœuvred so skilfully that
more than once Hyder only with difficulty escaped
disaster.

Resolved to bring matters to a crisis, Hyder at
last formed a chosen corps of two hundred infantry
and six thousand cavalry, and marching one hundred
and thirty miles in eighty-four hours appeared suddenly March 29.
before the gates of Madras, where he desired that a
messenger should be sent to discuss with him terms of
peace. Smith instantly followed him up, but Hyder
declined to proceed to further negotiations unless Smith
remained at least twenty-five miles distant from him.
A treaty was finally concluded on the 2nd of April, on April 2.
the basis of mutual restitution of all captured places
and prisoners, with an engagement that each party
should assist the other in case of invasion by a third
power.

Thus dishonourably ended the first contest with
Hyder Ali, owing to the folly, perversity, and corruption of the Council of Madras. There is, I think, no
other instance in our history of so close, minute, and
persistent interference of civilians with military operations as is recorded in this campaign; and yet the
soldiers went near to achieve great triumphs in the
face of these obstacles. Wood, who owed his position
entirely to the ignoble court which he paid to the
Council and field-deputies, did indeed display an incom-
petence which was worthy of his patrons, and, being
found later to have caught from them the taint of

1769. corruption, was tried and cashiered. There was yet another reproach of still baser kind which could be levelled against the military, for there was an instance of that rarest of rare occurrences, the desertion of an officer.[1] But setting these two incidents aside, the behaviour of both officers and men in most trying circumstances was beyond praise ; and, tedious though I fear that the account of the operations has been, there are few nobler scenes in the history of our Army than that of the wounded Brooke with his handful of crippled British and his tiny force of Sepoys dragging himself to the battlefield at Mulwagal, to save a whole army by raising the cry of Smith. As to Smith himself, his only fault as a man seems to have been excess of good temper and of diffidence,[2] which prompted him to obey too readily, even for evil, the orders of incompetent superiors. A more masterful man might have borne down the Council of Madras by sheer force of character ; a worse disciplined man might have ended their rule by violence. Smith did neither of these things. He was no politician ; but as a commander in the field he seems to deserve the rank assigned to him by the historian of Mysore, as among the first of the age in which he lived. He was hampered by want of cavalry, by want of supplies, by want of authority, by needs and difficulties and encumbrances which might have reduced a Marlborough to despair ; yet Hyder Ali, the born soldier and daring cavalry-leader, was a plaything in his hands, and Hyder's army trembled at his very name. There are few who know that one of the greatest of Indian warriors was daunted in the moment of victory by the sound of the homeliest of British patronymics ; but the fact is sufficient to

---

[1] Wilks, ii. 31. There had been another case in 1761, when a Captain Coulson disappeared with a small party of fifty Sepoys and Europeans, and was supposed to have taken service with Hyder Ali. Recent years furnish the case of the French officers Voulet and Chanoine in Africa.

[2] Wilks, ii. 62, 63.

place Joseph Smith by the side of Forde and Knox 1769. and Adams among the great officers of the school of Clive.

AUTHORITIES.—Wilks's *History of Mysore;* Wilson's *History of the Madras Army;* Reports *of the Secret Committee of the House of Commons.* Malleson's *Decisive Battles of India* (Porto Novo) is simply an abstract of Wilks as regards these campaigns, but needs to be very carefully checked.

CHAPTER VII

1769. THE corruption in the Civil Service of Madras had already borne evil fruit, but the axe was not yet laid at the root of the tree, and there was to come to maturity a crop even worse than had yet been gathered. It has been seen how the whole Council, with the one exception of Governor Du Prè, was at the beck of Mohammed Ali throughout the past campaign; but it has yet to be told how such a man contrived to lure even the Government in London to his aid. Mohammed Ali's great ambition, it must be repeated, was to gain sovereignty over the whole of Southern India, and to this end he had cleverly contrived in 1767 to open negotiations directly with King George the Third. His design was to render the Madras Government subordinate to himself, to use French and English alike for the purpose of his own aggrandisement, then to turn them against each other, and ultimately to expel them both; and it is a degrading fact that he received offers of service from many Englishmen both in England and in India who, though ignorant of his ulterior aim, were very well content to take his money and to further his apparently innocent desires. The whole story, more particularly that portion of it which concerns the usury and extortion practised by certain civil servants in India, may be read in Burke's speech on the Nabob of Arcot's debts, though it is hinted not obscurely by the historian of Mysore that Burke himself took more than a spectator's share in some of the transactions which he afterwards condemned.[1] The main point, however, is that Mohammed Ali did succeed in opening negotiations directly with the British Government, and that the Duke of Grafton was persuaded, though by no dishonourable means so far as he personally was concerned, to send an ambassador, Sir John Lindsey, from England to this paltry though aspiring potentate.

After the conclusion of his treaty with the British, Hyder Ali found himself confronted once more with the immediate prospect of a Mahratta invasion from the north. The restless craving of the Mahrattas for empire was a perpetual menace to the peace of India. It is true that in 1761 they had received a terrible lesson at Paniput, that the defeat had caused endless dissensions among them, and that the Peishwa, the nominal head of the confederacy of Poonah, had died of a broken heart. Yet they had defeated Nizam Ali in 1763, when he attempted to take advantage of their quarrels, and Hyder himself, whose rise had provoked their jealousy in 1764 and 1765; and now the new Peishwa, Madoo Rao, a prince of conspicuous ability, was again descending upon Hyder's new conquests to the north of Mysore. Hyder, in pursuance of the treaty of 1769, made application to Madras for assistance against the Mahrattas, assistance which it was not only the duty but the policy of the Council to grant. But Mohammed Ali, to whose designs the extinction of Hyder was a prime necessity, refused to provide funds for the campaign, and was supported in his refusal by Sir John Lindsey, who had recently arrived on the spot. Not content with this, Mohammed Ali and Lindsey tried hard to persuade the Council to fly in face of the treaty and to assist Madoo Rao against Hyder; but this Governor Du Prè refused to do, though he was compelled to give Hyder an evasive reply, to the effect

[1] Wilks, ii. 213. He says that the proof lies open to every one in printed official documents, which I take to be the *Reports of the Secret Committee of the House of Commons.* But though I have used these reports much, I have not been at pains to verify this hint.

1770.	that the whole matter had been referred for decision to England. Hyder, therefore, encountered Madoo Rao alone, and after several minor engagements sustained a
1772.	severe defeat, which obliged him to purchase peace by the concession of considerable territory to north and east of Mysore. Thus, in reward for their infraction of the treaty, the British found the Mahrattas, the very neighbours that Clive had always striven to keep at a distance, extended along the whole western frontier of Arcot, from the Palar to the Damalcherry pass.

For some time after the rejection of his proposals Mohammed Ali remained sulky, until at the beginning of 1771 he required from Madras a body of British troops to enforce payment of tribute by the Rajah of
1771. Tanjore. A corps was accordingly despatched under
Nov. 15. Smith, who laid siege to Tanjore, and only raised it on
1772. the Raja's agreement to pay Mohammed Ali a contribution. Mohammed Ali, however, declared to the Mahrattas at Poonah, who were lords paramount of Tanjore, that he had ordered the operations to cease out of pure consideration for them; for the destruction of Hyder was always uppermost in this treacherous man's mind. At the same time there arrived envoys from Hyder at Madras, saying that the Mahrattas had proposed a league with him for joint conquest of Arcot, that he had refused the offer, and that if the British would come to his aid at once he would cede to them Baramahal, besides other territory; but, if not, he would be obliged to throw himself into the arms of the French. Instructions from England, however, forbade the Madras Council to give help either to Hyder or to the Mahrattas, and this second opportunity of securing one dangerous enemy and of crippling another was lost.

On the 18th of November 1772 Madoo Rao died, and the certain prospect of intestine discord among the Mahrattas over the succession to his throne offered welcome opportunities both to Hyder and to Mohammed Ali. The latter at once urged the Madras Government once more to conquer Tanjore for him;

and in August 1773 General Joseph Smith laid siege 1773. to the city and captured it by assault. In September of the same year Hyder Ali took the field against the Mahrattas, and by February 1774 had recovered all 1774. that they had wrested from him two years before. He had not ended his campaign before he again made Dec. proposals to Madras for renewal of the treaty of 1769, encouraged by the fact that Mohammed Ali, through the capture of Tanjore, had definitely committed himself against the Mahrattas. But Mohammed Ali continually evaded any definite arrangement; and, since the Madras Government was bound by a new Act of Parliament to refer all such matters to the supreme Government at Calcutta, the negotiations were protracted to such length that Hyder finally abandoned them in disgust. Therewith vanished the last chance 1775. of gaining his friendship.

Meanwhile the action of the Mahrattas in other quarters had raised new difficulties both in Bengal and Bombay. By the treaty concluded by Clive in 1767 the districts of Corah and Allahabad, as well as an annual allowance of a quarter of a million sterling, had been awarded from the territory of the Nabob of Oude to Shah Alum, in the hope that with such liberal indemnity he would be content to abandon further aspirations to the throne of the Moguls. But such was by no means Shah Alum's intention. He never ceased to entreat the Government at Calcutta to escort him to Delhi, and, failing to persuade them, fell back upon the Mahrattas. In 1769 Madoo Rao had made a very 1769. successful inroad upon the Jats of Agra, and had 1771. then turned his arms against Rohilcund, the Mahrattas bearing a grudge against the Rohillas for fighting against them at Paniput. Finally Madoo Rao had penetrated into Corah itself, demanding contributions from the Nabob Shuja Dowlah of Oude, and alarming the British with a menace of invasion. Shuja Dowlah, always tortuous, was in reality in correspondence with the invaders for his own ends; and then it was that Dec.

1771. Shah Alum withdrew himself from the protection of the British, and was escorted into Delhi by a great Mahratta chief, of whom we shall see much in coming years, the famous Madajee Sindia.

1772. This done, the Mahrattas, hounded on both by Shuja Dowlah and Shah Alum, turned again upon the Rohillas and seemed likely to destroy them utterly. The unlucky people threw themselves on the mercy of Shuja Dowlah, who agreed to protect them for a subsidy of four hundred thousand pounds, and did not fail to take bond for that sum. The Mahrattas likewise set themselves to extort from Shah Alum the provinces of Corah and Allahabad, a proceeding which so greatly alarmed Shuja Dowlah that he applied to Bengal for assistance, and was answered by the despatch of the First Brigade to join him, though with strict orders to the commander to act on the defensive only.

Nov. 18. The death of Madoo Rao then intervened to hasten the withdrawal of the Mahrattas from Hindostan, and Shuja Dowlah was left with the field clear for his favourite design, namely, to gain possession of Rohilcund. What followed is well known. Warren Hastings, the Governor-General at Calcutta, had received particular instructions from the East India Company to reduce expenditure and augment receipts. The districts of Corah and Allahabad were treated as forfeited by Shah Alum, and were sold to Shuja Dowlah; and in return for a sum of four hundred thousand pounds British troops were placed at the Nabob's disposal for the reduction of the Rohillas.

It was late in the year 1773 before the final arrangements were concluded; and not until February 1774 did a complete brigade of the Bengal Army, under command of Colonel Champion, arrive in Oude. On the 17th of April the invaders crossed the border into Rohilcund. The Rohillas for their part had taken up a strong position at Kutra, on the Babul Nullah, where, with a strength of about forty thousand men, they resolved to defend themselves to the last. By skilful

1774.
Feb. 24.

April 17.

manœuvring Champion contrived to entice them from their stronghold into the plain, where they encamped in careless security with the Babul Nullah in their rear, the British force being separated from them by the river Gurrah. Champion having good intelligence of the defects of their new position, resolved to attack without delay; and not all the remonstrances of Shuja Dowlah, who was most reluctant to fight, could dissuade him. Accordingly, early in the morning of St. George's day, Champion crossed the Gurrah with his own brigade, five battalions of Shuja Dowlah's regular infantry, and four thousand matchlock-men, and advanced upon the enemy's left flank. After a march of five miles, he came upon a rising ground, within twelve hundred yards of their camp, which he at once occupied with the matchlock-men as a resting-point for his own left, and with the rest of his force continued to file rapidly across the enemy's flank to the Babul Nullah, with which he designed to cover his right. Before the movement could be completed the Rohillas opened fire upon him with their artillery; and Champion, pushing forward two guns to answer them, deployed to the left for battle in the usual two lines, leaving his right flank for the moment in the air until Shuja Dowlah's cavalry should come up, pursuant to arrangement, to protect it. But the promises of so treacherous an ally were worth little; the cavalry never appeared; and the Rohilla general, though completely surprised by Champion's attack, lost no time in sending rocket-men to the Nullah to enfilade Champion's line, while at the same time posting a large force in the jungle that covered its banks in readiness for a counter-attack on his right flank. To foil this movement Champion was obliged to bring forward the whole of his second line, so as to clear the Nullah and to protect his right; but when this had been accomplished the issue of the action ceased to be doubtful. The Rohillas fought gallantly, but, surprised as they were in flank and rear, they could offer no effective resistance to the steady advance of the British and the superior fire

1774.
April 21.

April 23.

1774. of Champion's artillery. Fifty of their guns were taken and two thousand of their bravest warriors laid dead on the field; and had Shuja Dowlah's cavalry been on the spot, as it should have been, the Rohilla army would never have been heard of again. The loss of the British troops was less than one hundred killed and wounded, while that of Shuja Dowlah's detachment did not exceed two hundred and fifty; and it is probably from this cause, as well as from the indignation which has been lavished upon this first Rohilla war, that the action has received little notice. But the battle was won, not because the Rohillas were a body of gallant but unskilful men, who lay at the mercy of any handful of disciplined troops, but because Champion was an extremely skilful, daring, and resolute officer. In the first place, he manœuvred his enemy out of an impregnable position; in the second, he contrived to lull them into false security on the plain, and to surprise them by a most effective and sudden attack; and in the third, though disappointed of a great part of the force upon which he had counted, he modified his dispositions under fire, drawing the whole of his reserve forthwith into the fighting line, and pressed his attack without hesitation with a slender array of no more than eight battalions [1] against forty thousand men. That a difficult task should have been accomplished with ease is only the greater testimony to the skill of the general, and the presumed injustice of the politician's design should not be allowed to obscure the soldier's merit in execution.

The battle over, Champion enforced the strictest order and discipline to keep his troops from plunder, whereupon Shuja Dowlah, who had not even crossed the Gurrah until the action was over, let loose the whole of his rabble to pillage and destruction. "We had the honour of the day," wrote Champion, "and these banditti the profit." The whole country was laid waste in spite of Champion's repeated protests; and the disgust of the British with their allies found loud

[1] The 101st took part in the engagement with great distinction.

expression among all ranks. One of the Rohilla chiefs, 1774. Fyzullah Khan, who had escaped from the battle, threw himself into a fortress from which he defied the invaders anew; and Shuja Dowlah, not ignorant of the feelings of the British, thought it prudent to come to terms with him by ceding to him the district of Rampore, with a large annual revenue. So ended the campaign, which has probably been painted in blacker colours than it merits, called the First Rohilla War.

From Bengal it is necessary to turn next to Bombay. This Presidency, which in earlier times had been the most important of the three, had for years remained almost stationary, while Bengal and Madras were making extraordinary progress; wherefore the Government thought it time to make some movement. In 1759 a state of anarchy at Surat had enabled the British to possess themselves of the castle, and to retain, under the nominal protection of the Moguls, the right to defend the place. In 1771, in consequence of a quarrel with the neighbouring Nabob of Baroach, at the mouth of the Nerbudda, the Bombay Government sent a force against that city, which accomplished nothing; but in 1772 a second expedition under General David Wedderburn after a short siege[1] took Baroach by storm on the 18th of November, the very day of Madoo Rao's death. The aggressive policy of Bombay had made its Government anxious to cultivate good relations with the Mahrattas, and in April 1772 the East India Company had given orders for the despatch of a British resident to Poonah. The object was not only to gain intelligence as to the intentions of the Mahrattas, for the safety of all the Presidencies, but to obtain certain commercial privileges, and in particular the possession of the Island of Salsette, the port of Bassein, and the islets of Hog Island, Canara,

[1] This siege has an interest of a curious kind, since it enriched English military terminology by a useful word. The soldiers in the trenches, we are told, put their hats on the parapet for the enemy to shoot at, and "humorously called it *sniping*." Letter from India, *General Evening Post*, 15th June 1773.

1774. and Elephanta—all of them in Mahratta hands—for the greater security of Bombay harbour. The envoy arrived at Poonah a few days before Madoo Rao's death, which was of course followed by a dispute as to the succession. Narain Rao, the son of Madoo Rao, was murdered before

1773. he had held his father's place for more than eight months;
Aug. 30. and his uncle, Ragonath Rao, better known as Ragobah, was then invested as Peishwa in his stead. Ragobah's first design was to recover the territory taken by Hyder Ali, and to punish Mohammed Ali and the British for their recent seizure of Tanjore; but being speedily recalled by a dangerous conspiracy at Poonah, he sought to strengthen his position by negotiations with the powerful Mahratta chiefs Sindia and Holkar in Malwa, and also with the British.

The Bombay Government on the first news of dissension among the Mahrattas had made up their minds to take Salsette by force of arms; but on receiving promises of great advantage from Ragobah, if the British would give him troops to establish his rule at Poonah, they determined to entertain his overtures and to try the effect of
Sept. negotiation. They accordingly formulated demands for the coveted islands, to which, however, Ragobah was by no means disposed to accede; and after long haggling the Bombay Council was inclined to accept other territory in lieu, when information reached them that the Portuguese had sent an expedition from Europe to recover their lost possessions in India, and among them Salsette and Bassein.

The Council thereupon decided that the Portuguese must be anticipated at all costs, and with this object despatched an expedition of eighteen hundred men, one-third of them Europeans, and fifteen guns, under command of Brigadier Robert Gordon, together with a squadron under Commodore Watson. The
Dec. 12. troops sailed on the 12th of December, and on the 13th the Portuguese fleet anchored at the mouth of the harbour to remonstrate. The Council, however, took no notice of the protest. The troops broke

ground before Tannah, the chief fortress of Salsette, 1774. opened fire on the 20th, and on the 27th delivered an assault which was repulsed with very heavy loss. The attack was, however, renewed on the following evening, Dec. 28. and the fort was carried by storm. A separate detachment, under Lieutenant-colonel Keating, was sent to occupy the fort of Versovah; the Island of Caranga, a few miles to south-east of Bombay, was likewise occupied, and by New Year's day the British had 1775. reduced the whole island of Salsette.

Negotiations with Ragobah continued during these operations; but meanwhile his cause received a serious blow from the defection of Holkar and Sindia, who for a time had embraced it. This incident should have set the Bombay Government doubting whether it might not have espoused the wrong cause in the intestine quarrels of the Mahrattas; but the desire to gain territory and so to ingratiate itself with the Company was too strong. The treaty was finally concluded on the 6th of March 1775, when the Bombay Government engaged itself to send at once to Ragobah's assistance five hundred men, and later on one thousand more. In return for this Ragobah agreed to pay fifteen thousand pounds a month, besides further sums amounting to nearly two hundred thousand pounds, and to cede Bassein, Salsette, and the rest of the desired islands, together with certain other districts, to the East India Company for ever. Thus were the British definitely committed to the First Mahratta War.

Even before the final conclusion of the treaty the Bombay Government had made ready fifteen hundred men, one-third of them Europeans, which embarked under command of Lieutenant-colonel Keating towards the end of February, and on the 27th arrived at Surat. Feb. 27. There they learned that Ragobah had been completely defeated by Holkar and Sindia, and had retreated with no more than a thousand men to Cambay. Thither the British accordingly followed him, disembarking on the 17th of March, for Keating was quite confident of March 17.

1775. his ability to subdue the entire Mahratta host with his handful of men. Reinforced by two additional companies of Europeans and by another battalion of Sepoys, he moved out from Cambay north-eastward for eleven
April 19. miles, and there on the 19th of April joined Ragobah, who had contrived to collect a motley host of some twenty thousand mutinous, discontented men. From thence the whole force moved northward, though but slowly, owing to defective commissariat. The objective desired by Ragobah was Ahmedabad, and several marches were accordingly made north-westward as far as Malitur, when, in deference to repeated orders from
May 5. the Bombay Government, the army turned eastward upon Neriad and thence to the river Myhie. So far little opposition had been encountered beyond a few trifling attacks of Mahratta horse; but after leaving Neriad the march of the army lay along a deep, narrow, sandy road with high hedges on either side, through a strongly enclosed and highly cultivated country. The wheeled carriage being confined to this one road, the movements of the baggage were very slow; and so timid were Ragobah's troops in escorting it that Keating had been compelled to add to them two guards of two hundred men each, half Sepoys, half Europeans, with two guns. One of these guards was posted in rear, and the other on the reverse flank of the army, with orders to give each other mutual support in case of attack.
May 18. The army was advancing thus near Arass in sweltering heat on the morning of the 18th of May, when six guns suddenly opened fire upon its rear from a grove upon the left side of the road, while a large band of the enemy were seen to be advancing from the same point. Keating at once halted the column and, reinforcing his little rearguard with two guns, speedily silenced the Mahratta artillery and drove back the advancing body. Two of the enemy's guns, however, were not withdrawn with the rest, and in an evil moment Keating granted the request of some of his officers to make a dash at them. Accordingly Captain Myers led two companies

of Europeans and another of Sepoys up a sandy lane 1775. between high hedges to the field where these guns were posted, but had no sooner formed his men for attack than he was charged by the Mahratta horse. The little knot of infantry stood firm and repulsed the onset, which, however, was presently repeated with great fierceness and only repelled at the cost of Myers and another officer, besides several men, killed. The Mahrattas then posted a couple of elephants in the lane, so as to cut off the isolated party, and charged it in rear; but the three companies coolly faced about and drove them off once more. Meanwhile several bodies of Mahratta horse had pushed on between them and the main body, and careering up and down the column threw the whole of it into confusion. Then suddenly one of the isolated companies of grenadiers was seized with panic and ran back to the main column. The infection spread to the Sepoys, and presently all three companies came flying back in disorder, broke up on reaching the hedges by the main body, and would not be rallied. It was an awkward and dangerous moment, but the troops of the main body fortunately were unshaken, and Keating, handling his artillery with great skill, drove back the enemy at last with very heavy loss. The action, however, cost him two hundred and seventy-two killed and wounded; while of fourteen British officers engaged, seven were killed and four wounded. In fact, the engagement approached dangerously near to a great disaster; but the loss of the enemy was set down as at least a thousand men, and by their testimony the combat of Arass was undoubtedly a victory for the British.

So greatly were the Mahrattas discouraged that they made no attempt to dispute the passage of the Myhie, which was both difficult and dangerous; and May 29. Keating pursued his march to Baroach, from whence, after a fortnight's halt, he made a forced march to surprise the Mahrattas, and failed of brilliant success only through the misconduct of Ragobah's rabble.

1775. Keating then moved to Dubhoy, about twenty miles south-east of Baroda, where, by gaining over Futteh Singh, who had been one of Ragobah's chief opponents, he brought about a temporary pacification, decidedly in Ragobah's favour and to the advantage of the Bombay Government. Soon afterwards there arrived from the Supreme Council at Calcutta a letter condemning the war and every other proceeding of the Bombay Council, and ordering hostilities to cease; and finally, after much
1776. controversy between the two Councils, the Supreme
March 1. Government negotiated the foolish treaty of Poorundur, practically throwing over Ragobah and renouncing the best part of the concessions granted by him. For the present, therefore, there followed a period of inaction during which the rival chiefs of the Mahrattas drew breath for a fresh struggle; though it was evident that such a peace could not be of long endurance.

At this point, then, I close for the present the narrative of events in India. The brief period that has been reviewed in the foregoing chapter is one that can be regarded only with mixed feelings even by the most prejudiced of Englishmen. It reveals his countrymen abandoned to the intoxication of great success, deaf to all warnings, blind to all dangers, careless of all responsibilities. It is said in the world of commerce and speculation that the test of success is not the making a fortune but the keeping it; and the adage is but an illustration of the craving, as strong in nations as in individuals, to sit down and rest after a great task done. An individual can retire from business, committing the management to other hands; a nation never. It must retain full control or none. The Governments of the Presidencies sat down to eat, drink, and be merry; and the East India Company, while deprecating any extension of responsibility, sought strenuously and unceasingly an increase of profit. Hence the sacrifice of future security to present gain, the tortuous and shortsighted negotiations with native princes, the hiring out to them of British troops, and the dangerous and selfish fiction of exerting authority only as deputed by native 1775. sovereigns. Most demoralising perhaps of all was the constant deliverance of the civil governments from their difficulties by the astonishing talent of their military commanders. Again and again officers were sent forth to accomplish the impossible, and again and again almost by miracle they achieved it. The relief of Patna by Knox, the amazing campaign of Adams, the hardly less wonderful operations of Joseph Smith—all these, notwithstanding the warnings of occasional failure, were so many encouragements to the civil authorities to persist in a policy always of recklessness and sometimes of rascality. No matter to what pitfalls their follies might lead them, there was always a soldier who would pluck them out. Such was their feeling, which was not and is not confined to them among British politicians.

So, though a far-sighted soldier and statesman like Clive perceived that, apart from the internal peril of their own corruption, the two principal dangers that threatened British power in India were Hyder Ali and the Mahrattas, yet the Presidencies in their selfish blindness deliberately made enemies of both. It was not long before they began to pay the penalty, nor much longer before they found that they had to deal not only with Hyder and Mahrattas, but with the fleets and armies of France in league with them, and that the contest in India was but part of a gigantic struggle wherein England was involved first for retention of empire and at last for sheer national existence. Leaving then these two clouds of Hyder Ali and the Mahrattas still darkening over the East, I return to the storm that was about to burst on the British Empire in the West.

AUTHORITIES.—For affairs in Madras, see the close of the preceding chapter. For Bengal, the fullest accounts are in the *Report of the Secret Committee*, to which may be added Gleig's *Life of Warren Hastings*. For Bombay and for everything connected with the Mahrattas Grant Duff's *History of the Mahrattas* is invaluable, and there is much good material in Forbes's *Oriental Memoirs*. Official despatches and the *East India Military Calendar* of course enter into every phase of warfare in India at this period.

CHAPTER VIII

1774. WE left General Gage in Boston at the close of 1774 with the people of Massachusetts drilling all round him, and with the news arrived from New Hampshire and Rhode Island that the King's fort and cannon had been seized by the populace. Meanwhile the British Parliament had met on the 29th of November, and, after passing certain additional coercive Acts, had voted to increase the troops in Boston to ten thousand men. Chatham, on the other side, brought forward the draft of a bill "for settling the troubles in America," which is remarkable only as evidence of his total misapprehension of the situation. Burke likewise moved resolutions in favour of conciliation, wise enough in themselves, but quite inadequate to meet the case. Whatever the American party in England might think, the revolutionary leaders in Boston had long been working for independence, would be satisfied with nothing less, and were quite prepared to fight for it. At least one shrewd observer, the historian Robertson, had detected this from the first, while there was another very able writer, no very friendly critic of America, who advocated the concession of independence; but this was a length to which Burke could not go, while the bare thought of it would have made Chatham furious. The only alternative seemed to be force; but with the exception of a few who, like Lord Sandwich, talked with blind and insolent ignorance of the Americans yielding at the sound of the first cannon, there was not a man in England, least of all the King himself, who desired war. Faction was too busy, the memory of the last war too fresh, the debt 1774. bequeathed by it too grievous, the disturbance of trade already too distressing, the issue of a struggle with America too problematic, for any thinking man to desire to plunge lightly into such a conflict.

The British Government therefore tried hard to avert war by blinking facts. Gage had written that a policy of coercion would mean the reconquest of New England and would require twenty thousand men. "It is impossible," wrote Lord Dartmouth almost hysterically, "without putting the Army on a war-establishment; and I am unwilling to think that matters have come to such a pass yet."[1] No effort, therefore, was made to comply with the recommendation of the General on the spot; but a new measure of conciliation was passed, bringing back the dispute to its original issue by the promise to exempt from Imperial taxation any province which would of its own accord make a proper contribution to the common defence of the Empire, and a fixed provision for the support of the civil Government. This proceeding was of course violently denounced by the Whigs, though it was far more practical than anything that had been suggested by Burke or Chatham; but before the new proposal could reach the Colonies the first blood had already been shed.

In February the Provincial Congress, which had assumed the functions of government in Massachusetts, met in session at Cambridge, issued an inflammatory address exhorting the militia to perfect themselves in discipline, and passed resolutions for the collection and manufacture of arms. This example was presently followed all over the country. Seeing what he must expect, Gage on the 18th of April despatched the flank- April 18. companies of his garrison to Concord, some twenty miles from Boston, to seize a quantity of military stores which had been amassed there by the agents of the Provincial Congress. Boston being full of spies and the revolutionists' system of intelligence very perfect,

[1] Dartmouth to Gage, 27th January 1775.

1775. all egress from the town was forbidden on that night, and the troops moved off with all possible silence and secrecy at ten o'clock. Rowing across the harbour to Charles River, they followed that stream upward for some distance, when they landed and pursued their march through the darkness. They had not proceeded many miles before the ringing of bells and firing of
April 19. guns warned them that the alarm had been given. Colonel Smith, who was in command, at once pushed forward six companies under Major Pitcairne in order to secure the bridges on the other side of Concord; and this advanced detachment on arriving at Lexington at about five o'clock found a body of American militia drawn up for drill on the village green. Pitcairne ordered them to disperse, whereupon they moved off; but, as they retired, several shots were fired from behind a wall and from adjacent houses, which wounded one man and struck Pitcairne's horse in two places. Some of the British Light Infantry answered by a volley, by which eighteen of the Americans were killed and wounded and the remainder effectually broken up.[1] Pitcairne's detachment was, however, detained by this incident sufficiently long for Smith's party to join it, when the whole body moved on together to Concord. As they approached it they found another body of militia drawn up in their front, which, however, retired

[1] It is only fair to give the American version as stated by Mr. Fiske, namely, that Pitcairne, on the militia refusing to disperse, ordered his men to fire, and that his men declined to do so until he set the example by firing his pistol. Colonel Smith in his report says expressly that the British did not fire until fired upon, that Pitcairne's troops had not loaded until they found armed men formed to oppose them, and that his own detachment had not loaded at all. Whether this be true or not (and I see no reason for doubting its truth), the proved good discipline of the British makes it absolutely incredible that the soldiers should have refused to fire when ordered; so on this ground alone, if on no other, I must reject Mr. Fiske's story. Pitcairne's pistols are shown in the town-library of Lexington as having fired the first shot of the war, which sufficiently accounts for the rise of this legend. The matter is really of trifling importance.

across a river on the further side of the town without 1775. resistance. The bridges over this river were then April 19. occupied by the Light Infantry, while the Grenadiers destroyed such of the stores as had not been concealed or carried off. While they were thus employed, the American militia, reinforced to a strength of some four hundred men, attacked the Light Infantry at one of the bridges, and after a sharp exchange of fire carried the passage by sheer weight of numbers, driving the British back upon Concord. Though for the present they refrained from pressing their advantage further, Smith speedily realised that it was high time for him to retreat.

Then the day's work began in good earnest. The entire population had turned out in arms, and along the whole line of march a continual fire of musketry rained on the British troops from an invisible enemy concealed in houses or behind walls and trees. Not Braddock's column itself was in a more desperate situation. It was useless to attempt a counter-attack; and the men were weary after fourteen hours afoot and a march of twenty miles without food. As far as Lexington Smith's soldiers were driven along like a flock of sheep, and, but for the fact that a few of the dead and wounded had been scalped by some rough Americans at the bridge, it is probable that they would not have struggled even as far as Lexington. There, however, a party of about fourteen hundred men[1] with two guns, which had been despatched under command of Lord Percy to their support, was awaiting them; and Percy forming a hollow square received the survivors of the detachment, who threw themselves down on the ground in utter exhaustion. Having refreshed them, Percy resumed the retreat, harassed for fifteen miles by the same incessant, irregular fire from front, flanks, and rear. The numbers of the enemy increased at every point on the road, and it was only by great energy, considerable skill, and some good fortune that Percy saved his force

[1] Eight companies each of the 4th, 23rd, 47th, and Marines.

1775. from annihilation, and at sunset brought it, quite worn out with fatigue, into Boston.

The casualties of the eighteen hundred men who took part[1] in this disastrous expedition amounted to nineteen officers and two hundred and fifty men killed and wounded. The loss of the Americans, who for the most part were in the happy position of giving without receiving fire, did not exceed ninety; and all that can be said of the affair is that, bad though it was, it might easily have been far worse. To blame Gage for attempting the enterprise and Smith for not abandoning it when he found that the alarm was given, is mere wisdom after the event. The whole incident was a revelation to the British, and a sufficiently unpleasant one, since it showed the nature of the warfare that was to be expected, and the efficiency, for short and sudden effort, of the levies of the New England townships. The Americans were naturally much elated by their success; and within a very few days from sixteen to twenty thousand men from the several provinces of New England were drawn round Boston from north to south, holding Gage and his eleven weak battalions in strict blockade. There was nothing further for him to do but to await reinforcements from England.

The effect of the skirmish at Lexington made itself felt far beyond New England. In New York, where there had been symptoms of a return to loyalty, the populace seized the magazines and two provision-ships, erected a Provincial Congress, and began to arm and organise a military force. In Philadelphia and New Jersey the same spirit was at work, and the conciliatory proposals of Lord Dartmouth were everywhere rejected. And meanwhile New England, not content with defensive measures, resolved with great promptness, while the British were still weak, to make a sudden attack upon the British posts on the Lakes. Benedict

---

[1] Flank-companies of the 5th, 10th, 18th, 23rd, 38th, 43rd, 52nd, and 59th. The whole of the 4th, 23rd, 47th, and ten companies of Marines.

Arnold, a man of inborn genius for war who had lately 1775. joined the American army before Boston, was the person who suggested this stroke and received a commission to deliver it; but the same idea had occurred also to the Government of Connecticut, which, after carefully proposing to Gage a cessation of hostilities, had already sent Ethan Allen of Vermont to surprise Ticonderoga. Allen characteristically refused to serve under Arnold; and since few of Arnold's men had yet joined him, Arnold accompanied Allen's force as a volunteer. Early in May the little party, numbering but eighty- May. three men in all, arrived before Ticonderoga. The garrison counted but forty-eight men; and Allen had observed that its commander was incompetent, its discipline relaxed, and the most ordinary precautions unobserved. With great cunning he paid an innocent visit to the officer in command, borrowed twenty men of him for certain heavy work on the lake, made every man of them drunk, and on the same night captured the post without firing a shot. Over one hundred and twenty cannon, besides large stores of ammunition, which were sorely needed by the Americans, thus fell into their hands. Crown Point having neither guard nor garrison, was of course taken without trouble; and Arnold, seizing the one British vessel on Lake Champlain, sailed at once to St. John's, where he quickly overpowered the garrison. General Carleton, who was in command at Montreal, presently sent a force to recover it, but Arnold, ascertaining that the entire British force for the defence of Canada consisted only of the Seventh and Twenty-sixth Foot, both of them weak battalions, speedily conceived a scheme for the reduction of the whole province.

Meanwhile the preparations in England had gone forward very slowly, chiefly owing to the extreme difficulty of obtaining recruits. The Highlands of Scotland had hitherto been a recruiting-ground that had never failed; but in recent years the Americans had offered such inducements to emigrants as had tempted large numbers to the New World, and not all

1775. the measures of the British Government could keep emigrant ships from entering every creek on the western coast and carrying off whole families.[1] Seven battalions of infantry and one regiment of light dragoons were ordered to embark from Ireland and England during January and February, but all were so weak that they could only be raised to passable strength by heavy drafts from other corps. The Seventeenth Light Dragoons, even after receiving one hundred drafts, embarked less than three hundred strong. From this and from other causes the embarkation was long delayed; and Captain Delancy, who had been sent forward to New York to buy horses for the dragoons, found the city in the hands of the revolutionary party and was compelled to abandon his mission. Thus it came about that the reinforcements did not arrive at Boston until late in May. With them came three officers in particular, of whom we shall see much. General William Howe, younger brother of Lord Howe, was the senior of them, being the same man who, as Colonel Howe, had led the forlorn hope up the cliffs to the Plains of Abraham. General John Burgoyne also we have seen before in Portugal with the Sixteenth Light Dragoons, since which time he had made himself conspicuous chiefly by ornate speeches in the House of Commons and by violent attacks on Lord Clive. General Henry Clinton had served with distinction in the Seven Years' War, and had been aide-de-camp to the Hereditary Prince of Brunswick. The subsequent narrative will show the quality of their military talent.

During this interval the American Continental Congress had met and had adopted the troops before Boston as a Continental Army. It was rather a remarkable force. A great number of the men had seen service against the French, and the majority were, through the nature of their life, good marksmen trained in the

[1] *H. O. S. P. Scotland*, 47. Lord Justice Clerk to Secretary of State, 14th August 1775. Nearly four thousand emigrants had sailed since the beginning of 1774.

excellent school of sport. Their equipment, however, was deficient, and their discipline very faulty indeed. Several companies, owing to a quarrel with their commissaries, had threatened to march home even while the British transports were entering Boston harbour, and had only with difficulty been kept to their duty.[1] Their officers were of varying merit; but in command of the Rhode Island contingent there was one who, though untrained except by books and by constant study of the British regiments in Boston, was brave, far-seeing, single-minded, and skilful, by name Nathaniel Greene. The object of the Americans was to drive the British from Boston; but though they had already given Gage much trouble to collect supplies, they could only dispossess him by seizing some of the hills which commanded the town. The situation of the two armies, dictated of course by the configuration of the ground, was somewhat peculiar. The Americans occupied a line of heights in a semicircle from north to south, with the curve to westward, around the inner harbour; while the British held the peninsula of Boston, which forms, roughly speaking, the southern half of the base of that semicircle. There were two eminences from which Boston could be commanded by artillery: one called Dorchester Heights to the south-eastward, the other in the peninsula of Charleston, which forms the northern half of the base of the semicircle, called Bunker's Hill. The latter, being the nearer, was the more important of the two; and Gage, soon after the arrival of the reinforcements, resolved to occupy it.

So perfect was the American system of intelligence that every design of the British was known at once at their headquarters; and thus it came about that on the evening of the 16th of June a strong party of Americans stole out with entrenching tools, not to Bunker's Hill but to Breed's Hill, a height on the same range still nearer to Boston, where with great industry they threw up a strong redoubt on the summit of the hill, and a

1775.

June 16.

[1] Johnson, *Life of Greene*, i. 31.

1775. line of trenches reaching for a hundred yards from this redoubt to the water on the northern side. So silently was the work done that no sound of it was heard in the transports and men-of-war that surrounded the peninsula;

June 17. and when the day broke Gage found that he had been forestalled, and that the entrenchment was well-nigh completed. He was in luck if ever general was, only less lucky than Abercromby when Montcalm resolved to stand his ground at Ticonderoga. The water all round the peninsula was navigable for vessels of light draught, and the command of that water lay with him, so that he could land troops wherever he would in the flanks or rear of the entrenchment, or, simpler still, he could either occupy the neck of Charleston peninsula, which was not two hundred yards wide, or station a gun-boat on each side to rake it with cannon. In a word, the American detachment on Breed's Hill lay practically at his mercy.

The vessels of war in the harbour soon opened a lively fire on the entrenchment, but with little effect owing to the extreme elevation; and as the Americans still stuck with creditable pertinacity to their work with the spade, Gage after much discussion decided, with a contempt which was quite unwarranted by previous exploits of the Americans,[1] to make a frontal attack. Accordingly, twenty companies of the Grenadiers and Light Infantry of the army under General Howe, together with two battalions under General Pigot, were landed at the extreme east of the Charleston peninsula and to the north of Charleston, when the generals after reconnoitring the position decided to ask for a reinforcement of two battalions more. The whole detachment was drawn up in three lines; the Grenadiers, Fifth, and Fifty-second in column of battalions forming the left wing under Howe, and the Light Infantry, Thirty-eighth, and Forty-third the right wing under Pigot. The action then opened with a sharp cannonade from eight British field-pieces and howitzers, directed chiefly

[1] See *e.g.* Vol. II. of this *History*, pp. 283-84.

but ineffectually against the redoubt, under cover of 1775. which fire the infantry slowly advanced. The day was June 17. intensely hot, the grass rose up to the men's knees, the ground was broken by a succession of fences ; and yet the men were burdened by their heavy packs and by three days' provisions, which, supposing that they were needed at all, had much better have been conveyed by water. During the advance of about six hundred yards the regiments deployed, and the plan of attack developed itself, the Light Infantry being directed against the extreme left of the Americans, while the Grenadiers, Fifty-second, and Fifth, with the Thirty-eighth and Forty-third in support, were turned against the entrenchment and redoubt, to the left of the Light Infantry. It should seem, indeed, that the advance against the redoubt was designed to be more or less of a demonstration, the British commanders really counting for success on the turning of the enemy's left. In this case a vessel of light draught might have raked the American left from end to end without need to employ any infantry whatever.

Be that as it may, the attack was delivered with equal strength or weakness against the entire American front ; and the fire of the British—a very rare fault with them—was opened at too great a range. The Americans, with the good judgment of old soldiers, as indeed many of them were, held their fire until the British were within fifty yards, and then poured it into the scarlet ranks with the greatest effect. Groups of riflemen had been specially detailed to pick off the officers, whose glittering gorgets made an excellent target, and the best of the American marksmen were kept supplied with a succession of loaded weapons, so that they should do the greatest possible execution. The fire was so terrible that the British, after a gallant attempt to reload and return it, gave way, broken to pieces by their losses, and fell back out of range, when they quickly rallied and reformed for a second attack.

The left wing having been galled during its advance

1775.
June 17.
by a flanking discharge of musketry from the houses of Charleston, a heavy fire had been poured into the town from a battery on the outskirts of Boston; and the houses being thus kindled burned fiercely, sending up columns of smoke, which were borne by the wind straight into the eyes of the British. But on the field the British guns were silent, because, through mere carelessness, shot of the wrong calibre had been sent from Boston, while the officers declared it impossible to advance their pieces within range of grapeshot owing to a patch of swampy ground. None the less Howe now led a second attack, exactly similar to the first, though it seems that the battalions were now extended from end to end of the American line, the Light Infantry as before holding their place on the extreme right of the British, with the Grenadiers, Fifty-second, Forty-third, Thirty-eighth, and Fifth aligned with them in order as named. Once again the same scene was repeated. The British advanced with all possible gallantry over the bodies of their fallen comrades, only to be swept down by the same rain of bullets. A brick-kiln, with some other obstacles within a hundred yards of the redoubt, kept the Fifty-second in particular exposed to the worst of the fire; and the second attack, like the first, was driven back with very heavy loss.

But neither Howe nor his troops were yet beaten. The General was still untouched, though every officer of his staff had been shot down; and he now ordered the men to throw off their packs and to trust for the next assault to their bayonets only. Clinton observing two battalions on the beach in great disorder, doubtless from loss of officers, hurried across the water from Boston to rally them, while a reinforcement of the Forty-seventh and Marines had already arrived in the course of the engagement. Howe now abandoned the attack on the American left, converting it into a mere feint, and turned all his strength upon the breastwork and redoubt. The British advanced without firing a shot, and the Americans as before let them come close before they drew trigger, but having exhausted their ammunition they shrank from before the British bayonets. Not a few of them stood bravely to the end, but the mass gave way, and, coming under the fire of the British warships in their retreat across the Isthmus, suffered very heavily. Thus the redoubt and entrenchments were gained, but beyond this the British advantage was not pressed ; and the day closed leaving the redcoats in possession of the fatal hill.

1775.
June 17.

The losses of the British were terribly severe. Of about twenty-five hundred troops nineteen officers and two hundred and seven men were killed, and seventy officers and seven hundred and fifty-eight men wounded, making a total of one thousand and fifty-four casualties in all, or over two-fifths of the force engaged.[1] Indeed, the regiments that took part in all three of the attacks lost little if any less than half of their numbers, and it is pitiful to read of the havoc wrought among the several battalions, not one of which had brought more than four hundred men into the field. The Fifth lost one hundred and fifty-eight killed and wounded ; and it is noteworthy that the grenadier-company of this regiment was led first by Captain Harris, and after his fall by Lord Rawdon, both of whom we shall know better in later days, the one as Lord Harris of Seringapatam, the other as Marquess of Hastings. The Thirty-eighth can have lost little fewer men than the Fifth ; the Forty-third lost one hundred and eight, the Fifty-second one hundred and eleven. The grenadier-company of the Twenty-third went into action with forty-nine of all ranks and returned with five ; and the flank-companies of the Thirty-fifth alone lost five officers and sixty-four men.[2]

[1] This does not include the wounded of the 38th, which were accidentally omitted from the official list. These probably numbered at least 100, as this regiment lost a greater number killed (25) than any other. This would raise the total casualties to 1150.
[2] The troops engaged were the flank-companies only of the 4th, 10th, 18th, 22nd, 23rd, 35th, 59th, 63rd, 65th ; the entire strength of the 5th, 38th, 42nd, 47th, 52nd, and two weak battalions of Marines.

1775. In truth, the return of the British infantry to the third attack after two such bloody repulses is one of the very greatest feats ever recorded of them, and points to fine quality among the men, grand pride in their regiments, and supreme excellence of discipline. Equally does the coolness and steadfastness of the Americans, thanks to the example of a few brave and experienced officers, call for our warm admiration; though of course it is fallacious to look upon them simply as raw peasants, for a large proportion of them had been in action before. British writers for the most part estimate the American numbers as superior to our own, but it seems probable that not more than seventeen hundred of them were engaged at Bunker's Hill at any one time, though there may have been more on the peninsula. Their acknowledged loss was four hundred and fifty killed and wounded, and there seems to be no reason to doubt that this figure is substantially correct. Of the action of the general officers on both sides, the less said the better. There is no need to expatiate on the folly of Gage; and it must be confessed that the apathy or indiscipline which denied reinforcements to the American detachments on the peninsula was anything but creditable to the American commanders. For the rest, the combat produced a remarkable effect on the future operations of the war. It shook the nerve of Howe, and showed the British that the subjugation of the Colonies would be no child's-play. On the other hand, it not only elated the Americans, as was but natural and just, but encouraged them to a blind and fatal trust in undisciplined troops, which went near to bring ruin to their cause. Notwithstanding the mistakes of generals and the deplorable waste of excellent troops, Bunker's Hill was probably a greater misfortune, taken altogether, to the Americans than to the British.

The captured position on the hill was entrenched and occupied by Gage, after which there remained nothing for him but to sit still and await what might come. Meanwhile great events had been going forward in Congress. Just two days before the action, 1775. George Washington had been chosen unanimously to be Commander-in-Chief of the Continental Army— the only man, as events were to prove, who could possibly have carried the war to a successful issue. On the 2nd of July he arrived in the camp before Boston to take command; and shortly after him came a contingent of three thousand men from Pennsylvania, Maryland, and Virginia, to swell the ranks and give better justification for the title of Continental Army. Other officers in that camp who now claim our attention were Major-general Horatio Gates, who had long held a commission in one of the King's independent companies at New York, and had recently retired on half-pay as Major in the Sixtieth; and Major-general Charles Lee, who had served in the war against the French, had risen to the rank of Lieutenant-colonel in the King's service, and was still on half-pay. Both, though English by birth, owned property in America, and both were a discredit to the country alike of their birth and of their adoption. Two more remarkable officers, Brigadier Richard Montgomery, who had also held the King's commission in the regular army, and Benedict Arnold, were absent on an expedition to which we must follow them.

The attack on Ticonderoga by Ethan Allen is said to have been viewed at first with mixed feelings by Congress, as at variance with its professions of acting solely on the defensive.[1] Why the members should have felt these scruples, if indeed they did feel them, is not very clear, since American emissaries had already been despatched to Bermuda and to the Bahamas to stir up sedition; which step was now followed up in Bermuda by a raid of American sloops upon the forts and Aug. 14. by the abstraction of all the powder in the magazines. It may easily be guessed, therefore, that means were found to quiet uneasy consciences, as well as pretexts to justify an attempt at the conquest of Canada. The

[1] Fiske, i. 164.

1775.
Aug.

enterprise was accordingly approved, and entrusted to Montgomery and Benedict Arnold. The former, a very capable officer, therefore started at the end of August from Ticonderoga with two thousand men for an attack on Montreal; while Arnold set forth a week or two later with fifteen hundred men to advance up the rivers Kennebec and Chaudière and through the

Sept. 12.

forests of Maine upon Quebec. On the 12th of September Montgomery laid siege to St. John's, which however held out stoutly, for Carleton had thrown five hundred out of his eight hundred regular troops into the fort, together with one hundred Canadian volunteers. Finding that he could make little impression and that his ammunition was running short, Montgomery detached three hundred men with two guns five miles down the river to Chambly, which post, though held by one hundred and fifty men, made a most discreditable

Oct. 20.

surrender. This was the saving of Montgomery's campaign. The fall of Chambly gave him stores sufficient to renew the siege of St. John's, which after a very gallant defence of fifty days was forced on the

Nov. 3.

3rd of November to capitulate. Carleton, who had been repulsed in an attempt to march with a handful of troops to its relief, now evacuated Montreal; and on the 12th of November Montgomery entered that town in triumph.

Nov. 5.

Just a week earlier Arnold's force had appeared before Quebec. His troops had suffered much from a terrible march of thirty-three days through a wilderness of forest. They had endured indescribable toil and hardship through lack of supplies, and had been forced to devour even their dogs. Two hundred men had died of starvation and hard work, as many more had been sent back sick, and quite three hundred more had deserted with a colonel at their head; but still Arnold with magnificent tenacity pushed on to the St. Lawrence, and encamped his exhausted force at Point Lévis. The alarm at his coming was intense, for the fortifications of Quebec were weak and the garrison trifling. The Canadians, in whom Carleton had reposed 1775. such confidence that he had sent nearly all of his regular battalions to Boston, remained loyal indeed to the King, but would not serve him in the militia. Fortunately there was stationed at Sorel a very capable officer, Colonel Allan Maclean, with nearly four hundred recruits for a regiment which he was then raising, who no sooner heard of Arnold's arrival at Point Lévis than he made a forced march on Quebec, reaching it safely on the 13th of November. On that same day Arnold Nov. 13. had climbed the Heights of Abraham and challenged the garrison to come out and fight, or surrender. Since the garrison declined to oblige him, he made an attack on the same night, but was beaten off with loss. He then resigned himself to await Montgomery's arrival; but there was no sign of his coming for a full fortnight, in the course of which Carleton slipped down the river in disguise, and began vigorous preparations for the defence of Quebec.

At last, on the 3rd of December, Montgomery Dec. 3. appeared with a small body of troops, which, joined to Arnold's, raised the American force to twelve hundred men. Carleton had about as many of one kind and another, but sixty only were British regular troops, and a large proportion of the rest were anything but trustworthy. After a feeble bombardment of field-guns which produced no effect, Montgomery came to the daring resolution to attempt a storm. The time chosen was two o'clock on the morning of the 31st of De- Dec. 31. cember, when by signal of rocket four simultaneous attacks were to be delivered, two of them false, and two of them, led by Arnold and himself at opposite ends of the town, real and earnest. A blinding snowstorm favoured the adventure, but the false attacks were begun prematurely, and, their actual character being thus revealed, the garrison was concentrated to meet the real danger. Montgomery's column was met at fifty yards' range by a withering blast of grape which laid him dead among the first; and his followers, though they

1775.
Dec. 31. did not at once retreat, after half an hour abandoned the assault. Arnold, being opposed at first only by Canadian volunteers, forced his way into the fortress, and, when he was himself wounded, found a brave successor in General Morgan to lead his men on. But the arrival of Maclean quickly turned the tide; the foremost of the Americans were surrounded and taken, and the rest easily driven back. The casualties on the British side did not exceed twenty in all, while those of the Americans were far heavier.[1] Thus Quebec was saved, and with Quebec the whole of Canada.

So ended the boldest attempt made by the Colonies to add to their territory during the war. It was a daring enterprise, conducted with remarkable ability both by Montgomery and by Arnold; yet it was a foolish one, for even if the Americans had taken Quebec they could not have held it without an adequate naval force. Nor is there the least ground for supposing that the Canadians, cold though they were in the cause of Britain, would have warmed towards the Americans. By promises and proclamations the invaders succeeded indeed in instilling a spirit of lawlessness and insubordination into the Canadian peasants; but such a spirit is as unfavourable to usurped as to displaced authority; and the priests and upper classes remained on the side of the British. The Americans actually attempted to raise two regiments in Canada; but, in the words of an American historian, the Canadians proved themselves nowise inclined to be conquered into liberty. Montgomery had taken great pains to avoid offence to the religious scruples of the Canadians, and Washington had issued special orders with the same object; but orders are one thing and obedience is another. It would be unjust to hold the American officers responsible for the fact, but a fact on their own showing it is, that Montgomery's men were a gang of undisciplined ruffians. They would fight boldly under

[1] Carleton gives them as 750 killed, wounded, and prisoners; but this must be an exaggerated estimate.

shelter, but they would not stand in the open ground. 1775. They broke almost into open mutiny because they were forbidden, according to the terms of the capitulation, to strip the clothes off their prisoners at Montreal and take them for themselves; while by fraud and by robbery of the Canadians they did more to strengthen their loyalty to England than all the blandishments of Carleton.[1] The invasion of Canada ought therefore to have been pure loss to the Americans; and so it might have been had the British Ministry taken the advice of Sir William Howe, the Commander-in-Chief of its own choice. Indirectly, however, as shall be seen, it lured the British Government into a false plan of operations, and to a disaster which, less for its strategic consequences than from its moral effect in Europe, virtually decided the issue of the war.

[1] Washington's *Works*, iii. 180, 277, 362.

CHAPTER IX

1775. In the course of the summer the British Government gradually opened its eyes to the fact that a war, and a serious war, was actually staring it in the face. On the 12th of June, five days before Bunker's Hill, Gage had written that it was inevitable, adding that fifteen thousand men would be required on the side of Boston, ten thousand at New York, and seven thousand on the side of Canada. The statement reveals the plan which was in the mind of Gage, and indeed of many officers. Though there was not a province in which the King's authority had not been overthrown by the end of 1775, yet the heart of the rebellion lay in the New England Colonies, situated between the Hudson River and the sea. By occupying the line of the Hudson these Colonies could be practically isolated and reduced; and this operation, if conducted by simultaneous advance of three corps from Boston, Lake Champlain, and New York, could hardly be prevented by the enemy.[1] This scheme of isolation was likely to be the more effective since the New England provinces drew most of their supplies from the more fertile provinces of the south. On the other hand, it would require from thirty thousand to fifty thousand men, almost all of whom must be transported from the British Isles over three thousand miles of ocean, a distance which made America in those days practically more remote than the Antipodes at the present time.

Thus, when critically examined, the task of sub-

[1] Lloyd's *War in Germany*, i. 182-186.

duing the whole of the American Colonies by force appeared to military men an impossibility. It was reckoned that the population of the thirteen provinces numbered from two to three millions, scattered over a vast extent of territory. The principal towns were of course on the coast; and even if one of these were captured as the base for the British, there was no stronghold inland which could command any great tract of country, and therefore no certain line of operations. The enemy had but to retire inland, if pressed, and the invader could not safely follow them, from the impossibility of maintaining his line of communications. The one exception to the rule was the line of the Hudson above mentioned; but even there the American force that could be brought forward against the British was an extremely uncertain quantity. General Conway reckoned that the American Colonies could raise an army of one hundred and fifty thousand men; and this number, viewed merely in its proportion to the total population, was no extravagant estimate. Moreover, the reduction of New England might not necessarily mean the conquest of America. "Taking America as it at present stands," wrote General Harvey, who as Adjutant-general was, in the absence of a commander-in-chief, the highest military official in the kingdom, "it is impossible to conquer it with our British Army. . . . To attempt to conquer it internally by our land force is as wild an idea as ever controverted common sense."[1] It was therefore the opinion of many, and among others of the Secretary at War, that the operations should be entirely naval, that the principal ports of America should be occupied as naval bases, that the external and coasting trade of the Colonies should be cut off, and that occasional predatory expeditions should be made upon the enemy's stores and depots of merchandise. This, it was thought (and probably with sound judgment), would bring the revolted

[1] *Commander-in-Chief's Letter Books.* Harvey to General Irwin, 30th June 1775.

1775. Colonies speedily to reason and induce them to listen to proposals for conciliation.

On the other hand, the Governors of various provinces reported, not without good reason, that the loyalists were in such a majority as to be able with very little help to overcome the disloyal. Governor Martin wrote very strongly in this sense as to North Carolina, and Governor Lord Dunmore, though driven from Virginia, pledged himself to recover the province with three hundred men.[1] Such a pledge was of course ridiculous, but it was not considered to be so at the time. It was therefore concluded that the mere presence of British troops in certain quarters would be sufficient to rally the entire population to the royal standard; and it was resolved in effect to base the military operations on the presumed support of a section of the inhabitants. Of all foundations whereon to build the conduct of a campaign this is the loosest, the most treacherous, the fullest of peril and delusion; yet, as shall be seen in the years before us, there is none that has been more in favour with British ministers, with the invariable consequence of failure and disaster. I know of but one instance of the success of such a design, namely, the invasion of England by the Prince of Orange; and this is perhaps the reason why the English are so firmly wedded to the principle. The temptation to the British Ministry in 1775 was great, for the loyalist party was very strong in America; and it is, I think, unquestionable that the American Revolution was, as is generally the case, the work of a small but energetic and well-organised minority,[2] towards which the attitude of the mass of the people, where not directly hostile, was mainly indifferent. In truth, there was no tangible issue which should unite the Americans against England. The Mother Country had pledged herself to abjure the right of imposing taxation, in return for a very

[1] Secretary of State to Howe, 22nd October 1775.
[2] The fact was recognised eighty years ago by Johnson, the American biographer of General Greene.

reasonable equivalent; and the Acts of Trade and Navi- 1775.
gation, which furnished the only pretext for discontent,
had been so long accepted in principle even by the revolutionary leaders that they could hardly be called a grievance.
The British Government therefore counted on internal
divisions, and on provincial jealousies and prejudices to
weaken the spirit of revolt among the Americans; while
the Americans, encouraged by the Whig Opposition,
counted not less on faction in Great Britain and Ireland
to paralyse the arm of the British Government. It may
fairly be said that neither party reckoned in vain, and
that both were brought to the verge of ruin by intestine
discord.

The mere fact that the British Ministry rested its
hopes on the co-operation of the American loyalists was
sufficient to distract its councils and to vitiate its plans.
Their purpose being vague and undefined, the Ministers
proceeded without any idea of what an army could or
could not do, or of the force that was required for any
given object. General Harvey's impatience with them
passed all bounds. "Unless a settled plan of operations
be agreed upon for next spring," he wrote, with all the
vigour of a veteran of Flanders, "our army will be
destroyed by damned driblets . . . America is an
ugly job . . . a damned affair indeed."[1] In July Gage
had written that Boston was a disadvantageous base for
all operations; and a month later he strongly urged
that it should be evacuated. But it was not until September that Howe was authorised to remove the army
before the winter, unless the situation should improve;
and, when this conditional order arrived, he could not
collect ships enough for transport of the troops.[2] Nor
was it possible for the generals on the spot to broach
plans of their own, for they knew not—nor indeed
in the prevailing confusion were the ministers in a

[1] *Commander-in-Chief's Letter Books.* Harvey to Howe, 30th
June; to Lieut.-Col. Smith, 8th July 1775.
[2] Secretary of State to Howe, 5th September; Howe to Secretary of State, 26th November 1775.

1775. position to inform them—what number of men would be placed at their disposal.

The weakness of the armed force of Great Britain had indeed revealed itself at last in all its naked peril. The Navy had been suffered by successive Ministries to decline; and as late as in December 1774 the establishment of seamen had been reduced from twenty thousand to sixteen thousand men. The minister now at the head of the Admiralty was Lord Sandwich, a politician of evil reputation and an inveterate jobber; but though he was the best-abused man of his time, and though everything that concerned him, from the conduct of the war to the misconduct of his mistress, was virulently assailed, he was by no means solely to blame for the state of the Navy. The Army likewise had been left in December 1774 with an unchanged establishment, nor was it until the spring of 1775 that it was augmented by a paltry four thousand men, of whom one-half were invalids. The King had long since condemned the dangerous weakness of the country in time of peace, and early in the summer of 1775 had pleaded that recruiting should begin at once, but in vain;[1] and when at the end of August it was at last resolved to increase the Army from thirty-three thousand to fifty-five thousand men, much valuable time had already been lost. But even this increase, supposing it to be realised, was far too small to provide for the conquest of America; and the King therefore agreed to transfer four Hanoverian battalions to Minorca and Gibraltar in order to release as many British battalions from those garrisons. Simultaneously he entered into treaty with the rulers of Brunswick and Hesse-Cassel for the supply, in return for a liberal payment, of some eighteen thousand mercenary troops.

The bargain was quickly struck; and at once there arose a storm of indignation against both parties to the contract. Natural and even commendable as this indignation now appears, it was really rather ridiculous,

[1] King to General Conway, 11th August 1765. *Correspondence of George III. and Lord North*, i. 265, 266.

for there was nothing new in this hiring of German soldiers. Apart from the constant employment of mercenaries by England,[1] particularly during the conquest of Canada in Germany, foreign troops had been called into Britain itself to suppress the Highland rebellions both of 1715 and of 1745. The Sixtieth or Royal American Regiment, which by the last augmentation had been again increased to four battalions, was composed almost entirely of foreigners, both officers and men; yet no American province would have hesitated to employ it, if she could, against her neighbour in a quarrel over boundaries. As a matter of fact, the Sixtieth had already been used to keep order among the turbulent frontiersmen of Virginia and Pennsylvania; yet neither province had uttered a word of complaint. Moreover, the aggressive attack of the Americans upon Canada had altered the entire complexion of the quarrel. The Colonists might or might not be justified in taking up arms against British authority within their own boundaries, but they could have no excuse for attempting to annex British territory. Now, judging by the account given by Lord Barrington to Parliament in October 1775, it was extremely doubtful whether even Canada could be recovered without the hiring of foreign troops. The existing fragment of a British Army was far below its establishment, and few recruits, even among Irish Catholics, were obtainable, in spite of bounties raised and of standard lowered.[2] Barrington had long ago foreseen the impossibility of raising the force in America to twenty thousand men by the spring of 1776; and he complained in private that in England there were but thirteen thousand regular troops, and in Scotland no more than a single regiment of foot and a single regiment of dragoons. Worst of all, the Militia had decayed so rapidly in efficiency since the peace, that it was hardly safe to call them

[1] It is hardly necessary to add that mercenaries were as freely employed by other nations as by the British.
[2] *Parl. Hist.*, xviii. 870.

1775. out.[1] In a situation of such peril the Government can hardly be blamed for resorting to the hire of mercenaries.

It is interesting and important in its bearing on the history of the Army to observe the behaviour of the Whig Opposition at this crisis. First it must be noted that since 1772 the Opposition had gained an important recruit in the person of Charles James Fox, a young man of considerable talent, great eloquence, and singular charm. Principles, as shall be seen, he had none, but he found a substitute sufficient for his purpose in three dominant passions—for women, play, and politics—which he indulged with impartial recklessness at enormous cost to himself and to his country; though it is fair to add that he accepted his own losses always with good humour and his country's even with exultation. The reader must bear in mind that there were already rumours, disseminated by a vile and seditious press, of disaster to Gage's force and of the fall of Quebec, and that the question immediately before the country was not whether we should impose our will upon the Americans, but whether they should impose their rule on Canada. The Whigs then, with almost indecent ignorance of their country's history, began by railing furiously against the despatch of Hanoverians to Minorca and Gibraltar as unconstitutional and illegal, a charge which was easily rebutted by the adduction of indisputable precedents. Next, Fox violently opposed a bill which was introduced for the embodiment of the Militia, protesting that he saw no difference between a standing Militia and a standing Army. Next, a Militia Bill for the embodiment of six thousand men in Scotland was as vehemently combated by Burke, on the ground that the number was excessive. But the most shameful utterance was that of Barré, himself not long since a good and gallant officer, who accused the heroic troops of misbehaviour at Bunker's Hill, owing to their aversion to the service. Barré had a real grievance,

[1] *Political Life of Lord Barrington.* Barrington to Dartmouth, 31st July, 26th October 1775.

since he had been unjustly deprived of his commission 1775. for political reasons; but such a speech as this makes one ashamed that he should ever have held a commission at all. Such was the Whig Opposition; such had been the Tory Opposition in Marlborough's time; such, it should seem, are all Oppositions at all times; and yet the country looks for success in war.

However, the money for the augmentation was voted, and the recruiting sergeants were set to work, in the hope that strict enforcement of the Act against Vagabonds, aided by enlistment for short terms, might further their efforts.[1] One new regiment only was raised, namely, Major-general Fraser's of two battalions of Highlanders, which, though it no longer survives, we shall see on many fields.[2] Five battalions had already been despatched to Boston in August 1775;[3] and by the end of November five more,[4] besides the Sixteenth Light Dragoons, were under orders to take ship. Eight more were directed to embark from Ireland, but in deference to the protests of the Irish executive the number was reduced to six,[5] which when finally despatched in April 1776 did not muster as many as three thousand men. There was great show of activity but very little progress. The naval preparations were much retarded by the severity of the winter; and everything was behindhand. Worst of all, Lord Dartmouth had suffered himself to be persuaded by Governor Martin to send an expedition to Cape Fear,[6] in order to rally the loyalists of North Carolina and Virginia, though this was directly contrary to the opinion of the military authorities.[7] Howe, who by the recall of Gage in

[1] *Miscellaneous Orders*, 16th December 1775.
[2] *Secretary's Common Letter Book*, 27th November 1775. Fraser's Highlanders while it lasted bore the number 71st.
[3] 17th, 27th, 28th, 46th, 55th.
[4] 15th, 37th, 53rd, 54th, 57th.
[5] 9th, 20th, 24th, 34th, 53rd, 62nd.
[6] Dartmouth to Howe, 22nd October, 8th November 1775.
[7] *Commander-in-Chief's Letter Books.* General Harvey to General Cunyngham, 13th February 1776.

1775. September had been left in command at Boston, deplored this dispersion of force as likely to reduce him to a defensive campaign in 1776, and urged earnestly that all efforts should be concentrated on the side of New York. Not even the American conquest of Canada, which at one moment seemed inevitable, could turn him from this purpose. No doubt, as he wrote, the reconquest of Canada could be accomplished; but he added, with strong conviction, that the enemy could be more distressed by adherence to the original plan of seizing the line of the Hudson.[1] No better proof could be produced of the soundness of his judgment.

Nov. 10. Dartmouth had hardly initiated this most foolish scheme of operations before he was displaced to make room for the minister who, by adherence to the same false methods, was destined to end British rule in America. This was Lord George Germaine,[2] better known to us as the Lord George Sackville who had brought such a disgrace on himself and on the Army at Minden. There can be no question but that he was a man of more than ordinary ability, though, owing to the persistent English mistake of confounding a certain dexterity in Parliamentary management with genuine administrative power, his capacity has been rated more highly than it deserves. In any case it was a disgraceful thing that one who had been publicly degraded for misconduct and struck off the list of the Privy Council should have been restored to high office; still more that he should have been appointed to a department which gave him control of the Army abroad, from which he had been expelled as unworthy to hold a commission. It was asking very much from the loyalty of brave officers that they should receive their orders from one whose name they could never hear without shame; and the evil of the appointment

[1] Howe to Dartmouth, 3rd December 1775, 16th January 1776.
[2] He had assumed the name of Germaine on inheriting property from Lady Betty Germaine.

was not diminished by the fact that Germaine nourished an old grudge against Carleton, and was not too well disposed towards Howe.[1] The only excuse for the selection of such a man to direct the operations in America would have been exceptional ability as a minister of war; and this talent Germaine most assuredly did not possess.

Throughout the long, dreary winter Howe remained blockaded in Boston, his troops distressed by cold and by want of fresh provisions, and consequently suffering greatly from sickness. Washington on his side had passed through even greater difficulties than Howe. His troops were enlisted only until the 1st of January 1776, some of them indeed for still shorter terms, so that he was confronted with the prospect of a gradual dissolution of his whole army. Moreover, his ammunition was so scanty that for a time he could raise but three rounds for each musket; while the arrangements for the feeding of his army were of such haphazard description as to drive the troops that remained in camp almost to mutiny. Meantime his men came and went very much as they pleased, returning sometimes to their own farms, sometimes to those of their officers, to work there for days together. As the term of engagement drew nearer its close, desertion and malingering became more and more frequent, and the re-enlistment of troops a matter of increasing difficulty. Men would not engage themselves until they were sure of their field-officers and captains. Officers belonging to the same regiment but to different provinces declined to mix together, while some openly dissuaded their men from re-enlisting. "Such a dearth of public spirit," wrote Washington on the 28th of November 1775, "such stock-jobbing and fertility in all the low arts to obtain advantage of one kind or another in the great change of military arrangement I never saw before, and pray God's mercy I may never be witness to again. . . . To enlist five hundred men I am obliged to furlough

[1] *Correspondence of George III. and Lord North*, i. 44, 119.

1775. fifty to a regiment. Such a mercenary spirit pervades the whole that I should not be surprised at any disaster. . . . Could I have foreseen what I have experienced and am likely to experience, no consideration on earth would have induced me to accept the command."[1]

Such defects were so obviously to be expected from the composition of the American forces and the factitious nature of the quarrel with England, that it is difficult to imagine how Washington could have felt surprise at them. Our own Civil War, and probably every civil war, could furnish abundance of parallels to the state of things of which he complained. But with Washington a difficulty once realised was half conquered ; and he would speedily have converted the rough material before Boston into excellent troops, but for the obstruction of Congress. That Assembly, mindful of Cromwell the dictator but forgetful of the work first done by the New Model Army, was insanely jealous of all military power. In vain Washington and Greene urged upon them that discipline was essential to success, that time was needed to make a disciplined soldier, that short enlistments placed officers at the mercy of their men ; nothing would induce the lawyers and praters at Philadelphia to sanction the making of an American New Model. Nevertheless, by hook or by crook the indomitable Washington succeeded (to use his own words) in disbanding one army and raising another within distance of a reinforced enemy ; so that by February 1776 he was once more in command of nearly eighteen thousand men, with the cannon captured at Ticonderoga and a sufficiency of ammunition, ready to drive the British from Boston.

1776. Howe has been much blamed for his inactivity during these months, but, as it seems to me, without due consideration of his position. He could know nothing of Washington's lack of ammunition, whereas Washington had the best of information as to all that went forward in Boston. He knew that all operations

[1] Washington, *Works*, iii. 148, 156, 165, 176, 178, 182.

undertaken from the town must be futile and indecisive; 1776.
for even if he drove the enemy from their entrenchments, he could not follow them from want of transport, which the British Government had declared itself unable to furnish,[1] nor could he hold their works from want of troops. A successful attack therefore could lead to nothing, and an unsuccessful attack to worse than nothing; and in fact he awaited only the arrival of sufficient shipping to evacuate the town. This, however, was not to be. On the 2nd of March Washington March 2. opened a heavy bombardment, which on the 4th he prolonged until far into the night, landing under cover of the fire a considerable force on Dorchester Heights, which entrenched itself with remarkable rapidity and by daylight had rendered its position impregnable. Howe prepared to attack the entrenchment on the night of the 5th, but the enterprise was prevented by a heavy storm; and probably this was fortunate, for the ascent to the position was almost perpendicular, and the Americans with great ingenuity had prepared barrels, filled with stones and chained together, to roll down upon the attacking columns. The Americans pushed their new works rapidly forward to Nook's Hill, a promontory which flanked the British lines on Boston Neck; and Howe decided to evacuate the town while yet he might. The operation was accomplished without loss on the 17th of March. The troops, though re- March 17. duced to nine thousand men,[2] were much crowded on the transports owing to the presence of several hundred loyalists with them; and, for want of shipping, large quantities of guns and stores were left behind, of which it seems that a great proportion were, despite Howe's orders, undestroyed.[3] Howe then sailed for Halifax, where the transports arrived on the 2nd of April; and the Americans marched triumphant into Boston.

[1] Germaine to Howe, 5th January 1776.
[2] Twenty battalions of Infantry and Marines, Royal Artillery, 17th Light Dragoons. Howe to Secretary of State, 7th May 1776.
[3] Stedman, i. 167.

1776. Meanwhile, in England disappointments and delays were multiplied. There had been some improvement in recruiting, but in spite of remorseless drafting it was necessary to contract for recruits from Germany to raise several regiments to even a decent strength.[1] The expedition to Cape Fear, though ordered in October, did not sail till the middle of February. It was the end of April before the reinforcements for Canada were embarked; and only the beginning of May saw the first division of Hessians and a composite battalion of Guards start on their voyage across the Atlantic. And all this time Howe lay helpless at Halifax, waiting for provision-ships, which were so long belated that he trembled for the subsistence of his army, to enable him to proceed to New York. June was actually come before he received his orders for the campaign.

It was therefore in Canada, where the first British transports began to arrive in the St. Lawrence at the end of April, that the operations of 1776 were opened. Since his repulse of the 31st of December, Benedict Arnold had received reinforcements sufficient to maintain the blockade of Quebec. His troops, however, had been so much reduced by small-pox and desertion that he was on the point of retiring, when three small British vessels made their way unexpectedly through the ice, severing all communication between the two divisions of his force which lay on the opposite banks of the river. Carleton waited only to dis-
May 6. embark two hundred men, and at once sallied out against the Americans on the Plains of Abraham, who fled almost without resistance, abandoning the whole of their artillery and stores. No immediate pursuit was undertaken, for Carleton wished first to receive his reinforcements, which would raise his numbers to thirteen thousand men;[2] but as soon as these had been landed he pushed up the river to Trois Rivières, only

[1] *Secretary's Common Letter Book*, 27th February 1776.
[2] 9th, 20th, 21st, 24th, 34th, 47th, 53rd, 62nd.   4300 Brunswickers. The 47th was sent by Howe from Halifax.

to find that the Americans had fallen back to Sorel, 1776. where reinforcements under General Tomson had joined them. Tomson, hoping perhaps to stem the adverse tide, attacked General Fraser's division at Trois Rivières with two thousand troops, but was repulsed with heavy loss and was himself captured together with two hundred of his men. Carleton pursued the enemy up the river as far as Sorel, the junction of the routes to Lakes Ontario and Champlain; but there he halted, although the wind was favourable, and only later despatched columns along June. both routes. The western column was entrusted to General Burgoyne, but with strict orders not to fight without the support of the eastern column; and it was thought that except for this caution Burgoyne might have reached Chambly before the retreating Americans and compelled the whole of them to surrender; but as things were, the enemy was not pressed beyond Crown Point. Still, the American troops employed on this service lost no fewer than five thousand men from sickness and other causes during June,[1] and were driven absolutely out of Canada.

None the less, Benedict Arnold, having gained for the present a short respite, worked with indefatigable activity to build and equip a flotilla for the protection of the lakes, and by the end of September had actually completed sixteen vessels mounting seventy guns. Carleton likewise had been dragging up to Lake Champlain gunboats, which had been sent out in sections from England; and by the beginning of October he was ready to meet Arnold with a flotilla of far superior strength and a force of twelve thousand men. On the 11th of October the British attacked Arnold, who had Oct. 11. skilfully taken up a very strong position, and handled his ships so roughly that Carleton doubted not to capture his entire force on the following day. Arnold, however, slipped away in the night, and the British did not overtake him until the 13th, when he very gallantly turned with a fraction of his force to cover the retreat

[1] Washington, *Works*, iv. 13.

1776. of the rest; and though he was finally overpowered
and seven of his ships were taken, he contrived to land
the survivors near Crown Point and retire with them to
Ticonderoga. Carleton also landed at Crown Point on
Nov. 3. the 3rd of November, but, contrary to the advice of his
officers, declined to advance over the fifteen miles to
Ticonderoga, which he could certainly have captured in
three or four days. This was a grave mistake, for it
delayed the operations of the ensuing year and disheartened the loyalists, of whom there was a respectable
nucleus about Albany. Very different would it have been
if the British had been commanded by such a man as
Arnold, whose amazing skill, gallantry, and resource
make him undoubtedly the hero of this short campaign.

From Canada I return to the operations in the south.
The belated expedition to Cape Fear, under command
of Lord Cornwallis, reached its destination almost
May 3. simultaneously with the reinforcements for Canada,
having consumed three months in crossing the Atlantic.
For its particular purpose it arrived just five months
too late, for, since it had been expected in January, and
General Clinton had actually left Boston in December
to take command of it, the loyalists in the district had
made all their preparations for that month. Unable to
defer their outbreak, they began operations in January
accordingly, but, being unsupported and divided among
themselves, were very easily dispersed. Clinton had
strict orders not to linger in the south beyond a certain
day, after which he was to join Howe at New York;
but since his time was still unexpired and his force
amounted to two thousand men,[1] with a squadron of
eight frigates under Sir Peter Parker, he thought that
at least he might attempt something. Misled by false
information, he selected the object recommended by his

[1] The 15th, 28th, 37th, seven companies of the 46th, the 54th,
and 57th. Mr. Fiske and Sir George Trevelyan, misled by the
fact that Clinton came from Boston to command, say that this force
was brought from Boston, add to it six imaginary battalions from
England, and, having thus doubled Clinton's strength, found on this
fictitious basis a necessarily unstable superstructure of criticism.

instructions, namely, the capture of Fort Moultrie on 1776. Sullivan's Island, which dominated the harbour of Charleston. Accordingly, after long waiting for missing transports he sailed to Charleston, and on the 28th of June 28. June the squadron engaged the American batteries at long range, the intention being that the troops should wade ashore through the shoals and carry the fort by storm. The result was a serious reverse. The shoals were found to be unfordable, and the squadron after ten hours firing withdrew, heavily punished by the great guns of the fort, with the loss of one ship burned and over two hundred men killed and wounded. The loss of the Americans was trifling, and they might justly plume themselves on their success. After lingering three weeks longer in the hope of finding means to achieve the impossible, Clinton sailed for New York. July 21.

There, or rather at Staten Island, Howe was already awaiting him. After long and vexatious delay, due to the tardy arrival of his stores and the need for repairing his transports, he had at last embarked his troops at Halifax on the 7th of June, on which very day he June 7. seems to have received his instructions from Germaine. On the 11th a fair wind enabled the transports to sail, June 11. and on the 29th they reached Sandy Hook at the mouth June 29. of the Hudson River, leading to Howe's first objective, New York. The approach to the river, as is well known, lies between Staten Island on the west and Long Island on the east, the straitest point of the passage betwixt them being known as the Narrows, six miles above which stands New York. The city at that time covered only the south-western extremity of the slender slip of land which, enclosed between the Hudson or North River on the west, and a strait called the East River to south and east, bears the name of New York or Manhattan Island. Having information that the Americans were endeavouring to block both the North and East Rivers by strong batteries on Long Island and Manhattan Island, as well as by lines of sunken vessels, Howe decided to land at once on Staten Island, from

1776. which he could watch their motions. He did so
July 3. accordingly on the 3rd of July, just one day before the American declaration of independence. So far he had parted with one battalion to Carleton, and had received no reinforcement except half a battalion of Fraser's Highlanders, of which the other half had been captured at sea by an American privateer; but on the 1st of July the transports from England, convoyed by a squadron under his brother Lord Howe, began to arrive at Sandy Hook, and kept dropping in day after day. On the
Aug. 1. 1st of August Clinton arrived from Cape Fear, and Howe proceeded to organise his force into seven brigades and a Reserve, the Grenadier and Light Infantry companies being as usual massed into distinct battalions.[1] Late, however, though the reinforcements had arrived, action was still delayed by the want of camp-equipage, which had not been sent out with the troops; and though Howe could now muster in British and Hessians a force of some five-and-twenty thousand men, the best part of the year was past, through no fault of his own, before he could open the campaign.

Washington on his side had about eighteen thousand men, five thousand of them distributed among the defences of New York and in the forts commanding the North River, and from nine to ten thousand concentrated in an entrenched position on Brooklyn Heights and in some very strong lines outside them. This latter force, under the command of General Putnam, was designed to cover the approach to New York from
Aug. 22. the side of Long Island. On the 22nd of August a first

[1] *Reserve.*—Four battalions of Grenadiers, 33rd, 42nd.
First Brigade.—4th, 15th, 27th, 45th.
Second Brigade.—5th, 28th, 35th, 49th.
Third Brigade.—10th, 37th, 38th, 52nd, 55th.
Fourth Brigade.—17th, 40th, 46th, 55th.
Fifth Brigade.—22nd, 43rd, 54th, 63rd.
Sixth Brigade.—23rd, 44th, 57th, 64th.
Seventh Brigade.—Fraser's Highlanders. New York Companies. Hessian troops.
Light troops.—Three battalions of Light Infantry. 16th and 17th Light Dragoons.

division of the British landed at Gravesend Bay on Long 1776. Island, close to the Narrows, whereupon the American advanced parties retired, burning all houses and barns as they went, to a ring of wooded heights which barred the approach to their lines at Brooklyn. The greater part of Howe's army was then landed at the same point, and Lord Cornwallis was at once pushed three miles forward, with the Grenadiers, Light Infantry, Thirty-third and Forty-second, to the village of Flatbush. Since it was clear that the enemy intended to defend the wooded heights before mentioned, Flatbush was occupied as an advanced post, and the rest of the army encamped between the villages of Utrecht and Flatlands, two miles in rear. Four days were then spent in reconnoitring, and on the 26th of August Howe's plan had been thought out. There were three roads whereby to pass the wooded hills which blocked the way to Brooklyn, of which the westernmost, or Gowan's Road, skirted the western base of the hills close to the coast, and was defended by an American detachment under a New Jersey man, who claimed the title of Earl of Stirling. Nearly three miles to north-east of this was the Flatbush road, leading over the very centre of the hills, astride of which was the main body of the Americans under General Sullivan. But Sullivan's camp, though extending for some distance to eastward, did not reach the easternmost, or Jamaica road, which traversed the hills a mile from their eastern extremity and descended from them on to the village of Bedford. Howe judged that he could turn the whole of these roads to good account.

At nine o'clock on the evening of the 26th Clinton Aug. 26. moved off with the Seventeenth Light Dragoons, Light Infantry, Grenadiers, First Brigade, Fraser's Highlanders, and fourteen guns along the Jamaica road to turn the American left. Halting two hours before daybreak, he Aug. 27. learned from a captured patrol that the pass over the hills was not guarded, and at once sent a battalion to occupy it. The Guards, Second, Third, and Fifth brigades, under Lord Percy, following hard upon

1776
Aug. 27.
Clinton, with the baggage of the army in rear, halted close behind him an hour before dawn. Both Clinton's and Percy's divisions, with Howe in supreme command, then passed over the heights unopposed, and pushing on to Bedford pursued the turning movement round the enemy's left flank and rear. Meanwhile General von Heister with two German brigades had advanced along the Flatbush road, confining himself to a cannonade only until the turning movement began to make itself felt, when he threw his infantry against the heights. Sullivan's division had already begun to retire from the hill; but his retreating troops were checked by the Light Dragoons and Light Infantry until the Grenadiers and Thirty-third had actually pushed on to within musket-shot of the fortified lines in rear of the hills; and the British were only with difficulty restrained from storming them on the spot. Nearer to the hills another battalion of Light Infantry engaged a force of Americans who were retiring before Heister's attack, and being outnumbered were for a time hard pressed; but being joined by the Guards they continued the struggle, even capturing three guns, until at last the arrival of the Hessians put the Americans to utter rout. Thus Sullivan's division was beaten and dispersed; and meanwhile at daybreak General Grant with nine battalions and ten guns had opened his attack upon Stirling's division. The Americans at this point were strongly posted and held their own stoutly for four hours, until Cornwallis came up with troops in their rear, when they gave way; but the greater part of them seem to have made their escape to their lines, though with considerable loss, while Stirling himself was taken prisoner. With the rout of Stirling's men the action of Brooklyn came to an end.

The loss of Howe's force in the engagement was slight, the casualties numbering less than four hundred in all.[1]

[1] British—5 officers, 56 men killed; 13 officers, 275 men wounded and missing. Hessians—2 men killed; 3 officers and 23 men wounded.

That of the Americans seems never to have been 1776. ascertained; but close on eleven hundred officers and Aug. 27. men were taken prisoners, so that with the addition of those killed and wounded in the action and drowned in a swamp which obstructed the retreat, the total of American casualties can have been little less than two thousand men. Six field-guns and twenty-six heavy guns were also taken. Yet it should seem that the victory should have been far more crushing; for when once Howe and the turning columns were fairly astride of the Flatbush road on the reverse side of the heights, the only retreat to the American entrenchments lay across a morass, traversed by a single causeway, at the western end of the lines. Grant bears the blame of having neglected to push forward to this causeway, though with what justice it is impossible to decide. Howe, too, was much criticised for checking his men when, by his own admission, they could have stormed the American lines. But against this he urged with some force that the said lines were strongly constructed and strongly held, the troops on the hills being but an advanced detachment, and that, even if these works had been carried, the enemy's retreat was still secured by the entrenchments on Brooklyn Heights and by floating batteries on the water. It is less easy to defend the American general who, for no possible advantage, deliberately exposed an advanced detachment to the certainty of destruction by a superior force.

Complete or incomplete, the victory was at any rate telling. Washington on the next day reinforced the Aug. 28. troops left on the side of Brooklyn to a strength of ten thousand men; whereupon Howe broke ground for the siege of the entrenchments in form. This was not what Washington desired, who had hoped for a repetition of Bunker's Hill. British ships could not lie off Brooklyn Ferry without exposure to his batteries, but they had only been prevented by foul winds from entering the channel and cutting off his retreat. He resolved there-

1776. fore to retire while yet he might. Accordingly, having collected every vessel that he could lay hands on from the North and the East Rivers, he embarked his whole force after nightfall of the 29th, so quietly and swiftly that, by seven o'clock on the morning of the 30th, he had transferred every man and every scrap of his stores safely across a mile of water to New York. Howe was early apprised of the retreat, but took no measures to interfere with it until too late, the British picquets arriving in time only to fire a few shots at the rearguard. Washington was so far fortunate that his movements were for some hours concealed by a fog; but there seems to be little doubt but that Howe might have cut off a part, if not the whole, of the American army. Indeed, so obvious was the opportunity that Howe's neglect of it was ascribed less to incapacity than to desire to promote certain negotiations for peace, which had been recently opened by Lord Howe, under special powers, with Congress. Lord Howe's overtures were of course rejected. The capture of Washington's army might have made them welcome: not so its escape. No mistake is more common nor more fatal in British statesmen than the attempt to wage war on the principles of peace.

The Americans, however, were much dispirited by the reverse at Brooklyn. The Militia at once became eager to return to their homes, and deserted in whole companies. Washington by his own confession had no confidence in the generality of his troops,[1] and there was considerable distraction of counsel among his officers. Washington and Greene were very rightly for evacuating New York, burning the city, and retreating without delay; for the creek which divides Manhattan Island from the mainland on the north had but two bridges, not a mile apart, and if Howe should succeed in seizing Kingsbridge, the more northerly of these, he would accomplish the work which he had failed to complete at Brooklyn. The American Council of War, however,

[1] Washington, *Works*, iv. 72.

decided to keep five thousand men in New York and 1776.
nine thousand at Kingsbridge, disposing the remainder
of their force in the intermediate space; and meanwhile
their troops were employed in throwing up entrenchments in every direction. Such a disposition was of
course fatuous. On the 15th of September British men- Sept. 15.
of-war sailed up the North River as far as Bloomingdale, and up the East River as far as Turtle Bay, and
opened a heavy fire which sent the Americans flying out
of their entrenchments.[1] Under cover of this fire the
British troops landed at Kip's Bay, about three miles
above New York, and took post across the island, little
more than a mile broad at that point, from Horen's
Hook to Bloomingdale. Washington succeeded in
drawing off a number of his fugitive troops to Haarlem
Heights, some two miles away, with little loss but that
of their baggage; but there were still from three to four
thousand men in New York, who ought to have been
cut off and taken by Howe. Nevertheless, these troops
retired with little loss; and it seems that they owed
their escape chiefly to an astute American lady, who
invited Howe at the critical moment to luncheon. But
whatever the reason, it is certain that little more than
three hundred of them were captured. Still, New York
was thus recovered by the British; sixty-seven guns,
mounted and unmounted, were taken with it; and the
demoralisation of the Americans was considerably increased.

Nevertheless, the problem set to Howe was still un-
solved. The Americans were entrenched just above
Haarlem so strongly as to prohibit a frontal attack,
while their flanks were protected against the fleet by
batteries commanding Haarlem Creek on the east and
by Fort Washington and Fort Lee, on opposite banks
of the Hudson, to the west. So unpromising seemed
the outlook that Howe was disposed to close the campaign on the side of New York there and then. On
the 16th there was sharp skirmishing between detached Sept. 16.

[1] Washington, *Works*, iv. 72-94.

1776. parties of the two armies, but with no result;[1] and from that day for fully four weeks Howe remained motionless, throwing up strong entrenchments across his position at Macgowan's Hill so as to cover New York from the north. A great fire, beyond all doubt Sept. 21. the work of American incendiaries, which destroyed one-third of the town of New York, certainly caused delay and difficulty to the British General for several days; but the only acceptable excuse for his inactivity was that the American army was likely to break up more rapidly if left to itself than if attacked. To judge from Washington's letters at this period, such a dissolution was by no means improbable.[2]

There was, however, a vulnerable point in Washington's armour of which Howe might well have taken earlier advantage, namely, by operating against his communications to eastwards with Connecticut, from which most of the American supplies were drawn, and using the same route to threaten his rear at Kingsbridge. This was the plan which, after long delay, he at last Oct. 12. adopted. Accordingly, on the 12th of October, leaving Percy with one Hessian and two British brigades to hold the lines at Macgowan's Hill, he embarked the rest of his army in boats, and passing through the dangerous and intricate channel of Hell Gate landed at Throg's Neck, a peninsula jutting out into the East River from the mainland and connected with it by a Oct. 17. bridge. This operation was not concluded until the 17th; and meanwhile Washington had detached a force to break down the bridge and to take up a strong position commanding the morass beyond it. Howe therefore Oct. 18. re-embarked his troops on the 18th, and landed them again a mile to eastward at Pell's Point.[3] An American

[1] It is instructive that Howe gives the British casualties (in detail) at 92, and estimates the American at 300; while Mr. Fiske quotes the American casualties at 60, and the British at 300. It is safe to assume that the smaller number in each case is the correct one.
[2] Washington, *Works*, iv. 110-121.
[3] He explained that there would have been unnecessary risk in landing first at Pell's Point.—Howe's *Narrative*, p. 6.

party which guarded a pass on the road was dislodged 1776.
after a sharp skirmish; and on the 21st Howe's army Oct. 21.
advanced six miles to New Rochelle, where it was joined
by a division of Hessians which had just arrived from
Europe. But the delay of the double disembarkation
had given Washington ample time to shift his position.
Leaving two thousand men in Fort Washington, he
changed front from south to east, extending his army
in detached camps, each of them strongly entrenched,
for some eighteen miles along a line of hills that runs
northward from Kingsbridge to White Plains; his
front being everywhere covered by a deep river called
the Bronx, of which every ford was defended by strong
works. At the same time he prepared another
entrenched camp at White Plains, fronting to the
south, so as to check the march of the British to
northward.

Meanwhile, Howe advanced slowly with his thirteen
thousand men in two columns, and on the 25th en- Oct. 25.
camped on the Bronx, about four miles from White
Plains. Washington therefore on the 26th shifted into Oct. 26.
his new camp on that spot, leaving, however, a division
of four thousand men under Colonel Spencer in a bend
of the Bronx to his right front, and separated by that
river from his main body. On the 28th Howe con- Oct. 28.
tinued his advance; and Colonel Rahl of the Hessians,
perceiving that this isolated corps had omitted to
occupy a hill which commanded its flank, at once sent
a battalion across the river to seize it. Howe then
directed the Second Brigade with two Hessian battalions
against the front of Spencer's division, while Rahl moved
upon its flank; but, the frontal attack being prematurely delivered, the losses of the British were unduly
heavy,[1] and though the Americans were driven gallantly
from this very strong post, no solid advantage was
gained. Howe had ordered a simultaneous attack on
the American main position; but this movement, for

[1] British loss—214 killed and wounded, 99 Hessians killed and
wounded. American loss (Fiske)—140 killed.

1776. some unexplained reason, was never executed;[1] and indeed it seems that Washington's left was so strongly posted as to ensure his retreat to Connecticut with, at any rate, the greater part of his army. Meanwhile, Washington exerted himself strenuously to strengthen

Oct. 29. his entrenchments, and on the 29th Howe sent to Percy for a reinforcement of six battalions; but a general
Oct. 31. attack, which he had ordained for the 31st, was rendered impossible by a heavy storm of rain, and on the 1st of November Washington retreated across the river Crotton to a position from which it was impracticable to dislodge him.

But the driving of Washington behind the Crotton was no barren nor purposeless operation. On the day
Oct. 28. of the combat at White Plains the German General Knyphausen had marched with six Hessian battalions, which had been left at New Rochelle, upon Kingsbridge, to secure the passage from Manhattan Island; and Howe himself now fell back to Dobbs's Ferry, on the eastern bank of the Hudson, ready either to attack Fort Washington or to cross the river into New Jersey. This movement was extremely embarrassing to Washington. His operations had been dictated by the effort to secure three principal objects, namely, his safe retreat northward into the highlands on the east bank of the Hudson, his communications with the north-east, from which he obtained his supplies, and his communications with the country on the west of the Hudson. This last had already been seriously imperilled by the passage of British frigates beyond Forts Lee and Washington, and was now still more seriously threatened by the menace to those forts themselves. Howe's position was such that the slightest false step on the American side might give him an opportunity to strike a telling blow in any one of three or four quarters; in a word, it was very well and skilfully chosen. Washington now left General Lee with seven thousand men on the Crotton, detached

[1] Howe, "for political reasons," declined to account for this in his examination before the House of Commons.

three thousand to Peekskill to guard the passes into the highlands, and sent General Putnam with another detachment across the Hudson to take post at Hackinsaw, about seven miles south-west of Fort Lee, in New Jersey. His perfectly correct instinct was to evacuate both Fort Lee and Fort Washington, but in deference to his generals he hesitated to do so, and finally he gave General Greene, who lay close to Fort Lee, the option of evacuating or of reinforcing Fort Washington, as he might think best. Greene was of opinion that the post should be held, and, receiving an order from Congress that it must on no account be abandoned, decided to reinforce it. Washington, who joined Greene on the 14th of November, did not alter these dispositions; and Howe was not slow to use his opportunity against the forces thus dangerously dispersed.

1776.

Fort Washington with its outworks occupied an area of oblong shape about three miles long by one and a-half miles broad, consisting of two parallel ridges running north and south between the Hudson and Haarlem Creek. The ascent of these ridges, both on the north side and from Haarlem Creek, was extremely steep and rugged, and much of the ground was also covered with dense forest, while every point of vantage was strengthened by batteries and entrenchments. On the south side the approach was obstructed by three lines of entrenchments with strong abatis, which had been thrown up on Haarlem Heights to check Howe's original advance from New York. The innermost of these lines lay about a mile and a-half from Fort Washington itself, which was a work of five bastions, crowning the highest point of the western ridge. The position was in fact exceedingly strong, so much so that the American generals seem one and all to have regarded it as impregnable.

Howe had already constructed redoubts and batteries on the eastern bank of Haarlem Creek, to cover an attack from that side; and on the 15th of November he summoned Fort Washington, threatening to put the

Nov. 15.

1776.
Nov. 16.
whole garrison to the sword unless it were surrendered. The answer was of course defiant; and accordingly, at daybreak of the 16th, the guns of the redoubts on Haarlem Creek and of H.M.S. *Pearl* on the North River opened a heavy fire. Meanwhile, the attacking columns made ready to advance; the first, of five thousand Hessians under Knyphausen, against the north front from Kingsbridge; the second, of the Guards, Grenadiers, Light Infantry, and Thirty-third, under Generals Matthews and Lord Cornwallis, against the eastern side from Haarlem Creek; and a third, of the Forty-second Highlanders, which was directed to make a feint attack only, against the same side but a little further to the south. The fourth column, which had been sent down Haarlem Creek in the night to the south of the American position, consisted apparently of nine battalions[1] of British and one brigade of Hessians under Lord Percy. One and all of the columns made their way forward with incredible difficulty owing to the rugged character of the ground and the obstacles, especially abatis, opposed by art and by nature to their advance. The Americans made a very stubborn resistance, particularly on the northern side, where the Hessians suffered heavily in the task of forcing their way through the forest against skilled riflemen. Indeed, the turning-point of the action appears to have been the reinforcement of the Forty-second by two more battalions, and the conversion of their feint into a real attack. Colonel Stirling, who was in command at this point, made his way doggedly under a very heavy fire to the shore, and thence over a wooded promontory, at the summit of which he stormed the redoubt opposed to him after very hard fighting and captured two hundred prisoners. The British having thus broken into the lines, the Americans gave away at all points and crowded into Fort Washington, which presently surrendered. The American loss amounted to about

[1] 4th, 10th, 15th, 23rd, 27th, 28th, 38th, 52nd, Fraser's Highlanders.

three thousand three hundred killed, wounded, and prisoners; for Howe had no thought of executing his threat, and at once checked the Hessians who, maddened by the resistance of the American riflemen, had begun to ply their bayonets. The total loss of Howe's army was four hundred and fifty-eight killed and wounded,[1] two-thirds of the casualties falling upon the Hessians, while half of the fallen British belonged to the Forty-second Highlanders. Altogether it was a pretty little action, neatly designed and very neatly executed; for Howe at his best was no contemptible commander.

He lost no time in following up this blow by a second. On the 18th Lord Cornwallis landed about eight miles above Fort Lee on the Jersey shore, with a flying column of some forty-five hundred men,[2] and marched down with great swiftness and secrecy to surprise the fort. The movement was unfortunately betrayed by a deserter, or the entire garrison would certainly have been captured. Even as things were, Greene had only just time to withdraw his two thousand men across the Hackinsack, leaving his tents standing and abandoning the whole of his provisions and stores, together with one hundred and forty cannon. Cornwallis followed hard on his track, untroubled by further resistance than an occasional bullet from some skulking patriot concealed behind a bush; and meanwhile matters elsewhere were going ill with Washington. Lee, whom he had summoned from the Crotton on the 17th and again on the 21st, refused for the present to move, having his own treacherous objects in view; the militia of New Jersey declined to come forward, and that of Pennsylvania openly exulted over the success of the British.[3] On

1776.

Nov. 18.

---

[1] Hessians, 330 killed and wounded; British, 128 killed and wounded.

[2] Two battalions of Grenadiers, two battalions of Light Infantry, Guards, 42nd, 33rd, detachment of 16th Light Dragoons, four companies of Hessians.

[3] Washington, *Works*, iv. 202, 223.

1776.
Nov. 24.
the 24th Cornwallis was reinforced by nine battalions of the Second and Fourth Brigades and Fraser's Highlanders; and Washington, who had joined Greene, could only retreat before far superior numbers. Howe, naturally not counting on Lee's inactivity, had, in view of the lateness of the season, instructed Cornwallis to pursue no further than Brunswick. Washington broke down the bridge over the river Rariton after passing it, and Cornwallis, whose troops were half starved, and quite worn out with fatigue, was fain to halt.[1] Mean-

Dec. 2. while Lee's division had at last started on its march towards Washington, and required watching; but Howe, alive to the advantage of pushing on to the Delaware,

Dec. 6. joined Cornwallis on the 6th of December at Brunswick and continued the advance. Washington's army was fast dwindling through desertion, and when he reached Princeton he had with him but three thousand men; nor had he left that place an hour before Howe's advanced guard entered it, close upon his track. But, instead of hurrying on, Howe for some reason halted for seventeen hours, and reached Trenton, on the Delaware, just as Washington's last boatful of troops touched the

Dec. 8. opposite bank. Cornwallis started very early on the
Dec. 9. following morning and marched for thirteen miles up the river in the hope of finding boats, but in vain, for Washington had taken good care that every one should have been removed. The pursuit was therefore abandoned, and Washington was left to recover himself in Pennsylvania.

Even thus the British successes were not wholly ended. Lee, after doing his best to ruin his commanding officer, had taken up comfortable quarters at some distance from his army, where he was surprised

Dec. 13. and taken prisoner by a patrol of the Sixteenth Light Dragoons. This was considered a great misfortune by the revolutionary party, and in itself could not but be a discouragement. Moreover, on the 1st of December, General Clinton had sailed for Rhode Island with six

[1] Cornwallis's evidence before the House of Commons.

thousand men[1] under convoy of Sir Peter Parker's 1776. squadron, and had occupied it without resistance. Nearly all, therefore, had been prepared for carrying out the original plan of campaign. New York had been taken as a base for the advance up the Hudson from the south, and Rhode Island for the movement from the east. Canada also had been cleared—though by grievous error Ticonderoga had not been captured—for advance upon the Hudson from the north. Further, the British arms had been carried not only into New Jersey, which had been the furthest limit of Howe's expectation, but even to the Delaware. But for the tardiness of the preparations in England, which kept both Howe and Carleton so long inactive, the campaign of 1776 might almost in itself have sufficed to end the war.

It remained for Howe to settle his cantonments for the winter. His original intention (and it had been well if he had adhered to it) was to have made Brunswick the left and Newark the right extremities of his line; but, at the suggestion of Cornwallis, Trenton and Bordenton were included, although the chain of posts was thereby unduly prolonged, for the sake of giving protection to the loyal inhabitants. Loyalty had increased amazingly in New Jersey during the victorious advance of the British, and the inhabitants had come in by hundreds together, in response to a proclamation by Howe, to take the oath of allegiance to the King. In a very short time numbers of these people were to be captured in arms against the British, with General Howe's protections and certificates of loyalty in their pockets.[2] It is not by oaths but by arms that men should wage war.

[1] 10th, 22nd, 37th, 38th, 43rd, 52nd, 54th, 63rd, Light Infantry, Grenadiers, detachment of 17th Light Dragoons, six battalions of Hessians.
[2] Howe's *Observations on a Pamphlet*, p. 51.

CHAPTER X

1776. THE general results of the campaign of 1776, so far, could not but be satisfactory to the British Government and correspondingly depressing to the Opposition. Fox wrote in anguish of the "terrible news"[1] of Howe's success at Brooklyn ; and, when Parliament met, Burke could find nothing cheering in the course of the operations except the burning of New York, which, for reasons best known to himself, he thought fit to celebrate as an heroic achievement in sounding periods of incomparable nonsense. Unfortunately for Burke, an
Dec. 7. emissary of Silas Deane, the American agent in Paris, was shortly afterwards caught in the act of emulating this particular form of heroism in Portsmouth Dockyard, with the result that the whole of the rope-walk was destroyed, and that the culprit was hung in chains. The session, in such circumstances, passed off favourably enough for the Ministry ; and the only cause for alarm to its supporters was the inadequacy of the military preparations for the next campaign. The military establishment voted for 1777, including twenty-four thousand foreign troops, was just short of eighty-nine thousand men, which, after deducting a very insufficient force for the protection of the British Isles and for the Mediterranean stations, left but fifty-seven thousand men for the service of colonial garrisons and for the prosecution of the war. It must be remembered too that these figures, small enough in themselves, existed on paper only and were very far from realised in fact.

[1] *Fox Correspondence*, i. 145.

It was above all things necessary to end the war as early as 1776. possible; and this could only be accomplished by a great effort and by the employment of an overwhelming force.

Recent events had shown the urgency of the need. Spain supplied the revolted Colonies freely with money and with gunpowder. Holland sold them endless stores, which were sent, with great show of innocence, to the Dutch island of St. Eustatius. Frederick the Great threw every possible obstacle in the way of enlisting Germans for the British service. Above all, France, outwardly friendly, was full of enmity and malice. The Declaration of Independence had altered the footing upon which the American Congress could approach her to seek her alliance; but long before the arrival of the American emissaries in Paris in 1776 the French had sent a million livres to the Colonies, while Silas Deane in the course of the year obtained for them gifts of thirty thousand stand of arms, as many suits of clothing, two hundred and fifty cannon, and vast quantities of military stores. Further, American privateers were sheltered, equipped, and allowed to sell their prizes in French ports, while the Caribbean Sea swarmed with ships flying American colours, but manned, fitted out, and owned by Frenchmen, and in truth little else but pirates. Beyond this point the French Court for the present hesitated to go; but there could be no doubt that the first favourable opportunity would be seized for a war of revenge against England.

Moreover, yielding to the bitter complaints of Washington, Congress had actually bestirred itself a little to create an American army. Discipline, so Washington had urged, was impossible while men treated their officers as equals and regarded them "no more than a broomstick"; and when we read that many American corps would elect no officers who did not consent to throw their pay into the common stock, that officers were often leaders in plunder, that one captain was also barber to his company, and that another had been tried and cashiered for stealing his

1776. soldiers' blankets, it is easy to understand why he should have begged for the preference of "gentlemen and men of character" in the allotment of commissions. Even the officers nominated by the different provinces were "not fit to be shoeblacks," being chosen according to the favour and interest of members of the Assemblies. Above all, the system of enlistment for very short terms must dissolve his army regularly every Christmas with much greater certainty than any operations of the British.[1] Such was the burden of Washington's representations. The simple truth was, that so long as the quarrel with England meant no more for the Americans than town-meetings, demolition of houses, tarring and feathering of defenceless individuals, assaults on soldiers who were forbidden to defend themselves, and even shooting at convoys from behind walls—so long every man was a patriot; but when it came to taking as well as dealing blows, the number of patriots was woefully diminished.[2] It is no reflection on the Colonists that this should have been so, for it means only that they were neither better nor worse than other people; but our admiration is increased for such men as Washington and Greene, who had not only the unselfishness to devote their whole strength without reward to the cause which they had embraced, but the ability to perceive the remedy for these dangerous evils and the tenacity to force them upon such an assembly as Congress. The outcome of Washington's repeated remonstrances was that in September 1776 Congress agreed to vote an army of sixty-six thousand men, enlisted for three years or for the war; authorising Washington also to raise fifteen thousand more, if he thought fit, and at the same time greatly extending his powers as Commander-in-chief. This army, of course, like the British establishment existed on paper only, and, since its pay was also likely to consist of paper only, there was no saying how

[1] Washington, *Works*, iv. 110-121, 184.
[2] See letter of Robert Morris, Member of Congress, 21st December 1776.

far it could be realised in the field; but the step was at 1776. any rate full of significance for the future of the war.

At the end of November, Howe, still intent on the original plan for the isolation of New England, had written to England proposing that his force should be made up to thirty-five thousand men, eight thousand of them to cover New Jersey, twenty thousand to advance in two armies upon Albany from Rhode Island and New York, and the remainder to garrison the bases of operations. For this design he requested reinforcements of fifteen thousand men and ten ships of the line.[1] But after reaching the Delaware he became more anxious to gain possession of Philadelphia, and proposed to hold Rhode Island, New York, and the lower Hudson defensively only, employing ten thousand men for the invasion of Pennsylvania.[2] He had, in fact, every intention of advancing on Philadelphia as soon as the Delaware should be frozen, and had returned with Cornwallis to New York to mature his plans, when his security was disturbed by a rude shock.

Washington's force had lately been raised to six thousand men by the remnants of Lee's division and by reinforcements from the north, but was about to suffer its annual dissolution on expiration of its term of service. The state of the revolutionary cause was so desperate that, in order to hearten his despondent followers, he resolved to hazard a sudden blow at Howe's frontier-posts. These posts, as Howe himself had confessed, were too much extended; and Trenton and Bordenton, which formed the extreme left of the line, were, pursuant to etiquette, garrisoned entirely by Hessians, Trenton by thirteen hundred men under Colonel Rahl, and Bordenton by two thousand men under Count Von Donop. Moreover, despite Howe's express orders, Rahl had neglected to throw up redoubts for the defence of Trenton. Fully alive to this omission, Washington selected Rahl's post as the object

[1] Howe to Germaine, 30th November 1776.
[2] *Ibid.* 20th December 1776.

1776. of his attack. Having drawn Von Donop southward to Burlington by a clever feint movement, he divided his own force into three corps and arranged that all three should cross the Delaware upon Christmas Day, the first near Bordenton to attack Von Donop, the second at Trenton Ferry, and the third, under his own command, nine miles above Trenton, in order to converge with the second corps against that post. So severe was the
Dec. 25. weather that Washington's own column alone succeeded in passing the river, after which it marched through a storm of sleet upon Trenton. Rahl had full warning of the coming attack, but he had allowed his men to lose discipline and to go plundering, with the result that he could not assemble them. Having no entrenchments, he could make little resistance against odds of two to one, for Washington had brought artillery with him. Hence, Rahl himself being mortally wounded early in the attack, his troops laid down their arms, though they had suffered but trifling loss. Von Donop, on learning what had happened, at once fell back to Princeton, abandoning his sick and his heavy baggage. Washington judged shrewdly, when he fell upon the Hessians on Christmas Day.

1777. Cornwallis had been on the point of embarking for England, but the news of the mishap brought him hastily back from New York to Princeton. On the
Jan. 2. morning of the 2nd of January he advanced against Trenton, which Washington, after safely depositing his thousand prisoners at Philadelphia, had reoccupied on the 29th of December. The march of the British was much harassed by small parties lurking in the woods and by a force of six hundred men under Greene; and it was not until late in the afternoon that Cornwallis reached Trenton, to find Washington drawn up a little beyond the town, in a good position behind a stream called the Assunpink. After a sharp cannonade from both sides, Cornwallis decided to send for reinforcements and to renew the attack on the following morning; but Washington was not so easily to be caught. Leaving his camp-fires burning and a few small parties to make

a sound of work in throwing up entrenchments, he stole away with the rest of his force at two o'clock in the morning, fetched a wide compass to south-eastward in order to clear Cornwallis's left wing, and marched upon Princeton to capture by surprise the stores which he guessed to be there. At sunrise his leading column met a British detachment, consisting of the Seventeenth and Fifty-fifth regiments, under Colonel Mawhood, which by Cornwallis's orders were on march towards Trenton. The morning was foggy, and Mawhood at first mistook the Americans for Hessians;[1] but discovering his error, and being unable to discern their numbers, he conjectured that Washington was retreating before Cornwallis, and resolved at all hazards to check him. Summoning, therefore, the Fortieth Regiment from Princeton to reinforce him, he took up a position; and after some sharp play with the artillery, which did considerable execution among the Americans, the Seventeenth charged with the bayonet, killing the American General Mercer and driving back his column in confusion. But Washington now came galloping up to rally Mercer's men, with the rest of his troops close after him, and the British were quickly driven back by superior numbers. Yet even so the Seventeenth fought their way through the enemy to Cornwallis, escaping with the loss of sixty-six killed and wounded and five-and-thirty prisoners. Since the battalion could not have taken more than two to three hundred men into action, this feat was rightly judged to be one of the most gallant exploits of the war. The two other regiments lost several prisoners, the casualties of the whole force amounting to two hundred and seventy of all ranks,[2] while Mawhood lost also all of his guns. It is said that he might well have made good his retreat, but in the circumstances he can

1777.
Jan. 3.

[1] The same mistake was made at the action of Brooklyn, and thirty British became prisoners in consequence.
[2] So say Howe's official figures. Stedman says that the 40th and 55th lost half of their numbers, but the battalions were so weak that probably the three together on this occasion did not muster 700 bayonets.

1777. hardly be blamed for risking an action; for it was difficult for a man to divine that Washington, who was credited with the glaring blunders of the past campaign, could be capable of movements so brilliant and so audacious.

Cornwallis, on discovering how he had been duped, hastened back with all speed to save the stores at Princeton; but Washington reckoned it prudent to abandon his design against that place and to retire to Morristown, where he could be sure of obtaining supplies, while Cornwallis pursued his retreat to New Brunswick. Washington then extended his chain of cantonments from Peekskill southward to Morristown, and thence eastward to Newark, leaving Howe with no more of New Jersey than the slip of land enclosed within a line drawn from Paulus Hook southward to Jan. 25. New Brunswick and thence to Amboy. Washington now issued a proclamation in counterblast to Howe's, calling on the people to swear allegiance to the United States. To this there was naturally a willing response. The people flocked in and took the oath cheerfully, not however omitting, as has been told, to keep their certificates of loyalty to King George in their pockets. Herein doubtless they displayed strong common sense, for they cared very little about the quarrel though a great deal about their farms, and were quite ready to swear allegiance to any one for the sake of peace. It is said that the people of New Jersey were alienated from the British by the misconduct of the troops, who gave themselves up without restraint to violence, plunder, rape; and there seems to be no doubt that the Hessians were guilty of great excesses while in cantonments. But Howe strenuously denied the charges of misbehaviour against the army in general, and proved conclusively that he and Cornwallis took every precaution, and with success, to maintain order.[1] Of course endless accusations,

---

[1] Howe's *Narrative*, pp. 58, 59. Stedman presses the charges against the troops, but his strong bias against Howe and his favourable contrast of the behaviour of the Americans, which was condemned by Washington himself, seem to me to render his statements valueless.

accompanied by endless affidavits, were circulated for 1777. the purpose of rousing animosity against the British; but affidavits, never a very costly article, are remarkably cheap in times of revolution,[1] while the denigration of adversaries, political or belligerent, by wholesale lying is so common a matter that I see no reason why Howe's statement should be doubted. On the other hand, Washington, who never told a lie, complained bitterly that his own militia plundered all inhabitants indiscriminately, on the specious pretext that they were loyalists, or, to use their own expression, Tories.[2] The truth seems to be that the people of New Jersey were for the most part heartily sorry to see either army among them, which is neither more nor less than might have been expected from ordinary human nature.

It is probable, therefore, that Howe was wise in making no immediate attempt to recover the lost ground. Had Rahl obeyed his orders there would have been no mishap; had Von Donop, on the first news of his defeat, marched at once to recover Trenton, the mischief might have been repaired; but, as things fell out, the whole cause of the revolution in America was saved by Washington's very bold and skilful action. The spirits of the revolutionary party revived; and an advance of five thousand militia upon Kingsbridge showed Howe that enemies were ready to swarm upon him from every side at the first sign of a British reverse. In a word, the moral effect of the past campaign was in great measure cancelled, and the whole of the work, excepting the capture of New York, required to be done again.[3] The situation was extremely embarrassing. The operations

The whole of his criticism is based on the allegations of Joseph Galloway, who, as a renegade member of Congress, had every motive to try to ingratiate himself with the public and the Government at the expense of Howe. The statements of such a character are *prima facie* open to suspicion.

[1] I speak not without experience of American affidavits in particular, having examined and abstracted many hundreds of the troublous period 1678-1694. [2] Washington, *Works*, iv. 296.

[3] Cornwallis to Germaine, 20th January 1777.

1777. had been based on the assistance of the loyalists; but the loyalists, as might have been anticipated, had not fulfilled the requirements expected of them. In New York, during the winter of 1776, certain gentlemen, notably Mr. Delancy and Mr. Skinner, offered to raise troops to the number of more than six thousand men; but only eleven hundred of them were ready for the campaign of 1777, while even of these but a small proportion were Americans.[1] There were, however, great promises of solid help from Pennsylvania; and in that direction Howe had accordingly turned his thoughts. Any advance towards that quarter, however, necessarily implied the abandonment of the scheme for isolating New England; so Howe recalled three thousand of the six thousand troops in Rhode Island, though, for the advantage of the fleet, he still held Newport instead of evacuating the island altogether. Meanwhile he was absolutely in the dark as to the prospect of obtaining the reinforcements for which he had asked, and as to the general scheme of operations which might be favoured in Downing Street.

Very strange designs, from a military point of view, were under consideration in London during those first weeks of 1777; and, intricate though they may appear, they demand the reader's close attention. In the first place, Germaine's dislike towards Carleton had ripened into rancour,[2] and the minister was urgent for the general's recall. On military grounds Carleton's failure to advance to Ticonderoga might have justified this step; but since Germaine's hatred arose less from military than from political and personal sources,[3] the King was for retaining Carleton at Quebec, though he was disposed, with Germaine, to entrust any expedition

---

[1] Howe's *Observations on a Pamphlet*, p. 52.
[2] *Correspondence of George III. and Lord North*, ii. 44, 56.
[3] Chatham had sent young Lord Pitt, who had joined the 47th Foot, to Carleton in Canada. Carleton sent him home with despatches in September 1775, and on his arrival Chatham withdrew him from the service. Unfortunately, as we shall see, the young man re-entered the Army at a later period and rose, through no merit of his own, to high command.

from Canada to Burgoyne as being an officer of greater enterprise. For as yet nothing was known of Howe's misfortunes on the Delaware; and the latest letter from him before the Ministry was of the 30th of November, in which, as will be remembered, he had asked for thirty-five thousand men to cover his conquests and to pursue the plan of campaign against New England. This letter reached England on the 30th of December; and a few days earlier Burgoyne himself, as was the custom for officers who were also members of Parliament, had arrived to take up his winter quarters in England, bringing with him full details of the situation on the side of Canada. Howe's request for fifteen thousand additional troops staggered Germaine, who declared it impossible to send more than at most eight thousand; but he answered Howe by calmly assuming that this reinforcement would raise his numbers to thirty-five thousand, or in other words that one is equal to two, and left him to draw his own conclusions.[1] He then proceeded to compose a scheme for the invasion of New York from Canada, which Howe had never suggested and had formerly disapproved.

On the 28th of February Burgoyne submitted a memorandum on this subject, working out in full and careful detail the advance from Crown Point to the Hudson, either by way of Lake George, or by South Bay and overland to Skenesborough. He pointed out clearly the difficulties of the latter route and the danger to any force that might adopt it, through the necessity of leaving a chain of posts to guard the line of communication with Canada. Concurrently he suggested that a diversion by a small body of British and Indians should be made from Oswego upon the Mohawk River, putting forward Colonel St. Leger for the command of this force; but he was careful to add that he doubted whether the strength of the army would justify even so small a detachment. Finally, he pleaded the expediency of allowing to the general who should command the expedition to Canada the option of moving eastward

[1] Germaine to Howe, 14th January 1777.

1777. from Ticonderoga to the Connecticut River, in order to co-operate with the force at Rhode Island; and above all, he urged that the general should have the latitude to embark his force and join Howe by sea, if he should think it prudent. None the less he decidedly advocated an advance from Ticonderoga as the most effectual measure for ending the war; and this was the true flaw in the scheme. Burgoyne indicated the purely military difficulties and risks of an advance to Albany from Canada by land so clearly, that a wise man might well have hesitated to incur them; but he omitted to take into account the supreme peril of a march in a very wild country through the midst of a hostile population, of which every man was a rifleman trained by sport in the forest. Indeed, at the bottom of the whole design lay the fundamental error of reliance on the help of the loyalists; while no notice was taken of the fact that the New England militia, though unwilling to sacrifice themselves for other provinces, had shown themselves ready enough to fight in defence of their own homes. Again, viewed from a purely military standpoint, the convergence of three distinct columns upon Albany from three points, each over one hundred miles distant from it to north, south, and east, must necessarily give the Americans the advantage of operating on interior lines—of massing their forces, so to speak, at the centre of a circle, ready to overwhelm in detail the columns directed upon that centre, before they could effect their junction with one another. The virtual impossibility of communication between the convergent armies in those days made such movements the more hazardous; while the situation in America was widely different from that which had enabled Amherst and Wolfe to close in from Lake Ontario, Lake Champlain, and Quebec upon Montreal. Moreover, as has already been seen, it was more than doubtful whether any advance would be made from Rhode Island at all. Finally, it was quite certain that to attempt to direct the operations from London was simply to court disaster.

Either just before or simultaneously with the delivery of this memorandum, Howe's letters of the 20th of December 1776 and of the 20th of January 1777 reached Germaine, the former of them favouring offensive operations on the side of Pennsylvania, the latter reporting the complete change wrought in the situation by the disaster at Trenton. A letter from Lord Cornwallis of the same date in January pressed urgently for a reinforcement of at least fifteen thousand men. Germaine answered[1] by approving an attack on Philadelphia; but simultaneously he reduced the promised reinforcement from eight thousand to three thousand men, and yet at the same time recommended a "warm diversion" on the coasts of Massachusetts and New Hampshire. The obvious inference was that he had abandoned all idea of an expedition to the Hudson from Canada; but it was not so. On the 26th of March he sent instructions, insulting in their minuteness, to Carleton, bidding him furnish Burgoyne with seven thousand regular troops for the advance on Albany, and St. Leger with seven hundred men for the diversion on the Mohawk, according to the plan of Burgoyne's memorandum. But Germaine made an important divergence from Burgoyne's recommendations, in that he allowed no latitude to him to strike eastward to Connecticut, nor to Carleton to send the expeditionary force to New York by sea; and this although the ostensible purpose of the whole movement was the junction of Burgoyne's army with Howe's. This done, Germaine sent a copy of these instructions to Howe, but without a word to modify his former directions to that General. Meanwhile Howe had received Germaine's letter of the 14th of January, when, perceiving that he would obtain few or no reinforcements, he wrote at once to Carleton warning him that he could do little to help the advance of the army from Canada, since he would probably be in Pennsylvania. He then enclosed a copy of this letter to Germaine, adding that all offensive

1777.

April 5.

[1] Germaine to Howe, 3rd March 1777.

1777. operations from the side of Rhode Island must now be abandoned, and that even those against Philadelphia must be conducted by sea. This letter reached Germaine some weeks after the departure of Burgoyne for Quebec, so that it was too late to alter plans except by sending a messenger across the Atlantic; but Germaine, far from altering them, only repeated his assent to Howe's embarkation against Philadelphia, adding vaguely that he hoped that Howe's projects might be accomplished in time for him to co-operate with the army moving May. southward from Canada.[1] A few days later it seems that a despatch was drafted giving Howe positive orders to march up the Hudson, but that Germaine, finding it unready for signature when he called at the office on his way to the country, left it to take care of itself.[2] The natural result was that this despatch was never sent at all; so that Howe was left with directions to attack Philadelphia, and Burgoyne with positive and unconditional commands to advance to Albany and there to place himself under Howe's orders. The reader will, I fear, have grown impatient over this confusion of dates, orders, and letters; if so, he will the more readily understand the distraction of the generals. Never was there a finer example of the art of organising disaster.

The necessity for this preliminary explanation having led me in some measure to anticipate events, I shall for the present forsake Burgoyne, merely premising that he embarked on Lake Champlain on the 17th of June; and shall return to follow the fortunes of Howe. Since he had first conceived the design of an attack on Philadelphia, Howe had been strengthened therein by the advice of the American General Lee, who while a prisoner at New York had turned traitor, and had represented that both Maryland and Pennsylvania were full of loyalists, waiting only for the arrival of the King's army to rise against the party of revolution. Meanwhile the preparations of the Americans to northward of New York

[1] Germaine to Howe, 18th May 1777.
[2] Fitzmaurice's *Life of Shelburne*.

demanded his immediate attention; for Washington, 1777. fully aware of the British plan to master the line of the Hudson, was amassing large quantities of stores at Peekskill and at Danbury, on the eastern and western confines of the Eastern Highlands. On the 22nd of March 22. March a small British detachment was sent to Peekskill, which, meeting with no resistance, destroyed such few stores as were found in that post. A month later a far April 25. stronger force of two thousand men was sent up to Danbury, which met with better success so far as regarded the destruction of supplies, but was intercepted on its return and subjected to much the same treatment as the expedition to Concord in 1775. It was, in fact, compelled to fight for every yard of its retreat, and escaped only with the loss of three hundred and sixty men killed and wounded.[1] Throughout the spring also petty warfare never ceased before the cantonments in New Jersey, with varying fortune, but never without loss, which, though fairly even on both sides, could not from the nature of the case but be more injurious to the British than to the Americans.

Yet Washington's difficulties were seldom greater than at this time; for his old army had as usual disappeared, and his new army was yet in the making. In the middle of March he had but three thousand men, two-thirds of them militia; for the various provinces seemed, as he said, to think it a matter of moonshine whether they furnished their contingents to-day, to-morrow, or a month later. "If Howe does not take advantage of our weak state," he wrote on the 12th of April, "he is very unfit for his trust"; but Howe's only effort at an offensive movement had been foiled by a heavy fall of snow, while his information, doubtless carefully inspired by Washington himself, reported the strength of the Americans to be not less than eight thousand men.[2]

On the 8th of May, Howe received Germaine's letter May.

[1] Parties of the 4th, 15th, 23rd, 27th, 44th, and 64th were the troops engaged.
[2] Washington, *Works*, iv. 387.

1777. of the 3rd of March, approving of his project for invasion of Pennsylvania; and on the 24th there arrived drafts from England which raised his total strength to about twenty-seven thousand men. At about the same time Washington, having at length increased his numbers to eight thousand men, moved southward from Morristown and took up a strongly entrenched position at Middlebrook, about ten miles west of New Brunswick. Then, to embarrass Howe still further, there arrived on the 5th of June the copy of Carleton's instructions for the Canadian campaign, without a word of direction to himself. However, he decided to follow his own plans, and having concentrated

June 12. his force at New Brunswick, advanced on the 12th of June along the southern bank of the Rariton, in the hope of tempting Washington to forsake his stronghold at Middlebrook. Failing in this he withdrew to Amboy,

June 19. and had completed his preparations for crossing to Staten Island for the embarkation of his troops, when he was made aware that two American divisions, numbering in all some four thousand men, had come down from the hills in pursuit of him, and that Washington with the main body had also moved eastward to Quibbletown so as to remain in touch with these detachments. Observing the success of his retrograde movement in luring Washington from the hills, Howe very warily laid his plans to force him to a general engagement. After lying inactive for a while so as to lull his enemy into false confidence,

June 26. he marched early on the morning of the 26th with eleven thousand men in two columns, to fall upon Washington's flank at Quibbletown. But the American General made haste to retreat with the main body on the first sound of firing, though Cornwallis engaged one of the detachments with considerable success, killing and wounding two hundred and fifty Americans and capturing three guns with trifling loss to himself.[1]

[1] Mr. Fiske (*American Revolution*, i. 306, 307) put forward Washington's movements of 12th-28th June as one of the most remarkable examples of his skill; assuming that Howe's object was

But so slight an advantage was not worth the loss of precious time. On the 28th Howe withdrew again to Amboy, and in the first days of July he embarked some fourteen thousand men[1] for the expedition to Philadelphia. 1777. June 28.

He did not, however, at once set sail, waiting first to see Clinton, whom he was about to leave in command at New York with about nine thousand men, and desiring also to hear something of the army in Canada. Clinton duly arrived on the 5th, and a letter from Burgoyne, reporting all to be well, reached him on the 15th; but foul winds delayed the fleet until the 23rd, when at last it got under way. Meanwhile Washington remained in painful doubt and embarrassment. He had information of the intentions of Burgoyne, which indeed had been long the talk of Montreal,[2] but could not believe that they could be seriously entertained; and he came to the conclusion that Burgoyne's advance must be a mere feint, or that Howe would move up the Hudson to meet him. For a full fortnight he marched and counter-marched, until on the 31st of July he learned that Howe's transports were off Delaware Bay. Still the idea of Howe's deserting Burgoyne remained inexplicable; and further news that Howe had again put to sea from the Delaware Capes made Washington tremble for Charleston. At last, on the 22nd of August, came definite intelligence that Howe was in Chesapeake July 5.

to march to Philadelphia by land, and that Washington's manœuvres prevented him. Howe's letters, however, prove conclusively that as far back as in April he had decided that he must sail to Philadelphia; and the little action of the 26th (of which Mr. Fiske says nothing) seems to me to show that Washington for once was off his guard. Moreover, Washington had as far back as the 9th of May convinced himself that Howe had no designs on the Delaware. *Works,* iv. 409.

[1] Howe's *Narrative,* p. 60. His exact numbers were 13,799 rank and file.

[2] "I had the surprise and mortification to find a paper handed about at Montreal, publishing the whole design of the campaign almost as accurately as if it had been copied from the Secretary of State's letter." Burgoyne to Harvey, 19th May 1777.

1777. Bay. "Now," wrote Washington exultingly, "let all New England turn out and crush Burgoyne."[1]

The mystery of Howe's movements is very easily explained. He had made up his mind originally to land in the Delaware,[2] so as to be nearer to New York and to Burgoyne, but gave up the attempt on the remonstrances of the naval officers, and sailed on to the Chesapeake. Whether the naval officers may have exaggerated the risks of disembarkation in the Delaware I cannot pretend to decide;[3] but the fact remains that the voyage to the Chesapeake was disastrous, since contrary winds prolonged a passage of three hundred and fifty miles over no fewer than twenty-four days.

Aug. 25. Then the army was disembarked at the head of Elk River, unopposed indeed, but actually only thirteen miles west of Delaware Bay. By a strange irony it was not until he reached the Chesapeake that Howe received Germaine's letter, wherein was expressed the hope that his work in Pennsylvania would be finished in time to allow him to co-operate with Burgoyne's army.

Immediately on learning of Howe's true destination
Aug. 22. Washington had marched southward to Wilmington; while Howe, having landed on the 25th of August, moved
Sept. 3. slowly and cautiously north-eastward till, on the 3rd of September, the advanced parties of both armies came into collision. Manœuvring always to turn the right or northern flank of the Americans, Howe continued his march in two columns, driving Washington's scouts
Sept. 9. before him. On the 9th the American army was concentrated in its selected position in rear of Brandywine Creek, barring the road to Philadelphia where it crossed

[1] Washington, *Works*, iv. 466, 475, 480, 489, 501.
[2] Howe to Germaine, 16th July 1777.
[3] Mr. Fiske regards Howe's defence of his action as "trumped up and worthless." It may be so; but he certainly intended to land in the Delaware when he started, and threw himself on the naval officers for his defence. The evidence of the naval officers is so highly technical that I am quite incompetent to weigh it; and I greatly doubt whether Mr. Fiske ever cast eye over it, or he might have been more cautious in giving his opinion.

that stream by Chad's Ford; and on the 10th the British encamped within four miles of it at Kennett Square. Washington, who had with him a force nominally of fifteen thousand men, but probably not exceeding twelve thousand effective soldiers, had as usual prepared his ground with skill. The passage of the Brandywine at Chad's Ford was commanded by batteries and entrenchments, while just below the ford the stream became a torrent, pent in between high, steep cliffs, which effectually forbade any attempt upon his left. Behind these cliffs therefore he stationed his militia, taking command himself of the centre at Chad's Ford, while his right, under General Sullivan, was extended for some two miles up the stream in broken, wooded, and difficult country. A frontal attack was out of the question, for Howe's numbers were probably inferior to Washington's; and the only hope of success lay in the turning of the American right flank.

1777. Sept. 10.

Howe's manœuvres for this end prove how great was his ability when he chose to exert himself. Hitherto in all marches and movements since the disembarkation Cornwallis had commanded the right column and the German General Knyphausen the left.[1] At daybreak of the 11th of September the whole army advanced from

Sept. 11.

[1] *Knyphausen's Column*—
1st Brigade, 4th, 5th, 23rd, 49th, Major-general Vaughan.
2nd Brigade, 10th, 27th, 28th, 40th, Major-general Grant.
Four Hessian battalions.
Three battalions Fraser's Highlanders.
Queen's Rangers (Irregulars).
One squadron 16th Light Dragoons.
Six 12-pounders, 4 howitzers, and battalion-guns.

Cornwallis's Column—
3rd Brigade, 15th, 33rd, 44th, 55th, Major-general Grey.
4th Brigade, 17th, 37th, 46th, 64th, Major-general Agnew.
Two battalions Guards, 2 battalions Light Infantry, 2 battalions Grenadiers, 2 squadrons 16th Light Dragoons.
Three battalions Hessians, mounted and dismounted chasseurs, four 12-pounders, and battalion-guns.

Note.—The English brigades are given as organised in May 1777, with corrections from Howe's subsequent returns, but they may have been changed.

1777. Kennett Square; but while Knyphausen took the direct
Sept. 11. road eastward upon Chad's Ford, Cornwallis's column
filed off in rear of it to the left, making for the upper
forks of the Brandywine, some twelve miles to the
north-east. After a march of seven miles, prolonged
by continual skirmishes with Washington's light troops,
Knyphausen reached the creek at ten o'clock, when he
unlimbered his guns, deployed his columns, and opened
a vigorous cannonade, as if about to force the passage
of the ford. Washington appears to have taken steps
to ascertain the safety of his right flank; but his parties
either failed to discover Cornwallis's turning movement
or were checked in the attempt by Knyphausen's light
troops. It was not until noon by Howe's report, not
until two o'clock by American accounts, that he realised
what was going forward; and by two o'clock Cornwallis had forded both branches of the upper Brandywine, and was marching upon Dilworth, to the right
rear of the Americans. Washington's first impulse
was to make a counter-attack with his whole force upon
Knyphausen; and he actually sent two thousand troops
across the creek for that purpose,[1] which were driven
back without difficulty. Then contradictory reports
from his right induced him to withdraw them, and
fortunate it was for him that he did so. For Knyphausen
was an able commander, his troops were far superior to
Washington's in training and discipline, and by Howe's
forethought he had been supplied with plenty of guns,
so that he could certainly have held his own until Cornwallis came up in the enemy's rear and destroyed the
Americans utterly. So unobservant were Washington's
officers that he only by mere chance gained accurate
information that Cornwallis's turning movement was
not merely in progress but actually accomplished.

[1] Most narratives give the impression that the counter-attack was
only contemplated, but Major André's *Journal* states that it was
actually made and defeated. I take this opportunity of acknow-
ledging my obligations to Lord Grey for kindly giving me access
to this *Journal*, which is still in MS.

Washington then detached Sullivan's division farther to his right, where it took up a position on some heights above Birmingham Church, at right angles to the original line of battle. There, with his left close to the Brandywine, both flanks protected by dense forest, and his artillery advantageously posted, Sullivan hoped to check the British, at any rate for a time. At four o'clock, after a march of eighteen miles, Cornwallis appeared, and deployed with a front of eight battalions[1] in first line, seven more in support, and four in reserve. After a sharp struggle the Americans were driven back in confusion, and retired two miles to Dilworth before they rallied; but unfortunately two battalions of Guards, besides two more of the first line, became entangled in the woods during the pursuit and to all intent passed for a time out of action. In fact, as is usual in woodland fighting, the troops seem to have become much scattered, though the Light Infantry and Hessian Chasseurs were able by themselves to disperse Sullivan's rallied battalions; but meanwhile Washington with excellent judgment had ordered the two brigades of his reserve, under General Greene, to a strong position about a mile in rear of Dilworth, so as to cover Sullivan's retreat to Chester. Greene was here attacked by two battalions of Cornwallis's first line, and by a brigade of the second, but held his own skilfully and gallantly until nightfall, when he made his retreat in safety.

1777. Sept. 11.

Meanwhile, as soon as Cornwallis's movements began to make themselves felt, Knyphausen attacked the position at Chad's Ford in earnest, and the Fourth and Fifth regiments crossing the ford quickly stormed the first entrenchment and captured four guns. The Guards then came blundering through the woods—accidentally but most opportunely—upon the uncovered flank of the American centre, and the retreat of the enemy became general; but darkness came on before Knyphausen and Cornwallis could join hands, and thus saved the

[1] Two battalions each of Guards, Grenadiers, Light Infantry, and Hessians.

1777. Americans from absolute destruction. Sullivan's division had been utterly routed; and though the rest of Washington's army seems to have retired for a time in tolerable order, the road to Chester soon became a scene of the greatest confusion.[1] But Cornwallis's troops after such a bout of hard marching and hard fighting were in no condition to pursue, and the ground was not such as to give any opportunity for cavalry; so Washington escaped with an army shaken indeed but not demoralised. Howe's losses did not exceed five hundred and seventy-seven killed and wounded,[2] nearly all of whom were British; the loss of the Americans exceeded one thousand, four hundred prisoners having been taken, besides eleven guns. Though far from decisive, Brandywine was a skilful action, very creditable to Howe considering that he had little or no superiority of numbers. There has always been a conspiracy to belittle Howe, but, whatever his failings, he could fight a battle and handle his troops on occasion with uncommon ability.

Sept. 12, 13. The British bivouacked on the battle-field; and on the two following days detachments were pushed forward to Ashtown on the road to Chester, to Concord and to Wilmington, in which last, on its evacuation by the Americans, Howe on the 14th established his hospital.

Sept. 16. On the 16th, since the Schuylkill was impassable by the direct route, the whole army moved north-eastward towards Goshen, whither Washington was himself on march by way of Derby, with intent to offer battle. But a general action was prevented by a deluge of rain, and the British pursued their advance eastward by the Lancaster road, the Americans retiring rapidly before

[1] Chastellux, i. 247.
[2] British—8 officers and 73 men killed; 45 officers and 411 men wounded. Hessians—8 men killed; 4 officers and 28 men wounded. Mr. Fiske (*American Revolution*), i. 317, says that, according to British rolls captured at Germantown, the British loss far exceeded the American. What these rolls may have been I do not know, nor how they fell into American hands; but I prefer the evidence of Howe's casualty-list to that of these apocryphal rolls.

them. Washington now passed the Schuylkill, distributing his troops about the fords so as to delay Howe's passage for as long as possible, and at the same time detaching a force under General Wayne to harass Howe's left flank and rear. Howe promptly sent Major-general Grey with three battalions[1] to deal with Wayne, which that officer very effectually did. Removing the flints from every musket in his force so that there could be no possibility for a shot to be fired, Grey fell upon Wayne's camp at night by surprise, killing and wounding three hundred of his men and capturing one hundred more, with the loss of no more than eight British killed and wounded. From that day forward Grey was known by the name of "No-flint." On the 21st Howe's whole force encamped on the Schuylkill from Flatland Ford to French Creek, and on the next day Howe, having by a variety of perplexing manœuvres[2] lured Washington higher up the river, crossed it unopposed at Flatland Ford, and captured six guns in one of the American redoubts. There was nothing now to bar the entry of the British into Philadelphia, which was accordingly occupied on the 25th. In one respect the invasion of Pennsylvania seemed to justify itself, for the people were sufficiently well affected to the British to give intelligence to Howe and to withhold it from Washington.[3]

It remained now to remove three lines of heavy *chevaux de frise*, which had been sunk by the Americans to obstruct the navigation of the Delaware, and to open the river to the British fleet. For this purpose it was necessary first to capture a fort on Mud Island, near the Pennsylvanian shore, and a redoubt and entrenchment called Red Bank, together with a smaller stronghold at Billingsport, on the opposite shore; these works having been constructed to cover the sunken obstacles with their cannon. Accordingly, on the 29th three battalions

1777.

Sept. 20.

Sept. 21.

Sept. 22, 23.

Sept. 25.

Sept. 29.

---

[1] 2nd battalion Light Infantry, 42nd and 44th regiments.
[2] Washington's own expression, *Works*, v. 69.
[3] *Ibid.*

1777. were sent across to Billingsport, which being abandoned by the Americans was at once dismantled; but as the navigation of the river was still blocked, Howe was obliged further to detach three thousand men to escort his supplies overland from the Chesapeake, thus reducing his main body to less than nine thousand men. Of these the greater part were encamped at Germantown, then a long, straggling village of widely detached houses extending for some two miles along the road from Philadelphia northward to Skippack Creek, where Washington was encamped. At about the middle of the village was a four-cross-way, formed by the junction of the Limekiln Road from the north-east and the Old School Lane from the west with the main road; and it was astride of this main road, in rear of the four-cross-way, that the British troops were encamped, with detached posts in front and flanks. Yet another road, called the Old York Road, ran from the north-east, parallel with the Limekiln Road and to southward of it, falling into the main road two miles in rear of the encampment.

Oct. 3. Observing the detachments made by Howe, and having himself reinforcements which raised his strength to eight thousand regular troops and four thousand militia, Washington determined to attempt the surprise of the camp at Germantown. To this end he marched on the evening of the 3rd of October, directing five brigades[1] under General Sullivan down the main road upon Howe's centre and left, two brigades of militia along the Old School Lane to make a feint attack on his left flank, three brigades down the Limekiln Road to fall upon his right flank, and two more down the Old York Road to sweep round upon his right rear; these last five brigades being under command of General Greene. Howe had full information of the intended attack, but resolved to await it without entrenching his position, only pushing his advanced posts rather farther

[1] These brigades were of course very weak, not exceeding 1000 bayonets at most.

forward and enjoining special vigilance on his patrols. At three o'clock in the morning the American advance was duly reported by the outposts, and the British troops stood to arms. About sunrise, however, there came on a dense fog, which involved the whole engagement in perplexity and confusion. At four o'clock Sullivan's division opened the attack on the main road, and was met by a vigorous resistance from a battalion of Light Infantry and from the Fortieth Foot, which were in advance. Fighting at every step the two battalions withdrew slowly to a house belonging to a Mr. Chew, a little to northward of the village, when Colonel Musgrave occupied the building with six companies of the Fortieth, while the Light Infantry fell back on the main body. Musgrave at once opened so sharp a fire that Sullivan's whole line was for some minutes stopped; and Howe, looking for the most serious attack to fall on his left flank, reinforced his troops in that quarter so as to hold the militia at bay. But it was really on the British right that the danger was greatest. There the picquets had been driven back on their supports, though these had retired very steadily, contesting every yard of ground; and Greene was pushing his advance gradually forward when the sound of tremendous firing about Chew's house led him to believe that a general action had begun. In truth, Washington's attack on the centre had been abruptly checked by the little band of the Fortieth in the house, who held on stoutly to their stronghold in utter contempt of the American artillery. Washington therefore decided to mask the house and to continue his advance; but, the ground being strongly enclosed, this was a matter of some difficulty. The result was that Sullivan's division deployed prematurely on both sides of the road, and not, as had been prearranged, on the west side only. Greene, knowing nothing of this and unable to see anything in the fog, also deployed, as his orders bade him, with his right resting on the main road. Wholly unconscious that he was thus overlapping Sullivan's left, he then opened his

1777.
Oct. 4.

attack with vigour, guided only by the flashes of the musketry through the mist; and thus it came about that while Sullivan's left brigade was hotly engaged with the British in front, it found itself harried by bullets from Greene's brigade in rear. Very pardonably the unlucky battalions were smitten with panic, and the disorder quickly spread to the whole of the American right, where it was increased by the action of General Grey, who, always calm and cool-headed, had wheeled up a brigade from the extreme British left upon Sullivan's right flank. Almost simultaneously General Grant brought up the Fifth and Fifty-fifth from the British right centre upon Sullivan's left flank, and completed his discomfiture. This movement was the more important since the American brigades on the Old York Road had forced back the Guards, Twenty-fifth, and Twenty-seventh from their camp to the village, where they held them hard pressed, capturing even several prisoners. By Grant's advance these brigades of the extreme American left were isolated, in spite of their success; and Grey, withdrawing to the assistance of the Guards the bulk of the force which had been opposed to the militia on Howe's left flank, speedily restored the balance of the scale in that quarter. Cornwallis too now hurried to the sound of the cannon with two more battalions from Philadelphia, and the Americans were soon in full retreat, though their left wing was recalled too late to save one regiment from being cut off. Thereby not only were the whole of the British prisoners recaptured, but four hundred Americans were taken in their stead.

The action lasted for two hours and a-half, and was sharply fought throughout. The loss of Howe's army was five hundred and thirty-seven killed and wounded, and fourteen prisoners;[1] that of the Americans was

---

[1] British—4 officers and 66 men killed; 27 officers, 396 men wounded; 14 missing. Hessians—1 officer and 23 men wounded. Mr. Fiske (*American Revolution*, i. 322) says that the Americans captured several guns. It may be so; but Howe says nothing of it,

six hundred and seventy-three killed and wounded, 1777. and four hundred prisoners. The result was a great mortification to Washington, who declared that the Americans retreated in the moment of victory; but the truth is that the plan of attack was too intricate for inexperienced officers and imperfectly disciplined troops, while the fog was an accident wholly to the advantage of the better disciplined army. In effect the resolute defence of a single well-built house was sufficient to upset the whole of Washington's combinations; while even though Sullivan's advance was thus delayed by Musgrave's handful of men, Greene's right brigade arrived so late in the field that Sullivan's division was already deployed in front of it. Moreover, the feint attack of the militia was so feeble that Grey was able to use the battalions of the left wing as if they had been the reserve rather than part of the fighting line. Lastly, Washington's plans were not furthered by the fact that many of his officers and men had been stimulating their valour at the expense of their understanding and were exceedingly drunk.[1] Howe was not unreasonably blamed for not entrenching himself, but, as he frankly confessed, he did not look for so vigorous an onslaught after such a success as Brandywine. He therefore made his dispositions to invite attack, relying on the superiority of his troops; and it is fair to add that the result fully justified his confidence.

On the 8th of October Lord Howe's fleet anchored Oct. 8. in the Delaware below Newcastle, and General Howe withdrew his army to Philadelphia to cover the operations for opening the navigation of the river. A fortnight later an assault was delivered upon the fort at Red Oct. 22. Bank by a party of Hessians under Von Donop, but was beaten off, in spite of the gallantry of the assailants,

nor Washington, nor Stedman in his *History of the American War*, nor Johnson in his *Life of Greene*. Washington says, indeed, that he is uncertain as to the fate of one of his own guns, which though dismounted was saved; but this is not quite the same as several British guns captured.

[1] André's *Journal*, which is corroborated by Mr. Fiske's account.

1777. with very heavy loss to them [1] and at trifling cost to the defenders. Howe had already sent to Clinton for five additional battalions from New York; but it was not until the 15th of November, and after immense labour, that the Americans were driven by the British batteries from Mud Island and Red Bank, and that the navigation of the Delaware was opened for the supply of the army.

Dec. 4. Howe then marched out towards Washington, who was entrenched in a strong position at Whitemarsh, fourteen miles from Philadelphia, but the American general was too wary to be drawn into an engagement; and after a skirmish or two Howe withdrew to winter quarters in

Oct. 22. Philadelphia. Already he had written to Germaine [2] that without ten thousand additional troops it was hopeless to think of ending the war in the next campaign, and that since his former requests for reinforcements had been disregarded he begged to resign his command. Not yet did he know what had happened just five days before at Saratoga.

[1] 127 killed, 105 wounded and prisoners.
[2] Howe to Germaine, 22nd October 1777.

CHAPTER XI

On the 6th of May, as has already been told, Burgoyne 1777. arrived at Quebec with Germaine's instructions to Carleton, prescribing the exact numbers and the precise units which were to be employed in the projected expedition. Deeply hurt that the command of this enterprise should be taken out of his hands, Carleton at once sent his resignation to England, but meanwhile exerted himself loyally to give all possible assistance to Burgoyne. The number of regular troops allotted to the service was seven thousand two hundred and thirteen, to which it was designed to add two thousand Canadian levies and a large body of Indians. As a vast deal of false sentiment and a still larger allowance of false statement has been lavished over this employment of Indians by the British, it is as well to mention that the British hesitated to use them until the Americans set the example in 1775.[1] Nor are the Americans the least blameworthy in this respect, since any attempt to exclude the Indians from a share in the war was, in the words of an excellent judge,[2] dangerous, delusive nonsense. The Indians were ready enough to join the British, but the Canadians hung back. Only one hundred and fifty would serve as soldiers, while even for employment in the matter of transport they were backward and unwilling. Nevertheless, by sheer energy and perseverance Carleton and Burgoyne pushed the preparations forward; and at

[1] Gage to the Secretary of State, 12th June 1775. And see Adolphus, *History of England*, ii. 463.
[2] Mr. Pownall, ex-Governor of Massachusetts.

1777.
June 20.

July 1.

July 5, 6.

July 6.

length, despite bad weather, foul winds, and all other impediments, the army assembled on the 20th of June at Cumberland Point on Lake Champlain. A short time before this Colonel St. Leger had also been despatched with a small force of light troops and of Indians to make a diversion on the Mohawk.

Halting for three days at Crown Point to establish magazines, Burgoyne marched from thence by land, and on the 1st of July came before Ticonderoga. The American garrison of the place numbered three thousand men under General St. Clair, and occupied not only Ticonderoga on the western shore but a hill called Mount Independence on the eastern shore, of which the sides had been strengthened by entrenchments and batteries, and the summit crowned by a starfort. The two fortresses were connected by a bridge, constructed with infinite labour and protected on the northern side by a boom. Advancing with great caution, Burgoyne wound his troops round the whole position and began to throw up trenches so as to invest it completely; but an eminence called Sugar Hill had caught the eye of an old artilleryman, Major-general Phillips, who, finding that it commanded the whole of the enemy's works, lost no time in erecting a battery on the summit. The Americans, seeing the hopelessness of the position, embarked such stores as they could in their bateaux, and, since communication with Lake George was cut off, sent them up the South River to Skenesborough, while the army retired by way of Castleton upon the same point. Brigadier Fraser, anticipating Burgoyne's orders, at once started in pursuit with his own brigade of Light Infantry and Grenadiers by land, while Burgoyne set about forcing the boom so as to carry on the chase by water. By nine o'clock on the morning of the 6th July a passage had been broken through the boom, when the British gunboats hurried on with such speed that they overtook the enemy's rear and destroyed a number of galleys and bateaux. Fraser, meanwhile, had pushed on with all possible haste from tour in the morning until one in the afternoon, when he halted to await General Riedesel, who was advancing to his support. He then started again, bivouacked for the night within three miles of the enemy, renewed his march at three o'clock next morning, and in two hours came upon the American picquets, which fired on him and instantly retired. Anxious above all things to delay the American retreat, Fraser at once attacked, though with no more than eight hundred and fifty men against nearly, if not quite, twice that number. The Americans made a very fine fight, being picked troops and skilled marksmen under a most gallant leader, Colonel Francis. They had further every advantage of position, the forest being so thick that the British could not advance to the attack in regular order; but none the less the red-coats, for all their rigid training, faced the new conditions with perfect readiness and resource. For two hours the unequal contest went on, until Riedesel's division at last came up and decided the action in Fraser's favour. The Americans left Colonel Francis and over two hundred men dead upon the field, and about the same number prisoners in Fraser's hands. The British loss did not exceed one hundred and forty killed and wounded, nor would the figure have been so high but for an unfortunate occurrence. In the course of the action about sixty Americans approached two companies of grenadiers with rifles clubbed in token of surrender, and were allowed to come within ten yards unharmed; when they suddenly stopped, fired a volley, disabling many of the grenadiers, and ran away to the shelter of the forest.[1] Such methods of warfare, though not unusual among half-disciplined men who have lost touch with civilisation during long life in a wild country, never fail to rouse bitter indignation among regular troops.

Burgoyne now detached the Ninth Foot to Fort Anna, some fifteen miles south of Skenesborough, to intercept any fugitives that might be making their way

[1] Anbury, *Travels in America*, i. 330.

1777.
July 9.
by water up Wood Creek. The regiment was heavily attacked on its way, but held its own against very superior numbers until reinforced; and the Americans in Fort Anna then set fire to it and retreated. Their main body also retired southward to Fort Edward on the Hudson, using their axes skilfully as they went, so as to drop a tree at every few yards along the road.

July 10. Meanwhile, on the 10th, Burgoyne's whole force assembled at Skenesborough, where the men were employed for many days in clearing the track to southward and in opening up the communications by Lake George and Wood Creek for transport of artillery and stores. Some hundreds of loyalists joined Burgoyne at this time, both armed and unarmed, with offers of service; but to southward the revolutionary committees threatened death to all who would not remove their cattle and stores and take up arms against the British. Considering the immense difficulties of the road through the forest, and the fact that no fewer than forty bridges, some of them of great length, needed to be constructed, it was no small feat that Burgoyne should have reached Fort Edward

July 30. on the 30th of July, having accomplished the twenty miles from Skenesborough in exactly twenty days. Slow though his progress was, he only narrowly missed intercepting the American garrison of Fort George, which, finding its rear threatened, had fallen back from the head of Lake George to join the main body under General Schuyler.

Meanwhile Schuyler with the soundest judgment withdrew his army still farther southward to Stillwater, some thirty miles above Albany; Burgoyne being again detained at Fort Edward by the extreme difficulty of transporting his supplies and bateaux overland to the Hudson. The number of his baggage-animals was inadequate to his needs, the Canadian contractors having failed to fulfil their engagements, and he dared not advance without plenty of artillery against an enemy who in a few hours could throw up wooden forts and abatis that defied any but heavy metal. Had any latitude of enterprise been permitted to him he would probably have turned eastward into New England; but as matters stood he was committed by positive orders to operations in which rapidity of movement, though essential to success, was impossible. St. Leger he knew to be moving on the Mohawk, and, if any good was to come of the diversion, it was of the greatest importance that his own advance should correspond with St. Leger's. Then trouble sprang up with the Indians, owing to Burgoyne's stringent regulations against pillage and murder, and several of them left the camp in a rage. Every cause conspired to increase the General's anxiety, for nothing was more certain than that the enemy's numbers were augmenting in his front and flank. The New Englanders had been roused to madness by an outrage of the Indians, and every day's delay meant accession of strength to the Americans. His army, it is true, was in grand condition and spirits, his operations so far had been brilliantly successful, and he had captured considerably over one hundred guns; but advance without provisions he could not. The problem of supply seemed indeed insoluble. Every day showed him more clearly the hopelessness of attempting with the transport at his command to form magazines; while his weakness in numbers forbade him to establish posts or to furnish escorts for convoys between the line of his advance and Lake George.

The only alternative was to endeavour, like Major Thomas Adams, to supply himself at the enemy's expense. A magazine had been established by the New England militia at Bennington, about thirty miles south-east of Fort Edward, where many hundred horses had been collected, besides ample stores of food and ammunition. Accordingly, on the 13th of August, a motley detachment of about five hundred men was placed under the orders of Colonel Baum, a very competent German officer, for the surprise of Bennington.[1]

[1] 150 Brunswick dismounted dragoons, 50 picked British marksmen, 150 Provincial soldiers, 56 Provincial and Canadian Volunteers,

1777. The force had been made thus small because Major Skene, a loyalist who acted as its guide, had assured Burgoyne that the country swarmed with men who wished to take up arms for the King. At the same time, to make a diversion, the army moved down the east bank of the Hudson, an advanced corps crossing the river to Saratoga, and a detachment taking post at Battenkill, five miles above Saratoga, on the direct road to Bennington. Baum was soon aware that his march had been discovered and that the surprise of Bennington was impracticable; but he pushed on to within four miles of it, at which point he was met by a party of professed loyalists, who cheerfully took the oath of allegiance and invited him to proceed farther. Presently, however, he found himself opposed by a strong force of militia, and was obliged to take up a strong defensive position as his bivouac for the night. On the next morning about five hundred militia attacked him in front, while five hundred men in rustic attire, many of whom had sworn allegiance on the previous day, came round upon his rear. The disparity of numbers added to the treachery was too much for Baum's party, with its nucleus of only three hundred regular troops. The Indians fled at the first fire, but the little handful of soldiers fought gallantly until, their ammunition failing, they were overpowered, when all who were not killed or captured ran away into the forest. The American militia had just dispersed to the plunder of Baum's camp when a party of five hundred Germans with two guns, under Colonel Breyman, appeared on the scene. These had been despatched to the assistance of Baum, but for some reason had consumed sixteen hours in marching twenty-four miles. Most fortunately, however, for the Americans, a reinforcement of five hundred additional militia had just come up, which checked Breyman's advance. The same tactics were then re-

Aug. 15.

Aug. 16.

80 Indians. Mr. Fiske (i. 283) describes Baum's force as consisting entirely of German veterans; but the above is Burgoyne's list, and I conceive that Burgoyne was in a position to know.

peated against him as against Baum, with the same result. The Germans fought bravely and held their own until their ammunition was expended, when all but sixty or seventy men were captured. Thus disastrously ended the attempt upon Bennington, with a loss to Burgoyne of about five hundred men and four guns.[1]

The blow was a heavy one to the General, for had the enterprise been successful he had hoped to push an advanced corps forward to Stillwater, and thus to ensure his junction on the Mohawk with St. Leger's column. Meanwhile his news of that force was not reassuring, and was soon to be disquieting. St. Leger, in obedience to his instructions, had landed about the middle of July at Oswego, where he had been joined by two small parties of loyalists and by some Indians, which raised his total strength to seventeen hundred men. But of these not six hundred were regular troops, and of the six hundred not one-half were British. His first task was to capture Fort Stanwix and so to open to himself the navigation of the Mohawk ; and accordingly, after a cautious march through the forest, he on the 3rd of August invested the fort, which was garrisoned by six hundred men. On the 5th, hearing that eight hundred American militia had arrived within twelve miles of him for the relief of the fort, St. Leger determined to sally out and attack them, and, since he could spare no more than his Indians and eighty white men for the service, to try the success of an ambuscade in a ravine on the line of the enemy's march. It had been arranged that the Indians should not show themselves on the flanks and rear until the white men should have engaged the Americans in front ; but the savages were hurried by their impatience into a premature attack, with the result that the American rearguard was not entrapped, but was able to retreat.

[1] Mr. Fiske gives the British loss in the two engagements at 207 killed and wounded and 700 prisoners, making a total in excess of the entire force engaged. He admits also the escape of 60 men. Burgoyne's official list of casualties is undiscoverable. He reckoned his losses in the two actions at about 430 men, but added that missing men were dropping in daily.

1777. The main body of the Americans though surrounded made a most gallant fight, and succeeded at length in driving off the Indians, but with such heavy loss to themselves that they were obliged to abandon all hope of raising the siege. During the engagement the garrison of the fort seized the moment to make a sortie, and succeeded in pillaging part of the camp,[1] including that of the Indians. This misfortune, added to the loss of many of their bravest warriors, roused deep discontent among the savages. The siege also went forward but slowly, for St. Leger's guns were too light to make any impression upon the fort, so that he was compelled to proceed by regular approaches.

Meanwhile Benedict Arnold had collected twelve hundred volunteers from Massachusetts and was advancing up the Mohawk from Albany. Finding that he made little progress, he very artfully contrived to spread reports in St. Leger's camp that Burgoyne's army had been cut to pieces, and that an overwhelming force was on its way to relieve Fort Stanwix. St. Leger was not to be deceived, but the Indians were greatly discouraged, and presently broke into open mutiny. Finally a large party of them deserted, and the rest threatened to do the like unless St. Leger should retreat; and with practically no other force at his disposal, St. Leger was obliged to comply. But now the savages laid violent hands on the liquor, and turned the camp into a pandemonium. It was only with immense difficulty that St. Leger was able to protect his boats and withdraw his regular troops, abandoning his camp and the whole of his artillery. No blame can be attached to him for his failure, which was due entirely to the insufficiency of the force and of the guns allotted to him.

Thus the diversion on the Mohawk had gone to

[1] Mr. Fiske mentions that five British standards were captured. I know not what they can have been, since but 200 men of the 8th and 34th were with St. Leger, and such detachments were not likely to have taken the colours with them.

wreck ; and even apart from this Burgoyne was already 1777. in a very critical situation. "Wherever the King's forces point," he wrote, "militia to the number of three or four thousand assemble in a few hours. . . . Had I a latitude in my orders, I should think it my duty to wait in this position near Saratoga, or perhaps as far back as Fort Edward, where my communication with Lake George could be perfectly secure until some event happened to assist my movement forward." His force too was so seriously reduced by casualties and by the detachment of a garrison for Ticonderoga, that his regular troops amounted to little more than five thousand men ; but since his instructions were imperative, he decided to continue his advance after collecting thirty days' provisions, a task which, with his limited resources of transport, occupied him until the 13th of September. Sept. 13 On that and the following days he threw his whole and 14. army across to the western bank of the Hudson by a bridge of rafts, and encamped on the heights and plain of Saratoga. There heavy rain delayed him until the 19th, when he resumed his march by the road along the river upon the American encampment near Stillwater.

The enemy had taken up a strong position on Bemis Heights, which had been skilfully entrenched and fortified by a Polish engineer, later to become famous, named Kosciusko. Burgoyne, however, was a better soldier than the Pole. He remarked very quickly that there was a hill on the American left which commanded the whole of their position, but which was still unoccupied. Could he but seize this hill by a vigorous attack, he could haul his heavy guns to the summit and rake the American trenches from end to end. For this object accordingly he laid his plans. The army was to advance in three columns ; the left column under General Riedesel, with General Phillips in charge of the artillery, being appointed to follow the road by the river and engage the American right ; the centre column, under Burgoyne himself, to advance parallel with Riedesel's upon the enemy's left centre ; and the right column,

1777. under General Fraser, to make a wide detour and, on regaining touch with Burgoyne's, to fall upon their left flank. Since the whole of the ground was clothed with dense forest, the discharge of three heavy guns was to be the signal to Riedesel that Fraser and Burgoyne had joined hands and that the attack should begin.

Sept. 19. The officer in command of the Americans at this time was Horatio Gates, who had recently been appointed in place of the far more capable General Schuyler; but he had with him a force of fourteen thousand men, and at least one very able subordinate in the person of Benedict Arnold. Burgoyne's march was quickly perceived by the American scouts, and Arnold, who had at once divined Burgoyne's intentions, was anxious to move forward with the whole army and attack him on the march; but it was long before Gates, a thoroughly incompetent officer, could be induced to give Arnold even a detachment. The idea of Gates was to await attack within his entrenchments, he being too slow-witted to perceive that Burgoyne could turn them. Meanwhile the British columns steadily pursued their advance, Burgoyne reaching his station first and deploying his four battalions, the Ninth, Twenty-first, Sixty-second, and Twentieth, in due order of precedence from right to left. The whole four of them mustered fewer than eleven hundred men,[1] but they were no ordinary soldiers. Then Fraser appeared punctually with the Grenadiers, Light Infantry, and Twenty-fourth Foot, and took up a good position on some heights to Burgoyne's right. Between one and two o'clock the signal-guns roared out their message to Riedesel; and after another hour of march through the forest the attack began.

The action opened with the driving of an American picquet from a house, known as Freeman's Farm, in a cleared space immediately in Burgoyne's front. About three o'clock Arnold, who had at last succeeded in obtaining from Gates three thousand men, including a famous corps of marksmen, came upon the scene and

[1] Burgoyne's *Narrative*, p. 79.

attempted first to turn Burgoyne's right, but was beaten back with heavy loss by Fraser's brigade, whose position he had not yet discovered. Then quickly marking the weak point of the British line, Arnold turned all his strength upon Burgoyne's brigade in the centre, now reduced to the Twentieth, Sixty-second, and Twenty-first only; for the Ninth were held back in reserve. Never were troops more hardly tried, nor met their trial more grandly than these three noble battalions, with the forty-eight artillerymen who worked their four guns by their side. Attack after attack of far superior numbers was launched upon them without intermission for four hours; and it was only occasionally that Fraser's brigade could leave its station on the heights to relieve them, lest so valuable a position on the way to the coveted hill should be lost. Again and again the three battalions charged with the bayonet, but Arnold could always bring forward fresh troops to replace those who had fallen, while the American sharpshooters, perched aloft in the trees, picked off officer after officer with their rifles. At length support came to them from the left. General Phillips arrived first with four guns and took personal command of the Twentieth, as befitted a veteran of Minden; while a little later Riedesel came up on Arnold's flank and forced him to abandon his attack. Darkness closed the action, which was most gallantly fought on both sides. Had Gates sent to Arnold the reinforcements for which he asked, Arnold must certainly have broken the British centre, which, even as things were, could barely hold its own. The three devoted battalions suffered terribly, losing three hundred and fifty killed and wounded out of a strength of little more than eight hundred. The Sixty-second had scarcely sixty men standing at the close of the combat, while the gallant little detachment of artillery, which had served its guns to the very end, lost all its officers and thirty-six out of forty-eight men. The total loss of the British troops was over five hundred, or little less than one-third of the whole force engaged;

1777.
Sept. 19.

1777. that of the Germans seems to have been about fifty men.¹

That night the British bivouacked on the ground, only a few hundred yards in extent, which they had won, and on the next day they moved up almost to within cannon-shot of the enemy, fortifying their right and extending their left so as to cover their stores and bateaux. Gates likewise threw up new entrenchments to guard his left. But the Americans had already bethought them of sending a force in rear of Burgoyne
Sept. 18. to cut off his supplies, and on the 18th of September these troops surprised and took the British flotilla at the head of Lake George, together with three companies of the Fifty-third. Emboldened by this success, the Americans pushed on to the siege of Ticonderoga, which, however, they quickly abandoned. A further attack which they essayed upon an island on the lake was brilliantly repulsed by two companies of the
Sept. 24. Forty-seventh, who, following up their victory, retook the whole of their cannon and some of the shipping previously captured by the enemy. The news of the mishap to the flotilla might well have prompted Bur-
Sept. 21. goyne to retreat, had not intelligence reached him on the very same day that General Clinton was about to undertake a diversion in his favour. He waited therefore behind his entrenchments in hope of the promised relief.

Nor was Clinton worse than his word. Towards the end of September he had received a body of about

¹ It is extremely difficult to ascertain the number of men engaged. On the 3rd of September the British fit for duty were 2935; the Germans on the 1st of September numbered 1741; the artillery cannot be reckoned at more than 400. The Provincials, Volunteers, etc., numbered 830 on the 1st of July, but had been since greatly reduced by desertion. It seems therefore that when he crossed the Hudson, Burgoyne's force cannot have exceeded 5000 regular troops and 700 irregulars fit for duty; and there had been many casualties from skirmishes and "sniping" before the action. Until Reidesel came up, I think it unlikely that Burgoyne had above 1800 troops engaged or above 2200 on the field. With Riedesel's troops added, the numbers would hardly have exceeded 3000. See Evidence, etc., in Burgoyne's *Narrative*.

three thousand recruits, which enabled him at last to 1777. take the offensive on a small scale without endangering the safety of New York. The great object of the British was to open the navigation of the Hudson to the north, which was still barred about three miles above Peekskill by a boom, covered by two strong fortifications named Forts Clinton and Montgomery, on the western bank of the river. At Verplanks Point, some four miles below Fort Clinton and on the eastern bank, stood a weak breastwork with two guns, which had been erected by the Americans to cover the landing-place of the stores for their troops at Peekskill. Upon this work at Verplanks Clinton suddenly descended Oct. 5. with three thousand men, drove out the garrison and captured the guns. He then bivouacked on the Point for the night; whereupon the American General Putnam, who commanded at Peekskill, at once concluded that Clinton designed to attack the passes of the Eastern Highlands, and collecting two thousand men from the posts on the river hurried off to occupy them. This was precisely what Clinton wanted. At dawn of the following day he passed two thousand men over the Oct. 6. river to Stony Point, where they separated into two columns for simultaneous attack on Forts Clinton and Montgomery. The only road in that steep and rugged country was so narrow as to admit but three men abreast, and so circuitous and difficult that the march of twelve miles from Stony Point was not accomplished until near sunset. Then both attacks were delivered simultaneously with great precision. Fort Montgomery[1] being of no great strength was carried with little difficulty or loss, though most of the garrison made their escape. Fort Clinton was a more serious matter, the only possible approach to it lying over a space, about four hundred yards square, between a lake and the cliffs overhanging the river. The whole of this patch of ground was blocked by abatis and swept by the fire of ten guns

[1] The attacking force consisted of the 52nd, 57th, and detachments of Provincial corps, in all 900 men.

1777. from a central battery and two flanking redoubts. Clinton had brought no cannon with him, knowing that his only chance of success lay in a swift advance with the bayonet. The attack[1] was led by the flank-companies of the Twenty-sixth and of Fraser's Highlanders, together with one company of German Chasseurs, while the Sixty-third endeavoured to break in on the opposite or northern side. In perfect silence the men of the storming party pushed on through the abatis under a terrible fire, and on arriving at the foot of the fort itself very coolly hoisted each other into the embrasures. The American garrison, four hundred strong, made a very brave defence, but being at length driven from the ramparts fired a final volley and surrendered. The Americans in the two attacks lost about one hundred killed and three hundred prisoners, while the British lost eighteen officers and one hundred and sixty-nine men killed and wounded. Sixty-seven cannon, a sloop of ten guns, and a large quantity of stores were captured; while the American flotilla behind the boom, being unable to escape up the river owing to foul winds, was burned to prevent it from falling into Clinton's hands. On its own scale the enterprise was as well and skilfully conducted as any operation of the war.

Oct. 8. "*Nous y voici,*" wrote Clinton to Burgoyne from Fort Montgomery on the 8th, "and nothing between us and Gates. I sincerely hope this little success of ours will facilitate your operations." This short message, written on the thinnest of paper, was enclosed in a tiny silver bullet and entrusted to a single messenger for delivery. The British squadron then sailed up the river as far as Kingston, destroying stores and capturing petty batteries; but meanwhile Burgoyne's situation was growing desperate. He knew the difficulty, if not impossibility, of a retreat to Canada before the daily

---

[1] The attacking force consisted of the flank-companies of the New York garrison, the 26th, 63rd, one troop of the 17th Light Dragoons (dismounted), Hessian Chasseurs. The 7th Fusiliers and a German battalion formed the rearguard. Total, 1200 men.

increasing numbers of Gates's army, but on the other 1777.
hand he hesitated to set free even a portion of that
army to join Washington against Howe. At length,
on the 7th of October, he resolved to make a last Oct. 7.
attempt to turn the enemy's left. The overwhelming
numbers opposed to him forbade him to withdraw more
than fifteen hundred men from the protection of his
camp; but with these and with ten guns, under the
direction of Riedesel, Phillips, and himself, he moved
out between eleven and twelve o'clock in the forenoon,
so as to ensure the advantage of darkness for his retreat
in case of need. Posting the Germans in the centre, and
the British on either flank of them, he formed his line
within three-quarters of a mile of the American left,
while the very few Indians and Provincials that remained with his army defiled by secret paths through
the forest, to make a demonstration upon the American
rear. All hopes of success were instantly and rudely
dispelled by a sudden attack of the American General
Morgan upon Burgoyne's left. The British Grenadiers,
wheeling back at right angles to cover the left flank,
met this onset with great firmness; but the Americans,
bringing some four thousand men into action, speedily
extended their offensive movement to the Germans on
Burgoyne's left centre, where one battalion of Brunswickers gave way immediately. At the same time a
separate column came down in force to turn Burgoyne's
right flank, whereupon General Fraser withdrew the
Light Infantry and Twenty-fourth from Burgoyne's
right to cover the retreat. But meanwhile the Grenadiers
on the left gave way before overpowering numbers, and
Fraser was obliged to move his detachment hastily to
their support, during which movement he was mortally
wounded by a bullet from some hidden rifleman in a
tree. Burgoyne had early perceived that it had become
a question of saving not only his tiny attacking force but
also his fortified lines, and had ordered the artillery to
retire; but the aide-de-camp who carried the message
was mortally wounded before he could deliver it, and

1777.
Oct. 7.
thus much valuable time was lost. He therefore directed Phillips and Riedesel to cover the retreat as best they could, and withdrew his troops, hard pressed indeed but in good order, within his entrenchments, though at the sacrifice of six guns, which were perforce abandoned after every man and horse belonging to them had been shot down.

Had Gates been in true command of the Americans, the combat might have ended at that moment; but Benedict Arnold, with true military instinct, seized the opportunity to order a general attack upon the British entrenchments. The first assault was delivered against the British right centre, and was beaten back with heavy loss by Lord Balcarres and the Light Infantry; but the post next to the right of Balcarres, being defended only by Canadian irregulars, was easily carried, admitting the Americans to the flank of the extreme right of Burgoyne's line. This station was held by the German grenadiers and light infantry under Colonel Breyman, tried and gallant soldiers who fought hard until their commander was killed, and prolonged their resistance so late that Burgoyne only learned of their defeat after night had fallen. Realising then that the enemy had established themselves on his right flank, he withdrew his army during the night to some heights immediately above the river, where he showed a new front. That this change of position should have been accomplished in good order and without loss speaks highly for the General and for his troops, after so much gallantry expended in vain. Burgoyne offered battle in his new position on the next

Oct. 8. day; but learning that the enemy were on march to turn his right, found himself compelled to retire up the river to Saratoga, abandoning some five hundred sick and wounded men to the enemy. The retreat itself was accomplished without hindrance; but so heavy was the rain and so severe the weather, that the men on coming into camp had not strength to cut wood or make fires, but threw themselves down, old soldiers though they were, on the sodden ground to sleep. When the light

Oct. 9. came on the morning of the 9th, it revealed the

Americans in the act of entrenching the heights on the opposite side of the river, so as to prevent the British from crossing. Burgoyne therefore decided on the following day to abandon his artillery and baggage and to withdraw by a forced march to Fort Edward. Scouts, however, came in to report that the whole of the fords on the road were beset, and that the Americans were strongly entrenched, with cannon, between Fort George and Fort Edward. The British were in fact surrounded. Gates had by this time from eighteen to twenty thousand men; and there was no escape. For yet a few days Burgoyne waited in the vain hope of news from Clinton; but the message in the silver bullet had been intercepted and the messenger hanged. The army was not only surrounded but starving, and on the 14th Burgoyne made overtures for a capitulation, which was finally concluded on the 17th. It was agreed that Burgoyne's troops should march out with the honours of war, pile their arms, and be conducted at once to Boston for shipment to England, on the understanding that they should serve no more in America during the continuance of hostilities.

1777.

Oct. 17.

The army marched out accordingly, a bare thirty-five hundred men fit for duty, nineteen hundred of them British and the remainder of them Germans, all that were left of the seven thousand who had started from Canada four months before in all the confidence of perfect discipline and of reputation won on a score of fields.[1] Gates, with a chivalrous feeling which did him honour, kept his troops in camp while the British piled their arms; and all ranks of the victors vied with each other in showing to the vanquished that courtesy and consideration which is never denied by brave men to brave men. Not such was the behaviour of the Assembly of civilians, which was called Congress. With shameless ill faith they evaded the agreement to return

[1] The full total of men surrendered, including the sick and wounded abandoned on the 9th, Provincials, Canadians, bateaux men, etc., was 4880.

1777. the prisoners to England, under a series of pretexts, each flimsier than the last. In vain Washington and other of the American generals remonstrated, with all the indignation of gallant officers and honourable men. Burgoyne was indeed allowed to go home on parole, but the rest were retained, and every effort was strained to drive the British rank and file to enter the American service. As the American provinces had formerly thrust the burden of defending them upon sick and disabled Highlanders, so Congress now hoped to commit the battle of American independence to British deserters.

Transported first to New England, all ranks of the captured British were treated with the greatest indignity and even cruelty by the civil authorities. One individual, who bore the rank of Colonel of Militia, actually bayonetted a defenceless British corporal because of some trifling matter; and this example of brutality was speedily copied by his men. Burgoyne endeavoured to obtain redress before an American court-martial, but despite much eloquence was unsuccessful. A few weeks later a British officer was wantonly shot dead by a boy of fourteen who was standing sentry. The boy was tried and commended; and when the officer was buried in the Anglican Church at Cambridge, the mob entered the building during the funeral and plundered or destroyed every article on which they could lay hands.[1] Finally, after every kind of insult and ill-treatment suffered in New England, the troops were ordered by Congress to march down in the depth of winter to Virginia, partly to relieve New England of the burden of supporting them, partly in the hope of hastening the process of desertion. On arriving at their destination in Virginia, the troops found neither food nor shelter ready for them, although the snow lay thick upon the ground. The officers indeed received much consideration and generous hospitality from the gentlemen of the upper class, while the foreigners of all ranks were persistently

[1] Anbury, ii. 231 *sqq.*

favoured; but the British soldiers were still abominably 1777. fed and otherwise neglected. It is noteworthy that by this contemptible conduct Congress defeated its own object; for although there were a few men who purchased comfort at the price of desertion, the majority stuck faithfully to their officers, or escaped and made their way to the British army at New York. Finally, in 1781, the men, by direct infringement of the capitulation, were separated from their officers, and vanished no man knows whither. So ends this sordid story of meanness and ill faith, an indelible blot on the reputation of Congress.

As to Burgoyne's campaign at large, it seems to me that no more honourable attempt of British officers and men to achieve the impossible is on record. Burgoyne was denied the satisfaction of a court-martial, and was treated both by the King and by Germaine with great harshness and injustice; but he was allowed to defend himself before a Committee of the House of Commons, where in my judgment he vindicated himself completely. A stronger man might indeed have retreated, whatever his instructions, after the reverse at Bennington; but Burgoyne's instructions were undoubtedly positive, nor could he tell how far other operations might be dependent upon his advance. His movements were extremely skilful, and the quickness with which he hit the vulnerable point of Gates's position shows that he was a capable commander. Even more to his honour is the unfailing loyalty and confidence of his troops towards him, while their behaviour in the field was beyond all praise. In the whole history of the Army I have encountered no grander display of stedfastness and fortitude than the heroic stand of the Twentieth, Twenty-first, and Sixty-second, with their little handful of gunners, on the 19th of September; and it is surely a marvellous instance of gallantry and discipline that fifteen hundred men should have moved out cheerfully and confidently as they did on the 7th of October, in spite of much hardship and heavy losses, to attack an enemy of five times their number; that when forced back they should have retired with perfect order and coherence; and that though fighting all day and marching or entrenching all night, they should never have lost heart. Assuredly, too, it is not every commander who can command such unwavering devotion. In fact, what men could do, Burgoyne and his army did. Burgoyne's one stroke of good fortune was the substitution by Congress of Gates for the far more competent Schuyler as commander of the American Army; but this was neutralised by Washington's foresight in appointing Benedict Arnold to a subordinate command. But for Arnold, Burgoyne might have made his way to Albany; as things fell out, he failed; and the only pertinent comment on the capitulation of Saratoga is that of General Carleton: "This unfortunate event, it is to be hoped, will in future prevent ministers from pretending to direct operations of war in a country at three thousand miles' distance, of which they have so little knowledge as not to be able to distinguish between good, bad, or interested advices, or to give positive orders upon matters which from their nature are ever on the change."[1] Carleton was too sanguine. It was not until Germaine had received another such fatal lesson that he was to relinquish the direction of operations in America from his desk in Downing Street.

[1] Carleton to Burgoyne, 17th November 1777.

CHAPTER XII

Few events in our history have been more momentous 1777. their results than the disaster of Saratoga. In itself might have seemed to be nothing past repair. The ss of four thousand troops for service in America ly (for such were the terms of capitulation) was t so great as to be irremediable, and the operations the campaign had not been entirely thrown away. iconderoga had been recovered, and, though much aterial of war had been lost, infinitely more had been ptured and destroyed both by Burgoyne himself and Clinton. Nevertheless the fact remained that a itish army, or the remnant of one, had been beaten d captured; whereby a great blow had been dealt at e reputation of England, and great encouragement ven not only to the revolutionary party in America, t to that far more dangerous and unscrupulous enemy, e Opposition in the British Parliament.

The Houses met early in November, when the untry was still exulting over the capture of Ticonroga and the victory of Brandywine; but the news of nnington was also come, and newspapers and politicians re already croaking prophecies of disaster to Buryne. They spoke not from any military knowledge, r they had uttered the same sinister predictions as to ery movement of British troops during the war,[1] but

[1] On this ground I must very respectfully reject Mr. Lecky's bute to Chatham's military prescience when that statesman in bate predicted disaster to Burgoyne. Chatham could inspire men great deeds, but he was a very poor designer of a campaign; and

1777. from that heedless malignity of faction which would cheerfully wreck an Empire to pull down a Ministry. The estimates for the Army allowed for but trifling increase on the establishment of the previous year, an omission which, in the face of Howe's repeated remonstrances, can be characterised only as sheer madness. Then the usual dreary round of talk began, and Chatham, now drawing very near to his end, made the usual passionate appeals for peace and for withdrawal of the army from America, always on the fatally false presumption that American dependence and submission to the Acts of Trade and Navigation were matters not yet wholly obsolete. Then, as though he of all men had had no concern with the Canadian operations of 1759, he fell to wild denunciation of the employment of Indians in civilised warfare. The Duke of Richmond, himself once an officer, feebly echoed the thunders of Chatham, and declared that a British army associated with such allies would be a menace to liberty on its return home. Like Chatham, he ignored the fact that British troops had been associated with those identical allies for the best part of a century. A fortnight later, rumours of the surrender at Saratoga were noised abroad; and when the news of this national disaster was confirmed in the House of Commons, it was received by the Opposition with such a howl of insulting triumph as exasperated the Government once more into cheerfulness. Chatham once again opened his mouth, and, while very justly defending Burgoyne, condemned his campaign as "a mad, uncombined project," which undoubtedly it was, though it was not for Chatham to make such a criticism. Then returning in an evil moment to the question of the employment of Indians, he was remorselessly pinned to his own sanction, in 1759, of the very measure which he now condemned. In vain he wriggled and shuffled and raved: there was no escape from the facts. Never was seen a more pitiful exhibition of the wreck of a great mind.

he was simply repeating the commonplaces that had been current in the mouths of the Opposition for several weeks.

Happily, in other quarters there was more patriotism; 1777. for, from the moment when the news of Saratoga arrived, all thinking Englishmen were filled with apprehension for its possible influence on the policy of France. Very early in December the town of Manchester volunteered to raise a battalion of eleven hundred men at its own expense. Liverpool shortly afterwards followed this example, and was immediately imitated by Glasgow, Edinburgh, and Aberdeen; and the offers of all except Aberdeen were accepted. Birmingham, Warwick, and Coventry made like proposals, which however were not embraced. London, being still under the spell of the ignoble Wilkes, and Bristol, a great centre of colonial trade, held sullenly aloof; though private subscriptions of their citizens atoned in some measure for the studied apathy of their municipal councils. Simultaneously a number of Scottish noblemen and gentlemen offered to raise regiments, though not at their own expense. Lord Macleod, son of Lord Cromartie, and late of the Swedish service, came forward first to create the corps which now bears the famous title of the Seventy-first Highland Light Infantry. Five more Scottish gentlemen likewise raised regiments, of which the last, Lord Seaforth's, still survives as the Seventy-second Highlanders. Nor was this patriotic spirit confined to Britain, for in Ireland also Lords Ross, Granard, Lanesborough, and Bellamont, together with a Major Blakeney, all tendered their service to raise regiments or corps, though the proposal was in every case gratefully declined.[1] Finally, it was resolved to raise in Wales independent companies sufficient to be incorporated into a regiment.[2] In all, about fifteen thousand men were given by private subscription for the service of the State.[3]

[1] *S. P. Ireland*, Lord Lieutenant to Secretary of State, 16th September 1777, 7th January, 28th February 1778.
[2] Picton's, numbered then the 75th; afterwards disbanded.
[3] The following is the full list of the regiments raised in the spring of 1778, with the numbers which they then bore:—72nd

1777. It was indeed none too soon, for the disaster at Saratoga had decided the French Government to conclude a treaty with the revolted Colonies, whereby France agreed not only to acknowledge but to uphold their independence, on the sole condition that the States should make no peace with England that did not acknowledge that independence. The treaty was not immediately signed, and indeed the French ministers denied, with shameless mendacity, that it was even on foot; but the British ambassador at Paris knew enough to rouse his suspicions, while Fox and other members of the Opposition had early intelligence of the real state of affairs. In the face of an imminent rupture with France the behaviour of the Opposition is worthy of remark.

1778. First they attacked the raising of troops without consent of Parliament as unconstitutional; and Fox railed at Manchester and the Scottish towns for the example which they had set, affirming that "they were so accustomed to disgrace that it was no wonder if they pocketed instances of dishonour and sat down with infamy." Then Fox in the Commons and the Duke of Richmond in the Lords moved simultaneously that no more of the old regiments should be sent out of the kingdom, which, as they had already condemned the raising of new regiments, amounted practically to a motion for the sacrifice of all external British possessions whatever. Then Burke came forward with hysterical utterances about the employment of Indian allies; to which Governor Pownall, with the weight of long experience of America, answered decisively that the idea of Indian neutrality was dangerous, delusive nonsense. Meanwhile Lord North, after vainly pressing his resignation upon the King, brought forward proposals for conciliation, which included the suspension of all acts

---

(Manchester), 73rd (Macleod's, now the Seventy-first), 74th (John Campbell), 75th (Picton), 76th (John M'Donnell), 77th (James Murray, the Athol Highlanders), 78th (Seaforth's, now the Seventy-second), 79th (Liverpool), 80th (Edinburgh), 81st (William Gordon), 82nd (Francis M'Lean), 83rd (Glasgow).

relating to America which had been passed since 1763, 1778. and virtually conceded all that England had been fighting for since 1775. This forced the hand of France; and on the 6th of February her treaty with Feb. 6. the revolted Colonies was signed, though it was not until the 17th of March that the fact could be authenti- March 17. cally reported to Parliament.

At such a crisis it was felt that Chatham was the one man who was fit to take the helm, and some effort was made to place him at the head of an administration. But the King would not hear of Chatham except as subordinate to North; and, however hardly his resolution may be judged, there was very much to be urged in its favour. In the first place, Chatham's body was half dead and his mind probably more than half unhinged. It was under Chatham's administration that the crowning folly of Charles Townshend had been committed; and there was no certainty that similar disloyal action might not be repeated by some mutinous subordinate. There was no discipline among the Whigs, as was proved when Fox and Shelburne took office in 1782; and the Opposition was so much divided on the American question that all prospect of uniting it was hopeless. Chatham was still firm for British sovereignty over the Colonies and for the Acts of Trade,[1] which Rockingham and the Duke of Richmond with truer insight were prepared to sacrifice, as indeed already lost.[2] The attitude of the Colonies also was unpromising, for even with the depression of Burgoyne's success at Ticonderoga still heavy upon them, they had named the cession of Canada, Nova Scotia, and Newfoundland as essential conditions to the conclusion of a federal treaty, offensive, defensive, and commercial, with the Mother Country.[3] To such

---

[1] It was recognised by at least one shrewd observer in America, Thomas Paine, that Chatham's "plans and opinions towards the latter part of his life would have been attended with as many evil consequences and as much reprobated by America as those of Lord North." See Adolphus, iii. 3.
[2] *Chatham Correspondence*, iv. 490-493, 518.
[3] *Parl. Hist.*, xix. 930.

1778. a surrender the King, though anxious to end the war with America, absolutely declined to agree; nor can his refusal be called unreasonable.¹

Meanwhile the usual factious embarrassment of the Government continued. The egregious John Wilkes
April 2. brought in a bill, of course aimed at the gratuitous creation of regiments by patriotic men, to forbid subscriptions for giving money to the Crown without consent of Parliament; and it is significant that Burke, who posed as the apostle of liberty, actually supported
April 7. this monstrous and tyrannical proposal. A few days later Chatham delivered his last speech in Parliament, calling upon his countrymen to fight the whole of Europe rather than yield the independence of America from dread of foreign powers; but before he could end his oration he fell down in a fit, and a few weeks later
May 11. he was dead.

He was not a great minister of war, nor was he a great administrator; and his wild intemperance of speech, his incorrigible proclivity to faction, and his lordly contempt for all detail, impair his claim to the title even of a great practical statesman. But never has England produced one who was more emphatically a leader and a king of men. He is known as the Great Commoner; but his habits, his speeches, his writings were rather those of a king. His orders read like royal edicts; his letters, in outward form no less than inward substance, bear the semblance almost of royal charters; and in truth his passion for the grandiose amounted almost to a disease. His qualities, with the exception of what may be called his driving power, were, indeed, rather those of the poet than of the statesman. His deep insight pierced into the heart of things, his wide imagination delighted to compass great designs, his imperious will brushed aside all difficulties, his fiery enthusiasm kindled all subordinates to like energy with his own, his passion for the greatness of his country carried his countrymen with him on an irresistible wave of patriotic

¹ *Correspondence of George III. and Lord North*, ii. 161.

sentiment; but he trusted overmuch and too often to 1778. sentiment. His genius showed him the broad foundations on which to build; but he was impatient when the superstructure which his imagination had raised did not at once arise in obedience to sentiment; and it is not sentiment but patience which conquers all things. His reign was short, and possibly his reputation would have suffered had it been longer; but he was a king of men.

France having now joined the Americans in war, it was imperative to readjust the British plans so as to meet the entry into the situation of that new and important factor, the French fleet. The forces of England were widely dispersed. Setting aside India, there were troops in America at New York, on the Delaware, in Florida, Quebec, Halifax, and on the Lakes; in the West Indies at Jamaica, Grenada, St. Vincent, Tobago, Bermuda, and the Bahamas; in the Mediterranean at Gibraltar and Minorca. Amherst, being consulted, gave his opinion that forty thousand men would be required for offensive operations by land in America, and recommended a naval war only. Forty thousand men, at a moment when every British garrison needed reinforcement, was quite out of the question for America; and until Burgoyne's army could be replaced it was obvious that New York at any rate must stand on the defensive. There was also the question of keeping the French well occupied by some offensive movement, so as to distract them from sending succour to America. Every consideration pointed to the desirability of concentrating the British forces as far as possible; and the King early made up his mind that Pennsylvania must be evacuated. But he still clung tightly to every other post which he held in America, not only to Halifax and to New York, which were essential to naval operations, but also to Rhode Island, which was superfluous, and to the stations in Florida, which were of no value, commercial or strategical, and were most unhealthy for the troops. Most unfortunately too the Governors of North Carolina and Georgia had during the past summer urged upon

1778. Germaine the fruitlessness of operations in the north, and had begged that the British arms might be turned upon the Carolinas; arguing that not only would many loyalists be heartened to come forward for the King, but that the supplies of indigo and tobacco, with which the Colonies paid for their arms and ammunition, would be cut off. Germaine was not yet cured of reliance on the loyal section of the American population, and the King was tempted by the thought of retaining the southern provinces, even if he should be forced to part with New England. Thus the old fatal principle was once more made the pivot upon which all operations were to turn.

March 21. On the 21st of March the ultimate instructions to Clinton, who was to succeed Howe in command, were finally drawn up. The first duty enjoined upon him was to embark five thousand men, with artillery and stores, to attack St. Lucia, the significance of which operation shall presently be explained. He was then to detach three thousand more men, fully equipped with artillery and stores, to St. Augustine and Pensacola, and to withdraw the troops from Philadelphia to New York, until the result of Lord North's conciliatory proposals should be known. If these proposals should fail of their effect he was to evacuate New York, leave sufficient garrisons at Rhode Island and Halifax, and send the rest of the troops to Canada. Subsequent orders directed further small parties to be sent to Bermuda and to the Bahamas. As to reinforcements to fill the gaps created by these detachments, there were merely vague promises of ten or twelve thousand men to be despatched at some time in the course of the summer. The instructions indeed were throughout characteristic of Germaine. Canada, into which he was pouring fresh battalions, and bidding Clinton to pour yet more, was in little or no danger. Rhode Island could not be held if New York were evacuated, because it depended on New York for fuel; while after the deduction of all the detachments there were hardly men enough left to hold both. Yet

CH. XII   HISTORY OF THE ARMY   251

he wrote casually to Clinton about six months later, "I 1778. suppose that if you evacuate anything, it will be Rhode Island." It is hardly surprising that before this last missive reached Clinton the unfortunate General should have asked permission to resign.[1]

But before proceeding farther, it is necessary to refer 1777-1778. to General Howe and to take note of what had passed in Philadelphia during the winter of 1777-1778. The successful close of his campaign had given him and the army comfortable quarters in Philadelphia; and these he determined to enjoy to the utmost. Washington meanwhile encamped his army at Valley Forge, in order to narrow as far as possible the country that lay open to the British for forage, bidding his men build huts to shelter themselves during the severe weather. Never was he so hardly pressed by his own people as during this winter. Gates, always a jealous man, and other officers had formed a cabal to oust him from the chief command; and their intrigues had for a time been not unsuccessful with the ignorant civilians of Congress, who opined that Washington ought long ago to have ended matters by a short and violent war. Though ultimately the conspirators failed of their object, they yet caused such neglect and disorganisation of the army during the winter of 1777 that Washington was driven almost to despair. His force rapidly melted away through desertion; and by Christmas the small remnant of less than three thousand men, which remained with him, was driven by starvation into open mutiny.[2] Yet no adequate measures were taken for its relief; and throughout the long winter the men, ill clad, ill fed, and ill sheltered, suffered terribly from famine, cold, and sickness. Nevertheless Howe made no effort to drive Washington from his position; and it is fair to add that Major-general Grey, an excellent officer, declared

[1] Germaine to Clinton, 8th, 21st March, 1st July, 25th September 1778. Clinton to Germaine, 15th September, 8th October 1778.
[2] Washington, *Works*, v. 197.

1778. that an attack upon Valley Forge would have been wholly unjustifiable. Howe's own plea was that no great advantage could be reaped from success at that season of the year; and if by a great he meant a decisive advantage, he was undoubtedly right. But as to indirect gain, we have Washington's own statement that he himself used, though without success, the greatest severity towards the inhabitants to prevent them from furnishing the British with horses and with every kind of supplies;[1] and since the whole campaign rested on the support of the loyalists, it was certainly false policy in Howe to allow them to be oppressed. The truth seems to be that Howe's natural indolence and unwillingness to impose unnecessary hardships upon his men were increased by the thought that the command would shortly pass out of his hands, and that his action might be misconstrued if he should transfer to his successor an army enfeebled by severe winter operations, which at best could lead to no serious result. There was also much to be said for allowing the American army to go to pieces of itself, without risking the life of a single British soldier; and had it not been that a successful attack would have brought about the downfall of Washington, and interrupted one of his best foreign officers, Baron von Steuben, in the work of reorganising the staff and remodelling the discipline of the American army, Howe might well have put forward this plea in justification of his conduct. But he lies under the further and more serious charge of suffering the discipline of the British to become relaxed by neglect and inaction; and it is certain that the amount of sickness among the troops during the winter was alarming. These are accusations which are less easily rebutted, and which remain a grave reproach to Howe. It seems indeed that, weary of his whole task, realising the hopelessness of success without large reinforcements, and above all chafing against the constant interference of Germaine, he abandoned himself to

[1] Washington, *Works*, v. 300.

simple inertness pending the appointment of his successor. It is easy to censure him; and indeed Howe has been made the scapegoat for the failure of the war; but no war could have gone well under the direction of Germaine.

After the successful execution of a few petty operations in March, Howe received in April the acceptance of his resignation; and on the 8th of May Clinton arrived to take over the command. A few days later, after a very ridiculous festival held by his officers and by the prettiest women in Philadelphia in his honour, Howe sailed for England. Whatever might be said of him, he had at least beaten the Americans in several actions, and taken some five thousand prisoners besides a large number of guns. Clinton at once began to ship his stores for the evacuation of Philadelphia; but finding that he could not embark the troops at any point nearer than Newcastle, some forty miles away, and that his transports were insufficient to convey both the army and some three thousand refugees who claimed his protection, he decided to retreat to New York by land. Accordingly, at three o'clock on the morning of the 18th of June, he marched with his fifteen thousand men and an immense train of baggage, and crossed the Delaware at Gloucester Point before the Americans could molest him. His position was no enviable one, for Washington speedily set fifteen thousand well-trained and well-equipped men in motion to pursue him, while small parties of the enemy in his front broke down all the bridges in order to retard his progress. Pursuing a parallel course to northward of Clinton, Washington rapidly gained on him; and on reaching Allentown after five days' march Clinton learned that Gates was moving down from the north to bar the passage of the Rariton. He thereupon struck eastward for Sandy Hook instead of holding on his course for Amboy; and placing Knyphausen with ten battalions and the Seventeenth Light Dragoons in charge of his baggage, he himself took personal command of fourteen

1778. battalions and the Sixteenth Light Dragoons, which formed the rearguard. Washington meanwhile sent six thousand men under Lee, who had lately been released by exchange, with orders to attack the flank of the British rearguard and to hold it engaged until he should arrive with the main body.

June 28. At dawn of Sunday the 28th of June, Knyphausen and the baggage moved off from its encampment on the heights of Freehold, followed at eight o'clock by the rear division. At ten o'clock Lee's cannon opened fire on Clinton's rearguard, while parties of his men appeared on both of its flanks. A charge of the Sixteenth Light Dragoons drove back the American cavalry; and Clinton, after sending to Knyphausen for reinforcements, made his dispositions for attack. The Americans thereupon fell back, in obedience to Lee, who, it appears, was still playing a treacherous game; and Clinton pushed the Guards and grenadiers against their front, while his light troops fetched a compass to turn upon their flank. Lee continued to retreat before the Guards, who, however, coming upon the American main body under Washington, were obliged to retire, heavily pressed in front and flanks, until night put an end to the combat. At ten o'clock Clinton renewed his march and accomplished the remainder of his retreat without molestation. The action cost the British three hundred and fifty-eight officers and men, of whom no fewer than sixty fell dead from sunstroke owing to the overpowering heat of the day. The loss of the Americans was almost exactly the same; but Clinton's army was considerably reduced during this march by the desertion of some six hundred men,[1] three-fourths of them Germans, who had contracted attachments of one description or another to the town of Philadelphia. Washington, after the action of Freehold, abandoned the pursuit and marched to his own encampment at White Plains; while Clinton, after waiting two days on the

[1] Mr. Fiske gives the number of deserters at 2000, but this figure is irreconcilable with Clinton's returns.

Navasink in the hope that Washington would attack 1778.
him, embarked his troops at Sandy Hook, and on the
5th of July arrived at New York.

Three days later the French fleet from Toulon July 8.
under Count d'Estaing appeared with four thousand
troops at the mouth of the Delaware, marking the
entry of a new element which, as Washington had long
foreseen, was vital to the success of the Colonies. So far
British supremacy at sea had enabled the British generals
to transport their troops and to land them where they
would, without anxiety for the safety of their retreat.
From henceforth the loss of that supremacy even for a
week might bring about disaster. D'Estaing's design
had been to intercept Lord Howe's squadron in the
Delaware, which was of little more than half the strength
of his own; but he arrived too late, and sailed for Sandy
Hook, where a council of war was held. The British
forces were now separated into two divisions at New
York and Rhode Island, with no communication except
by sea; and it seemed feasible with a superior naval
force to overwhelm one or the other of them. New
York, as the more important, was first chosen for attention, but d'Estaing, who though a brave man was a
soldier and not a sailor, recoiled before the dangers of
the navigation and the extremely able dispositions of
Lord Howe. The allied force of French and Americans
was therefore turned against Rhode Island, which was
held by General Pigott with some five thousand troops.
The American General Sullivan had been watching
Pigott from Providence on the mainland since April;
and to him Washington now sent fifteen hundred of his
regular troops under General Greene and the Marquis
de Lafayette, in the hope that this force, added to four
thousand French and nine thousand New England
yeomanry, would suffice to make an end of Pigott.
D'Estaing duly arrived with his fleet before Rhode
Island on the 29th of July; and the British were com- July 29.
pelled to burn seven small men-of-war to prevent them
from falling into his hands. But Pigott, an active

1778. and vigilant officer, had by two sudden descents upon Providence already made such destruction of the American boats and other stores as greatly to retard their preparations for attack; and it was the 8th of August before d'Estaing and Sullivan were in a position
Aug. 9. to concert their plans for joint action. But on the 9th of August the indefatigable Lord Howe appeared on the scene with his squadron, and d'Estaing stood out to sea, where a storm of extraordinary violence separated and dispersed both fleets before they could come to a decisive engagement. A gallant battle was, however, fought between two British ships of fifty and two French ships of eighty guns, wherein the Light Company of the Twenty-third Fusiliers on board H.M.S. *Isis* bore a distinguished part.[1] Meanwhile General Sullivan crossed over from the mainland and invested Pigott's entrenched camp, but made little progress against it; and on
Aug. 20. the 20th d'Estaing, returning with his shattered ships, announced his intention of going to Boston to refit and of taking the troops with him. Thereupon the whole of the operations collapsed. The American yeomanry with their wonted indiscipline went back to their farms; and
Aug. 28. on the 28th Sullivan raised the investment and retreated.
Aug. 29. Pigott followed him up at once, and there was sharp fighting;[2] but the American rearguard, skilfully handled by Greene, made so steady and stubborn a
Aug. 30. resistance that Sullivan was able to retire safely to the mainland. He was but just in time, for on the very
Sept. 1. next day Clinton sailed in from New York with five thousand men, a force which, added to Pigott's, would have sufficed to cut off and overwhelm the whole of Sullivan's army.

Thus in impotent failure, with but narrow escape from disaster, ended the first enterprise of a superior French fleet on the coast of America. It will surprise no reader, who has watched the temper of the New Englanders, to hear that the result created much ill

---

[1] Lord Howe to Admiralty, 17th August 1778.
[2] The American loss was 211, and the British 260 of all ranks.

feeling between the French and their allies. There was 1778. a dangerous riot between French and American seamen at Boston, in accordance with the traditions of that peaceful and law-abiding city, and another yet fiercer at Charlestown ; while it needed all Washington's tact and patience to keep the peace between the superior officers. In truth, Washington had been considerably embarrassed by the arrival during the past twelve months of a number of French gentlemen, full of curious revolutionary ideas, which had been minted in the coffee-houses of Paris, and still fuller of their own importance and condescension. Lafayette, who had fought with him through the Pennsylvanian campaign, was welcome to the American General as a good and energetic soldier ; but the rest he would gladly have seen sail back to France by the first ship.[1] Moreover, to increase Washington's embarrassment, Clinton, though he had missed his prey at Rhode Island, made on his return voyage a series of raids upon sundry little ports which harboured American privateers, destroying large quantities of shipping and stores. It was during this season that the famous irregular corps of mixed cavalry and infantry known as the Queen's Rangers, commanded by Major Simcoe, the Legion under Major Tarleton, and another body of Rangers under Major Patrick Ferguson, first made their mark by sundry useful little enterprises in partisan warfare. One and all of them were recruited in America ; and we shall see much of their work in the years before us.

At this point serious operations in the north came to an end. Clinton, in the perplexity caused by Germaine's foolish orders, still forbore to withdraw the garrison from Rhode Island, where the troops were kept inactive to no purpose, the station being as much of a distraction to the British Navy as to the American generals.[2] It

[1] "There is a hundred times more enthusiasm for the revolution in any Paris café than in the whole of the United States put together." M. de Portail to the Comte de St. Germain, 12th November 1777. And see Washington's *Works*, vi. 15.

[2] Lord Howe to Admiralty, 31st March 1777.

1778. is true that Howe should long ago have been reinforced to superior strength by Admiral Byron's squadron, but Byron had met with the luck which had earned him the nickname of "Foul-weather Jack." Though he had sailed from England on the 9th of June, his squadron had been so frequently dispersed by storms that it was not finally assembled and refitted at New York until the 18th of October. He then sailed to blockade d'Estaing's fleet at Boston, but was once more driven away by a
Nov. 4. furious gale; and on the 4th of November d'Estaing slipped out of Boston and sailed for Martinique.

On that same day a force of over five thousand British troops under Major-general Grant also sailed from New York to the West Indies; and it is now necessary to follow their fortunes in the Caribbean Archipelago.

CHAPTER XIII

THE part played by the West Indian Islands during the 1778. American War of Independence has been so little appreciated as to demand particular attention in these pages. Then as now the British West Indies depended practically upon America for their supplies of food; for, with the exception of small quantities of yams, sweet potatoes, and the like, provisions were little cultivated in a soil which could more profitably be devoted to sugar, indigo, and spices. A war with America therefore threatened the islands with scarcity, or at any rate with increased cost of victuals, while at the same time depriving them of their best market for rum and molasses, and of their share in the vast profits of smuggling on the American coast. American emissaries were early despatched to magnify the fears of the West Indian planters, and to enlist their sympathy against the tyrannical British Government which designed to bind the Americans in chains. Their task was the easier since in each island the power of the purse was entrusted to a representative assembly composed chiefly of planters, who, having little knowledge of matters outside the management of their own estates, were controlled for the most part by a small knot of busy, unscrupulous lawyers, of the same type as, though with less ability than, the eminent Samuel Adams. Symptoms of a disloyal spirit, in the form of extremely insolent addresses from the Assembly, showed themselves in Jamaica early in 1775, and in Barbados a year later, the language employed being the same as that in favour

1778. at Boston. In Bermuda, where for a century and a-half the population had been incurably restless and turbulent, the Assembly sent delegates to the Congress at Philadelphia, while the people sold to the Americans ammunition, salt, and even the fast sailing-vessels for which the islands were famous. In fact, until troops arrived in 1779 to restore the King's authority, the Bermudians openly took sides with the revolted provinces, even passing a bill to tax prizes taken by British privateers. In the Bahamas it has already been told how the Americans successfully carried off the guns and ammunition. This was done by the deliberate connivance of the authorities, who refused to allow the ordnance to be embarked in the ships which Gage had sent for the purpose; and from that time forward the Bahamas were practically in open rebellion. In the Leeward Islands[1] the chance of plundering American traders proved so tempting that the inhabitants reverted eagerly to their old profession of piracy, and were only with much difficulty brought to accept commissions as privateers. But in September 1778 a disloyal faction grew up among the people and in the Assembly of St. Kitts, and thenceforward increased continually in power. The favour shown to American privateers by the French at Martinique, even before France took open part in the war, as also by the Danes at St. Croix and the Dutch at St. Eustatius, all worked for the strengthening of this American party. The Dutch indeed drove a roaring trade during the war, and freely granted the use of their credentials to American privateers. "If our cruisers were to spare everything with Dutch clearances and papers," wrote the Governor of the Leeward Islands, "there would not be a French or American vessel on the sea." St. Eustatius was neither more nor less than a huge depot for stores of all kinds on passage from Europe to America; and the trade in these goods was so profitable as to entice large numbers of British merchants, both in the West Indies and in the United

[1] Antigua, Montserrat, Nevis, St. Kitts.

Kingdom, into providing the wants of their country's 1778. enemies.[1]

Next, a word must necessarily be said as to the strategic position of the islands. In the days of sailing ships all naval operations in the West Indies were necessarily governed by the trade-wind, which blows, roughly speaking,[2] from east to west persistently for three parts of the year, and intermittently during the fourth part also. But from the beginning of August to the beginning of November the Archipelago is subject to hurricanes, for which reason it was customary for fleets to desert tropical latitudes during these "hurricane-months." The British West Indies were divided into two groups: first, the chain of islands to windward, that is to say to eastward, which runs, interspersed with certain French islands, from St. Kitts in the north to Tobago in the south; secondly, Jamaica, a thousand miles to leeward, to which were attached for purposes of defence the posts of Pensacola and Mobile, in the districts at that time comprehended under the name of Florida. Practically these two divisions were distinct; for though a ship could be sure of a good passage from Barbados to Jamaica, she could be equally sure that a voyage from Jamaica to Barbados would occupy as much time as a voyage from Jamaica to England.[3] In a word, a force once despatched from windward to leeward was

[1] *Jamaica*—Governor Keith to Secretary of State, 4th January 1775, 27th March 1776.
Barbados—Governor Hay to Secretary of State, 13th and 15th February, 25th July, 31st August 1776.
Leeward Isles—Governor Burt to Secretary of State, 30th September, 9th October, 2nd and 25th November 1776.
Bermuda—Governor Bruere to Secretary of State, 1st February, 21st July, 17th and 20th August 1775, *et passim*.
Bahamas—Governor Browne to Secretary of State, *passim*, 1775-1782.

[2] More truly south-east to north-west, shifting occasionally in certain months to north-east.

[3] Governor Russell wrote to the Board of Trade in 1697 that the voyage from Barbados to Jamaica was reckoned at six or seven days. A good sailer would beat back to Barbados from Jamaica in two months; a bad sailer would never reach Barbados at all.

1778. to all intent irrecoverable ; and this fact was one with which commanders, both naval and military, had always to reckon. The French on their side were in exactly the same case, having their two divisions of territory in St. Lucia, Martinique, and Guadeloupe to windward, and Haiti to leeward. But to leeward they had this advantage, that Haiti, being to windward of Jamaica, and within twenty-four hours' sail of it, was a perpetual menace to that island. Moreover, the harbour of St. Nicholas, which of late had been fortified to great strength, so dominated the Windward Channel between Haiti and Cuba—a very important passage for homeward-bound ships—that it was esteemed the Gibraltar of the West Indies. To windward, the British had somewhat of a corresponding advantage, Barbados being the most windwardly of the whole of the eastern group. But, on the other hand, Barbados has no safe harbour, nor was there any port in Grenada, St. Vincent, or any of the British islets to northward of it, where British ships could refit, excepting the royal dockyard at English Harbour in Antigua. Barbados, it is true, was an excellent depot for troops and stores, and could be used within certain limits for repair of ships ; but the true dockyard, as aforesaid, was in Antigua, some distance to leeward. The French on the contrary had three admirable harbours in St. Lucia, Martinique, and Guadeloupe, of which Martinique, the principal naval and military centre, was little further distant from France than Barbados from England. Henceforward I shall treat all to the east of Porto Rico as the windward, and all to westward of it as the leeward sphere of operations ; but it must be remembered that the law of the trade-wind is as inexorable between any two islands within each of these groups as between the two spheres taken at large. To recapitulate : Port Royal on the English side and St. Nicholas on the French were the naval stations to leeward ; Barbados and Antigua on the English side, and Martinique on the French, the principal stations to windward.

Not only were the British West Indies infected by the

spirit of rebellion, but their fortifications, where not in 1778. a ruinous condition, were sadly out of repair. This would have been no great matter if the troops could have been withdrawn from them; but the danger from Caribs almost compelled the retention of small parties in Grenada, St. Vincent, and Dominica, which made a grievous drain on the force, never of sufficient strength, which guarded the naval stations. It had been laid down a century before[1] that small garrisons in the West Indies were useless, and large garrisons, except for the protection of naval bases, an unnecessary expense, since security to the British and menace to the French could be very much better assured by superiority at sea. The only difficulty in the way of putting this very sound theory into practice was the outcry invariably raised by each island for a few troops for its individual defence, a clamour which, owing to the peril of negro insurrection, was always troublesome, and in times of disaffection became unpleasantly cogent.

In 1778 the French were beforehand in taking the offensive in the West Indies. On the 6th of September the Marquis de Bouillé, embarking a couple of thousand men at Martinique, dropped down upon Dominica, which was defended only by weak detachments of the Forty-eighth Foot and of artillery,[2] and by the offer of very favourable terms obtained the immediate surrender of the island. Bouillé then locked up fifteen hundred of his troops as a garrison to secure his prize, and hurried back to Martinique lest Admiral Barrington, who had arrived with a small squadron at Barbados, should reach Fort Royal before him. The loss of Dominica was of small importance, except that it was the one island where a fleet could conveniently obtain wood and water at one and the same time; and it was not long before the British counterstroke fell. Though encumbered with

Sept. 6.

Sept. 8.

[1] By Governor Christopher Codrington, *Cal. S.P. Col.* 1689-1692.
[2] These, added to the local militia, made up a force of less than 500 men.

1778. the fleet of fifty-nine transports whereon Grant's troops had been embarked, Admiral Hotham arrived from New York at Barbados on the 10th of December; while d'Estaing, who had sailed from Boston without encumbrance on the same day, reached Martinique only twenty-four hours before him. Barrington was not the man to lose precious time. Without permitting the disembarkation of the troops for one minute, he sailed
Dec. 12. within twenty-four hours of their arrival for St. Lucia, and on the afternoon of the same day anchored in Cul de Sac Bay.[1] Two brigades were immediately landed, one of which speedily forced the heights to northward, capturing a battery of four guns and opening the way to the next inlet, now known by the name of Castries
Dec. 13. Bay. On the next morning, the remainder of the troops were disembarked, and the famous mountain called the Morne Fortuné, which commands the south side of Castries Bay, was captured almost without resistance. Before evening the British were in possession also of the peninsula of Vigie on the north side of the harbour, with all the forts, batteries, magazines, and fifty-nine guns. Thus a fortified naval base was gained, so to speak, ready made, at a trifling cost.

The last of the white flags had not been struck for one hour when d'Estaing's fleet came into sight. On his arrival at Martinique he had been joined by transports containing nine thousand troops; and with these added to a superior fleet he hoped to give short shrift to the British possessions to windward. But the fate of St. Lucia determined him to recapture that island before going any farther; the task seeming easy to him, since his fleet outnumbered Barrington's by three ships to one. Nevertheless, so skilfully had Barrington drawn his squadron across Cul de Sac Bay, that d'Estaing after
Dec. 15. two attacks failed to make the slightest impression on it. Beating therefore up to windward, he landed his troops

[1] Grant's force consisted of the 4th, 5th, 15th, 27th, 28th, 35th, 40th, 46th, 49th, and 55th Foot, and just under 200 artillery; in all, about 5800 men.

in the Anse du Choc, immediately to northward of Castries 1778.
Bay, designing to force the British post at Vigie, and so
to open the harbour to his own fleet. Grant's force was
necessarily divided between Cul de Sac, Morne Fortuné,
and Vigie, the last named being entrusted to Colonel
Medows with thirteen hundred men of the Fifth Foot,
Grenadiers and Light Infantry, and four guns. It was
a strong position accessible only by an isthmus less than
three hundred yards wide; and Medows had disposed
the mass of his force in rear of this isthmus with five
light companies on two wooded hills in advance of it.
The sight of this isolated detachment was too much for
d'Estaing. On the morning of the 18th he directed Dec. 18.
two battalions against it, simultaneously moving the
rest of his force against Medows's main position; but
to his astonishment the five light companies made utter
havoc of his two battalions, and withdrew through a
belt of brushwood to the isthmus before he could cut
them off. He then launched his troops in heavy
columns against the isthmus itself, but was repulsed in
two successive attacks, and after three hours' fighting
retired, very heavily punished. The French were in fact
powerless before veterans trained in the American school.
The casualties of the British were thirteen killed and
one hundred and fifty-eight wounded. The French left
over four hundred dead on the field, and acknowledged
the further loss of twelve hundred wounded. In short,
their defeat was so bloody and so severe that d'Estaing
remained paralysed until the 28th, when he withdrew Dec. 28.
his shattered forces to Martinique. The original French
garrison, which had retired inland, thereupon surrendered,
leaving the British masters of St. Lucia.[1]

A more brilliant series of little operations by both
army and navy, under the favour of fortune, it would
be difficult to find. Had Barrington waited for a day
longer at Barbados, his squadron and transports must
have fallen a prey to d'Estaing's superior fleet. Had

[1] Details will be found in *Lives of the Lindsays*, iii. 331 *sq.*
See also "St. Lucia, 1778," in *Macmillan's Magazine*, April 1902.

1778. Grant delayed for an hour in landing and attacking the French posts, the French militia might have held their own till d'Estaing came to their relief. But for Barrington's very bold and skilful dispositions in Cul de Sac Bay, his squadron must have been dispersed, if not destroyed, and Grant's army cut off. But for Grant's equally skilful defence of his posts on Vigie, the French could have brought up guns to force Barrington's squadron from Cul de Sac Bay into the jaws of a superior fleet. As things fell out, d'Estaing was driven back with heavy loss to Martinique, and the British were left with the key of the Windward Islands in their hands. Thus installed on an excellent harbour to windward both of Martinique and Guadeloupe, "in a way looking into Fort Royal," as Grant wrote, his force was a standing menace to French power in the West Indies.

1779. On the 6th of January 1779 Byron's fleet arrived at St. Lucia, too late, by his usual bad luck, to cut off d'Estaing's retreat to Martinique, and so much shattered as hardly to restore the British even to equality at sea. Nevertheless, his presence sufficed to keep d'Estaing locked up tightly in Fort Royal; and meanwhile Grant was still strengthening his defences, for his troops were sickening rapidly,[1] and Byron's crews also were so much reduced by sickness that soldiers were required to make up the complement for the fleet. Grant fought with the climate as successfully as his limited supply of quinine[2] would permit him; but his principal struggle lay, as usual, with human stupidity. In May the disaffection at St. Kitts rose to an alarming height; the Assembly refused to pay for the provisions collected for the militia in case of need, and the Governor, Mr. Burt, begged in

[1] "850 sick in last week's state." Grant to Germaine, 5th February 1779.

[2] "Without bark we should not have a man fit for duty in three months; but the hospital at New York would not give so much as I looked for." Grant to Germaine, 4th April 1779. The returns for 5th April show 3300 fit for duty, 1350 sick. There were 100 deaths between 31st March and 24th April. *Ibid.* 24th April 1779.

abject terms for troops. No policy could have been more foolish, politically or strategically; for, as Burt himself admitted, the Assembly behaved properly so long as the French fleet threatened attack, and only became refractory when Byron promised protection.[1] In plain words, this nest of smugglers, pirates, and receivers of stolen goods was loyal only when threatened with the loss of its ill-gotten gains. Worst of all, Byron actually sailed to St. Kitts to quiet the incessant clamour of Burt; and, as luck would have it, a French squadron under Count de Grasse was able to join d'Estaing at Fort Royal unmolested during his absence.[2] Finally, as a climax, there came an order from the incorrigible Germaine[3] to provide garrisons for all the British islands, and to send back all the troops that could be spared, after this dispersion, to New York.

Fortunately, Grant was as outspoken to Germaine as to any West Indian Governor. "Small detachments are no security against invasion," he wrote; "if troops are not kept together in the West Indies the best of them will soon cease to be soldiers. I shall therefore send none to the islands. Their safety must depend on the fleet." With a just insight into the true position he declined to weaken the garrison of St. Lucia to no purpose, though he cheerfully lent Byron two additional regiments, the Fifth and Fortieth, to man the fleet. Now, however, luck turned against him. About the middle of June Admiral Byron was obliged to take his fleet to leeward in order to convoy the homeward-bound merchant-vessels beyond the islands; and in his absence d'Estaing sent a small expedition to capture St. Vincent. That island, though garrisoned by four hundred sickly men of the Sixtieth, who had much better have been at St. Lucia, surrendered without firing a shot; and on the 30th of June d'Estaing sailed with his whole fleet against Grenada.

[1] Burt to Secretary of State, 3rd May, 1st June 1779.
[2] Grant to Germaine, 13th May 1779.
[3] Germaine to Grant, 1st April 1779.

1779.
July 5. Byron on his return at once took the alarm, and on the 5th of July sailed with twenty-one ships of the line and one thousand troops under Grant's command to recapture St. Vincent ; but, hearing that the French had called the Caribs to them and were entrenching themselves, he decided first to rescue Grenada. D'Estaing,
July 4. however, had already mastered that island, though the tiny garrison of three hundred regular troops and militia made a gallant resistance ; and when at day-
July 6. break of the 6th Barrington, who was Byron's second in command, arrived off St. George's Harbour, the French fleet was anchored in disorder at its mouth. Unable to ascertain the numbers of the French owing to their confusion, Barrington made signal for a general chase, and only too late realised that he was pitting twenty-one ships against twenty-five. Readers must turn elsewhere for the story of the gallant but indecisive action that followed, and of the failure of d'Estaing to turn his advantages to account. Let it suffice that the British soldiers bore their part in the fight, losing seventy-four officers and men killed and wounded, and that Barrington, though he could not retake Grenada, brought off his fleet and transports in safety. Grant, after paying the highest compliments to the bravery of the fleet, thus pointed the moral of the operations. " If the troops had not been kept together we could not have made the attempt to recover the islands, which would have succeeded but for our inferiority at sea. If detachments had been stationed in the islands, they could not have saved them for a day. . . . Being inferior at sea, we cannot send back the troops to New York as ordered by you." [1] He therefore made a new distribution of the troops,[2]

[1] Grant to Germaine, 8th and 17th July 1779.
[2] *Ibid.* 29th July 1779 :—

St. Kitts, R.A., 15th, 28th, 55th . .	1500	men.
St. Lucia, R.A., 27th, 35th, 49th . .	1600	,,
Antigua, 6 companies 40th, detachment 60th	800	,,
Serving with the fleet, 5th, 46th . .	925	,,
Total	4825	,,

since the battalions intended for America remained 1779. at his disposal, and on the 1st of August sailed for England.

On his homeward voyage Grant crossed a letter of reproof from Germaine, containing an expression of the King's displeasure at the loss of St. Vincent, and definite orders to disperse the troops for the protection of all the islands. But Grant did not shrink from meeting the storm in London. While serving with Forbes in 1758 he had indeed on one occasion lost his wits,[1] but he was not now disposed to submit to the like reproach. "I do not think," he wrote, "that I can be blamed for the loss of St. Vincent. D'Estaing had a superior force and kept it together at Martinique, so I was obliged to do the like at St. Lucia. I knew that it was not in my instructions, but at a distance of three thousand miles from the capital one must act according to circumstances." To drive home these very shrewd thrusts, he demonstrated by a few figures to Germaine the absurdity of his orders and left him to make the best of them. I dwell on these matters with reason, for it was owing to Grant's firmness in holding on to St. Lucia at all costs, and to his boundless loyalty to the fleet, that Rodney was able in 1782 to turn the scale of arms against France in the West Indies. Otherwise all would have been lost by the folly and ignorance of Germaine, who forfeits all credit for the capture of St. Lucia by his readiness to risk the loss of it. It is refreshing to find that there was an officer who would stand up to this deplorable Secretary of State; and it is not too much to say that a few more generals of Grant's stamp in America would have altered the whole course of the war.

Here, therefore, for the present we take leave of Grant. While he was yet on his way to England, d'Estaing had sailed from the West Indies to the American coast; and it is now necessary to examine the events which led him thither.

[1] Vol. ii. of this *History*, p. 336.

CHAPTER XIV

1778. THE negotiations for conciliating the Americans having failed completely, Clinton, pursuant to his instructions, had even before Grant's departure taken steps to send an expedition to Georgia. The force selected for this purpose was two battalions of Fraser's Highlanders,[1] four of Provincial Infantry, and two of Hessians, in all about three thousand men, under the command of Lieutenant-colonel Campbell of Maclean's Regiment. It is worth remarking that among the provincial troops (of which Clinton had now some four thousand in all) there was one corps composed entirely of Irish deserters from the American army under the colonelcy of Lord Rawdon.[2] To co-operate with this detachment General Augustine Prevost had received orders to move up to Georgia from East Florida with such troops as could be spared, and on effecting his junction with Campbell to take command of the entire force. Campbell sailed on the 8th of November, but being blown back by a storm
Dec. 24. did not arrive in the Savannah river until the 24th of December; nor did the whole of his transports pass the
Dec. 27. bar until three days later. Having no information whatever as to the enemy's numbers or dispositions, Campbell utilised these days of inaction by seizing a few of the inhabitants, from whom he learned that the American General Howe had just returned from a predatory excursion into East Florida and was encamped, in daily expectation of reinforcements, with from twelve

[1] Then numbered 71st.
[2] Clinton to Germaine, 23rd October 1778.

to fifteen hundred men for the protection of Savannah. 1778. Accordingly, on the 28th, Campbell's transports moved up the river about twelve miles; and on the following day the disembarkation began about two miles below Dec. 29. the town.

From the landing-place the advance lay along a causeway between rice-swamps for some six hundred yards, at the end of which the ground sloped upwards; and at the top of this ascent was stationed an American advanced-post which fired upon the Highlanders as they moved forward, but speedily dispersed before an attack with the claymore. Campbell then went ahead to reconnoitre, and found Howe's troops drawn up about half a mile from the town and astride of the main road to it; their right protected by a thickly wooded morass, with a few buildings in advance of it, their left resting on the rice-swamps that bordered the river, and their front also covered by a marshy rivulet. Two field-guns were posted in the road before their line; and about one hundred yards in advance of the guns, at a point where the sound ground on each side of the road was no more than one hundred yards wide, a deep trench had been cut through it from swamp to swamp. The position seemed formidable; but Campbell, having learned of a practicable path through the morass on the enemy's right, determined to attack at once, though little more than half of his force had yet been disembarked. Advancing at about three o'clock in the afternoon within a thousand yards of the American line, he perceived that the enemy wished and expected his attack to be delivered against their left. Being desirous, as he said, to cherish that opinion in them, he at once pushed forward the Light Infantry against their left wing, and ordered the Highlanders to follow them in support. Then extending the Light Infantry until they were concealed by a fold in the ground, he passed them swiftly round his rear to the other flank, with orders to turn the American right by the path through the morass. His guns also he kept concealed behind

1778.
Dec. 29.

an eminence until the time should come for them to be shown with advantage.

Meanwhile the enemy opened fire with their artillery, and continued, in Campbell's quaint phrase, to amuse themselves with their cannon until the Light Infantry had fairly swept round to their right rear. Campbell then ran his four guns forward to the top of the eminence that had concealed them, and under cover of their fire ordered a general advance. The Americans quickly gave way under the double attack, suffering heavily as they passed the Light Infantry in their flight. Campbell, following in hot haste, pursued them into the town; and before nightfall he was master of Savannah, together with its artillery and stores and the whole of the shipping in the harbour. The Americans left eighty killed and eleven wounded on the field; whereas the British loss did not exceed twenty-six killed and wounded. On its own small scale this action, with its clever feint after the model of Ramillies, was a brilliant little affair. Numbers were equally matched, but the advantage of ground was on the enemy's side, while the British troops were in bad condition after many weeks on board ship, so that Campbell deserves as much credit for his audacity as for his skill.

1779.

Though the ships which carried his horses were not yet arrived, Campbell after only two days' halt advanced up the river, getting his guns and waggons forward as best he could, but meeting nowhere with resistance.

Jan. 1. Many inhabitants joined him, some with rifles and horses, who were at once organised as rifle-dragoons for duties of patrolling and scouting, and others on foot and unarmed, who were turned into militia. On the

Jan. 10. 10th of January, Campbell, having cleared the lower parts of the province of rebels with the exception of a small and unimportant body at Sunbury, returned to Savannah, where he learned that Prevost had completed his last piece of work for him. Prevost from lack of horses had been compelled to conduct all his transport by water along the creeks and water-courses of East Florida, and during his march his men had frequently been driven to live for days together on oysters. After 1779. entering Georgia, however, he heard of the party of rebels at Sunbury, and sent his brother, Mark Prevost, forward by a forced march to surround them. After a short resistance the Americans surrendered; and forty guns, great stores of ammunition, and two hundred prisoners fell into the hands of their captors. On the 17th Prevost and Campbell united their forces at Jan. 17. Savannah; for a new enemy had appeared on the scene in the person of General Lincoln, a brave and able officer, who on the 3rd had taken up a position with nearly three thousand men at Purysburg on the Savannah river, obstructing the navigation and watching his opportunity to do further mischief. With four thousand men[1] of his own, however, Prevost thought himself strong enough to pursue the reduction of the upper province; so Campbell again advanced fifty leagues up the river to Augusta. Thus by the end of February the communications of Augusta with Savannah were secured by a strong chain of posts, and to all intent the authority of King George was re-established in Georgia.

One serious mishap, however, occurred during these operations, namely, the rout and capture by some American militia of a band of loyalists who were on their way to join the British at Augusta. Seventy of the prisoners were tried for high treason by a civil court of the Revolutionary Government, and five of them were hanged. This was but an ordinary specimen of the extremes to which the quarrel between the loyalists and revolutionists had been pushed from the first in the Southern Colonies. Everywhere the revolution had been carried forward to a great extent by intimidation, but in the Southern Colonies, and particularly in Carolina, that intimidation had been of the most violent and barbarous kind. This naturally led to retaliation not less bloodthirsty; and so came a succession of reprisals and counter-reprisals which turned the quarrel

[1] He had brought with him detachments of the 16th, 60th, and provincial corps, in all 989 men.

1779. between the two factions into a strife so ruthless, savage, and indiscriminate, that it was the despair alike of British and of American generals. That there were grave faults on both sides cannot be doubted, and that many a personal revenge was wreaked and many a blood-feud prosecuted under colour of political differences, is unquestionable; but on the whole it seems that the excesses of the revolutionary party during the period of their first ascendency were primarily responsible for the internecine struggle which followed on the appearance of the British troops in Georgia and South Carolina.

Another terrible complication in these Southern campaigns was caused by the negro-slaves, who deserted the plantations in hundreds to follow the British Army, alleging that if they returned they would be shot by their masters.[1] To pretend that, in the abstract, the Briton was a man of greater humanity than the American, would be ridiculous; but it is still possible that the British, wholly ignorant of life among a teeming black population and therefore of the meaning of what is termed colour-feeling, may have dealt with them more kindly than their masters. The negroes were certainly valuable for what are called fatigue-duties; and it is extremely likely, if not absolutely demonstrable, that British officers were not indisposed on occasion to make profit out of their sale. Provincial officers would assuredly have been alive to the monetary value of slaves, and British officers would not have been slow to learn. But in any case the desertion of the negroes must have exasperated the revolutionary party to the utmost against the British; for even if the British had no intention of raising a servile rebellion — the haunting dread of slave-owning communities—they at any rate attracted to themselves costly property which they had no intention of restoring. Add to these elements of faction and colour the fact that, with the exception of their very few regular troops, the Americans conducted the war on the principle that the destruction

[1] Mark Prevost to Germaine, 27th November 1779.

of any single man of their enemies was a solid gain to be compassed by almost any means; and it is no matter for surprise that the struggle in the Southern Colonies was carried on with the bitterness which is to be found only in a civil war.

1779.

Having established his chain of posts for the security of Georgia, Prevost found himself crippled for further offensive operations by lack of men. It was the defect of all of Germaine's plans that he left garrisons and lines of communication entirely out of account; and Prevost was in want not only of men but also of money and provisions.[1] Lincoln, too, now became troublesome, detaching fifteen hundred men under General Ashe up the Savannah, with orders to cross the river and threaten Augusta. The British evacuated the town and retired southward at his approach, Ashe following them up as they retreated till they reached Briar Creek, where his pursuit was abruptly and effectually stopped. For Colonel Mark Prevost, taking a leaf out of Washington's own book, dexterously detached nine hundred men to make a wide detour and fall upon his rear by surprise, with the result that four hundred Americans were killed and wounded, two hundred prisoners, seven guns, and the whole of their baggage captured, and the rest of their force scattered to the four winds, at a cost to the British of no more than sixteen killed and wounded. But this brilliant little action, telling though it was, disabled Lincoln only for a few weeks. Reinforcements of regular troops and militia restored his army to a respectable figure; and towards the end of April he again marched up the river towards Augusta, leaving General Moultrie with a thousand men to guard the lower Savannah. Prevost, who through the capture of a British convoy at sea was threatened with scarcity of supplies, thereupon collected two thousand men and, passing the Savannah river below the American posts, boldly invaded South Carolina. But for an extraordinary and sudden rising of the waters

March 3.

April 23.

[1] See his letters enclosed in Clinton's to Germaine, 25th July 1779.

1779. which delayed his movements, he would probably have cut off Moultrie's retreat; but, as things fell out, Moultrie was able to escape with little loss, and fell back with all haste upon Charleston. Lincoln, rightly judging Prevost's march to be a mere feint to draw him to southward, continued his advance upon Augusta; but Prevost, hearing that Charleston was defenceless and finding much friendly feeling among the inhabitants, now resolved to turn his feint into a reality and to endeavour to seize the capital of South Carolina.

His march is described by American writers as having been a scene of wanton vandalism;[1] but Colonel Mark Prevost indignantly repudiated all charges of misconduct against the troops;[2] and if the stories of plunder and outrage be true, the explanation may be found in the fact that Prevost's force was composed chiefly of regiments raised in the Colonies themselves. Be that as it may, though every bridge over the innumerable creeks on the road had been broken down, Prevost covered the

May 5-10. distance between Beaufort Island and the Ashley river in five days, crossed the river on the 11th, and on the 12th summoned Charleston to surrender. The population was so far overawed that a proposal was made for South Carolina to preserve neutrality during the remainder of the war; but this overture was of course rejected. On examining the defences of the city, however, Prevost decided that an assault would cost him more men than he could spare, for the garrison, by the rapid collection of troops and militia from all quarters, had been raised to numbers far exceeding his own. He therefore recrossed the Ashley and occupied James Island and St. John's, where there were comfortable quarters and abundant supplies for his troops, while a flotilla of small vessels assured to him a safe retreat by sea.

[1] *E.g.* Fiske, ii. 69.
[2] Letter to Germaine, 27th November 1779. Augustine Prevost also wrote on 16th April, "The enemy treat loyalist prisoners very ill. Only the presence of Burgoyne's captured officers with the enemy keeps me from retaliation."

Notwithstanding the ability of his operations, Prevost was greatly chagrined by his failure to seize Charleston. "I am in bad health and too infirm for the command," he wrote some weeks later;[1] "had I possessed my old activity when pursuing the rebels through Carolina, I should have been at Charleston as soon as they, and have taken it without firing a shot." Meanwhile Lincoln, after reoccupying the principal posts in the upper portion of Georgia, had brought back his army in hot haste on the news of Prevost's advance; and on the 4th of June the Americans moved up in front of the British posts. They refrained, however, from attacking until a fortnight later, when Prevost began to withdraw his troops to Savannah. Lincoln then seized a favourable moment to fall with great superiority of numbers upon a remnant of five hundred men, which had been left under command of Lieutenant-colonel Maitland on St. John's Island; and the attack was only repulsed with great difficulty by Maitland's gallantry and skill after a full fourth of the British had fallen. The island was then evacuated; and Prevost's army fell back from islet to islet upon Savannah, a detachment being left at Beaufort on Port Royal Island as a perpetual menace to South Carolina.

1779.

June 4.

June 23.

By this time the heat was so great as to forbid all further operations;[2] and Mr. Rutledge, the revolutionary Governor of South Carolina, used the occasion to write to d'Estaing, who had arrived at St. Domingo with the French fleet, asking him to employ the hurricane season in recovering Georgia in co-operation with General Lincoln. D'Estaing willingly complied, although he had orders to return at once to Europe with certain of his ships; and indeed the time was not unpropitious, for the British had no naval force ready to meet him on the coast of Carolina. Setting sail accordingly, his first

---

[1] Prevost to Germaine, 21st August 1779.
[2] "The temperature for the last three weeks has been from 90° to 98°. At Ebenezer (twenty-five miles north of Savannah) it has been up to 103°." Prevost to Clinton, 14th July 1779.

1779.
Sept. 1-10.
ships arrived off the mouth of Savannah river on the 1st of September, and the remainder of the fleet on the following days; the whole force consisting of twenty-two ships of the line and eleven frigates, besides transports, with a considerable body of troops. The British were taken so completely by surprise that a fifty-gun ship, a frigate, and two store-ships fell at once, after a desperate resistance, into d'Estaing's hands. Prevost himself appears to have received no intelligence of his coming until the 4th of September, when he at once called in all outlying troops to Savannah, and set several hundred negroes to work on the defences of the town.

Sept. 10. On the 10th of September the lighter vessels of d'Estaing's fleet entered the river, compelling the four armed brigs which represented the naval force of Britain to move farther up the stream. The troops were then disembarked, and d'Estaing, without waiting for Lincoln, who was on the march to join him, moved straight upon

Sept. 15. Savannah and summoned Prevost in extravagant language to surrender. Prevost, anxious to gain time for the arrival of Maitland's detachment from Beaufort, asked for twenty-four hours to consider the matter, within which space Maitland by extraordinary exertions contrived to bring his eight hundred men safely into the town. His coming raised the garrison to a strength of

Sept. 16. thirty-seven hundred[1] men, of whom twenty-two hundred were fit for duty. Prevost thereupon returned an answer of defiance, and the siege of Savannah was begun.

The entire northern front of the city being covered by the river, and the western front by a morass, the whole circuit of the defences extended for little more than a mile, every yard of which had been made as strong as possible by abatis, entrenchments, and redoubts. Want of horses delayed the arrival of the French heavy guns for so long that d'Estaing did not break ground until the

Sept. 23. 23rd; and Prevost turned this time to the best account

[1] 200 of 2/60th, 720 of Fraser's Highlanders, 350 Light Infantry, a few Marines, a few men of the 16th, 2 battalions of Hessians, Provincial troops.

not only by mounting additional guns, but by making two lively and successful sorties. At length, on the 4th of October, the besiegers opened fire from sixty-seven cannon and mortars, and continued it until the 8th, though with little effect. D'Estaing now grew impatient, for there hung over him the danger that his fleet might be driven off the coast by the autumnal gales, or attacked by a British fleet from the West Indies; and he accordingly decided upon an immediate assault. The plan agreed upon was that the American militia should make a demonstration against the southern and eastern fronts, and that two columns, numbering together four thousand regular troops, should deliver the true attack. The first column, under Lincoln and d'Estaing in person, was to storm the Springhill redoubt at the south-west angle of the lines, while the other, hugging the swamp that covered the western front, should creep from thence into the rear of the defences.

1779.
Oct. 4.
Oct. 8.

Before dawn of the 9th the attacking columns advanced; but that which was designed to take the western front in reverse went astray at once in the swamp, and was unable to extricate itself before daylight exposed it to the full fire of the British batteries. The other column under d'Estaing made its way truly through the darkness and mist, and arrived close to the Springhill redoubt before it was discovered. The British batteries at once opened a tremendous fire, but the French and Americans came gallantly on, and reaching the redoubt closed with its little garrison—a mere hundred men of the Sixtieth and Provincial corps—in a fierce and desperate struggle. Captain Taws of the Sixtieth, who was in command of the redoubt, killed two of the assailants with his own hand, but fell dead with his sword deep in the body of a third; and for a moment the enemy's colours were planted upon the parapet. Then Maitland with the grenadiers of the Sixtieth and a party of Marines came up in the nick of time, and charged the attacking parties with a degree of fury that sent them flying in confusion back to their camp. No attempt was made to renew

Oct. 9.

the assault, nor, owing to the density of the mist, did Prevost think it prudent to pursue. So after two hours of bloody work the fight ended, the enemy leaving nine hundred[1] killed and wounded on the ground, whereas the British loss did not exceed fifty-four of all ranks. The siege was then raised, and after a great deal of angry recrimination between the Americans and their allies Lincoln retreated to South Carolina, while d'Estaing, after despatching part of his fleet to the West Indies, sailed himself with the remainder to Europe. So far things had gone well with the British arms in the south.

Meanwhile, since the end of 1778, Clinton had remained practically impotent at New York. It is true that Washington had no more troops than himself; but if New York with all its outlying posts was to be securely held, hardly a man could be spared for service in the field. Moreover, Clinton was often in deep anxiety, from want not only of men but of money and supplies.[2] Since he had assumed command Germaine had weakened his force by fully ten thousand men, detached to the West Indies and to the south; yet the incorrigible Secretary of State, as though Clinton's numbers were still undiminished, never ceased to plague him with suggestions for the coming campaign. Now he hoped that Washington would speedily be brought to action; now he recommended a raid of eight thousand men upon the coast of New England; now he urged the importance of recovering Carolina, and founded extravagant hopes on the successes of Prevost.[3] "For God's sake, my lord," wrote Clinton at last, "if you wish me to do anything, leave me to myself, and let me adapt my efforts to the hourly change of circumstances."[4] Meanwhile Germaine made great promises of newly

---

[1] 637 French, 264 Americans.
[2] Clinton to Germaine, 15th December 1778.
[3] Germaine to Clinton, 23rd January, 31st March, 1st April, 5th May 1779.
[4] Clinton to Germaine, 22nd May 1779.

raised regiments[1] to strengthen Clinton, as well as of 1779, three thousand recruits (which latter somehow shrank to thirteen hundred on embarkation) to fill the gaps in his ranks ; but this reinforcement did not sail until May, when the fleet that escorted them was delayed first by the alarm of a French attack on the Channel Islands and later by persistent contrary winds. The result was that these troops from England did not reach New York until the 25th of August, while those which should have been returned from the West Indies were, as we have seen, detained for want of a squadron to convoy them. In the face of these facts it is not difficult to guess that Germaine's breezy designs and lofty exhortations to action must have been more than ordinarily irritating to Clinton.

Necessarily restricted by his weakness to petty operations, Clinton did what he could. In May a small expedition to the Chesapeake took or destroyed vast quantities of warlike stores and of shipping, and in July a like descent was made for the same object upon Connecticut. American writers are loud in denunciation of these "barbarous raids," and of the brutality and wanton plundering of the British troops on these occasions ; but I find no support for these charges in English narratives, even among those authors who have not hesitated to record and to condemn such misbehaviour when it actually occurred. On the other hand, I do find that in Connecticut British sentries, who had been posted to prevent pillage, were shot down by the American inhabitants, which sufficiently accounts for any severity that may afterwards have been shown towards certain towns. But in truth the attitude of Americans in regard to certain operations of this war is to an Englishman not a little puzzling. For it seems that it was perfectly legitimate for Americans to invade Canada, for instance, to maltreat and defraud the people, and to violate capitulations towards prisoners, and not less legitimate for them to leave incendiaries to burn New York over

[1] Macdonnell's (then 76th), Edinburgh (then 80th).

1779. the heads of the British army, and to hire incendiaries to burn the British dockyards. Yet when the British in their turn destroyed American depots of stores or harried the nests of American privateers, they became by a curious transformation mere mediæval freebooters, and their actions the diabolical deeds of a brutal soldiery. It is perfectly clear from Washington's letters that these predatory raids were extremely embarrassing to him and that they possessed decided military value, more particularly in cutting off the resources of American privateers. But Washington was too good a soldier to take a blow without returning it, and accordingly we find him retaliating effectively from time to time. Thus July 15. in July he recaptured the fort at Stony Point on the Hudson, which had been taken by Clinton only a few weeks before, and carried off five hundred British Aug. 18. soldiers; and in August he made a like descent upon Paulus Hook and took one hundred and fifty prisoners. But for the most part the operations to northward were merely desultory, Washington rightly refusing to be drawn into a general action.

Nevertheless, there was one incident which possesses for us a peculiar interest. In view of the pitiful condition of the loyalist refugees at New York, it had been determined to form a settlement of them at Penobscot, on the coast about sixty leagues north of Boston. Accordingly, in June, General Francis Maclean, who commanded in Nova Scotia, was sent to Penobscot with six hundred men of his own and of Campbell's regiments [1] to build in the bay a fort which should serve as a protection at once to the settlement and to Nova Scotia. Intelligence of this design soon reached Boston, where the prevailing hostility towards the loyal New Englanders, who had left the city with Howe, at once suggested an expedition to mar the work of Maclean. By means of large bounties and an embargo three thousand troops were quickly raised, and nineteen ships armed and fitted out; for it was expected that the service would be brief,

[1] Then numbered 82nd and 74th respectively.

easy, and triumphant. The building of the fort was 1779. but little advanced when on the 21st of July Maclean July 21. heard of the preparations in Boston; whereupon, abandoning the completion of the permanent works, he employed his troops night and day in raising defences to secure them against assault. Four days later the July 25. armament from Boston appeared, and on the 28th the American troops were landed. The British picquets hastily fell back before them, with the exception of a single party of twenty men under the command of Ensign John Moore of Maclean's, a remarkably handsome lad of eighteen, of whom we shall see more. This young officer, though on that day he came under fire for the first time and had none but recruits with him, thought that the other picquets had retired too soon and held on stoutly to his post, until the General sent a party to bring him in, together with the thirteen of his twenty men that still remained unhurt. That night General Maclean gave young Moore the command of a reserve of fifty men, with orders to fall on the flank of any attacking column with the bayonet, as soon as it should reach the ditch. But the men from Boston were not so enterprising as to attempt an assault, preferring the safer methods of sap and cannonade. For a full fortnight they played their guns upon Maclean's little handful of men, interrupted by occasional sorties which retarded their operations not a little; until on the morning of the 14th of August the garrison to its surprise Aug. 14. found the American trenches deserted and its enemies re-embarked. The appearance in the bay of a British squadron under Sir George Collier quickly explained the mystery; and then there ensued a very curious scene. The American ships at first formed line as if for action, but before the shock could come they gave way, and every vessel sought safety for herself. Two put out to sea, but were promptly intercepted, one being taken and the other driven ashore. The rest fled up the river, transports mingled with men-of-war in panic and confusion, with the British in chase. A few were

1779.
Aug. 14. taken, but the greater number were driven ashore, where crews and troops took to their heels and fled into the forest, to find themselves a hundred miles from any base of supplies without a scrap of provisions. Soldiers and sailors soon fell to blaming each other for the disaster; from abuse they came to blows, and from blows to pitched battle. Fifty or sixty were killed on the spot; a far larger number perished of hunger and fatigue; and only an exhausted remnant found its way back to the settled districts of the province. Of the American fleet every one of the nineteen armed vessels was taken or burnt, and twenty-four transports were likewise destroyed. The success, in a word, was very complete, and taught a very wholesome little lesson to the city of Boston.

But this little affair could give small comfort to Clinton. Admiral Arbuthnot, with the reinforcements
Aug. 25. from England, arrived at New York simultaneously with Collier's return thither from Penobscot; but he brought also news that war with Spain was imminent, and a fresh suggestion from Germaine for an attack on New Orleans.[1] Only five days earlier Clinton had written[2] asking permission for the second time to resign his command and to make it over to Lord Cornwallis, who was just returning from a visit to England; and a glance at the embarkation returns could not but confirm him in his desire. He was never more in need of reinforcements, for General Haldimand had written[3] from Canada that a change had come over the people since the war with France, and that he required two thousand men, which Clinton, though ill able to spare them, most
Sept. 10. loyally sent to him. Yet the long-expected succours from Europe, which Germaine had reckoned at four thousand recruits, besides two new regiments,[4] now reduced themselves to less than thirty-four hundred men all told. Over one hundred men had died on the voyage

[1] Germaine to Clinton, 25th June 1779.
[2] Clinton to Germaine, 20th August 1779.
[3] Haldimand to Clinton, 26th May 1779.
[4] Macdonnell's (76th), Edinburgh (80th).

and nearly eight hundred more were ill of a fever, which 1779. spread so rapidly through the garrison that within a month five thousand men and within six weeks six thousand men were on the sick list in New York. Simultaneously there came appeals for help from Jamaica, which was trembling under the presence of d'Estaing's fleet at St. Domingo, in ignorance that his true destination was Georgia; and Cornwallis was on the point of sailing for Jamaica with four thousand men, when the news of d'Estaing's appearance at Savannah arrived just in time to stop him. Clinton took the opportunity to Oct. 28. evacuate Rhode Island and to concentrate all the troops in the northern colonies at New York; but he remained in cruel suspense as to the fate of Georgia until the middle of November, when the welcome news of d'Estaing's repulse left him free to form his plans for a campaign in Carolina.[1]

Fortunate it was for him that Washington had as bad a master in Congress as he himself in Germaine. All through the summer of 1779 the American General chafed against the paucity of numbers which kept him on the defensive and left him powerless to check the raids of Clinton; nor was he less annoyed at the waste of d'Estaing's power at Savannah, when the true point of attack should have been New York. Again, there was always the jealousy of the various provinces to contend with, and their selfish care for their own safety, to the neglect of the common advantage. It was vain for Congress to offer bounties to raise a Continental Army, since the different States would always outbid them to ensure levies for their own security. This same difficulty had borne hardly on Amherst when driving the French from the Continent twenty years before; but Amherst had all England at his back, and by her help had accomplished his task. Now Washington, who of all men least deserved it, was to feel the stress of the same trouble, and to discover that as his countrymen had left

[1] Clinton to Germaine, 21st August, 4th, 26th, 30th September, 9th, 26th, 28th October, 10th, 17th, 19th November 1779.

1779. the expulsion of the French mainly to England, so they now purposed to leave the expulsion of the English to France, while they busied themselves in making money. The depreciation of the paper-currency issued by Congress had now become formidable, for the value of the paper in proportion to specie had sunk to forty and even fifty to one; and nearly the whole of the Americans had given themselves up to gambling and stock-jobbing. "Speculation, peculation, and an insatiable thirst for riches seem to have got the better of almost every order of men," wrote Washington in December 1778. "The depreciation of our Continental money is alarming," he wrote again a year later, "the only hope, the last resource of the enemy; and nothing but our want of public virtue can induce a continuance of the war.... Virtue and patriotism are almost extinct. Stock-jobbing, speculating, engrossing seem to be the great business of the multitude."[1] Such seem ever and in all countries to be the first-fruits of revolution, and it is remarkable that the issue of paper-money was a liberty very dear to the birthplace of revolution in America. In the early days of the seventeenth century the godly community of Boston had set up a mint and coined base money, but had been checked by the cancelling of her charter. Twice since that time, in 1751 and 1765, the British Parliament had been driven to intervene lest New England should defraud her creditors by paying her debts in depreciated paper. Now the gates of the temple of fraud, so carefully closed by Parliament, were flung wide open by Congress, and the multitude of worshippers formed the only hope, the last resource of Britain.

Truly the contest appears in a ludicrous aspect under such illumination, neither side seeing hope of success except in the divisions of the other. It is time now to return to the arena of faction on the other side of the Atlantic.

[1] Washington, *Works*, vi. 151, 159, 287, 394, 397.

CHAPTER XV

THE declaration of war by France had, as we have seen, 1778. done much to unite the people of England, despite the efforts of Fox and of his kind; but unfortunately faction had made a new nest exactly in the quarter where it would work most mischief, namely, in the Royal Navy. The first action against a French fleet had taken place off Ushant, on the 27th of July 1778, and had been indecisive; but unfortunately some remarks in the despatch of the Commander-in-Chief, Admiral Keppel, were construed by his Rear-admiral, Sir Hugh Palliser, as a reflection upon himself. A court-martial was held, which might have settled the whole matter quietly and amicably but for the insane violence of partisans on both sides. For, Keppel being a Whig and Palliser a Tory, the politicians of course turned the controversy into a party question, and carried their extravagance to such a height that the Navy itself grew dangerously infected with the spirit of division. It became a point of honour that no Whig Admiral should accept command from Lord Sandwich; and this was a serious matter, since by chance the ablest flag-officers, with the notable exception of Rodney, were Whigs almost to a man, while many of them also held seats in the House of Commons. The effects of this fatal spread of the disease of faction will be seen all too clearly in America.

As regards purely military matters the necessities of internal defence required first consideration, owing to the incessant alarms caused by Paul Jones and by other

1778. American privateers on the Scottish coast.[1] Accordingly, in April 1778, orders were given for raising in Scotland three regiments of Fencible Infantry, that is to say, of regular troops enlisted for service in Great Britain only, with special exemption from the curse of drafting.[2] The strength of each regiment was fixed at eleven hundred and twenty men, and their Colonels were the Duke of Buccleugh, the Duke of Gordon, and Lord Frederick Campbell; a fourth regiment under Colonel Wemyss being added in February 1779. But while these regiments were raising, the seaports of Scotland began to form voluntary associations of armed men for defence, which proceeding raised an awkward constitutional question; for, however praiseworthy their object, and whatever their value in times of emergency, such combinations were illegal. In the sister-kingdom precisely the same difficulty presented itself a few months later. Ireland was dangerously denuded of troops at this time, the regular forces numbering barely nine thousand men, while all efforts to raise a militia were defeated by the alarming depletion of the Irish Treasury. In this dilemma, the Irish Protestants, especially those in the coast-towns, began likewise at the end of 1778 to form voluntary associations for defence, a movement which rapidly spread, and was shortly to produce the famous Irish Volunteers. Though these associations also were contrary to law, they professed every good intention, the Irish Protestants having been rallied to loyalty by the war with France; hence the Lord Lieutenant, though unable to recognise them, took no steps to suppress them.[3] Here, therefore, both in Scotland and in Ireland were organised bodies of armed men, all of them rabid Protestants, established in defiance of the law; and it is noteworthy that just a month after the inception of the

---

[1] *S.P. Scotland*, General Oughton to Secretary of State, 27th April 1778.

[2] *Secretary's Common Letter Book*, 14th April 1778.

[3] Lord Lieutenant to Secretary of State, 21st and 30th April, 10th December 1778.

movement in Scotland, Parliament removed many of the disabilities imposed by an Act of King William the Third on Roman Catholics. 1778.

On the meeting of Parliament in November, the estimates provided for an establishment of one hundred and twenty-one thousand men, twenty-four thousand of them foreigners, besides forty thousand embodied militia. It was none too large a force, considering the certainty that Spain would soon be added to the open enemies of England. No new regiments were provided for under these estimates except a single corps called the Royal Highland Emigrants, which was to be raised in America. As the aspect of affairs became more menacing, three new regiments of Light Dragoons, under Colonels Manners, Philipson, and Douglas,[1] were formed out of the light troops of other regiments of dragoons, but no further steps were taken. Then on the 16th of June 1779 Spain declared war, and the British people braced itself in earnest for the work of defence. The need indeed was urgent, for the French fleet from Brest had been careful to join the Spanish fleet before the declaration of hostilities, in order to accomplish the invasion of England. There was, however, long delay before the full strength of the joint armament could be assembled; and though at length it entered the British Channel with sixty-six ships of the line and rode there triumphant for a few weeks, it accomplished absolutely nothing but the capture of a single ship of the line off Plymouth Sound. Had an attack upon Plymouth been really pressed, the allies could, in the opinion of the general in command at the port,[2] have taken the dockyard in six hours, so culpably had the defence been neglected by the Government. The danger, however, fortunately passed away. The allied fleets, half disabled by the sickness of their crews, were driven out of the Channel by an easterly gale, and the panic-stricken 1779. June 4. July 22. Aug.

---

[1] Then numbered 19th, 20th, and 21st; disbanded in 1783.
[2] *S.P. Dom.* General Lindsay to Secretary of State, 31st August 1779.

1779. people on the British coast drew a long sigh of thankfulness and relief.

June-Aug. Meanwhile there had been feverish activity in raising levies for defence of the country. A bill was brought into Parliament at the end of June to double the strength of the Militia and to enable individuals to raise loyal corps of volunteers; and though the clause for doubling the Militia was struck out by the Lords, the rest of the bill was passed. But long before volunteers could be thought of, noblemen and gentlemen came forward with offers to raise regular regiments at their own expense; and within two months thirteen regiments of infantry for general service, three regiments of Fencible Infantry, a twenty-second regiment of Light Dragoons, and yet another small corps of cavalry [1] were all raising without cost to the country. Simultaneously Lord James Murray at his own charge added a second battalion to the Forty-second Highlanders, which after long independent existence as the Seventy-third Highlanders has in later days reverted to its old place with the Black Watch. At the same time corps of Volunteers sprang into life all over England. Middlesex led the way with twenty-four companies, the Tower Hamlets followed with six, and the Board of Works and Artificers of Somerset House with four more. Then the remoter counties came forward, Devon with twenty-four companies and Sussex with seventeen, while the provincial towns, and even a regiment or two of Militia, added further companies of their own, so that before the end of 1779 there were close upon one

[1] 1st July. Lord Harrington's (85th), Duke of Rutland's (86th), Duke of Ancaster's (87th).
10th July. Lord Winchilsea's (87th), James Stuart's (92nd), White's (96th), Sir T. Egerton's Fencible Infantry, Lister's Corps of Light Dragoons.
23rd July. Keating's (88th), Cary's (89th), Acland's (91st), M'Cormick's (93rd), James Dundas's (94th), Reid's (95th), Stanton's (97th), Lord North's Fencibles.
6th August. Lord Fauconberg's Fencibles.
18th August. Holroyd's (22nd) Light Dragoons.
The whole of these corps were afterwards disbanded.

hundred and fifty companies, each with a strength of at 1779. least fifty men. In some counties the gentlemen preferred to devote their subscriptions to the gaining of recruits for the regular Army. Oxfordshire alone helped to supply some ten regiments, while Nottinghamshire devoted itself to the Forty-fifth Foot,[1] the King engaging to honour the corps with the name of the Nottinghamshire Regiment as soon as the county should have raised three hundred recruits. Thus was initiated that which is known as the Territorial System.

But amid the general harmony of patriotic feeling there were not wanting discordant notes. Fox was still unable to look at any military operation, successful or unsuccessful, except with an oblique eye to its effect on the Government,[2] being apparently quite unable to realise that a nation is something greater than even the noisiest party within it. The Duke of Richmond, who was the Fox of the Lords, behaved even worse. The Government had issued a very proper proclamation as to the removal of cattle and supplies in case of an invasion; the Duke, though Lord Lieutenant of Sussex, and therefore responsible for the defence of the county, actually summoned a public meeting, wherein he declared his disapproval of the proclamation and his intention not to execute it.[3] A private soldier who uttered such sentiments would have been rightly tried for mutiny and shot without mercy; and the punishment would not have been extreme in the case of the Duke himself, though unfortunately it was not applied. In Scotland there was a spirit abroad more dangerous than the envenomed conceit of such men as Richmond and Fox. In April 1779 a draft of sixty men for Fraser's Highlanders mutinied and refused to embark for America. A Fencible Regiment was brought down to coerce

[1] It is now the 1st Battalion of the Derby Regiment.
[2] "If we really wished nothing but the destruction of those we hate, the extraordinary Gazette we have just received [of the defeat of the Americans at Penobscot] would be very good news." Fox to Fitzgerald. *Fox Correspondence*, i. 235.
[3] *Correspondence of George III. and Lord North*, ii. 278.

them; and there ensued a regular fight which did not end until thirty of the mutineers had been killed and wounded, and an officer of the Fencibles killed, together with several men.[1] The next incident was a mutiny of the Fencible Regiment itself in Edinburgh, which was checked in the nick of time by the firmness of General Oughton, who contrived to surround and disarm five companies, and vowed that he would show no mercy to the rest unless they surrendered instantly.[2] These incidents aroused the jealousy of the Volunteer Associations, which pleaded with much reason that in such circumstances their services should be accepted and arms placed in their hands. But the Government still refused to listen to them, and with excellent cause. Highlanders in those days, though splendid troops on active service, were dangerous at home owing to their capricious, obstinate, and mutinous temper;[3] and there lay something more than mere caprice behind the insubordinate spirit of Scotland just at that time. Great numbers of the clergy of all denominations were avowed Americans and Republicans, and, exasperated by the repeal of the penal laws against Roman Catholics, had been inflaming the minds of the populace with the cry of No Popery. Lord George Gordon, a gentleman of greater vanity than intellect, sought notoriety by placing himself at the head of this intolerant party; and it was obviously not in the interest of peace and order to arm his followers by the distribution of muskets to the Volunteer Associations. The case of the Scottish seaports was undoubtedly very hard, but they had no one to thank for it except their ignorant and bigoted ministers of religion. The reader may judge of the extreme difficulty, in such circumstances, of the organisation of national defence.

Hence, in spite of the vigour and self-abnegation with which the nation as a whole had risen to bid

[1] General Oughton to Secretary of State, 20th April 1779.
[2] Same to same, 9th October 1779.
[3] *Ibid.*

defiance to Spain, the winter session of 1779 showed an increase rather than a diminution of factious feeling in Parliament. The speech from the throne spoke in moving terms of the dangerous European confederacy against Britain ; and the estimates provided for a British establishment of one hundred and four thousand regular troops, which, added to forty-two thousand embodied militia, twenty-five thousand foreigners, and the forces on the Irish Establishment, made up a total of about one hundred and ninety-four thousand men for the service of 1780. The men were duly voted, and three new regiments were raised in the course of the winter ;[1] but the animosity of the Opposition had lost none of its violence, and had discovered a new vent in general criticism of the military operations. This was doubtless due to the examination of Howe and Burgoyne in the previous session. No worse tribunal than a Committee of the House of Commons can be imagined for trial of military men ; but none the less both naval and military officers had been summoned to give evidence and had been tormented with questions, many of which, being propounded merely for factious objects, they, to their honour, had declined to answer. The result was that several members of both houses began to esteem themselves fit judges of the conduct of a campaign. Undoubtedly there was very much in the military operations that lay open to criticism ; and strong censure of the neglect that had left Plymouth defenceless was perfectly justified. But the purpose of the Opposition was not to improve matters but to make them worse, and to that end accordingly all its energy was devoted. First, therefore, Lord Shelburne rose and condemned General Grant for concentrating his force at St. Lucia instead of distributing it among the islands for their defence. In other words, Lord Shelburne, by his own showing, was for permitting the whole of the British troops in the West Indies to be captured piecemeal, together with the islands on which he would have had them stationed ;

1779.

Nov. 25.

---

[1] Rainsford's (99th), Fullerton's (98th), Humberstone's (100th).

1779. which gives us a pretty accurate idea alike of his patriotism and of his sense. Then the Duke of Richmond gave expression to the jealousy and alarm with which he viewed the increase of the military force in the kingdom, arguing that if England had a fleet the number of troops was excessive, and that if not the number was insufficient. The Duke had once been a soldier, and he knew perfectly well that the function of a British fleet is not to lie at anchor in British ports; but such is the puerility of faction that both he and Shelburne deliberately urged the Government to a false military policy, towards which it was already far too much
1780. inclined. After the Christmas recess there followed bitter personal attacks over the appointment of several of the colonels of the new regiments, particularly of such as happened to be Scotsmen. So fine an opportunity of making mischief was not lost upon Fox, who spared no ignoble or malignant taunt against the Scots.

Meanwhile, a new weapon had been placed in the hands of the Opposition by the condition of Ireland, which had rapidly become more and more serious. In
1779. April 1779 an Assembly, which gave itself the name of the Citizens of Dublin, passed resolutions after the American model against the importation of British goods, a movement which was evidently quickened by American and French emissaries.[1] Such resolutions might have passed as comparatively harmless, had not the Volunteer Associations greatly increased their numbers, and showed pretty clearly that they hoped by a parade of strength to awe the British Government into political concessions. These Associations, it is true, made fervid protestations of loyalty and of zeal for the defence of the country; and several offers to raise regiments, together with large subscriptions towards the expense of gaining recruits for the Army, were good proof that these professions were genuine. At length, therefore, in July[2] the Lord Lieutenant consented to issue arms to the Volunteers, and thus gave them by implica-

[1] Lord Lieutenant to Secretary of State, 29th April 1779.   [2] *Ibid.*

tion a legal standing. Fox, it need hardly be said, at 1779-80. once encouraged the Irish to abuse the power thus entrusted to them. "Legal or illegal, I approve of the Irish Associations," he said. "I approve of the manly determination which in the last resort flies to arms for deliverance." No doubt there was very much to command sympathy in the efforts of Ireland to free herself from the commercial trammels wherein England had bound her; but it is significant that Fox's fellow-feeling for those who flew to arms for deliverance did not extend to the Scots, who only asked for liberty to defend themselves against French privateers. In a word, the man acted not from principle, but from mischief. Unfortunately it was not only Volunteer Associations and restrictions on trade that caused trouble in Ireland; otherwise the commercial concessions, now hastily granted by the British Parliament, might have proved a sufficient remedy. There was a constant traffic from Irish ports in provisions which were beyond question destined for the French fleet, but which, being loaded in Dutch ships and consigned to Dutch ports, could not be stopped by any legal process. Thus, while the enemies of England were drawing most important stores of war from Ireland, the Government was obliged to look on in utter helplessness, without legal powers to confiscate the ships that carried them, and without strength to check the delivery of the goods at the ports from fear of an insurrection.[1] Moreover, the Irish Parliament, taking the happy tide at the flood, left the Government no time to deal with any such matters. Seizing hold of the concessions proffered by England to America, and arguing not unreasonably that they should be extended also to Ireland, the Irish patriots claimed that English Acts of Parliament were no longer binding in Ireland, and that in consequence the English Mutiny Act, among others, was of no force. Nor was this contention idly put forward, for the magistrates took upon themselves to discharge deserters; and it was made perfectly clear

[1] Lord Lieutenant to Secretary of State, 12th and 30th January 1780.

1780. that juries would find indictments against officers who should take action under any clause of the English Mutiny Act.[1] The only alternative was that the Irish Parliament should itself pass a Mutiny Act, which, notwithstanding the opposition of the British Cabinet, it proceeded to do, lest all military discipline should come to an end. But lest the power of raising fresh difficulties should also come to an end, the Irish Parliament actually refused to pass the Act except as a perpetual Act, leaving the British Government with the unpleasant alternative of acquiescing in the violation of a great constitutional principle, or, practically, of forfeiting all executive control in Ireland. The whole proceeding was ludicrously characteristic of the Irish. It could never have occurred to any other nation to deprive itself of its own liberty simply for the sake of embarrassing its rulers; but it is certain that the embarrassment thus caused was extreme.

June 2-9. In the midst of all these difficulties in Ireland came the insurrection against Roman Catholicism, known as the Gordon Riots, which placed London for several days at the mercy of the mob. These disturbances could have been suppressed without difficulty if military force had been employed at once; but London now paid the penalty for the weakness of successive governments in dealing with the riots which are associated with the names of Porteous and Wilkes, and with the late tumults at Boston in New England. Officers had been tried for their lives for firing on a mob; hence no officer would act without a magistrate. A Surrey justice had been tried for his life in 1768 for suppressing a riot; therefore no magistrate would move without orders from a superior. The Government with deplorable feebleness hesitated to give such orders; and had not the King taken matters into his own hands as Chief Magistrate, there is no saying where the work of violence and of destruction would have ended. The Opposition of course abetted the mob. It was nothing to them that

[1] Lord Lieutenant to Secretary of State, 8th and 22nd April 1780, and *S.P. Ireland*, April-August 1780, *passim*.

London should be burned down, so long as the Government perished in the flames. "No, by no means call out the military," cried Shelburne, when the scum of London was actually seething round the gates of the House of Lords. The Duke of Richmond, after the danger was over, moved a resolution of censure against Lord Amherst for ordering the troops, at the height of the riots, to disarm all unauthorised persons who carried weapons in the streets. Such behaviour was natural in a man who could ascribe the insurrection to the Quebec Act; but it is remarkable that when the Duke of Richmond again called attention to the order of Amherst, as an infringement of the Bill of Rights, he actually found a supporter in the Duke of Grafton.[1] Thus, whatever the divisions of the Americans among themselves, the revolutionary party could count with good hope upon similar divisions in Great Britain.

With such distractions at home, both present and impending—for I have been led by convenience of arrangement somewhat to anticipate the course of our domestic history—the British Government was required to face the new problems set to it by the Spanish declaration of war. There could be no doubt that Spain's only excuse and object was the recovery of possessions lost in previous wars, Gibraltar, Minorca, Florida, and even Jamaica; and it might well be questioned whether it might not be advisable for England to abandon some of them in order to secure the rest. Already, as I have pointed out, great opportunities had been lost, great losses had been incurred, and still greater risks had been run, owing to the excessive dispersion of the limited British force; and it was incontestable that these risks were now doubled, and that each petty, isolated garrison abroad was more than ever a hostage to fortune. Whether the military policy of England, in face of the great coalition formed and forming against her, was to be purely defensive, or what is called the defensive-offensive, the one hope of success lay in concentration.

[1] *Parl. Hist.*, xxi, pp. 671, 691, 776.

1779. Everything turned upon the command of the sea ; and a multiplicity of scattered garrisons, all of them dependent on the fleet for their safety, was a source not only of military but of naval weakness, since it entailed the constant detachment of ships, and consequently the enfeeblement of squadrons, to convoy to the various stations their reinforcements and supplies. On the other hand, a respectable military force, concentrated at a single naval base in each sphere of operations, would not only leave the fleet free to act against the naval force of the enemy, but would enable it at any moment to throw a sufficient body of men upon any one of his isolated posts, to overwhelm it, and, after due havoc wrought, to withdraw the troops once more to the base. Barrington, by adhering to this principle on a small scale, had conquered Guadeloupe in 1759; Grant, by cherishing it in defiance of both Government and Opposition, and in contempt of the loss of less important islands, had preserved the key of the windward group of the Antilles. It is characteristic of Germaine that he tried to combine the two methods at once, and both of them on a wrong principle, namely, the purely defensive, which he conceived to be identical with a multiplicity of garrisons, and the defensive-offensive, which he interpreted as the acquisition of useless posts requiring yet more garrisons. Finally, to these glaring faults he added the crowning error of continuing to found his operations on the assumed disaffection of foreigners and of colonists towards their rulers for the time being.

In a war with Spain the British stations which called for first attention were, of course, those in the Mediterranean. Alarms of a Spanish attack upon Gibraltar had been current as far back as in 1775,[1] and a respectable sum of money had then been spent upon the improvement of the defences. With the arrival of General Eliott as Governor in May 1777, yet more vigour was infused into the work of fortification, and by

[1] Lord Rochford to Lieutenant-Governor Boyd, 25th May 1775.

the spring of 1778 the General had planned his scheme of defence, and resolved to try the effect of red-hot shot in case of an attack.¹ In June 1779 the Spaniards began the blockade, or, as it is inaccurately termed, the siege of Gibraltar, and before the end of the year fuel and ammunition were already running short in the fortress, while the daily duty pressed very hard on the insufficient numbers of the garrison.² At the end of November Rodney sailed from England with a convoy and with reinforcements, engaged and defeated a Spanish squadron, capturing six ships and burning a seventh, and brought much-needed succour into Gibraltar. But with less than forty-five hundred men fit for duty, and daily work requiring the services of twenty-two hundred of them, Eliott felt himself obliged to detain the second battalion of the Seventy-first, which had been intended to reinforce the garrison of Minorca.

Now Minorca also was in charge of a good and able soldier, General James Murray, sometime brigadier to General Wolfe, and commander of the British troops at the action of St. Foy. He too had begun his preparations for defence as far back as in 1775; but the spring of 1779 found his garrison, already too weak in numbers, still further enfeebled by tertian fever. "The two British regiments," he wrote, "look more like ghosts than soldiers. The invalids and drafted men are quite worn out, and in a siege would be useless. If in March I can muster fourteen hundred able rank and file fit to go through the hardships of a siege, we shall be stronger than our present condition promises."³ Yet it was from this garrison that Eliott felt it his duty to withhold the whole of a strong battalion, though warned⁴ that the safety of Minorca might depend upon its arrival there. For so doing Eliott deserves praise rather than blame. It was perfectly clear that England could not provide

---

¹ Eliott to Lord Weymouth, 10th April 1778.
² Same to same, 27th October 1779, 28th January 1780.
³ Murray to Secretary of State, 13th January 1779.
⁴ Lord Weymouth to Eliott, 4th December 1779.

1779. the troops to hold both fortresses; and since Fort St. Philip at Minorca, though immensely strong, was extremely unhealthy, owing to the foul air of the subterranean defences, it would have been better to have blown up the works and to have evacuated the island, even at the sacrifice of so good a harbour as Mahon. Such a course was rendered the more expedient by the fact that the fleet which relieved the Mediterranean fortresses generally passed on from thence to the West Indies, but instead of proceeding thither direct from Gibraltar was obliged to wait until a convoy had been escorted to Minorca and back again, whereby much valuable time was lost. Nevertheless, the Government held on firmly to both fortresses, with results which were fatal to one and very serious to the other.

In the Windward Islands of the West Indies the capture of Dominica, St. Vincent, and Grenada had to a greater or less extent forced concentration, though at the cost of many prisoners, upon the Government; but there was still far too much dispersion of troops. Barbados was always worth holding as a depot, not only for its position, but for its comparative healthiness, while its situation, well to windward of Martinique, almost ensured its immunity from a French attack. But there were still at St. Kitts troops too few for its protection, though too many to be conveniently spared; to say nothing of the fact that the loyalty of these islands was best secured by abandoning them to their own resources.[1] Again, there was a detachment at Tobago, in which island some perfectly useless fortifications had been constructed at great expense, with more guns than there were men to work them; a piece of folly which was very profitably revealed to Parliament by Colonel Barré.[2] To keep such bodies of men and such numbers of guns

---

[1] Governor Burt (Leeward Islands) to Secretary of State, 3rd May, 27th September 1779. Governor Cunyngham (Barbados) to Secretary of State, 18th September 1780.

[2] *Parl. Hist.*, xx. 46. There seem to have been 180 guns and mortars and 41 men.

in indefensible stations was simply to court attack by 1779. the French; yet there they were kept, and, as shall be seen, the French did not overlook them.

But it was to leeward rather than to windward that Spanish hostility threw its weight into the scale in the West Indies. There England, besides her naval base at Jamaica, had her outlying posts in Florida and on the Mississippi. So burdensome were these last from their unhealthiness and their absolute dependence on supplies from without, that they might well have been abandoned at the beginning of the war. But when Spain became an open enemy, it was more than ever expedient to evacuate them, since the Spanish naval base at Havannah was five hundred miles nearer to Florida than Port Royal, while the Spanish port of New Orleans commanded the whole of the British settlements in the province.

Germaine, as has been told, had on the contrary recommended an attack on New Orleans; and for this purpose Brigadier John Campbell had been despatched by Clinton to Pensacola at the end of 1778, so as to be ready for offensive action immediately on the declaration of war. The state of things which Campbell found on his arrival was not, however, encouraging. There were neither money nor credit for the payment of his troops, nor tools nor other materials for fortification, nor vessels nor bateaux for communication with his outlying posts. Provision ships arrived but once a year, bringing supplies for twelve months and for no longer, and there was no stock on which to fall back in case of failure. The troops which Campbell found there consisted of seven companies of the Sixteenth Foot, chiefly worn-out veterans, and eight companies of the Sixtieth,[1] composed principally of Germans, condemned criminals, and " other species of gaol-birds." The troops which he brought with him were a battalion of Waldeckers, unfit in dress, equipment, and discipline for service in the wilds, and two battalions of Provincial Infantry, raised in Maryland

[1] Of the 3rd and 4th battalions.

1779. and Pennsylvania from Irish vagabonds who had deserted from the American army, and were quite ready to desert from the British. Lastly, the harbour of Pensacola was unprotected, and lay at the mercy of a single privateer.[1]

With such a force it was evident that the only hope of a successful attack on New Orleans must lie in suddenness and rapidity of movement; but such was Germaine's mismanagement that the news of the rupture with Spain did not reach Campbell until September. Consequently, when just about to march against New Orleans he learned that the Spaniards, having earlier information, had already overwhelmed the isolated posts on the Mississippi and taken four hundred and fifty prisoners. The Spaniards were able, as Campbell wrote, with their united forces, to attack the dispersed forces of the British; but still the British force was divided between Pensacola and Mobile, though of no possible service in either.

Sept.

Nor was Florida the only quarter to leeward where the Spaniards were beforehand with the British, for almost simultaneously with the descent on the Mississippi the Spanish Governor of Honduras made an unexpected attack upon the British logwood-cutters in that bay, took many of them prisoners, and expelled the rest from their settlement at St. George's Key. Admiral Sir Peter Parker, however, had already reported to Governor Dalling[2] of Jamaica an offensive movement upon Omoa, the key of the bay of Honduras, which enterprise was promptly undertaken by three ships of the Jamaica squadron and a mere handful of troops from Jamaica, under Major Dalrymple. This force at once recaptured St. George's Key, and then laid siege in form to Omoa; but Dalrymple found the work progressing so slowly, the walls of the port of Omoa being eighteen feet thick,

Oct. 16.

---

[1] Campbell to Secretary of State, 22nd March 1779, and to Clinton, 20th February 1779.
[2] *Admiral's Despatches*, Jamaica. Parker to Dalling, 3rd September 1779.

that he resolved to risk an assault. One hundred and fifty seamen, mariners, and soldiers were accordingly told off for this duty, which, marvellous to say, they accomplished, though the garrison was of more than twice their strength. The Spaniards were in fact paralysed with fear by the sheer audacity of the enterprise. Two only of them were wounded, while three hundred and sixty-five were taken prisoners; and Omoa, the storehouse for the gold of Guatemala, together with ships and cargoes worth three millions of dollars, passed bloodlessly into the hands of the British.[1]

Dalrymple then sailed away to take Rattan, leaving a garrison in Omoa, while Dalling in vain wrote orders for the blowing up of the fortifications and the evacuation of the place. Omoa was, however, abandoned in December at the mere menace of a Spanish attack, the garrison being hopelessly reduced by fever and disease. But unfortunately it was on no sound principle that Dalling hastened to leave an unhealthy spot after a successful raid, for he was bent upon an immediate expedition to Nicaragua. The design was that troops should advance up St. John's River from the east coast to the lake, should seize the Spanish fort at the head of it, and pushing on to Grenada and Leon should draw a chain of posts from sea to sea, and so cut Spanish America in twain. Such was the plan of a defensive-offensive attack, suggested to Dalling and Germaine by Mr. Hodgson, late Governor of the British settlements on the Mosquito Coast, in reliance, as usual, on an insurrection not only of Indians, but of the whole body of Spanish colonists against the rule of Spain. Four hundred troops would suffice to make a beginning, according to Dalling's calculation, with four hundred more to reinforce them as soon as the lake of Nicaragua should have been taken. A small squadron of frigates would co-operate, and

---

[1] It was at the storm of Omoa that a British sailor, having two cutlasses himself, offered one to an unarmed Spanish officer that they might meet on equal terms. Dalrymple to Germaine, 21st October 1779.

1779. Captain Horatio Nelson, of H.M.S. *Hinchinbrooke*, a very zealous officer, would accompany the expedition up the river to the lake.

Such was the grand scheme of operations to leeward for the year 1780; and at this point it is necessary for the present to leave it, in order to follow more important occurrences in other quarters. The reader need only bear in mind that from this time the naval base to leeward at Jamaica, together with the squadron and the troops attached to it, was charged not only with the maintenance and succouring of the weak detachments at Pensacola and Mobile, but with an offensive expedition against Central America, involving, if successful, the establishment of posts across the whole width of the isthmus. Meanwhile it was Admiral Rodney's duty to deal with the French fleet to windward and on the American coast; and it was General Clinton's task to conquer Carolina. Let us first revert to Clinton, who for the second time within two years had asked in vain for permission to resign his command.[1]

[1] Germaine to Clinton, 4th November 1779.

CHAPTER XVI

THE withdrawal of d'Estaing's fleet after his repulse 1779. before Savannah left the sea open to Clinton to transport troops whither he would. Prevost's successes in Georgia had raised Germaine's hopes to an unwonted height, for their effect had been immediate. The southern provinces could no longer send remittances to France and to the West Indies; French merchants trading with them had become bankrupt, and American credit in France at large had been seriously shaken.[1] The conquest of Carolina became, therefore, in his eyes an object of extreme importance, in order to reduce American exports and American credit still lower; nor was the design altogether without merit, provided that men enough were given to Clinton to execute it. But this was precisely the difficulty which had hampered the British operations throughout. Germaine's reckoning on a large enlistment of Americans had proved delusive during Howe's period of command, and promised to be little better realised under Clinton.[2] At the end of 1779 the entire force at that General's disposal, including the troops in Florida and Georgia, did not exceed twenty-seven thousand rank and file fit for duty; and since the posts at New York and Long Island demanded from twelve to fifteen thousand men for their security, the balance remaining for service in other quarters was dangerously small.

It may be asked why, since the number of troops to

---

[1] Germaine to Clinton, 5th May 1779.
[2] Clinton to Germaine, 15th December 1779.

1779. hand was so scanty, they should not have been withdrawn altogether from the American Colonies, and Halifax made the headquarters for all naval operations. To this the answer is that in such a case the Americans would have been left free to turn all their force against Canada and the West Indies; and it is certain that Congress cherished no enterprise more closely at heart than the conquest of Canada. The presence of a considerable force at New York, in itself a standing menace to New England, was necessary to paralyse any such offensive movement of the Americans to the northward; and events showed that it did so effectually. The same reasoning applies with equal force to another question, namely, whether the base should not have been shifted to the south, since the south had become the principal sphere of operations. It was of course certain that, wherever the main body of the British might go, Washington and his regular troops were bound to follow; but outside the Continental Army there was always that incalculable factor the American militia, a factor which could never be counted on by its friends, but equally could never be ignored by its enemies. It was therefore imperative that New York should be held; and, this being so, it was plain that any expeditions undertaken from thence, with the force at Clinton's disposal, could be no more than predatory.

It can hardly be doubted that raids upon the coast were the best means of harassing the Americans, of widening their internal divisions, and of keeping their forces apart; for the provinces were still far too selfish to help each other, or to use their own troops for any purpose but for their own individual defence. Moreover, the British could be sure of working much mischief by such inroads, whereas the Americans could do nothing except by attack on New York, which implied a great and formidable effort. But if the British undertook serious operations to southward, or at any point remote from New York, the whole situation was altered, since each new British post offered to the enemy a fresh point for attack. A new base must first be taken and held; 1779. and if any advance into the interior was to be effective, the captured territory and the lines of communication must be sufficiently guarded. In a word, two complete armies would be needed, one at New York to hold the forces of New England in check, and another in the south. The task set to Clinton was to make one army do the work of two, relying on the sea for communication between the different sections of the force. If the command of the sea were kept, the operations might be successful but could hardly be decisive ; if the command of the sea were lost—and Clinton trembled night and day before the thought—they could hardly fail to be disastrous.

On the 26th of December 1779 Clinton sailed with a force of seven thousand six hundred men [1] for the capture of his new base at Charleston, leaving General Knyphausen in command at New York. He was not in the best of spirits, having little trust in the service of the loyalists in Carolina. Many of his best officers were gone. Vaughan and Grey had sailed home sick ; Campbell, the victor of Savannah, was dead; Francis Maclean, the hero of Penobscot, was dying at Halifax ; worst of all, Lord Howe and Sir George Collier had gone to England, and the fleet was under command of Admiral Arbuthnot. He had, however, still Cornwallis, Rawdon, and other good officers of high rank, besides Simcoe of the Queen's Rangers and Banastre Tarleton of the "Legion," both of them fine leaders of irregular troops. In any case, he had no misgivings as to his ability to capture Charleston.

The voyage was exceptionally stormy, and the fleet 1780. was utterly dispersed. One vessel loaded with heavy cannon foundered, two or three more fell into the hands of American privateers, almost the whole of the horses perished, and it was not until the end of January 1780

---

[1] 1 battalion of Light Infantry, 2 battalions of Grenadiers, 7th, 23rd, 33rd, 42nd, 63rd, 64th, Queen's Rangers, 6 battalions of Germans.

1780.	that the transports arrived singly or in small groups at Tybee in Georgia. The delay gave General Lincoln time to improve the defences of Charleston and to receive from Washington reinforcements which raised the troops for defence of the town to about seven thousand men. Clinton, without waiting for any of the missing transports, summoned reinforcements from Savannah
Feb. 10.	and New York and sailed again on the 10th of February for the Edisto River, where landing on John's Island
Feb. 11.	he pushed forward slowly to James's Island. Being inferior in numbers, he moved with extreme caution, fortifying his line of communication with the sea as he advanced, till at length he established himself on the south bank of the Ashley River over against Charleston. The city then stood at the tip of a tongue of land running, roughly speaking, east and west between the Cooper River on the north and the Ashley River on the south. To landward Charleston was defended by a chain of strong entrenchments and redoubts, covered by a double abatis ; the line of fortifications extending from river to river except at certain points adjoining the Ashley, where a deep morass provided a sufficient natural protection. To seaward the entrance to the harbour was guarded on the south side by Fort Johnston on James's Island, and on the north side by Fort Moultrie on Sullivan's Island, by which latter the British squadron had been repulsed in 1776. But more formidable than these forts to seaward was the bar beyond them, which was impassable by ships of the line and dangerous for frigates ; while a patch of deep water just within it furnished a convenient anchorage from which the nine ships of the American squadron could play upon any British vessel that attempted the entrance.
March 20.	However, at the first approach of the British squadron to the bar the American Commodore withdrew his ships to Cooper River, where he sank some of them to obstruct
March 29.	the navigation. Some of the British frigates then passed the bar, and nine days later Clinton, now strengthened by the arrival of his mounted troops from Georgia,

moved twelve miles up the Ashley, crossed it un- 1780.
opposed, and on the next day invested the city from
river to river. On the 9th of April the British April 9.
squadron ran past the batteries of Fort Moultrie with
trifling loss, effectually isolating the city from the
country to southward ; and on the 10th Clinton summoned Lincoln to surrender, and was answered by the
usual defiance.

The first thing needful, therefore, was to sever the
communications of Charleston with the north, which
were kept open by three regular regiments of American
cavalry under General Huger, at that time encamped
some thirty miles up the Cooper at Biggin's Bridge.
On the 12th of April Tarleton with his Legion[1] and April 12.
Ferguson's Rangers surprised this corps at night, and
dispersed it completely, with loss of all its stores and
ammunition, four hundred horses, and one hundred
prisoners. This brilliant little success, won at the cost
of but three men wounded, was marred by a wanton
brutality, too common among Tarleton's irregulars,
which provoked Ferguson to such wrath that he was
hardly restrained from shooting some of Tarleton's
dragoons on the spot. The defeat of Huger effectually
cleared the enemy from the ground north of the Cooper,
which was now occupied by a strong force under Cornwallis. Meanwhile, with the help of the reinforcements
from New York, the besieging army pushed its trenches
steadily forward, and on the 6th of May the third May 6.
parallel was opened within two hundred yards of the
abatis. This was a day of misfortune for the Americans.
Fort Moultrie, heavily battered by sea and threatened
by a strong force ashore, surrendered to the British,
while Tarleton by a forced march of thirty miles
northward to the Santee surprised the remnant of the

[1] The Legion included both cavalry and infantry. The only
regular troops attached to it were one troop of the Seventeenth
Light Dragoons, who seem to have held the irregulars in some contempt, since they refused to wear the green uniform of the Legion,
but stuck to their own scarlet.

1780.
May 9.

cavalry that had escaped from Biggin's Bridge, killing or capturing one hundred men and carrying off the whole of the horses. Three days later Charleston surrendered, and Lincoln with his army of five thousand six hundred men, besides one thousand sailors, became prisoners of war. The losses of the British during the siege did not exceed two hundred and sixty-five killed and wounded.

Having thus gained his first great object, Clinton prepared at once to return with a portion of his army to New York, for he knew that a French fleet with reinforcements was on its way across the Atlantic, and he wished to be ready to meet it. He decided therefore to leave the completion of his task to Cornwallis, and meanwhile issued a proclamation, offering pardon to all Americans who should return to their allegiance, threatening confiscation of estates to those who should in future take up arms against the King, and inviting all well-disposed people to form a militia in order to suppress any further attempts at rebellion. Concurrently, he arranged for the advance of three separate columns into the interior, of which the first, under Cornwallis, was to move up the north bank of the Santee upon Camden, while the second should march to south-west of the Santee upon Ninety-Six, and the third up the Savannah River to Augusta.

May 18.

Accordingly, on the 18th Cornwallis started with twenty-five hundred men, including Tarleton's Legion; and on the 27th, hearing that a Continental regiment of infantry under Colonel Burford, which had been ordered to march on Charleston, was now retreating in all haste

May 27. before him, he sent Tarleton in pursuit. Taking with him only two hundred and thirty mounted infantry and dragoons of the Legion, and forty men of the Seventeenth Light Dragoons with one light gun, Tarleton hurried with all speed to the chase. Such was the rapidity of his march that many of his horses succumbed to fatigue and to the intense heat; but he impressed others on the road to take their place, and went on.

May 28. Reaching Camden next day, after traversing more than

sixty miles, he learned that Burford had already left 1780.
Rugeley's Mills, fifteen miles ahead, and was straining
every nerve to join a corps that was on its way to him
from the westward. After a short halt Tarleton started
again at two in the morning, and by dawn was at May 29.
Rugeley's Mills, where he obtained fresh intelligence of
Burford, still twenty miles ahead. He now sent forward an officer to summon Burford to surrender; but
the American, far too shrewd to be delayed by such a
trick, merely returned a defiant answer, and continued
his march without halting for a moment. There was,
therefore, nothing for Tarleton but to push on after
him with exhausted men and exhausted horses. Many
dropped to the rear unable to proceed farther, and the
one British gun came to a standstill; but some of the
men still rode on, and at three o'clock in the afternoon
Tarleton's advanced party overtook Burford's rearguard
and took four prisoners.

Then at last Burford faced about with his little
body of infantry, less than three hundred and eighty
men strong, and drew it up in a single line in an open
wood, sending on his convoy and guns under protection
of a small body of cavalry. Tarleton on his side sent
one hundred and twenty men to open fire on Burford's
left flank, selected thirty more to fall under his own
leadership on his right flank and rear, and posted the
remainder, including the men of the Seventeenth, in
the centre, with orders to charge home. The centre
moved rapidly to the attack; and the Americans with
excellent discipline held their fire, by Burford's order,
until the British were within ten yards of them. The
mistake though gallant was fatal. The volley was fired
too late to check the rush of the horses, and in an
instant the American battalion was broken up and the
sabres were at work, the more fiercely since Tarleton,
whose horse had been killed under him, was reported to
have fallen. Over one hundred of the Americans were
killed, and some two hundred more, together with two
guns and all of their waggons and stores, were captured,

1780. at a cost to the British of three officers and sixteen men killed and wounded. Thus brilliantly closed an extraordinary march of one hundred and five miles in fifty-four hours.[1]

This success practically extirpated for the time the Continental forces in South Carolina. Cornwallis arrived at Camden a few days later, and on the 5th of June Clinton sailed for New York. His last act in Carolina was to issue a proclamation freeing all prisoners, except military men, from their paroles, but declaring also that unless they returned to their allegiance they should be treated as rebels. To this measure was ascribed much of the treacherous dealing that was shortly to follow. Meanwhile Cornwallis was left with about four thousand men to complete the recovery of South Carolina, and in due time to carry his arms into North Carolina also.

The inhabitants of South Carolina were of curiously diverse origin. Settled first by a handful of adventurers from England in 1669, the country received in succession between 1685 and 1763 immigrations of Protestants from France, of discontented Dutch from New York, of Swiss, of Palatines, and of Highlanders; while after 1763 the medley of immigrants was varied still further by the offer of bounties to all foreign Protestants who would settle in the province, and by the arrival of colonists from Virginia and Pennsylvania. The natural tendency of the different races was to segregate themselves into distinct communities; and, since inland communication depended chiefly on navigable rivers, the various settlements were distributed for the most part along one or other of the great waterways which, with their innumerable tributaries, cut their way down in parallel courses from the Blue Mountains to the sea. The rivers with which the reader will be chiefly concerned are the Savannah, which forms the boundary between South Carolina and Georgia, the Edisto, the Santee, with its two tributaries of the Congaree and

---

[1] Tarleton had once before covered sixty-four miles in twenty-three hours. Clinton to Germaine, 25th July 1779.

Wateree, the Peedee, and, across the border of North 1780.
Carolina, the Cape Fear River. The sympathies of the
people naturally varied according to the race to which
they belonged, but it is noteworthy that the most
prominent leaders both of loyalists and rebels bore,
with a few exceptions, British or Irish names. The
Highlanders were almost to a man loyalists, as were
also the Irish who had emigrated direct from Ireland;
while the Irish who had moved down from other
provinces were staunch for the revolution. The settlers
in the hinder country were chiefly royalists, partly, as
in the case of the Dutch, from a predilection for
monarchy, and partly owing to the very sharp lesson
against rebellion which some of them had received in
1771. In the majority of districts loyalists and revolutionists were pretty evenly divided; but there was one
tract between the Broad and Saluda rivers on the upper
forks of the Congaree, generally known as the district
of Ninety-Six, which was a great stronghold of royalism
and therefore a factor not to be ignored in any British
general's plan of campaign.

In the course of the revolution South Carolina had
in some respects led the rest of the Colonies in revolt
She first had shown the way towards united action, and
had framed an independent provincial constitution; but
the main encouragement to rebellion had been the
failure of the British attempt on Charleston in 1776
Since that year until the invasion of Prevost the
province had enjoyed extraordinary prosperity, the
war having made Charleston the centre of supply for
all the Colonies south of New Jersey. The loyalists had
risen at least once in serious insurrection against the
revolutionary government; but, their efforts being dis-
jointed and uncombined, they had always been put
down with little difficulty, and had been forced in great
measure to efface themselves. All this was changed by
the capture of Charleston. The loyalists began to come
forth from their hiding-places and to take revenge for
the sufferings which they had endured during the long

1780 ascendency of the revolutionary party. Both factions being made up in great measure of lawless, vindictive, half-civilised men, accustomed to settle all differences and to prosecute all feuds with the rifle, the contest between them could not but be of the bitterest.

It was in the midst of such a people, agitated with such passions, that Cornwallis found himself set down with four thousand men. His task for the present was so to canton his troops as to preserve order, while the militia was forming for the maintenance of royalist supremacy; for until the harvest should be gathered in and the heat of the summer should have passed away, active operations were impossible. His bases upon the sea were secured by garrisons at Savannah, Beaufort, Charleston, and Georgetown. Up the Savannah there was an intermediate post at Augusta and an advanced post at Ninety-Six, which latter was not only the controlling centre of the stronghold of loyalism, but dominated the upper waters alike of the Savannah and the Congaree. Up the Santee the principal station was Camden, with a strong advanced post at Rocky Mount, on the eastern border of the loyalist district; the communication between Rocky Mount and Ninety-Six being secured by a moving column. On the Peedee the most important post was Cheraw Hill, communicating not only with Camden on the west but with Cross Creek, a settlement of loyal Highlanders on Cape Fear River, to the east. The entire area to be comprehended within these points was a tract of nearly one hundred and fifty miles square.

Having chosen these cantonments, Cornwallis returned to Charleston to settle the civil administration and to prepare for opening the campaign in September. The loyalists of North Carolina were in correspondence with him, and had been entreated to bide their time in patience until the British troops should enter the province; but with the precipitation of undisciplined June. men a party of them rushed into a premature and isolated insurrection, which brought not only defeat

upon themselves, but oppression upon all who sym- 1780.
pathised with them, at the hands of the revolutionists.
Then the results of Clinton's second proclamation began
to be revealed. Revolutionists who desired to remain
neutral on parole, finding themselves compelled to swear
allegiance to the King or to leave the country, took the
oath with bad grace and bad faith, while the loyalists
complained that notorious rebels needed only to take
the said oath in order to receive as good treatment as
the King's friends. The spirit of unrest was increased
by the news that a detachment of two thousand men
from Washington's army had reached Hillsborough,
near the upper forks of Cape Fear River, and that rein- June 20.
forcements were on their way to join them. Finally, the
hidden refugees of the revolutionary party reappeared
from their lurking-places as guerilla-bands, under
leaders whose skill, activity, and daring were destined
to change the whole face of the war in the Carolinas.

Thomas Sumter, a Virginian who had served with
Braddock and had seen much fighting on the Indian
frontier, was the first of these leaders to enter the arena,
midway between the upper waters of the Peedee and July.
Santee. Then the value of oaths was sufficiently tested.
A rebel, who had sworn allegiance and obtained from
Cornwallis not only a certificate of loyalty but a commission in the loyal militia, seduced his regiment from
its colonel and led it to join Sumter. Meanwhile, at
the first menace of Sumter's advance Lord Rawdon had
ordered the post at Cheraw Hill to be evacuated ; and
accordingly the sick men of the garrison were sent
down the Peedee under escort of another body of loyal
militia, which likewise rose against its colonel and carried
the helpless invalids away as prisoners to North Carolina.
Reinforced by these deserters, Sumter made two attacks July 30.
in quick succession upon the British posts at Rocky Aug. 6.
Mount and at Hanging Rock, which commanded the
northward roads on the eastern and western banks of
the Catawba ; and though he was beaten off in both
cases, it was not without heavy loss to the British. His

1780. advance was, moreover, sufficient to stir the entire district between the Santee and the Peedee to rebellion, while the revolutionary spirit was encouraged by the news, which had not yet reached Cornwallis, of the arrival of
July 10. French reinforcements at Rhode Island. Meanwhile the main body of the American army still lay at Hillsborough, with Gates, the reputed conqueror of Saratoga, in command; and though no information as to his movements was obtainable from any quarter,[1] there could be little doubt that he would advance upon
Aug. Camden. Cornwallis was painfully embarrassed. The harvest was nearly over, but the magazines for his coming campaign were not yet ready at Camden; and yet he was convinced that active operations were an imperative necessity—that in fact the invasion of North Carolina, however imprudent, was the only alternative to the abandonment of South Carolina and Georgia and the withdrawal of the British troops within the walls of Charleston.[2] Rawdon, who held command at Camden, was in an even more anxious position. He saw the necessity for contracting his posts and concentrating at Camden, but he dared not remove the garrisons from Hanging Rock and Rocky Mountain, lest Sumter should slip past him and either cut his communications with Charleston, or move rapidly westward and overwhelm his posts on the Broad River. He could, therefore, do nothing but wait and be vigilant; while Cornwallis wrote to Clinton, begging urgently that he would make a diversion in his favour on the Chesapeake, in order to draw Gates's army back to northward.

Gates meanwhile had marched from Hillsborough
July 27. on the 27th of July. Two routes lay open to him for his advance on Camden, one of them following the arc of a circle by Salisbury and Charlottetown, but passing through a fertile country and a friendly population, and the other crossing the chord of that arc, which would lead him through a barren district wherein the few

[1] Rawdon to Clinton, 29th October 1780.
[2] Cornwallis to Clinton, 6th August 1780.

inhabitants were chiefly loyalists. Notwithstanding that 1780. he was deficient in transport and supplies, he chose the latter route, rejecting the counsel of wiser men than he, and, picking up sundry reinforcements on his way, arrived on the 10th of August at Lynch's Creek, some Aug. 10. fifteen miles north-east of Camden. To this same point Rawdon had already advanced with the few hundred troops[1] at his disposal, on the news of Gates's approach, and had taken up a position in rear of the creek in order to bar his advance ; but he was only too painfully aware that a forced march of ten miles up the stream would enable the Americans to turn his left flank and to come down upon Camden by the road from Charlottetown. Gates, however, instead of making this movement in force, remained for two days inactive with his main body and sent only weak detachments to his right; thus giving Rawdon time to withdraw the whole of his outlying posts to Camden, and to fall back in safety to join them. Gates then moved slowly westward to Aug. 13. Rugeley's Mills, about fifteen miles north of Camden on the road to Charlottetown, and on the next day detached a party of his best troops to join Sumter in a Aug. 14. raid upon the British communications.

Early on the same morning Cornwallis arrived at Camden from Charleston with a fixed resolution to attack Gates at all hazards.[2] He could indeed have retreated with ease to Charleston, but only at the sacrifice of some eight hundred sick men and of a vast quantity of stores at Camden, which he could not bring himself to abandon without a fight. His force was pitifully small, numbering but fifteen hundred regular troops, many of them Provincial corps, and from four to five hundred militia ; but Gates, though he had thrice that number of militia, could muster no more

[1] 23rd, 33rd, Fraser's Highlanders, Volunteers of Ireland.
[2] Mr. Fiske assumes that Cornwallis brought reinforcements with him, but this was not the case, for he brought only his staff. This mistake in great measure vitiates Mr. Fiske's criticism of the operations.

1780.
Aug. 15.

regular troops than Cornwallis, and those of inferior quality. At ten o'clock on the night of the 15th Cornwallis marched northward from Camden, for he had intelligence that Gates was meditating an attack, and had resolved to anticipate him. At precisely the same hour, by a ludicrous coincidence, Gates moved off to southward in the hope of surprising Cornwallis. By his own account he designed to take up a strong position on the road, about seven miles from his camp; but in this case Cornwallis outmarched him, for at two o'clock

Aug. 16. in the morning, when the British had traversed about nine miles, the advanced parties of the two armies came into collision. The examination of a few captured Americans speedily satisfied Cornwallis that Gates was before him in force; and since the ground whereon he stood was narrowed by huge swamps on each flank, Cornwallis at once called in his advanced parties, halted, and made his dispositions to attack as soon as dawn should break. His line of battle, which extended from swamp to swamp, was made up of two brigades—the Right Brigade, under Colonel Webster, consisting of three companies of Light Infantry, the Twenty-third Fusiliers and Thirty-third Foot, and the Left Brigade, under Lord Rawdon, of the Volunteers of Ireland, the infantry of Tarleton's Legion, and a third Provincial corps. The whole were drawn up in the order here given, from right to left, with two six-pounder and two three-pounder guns. Two weak battalions of Fraser's Highlanders, each with one gun, stood as a support in rear of these two brigades, while the cavalry of the Legion under Tarleton was posted in rear of all. Gates formed his army into two lines, the right brigade in each line being composed of regular troops, and the left brigade of militia, with seven guns divided among the battalions. In all, his force numbered about fourteen hundred regular troops and sixteen hundred militia.

The action opened with an order from Gates to his militia to attack the British right. Addressed as it was to ill-disciplined and half-trained men, this command

produced rather a confused wavering than a regular 1780.
advance; and Webster promptly seized the moment to Aug. 16.
attack, while Rawdon engaged the regular troops
opposed to him. The American militia thereupon
flung down their arms and fled; and Webster, dis-
daining to pursue, at once wheeled up his brigade and
fell full upon the flank of the American regular troops.
So far these had held their ground against Rawdon
with great steadiness and obstinacy, and even now they
maintained a brave resistance for some three-quarters
of an hour. The day was so still and hazy that little
could be seen through the smoke, and, the flight of the
American militia being unknown to their regular troops,
the latter never doubted but that the day was going
well for them. But meanwhile Tarleton's cavalry,
moving unseen round their flank, plunged down upon
their rear; and then they broke and fled in all directions.
The mounted troops promptly took up the pursuit;
Tarleton pushed the chase relentlessly for twenty miles,
and the rout was complete. About a thousand of the
Americans were killed and wounded, and over a thousand
prisoners, together with seven guns and the whole of their
baggage, transport, and stores, were taken. Baron von
Kalb, a German officer of great ability in the American
service, was killed, and Gates was swept away in the
rush of fugitives, to find himself, when he drew rein,
without an army. The loss of the British was three
hundred and twenty-four of all ranks[1] killed and
wounded, of whom one hundred belonged to the
Thirty-third Foot.

The defeat was fatal to the spurious reputation of
Gates, and, so far as it went, was crushing in itself.
Yet it is noteworthy that on the day before the action Aug. 15.
Sumter had already passed to south of Camden, and had
captured a British convoy with its escort, which was on
its way to Camden from Ninety-Six. There could,
however, be no doubt that Sumter must retire when he

---

[1] 2 officers and 66 men killed; 18 officers and 238 men wounded.

1780. heard of the rout of Gates; and accordingly Tarleton was at once sent northward with all speed to overtake him, while Cornwallis followed more leisurely in his rear.

Aug. 17. Advancing up the eastern bank of the Wateree with three hundred and fifty men, Tarleton learned from stragglers that, as he had expected, Sumter was in full retreat along the western bank; and on reaching Rocky Mount Ferry at dusk he descried the fires of Sumter's bivouac a mile away on the opposite shore. The boats on the river were at once secured, and all fires were

Aug. 18. forbidden; but at dawn it was discovered that the enemy had decamped. Tarleton forthwith crossed the river and resumed the chase, but at noon he had still failed to overtake his quarry, while his men, owing to the heat of the day and to incessant work since the action of Camden, were but few of them able to proceed. Selecting, therefore, one hundred mounted men and sixty infantry from among them, Tarleton followed the tracks of Sumter with all possible caution, until the neighbourhood of the enemy was revealed by a shot from an American vedette, which killed one of Tarleton's dragoons. Both men of the vedette were at once cut down; and in the American camp, where there was no suspicion of the approach of the British, the shots were interpreted to signify nothing more serious than the slaughtering of cattle. So Tarleton's handful of men stole quietly on, and were rewarded by finding the whole of Sumter's eight hundred men lying at ease about their camp, and Sumter himself but half dressed. Before the alarm could be given, Tarleton's men had secured the enemy's arms; and though some militia concealed among the waggons made some attempt at resistance, these were speedily overpowered. About one hundred and fifty of the enemy were killed and wounded, over two hundred were taken prisoners, two guns, together with the whole of their waggons and stores, were captured, and one hundred British prisoners were released, all at a cost to Tarleton of one officer killed and fifteen men wounded. Sumter in the general confusion made his escape, which was unfortunate, for so able a leader would have been a valuable prize. Tarleton was not destined again to catch him unawares.

This brilliant success, due entirely to the indefatigable energy of Tarleton, seemed at the moment to have crushed American resistance in South Carolina. The moment appeared propitious for pushing forward the invasion of North Carolina; and Cornwallis, sending emissaries to call the loyalists in the province to arms, hastened his preparations for an immediate advance on Hillsborough. Yet his situation was in too many respects disquieting. In the first place, the amount of sickness among all ranks of his army was positively alarming; in the second place, it was speedily manifest that Sumter, far from being killed, was hardly even scotched, and that besides him there were many other guerilla leaders in the field. Above all, it became more and more apparent that no trust whatever could be reposed in the local levies, miscalled loyal. On the 19th of August, a small party of British was overwhelmed on the Broad River, owing to the desertion of its militia; and on the 24th a detachment of the American prisoners captured at Camden was actually betrayed, together with its escort, into the hands of the guerilla leader Marion, by a treacherous officer of this same militia. Cornwallis tried and executed several men who had voluntarily enrolled themselves with the British and had then turned against them; but though without doubt he was justified in so doing, the revolutionists could always answer by reprisals.[1] Lastly, as Cornwallis was aware, an invasion of North Carolina must depend for solid and permanent success on a diversion by Clinton in the north; and Clinton had long ago given warning that any such movement must be contingent on British supremacy on the sea. Nevertheless, an advance would benefit the health of the troops, not only by keeping them employed, but by moving them into a better climate; and Cornwallis determined to take the risk.

[1] Cornwallis to Clinton, 21st and 29th August 1780.

1780.
Sept. 7.   Accordingly, on the 7th of September, he advanced from Camden in two columns, the main body[1] under his own command moving up the eastern bank, and the light troops and cavalry up the western bank, of the Wateree. A third detachment under Major Ferguson at the same time moved up wide to the westward from Ninety-Six, with the object of raising recruits for the militia, in which Ferguson still reposed a confidence which no one else could share. The progress of the main body was slow owing to scarcity of forage, and it was not until the
Sept. 22. 22nd that Cornwallis arrived and halted at Charlotte-town. This district was a hotbed of revolution, and the British while they remained in it were harassed by incessant attacks on outposts and on convoys, while communication was rendered most difficult by the incessant waylaying or shooting of the British despatch-riders. Then, as usual, guerilla operations began again in rear of Cornwallis, and a fierce attack was made upon the post of Augusta, in Georgia, but was successfully repulsed with heavy loss to the Americans. The officer in command at Ninety-Six at once conceived the hope of cutting off this American party on its retreat to northward; but finding that the chase led him too far afield, suggested the same idea to Ferguson. Eagerly embracing the project, Ferguson hurried to westward until he had placed at least seventy miles between his detachment and Charlottetown, when he suddenly found himself threatened by a new and wholly unexpected enemy in the shape of three thousand settlers from the extreme backwoods, rough, half-civilised men whom no labour could tire, and whose rifles seldom missed their mark. Realising his danger, Ferguson instantly sent messages for help to Charlottetown, and retreated towards that place with all haste. But every one of his messengers was shot down; and the backwoodsmen, sending forward fifteen hundred picked men to ride after him, made so swift a pursuit as to leave him no hope of escape.

[1] 23rd Fusiliers, 33rd Foot, Provincial troops.

On the 6th of October, therefore, he chose a strong 1780. position on a hill known as King's Mountain, and Oct. 6. turned to bay. This hill was covered with tall forest, beneath which the ground was strewn with huge boulders, while on one side it was rendered absolutely inaccessible by a precipice; and Ferguson seems never to have dreamed that he could not hold it for ever. On the following afternoon the advanced party of the back- Oct. 7. woodsmen arrived, about a thousand strong, and, having tied up their horses and divided themselves into three bodies, began to ascend the hill from three sides. Creeping up in silence, every man confident in his skill as a stalker and a marksman, the central division made its way up to the crest, where Ferguson's men met them with a volley and a charge with the bayonet. The backwoodsmen then fell back slowly, keeping their pursuers in check by a biting fire from behind the trees and boulders, until a storm of bullets in Ferguson's flank showed that a second division of his enemies was lying in wait for him. Turning at once upon them, Ferguson found that the third division of backwoodsmen, which had been hidden on the opposite flank, was firing steadily into his rear. Thus entrapped, the militia found the odds too many against them. Still they fought hard until Ferguson was killed; and nearly four hundred of them had fallen killed and wounded before the remainder, rather more than seven hundred, laid down their arms. The whole loss of the backwoodsmen was eighty-eight killed and wounded, and the only marvel is that it should have been so great, for their exploit was as fine an example as can be found of the power of woodcraft, marksmanship, and sportsmanship in war. The victors celebrated their success by hanging a dozen of their prisoners before they dispersed, in revenge for the execution at Augusta of certain militiamen who had been taken in arms against the British after accepting service with them. The victims were of course Americans, for it was not Mother Country and Colonies but two Colonial factions that fought so savagely in Carolina.

1780. This unexpected blow shattered Cornwallis's whole plan of campaign at a stroke. The disaster fell the more hardly upon him since he had given Ferguson orders to retire,[1] not wishing him to wander beyond reach of support on the other side of the Catawba; though it must be added that the very existence of such a force of backwoodsmen was unknown to him or to his staff. But none the less he acquitted his unlucky subordinate of all blame, and, as became a brave and chivalrous gentleman, took upon himself all responsibility for his defeat. The loss of Ferguson himself, the most expert rifleman in the British Army and an admirable partisan leader, was a great misfortune; but that of his eleven hundred men was for the moment irreparable. There was nothing for it but to retreat;
Oct. 14. and accordingly on the 14th Cornwallis fell back on Winnsborough, his troops suffering much from scarcity of food and from exposure to incessant rain during the retreat. Sickness increased, and Cornwallis himself was among those that were stricken. He therefore committed his pen to Lord Rawdon,[2] who wrote on his behalf to Clinton, setting forth with great ability the hopelessness of reliance on the loyalists of North Carolina, the certainty that a junction with them was not worth the risk of losing South Carolina, and his conviction that, whatever the difficulties and dangers of a defensive war, these were preferable to the perils of adherence to the original scheme of invasion. Beyond all doubt these views were wise and sound, though the reader before long will ask himself whether they were as much those of Cornwallis as of Rawdon. Still, for the present, further advance towards North Carolina was suspended.

[1] *Cornwallis Correspondence*, i. 315-316.
[2] Rawdon to Clinton, 29th October 1780.

CHAPTER XVII

IT is now time to return to Clinton, who had reached 1780. New York on the 17th of June, six months after his first departure for Charleston. During his absence the usual neglect of Congress, added to the rigour of a terrible winter, had done more than any operations of the British to dissolve the American army. The country near New York had been exhausted of all supplies; transport, owing to the depth of snow on the roads, was extremely difficult; and finally the depreciation of the American paper-money was such that the people would not accept it in payment for provisions. Washington wrote in January 1780 that his army had never been in so distressing a state since the beginning of the war; and in fact he was compelled to levy contributions lest his troops should disband themselves from sheer want of food.[1] In April things had improved but little. The officers of the Continental regiments had never been so much dissatisfied; the men were constantly on the point of starving from dearth of food and forage, and the patience of both was very nearly exhausted.[2] At length Lafayette appeared on his return from a flying visit to France, with the news that French reinforcements would arrive shortly, together with a sufficient fleet; and Washington was not a little comforted, for Clinton's successful attacks on points remote from each other had forced him to confess that such a system, if continued, might be fatal. In May, however, his former troubles

---
[1] Johnson's *Life of Greene*, i. 146.
[2] Washington, *Works*, v. 432, 439; vi. 13, 20-25.

1780. began again. His army was once more reduced to extremity by want of provisions; and the insubordinate and seditious spirit within it finally culminated in the mutiny of two Continental regiments. Yet still the revolted provinces remained insensible and indifferent, and there was little hope of a change for the better; on the contrary, there was rather new danger ahead in the rapidly and deservedly declining power of Congress. There is no more ruthless commentary on the glowing narratives of the struggle of the Colonies for independence than the letters of Greene and of Washington.

July 10. On the 10th of July the French Admiral de Ternay arrived off Newport, Rhode Island, with seven ships of the line, three frigates, and transports containing six thousand troops under Count de Rochambeau. This squadron, however, gave the French supremacy at sea July 13. for only three days, since on the 13th Admiral Graves arrived from England with a reinforcement for Admiral Arbuthnot; but it should seem that Graves, if he had done his duty, would have arrived on the coast before de Ternay and enabled Arbuthnot to gain a signal advantage.[1] Nevertheless, since British supremacy at sea was established, the British commanders determined to attack the French in Rhode Island forthwith; and on July 27. the 27th of July Clinton, having embarked the necessary troops, sailed with them into Long Island Sound. Washington thereupon at once marched upon Kingsbridge with twelve thousand men, a force which compelled Clinton, weakened as he was by the detachments in Carolina, to turn back on the spot; so that Arbuthnot sailed with the fleet alone to blockade the French in Newport. This was a bitter disappointment to Clinton, whose complaints against the two Admirals seem to show that dissension between the two services, rather than Washington's movements, was responsible for the collapse of the enterprise. None the less, the blockade of Narragansett Bay sufficed to neutralise every effort of

[1] Germaine to Clinton, 4th October 1780.

the French and Americans on the side of New York; 1780.
for a second division of French troops and ships, which
should have joined de Ternay, had been shut up in
Brest by the British Channel Fleet.

Thus for the third year in succession the French
alliance had accomplished nothing for the Americans;
and Washington was almost in despair. His levies
came in but slowly, provisions were still scarce, and
patriotism was almost extinguished, while the depreciation
of the paper-currency was such that his troops absolutely
declined to receive it. "To me," he wrote in August,
"it will be miraculous if our affairs can maintain themselves much longer in their present train." The news of
Gates's defeat at Camden could not but increase his
discouragement. "The fate of North America," wrote
de Ternay at this time, "is still very uncertain,
and the revolution is not so far advanced as has
been believed in Europe"; which is a singular confirmation of former expressions of French officers, as
to the comparative enthusiasm over the revolution in
Paris and on the American continent. At his wits' end,
Washington wrote to Admiral de Guichen, who commanded a French squadron in the West Indies, setting
forth his situation and entreating for help; but de
Guichen, as shall presently be explained, was busy enough
over his own affairs. Meanwhile the intrigues of unscrupulous men in Congress, Samuel Adams among
them, had driven Greene, one of Washington's best
officers, to resign his post as quartermaster-general.
"I have lost all confidence in the justice and rectitude
of the intentions of Congress," Greene had written so
far back as in April. "Honest intentions and faithful
services are but a poor shield against the machinations of
men without principles, honour, or modesty," he now
added with yet fiercer indignation.[1] Such machinations,
though powerless to provoke so upright a man as Greene
to reprisals, were not without effect upon another

[1] Washington, *Works*, vii. 125, 159-160, 178, 195, 206;
Johnson's *Life of Greene*, i. 170, 171.

1780. more brilliant but less scrupulous character among the American Generals.

After the great American success at Saratoga, Benedict Arnold, to whom it was principally due, had been placed by Washington in command at Philadelphia, since a wound for the time disabled him from further service. It is a singular fact that luxury and extravagance never reigned with such unbounded licence in Philadelphia as in the years when the Americans, according to the narratives of their historians, were struggling to throw off the chains of despotic England. Arnold, penniless though he was, outdid all others in Philadelphia in ostentation, particularly in the matter of his stable; for he was a great lover of horses, and indeed had at one time been a horse-dealer, which is a calling not usually associated with scrupulous honesty or with loftiness of principle. Naturally he ran into debt, and as naturally he resorted to speculation to clear himself; nor is it difficult to believe that he may have abused his high position to further the success of his ventures. Further, he betrothed himself to the most beautiful girl in the city, who happened to belong to a loyal family; and thus he brought himself into closer relation with loyalists, whom possibly he may have found to be pleasanter company than the contrary party. Having thus tasted the pleasures of peace and quietness, he announced his intention of leaving the army, of obtaining a grant of land near New York, and of retiring into private life. But a man who in virtue of natural military genius has outshone incapable superiors in the field, who keeps the best table and the best horses at a time when ostentation is most fashionable, who enjoys and uses peculiar facilities for making money by crooked methods when the competition in that particular field is at its keenest, and who finally carries off the most beautiful girl of his society for his wife—such a man cannot fail to make enemies. Thus when he went to New York with a view to acquisition of the land which he desired, his back was no sooner turned than the Council of Pennsylvania formu-

lated a series of accusations against him, and published 1779.
them far and wide in all the provinces. After long
delay, due to much tortuous dealing on the part of the
Council, he was tried by court-martial and acquitted of
all but two very trivial charges ; but meanwhile he had
entered into anonymous correspondence with Clinton, in April.
order to be revenged upon his enemies. With the same
object he abandoned all idea of leaving the army, and 1780.
sought and obtained from Washington, who was anxious July.
to give proof of his confidence in him, the command of
the fortress of West Point on the Hudson River.

The correspondence with Clinton, always conducted
through his Adjutant-general, Major André, now
became more frequent and more definite ; and it became
pretty certain that Arnold was the correspondent when
he proposed to betray West Point, a new stronghold
which secured to the Americans the command of the
Hudson, and which, it was reckoned, could not be
taken by a smaller force than twenty thousand men.
The plot thickened ; and most opportunely, though
unexpectedly, on the 16th of September there arrived Sept. 16.
from the West Indies not de Guichen, as Washington had
hoped, but his opponent, Sir George Rodney, with half
of his squadron. Clinton at once embarked troops,
spreading everywhere the report that they were bound
for the Chesapeake ; and on the 18th Washington
started for Rhode Island to consult with Rochambeau
as to this unlooked-for complication. Advantage was
at once taken of his absence for André and Arnold to
meet ; and the former accordingly went up the river in
a frigate and arranged with Arnold the final details for
the capture of West Point. But by the merest accident
the American batteries opened fire on the frigate and
compelled her to drop down the stream, so that André
was compelled to return to the British lines disguised as
a countryman. On his way he was stopped by a party
of banditti, and, betraying himself by sheer bad luck to
be a British officer, was arrested and carried into the
American lines. The report of his arrest was in due

1780. course reported to Arnold, who with marvellous presence of mind effected his escape; but André was tried by court-martial as a spy, and, on the damning evidence of certain documents found in his boots, was sentenced to be hanged.

Beyond all doubt this sentence was perfectly justified by the rules of war, but equally beyond all doubt it was pronounced in the hope that Clinton, in order to save André, would surrender Arnold. Indeed, it was covertly whispered to Clinton that if Arnold were allowed to slip into the hands of the Americans, André would be set free. Moreover, the Americans at large had not shown themselves particularly scrupulous in the observance of the rules of war, and Washington himself little more scrupulous than others. He had indeed discountenanced the use of split bullets by his men, as well as wholesale breach of parole by his officers; and he had strongly reprobated the sale of British medicines, which had been supplied for the benefit of American prisoners, by American doctors for their own profit.[1] Yet we find him suggesting of his own motion that a party of an American regiment, which happened unlike other corps to be dressed in scarlet, should be furnished with the buttons of some English regiment, in order that they might pass for English soldiers and kidnap General Clinton.[2] Now, had these American soldiers, thus attired, been caught in the act, Clinton would have been perfectly justified in hanging every one of them; and their blood would have been upon Washington's head. It seems to me, therefore, unquestionable that the rigorous execution of André's sentence was employed chiefly as a means of putting pressure of a peculiarly cruel kind upon Clinton; and it was for this reason and for no other that it was so much resented by the British Army[3] and the British nation. Meanwhile, the fact remains unshaken that Washington acted within his right in confirming the

[1] Washington, *Works*, iv. 406, 557.
[2] *Ibid.*, v. 261.
[3] See Simcoe's *Queen's Rangers*, Appendix.

sentence. Any charges of ungenerosity against him are entirely beside the mark ; for it is not the business of a general to show generosity to his enemies, rather it is his duty to withhold it if he think generosity impolitic. André therefore, having petitioned in vain to be shot, went to the gallows without flinching, as became a British officer and a British gentleman. He had done his duty with full knowledge of the risk, so could not be dishonoured in his death.

The failure of Arnold's treachery and the arrival of Rodney's squadron left Clinton free to comply with Cornwallis's request for a diversion on the Chesapeake, for which Arbuthnot had declared himself unable to spare ships.[1] Not that Clinton viewed inland operations in Carolina with any favour, for he was persuaded that all hopes founded upon the loyalists were visionary. "An inroad is no countenance," he wrote to Germaine, "and to possess territory demands garrisons."[2] Nevertheless, Cornwallis's situation appeared so critical that he embarked between two and three thousand troops[3] under Major-general Leslie, with orders to sail to the Chesapeake, thence to proceed as far as possible up James River, destroying any magazines at Petersburg or elsewhere, and, after establishing a post on Elizabeth River, to communicate with Cornwallis. By these means he hoped to sever the American communications between Virginia and Carolina, and to ruin at any rate some of the enemy's chief depots of supplies. Leslie accordingly sailed for his destination on the 16th of October, just two days after Cornwallis's retreat from Charlottetown ; but very soon after arriving in the Chesapeake he received a letter from Rawdon in Cornwallis's name, which altered for him the whole aspect of the situation. The document simply showed that the tranquillity of South Carolina, upon which the whole plan of a diversion

1780.

Nov. 9.

---

[1] Clinton to Germaine, 30th August 1780.
[2] *Ibid.*, 25th August 1780.
[3] Guards, Maclean's (82nd), 1 German battalion, 2 Provincial corps ; in all a nominal 2500 men.

had been based, was illusory, and begged Leslie, if his instructions permitted him, to move his force to Cape Fear, where his co-operation would really make itself felt.[1] Clinton approved of this, thereby committing himself more deeply to inland operations in Carolina, towards which he now further engaged himself to contribute another diversion on the Chesapeake.

It was an unfortunate time for such a decision, since Washington had just submitted to Congress a scheme for reorganising the American army, which measure could not but modify the whole of Clinton's plans. Arnold was for meeting Washington's new designs with a counter-stroke, which would probably have defeated them. "The troops of the enemy engaged for the war," he wrote to Germaine,[2] "have received a promise of half-pay for seven years after its close, of one hundred acres to every private and eleven hundred acres to every general. Why not offer to make good to them all arrears, equal to about £400,000, to give half-pay for seven years, two hundred acres to every private and ten thousand acres to every general, as also a bounty of twenty guineas to every deserter who enlists for the King? It would be cheaper than importing men from England. Authorise me to do this, and I have no doubt of recruiting two or three thousand of as good soldiers as there are in America. Money will go farther than arms in America." There was shrewd worldly knowledge, whatever the cynicism, in these proposals; nor were Arnold's plans for a future campaign less sensible. "There are two ways of ending the war. The first is to collect the whole army and beat Washington, secure the posts which command the Hudson, which could be done in a few days by regular approaches, and cut off the Northern from the Southern Colonies. The supplies of meat for Washington's army are on the east side of the river and the supplies of bread on the west; were the

---
[1] Rawdon to Leslie, 24th October 1780.
[2] Arnold to Germaine, 28th October 1780. *S.P. Col. America and West Indies*, 306.

Highlands in our possession, Washington would be 1780. obliged to fight or to disband his army for want of provisions. The second way is to concentrate the whole army, except the garrison of New York, to the southward; but instead of marching three or four hundred miles from South Carolina to Virginia, we ought to seize Baltimore, which would overawe Virginia and Maryland, and proceed thence to Pennsylvania and New Jersey. But an army of fifty thousand men, wherever placed, will do nothing without energy and enterprise." Other soldiers besides Arnold had long striven to din the principle of concentration into the deaf ears of Germaine.

Such, therefore, was the position in America at the close of 1780. Cornwallis had been forced back to Winnsborough in South Carolina, with his communications everywhere threatened, and with his whole plan of invasion wrecked by the defeat of Ferguson; while Clinton, always apprehensive as to the movements of Washington and of the French at Rhode Island, was weakening his force by constant detachments to the south, for inland operations which at heart he disapproved. So far superiority at sea had enabled him to carry on the war on these terms; but how long that superiority might endure was another question.

It is now necessary to turn to the West Indies, in 1779. order to trace the course of events which brought Rodney so unexpectedly to New York. It will be remembered that General Grant had sailed from St. Lucia for Europe in August 1779, leaving General Prescott at St. Kitts to command the troops in that island and in Antigua, and Brigadier Calder at St. Lucia. His departure was followed by a general confusion of all military arrangements to windward. Troops there were in abundance, for British inferiority at sea had prevented the return of four battalions to Clinton at New York; but the sickly season was at its height. At St. Lucia the soldiers began to fall down fast from want of proper shelter; for the planters, directly that

1779. Grant's strong hand was withdrawn, refused to spare their negroes to repair the temporary barracks, doubtless in the hope of hastening the recapture of the island by the French.[1] In St. Kitts and Antigua, though sickness was less prevalent, there was almost more danger owing to the disloyalty of the population and the encroachment of the civil governor, Mr. Burt, on the province of the military commander. St. Kitts itself is an island on which, from the multitude of practicable landing-places, it was impossible to prevent an enemy from disembarking and laying waste the country. The island, further, so far differs in conformation from its sisters that the mountains, instead of extending to the sea on all sides, are surrounded by a belt of plain, with but one position that offers advantage to a defending force of inferior numbers. This position, famous in the annals of West Indian warfare, is an isolated eminence called Brimstone Hill, which lies near the south-western corner of the island, fully nine miles from the chief town of Basseterre and therefore of no protection to it. Here accordingly Prescott resolved to make his citadel for final resistance in case of a French attack, but found himself thwarted at every turn by the ignorant and conceited interference of Governor Burt. The relations between the two were strained almost to rupture when Burt, as a climax of folly, ordered two battalions to be moved from Antigua to St. Kitts, that is to say, from windward to leeward, leaving the whole of the naval stores and the only good harbour in that group of islands exposed to capture by any enemy.[2]

Happily this state of things was presently ended. In December 1779 Major-general Vaughan, who had just returned from America with high commendations

[1] Calder to Germaine, 19th September, 26th October 1779. *Returns of troops*—19th September, 1137 fit for duty, 510 sick; 29th October, 933 fit, 500 sick; 30th December, 685 fit, 576 sick. The gradual diminution of numbers is of course due to deaths.

[1] Prescott to Germaine, 30th August, 29th December 1779; 17th January 1780.

from Clinton, was appointed Commander-in-chief in 1779.
those islands and ordered to sail to the West Indies with
Rodney's squadron. He sailed accordingly in January 1780.
with two complete regiments[1] and drafts of recruits ;
and while Rodney defeated the Spanish fleet and threw
succours into Gibraltar, as has been already narrated,
Vaughan proceeded with the transports to Barbados,
and on arriving there in February found Sir Hyde Feb. 14.
Parker awaiting him with a fleet of sixteen sail of the
line. Germaine had left Vaughan a free hand, but had
recommended the recovery of Grenada and St. Vincent
as objects of prime importance ; only suggesting further,
in his usual airy fashion, that an attack should be made
on Porto Rico, though without a word as to the means
whereby that island should be held, if captured.[2] Meanwhile the policy of dispersion, enforced by Germaine in
the face of Grant's advice, had produced its inevitable
effects. Scattered as they had been all over the islands,
the troops had been practically useless for purposes of
defence, and now they were found to be useless also for
attack ; while want of transports made concentration a
work of great difficulty. Having first despatched a
part of his reinforcements to Jamaica, Vaughan sailed
without delay to Antigua, and found the regiments there
and at St. Kitts sickly, spiritless, and lifeless. " If
troops are not kept together in the West Indies the
best of them will soon cease to be soldiers." Such had
been Grant's warning to Germaine in the previous year ;
and Vaughan had now to pay for Germaine's perversity.
With great difficulty he contrived to embark the majority
of the men, and, leaving twelve hundred only at St.
Kitts, sailed with the remainder to St. Lucia. The March 10.
voyage of two hundred and fifty miles against the
trade-wind occupied ten whole days, from which the
reader may judge of the risks incurred by Germaine's
insane policy of scattering troops to leeward.

Vaughan arrived in St. Lucia only just in time ; for

[1] Keating's (88th), Cary's (89th).
[2] Germaine to Vaughan, 7th December 1779.

1780. on the 22nd of March a strong reinforcement for the
March 22. French fleet and army arrived at Martinique under
Count de Guichen, and on the 23rd a powerful force,
escorted by twenty-two ships of the line, came before
Port Castries to attempt the recapture of St. Lucia.
Sir Hyde Parker had but sixteen ships; but so skilful
were his dispositions at his anchorage, and so strong
were Vaughan's defences on Morne Fortuné and Vigie,
that de Guichen put back into Martinique without
venturing to attack. Here, however, was the command of the sea lost to the British, while five precious
weeks, which might have been turned to good account
before de Guichen's arrival, were wasted in the concentration of troops which ought never to have been
dispersed. Meanwhile Rodney, having finished his work
in the Mediterranean and sent home the bulk of his
fleet, had arrived at Barbados with four ships only;
Germaine having promised that he should be reinforced
by three of Arbuthnot's ships from the North American
station. Since, however, these ships never appeared, the
British fleet necessarily remained inferior in strength; and
Vaughan, seeing that offensive operations were out of
the question, reinforced the garrisons of Antigua and
April 17. St. Kitts and prepared to stand on the defensive. A
month later Rodney gallantly engaged de Guichen with
twenty ships against twenty-three. Vaughan was on
the flagship with him, and large numbers of troops
were serving as marines in the action, which, notwithstanding the disparity of force, bade fair to be a brilliant
victory for the British. But the unfortunate misinterpretation of a signal deprived Rodney of his reward;
and the battle was indecisive. Correct reading of a few
fluttering rags of bunting might have altered the whole
course of history; but such is the fortune of war.

The failure of this engagement extinguished all
hopes of an active and successful campaign to windward.
Fragments of four regiments [1] had begun to drop into

[1] St. Leger's (86th), Clinton's (87th), Tottenham's (90th),
Acland's (91st).

various ports of the West Indies, the intention having 1780. been that they should do service first in that quarter and pass on during the hurricane season to New York. But the transports had been dispersed by a gale off the Lizard, and, since by some extraordinary oversight no port of rendezvous had been indicated to the masters before they sailed, fully a quarter of them put into Cork, about half went to Barbados, and the rest sailed to Antigua.[1] Thus, when there were ships enough for an attack there were no troops to act with them, and when there were troops enough to act there were no ships to escort them. The arrival in June of a Spanish squadron, which raised the allied fleets in the West Indies to a strength of thirty-four ships against Rodney's eighteen, threatened destruction to the whole of the British islands, the more so since there was alarming sickness among the troops in St. Lucia.[2] But on the ships of the Allies also there raged a terrible epidemic, and after some weeks of delay and vacillation they broke up about the middle of July. In August de Guichen sailed to Europe with fifteen ships, which had been badly shattered in the action of the 17th of April; and the danger for the present passed away. Ignorant, however, of de Guichen's destination, Rodney sailed, as has been seen, to New York. He was in no amiable temper, and had already sent a letter to Arbuthnot to tell him that, but for his omission to reinforce the West Indian fleet, both the French fleet and the Spanish auxiliary squadron would have been destroyed.[3] Yet, as shall be seen, Arbuthnot was by no means to blame.

How Rodney was employed at New York has already been told, nor for the present need we follow him farther; but it is remarkable that his proverbial good luck, by drawing him to America, saved him from

[1] Germaine to Vaughan, 20th January; Vaughan to Germaine, 22nd and 23rd March 1780.
[2] 882 men out of 2086 on the sick list. Vaughan to Germaine, 31st May 1780.
[3] Rodney to Arbuthnot, 18th June 1780.

1780. a great disaster. On the 10th of October a hurricane of appalling violence broke over a part of the Windward Islands and wrought frightful destruction. In Barbados, where the fury of the storm was fiercest, the whole island was laid waste, four thousand inhabitants, over nine thousand horned cattle and horses, and smaller stock without number were killed, and the damage to property was reckoned at over a million sterling. In St. Lucia, where close on six hundred soldiers had died during June, July, and August, every building was unroofed, the sick were lying in pools of water, most of the ammunition was spoiled, and the whole of the transports were driven ashore. Nor was the mischief to be reckoned only by damage to property and shipping. Over and above the terrifying influence of the hurricane itself, there was the danger of a large servile population suddenly freed from all restraint and let loose to plunder and destroy; and the task of restoring order, which necessarily fell chiefly on the troops, bore heavily on bodies already weakened by sickness and now further enfeebled by exposure. So miserably ended the campaigning season in the Windward Islands for the year 1780. Yet, strangely enough, the hurricane proved to be a blessing in disguise; for the levelling of the tropical forest by the storm converted St. Lucia by magic from a deadly into a healthy station.

To leeward matters went little better than to windward. Pursuant to the grand scheme for drawing a chain of posts across the Central American isthmus from ocean to ocean, a force of four hundred regular troops[1] under Captain Polson of the Sixtieth had sailed
Feb. 3. from Port Royal on the 3rd of February for the Bay of Honduras. Polson's orders were to make first for Cape Gracias a Dios in order to pick up a contingent of Indians, who were supposed to be disaffected towards Spanish rule, together with a flotilla of small sailing craft which was expected from the English settlement

[1] Detachments of the 60th, Liverpool Regiment (79th), and of Dalrymple's Jamaica Corps.

at Black River. On arriving at his destination, however, he found that Spanish agents had been tampering with the Indians and that the flotilla was not arrived. Three weeks passed away before the boats came in, when the expedition continued its voyage southward, stopping at Sandy Bay and at Pearl Cay lagoon to collect more Indians, which involved a stay of four or five days at each of these places. Finally, when Polson at length arrived in St. John's Harbour, Nicaragua, there was more delay, owing to unskilful loading of the small craft, so that April was come before the flotilla could start up the river for the Lake of Nicaragua. For a week the little force, urged on by the impetuous energy of Nelson, moved from five to ten miles a day against a rapid current in stifling heat ; and then it was found that further progress by water was impossible. The troops were accordingly landed and warily drawn round Fort St. Juan, the work which guarded the outlet from the lake to the river. One officer, whose enterprise could not be subdued even by sweltering heat in a pestilent climate, offered to lead a storming party against the fort on the spot ; but it was thought expedient to proceed to a cannonade in form. Accordingly, with immense labour the heavy ordnance was brought up, and fire was opened on the 13th ; but so low was the strength of the party reduced that almost every gun was laid either by Nelson or by Lieutenant Despard, the chief engineer. At last, after six weary days, the garrison was reduced by want of water to capitulate.

1780.
Feb. 14.

April 1.

April 10.

April 13.

April 29.

"Thus the door to the South Seas is burst open," wrote Governor Dalling grandiloquently from Jamaica, but to what advantage he did not explain. Owing to constant delays, which must be attributed to blind faith in the stories of Indians and to profound ignorance of the country to be traversed, the expedition had occupied three whole months instead of the four weeks which had been thought sufficient for it ; and the rainy season was drawing dangerously near. Dalling had sent a reinforcement of three hundred and fifty men close on the heels

1780. of the first detachment; but sickness was so general and so deadly among the troops that Colonel Kemble, who had now assumed command, had no energy to continue the advance to the lake, where the climate was said to be healthier. The very Indians were sickly and began to desert in numbers. By the middle of May there were not men enough to do the duty of the camp, and the guards remained unrelieved for forty-eight hours.[1] Kemble, therefore, left a garrison at Fort St. Juan, and sent the rest of the force back to St. John's Harbour. But the troops were as sickly by the sea as on the river, and at the end of June but ten men out of two hundred and fifty were fit for duty.[2] Still, Dalling continued to pour in such reinforcements as he could, though he could send few except privateersmen from Jamaica, unruly and insolent fellows who gave a great deal of trouble and were useless for any military purpose. Altogether some fourteen hundred men of one kind and another seem to have been sent to Nicaragua; but by the end of September only three hundred and twenty of them, blacks and whites, were left alive, while of these not one-half were fit for duty.[3] Officers who were sent out to report on the situation declared that with greater activity the object of the expedition might have been accomplished,[4] but they did not mention how the garrisons at each end of the isthmus were to be maintained. Finally, on the 8th of November, Dalling ordered Fort St. Juan to be blown up and Nicaragua to be evacuated; and so ended this disastrous enterprise, which is remembered chiefly by the fact that Nelson took part in it and came out of it alive.[5]

While Dalling, faithful to the example set by

[1] Polson to Dalling, 30th April 1780. Kemble to Dalling. 19th May 1780.
[2] Sir Alex. Leith to Dalling, 26th June 1780.
[3] Captain Clarke to Dalling, 27th September 1780.
[4] Sir Alex. Leith, enclosed in Dalling to Germaine, 2nd November 1780.
[5] Judging by the medical certificate upon which he was invalided, it was almost a miracle that Nelson recovered.

Germaine, was thus frittering away the lives of his men, 1780. the Spaniards had not been idle. In March a Spanish force of no great strength appeared at its leisure before Mobile, escorted by a single armed vessel, and swept away the little garrison of three hundred men. Pensacola only narrowly escaped the same fate through the timely arrival of the British squadron; yet the warning of the mishap at Mobile was not laid to heart. A feeble little force was still maintained at Pensacola, as a standing invitation to the Spaniards and a perpetual source of anxiety to the Commodore at Jamaica. Unfortunately, also, Jamaica during this season was proving itself little less deadly to the troops than Nicaragua. Four of the newly raised regiments [1] in England had been ordered to the West Indies in February, but through some mismanagement had not arrived at St. Lucia until July, just at the opening of the sickly season. From thence they sailed to Jamaica, arriving there on the 1st of August, by which time out of twenty-three hundred men one hundred and sixty-eight were dead and seven hundred and eighty on the sick list.[2] The mortality rapidly increased; and between the 1st of August and the 31st of December 1780 eleven hundred men out of seven and a-half battalions in Jamaica died outright, while half of the three thousand that remained were sick. The cause was easily to be traced. The barracks were built on low and unhealthy ground, and were continued there because neither the Assembly of Jamaica nor the British Government would be at the expense of reconstructing them in the higher and more salubrious districts of the island. Yet the outlay would have recouped itself within a year by the saving in the cost of transporting recruits. "Considered only as an article of commerce," wrote Dalling, in a sentence of terrible bitterness, "these eleven hundred

---

[1] Harrington's (85th), Jas. Stuart's (92nd), M'Cormick's (93rd), Dundas's (94th).
[2] Governor Dalling to Secretary of State, 12th August. Major-general Garth to same, 11th August 1780.

1780. men have cost £22,000, a sum which if laid out above ground might have saved half their lives."

Here then for the present let us leave the army in the West Indies, little injured by the enemy, but so much reduced by disease as to be powerless, both to windward and to leeward, for offensive movement. Cornwallis also we have left in Carolina, too weak to move, and Clinton in New York likewise. It is necessary now to return to Europe before entering upon the fateful year 1781.

CHAPTER XVIII

On the 1st of September 1780 Parliament was suddenly and unexpectedly dissolved, with the result that the elections as a whole turned greatly to the favour of the Government. At the meeting of the new Parliament in October, the speech from the throne was more cheerful than for some sessions past, owing to the successes in Georgia and Carolina. Thanks were voted to Clinton and to Cornwallis; and even Fox, though predicting fresh disasters to follow the success at Camden, thought that the victory might be made the foundation of an honourable peace with the Colonies. But meanwhile the past year had been marked by a new sign of hostility on the part of the European powers, namely, by a declaration to the effect that "free ships made free goods," that neutral vessels had the right to maintain the coasting trade of a belligerent, and that no articles were contraband except arms, equipments, and ammunitions of war. This declaration, issued first by Russia, was very soon subscribed by Sweden and Denmark, and later by all the powers of Europe; and, since the contracting parties bound themselves to uphold their principles by a combined fleet, the agreement received the name of the Armed Neutrality.

This convenient euphemism, however, could not conceal the fact that the declaration was a threat directed at England only; and England answered by retaliation upon Holland, the power that had used her rights as a neutral most unscrupulously to the prejudice of the British arms. St. Eustatius, as has already been

1780. told, was neither more nor less than a depot and arsenal for the Americans and French. The Dutch flag had been used from the first to cover French and American goods, and Dutch men-of-war had been employed to convoy American privateers. In September 1780 the capture of an American packet revealed the fact that a formal treaty between Holland and the United Colonies, greatly to the prejudice of Britain, had long been in progress and was now on the point of conclusion. This line of conduct on the part of the Dutch was due to the influence of France and of the French faction in the Netherlands; while France in her turn had been stirred to increased bitterness against England by Frederick the Great, who rejoiced alike to damage the English and to hurry the French on their road to ruin. An open enemy being always preferable to a secret one, the

Dec. 20. British Government demanded satisfaction of Holland, and, when this was refused, without further delay declared war.

Though the number of England's overt enemies was thus increased, the establishment of the military forces showed little augmentation, the only addition being that of forty independent companies which were raised in Ireland at the private cost of individuals, and which brought the nominal total of the British troops, including embodied militia, to about one hundred and eighty-two thousand men, besides twenty-five thousand foreign troops hired on the Continent. More troops were undoubtedly wanted, and in March orders were issued for the raising of six new regiments in Ireland,[1] which, however, do not all of them seem to have come to birth. In truth, the drain of men was so heavy in North America, in the West Indies, and in the East Indies, that it was difficult to keep the ranks filled. Nevertheless, in the face of the European coalition, the country

[1] Cunningham's, Ross's, Rowley's (102nd), Douglass's (104th), Burgoyne's (23rd Light Dragoons), Maunsell's. *S.P. Irelana.* Secretary of State to Lord Lieutenant, 22nd March 1781. Only those which are numbered were ever formed.

still held her head high. The eagles might be gathered together, but the carcase was not yet at their mercy. 1780.

It was just at this time, significantly enough, that the Spaniards, after a blockade of seventeen weeks, gave signs of more serious attack on Gibraltar. For several months they had been employed in drawing fortified lines of great strength across the isthmus, erecting batteries, and mounting guns; but on the 23rd of November they at last broke ground in earnest, and began to carry their trenches forward against the Rock. Eliott had worked unceasingly to strengthen his defences, but in December he wrote that supplies were running short and that he needed two thousand more men. The reply of the Secretary of State was ominous; he promised supplies immediately, but said plainly that not a man could be spared.

Even more serious to the besieged was the fact that the Spanish Government had outbid the British for the favour of the Emperor of Morocco, thereby cutting off supplies of provisions which hitherto had frequently found their way into the fortress. The distress of the garrison was thus greatly increased. Scurvy broke out and food rose to famine prices, till at length, on the 12th of April, Admiral Darby's fleet sailed safely into Gibraltar Bay with a convoy of nearly one hundred store-ships. On that very day the Spanish batteries opened a furious bombardment, which was thenceforth continued without intermission for thirteen months. But though from that moment the attack upon Gibraltar entered upon a new phase, the fortress was safe for twelve months against starvation; so the reader need only bear in mind for the present that throughout the year 1781 the rain of projectiles upon Gibraltar was ceaseless, though its effect was remarkably small upon either the batteries or the nerves of the garrison. Of Minorca there is no more to be said than that Murray, though still without reinforcements, continued with all diligence his preparations for defence. 1781. April 12.

One more incident alone need detain us before we

1781. leave Europe to follow the operations on the other side of the Atlantic, namely, a French attack upon the island of Jersey. For this service about two thousand French troops were embarked under the command of Baron de Rullecourt, who put to sea in dark and stormy weather with the hope of descending upon the island by surprise. Half of his transports were blown back to France, and some of his vessels were wrecked upon a shoal; but about
Jan. 6. eight hundred troops seem to have reached Jersey in safety. Of these the larger portion landed at Banc du Violet, about four miles from St. Heliers, marched straight up to the town under cover of night, and having surprised two outlying posts, occupied the market-place, with its avenues, and took the Lieutenant-governor, Major Corbet, prisoner. The alarm, however, was quickly given; and though Corbet, under threats of burning and massacre, had signed a capitulation for the whole island, the senior officer, Major Pierson, refused to recognise it. Assembling his troops round the town, Pierson quickly drove the French into the market-place and there surrounded them. Rullecourt dragged Corbet with him into the midst of the fire, but was quickly shot down, while Corbet escaped with two bullets through his hat. The French in the town then surrendered; two detachments which had been disembarked at other points were also overpowered, and the entire force of the French was captured with no greater loss to the British than eighty men killed and wounded. Among the slain was Pierson; and it is probably to a well-known picture of his fall in the moment of victory that the majority of Englishmen owe their knowledge of this futile descent upon Jersey.

1780. Let us now pass to operations across the Atlantic, and first to the windward group of the West Indian Islands. After two months' stay on the American coast Rodney sailed for St. Lucia, where he arrived at
Dec. 16. the beginning of December 1780. On the 16th he opened the campaign by escorting a force under General Vaughan to St. Vincent, where, however, the enemy

were found to be too strongly posted to warrant an attempt to recapture the island. Shortly afterwards a reinforcement consisting of the First, Thirteenth, and Sixty-ninth Foot arrived at Barbados ; and a fortnight later came the news of war with Holland. Without a moment's delay Vaughan embarked a sufficient force and sailed under Rodney's escort for St. Eustatius, which, with the adjacent islands of Saba and St. Martins, at once surrendered. Then for the first time the value of St. Eustatius to the enemies of England was fully realised. The whole island was one vast store of French, Dutch, and American goods, the very streets being piled with bales for want of space in the warehouses. Over one hundred and fifty sail of merchantmen and six men-of-war were taken in the bay, thirty more merchantmen with their armed escort were also pursued and taken, and, the Dutch flag being kept flying for some time over the island, yet more vessels were decoyed into the familiar roadstead and captured likewise. The total value of the captured goods was reckoned at four millions sterling.

1781.
Jan. 15.

Jan. 27.

Feb. 3.

The capture of the island was regarded by many as a deathblow to the American rebellion ; and there arose not only from the Americans, but from all quarters in the West Indies and in England, a storm of impotent rage, which even after a century and a-quarter has not yet wholly died away.[1] For the capture of St. Eustatius

---

[1] See, for instance, the pages devoted by that usually impartial writer, Mr. Fiske, to what he describes as the work of robbery, treachery, and buccaneering. It is really inexplicable why the destruction of a great depot of stores of war by the British should always be stigmatised as an act of wanton barbarity. The capture of St. Eustatius was as legitimate an operation of war as the capture of Ticonderoga, and the confiscation of the goods by no means an extreme measure considering the provocation. Washington could never find language hard enough for Americans who helped the English, and did not spare them when he caught them in the act. Why Rodney and Vaughan should not have meted out like measure to English who helped not only the Americans, but the enemies of their country generally, is to me an insoluble problem. The truth seems to be that such strictures as Mr. Fiske's are an echo of the

1781. was a stab to the heart of the contraband trade in the West Indies. Thither it was that Franklin from the first had consigned munitions of war from Europe, that the Colonists of St. Kitts had exported provisions and ammunition for French and American privateers, that the Bermudians had sent their famous schooners which could outsail all craft on the sea, that the enterprising traders of Holland, France, and Portugal, and the greedy, traitorous merchants of Barbados, Jamaica, and of London itself, had consigned every kind of supplies that could benefit the enemy. So enormous were the profits of these gentry, that the annual rents of the lower town in St. Eustatius—that is to say, of a space not greater than eighteen hundred yards long by two hundred yards broad—exceeded a million sterling. "But for the treasonable practices of these people," wrote Rodney, "I am convinced that the Southern Colonies of America would long ago have submitted"; and he confiscated the whole of their goods with the less mercy, since the merchants of St. Eustatius, though nominally neutral, had refused to sell him naval stores, while vending them freely to the French and Americans. It need hardly be added that Burke and Fox raved like madmen in Parliament against Vaughan and Rodney for this stroke against their country's enemies; but since it was revealed in the course of debate that over six score merchants of Liverpool, including at least one member of Parliament, had lost very heavily over St. Eustatius, the source of their indignation is not very difficult to trace. However, those merchants comforted themselves by plaguing Vaughan and Rodney considerably by litigation; and inasmuch as there was hardly a British trader in the West Indies without some venture in St. Eustatius, it may be guessed that the West Indian prize-courts raised many difficulties as to the condemnation of the prizes.

ravings of Burke over the affair; but Burke, though a very great man, allowed himself a lamentable latitude in the matter or talking nonsense.

The captured islands were secured by a small garrison; 1781. and very shortly afterwards the Dutch settlements of Demerara and Essequibo were captured by a squadron of British privateers. These, since they had given no such provocation as St. Eustatius, were treated by Rodney with all possible gentleness and liberality. Meanwhile, at the end of March, the Count de Grasse sailed from Brest for the West Indies with twenty-one ships, and, despite all the efforts of Admiral Sir Samuel Hood, contrived to effect his junction with the French April 29. squadron of four ships at Martinique. Though he had thus twenty-five ships against the British eighteen, de Grasse declined to come to an action with Rodney. A partial engagement was, however, forced upon him, after which he retired to Fort Royal, while the British bore away to Antigua to refit, and from thence returned to Barbados. Taking advantage of their absence, de Grasse, on the night of the 10th of May, landed troops on three different points of St. Lucia, and even captured a few sick men at Gros Islet; but General St. Leger's dispositions for defence were such that he re-embarked his troops on the following day, and abandoned the May 11. attempt to recapture the island.

A few days later, however, de Grasse despatched a May 23. small squadron with twelve hundred troops to Tobago, where they effected their landing unopposed. The Governor, who had but one hundred and eighty regular troops,[1] and about twice that number of militia and armed negroes, at once took up a strong position on the hills, and sent a message to Rodney at Barbados for help. Rodney thereupon despatched six ships of the line May 28. and some smaller vessels under Rear-admiral Drake to the relief of the island; but meanwhile de Grasse had moved to the assistance of the attacking force with his whole fleet, so that Drake had no option but to retire to Barbados. The Governor of Tobago, wholly undaunted by the display of force by the French, withdrew his

[1] Five companies of the Duke of Rutland's Foot (86th), of which 116 men were sick.

1781. garrison to a yet stronger position which defied attack; whereupon the French General began to burn the plantations, and the colonial militia, unable to endure
June 2. the trial of seeing their houses in flames, prevailed upon
June 4. the Governor to surrender. Two days later Rodney appeared on the scene with his whole fleet; but it was too late. Altogether the affair was vexatiously unlucky, for the garrison might very well have held out for several days longer; and the mishap was the more exasperating to Rodney since de Grasse, notwithstanding a superiority of five ships, still refused to come to a general action. Shortly afterwards the French Admiral sailed to Haiti, where he found despatches awaiting him from Washington, of which the purport will soon be too plainly seen. Rodney, for his part, sent fourteen ships under Sir Samuel Hood to the American coast, and himself returned to England for the recovery of his health. So ended the campaign of 1781 to windward.

To leeward affairs presented a still more unpromising aspect. The safety of Jamaica was seriously endangered by the behaviour of the Assembly, which, though always clamouring for military stores, refused to make any provision for housing them, and would not vote a penny even for repair of the fortifications.[1] Herein there was treachery as well as faction, with greed of gain, as usual, at the root of both. Again, most of the merchants had ventures in privateers, American as well as British, and spared no pains to seduce sailors from the Royal Navy to man them. It was vain for the Admiral to invoke the protection of the law, for the judges and juries on the island, being all of them interested parties, never failed to decide against him.[2] In fact, in Jamaica, as in the rest of the islands, the military measure which was most sorely needed was the hanging of half a dozen members of Assembly. Meanwhile the troops had

[1] Dalling to Germaine, 16th February; Brigadier-general Campbell to Germaine, 27th September 1781.
[2] Admiral Sir Peter Parker to Admiralty, 23rd September 1780.

dwindled to such weakness through disease that Governor 1780. Dalling had been compelled to apply to Cornwallis for some of his local levies from Carolina, and even to send an officer to enlist American prisoners for service against the Spaniard. Nor were these efforts without success, for the whole of the Continental troops captured at Camden, after a little hesitation, took service under the flag of the brutal oppressor, and became part of the garrison of a British Colony.[1] The fact forms a curious comment on the zeal of the Americans for the revolution.

Dalling's anxiety, however, was not only for Jamaica but also for Florida, for he knew the defencelessness of Pensacola and yearned to relieve it, if possible, by the capture of New Orleans. With this object he embarked a regiment of American loyalists in February, but was Feb. unable to despatch it, since the Admiral could not spare him a single man-of-war for an escort. His apprehensions proved to be well founded, for on the 9th of March a Spanish squadron appeared before Pensacola, and on the following day a Spanish army began to disembark. March 10. Then, proceeding in their own leisurely fashion, the Spanish forces by land and sea increased, until at last from eight to ten thousand men were encamped around the forlorn British post. The British garrison, under command of Brigadier Campbell, numbered no more than nine hundred men, but defended itself so stoutly, that on the 28th of April the Spaniards actually broke ground in form, and a few days later opened fire. For a May 2. week afterwards the siege made little progress, until the Spanish gunners, guided by a deserter from one of Campbell's American regiments, succeeded in dropping a shell into the principal magazine. The explosion May 8. killed or disabled over a hundred men, and utterly demolished one of the principal redoubts; whereupon the Spaniards at once advanced to the assault. The garrison met them gallantly and repelled the first attack; but the enemy, despite all their efforts, succeeded in establishing

[1] Dalling to Germaine, 10th August, 10th October 1781.

1781. themselves in the ruined fortifications, whence they could shoot down any man who attempted to work the British guns. With his defences thus paralysed, and his garrison reduced to six hundred and fifty men, Campbell capitulated; and Florida passed once more into the hands of Spain.

May 9.

Leaving now the West Indies, where, both to windward and to leeward, the British had suffered loss through their inferiority on the sea, let us return to Clinton at New York. There we discover at once the secret of Rodney's weakness in the West Indies. Arbuthnot had received Rodney's orders to detach ships to strengthen his squadron; but Clinton had pointed out that his own communications with Cornwallis depended entirely on the command of the sea, and that if de Ternay's fleet and de Rochambeau's army, which still lay at Rhode Island, were left free to act in Long Island Sound the safety of New York itself might be endangered. The remonstrance was so unanswerable that Arbuthnot could not but submit; but the incident shows how fatally Germaine's policy of dispersion reacted upon operations in every quarter. Meanwhile, though Rawdon had pointed out that the whole plan of a diversion in the Chesapeake had been based by Cornwallis on a fallacious trust in the loyalists of Carolina, Clinton, partly in deference to his instructions, partly from morbid fear of seeming disloyal to Cornwallis, now fulfilled his promise to send a detachment to that quarter. Accordingly, about fourteen hundred men, chiefly Provincials and irregular troops, were embarked under command of Benedict Arnold, who was instructed to make Portsmouth, at the mouth of Elizabeth and James Rivers, his base, and to prepare a flotilla in Albemarle Sound for the destruction of the enemy's shipping, and for the impediment of the navigation. Notwithstanding a stormy passage which cost him the loss of more than half of his horses, Arnold duly made his way up James River to Richmond, and in three weeks returned to Portsmouth, having captured several

1780. Dec.

1781. Jan. 20.

vessels, destroyed a cannon-foundry and vast quantities 1781. of stores, and inflicted generally much damage on the enemy with trifling loss to himself. Arnold, indeed, could be trusted always to do his work in the field with ability; but at the same time Clinton, by setting him down permanently in isolation with a mere handful of men, was giving him as a hostage to fortune, for the British squadron on the coast was little if at all superior to the French.

Washington, for his part, had opened the new year in the face of frightful difficulties. The discipline of his regular troops had been shaken by two serious mutinies, Jan. 1-20. which were due not to any fundamental disaffection, for the mutineers refused to enlist with Clinton, but to resentment against the ill faith kept with them by Congress. The execution of a few ringleaders sufficed to quell the rising, and Washington seized the opportunity to ask Congress to extend his powers of flogging to the infliction of five hundred lashes.[1] Thus the irony of fate retorted upon the American soldier the name of "bloody back," doubtless with great benefit to his discipline. Having thus restored order, Washington despatched Lafayette to Virginia by land with twelve hundred men; and on the 8th of March the French March 8. fleet and army sailed from Rhode Island to the Chesapeake in order to make an end of Arnold. Clinton, who had full information of the design, likewise embarked three thousand men under Major-general Phillips; while Admiral Arbuthnot's ships sailed to encounter the French squadron. The Admiral was so slow in getting under way that Clinton trembled for Arnold's safety; but, albeit late in starting, the British ships arrived before the French off the capes of the Chesapeake, and, though they gained little if any advantage over them in the action which followed, cut them off from the entrance to the bay, and so delivered Arnold.[2]

Washington was bitterly disappointed at the failure

[1] Washington to Congress, 3rd February; *Works*, vol. vii.
[2] Clinton to Cornwallis, 5th March 1781.

VOL. III 2 A

1781. of this stroke, for the fortunes of the revolutionists seemed at the moment to be desperate. His troops were naked through neglect, and starving because transport was no longer to be purchased with paper-money; his hospitals were without medicines, and all public undertakings were at a stand. "If France delays timely aid now," he wrote on the 4th of April, "it will avail us nothing if she attempt it hereafter.... We are at the end of our tether, and now or never our deliverance must come."[1] Beyond all doubt the capture of St. Eustatius was a thrust that had sped home; and yet, when we glance at the little group of the British Isles, torn by faction and insurrection, beset by enemies on every side, fighting desperately against overwhelming odds in Europe, in the West Indies, in America, and in India, we are tempted to ask, on meeting with this despairing lament of Washington, whether there was ever much real life at the heart of the American Revolution.

The French having been driven from the Chesapeake, the detachment under Phillips sailed at its ease on the 26th to join Arnold at Portsmouth. The operations prescribed for it by Clinton were only of a desultory nature, such as the destruction of magazines and stores, with the primary object of taking some pressure off Cornwallis; but, since Leslie's detachment had long since gone to Carolina, Phillips was instructed if possible to establish a post, which could be held by a small force, to command the mouth of the Chesapeake.[2] Clinton had no idea of entering upon solid operations in that quarter until reinforcements should arrive from England; and indeed the report of a great success, presently to be narrated, of Cornwallis, inspired him with the hope that not only Phillips's troops but Cornwallis's also would shortly be free to return to New York. Meanwhile, so long as the British retained superiority at sea, he

March 26.

[1] Washington, *Works*, viii. 7.
[2] Clinton to Phillips, 10th and 24th March 1781; to Germaine, 5th April 1781.

felt no anxiety over the temporary dispersion of his force.¹ Everything, as he wrote alike to Germaine, to Cornwallis, and to Phillips, depended on the command of the sea; and Germaine had held out every hope that it should remain in the hands of the British.

¹ Clinton to Phillips, 10th and 24th March 1781; to Germaine, 5th April 1781.

CHAPTER XIX

1780.
Oct.
WE left Cornwallis at Winnsborough, of one mind with Lord Rawdon to remain for the present in a position which should secure the frontier of Carolina without dividing his force. Since he had taken that resolution, events had conspired to strengthen rather than to weaken it. The partisan Marion had roused the whole district between the Santee and the Peedee to arms ; and it was necessary to despatch Tarleton to check him. But Tarleton had only just begun to press him hard, when he was recalled by news of a mishap in another quarter. Sumter was lying about forty miles north of Winnsborough, to cover the movements of certain marauding bands which were murdering and plundering the loyalists to westward, between the Tiger and Pacolet Rivers ; and it was important, if possible, to crush him. Accordingly, Major Wemyss, thinking that he saw a good chance of surprising Sumter, obtained leave from Cornwallis to march against him with the Sixty-third Foot, which had been converted for the nonce into Mounted Infantry. The attack was well planned and was not wholly unsuccessful, but Wemyss was unfortunately wounded early in the action, and the command devolved upon a very young officer, who, knowing nothing of his plans nor of the numbers of the enemy, abandoned the whole enterprise. Wemyss and a few more wounded men having been left behind in a house, the Americans at once proclaimed the fact as evidence of a great victory ; and the whole country rose to join Sumter, who now moved southward upon Ninety-Six.

He was on the point of overwhelming a small post 1780. about fifteen miles from that garrison, when he learned from a British deserter that Tarleton, having marched with his usual secrecy and swiftness, was close upon him. Sumter at once retreated, hoping to place the rapid river Tiger between himself and his pursuers; but finding escape impossible, took up a strong position on the bank Nov. 20. of the river by Blackstock House. Soon afterwards Tarleton came up with his mounted troops only, having made a long and fatiguing march. Since his infantry were several miles in rear, he dismounted his little party, fewer than three hundred men all told, within sight of the enemy, doubtless hoping to overawe Sumter by this parade of boldness. Sumter, however, quickly perceived the true state of affairs, and advancing his riflemen against Tarleton compelled him to deliver his attack against superior numbers in a strong position. By sheer skill and audacity Tarleton contrived to escape disaster till darkness came to deliver him, though he lost a fifth of his men; but fortune so far favoured him that Sumter was severely wounded, and his force for a time dispersed for want of a leader. Yet, in its general result, this little skirmish was damaging to the British, since it interrupted the sequence, hitherto unbroken, of Tarleton's successes.[1]

Mishaps such as these could not but be disquieting to Cornwallis; and now he found himself confronted with a new commander, aided by several able subordinates. Nathaniel Greene, who had been appointed by Washington to replace Gates, arrived at Charlottetown on the 2nd of December, and was presently joined by Dec. 2. his engineer Kosciusko, the Pole, by Daniel Morgan, who had so greatly distinguished himself against Burgoyne, and by Henry Lee and William Washington, the latter a kinsman of the great George, both of whom enjoyed great

---

[1] English and American accounts differ very greatly as to this action of Blackstocks, each side claiming a victory with heavy loss to the other. As usual, there is probably much exaggeration on both sides.

1780. reputation as leaders of cavalry. At his base in Virginia Greene possessed a very able Prussian officer, Baron Steuben, for the superintendence of transport and supplies; and there were yet more good men to whom he had committed the task of surveying the upper waters of the great rivers of North Carolina and Virginia, hitherto little explored, for purposes of navigation. On arriving at Charlottetown, Greene found that not more than eight hundred men of his army were properly armed and fit for duty, though by the energy of Lee, Steuben, and others he was soon reinforced to a strength of two thousand. But for the present it was plain that the chief hope of the Americans in Carolina rested on the guerilla bands which, under the leadership of such men as Marion and Sumter, never ceased to threaten Cornwallis's communications.

Meanwhile a change had come over the spirit of Cornwallis himself. So far he had worked well and loyally with Clinton, while Clinton on his side had granted to him all possible latitude, permitting him to correspond directly with Germaine and supporting him to the fullest of his power by diversions and reinforcements. In December Cornwallis's aide-de-camp, Captain Ross, who had carried home the news of Camden, returned to him from England; and from that moment Cornwallis's tone and bearing towards Clinton were completely altered. The fact was that Germaine, always crooked and purblind, and now dazzled by the success of Cornwallis at Camden, had decided virtually to give him an independent command and to make Clinton's operations subservient to those of his subordinate. In a word, since neither Howe nor Clinton would act upon his insane schemes of conquest without garrisons and of invasion without communications, he took advantage of the ambition and comparative youth of Cornwallis to thrust these disastrous designs upon him.

Dec. 14. On the 14th of December Leslie's detachment arrived at Charleston from the Chesapeake, and shortly afterwards began its march up country to Winnsborough; but before he had even seen these troops[1] 1780. Cornwallis wrote to complain of their quality in a letter of unbecoming and patronising tone.[2] He then sent a detachment under Major Craig to occupy Wilmington on Cape Fear, so as to secure the transport of his supplies into North Carolina; ordered the fortifications of Charleston to be dismantled, which was in the 1781. teeth of Clinton's orders; and on the 7th of January, Jan. 7. without a word to the Commander-in-chief of his intentions, began his advance northward with some two thousand men.[3]

Greene meanwhile had divined with quick penetration the only scheme of operations from which he could hope for success. Though too weak to oppose a front to Cornwallis's advance, he could keep the guerilla bands of Marion and Sumter playing on his flanks, and he now resolved to divide his army so as to second them. 1780. Accordingly, he himself moved with eleven hundred Dec. 20. men to Haly's Ferry on the Peedee, some eighty miles north-east of Winnsborough, to support Marion, and sent Morgan with nine hundred men across the Catawba to join with Sumter's troops in harassing Cornwallis's left flank. Thus Cornwallis could not march with his whole force against Greene, for fear of exposing the posts at Ninety-Six and Augusta to attack by Morgan, nor could he attack Morgan in real strength without leaving Greene free to march on Charleston. The situation was not only embarrassing but extremely irritating, owing to the incessant raids of the guerilla bands; and Cornwallis saw no other course open to him than to divide his own force. He therefore sent Tarleton with about a thousand men to the west of the

---

[1] They consisted of the Guards, a German battalion, six companies of Maclean's (82nd), and two Provincial regiments.
[2] Cornwallis to Clinton, 22nd December 1780.
[3] His force (including Leslie's detachment, which joined him on the 18th) consisted of the brigade of Guards, 7th Fusiliers, 3 companies of the 16th, the 23rd, 33rd, 2nd battalion of Fraser's Highlanders, 450 Germans, 700 Provincials, and Tarleton's Legion. Thus numbered about 4000 men.

1781. Broad River to drive back Morgan, and, advancing himself along the western bank of the Catawba, ordered Leslie's detachment to march upon Camden along the eastern bank, so as to guard his right flank.

Tarleton quickly gained touch of Morgan and forced him back northward before him. Then keeping himself well to westward, he urged Cornwallis to hug the eastern bank of the Broad River, in the hope of driving Morgan into his arms. Following up the enemy with Jan. 17. his usual diligence, Tarleton on the 17th January overtook Morgan, whom he found posted on a grazing ground, not yet wholly cleared of trees, which was known as the Cowpens, with the Broad River in his rear cutting off all hope of retreat. The position was not such as is generally favoured by military critics; but Morgan said boldly that he preferred to have an impassable river in his rear, since his militia would then understand that it was useless for them to run away. With excellent judgment he had posted the said militia, who were all of them good marksmen, in his first line, with strong exhortations not to give way until they had fired at least two volleys "at killing distance." On an eminence one hundred and fifty yards in their rear were drawn up his regular troops, few in numbers but of excellent quality; and behind a second eminence about the same distance in rear of these was concealed his cavalry under Colonel Washington.[1] The whole force numbered just under one thousand men. Tarleton, always eager for action, decided to attack forthwith, though his men were weary with marching for half the night along bad roads and wading through swollen creeks. His line was soon formed. A small body of Light Infantry stood on his right, and next to them in succession were the Legion Infantry and the Seventh Foot, with two three-pounder guns. A troop of fifty dragoons was posted on each flank of the infantry of the first line; and two hundred more cavalry, together

---

[1] The militia numbered 600, the regulars 290, the cavalry 80. Total, 970. Johnson, *Life of Greene*, i. 374.

with Fraser's Highlanders, formed the reserve. The entire force amounted to about eleven hundred men. 1781. Jan. 17.

Without any delay the infantry advanced rapidly in double rank at open files till, at a range of about forty yards, they received the fire of the militia, who, safely posted behind trees, picked off officers, sergeants, and corporals with unerring aim. After a short struggle, however, the militia, having made a very creditable resistance and wrought much havoc, gave way and retired round the left of Morgan's second line. Tarleton at once let loose his troop of the Seventeenth Light Dragoons upon them from his own right, but Washington's horse coming forward drove back the Seventeenth by sheer weight of numbers; and the American militia, on reaching the second hill in rear of Morgan's position, speedily rallied and reformed.

Meanwhile the British infantry continued their advance against Morgan's regular troops, but in no very good order, for the men were out of breath and a great number of their officers had fallen. Tarleton, hoping to bring the action to an end by a decisive stroke, now brought up Fraser's Highlanders to the left of the Seventh, and directed the squadron posted on that flank, together with his reserve of cavalry, to incline still farther to the left, so as to threaten Morgan's right. Morgan therefore ordered his right-hand battalion to wheel back at right angles to the line, in order to repel this flanking attack; whereupon the rest of his first line, seeing this battalion turn about, followed its example and retreated likewise, with perfect steadiness and discipline. This quite unpremeditated and accidental movement decided the issue of the action. The British infantry, confident that the day was won, hurried forward in ever-increasing disorder, with the Americans still retiring before them; when Colonel Washington, whom the pursuit of the British cavalry had carried to some distance in advance, sent a messenger to Morgan with the words, "They are coming on like a mob; give them a fire and I will charge them." At this moment

1781.
Jan. 17.

the rallied militia reappeared on the American right; and Morgan gave the word for the whole line to halt and fire. The Continental troops with perfect coolness turned about, the British being then within thirty yards of them, and delivered a destructive volley, which was the more demoralising because it was unexpected. Panic seized upon Tarleton's whole line. The Seventh was made up chiefly of recruits, the infantry of the Legion had never been well disciplined, the Light Infantry had suffered heavily; one and all were spent by a long march and breathless after a rapid advance, and after this staggering volley there was no spirit left in them. Fraser's Highlanders, in spite of heavy losses, fought hard for a time, but being presently attacked in front and on both flanks gave way like the rest. Tarleton in vain tried to save the day by a charge of the cavalry of the reserve. The dragoons of the Legion, ill disciplined at the best of times, and spoiled by the easy successes which Tarleton's energy had gained for them, were not the men to face so desperate a venture. They turned and galloped headlong from the field; and not a fraction of Tarleton's force showed a front except a tiny handful of British artillerymen who stuck indomitably to their two three-pounders, and the solitary troop of the Seventeenth Light Dragoons, which had rallied from its first repulse by Washington's horse. At the head of this troop, now reduced to forty men, Tarleton and a dozen mounted officers charged forward to extricate the artillery, but too late to save either the guns or the gunners, who had fallen almost to a man. There was then nothing left for Tarleton but to retreat with this little body of dragoons, the only men that retired from the field in order.

So ended the action of Cowpens, small in scale but momentous in result. The numerical superiority was slightly on Tarleton's side, but the quality inclined to the side of Morgan, whose militia were veterans in partisan warfare as well as practised marksmen, and fought, as violators of their oath, with halters round their necks. To Morgan, however, belongs the credit 1781. of making the most of their excellences while avoiding the dangers of their defects; and it is certain that the heavy slaughter of British officers by these marksmen at the beginning of the action contributed greatly to Morgan's ultimate success. Yet the turning-point of the whole engagement was the fortuitous retrograde movement of Morgan's second line, a manœuvre which was crowned with such success that, had not Morgan been too honest to claim praise for a mere accident, he might have credited himself with one of the most daring stratagems ever practised in war.[1] Blame is attached to Tarleton for making an attack when his men were wearied by five hours of arduous marching, whereas Morgan's troops were perfectly fresh and had breakfasted at their ease. But, on the other hand, Morgan's situation with an impassable river in his rear certainly invited attack, and the flanking movement whereby Tarleton strove to snatch the victory was well and boldly conceived, since, if successful, it must have driven Morgan across the line of Cornwallis's advance. It seems to me, therefore, that Tarleton deserves no blame, for the fortune of war was his chief enemy; though, looking to the behaviour of the dragoons of the Legion, there can be little doubt but that the best men won the day. The American loss did not exceed seventy-two killed and wounded: that of the British was close upon eight hundred killed, wounded, and prisoners, a very large proportion of those that fell being officers. Two British guns and the colours of the Seventh were also captured; and Tarleton's column, although he collected the best part of his fugitive cavalry on the day after the action, was to all intent annihilated.

Morgan halted no longer in the field than was necessary to secure his prisoners, but crossed the Broad River on the same evening and hurried eastward, lest Cornwallis should cut off his retreat. But Cornwallis,

[1] See Chastellux, ii. 62, 70. Chastellux, however, had never heard of Bouquet's action at Bushy Run.

1781. anxious for Leslie's detachment, which by an unfortunate error of judgment he had ordered to march on the east bank of the Catawba, had halted in order to enable it to join him; so that on the day of the action he was still at Turkey Creek, twenty-five miles south-east of Cowpens. Moreover, Leslie's march had been so much delayed by the passage of the swamps of the Catawba that he could not unite with the main army until the
Jan. 18. 18th. Tarleton had reckoned,[1] not without reason, that Cornwallis would have been parallel with him at King's Mountain on the day of the action, and had regulated all his movements according to that calculation; and since he had received no message from Cornwallis since the 14th, he had no reason to suppose that he was wrong in so doing. The General's action after learning of Tarleton's defeat was also questionable, for he hastened north-westward in the hope of intercepting Morgan, though by marching due north he would have taken the chord instead of the curve of the arc along which Morgan was retreating. The celerity of Morgan's movements and the swelling of the creeks by heavy rain defeated his object, and on reaching Ramsour's Mills,
Jan. 25. twenty-five miles north-west of King's Mountain, Cornwallis came to a halt.

It is not difficult to conceive of his embarrassment and mortification. He was now in exactly the same position as after Ferguson's defeat at King's Mountain, when, with Rawdon at his side, he had declared that the invasion of North Carolina must be abandoned. Like a good and chivalrous commander, he now acquitted Tarleton, as he had before acquitted Ferguson, of all blame; but the repetition of disaster, involving as it did the loss of the whole of his light troops, was sufficient to convince him of the peril of further advance. Nevertheless, the influence of Germaine seems to have been overpowering; and on the day after the fatal action Cornwallis wrote to Clinton that nothing short of the most absolute necessity should induce him to

[1] Tarleton's *Campaign*, pp. 245, 246.

CH. XIX   HISTORY OF THE ARMY   365

abandon his project for the winter's operations.[1] He 1781. had already committed himself deeply by ordering the destruction of the fortifications at Charleston, and by dragging up under Leslie's escort the entire material necessary for a campaign. He now resolved to destroy the whole of his superfluous baggage, to follow up Morgan and Greene, and to end the campaign at a blow.

Meanwhile Greene, on learning of the success at Cowpens, had set his army in motion at once to march Jan. 28. from Haly's Ford north-eastward to Salisbury, while he himself galloped for a hundred miles across country to take personal command of Morgan's force. In spite of the recent victory his lack of regular troops forbade him to be sanguine, though, to use his own words, he was not without hopes of ruining Lord Cornwallis if he should persist in his mad scheme of pushing through the country.[2] Unfortunately Cornwallis had every intention of persisting in it, for he too had marched eastward on the 28th, and on the 30th had reached the western bank of the Catawba, eighteen miles below the camp occupied by Greene on the opposite bank. Greene, on ascertaining the fact, gave up his former idea of checking Cornwallis's advance at the river Yadkin, and altered the destination of his main army from Salisbury to Guildford, in order to draw his adversary deeper into the country.[3] Meanwhile for two days the hostile armies lay separated by the swollen waters of the Catawba, until on the 1st of February the flood subsided; but the Feb. 1. fords along a length of thirty miles were still guarded by the American militia, though Morgan with his light troops had already retired. Accordingly, at dawn of the 1st, Cornwallis with one division of the army began the passage of the river at Cowan's Ford, sending the other division under Colonel Webster to another ford six miles above it. Webster was not opposed; but the

[1] Cornwallis to Clinton, 18th January 1781.
[2] Johnson, *Life of Greene*, i. 395, 404.
[3] *Ibid.* i. 407.

1781.
Feb. 1.
Guards, who led Cornwallis's column, were not more than half-way across the river when they were met by a biting fire. The American guide thereupon fled, and the Guards were left in the darkness, in the middle of a river five hundred yards wide and so rapid as to sweep even horses off their legs, with the bullets cutting the water into foam all round them. Yet still they advanced without heeding or returning the fire, Colonel Hall making his way at their head through an unknown depth of water towards the opposite bank. The flight of the guide was, as it happened, a piece of great good-fortune, for the Guards finally emerged from the river at an unprotected point, and the Americans were dispersed without difficulty. The British then continued their advance, but the roads proved to be so bad that Cornwallis on that evening made a further sacrifice of waggons and baggage so as to double his teams and increase his force of mounted men.

Heavy rain had warned Morgan to push on with all speed to the Yadkin, the next river to eastward, where Greene, with admirable foresight, had collected every obtainable boat at the principal ford. Cornwallis's mounted troops made a rapid advance to cut off his
Feb. 3. army, but succeeded only in intercepting his rearguard, the main body being already safe on the opposite bank. Cornwallis was now compelled to halt for two days at Salisbury to collect provisions, after which he turned north to a ford ten miles up the river; but he was so long detained by swollen creeks and bad roads that he
Feb. 8. did not pass the Yadkin until the 8th. With a start of five days, the Americans seemed unlikely to be overtaken; but Cornwallis, deceived by false information that the next river, the Dan, was impassable in winter and that few boats could be collected on it, hurried on in the vain hope of penning Morgan's force between the Dan and the Yadkin. He was, however, still twenty-
Feb. 10. five miles astern when Greene, on the 10th, effected his junction with his main army at Guildford. None the less, judging his numbers to be too weak for a general

action, Greene continued his retreat to the Dan, and 1781. crossed it at Boyd's Ferry in boats which he had caused to be collected several weeks before. Cornwallis, pursuing in hot haste, had the mortification, as usual, to see the last detachment pass over safely to the northern side of the river just as he arrived on the southern Feb. 15. bank. So often had this incident been repeated during the retreat that it is impossible not to attribute it to deliberate and well-calculated design on the part of General Greene.

Cornwallis now fell back by easy marches to Hills- Feb. 20. borough, where he hoisted the royal standard; but the loyalists of North Carolina had lost heart through long suffering, and Greene took care to keep his light troops hanging perpetually upon Cornwallis's rear. Thus it was never safe for large bodies of loyalists to join the British; and indeed one unfortunate party, which mistook the American cavalry for Tarleton's Legion, was Feb. 25. surrounded and cut to pieces. Cornwallis described his position as lying among timid friends and adjoining to inveterate enemies; but in the hope of giving better protection to his unlucky friends he now turned southwestward from Hillsborough to the country between the Deep and Haw Rivers, which he had appointed to them as a place of assembly. There he encamped at the junction of the roads from Salisbury, Hillsborough, Cross Creek, and Guildford, thus at once bestriding the line of his own retreat to Wilmington and commanding the avenues whereby he could take advantage of any opportunity that Greene might give him. Once he thought that he saw his chance, and with great readiness and skill made a spring upon an isolated American column; but fortune did not favour him, for Greene was able to concentrate in the nick of time. Meanwhile reinforcements had joined the Americans from Virginia, and Greene, being now strengthened to a force of fifty-five hundred men, pushed westward to Guildford Court-house, within twelve miles of the British army, and offered battle.

1781.
March 15.
Cornwallis hastened to seize the chance of closing with his redoubtable adversary. Leaving three hundred and fifty men to guard the baggage, he marched at daybreak with the remainder of his force, now reduced by fatigue, sickness, constant skirmishes, and desertion to about nineteen hundred soldiers.[1] The men started fasting, for provisions were scarce ; but though the numbers of the enemy were stated to be seven or eight thousand, they felt confidence in their leader and tramped cheerfully on, westward, until they struck into the road from Salisbury and then north-eastward upon Guildford. About four miles from Guildford the advanced cavalry of both armies met, and the Americans were driven back ; but no information could be obtained from the prisoners, while the accounts given by the people of the country were extremely inaccurate. Continuing his advance along the road, Cornwallis presently found himself in a narrow defile with thick copses on either hand, which continued unbroken to within half a mile of Guildford Court-house. At this point the ground had been cleared on both sides of the road, leaving an

[1] There is much controversy as to the number of British engaged at Guildford. Cornwallis wrote to Clinton that he had but 1360 regulars and 200 volunteers, but this he contradicted himself in a letter to Germaine of 17th March, wherein he said that these volunteers and 120 more men were detached to guard the baggage. A return of his troops of 1st March (Stevens, *Clinton-Cornwallis Controversy*, i. 376) gives his total numbers (without artillery) as 2213 rank and file fit for duty, or, allowing for artillery, say 2300 fit for duty. Deduct from these the volunteers (given in the return of 1st March as 232) and the rest of the baggage-guard, in all 352, and there remain 1950 men. But there were several petty skirmishes between the 1st and the 15th of March, wherein the losses may be reckoned as reducing the number to 1900 ; and since a field-return sent to Germaine gives the numbers at 1924, I think that 1900 may be taken as the likeliest figure. Stedman, however, quotes the Adjutant-general's return for the day, which states the force at 1445 exclusive of cavalry, or 1600 in all. For the American force I accept the careful computation of Johnson (*Life of Greene*, ii. 2, 3), which gives the numbers at 4300. Greene's regular troops of all arms were 1715, his militia 2600.

open space, broken only by fences, about five hundred yards square. Ahead of this first clearing the woods again closed upon the road for another half-mile, at the end of which there came another open space of cultivated ground, seamed by hollows, around the Court-house itself. When the British reached the southern skirt of the first clearing, two American guns opened fire upon them, whereupon Cornwallis deployed his troops into line, resolving that since the woods on the right of the road were less dense than those on the opposite side, he would attempt to turn the American left. It was perhaps a weak foundation whereon to base the plan of a general action, but there was none firmer to be discovered; and it is impossible not to admire the nerve of a man who would thus enter the lists, as it were blindfolded, against an enemy of twice his numbers, trusting to his own skill and to the discipline of his troops to tear the bandage from his eyes in sufficient time. His three guns he posted on the road itself, since they could not move elsewhere, to answer the American artillery; and the remainder of his force he disposed in the following order:—The right wing, under Majorgeneral Leslie, consisted of Bose's Hessian regiment and Fraser's Highlanders in first line, with the first battalion of the Guards[1] in support; and the left wing of the Twenty-third and Thirty-third under Colonel Webster in first line, with the Grenadiers and second battalion of the Guards under Brigadier O'Hara in support. A small corps of German Jägers and the Light Infantry were stationed in the wood to the left of the guns, while Tarleton with the cavalry remained in rear on the road.

1781.
March 15.

The dispositions of Greene, at which Cornwallis could only guess, were made with his usual ability. His first line, consisting of the North Carolina militia, was extended in the wood on the northern skirts of the first clearing, with two corps of picked riflemen thrown forward on each flank, the whole comprehending in all

[1] The Guards were drawn from all three regiments, but were sorted into two mixed battalions.

1781.
March 15.

nearly sixteen hundred men. Immediately in rear of these riflemen were two small bodies of cavalry, each of about eighty men, under Lee on the eastern and under Washington on the western side; and in advance of them upon the road were two field-guns. Three hundred yards in rear of this first line was a second line of Virginian militia, numbering about one thousand men, the right brigade being commanded by General Lawson, the left by General Stevens. These were deftly hidden in the woods on each side of the road, with picked marksmen behind them ready to shoot any man who should run away. Three hundred yards in rear of this second line, and rather to westward of the road, was a hill that formed a salient angle in the midst of the clearing round the Court-house; and here Greene had drawn up his regular troops in conformation with the ground, two Virginian brigades on his right and two Maryland brigades on his left, numbering together about fourteen hundred and fifty men, with two six-pounder guns in the salient angle between them. One point of vantage only was unsecured by Greene, namely, a height rising on the eastern side of the road, just at the point where the forest ended and the clearing about the Court-house began. It will be seen that he paid dearly for the oversight.

At about half-past one in the afternoon the action opened with the advance of the British across the first clearing, amid a storm of bullets from the invisible enemy in front and flanks. Perfectly unshaken, the redcoats pressed on to within close range and charged with the bayonet; but the North Carolina militia was not there to receive them, having fled away in panic, while Greene's two advanced guns had retired, in obedience to orders, to take post near the road with the American third line. But though the militia in front had disappeared, the American riflemen in the flanks of their first line still poured in a most destructive fire; whereupon the British line was halted, in order that the flank-battalions might turn outwards to

meet them. Bose's regiment accordingly wheeled off 1781.
to the right flank, the first battalion of Guards moving March 15.
into the line to take their place next to the Highlanders;
while on the other wing the Thirty-third, with the
Jägers and Light Infantry on their left, wheeled off in
like manner to the left flank, and the Grenadiers and
second battalion of the Guards advanced to the left
of the Twenty-third in their room.[1] Gradually the
American sharpshooters were forced back from tree to
tree before the bayonet's point, Lee and Washington
falling back likewise with their cavalry behind them;
and thus the British fought their way forward to the
Virginian militia in Greene's second line. These held
their ground with a stubbornness which contrasted
very favourably with the panic of their brethren from
Carolina, and, being most of them armed with rifles, did
great execution among the British. But the redcoats
were not to be denied, and gradually Lawson's brigade
on the American right began to give way before the
Light Infantry and Jägers, who were almost their peers
in bush-fighting. Farther and farther Lawson's brigade
retreated, though Stevens's brigade on their left stood
firm; and Webster's men bringing up their left
shoulders pressed them on and on till at last, on
reaching the road, Lawson's militia fairly broke and
retired in disorder through the wood to Greene's third
line. They were, however, protected from pursuit by
Washington's cavalry, which had retired with them to
the edge of the forest.

Webster now caught up the Thirty-third, Light
Infantry, and Jägers, and led them, thinned as they
were by their losses and wearied with hard marching
and hard fighting, against Greene's third line on the hill
by the Court-house. Selecting the nearest point for
his attack, he encountered, as it happened, the finest

[1] The order of the British line, from right to left, was now as
follows: Bose's Regiment, 1st battalion of Guards, Fraser's Highlanders, 23rd, 2nd battalion of Guards, Grenadiers. 33rd, Jägers,
Light Infantry.

1781.
March 15.

battalion in the American Army, the First Maryland, which awaited his assault with perfect steadiness, poured in its volley at close range, and, charging with the bayonet, drove the British back in disorder with very heavy loss. Had Greene followed up this stroke effectively, he might have made it fatal to Cornwallis, but he did not; and Webster, though severely wounded, drew off his men to the shelter of the forest, where they speedily rallied. Meanwhile, the three British three-pounders had advanced along the road, and were unlimbered with admirable judgment by Lieutenant Macleod on the rising ground at the edge of the forest, from which they kept up a steady and well-directed fire. Moreover, General O'Hara, observing that there were already troops enough to deal with Stevens's brigade of Virginian militia, now led the second battalion of Guards and the Grenadiers against the Maryland brigade in Greene's third line, while Leslie, finding the resistance of the Americans in the wood failing steadily before him, presently sent the Twenty-third and Highlanders to support him. The Second Maryland Regiment, however, gave way instantly before O'Hara's attack, and the second battalion of Guards was pressing on in triumph after them, when Washington with his cavalry galloped up from the wood and crashed into their rear, while the First Maryland Regiment also fell full upon their left flank. The Guards fought fiercely, but were utterly broken; and Cornwallis, who had come forward to rally them, was fain to hurry back to Macleod and bid him open with grape-shot upon the American horse. The fire checked Washington's onslaught, but dealt terrible destruction among the Guards, who were still mingled with his cavalry.

There was now a pause, during which Cornwallis reformed his line. The Highlanders and Twenty-third were halted; O'Hara, though very severely wounded, rallied the second battalion of Guards on their right, where the first battalion also joined them; and Webster again led up the Thirty-third, Jägers, and Light Infantry on their left. Bose's regiment was still hotly engaged with Stevens's brigade of militia on the American left; but these now began to retire in small parties, while Lee withdrew also his cavalry and a portion of his sharpshooters. Cornwallis therefore brought up Tarleton to make an end of the American resistance on his right, which was done by an effective charge of cavalry, delivered under the smoke of a volley. Bose's regiment and Tarleton then pressed upon the Americans' left flank, while the remainder of the British line engaged them in front; and Greene, seeing that the day was lost, gave the order to retreat, abandoning his four guns, together with their ammunition. There was little pursuit, for Cornwallis's troops were spent with long marching and heavy fighting; and thus came to an end the action of Guildford.

1781.
March 15.

Never perhaps has the prowess of the British soldier been seen to greater advantage than in this obstinate and bloody combat. Starting half-starved on a march of twelve miles, the troops attacked an enemy, fresh and strong, which not only outnumbered them by more than two to one, but which was so posted, by Greene's excellent judgment, as to afford every possible advantage to its natural superiority in bushcraft, armament, and marksmanship. Yet, though heavily punished, they forced the Americans from the shelter of the forest and drove them from the field; while the Thirty-third and Guards, though at one moment absolutely shattered—the latter indeed rent to pieces by Washington's well-timed charge—rallied at once and came forward again to the attack. American writers point with just pride to the fine behaviour of the First Maryland Regiment, and the still finer performance of Stevens's militia; but while doing justice to the valour of the British, they forget that the Guards and Thirty-third had already broken through two lines of Americans before they reached the Marylanders.[1] The losses of the victorious

[1] Thus Johnson puts down the 33rd at the moment of attacking the Maryland Regiment as 322 strong. But this was their strength

1781. army were very severe. The Guards went into action with nineteen officers, including brigadier and staff, of whom four were killed or died of wounds, and seven more were wounded; while of four hundred and sixty-two men, thirty-seven were killed and one hundred and sixty-nine wounded. Colonel Webster died of his wounds; Brigadier O'Hara was long disabled, and his son, Lieutenant O'Hara of the Artillery, was killed. In all twenty-eight officers fell, killed or wounded; and the total casualties of the army amounted to ninety-three killed and four hundred and thirty-nine wounded, making five hundred and thirty-two in all—more than a fourth of the whole number engaged, at the highest computation; more than a third, if the Adjutant-general's return be correct. Want of food—for not a man received a morsel until the following afternoon—and pouring rain during the night increased the sufferings of the injured, of whom no fewer than fifty expired before the morning came.

In truth, the victory, though a brilliant feat of arms, was no victory. Greene did indeed retreat, and the most part of his militia deserted to their homes, so that his losses were never actually ascertained; but Cornwallis had gained no solid advantage to compensate for the sacrifice of life, and he was now too weak farther to prosecute his mad design. Clinton, on hearing the first rumours of the action, wrote that Cornwallis seemed to have finished his campaign handsomely, but he was speedily undeceived by fuller intelligence; and Phillips truly described the engagement as the sort of victory

on the 1st of March, since which day they had been frequently engaged, to say nothing of their previous losses on the 15th. He also sets down the Second Battalion of Guards, with its Grenadier Company, as far exceeding the First Maryland (which he reckons at 285 men) in numbers. The Guards went into action 481 of all ranks, including brigadier and staff, and were divided into two battalions, a Grenadier Company, and a Light Infantry Company; so that one battalion and one company could not have exceeded 240 of all ranks at most, even supposing them to have suffered no loss (which is incredible) before they closed with Greene's third line.

that ruins an army. Cornwallis's troops had under- 1781.
gone hardships, fatigue, and starvation with cheerfulness,
since the officers, and most notably the General himself,
fared in every way as they did ; but they were now
terribly reduced in numbers, and almost destitute of
provisions. Cornwallis had no choice but to accept the
inevitable ; and on the third day after the action he March 18.
turned southward, and retreated down the Cape Fear
River through the Highlanders' settlement at Cross
Creek. But he found there neither provisions nor
forage ; while the navigation of the river, on which he
had counted for transport, was found to be impracticable,
the stream being narrow, the banks high, and the population hostile. Greene, who had followed him almost
to Cross Creek, now struck eastward upon Camden ;
but Cornwallis even so would not change his line of
retreat. He merely sent a message of warning to Lord
Rawdon at Camden, and then, leaving his sick and
wounded to the care of the inhabitants, with many
assurances that he would speedily return to them,[1] he
retired down the river from Cross Creek, and on the
7th of April arrived at Wilmington. April 7.

[1] Cornwallis to Germaine, 18th April.

CHAPTER XX

1781. THROUGHOUT the time since Cornwallis had advanced from Winnsborough there had been practically no communication between him and Clinton. Frigates, in spite of Arbuthnot's repeated remonstrances to the Admiralty, were scarce in the fleet; and, since the departure of Lord Howe and Sir George Collier, there had been sufficient friction between the naval and military commanders to compel the General to organise his own service of despatch-vessels.[1] Clinton was therefore quite in the dark as to the real scope and intention of Cornwallis's movements; and, though the force which he had sent to the Chesapeake under Arnold had diverted most of the Virginian troops from joining Greene,[2] yet, as we have seen, it had itself only narrowly escaped capture by the French fleet from Rhode Island. Of the disaster at Cowpens Cornwallis had indeed informed his chief, though the news had taken a full month to reach New York; and Clinton had written without reserve that he dreaded the consequences, that he was even then trembling for the safety of Arnold's detachment, and that without reinforcements from England and assurance of superiority at sea he should not undertake solid operations in the Chesapeake.[3] These letters reached Charleston on the 6th of April, but were not at once forwarded by the commandant, Colonel Balfour, to Wilmington. For what reason they were delayed it is not easy to explain; but it

---

[1] Stevens, i. 315, 331.   [2] *Ibid.* i. 339.
[3] *Ibid.* i. 341-344, 347, 2nd to 10th March 1781.

seems only too probable that Germaine's attitude to- 1781. wards Cornwallis had encouraged general disloyalty among subordinate officers towards the Commander-in-chief. The confusion caused by this tardiness of communication was incredible. Every one was working at cross-purposes. Clinton, with no information except from American sources, which could not conceal the fact of a British victory at Guildford, not unnaturally assumed that Cornwallis really had accomplished the subjugation of the Carolinas, and began to think of withdrawing all troops from the Chesapeake. In this intention he was strengthened by Phillips and Arnold, who pointed out that with their present strength they could do little except destroy tobacco, though with a small reinforcement they thought it might be possible to overwhelm a small force under Lafayette which lay at Baltimore.[1] Cornwallis, on the other hand, chose without the least warrant to assume that the presence of Phillips and Arnold in the Chesapeake signified solid operations in Virginia, to which he knew Germaine to be inclined. Germaine[2] for his part, though Clinton as yet knew it not, had airily assumed that the Carolinas had been reconquered by Cornwallis months before, and that Washington could now be driven to the eastern bank of the Hudson. Meanwhile, in these same first weeks of April, there came a messenger from Germaine to say that six regiments had been embarked to reinforce Clinton; whereupon Clinton, on the 13th of April, wrote to Cornwallis to come and meet him at the Chesapeake as soon as his arrangements for the security of the Carolinas were complete, in order to concert plans for the future. But at just about the same time Cornwallis was writing[3] to Clinton to tell him, not that he was on the point of abandoning the

[1] Phillips to Clinton, 15th to 19th April 1781.
[2] Germaine to Clinton, 7th March 1781 (received by Clinton, 27th June 1781).
[3] Cornwallis to Clinton, 10th April 1781.

1781. Carolinas altogether, which was actually the case, but that any hold upon those provinces must be precarious unless Virginia were first reduced, for which reason he advocated vigorous operations in the Chesapeake, even at the cost of evacuating New York. Having written thus to Clinton, he sat down to urge a serious attempt on Virginia upon Germaine,[1] rather, it must be feared, to justify his previous recklessness than from reliance on any well-conceived plan of operations. Finally, ignoring Clinton's instructions on no account to imperil Charleston, and forgetful of his promise to the loyalists at Cross Creek, he wrote to Phillips[2] that he saw no prospect of reaching Camden in time to relieve Rawdon, and should therefore march for the Roanoke, hoping that Phillips would be able to advance as far as Petersburg to join him, without exposing his army to ruin. In plain words, while fully conscious of the immense danger to which he would subject Rawdon and every garrison in Carolina, he resolved deliberately to abandon him, and this although Colonel Balfour had prepared a flotilla to carry his army down the Waccamaw River to the mouth of the Santee and so to Charleston. Accord-

April 25. ingly, on the 25th of April, without awaiting instructions from Clinton, he started on a march of two hundred miles to the north, perfectly aware that by so doing he was risking the safety of Phillips's force as well as of his own, but lulling himself with the false comfort that Greene might perhaps leave Carolina to follow him.

Greene, meanwhile, after pursuing Cornwallis as far
April 7. as Ramsay's Mill to eastward, had turned south upon Camden, detaching Colonel Lee to join with the partisan Marion in attacking some of the intermediate posts between Camden and Charleston. Moving with great rapidity, Lee appeared first before Fort Watson, about sixty miles north-west of Charleston. This post consisted merely of a stockade on the top of a mound which rose forty feet above the plain, and was held by a

---

[1] Cornwallis to Phillips, 18th April 1781.
[2] *Ibid.* 23th April 1781.

garrison of one hundred and twenty men. Neither side 1781. had any artillery, and Lee despaired of mastering the fort until one of Marion's officers suggested that a tower, after the classical model, should be constructed out of the forest hard by. Such was the expertness of the American axe-men, that in five days the trees were felled and shaped, while the tower itself was erected in a single night. In the morning the garrison, finding themselves commanded by rifles on every side, surrendered; and by this very ingenious expedient a first gap was made in Rawdon's communications with Charleston. Marion then moved northward to join Greene, who on the 19th had already appeared with his April 19. main body before Camden.

Greene had hoped to capture this very important post by surprise, and he was not a little chagrined to find that Rawdon, though he could raise no more than nine hundred men, was quite ready for him in a position which was unassailable except by means of heavy artillery. Having no heavy cannon, and judging himself too weak either to assault or to invest, Greene retired two miles northward to Hobkirk's Hill, where he took post astride of the northern road on rising ground covered with forest. His force numbered something over twelve hundred men,[1] five-sixths of them regular troops, and with the accession of Marion's detachment he might hope for a superiority which would enable him to deal decisively with Rawdon. But Rawdon had no intention of allowing the junction to come to pass unhindered. At nine o'clock on the morning of the 25th he marched April 25. out with every man that he could spare, about eight hundred men in all, and, making a wide circuit through the forest, came upon the picquet that covered the American left. Greene's force thereupon at once took up its allotted position, two Maryland and two Virginian regiments in first line, and the militia and cavalry in reserve. His three guns were concealed in rear of his first line, for Rawdon, thinking that Greene

[1] 850 regular infantry, 40 artillery, 90 cavalry, 250 militia.

1781.
April 25.

possessed no artillery, had brought no cannon against him, and Greene was not the man to undeceive his adversary. Rawdon then formed his own troops for action, the Sixty-third Foot occupying the right, the New York Volunteers the centre, and the King's American Regiment[1] the left of his line. Rawdon's own corps, the Volunteers of Ireland, stood in support of the right, a detachment under Captain Robertson in support of the left, and in rear of all stood a party of sixty Provincial dragoons. Taking a lesson from his enemies, Rawdon also sprinkled his flanks with loyalist marksmen to pick off the American officers.

Since his entire force did not number as many men as Greene's first line, Rawdon's line of battle necessarily presented a far narrower front; and Greene, coolly allowing the British to advance within close range, suddenly shifted his two centre battalions to right and left so as to unmask his guns, and poured in a heavy shower of grape. Then, seeing the British recoil under the unexpected rain of shot, he in one breath ordered his cavalry to move round upon Rawdon's rear, the flank battalions to close upon his flanks, and the two battalions of his centre to charge with the bayonet. But Rawdon was not so easily to be caught. Extending his supports to right and left of his first line, he allowed the Americans to advance, and then, closing in upon them in flanks and rear, caught them neatly in their own trap. The fall of one or two American officers under the bullets of Rawdon's riflemen shook the First Maryland Regiment, which occupied Greene's left centre, and caused it to retire in panic. The Second Maryland Regiment having lost its Colonel, retreated likewise, and in a very short time but one battalion of Greene's first line was holding its ground. Greene at once gave orders for it to cover the retreat, which it did with creditable steadiness, and then bestirred himself to save his guns; but it was not until he dismounted and laid hand to the drag-ropes

[1] A Provincial corps raised by Colonel Fanning in New York in 1776.

himself that his men would look to them. A resolute 1781.
little party of Americans kept Rawdon's cavalry at bay April 25.
while he did so, and Washington, who had been busy
with the task (rather strange in a leader of cavalry)
of capturing the British medical staff, at last came up
hurriedly to save the guns from jeopardy. Greene
then ordered a retreat to Rugeley's Mills, his men
being still too unsteady to renew the action; and
Rawdon, at the age of twenty-six, had won his first
victory. He had lost two hundred and seventy officers
and men in the fight, which was a heavy price to pay
for it, but he had captured one hundred prisoners
and, most important of all, had gained a moment's
breathing time.

Greene was much depressed by this reverse,[1] which,
though all praise must be given to Rawdon for his skill
and boldness, was anything but creditable to the American
troops. But Marion, Sumter, and other partisan-leaders
were still active in attacking the posts on the British
lines of communication, and it was evident to Rawdon
that he must fall back. A reinforcement of five
hundred men of the Sixty-fourth, which had made its
way to him in contempt of the American guerillas, did
indeed tempt him to advance to Greene's position; but
finding it unassailable he turned back, evacuated Camden
on the 9th of May, and retired rapidly to Monk's Corner, May.
thirty miles from Charleston. Within the same week
the British posts of Fort Granby and Fort Motte on the
Congaree, and of Orangeburg on the North Edisto, fell
in quick succession after a short resistance. Meanwhile
Greene on the 10th marched eastward to the Saluda, and
on the 22nd invested Ninety-Six, while Lee and one of the May 22.
partisan-leaders moved with astonishing rapidity to the
Savannah River and laid siege to Augusta. This latter
post was held by a body of Provincial troops under one
Colonel Browne, a loyalist whom the revolutionists in
the days of their ascendency had striven unsuccessfully
to convert to their opinions by roasting his feet at a

[1] Johnson, *Life of Greene*, ii. 117.

1781. slow fire. He had since taken his revenge upon his enemies without mercy, and being not only a desperate but a really brave man he now made a very fine defence; but the erection of a wooden tower again enabled the enemy's riflemen to shoot down all his gunners, and on
June 5. the 5th of June he was forced to surrender. Within two days one of his officers was murdered and another badly wounded while under confinement. The American officers were simply powerless to prevent such outrages, which indeed seem to have been as frequent on the part of loyalists as of revolutionists among these half-savage people of Carolina. Nor is the fact surprising, looking to the nature of the arguments first employed by the revolutionary party.

Nothing beyond Charleston now remained to the British in Carolina except Ninety-Six, the centre of loyalism, which was held by Colonel Cruger with rather more than five hundred loyal Americans, chiefly recruited in New York and New Jersey. Before he left Camden, Rawdon had sent orders for the post to be evacuated and for the troops to be withdrawn to Charleston; but every one of his messages had been intercepted, and the garrison, hating the revolutionists, was very well content to try conclusions with them. The defences of Ninety-Six consisted of a stockade strengthened by an earthen parapet and abatis, which enclosed the village on all sides, and of a star-fort adjacent to it. To this latter Greene, with the assistance of Kosciusko, laid siege in form, adding the now celebrated wooden towers to the ordinary resources of the engineer. The siege progressed slowly, not without heavy loss to
June 17. the besiegers; but on the 17th of June the garrison was compelled to evacuate the stockade, and matters would have gone hardly with them but for a strange accident. This was nothing less than the arrival at
June 4. Charleston of three[1] of the six regiments which had been sent to reinforce Clinton from England, and which, but for the interception of Cornwallis's orders by an

[1] 3rd, 19th, 30th Foot.

American privateer, would have sailed straight to New 1781. York. Rawdon at once marched with them to relieve Ninety-Six; whereupon Greene raised the siege, leaving Rawdon to withdraw the garrison in all haste to Orange- June 29. burg. So terrible was the heat during this retreat that fifty of Rawdon's men dropped dead on the march. Both parties then went into summer quarters, Greene retiring to the high hills of Santee, some forty miles north-west of Orangeburg. Broken in health, Rawdon was now obliged to hand the command to Lieutenant-colonel Stuart of the Buffs, and to return to England. Fortunate it was that a commander of such talent, constancy, and resource as Rawdon had been at hand to take charge of the scattered posts in Carolina after Cornwallis's reckless abandonment of them, and to bring at any rate a great part of them into Charleston.

Greene now awaited the arrival of reinforcements, which were slow in coming; but on the 22nd of August Aug. 22. he marched up to Camden, being unable to cross the Santee lower down, and moved from thence upon the Congaree. Stuart thereupon fell back from that river to Eutaw, to await the arrival of a convoy, while Greene marched down slowly towards him, collecting his guerilla parties as he went. It speaks ill for the vigilance of Stuart, who was only just arrived in the country, and well for the activity of the American patrols, that the British commander had little or no information as to Greene's movements; for it was only by the warning of two American deserters that he learned, on the morning of the 8th of September, that Greene was actually Sept. 8. on the march to attack him. So deeply was he lulled in false security that he had actually allowed a party of one hundred unarmed men, with only a slender escort of cavalry, to go three miles forward to gather sweet potatoes, which, since the army was without bread, were in great request. The whole of this party was cut off and captured, while the cavalry, galloping back in panic, threw the whole camp into consternation. Stuart's force, which numbered less than eighteen hundred

1781. effective men, lay in a cleared space amid high forest,
Sept. 8. with a house and garden in rear of the camp. He now
drew up his troops in a single line somewhat in front
of the clearing, and astride of the road by which Greene
was advancing. His right flank rested on a creek, a
body of three hundred men under Major Marjoribanks
being thrown slightly forward on the extreme right, at an
obtuse angle to the line. In echelon to his left rear he
posted his small body of cavalry to guard his left flank,
and in the road he stationed his three guns. Greene,
according to sound rule, formed his first line of militia,
about four hundred and fifty strong, with two small
bodies of light troops echeloned in rear of each flank
and two guns in the centre. The second line consisted
of three brigades of regular troops, rather over twelve
hundred strong, with two more guns; and in rear of
all came a reserve of cavalry and infantry under
Colonel Washington. In all his force numbered about
two thousand men.

The action opened with a slow advance of the
Americans, during which the artillery on both sides
carried on a duel of peculiar obstinacy, with the result
that one of the English and both of the American guns
were dismounted. The American militia behaved with
great gallantry, many of them being paid substitutes
who had served in the regular army and would fight
well when led by officers whom they admired and trusted.
They gave way at length before the British fire; and
in an evil hour the battalions of the British left rushed
forward in pursuit. They were met by Greene's regular
troops with a heavy volley and a charge of the bayonet
which drove them back in utter confusion, and Greene
seized the favourable moment to order a general charge of
his second line, while the British left was still uncovered.
The British right and centre stood firm for a time,
notably the Sixty-third and Sixty-fourth Regiments,
which had fought all through the war; but being
assailed on front and flank, and embarrassed by the
crowd of fugitives, the whole line, with the exception of

Marjoribanks's detachment, gradually gave way and fell back in disorder into the clearing where the British camp stood. Stuart, however, had instructed one of his officers to occupy the house in rear of it immediately in case of mishap; and this was now promptly done, while several companies rallied and took post in the garden to make further resistance.

1781. Sept. 8.

It now remained for Greene to sweep away Marjoribanks, who with troops strongly posted and skilfully handled still held his own upon the extreme right. Washington accordingly brought up his cavalry from the rear and charged with great gallantry, but was repulsed with very heavy loss and was himself wounded and taken prisoner. A renewal of the attack with infantry met with no better success, for Marjoribanks only fell back to a stronger position at the edge of the garden and maintained himself as stoutly as ever. Meanwhile Greene's victorious infantry poured into the British camp, where all tents were still standing, hurrying their two guns along with them; but while the officers ran on to storm the garden, the men stopped to plunder the camp, and, finding liquor in the tents, soon became unmanageable. The British in the house and garden quickly perceived their opportunity, and, having picked off most of the American officers, poured a most destructive fire upon the disorderly plunderers in the camp. Greene therefore ordered a retreat, and directed a party of cavalry to advance up the road in order to cover the movement. Stuart's small body of horse came forward to encounter this party, but, being borne back, drew the American troopers under the fire from the garden, by which they were almost annihilated. Marjoribanks snatched the moment to fall upon the American guns, which, together with two captured from the British, had been brought up to the garden, and carried the whole of them into a place of safety. Then collecting men from the house and garden, he attacked the Americans who hung about the tents, and drove them out, though he did not venture to pursue them

1781. into the forest; and so ended the very bloody and desperate action of Eutaw Springs.

Both sides vehemently claimed the victory, as is usually the case when neither has much to boast of; the only creditable features in the action being the steadiness of the American militia during the first onset, and the admirable skill and tenacity of Marjoribanks. The British captured two guns and the Americans one; and the losses on both sides were very heavy. Those of the British amounted to twenty-nine officers and six hundred and sixty-four men killed, wounded, and prisoners.[1] Those of the Americans, according to Greene's own account, numbered sixty officers and four hundred and ninety-four men killed, wounded, and missing; but the return is incomplete, and it is reasonable to assume that Greene lost at least as many men as Stuart.[2] In any case, both armies were for the present crippled. Greene fell back
Sept. 9. some seven miles forthwith, while Stuart on the 9th also withdrew to Charleston Neck, leaving seventy of his wounded behind him. Greene made a show of following
Sept. 12. him, but in a few days retired to the high hills of Santee, keeping the river between himself and the British. The action of Eutaw being the last serious engagement in the south, it is unnecessary to linger in Carolina. From the moment when Cornwallis marched northward, the recovery of the province by Greene was assured; and it was only through the courage, skill, and energy of Rawdon that Greene's advance was checked for so long. It is now, therefore, time to follow once more the fortunes of Cornwallis.

That officer, in accordance with his own design, had
April 25. marched from Wilmington on the 25th of April with

[1] 3 officers and 82 men killed; 16 officers and 335 men wounded; 10 officers and 247 men missing.

[2] Stuart's despatch says that over 200 dead Americans were left on the field; but, apart from this, Greene returned only 8 men missing, which, considering that the greater part of his force was dispersed among the British tents, plundering and drinking, is incredible. Moreover, the totals in his casualty list do not tally with the details.

sixteen hundred men¹ and four guns, taking part of the   1781.
garrison with him and ordering Major Craig to withdraw the remainder to Charleston as soon as he should himself have passed the Roanoke. Travelling almost due north, he encountered little resistance ; and on the
14th of May his advanced parties met those of the May 14.
British force in Virginia, a little to northward of the Nottoway River. On the 20th of May the junction of the two armies was completed at Petersburg, and Cornwallis took command of the whole, though with Arnold, not Phillips, for his second ; for Phillips had
died just a week before, leaving a gap which was not May 13.
easily to be filled. A few days later there arrived a reinforcement of seventeen hundred men² from New York ; for Clinton, on hearing of Cornwallis's retreat to Wilmington, had determined to sacrifice all other objects to the furtherance of his operations in Carolina.³ Not until after Cornwallis had entered Virginia did rumours reach the Commander-in-chief that Carolina had been abandoned. These reports caused him the greatest uneasiness. " I hope Cornwallis may have gone back to Carolina," he wrote, when Cornwallis was within two days' march of Petersburg. . . . " If he joins Phillips I shall tremble for every post except Charleston, and even
for Georgia." On the following day he received a May 21.
letter from Cornwallis, dated at Wilmington, which confirmed his worst fears ; but yet he wrote, " I still hope that Cornwallis may not join Phillips, for I doubt if he will affect Greene's movements." Whatever Clinton's merits or demerits, his calculation of the result of Cornwallis's manœuvres showed no little sagacity.⁴

Now, however, he stood face to face with the fact that Cornwallis, without the slightest regard for his orders, had abandoned Carolina for Virginia ; but

¹ Guards, 23rd, 33rd, 2nd battalion of Fraser's Highlanders, Bose's Hessians, Light Infantry companies of Maclean's (82nd) and of Hamilton's Provincials, and Royal Artillery with four guns.
² 17th, 43rd, two German battalions.
³ Clinton to Phillips, 26th April 1781.
⁴ Clinton to Germaine, 18th, 20th, 22nd May 1781.

1781. though he did not fail to censure the proceeding,[1] he left Cornwallis a free hand for further operations instead of ordering him to return forthwith to Charleston. Meanwhile his position in New York was an extremely anxious one. Though Germaine had long ago promised to remove Arbuthnot, the old Admiral still remained in command of the fleet, constantly changing his plans and hampering the General in a fashion which kept Clinton in terror of losing supremacy at sea.[2] Moreover, Cornwallis set at naught all projects that had been previously concerted for operations in the Middle Colonies. Phillips and Arnold had recommended an attack first on Baltimore and then on Pennsylvania; but Cornwallis would hear of nothing but a campaign in Virginia, and announced his intention of marching against Lafayette, who was then lying with a small force at Richmond. Accordingly, he

May 26-27. crossed the James River with that object; whereupon Lafayette at once crossed the Chickahominy and, retiring rapidly north-westward, defied the British general to overtake him. Finding that pursuit was hopeless, Cornwallis turned abruptly westward, and having destroyed a quantity of arms and ammunition at Charlottesville doubled back down James River through Richmond to Williamsburg. Meanwhile Lafayette, returning directly that he found himself unpursued, hung continually on Cornwallis's flanks and rear during the march. At Williamsburg, however, Cornwallis's wanderings were abruptly ended

June 26. by the receipt of new orders from Clinton. Enclosing an intercepted letter from Washington to Lafayette, the Commander-in-chief directed Cornwallis to establish a defensive post at Williamsburg or Yorktown, and to send back to New York every man he could spare as soon as the operations then in train should have been completed.

This letter from Washington, which was destined to exert a strange influence on the coming campaign, pointed to a design for a great attack upon New York, to which end he had, at the end of May, written to

[1] Clinton to Cornwallis, 29th May 1781.
[2] Clinton to Phillips, 30th April.

de Grasse at Haiti entreating him to bring the French 1781. fleet to his assistance. There can be no doubt that Washington at that time centred all his hopes in the capture of New York, and that the garrison of the city was then so weak as to justify Clinton's alarm for its safety. Cornwallis, however, received these orders at Williamsburg in no loyal nor kindly spirit. Some allowance may be made for the facts that he had long enjoyed practically independent command, that he had passed through a very arduous campaign with great strain to mind and body, and that he must have felt misgivings as to the absolute failure of his plans. But, be that as it may, he now deprecated the establishment of a defensive post in the Chesapeake, and begged, though rather late, for permission to return to Charleston in order to look to the safety of Rawdon.[1] Then, deciding that his force, after sending a detachment to New York, would be too weak to hold Yorktown together with the supplementary post of Gloucester on the opposite side of York River, he retired from Williamsburg to James River and prepared to cross it in order to fall back to Portsmouth. Lafayette at once followed him up with twenty-five hundred men, and Cornwallis July 6. with great skill contrived to draw him into an action which cost the Marquis a number of men and two guns. It was thought by some with the army that Cornwallis might have followed up this success and annihilated Lafayette's detachment without prejudice to his other arrangements ; and it is certain that the troops destined for New York might very well have been embarked in York River without retiring to James River at all.[2] No sooner had Cornwallis crossed the James River than there arrived a second letter from Clinton, July 8. ordering him to send him forthwith from two to three thousand troops, since he wished to make a raid upon Philadelphia and to destroy all the stores accumulated there.[3] Then, on his arrival at Portsmouth, he found

[1] Clinton to Cornwallis, 30th June 1781.   [2] Tarleton, p. 356.
[3] Clinton to Cornwallis, 28th June 1781.

1781. yet more letters from Clinton,[1] evidently written with the design of burying all unkindness and restoring the cordial relations that had once reigned between them. These last gave Cornwallis to understand that he was at liberty to keep the whole of his troops, but that it was the opinion both of Clinton and of Admiral Graves, who had lately superseded Arbuthnot, that a defensive post must be established at Old Point Comfort in York River, for the protection of the British cruisers.

If the reader be weary of this tangle of contradictory orders, he can the better understand the feelings of Cornwallis; and yet the blame for this confusion does not lie with Clinton. His own idea was not unsound, namely, to establish a post at the mouth of Chesapeake Bay which would serve at once as a refuge for the British ships employed in guarding the great waterways of Maryland and Virginia, and as a base for operations on a greater scale so soon as reinforcements should enable him to undertake them. No doubt he would have insisted on his first orders to Cornwallis, had he not just received positive commands from Germaine[2] that not a man was to be withdrawn from the Chesapeake, but that conquest should be pushed from south to north. This was nothing less than the rejection of the Commander-in-chief's scheme in favour of his subordinate's; yet by the irony of fate Clinton had hardly received this order before Germaine repented of it, and wrote again, though of course too late, to approve of Clinton's original plan.[3] The truth was that Clinton, Cornwallis, and Germaine were all of them in favour of a campaign in the Middle Colonies. Clinton, as has been seen, wished to await the arrival of reinforcements and of a covering fleet, and meanwhile to secure a naval base. Cornwallis was for evacuating New York, transferring the principal base of the British to the Chesapeake, and opening the campaign there at once. Germaine desired to combine both

---

[1] Clinton to Cornwallis, 11th and 15th July 1781.
[2] Germaine to Clinton, 2nd May 1781.
[3] Germaine to Clinton, 7th and 14th July 1781.

designs after some incomprehensible fashion of his own, 1781. with the result that he ordered the principal operations to be carried on from some vague external point inward towards the base, instead of from the base outwards upon some given objective. This ill-timed interference of Germaine was in every respect fatal. Not only was Clinton forced to abandon his own plans, but, being irritated beyond endurance by Germaine's disloyalty, he kept Cornwallis close at hand in order to resign the command to him, instead of sending him back, as he ought, to Carolina.

Cornwallis now proceeded to examine Old Point Com- July 29 to fort; but this station being condemned by his engineers, Aug. 2. he returned again to York River, seized Yorktown and Gloucester, and began to fortify them both. The evacuation of Portsmouth meanwhile proceeded gradually, though not a man except Benedict Arnold was sent back to Clinton, and on the 22nd of August the whole of his force was concentrated in these two new posts.

Meanwhile, on the side of New York all had been quiet. At the end of June Washington took post at White Plains, where on the 6th of July he was joined by July 6. the French force from Rhode Island under de Rochambeau. There the two commanders impatiently awaited news from de Grasse, making occasional demonstrations against the British posts at Kingsbridge. Clinton for his part was perfectly aware that de Grasse was expected, but felt little anxiety, since he had been assured that the French fleet would be followed by Rodney with a superior force. At the beginning of August two thousand German recruits reached New York from Europe; and Clinton at once conceived the design of dealing a sudden blow at Rhode Island before de Grasse should arrive. Admiral Graves was cruising to intercept a convoy at the time, but when he returned to New York Aug. 16. there was still ample time for the execution of the project, which Clinton broached to him with great eagerness. Nevertheless, to the General's great disappointment, Graves declared that the condition of his ships forbade

1781. any such operation; and the design was abandoned.[1] Meanwhile Washington, having received intelligence that de Grasse was sailing for the Chesapeake with his whole force, withdrew on the 19th behind the Crotton, and, crossing the Hudson four days later, advanced southward as if to take up his old position at Morristown in New Jersey. Clinton was puzzled, for he knew that Washington would not dare to move to Virginia without command of the sea, and he had long been assured that naval superiority would be on the side of the British.[2] Then there came to him a message, dated the 25th of August, from Sir Samuel Hood, saying that he had arrived off the Chesapeake with fourteen ships of the line, that he could neither see nor hear anything of de Grasse, and that he was sailing for New York to join Admiral Graves. He duly arrived on the 28th of August; and since there was intelligence that Admiral de Barras had sailed from Rhode Island with eight ships of the line and a convoy on the 27th, Graves on the 31st put to sea with eighteen ships to intercept him.

Aug. 19.
Aug. 23, 24.

Aug. 31.

Aug. 30.

Unfortunately de Grasse had already arrived in the Chesapeake on the previous day with twenty-eight ships of the line, had surprised two frigates at anchor, which should have been on the watch for him, and had captured the one and driven the other up York River. His appearance in such overwhelming strength was a surprise to every English commander, and upset all calculations. De Grasse lost no time in detaching four ships to convoy the troops which he had brought with him up James River to Lafayette, and anchored with the rest in Lynhaven Bay, just within the southern cape of Chesapeake Bay. There, on the 5th of September, Graves found him with twenty-four ships instead of de Barras with eight ships, as he had expected. An indecisive action followed, wherein Graves showed little skill; but after five days of manœuvring de Barras

Sept. 5.

---

[1] Clinton to Graves, 16th August; Graves to Clinton, 18th and 21st August.
[2] Clinton to Cornwallis, 27th August 1781.

passed safely within the Capes, while Graves sailed to 1781.
New York to repair damages.

It was not until the 2nd of September that Clinton Sept. 2.
realised that Washington was actually on the march for
Virginia, but still he felt little anxiety. He wrote to
Cornwallis that Admiral Digby's squadron was expected
shortly, and that he himself would send reinforcements
and make a diversion from New York, adding, in tragic
ignorance of the true state of affairs, that as Graves had
sailed Cornwallis need fear nothing.[1] True to his
promise, he sent an expedition under Benedict Arnold
against New London in Connecticut, which captured Sept. 6.
two forts and a number of ships; but the loss of men
was disproportionate to the object attained, and as a
diversion the enterprise was absolutely ineffective. Cornwallis, meanwhile, knew more of the true situation than
Clinton, who had no idea, until Graves's return to New
York, of the enemy's superiority at sea; and it must have
been clear to him that Clinton's promises were dependent
on the movements of the British naval force. Cornwallis
had about seven thousand troops, for the most part of
excellent quality, while Lafayette lay at Williamsburg
with no more than five thousand, many of whom, having
been just imported from the West Indies, were sickly and
inefficient. Obviously, Cornwallis could have attacked
this force and beaten it before the arrival of Washington's
army; and indeed, by his own account, he only refrained
from the enterprise in the expectation of speedy relief,
though he was fully aware that the French had thirty-
six ships against the British twenty-one.[2] There lay
open to him also the alternative of retreat into Carolina,
which would no doubt have been hazardous, and must
have led to great sacrifices, though to far less than the
loss of his whole army. He decided, however, to hold
his hand, and busied himself with the strengthening of
his position. Meanwhile, on the 14th, Washington and Sept. 14.
his staff arrived at Lafayette's headquarters. Four

[1] Clinton to Cornwallis, 2nd, 6th, 8th September 1781.
[2] Cornwallis to Clinton, 16th and 17th September 1781.

1781. days later the first division of his army marched in, and
Sept. 26. by the 26th the whole of it, some sixteen thousand strong, was assembled at Williamsburg. On the 28th
Sept. 28. Yorktown was invested, and the siege began.

The defences of the place were by no means contemptible. The little town was covered both to east and west by swamps, and the half-mile that lay in the centre between these two natural protections, as also the passages over the swamps themselves, were commanded by strong redoubts. Within this outer line was an inner line of defence drawn about the town itself, consisting of a stockade and a parapet of earth with redoubts and batteries; but the space included within this internal line did not exceed twelve hundred yards in length by five hundred in depth.

Sept. 29. On the 29th a messenger arrived from Clinton saying that Admiral Digby had arrived with three ships, and that he had every hope of sailing to his assistance with five thousand troops and twenty-six ships of the line on the 5th of October. Thereupon, for no apparent reason, Cornwallis abandoned the outer line of defences and retired within the works of the town, though these were actually commanded by the outer line. Accordingly, on
Sept. 30. the night of the 30th, the enemy broke ground on the eastern front, advanced their first parallel on the 6th of October, and on the 9th opened fire at a range of six
Oct. 11. hundred yards. Within two days the enemy's batteries had approached to within three hundred yards, their fire telling heavily, since, by Cornwallis's own confession, most of the inner defences could be enfiladed from the outer line. On the 14th the capture of two advanced redoubts made the British position almost hopeless. A gallant sortie on the 16th, though not wholly unsuccessful, was of little help, and an attempt to retreat across the river to Gloucester was defeated by a sudden storm of wind. There was no sign of Clinton's coming; and
Oct. 19. on the 19th, with a large proportion of his force disabled by wounds or sickness, and with hardly a gun able to fire, Cornwallis capitulated. On that same day Clinton, after long delay due to the defects of the fleet, sailed

to his relief, but on his arriving found that he was 1781. come five days too late, and sailed back, sick at heart, to New York.

The losses of the garrison during the siege were five hundred killed and wounded. The number that surrendered was six thousand six hundred and thirty men,[1] of whom twenty-five hundred were Germans and the remainder British; and it is noteworthy that no fewer than two thousand men were in hospital. The blow was, on the whole, perhaps the heaviest that has ever fallen on the British Army, and to all intent it put an end to the war in America. There was, indeed, occasional petty fighting from time to time in Carolina; but it was recognised that the contest was hopeless; and aggressive hostilities had long been abandoned in every quarter before Charleston was finally evacuated in December 1782. The story of the War of American Independence therefore ends practically with the surrender of Yorktown.

The immediate cause of the disaster was of course the arrival of de Grasse in such immense strength. No one dreamed that he would carry all his ships with him to America. Rodney reckoned that he would take at most ten, and supposed that by sending fourteen ships with Hood, and ordering six more, which for some reason never came, from Jamaica, he had made ample provision against all contingencies. The more credit is due to de Grasse for his energy and decision; and he was favoured, as he deserved, by the fortune of war. With the British Admirals everything went amiss. Apart from many mishaps which they could not have prevented, they made mistakes, and, worst of all, mistakes for which fortune exacted the utmost penalty. For in the conduct of war, as in the world at large, those sins only are unpardonable which are found out. But, setting the naval operations wholly aside, it seems to me

[1] Tarleton's list gives the total at 7247, including hospital staff and non-combatants. The above figure is from a return of 18th October 1781.

1781. that, judged by purely military standards, Cornwallis emerges by no means altogether with credit from this last phase of the campaign. Undoubtedly he contributed more than any one man, except only Germaine, to the final catastrophe by his mad invasion of North Carolina after Cowpens, and by his equally mad advance into Virginia from Wilmington. But even if this be forgiven to him, his behaviour at Yorktown seems to have been singularly weak. He knew that he was in a most perilous situation, and his better instinct prompted him to strike at Lafayette before Washington could arrive; but he resisted this impulse and abstained. Even so, all might have been well had he held fast to his outer line of defence, in which he could almost certainly have prolonged the siege for another week; whereas he knew that, by abandoning them, he rendered his inner line untenable. This proceeding has never been satisfactorily explained, and I confess that to me it wears no very pleasing aspect. Nevertheless, it is perfectly intelligible that Cornwallis, who at his best was certainly a good, skilful, and gallant soldier, might have been practically broken down by incessant anxiety and strain, and it is probably not less just than charitable to ascribe his shortcomings in great degree to physical causes. But the readiness of disloyalty with which he turned against his Commander-in-chief, the ill-temper which he showed when Clinton very properly called him to account for disobedience of orders and for the prosecution of unwise and unsound operations, and above all the impatience which he evinced at every stage in the miscarriage of his foolish campaign — these characteristics do not strike me as those of a good commander or of a well-conditioned officer. At the same time, he showed some very fine qualities. He shared every hardship with his men, he never hesitated to take the blame for any mishap that befell his subordinates, and he was rewarded by a devotion in his troops which gained for him the astonishing victory at Guildford, and kept his little force in heart through weeks of untold hardship, fatigue, and want.

As to Clinton, who was made the scapegoat for 1781, every misfortune that occurred during his period of command, it seems to me that no general was ever worse treated. With fewer troops than Howe, and with a French fleet constantly on the coast, he was expected to do fully as much as his predecessor. Had he been left to himself he might have won better success, for his letters show considerable insight into the realities of the situation, and he had a radical distrust of all operations based on the support of loyalists. Knowing his weakness in numbers, he would have relied on a system of raids on the coast, occasionally hazarding a heavier blow when he saw opportunity, but never attempting to conquer country which he could not hold. He could strike hard and swiftly, as he proved by his capture of Forts Clinton and Montgomery; but it was his misfortune, after brief and perfectly cordial intercourse with Lord Howe and Sir George Collier, to find himself harnessed with admirals who were neither good yoke-mates nor efficient commanders. Twice he was about to swoop upon Rhode Island and make it a Yorktown for the French, and twice he was thwarted by the Admiral. His views as to the conduct of the campaign were always sane, and he recognised, as Cornwallis did not, that the naval operations far exceeded the military in importance. Altogether he was an unlucky man, unlucky above all in the mistakes which were forced upon him by the minister at home.

For it is to Germaine, if to any one man, that the disaster of Yorktown as of Saratoga is to be ascribed: to Germaine with his blindness to facts, his deafness to wise counsel, his jealousy of commanders in the field, his appalling ignorance of the elements of war, his foolish ambition to direct all operations from Whitehall. In the matter of failure to furnish the recruits, supplies, and ships required by the generals, very much may be forgiven to one who had to deal with such a multitude of enemies in all quarters; but nothing can excuse the encouragement of disloyalty in a subordinate towards

1781. his Commander-in-chief, nor deliberate insult offered to a Commander-in-chief by ostentatious quotation of a subordinate's opinion against him.[1] He knew that Clinton would have resigned the command at once if the King would have permitted him, and therefore he took a cowardly delight in thwarting him. Then when he had driven him, as he had already driven Burgoyne, into disaster, he turned upon them both and rent them. There is, in fact, a malignity in the behaviour of Germaine towards all the principal commanders in America which bears very strong marks of personal vindictiveness. The man had never forgotten the court-martial after Minden.

Yet, in spite of Germaine in office, of Fox and Richmond in opposition, of Ireland on the verge of insurrection, and of all Europe armed against Britain, the fact remains that the American Revolution at the moment of its final triumph was on the eve of collapse. "We are at the end of our tether," wrote Washington in April 1781. "Great Britain desisted from the contest exactly when she ought most to have pressed it," writes the biographer of General Greene,[2] who gives abundance of facts to show that the Southern Colonies could not have maintained another campaign. Nor is the reason difficult to discover; for it is abundantly evident from the testimony of the Americans themselves that there was little enthusiasm in the Colonies over the quarrel. Unless their homes were invaded the people of America were unwilling to fight themselves, and except with paper money they were unwilling to pay others to fight for them. Everybody wanted to make money out of the war, but few wished to take any other share in it. Hence, dull to all sense of shame and honour, Congress violated the Convention of Saratoga and maltreated the prisoners simply in order to drive them into the American service. Joseph Galloway, a renegade member of Congress, averred that

[1] See Germaine to Clinton, 6th June 1781; a most insulting letter.
[2] Johnson, ii. 393.

scarcely one-fourth of the American regular troops 1781. were natives, one-half being Irish and the remainder British. Evidence from such a source should not, I think, be hastily accepted, for Galloway did not put forward such statements without purposes of his own; but, whether his calculations be exaggerated or not, there can be no doubt that they contain a strong leaven of truth. Again, it cannot be denied that desertion assumed extraordinary proportions at different periods of the war, chiefly of Germans from the British side and of Irish from the American. Greene was often heard to say that at the close of the war he fought the enemy with British soldiers, and that the British fought him with those of America;[1] and it seems certain that the Provincial troops in British pay exceeded, on an average, the permanent force of Washington. "Money will go further than arms in America," wrote the cynical Benedict Arnold, who knew his countrymen.

It is in view of these circumstances that the history of the war seems most remarkable. There were two great blows struck on each side, by the Americans at Saratoga and Yorktown, and by the British at New York and Fort Washington in 1776 and at Charleston in 1780. Minor successes on both sides, such as the repulse of the British before Charleston in 1776, and of the Americans at Penobscot and Savannah, leave little advantage to the credit of either. But in pitched battles the British were almost invariably successful; and though this is easily accounted for at Bunker's Hill and Brandywine, it is less easily explained after 1777, when the best part of the veteran troops sent from England had been used up in the campaigns of Howe and Burgoyne. Such of them as survived marched with Cornwallis through the Carolinas, but there can have been few of them left after the battle of Camden; and yet the remnant contrived to win the action of Guildford, when beyond doubt there must have been many Provincials in the ranks. Rawdon, again, won his

[1] Johnson, ii. 220.

1781. action of Hobkirk's Hill almost entirely with Provincial troops, which, by hypothesis, should have been no better than Greene's. Even at Eutaw, again, Stuart's Provincial troops rallied after their first defeat, whereas Greene's broke up to plunder before their work was half done. Cowpens was the one exception, for the action of King's Mountain was unique of its kind, and Cowpens was won, as many actions are, principally by an accident. Speaking generally, it seems to me certain that the British made far better troops of their Provincial recruits than the Americans themselves.

Regular pay was no doubt a principal cause of this, together with the better system of discipline which goes necessarily with an army of long standing and great traditions. No slur can be cast upon the gallantry of American officers, as their losses at Eutaw can testify; but even so they had rarely the hold possessed by English and loyalist officers over their men. The reason for this I believe to be that the loyal party was far more enthusiastic for its cause than the revolutionists. The most gallant feat of the whole war was the work of a little party of loyalists in one of the posts about New York, who, though no more than seventy strong and without a single cannon, held a block-house for three hours against several hundred of the enemy with seven guns. One face of the block-house was pierced by no fewer than fifty-six cannon shot, and the losses of this noble little garrison amounted to twenty-one killed and wounded; yet they held their post indomitably, beat the enemy off with heavy loss, and even took some of them prisoners.[1] Clinton also bore repeated witness to the excellent behaviour of his Provincial regiments; and I am driven to the conclusion, despite the presence of many brave and excellent officers in the American army, that the better class of American generally preferred the King's Commission to that of Congress, partly from a natural leaning to the side of loyalty,

[1] This happened on 21st July 1780. The King sent them his special thanks.

partly because, in Washington's phrase, the Americans 1781. regarded their officers, as such, no more than a broomstick. Nor is this in the least surprising when we reflect on the jealous and unclean intrigues of the self-seeking body named Congress. Had the British Government at the beginning of the war offered the inducements to enlistment which were afterwards suggested by Arnold, Washington's source of recruits would have been in great measure dried up. The fact is, as I must repeat, that the revolution was the work of a very small but busy and ambitious minority. Had the Americans really cared seriously about the quarrel with England, they would have raised the hundred and fifty thousand men of whom Conway spoke, and driven the British from the Continent in two campaigns. As it was, they left their work to be done mainly by the French.

How then, it will be asked, did the Americans contrive to achieve such successes as Saratoga and Yorktown? The answer is, that in the first instance they had their militia with them, and in the second a force of French troops in addition to the French fleet. It was, in fact, only when the militia came forward that the Americans achieved any important success apart from their allies; but the militia was an extremely uncertain element, both to friend and foe. "The collecting of the militia," wrote Washington[1] in 1781, "depends entirely on the prospects of the day; if favourable, they throng to you; if not, they will not move." This was strictly true, as the fate of Burgoyne can prove; and it was the knowledge of the fact that made the British commanders so extremely cautious and so averse as a rule to operations far inland, where the militia could waylay detachments or overwhelm posts on the lines of communication without going far from their homes. It was doubtless this consideration which prompted Amherst and Lord Barrington to urge that the war should be a naval war only. Against it there was of course the objection that the militia were of

[1] *Works*, vii. 467.

1781. value for the intimidation of loyalists; but as this terrorism soon degenerated into indiscriminate robbery and violence, it would necessarily have provoked retaliation, and would have brought about, as it actually did in Carolina, a civil war of unsurpassed ferocity.[1] By allowing Congress to work its will inland, while cutting off all communications by sea and making occasional raids on the ports which sheltered privateers, the British fleet would probably have brought the Americans back to the Crown without the expense of large forces from England and Germany; while if a Montrose had chanced to appear among the loyalists he might have shortened matters considerably. Even as things fell out, when the American war was a matter of but secondary importance in England's gigantic struggle with the powers of Europe all over the world, there was not vitality enough in the revolution to support it; and but for foreign assistance the whole movement would have collapsed.

In truth, as an eminent historian has written, the general aspect of the American people during the contest was far from heroic or sublime; and it is pleasanter to turn from it to the gallantry of their troops in the field, and to the indomitable patience and constancy of their leaders, Washington and Greene. Of their strictly military talents it is not easy to speak, for it is impossible to say how far Washington's earlier operations may have been marred by Congress. His fame as a military commander rests on the surprise of the German posts at Trenton, and on his march from the Hudson to the Chesapeake in 1781. The former, though a very brilliant and skilful feat, which led to great results, can hardly be rated more highly than a dozen similar exploits of the war; while the march to the Chesapeake was unopposed by Clinton less from any skill of Washington's in feint or manœuvre than from Clinton's reliance on Rodney's word that British supremacy at

[1] The process had begun in Pennsylvania. Washington, *Works*, iv. 296. New York also was full of brigands.

sea would be maintained. As a matter of fact, Washington would never have attempted this march with American troops only, since, by his own confession, they would have melted away on the road.¹ On the other hand, there were very grave flaws in his campaign of 1776 about New York, while he was completely outmanœuvred by Howe in Pennsylvania in 1777. From that time onward until 1781 he practically had no army with which to take the field, but was compelled to sit quietly on the defensive. It was in those long months of waiting in entrenched positions, and most notably in that bitter and desperate winter at Valley Forge, that Washington's finest qualities were displayed —his constancy, his courage, and his inexhaustible patience. Yet though every Englishman must admire him as a very great man and a brave and skilful soldier, it is, I think, doubtful whether he has any claim to be regarded as a really great commander in the field. He was not, it is true, a soldier by profession, but neither was Cromwell; and I take it that Washington hardly showed himself so great a general as Cromwell.

Greene's reputation stands firmly on his campaign in the Carolinas, his luring of Cornwallis into a false position, and his prompt return upon Camden after the retreat of Cornwallis to Wilmington. His keen insight into the heart of Cornwallis's blunders and his skilful use of his guerilla troops are the most notable features of his work, and stamp him as a general of patience, resolution, and profound common sense, qualities which go far towards making a great commander. One gift he seems to have lacked, namely, the faculty of leadership, to which, as well as to bad luck, must be ascribed the fact that he was never victorious in a general action. Washington's ascendency over his men was remarkable, but Washington had the advantage of being a gentleman. I am aware that this is now supposed to be no advantage; but Washington considered it to be essential to a good officer, and I am

¹ Washington, *Works*, viii. 108, 15th July 1781.

1781. content to abide by his opinion. Saving this one small matter, Greene, who was a very noble character, seems to me to stand little if at all lower than Washington as a general in the field.

But in natural military genius neither Washington nor Greene seems to me to approach Benedict Arnold. The man was of course shallow, fickle, unprincipled, and unstable in character, but he possessed all the gifts of a great commander. To boundless energy and enterprise he united quick insight into a situation, sound strategic instinct, audacity of movement, wealth of resource, a swift and unerring eye in action, great personal daring, and true magic of leadership. It was he and no other who beat Burgoyne at Saratoga, and with Daniel Morgan to command his militia Benedict Arnold was the most formidable opponent that could be matched against the British in America.

In justice to the Americans, too, it must be remembered that the British generals, taken altogether, were good and able officers. Howe and Clinton were fettered by Germaine, but Howe's brigadiers were all of them capable—some of them, indeed, such as Grey, Grant, and Vaughan, of unusual capacity. Many detachments were made in the course of the war, but few of them failed to do their work with success. Burgoyne and Cornwallis, for all their misfortunes, were excellent officers; so also were Cornwallis's brigadiers, O'Hara and Webster. Major Craig showed very great ability in his difficult post at Wilmington; and Ferguson, Tarleton, and Simcoe, though they had experience of mishaps, won deserved reputations as partisan-officers. But the ablest of all was Lord Rawdon, who received his baptism of fire at twenty-one, on Bunker's Hill, and at twenty-six contrived with great skill to save the position abandoned by Cornwallis. With him, together with James Craig and Ensign John Moore of Maclean's, we shall meet again in happier days.

AUTHORITIES.—The literature of the American War of Independence is of course boundless. For a simple narrative of the

operations the histories of Stedman, on the English side, and of 1781.
Mr. John Fiske, on the American side, strike me as the best. The
former is based chiefly on official documents, which are sometimes
too readily accepted. The latter is admirably written, and, though
naturally not without blunders, is free from the usual excessive
partiality of American writers, while retaining sufficient enthusiasm
for America to teach an English reader just sympathy with healthy
American sentiment. The official despatches of the British
Commander-in-chief in America are in the Record Office, *America
and West Indies*, 121-141; but these do not include Burgoyne's
despatches, which are only to be found copied in an Entry Book
(*America and West Indies*, 306), though all are printed in Burgoyne's
Expedition from Canada. There are a few details also in *W. O.
Orig. Corres.* 19-21. The naval operations can be studied in
Admiral's Despatches, North America, 5-10; but still better in
Captain Mahan's *Influence of Sea Power*. On the American side,
Washington's correspondence will be found in the *Life and Works
of Washington*, by Jared Sparks, and Greene's in Johnson's *Life of
Nathanael Greene*. Marshall's *Life of Washington* and other standard
works of American history are too well known to need mention.
Minor English authorities are Lamb's *Journal during the American
War*, Anbury's *Travels*, Chastellux's *Travels*, Moore's *Life of Sir John
Moore*, and the *Cornwallis Papers*. More important are Tarleton's
Campaigns in North America, Simcoe's *Journal of the Operations of
the Queen's Rangers*. The late Mr. B. F. Stevenson collected the
pamphlets of Clinton and Cornwallis, with all the official correspondence of the Carolina campaigns, into two volumes, entitled
the *Clinton-Cornwallis Controversy*. These are of special value from
the printing of Clinton's marginal annotations to the pamphlets,
annotations which I have verified from copies of the pamphlets
(unknown to Mr. Stevenson) which are in the library at Dropmore.
This mass of documents has been collated with a care such as is
usually bestowed only on St. Paul's Epistles. I have already
acknowledged my obligations to Lord Grey for access to Major
André's manuscript journal, and I must do the like to Colonel
Sackville West for placing at my disposal a similar journal by
an officer. Other works consulted will be found quoted in my
footnotes.

As to the West Indies, see, in the Record Office, *America and
West Indies*, 150-153 (*West Indies, Military*), and 155-158 (*Military,
Promiscuous*). For Pensacola, see *America and West Indies*, 267;
and for Nicaragua and Omoa the same; also *Colonial Correspondence,
Jamaica*, 12-22. For the West Indies at large, see *Colonial Correspondence, Jamaica, ut supra; Barbados*, 7, 8; *Leeward Islands*,
9-18; *Bermuda*, 5-7; *Bahamas*, 8-10. There is good material also
in the *Lives of the Lindsays*.

CHAPTER XXI

1781. THE news of Yorktown reached London on the 25th of November, and was announced by the King to Parliament. He made, however, no sign of yielding ; and indeed it was ridiculous to suppose that the disaster was irreparable. The tongues of the Opposition were rightly filled with condemnation of the Ministry's incapacity ; but estimates were duly passed for one hundred and ninety-one thousand men, including twenty-six thousand foreigners, for the service of the coming year. At the same time Lord North announced that no further attempt would be made to subjugate America by sending armies to march through it, which, if a wise resolution, was unfortunately taken a little too late.

1782. Feb. 11. Early in February 1782 Germaine resigned, and on the 27th General Conway carried a motion to stay further offensive hostilities against the Colonies, exactly at the same time when, as we have seen, they should have been pressed most vigorously. Had the motion been brought forward three months later, it would not have passed ; but history is made up of similar mistakes.

March 19. Three weeks afterwards Lord North resigned, and a new Ministry was installed with Lord Rockingham at the head of the Treasury, and Lord Shelburne and Fox as joint Secretaries of State. The first act of this enlightened Government was to send Rodney a curt letter of recall, his evil opinions as a Tory being held to outweigh his merits as the ablest of living admirals. Yet these were the men who had found no vituperation bitter enough for Sandwich.

It was well that this letter took long to reach its destination. The news of Yorktown caused much disaffection throughout the British West Indies, and the Assembly of Barbados actually refused to make any provision for the troops quartered in the island.[1] On the 27th of November the islands of St. Eustatius and St. Martins were surprised by a French expedition from Martinique ; and the garrisons, numbering about eight hundred men, were captured, together with large sums of money. This mishap was the more disgraceful since there was but one possible landing-place, and that easy of defence, on St. Eustatius, while the Governor, Lieutenant-colonel Cockburn, had received timely warning of the coming attack. Cockburn was tried by court-martial, found guilty of culpable neglect, and cashiered. The general opinion on the spot was that he had been bribed by the French.

Meanwhile, de Grasse, having left the Chesapeake on the 5th of November, arrived at Martinique on the 26th, and concerted with the Governor an attack upon Barbados. Foiled in the attempt by the violence of the trade-wind, they turned to leeward against St. Kitts, and on the 11th of January 1782 anchored off Basseterre with six thousand troops. The British garrison, consisting of about seven hundred men of the First and Fifteenth Foot under General Fraser, thereupon retired to Brimstone Hill ; in which position the French troops, being landed, prepared to besiege them. Meanwhile, Sir Samuel Hood had returned to Barbados on the 5th of December, where, on hearing of the attack on St. Kitts, he at once embarked the Sixty-ninth regiment and sailed to Antigua, picked up other reinforcements there under General Prescott, and arrived before Basseterre on the 25th of January. The manœuvres whereby Hood enticed de Grasse from his anchorage, and, taking it up himself, held it with twenty-two ships against twenty-nine, are famous in naval history ; but for our purpose their most notable result was that

[1] General Christie to Secretary of State, 30th November 1781.

1782. Prescott and his troops were able to land on the 28th.
Jan. 28. He was at once attacked by the French, who, however, were repulsed without difficulty; and then, sending forward two officers to Brimstone Hill, Prescott ascertained from Fraser that he needed no assistance, having a sufficiency of men and of provisions. Fraser was perfectly right. Brimstone Hill would have been quite safe but for the treachery of the inhabitants of St. Kitts, for Hood had taken or sunk the whole of the French ammunition-ships, so that the enemy had no material for prosecuting the siege. The Governor, however, had sent up artillery and ammunition to Fraser, which were intercepted by the inhabitants, and by them deliberately made over to the French. Thus provided with siege-guns, the French opened a heavy bombardment; and by the 12th of February Fraser's little garrison, having lost over one hundred and fifty killed and wounded, besides many men from sickness, was quite worn out by excessive fatigue. Many of his militia deserted, the remainder petitioned urgently that
Feb. 12. he would capitulate; and Fraser had no alternative but to comply. Not a word of intelligence of all this was sent by the inhabitants to Hood, who still lay at his anchorage, cutting off all communication between the French fleet and army; rather, all information was studiously withheld from him. On hearing at last of the capitulation, he made his escape adroitly enough, before the French could bring guns to play upon his ships from the shore; but he did not fail to write to General Christie at Barbados, and to the Admiralty at home, the true story of St. Kitts. It is really difficult to speak with patience of the behaviour of the detestable little oligarchy of planters in that island. But for their treachery the French troops would probably have been captured to a man. As things were, it was only by extreme promptness and skill that Hood averted a great disaster. It is some consolation to reflect that the Assemblies in the West Indies, which were answerable for so much folly and even crime, are, for the most part, no longer in existence.

Nevis and Montserrat, being defenceless, fell directly after St. Kitts ; Demerara and Essequibo were recovered, even as they had been captured, with little effort ; and now the French and Spaniards began to meditate the conquest of Jamaica, for which object fifty ships of the line and twenty thousand troops were to be concentrated at Haiti. But meanwhile Rodney had arrived from Europe with twelve ships of the line, and on the 25th of February effected his junction with Hood's fleet to the eastward of Antigua. De Grasse, therefore, sought shelter in Fort Royal, and Rodney put into Gros Islet Bay, St. Lucia, where day after day he climbed the rocks of Pigeon Island, watching for the signal which should tell of de Grasse's departure. It came at last on the 8th of April ; and on the 12th was fought the famous action of The Saints, which, though no such overwhelming victory as it should have been, brought de Grasse prisoner to England, saved Jamaica, and shook French naval power in the West Indies. While Rodney was on his way to Jamaica, the Spanish fleet and army in overwhelming force made conquest of the defenceless Bahamas, but with this the operations in the West Indies came to an end. Yet it must be recorded that in October a motley band of American rangers, British logwood-cutters, and Indians, under British officers, attacked the Spanish garrisons on the Black River, took the whole of them prisoners, and thus regained for New England her possessions in the Gulf of Honduras.

1782.

Feb. 25.

April 12.

May.

Oct.

The great blow planned by France and Spain for the humiliation of Britain in the West Indies had been parried by Rodney ; but there were vulnerable points for a like stroke in the Mediterranean. There also affairs had gone ill with the British at the opening of 1782. On the 20th of August 1781 a force of eight thousand Spaniards under the Duke of Crillon arrived before Minorca, bringing with it one hundred heavy guns for the siege of Fort St. Philip. Landing at the different points on the east and west coasts of the island,

1781.
Aug. 20.

1781. Crillon marched straight upon Mahon, which he took
without resistance, and opened further operations by
asking Murray to name his own price for the surrender
of the fortress. This overture having been indignantly
rejected, he began his preparations for a siege, wherein
he was presently joined by French troops from Toulon,
which increased his force to sixteen thousand men.
Murray, for his part, was ready and confident. His
garrison consisted only of the Fifty-first and Sixty-first
Foot, including a number of worn-out invalids, and of
two Hanoverian battalions; but he had organised a
body of seamen as gunners, and felt secure of his ability
to hold his own, since Fort St. Philip effectively kept
Sept.-Oct. open the harbour to friendly vessels. In vain the
enemy erected battery after battery in the effort to
close the port. Small craft could always creep in after
dark with men and supplies; and thus a full month
after the siege had begun a party of Corsican volunteers,
commanded by a nephew of the famous Paoli, came
into Fort St. Philip to take part in the defence.[1] Meanwhile Murray in September made a very daring sortie
against Crillon's headquarters, destroying one of the
Spanish batteries and capturing a hundred prisoners;
and altogether the progress of the siege was so slow,
that at the end of November Crillon decided to turn it
into a blockade.

In this state matters continued until the end of
December, the garrison maintaining an effective fire
varied by occasional successful sorties, when there
Dec. 20. appeared the one enemy that Murray dreaded—scurvy.
Half of his troops had lived on salt provisions for three
years, half for six years; there was no means of growing vegetables in the fortress, and the Government had
relied upon untrustworthy agents to supply them from
Italy. The sickness grew and spread with appalling
swiftness, its virulence being much increased by the
foul air of the casemates and of the subterranean
galleries. New difficulties were thrown in Murray's way

[1] Murray to Secretary of State, 4th October 1781.

through the insubordination of Sir William Draper, the conqueror of Manila, who as Lieutenant-governor claimed an equal voice with him in command. Still the garrison, though never strong enough in numbers for the extent of the fortifications, persisted manfully in resistance. The men concealed their ailments rather than go into hospital. Day after day they fell in for duty, mere shadows of soldiers, stood at their posts for the allotted time until the relief came round, and marched back uncomplaining to the guardroom, to await the hour which should summon them again to their work; nor was it until the roll was called that the sergeants, striving to rouse the men who had failed to answer, discovered that a sterner sergeant had been before them, and that the silent soldiers were dead. Others, too feeble even to walk, were borne to their posts while sound men were left to carry them, and finished their service under arms. And so for seven terrible weeks these simple, devoted men faced their unseen enemy in the gloomy, stifling casemates, until on the 1st of February the daily state showed but seven hundred and sixty soldiers fit for duty, whereas the daily guards required four hundred and fifteen. During the two following days over a hundred men were carried to hospital; and on the 5th Murray capitulated. Six hundred wasted, decrepit figures crawled out to lay down their arms; and so pitiful was the sight, as they staggered between the ranks of the besiegers' army, that the hardest veterans of France and Spain could not conceal their compassion. The officers of both nations vied with each other in giving succour to the captured garrison, Crillon in particular showing a generosity and gentleness well worthy of chivalrous Spain.

[margin: 1781. 1782. Feb. 1. Feb. 5]

Still, the stern fact remained that Minorca was lost; and poor Murray's misfortune was aggravated by the unseemly slanders of Draper and the vexatious litigation of malignant merchants. But Crillon was now to try his fortune against a more redoubtable fortress than Fort St. Philip. Our last sight of Gibraltar was on

1781.
April.

the 12th of April 1781, just after its relief by Admiral Darby and the opening of the bombardment by the Spaniards. From that day forward, as has been told, the bombardment continued without intermission for thirteen months; and it is said that in the first six weeks alone fifty-six thousand shot and twenty thousand shell were thrown against the fortress. The loss of life among the garrison was, however, comparatively slight, though the town was utterly destroyed. Curiously enough, the ruin of the houses brought about the most serious danger that menaced the safety of the fortress during the siege, for the fall of the buildings revealed large stores of wine and provisions which had been accumulated by the merchants. The hungry troops at once fell upon the booty, and for seven days they gave themselves up to an orgie among the wine-casks, and became absolutely unmanageable. By merciless use of the cat and of the gallows Eliott restored discipline and order; and the garrison returned to patient endurance of the bombardment. But Eliott was by no means content with patient endurance alone. He constructed new batteries to harass the Spanish camp, and finding that his guns, from their inferiority in numbers, could not arrest the progress of the enemy's works, he determined to destroy them by a sortie.

Nov. 27.

Accordingly, before daylight of the 27th of November some twenty-two hundred men in two columns stole across the six furlongs of ground between the Rock and the Spanish lines, drove out the Spanish guard, set fire to the elaborately constructed batteries in advance, which had taken fourteen months to build, spiked twenty-eight guns and mortars, blew up the magazines, and retired quietly, with the loss of no more than thirty killed and wounded. The feat was a brilliant one, though, as Eliott had rightly judged, it was attended by little real risk, for the Spaniards had based the whole of their plans and designed the whole of their

[1] The men were of the 12th, 39th, 56th, 58th, 2/71st, Manchester Volunteers (72nd), and Hardenberg's Hanoverian Regiment.

works on the assumption that they would have to do with artillery only. Thus their batteries, though internally of great height, were provided with no banquettes for the fire of musketry; there were neither guards nor picquets for protection against surprise; and the whole of the guns were pointed at great elevation against the Rock, so that the shot flew far over the heads of troops on the plain. For four days the batteries, carefully constructed of timber, continued to burn until they were burned out, when the Spaniards patiently began to build them again, while Eliott returned to the endless task of strengthening his own defences. Thus the year 1781 wore itself out at Gibraltar, the British losses during nine months of incessant bombardment numbering no more than five hundred and sixty-eight men, of whom not above a third were killed or permanently disabled. Scurvy, however, was alarmingly prevalent in December, abating only on the arrival of a cargo of lemons from Algiers. Two hundred and sixty men had died of sickness during the year, and in the spring of 1782 Eliott wrote, not for the first time, that the numbers of his garrison were insufficient.

After the fall of Minorca there was new activity on the part of the Spaniards and great preparations at Cadiz, to which the only counterpoise in Gibraltar was the arrival of a single battalion [1] in a very sickly state, and of a dozen gunboats, which were brought out in sections and rapidly put together by Captain Roger Curtis of the Royal Navy. On the 4th of May, for the first time since April 1781, the Spanish batteries were silent for twenty-four hours.

On the 26th one hundred Spanish transports, evidently loaded with reinforcements, appeared in the bay, and were followed in June by sixty French ships carrying five thousand troops. The activity in the Spanish lines was redoubled, and it is said that one work alone required for construction a million and a

[1] Stanton's Regiment (97th).

1782. half of sandbags. But the chief trust of the Allies was fixed on certain floating batteries of a new description, invented by the French engineer d'Arçon. These had been constructed by dismantling large vessels, and fitting the side of them which was to be exposed to fire with a sloping roof, composed of three layers of squared timber three feet thick, separated by wet sand and backed by a bed of wet cork. These roofs were further covered with wet hides and provided with central reservoirs of water, from which ran a network of pipes to every exposed part of the vessel's side. The armament of these floating batteries varied according to their size from ten to twenty-six guns, which were mounted on one side only, with crews of from two hundred and fifty to eight hundred men ; and, as d'Arçon claimed that they were indestructible and unsinkable, a great deal was expected of them.

Eliott was not without anxiety when he heard of these preparations, but he allowed no man to share it. His methods of dealing with insubordination or despondency were peculiar and effective. In October 1779 a man of the Fifty-eighth was charged before him with saying that if the Spaniards came into Gibraltar he would join them. Eliott declared that the man must be mad, and directed that his head should be shaven, that he should be blistered, bled, put into a strait-waistcoat, committed to the provost-marshal on a diet of bread and water, and prayed for in church. So now, when a private of the Seventy-first announced that the fall of Gibraltar upon a certain day had been revealed to him in a dream, Eliott ordered him to be confined by the provost-marshal until the day came, and then to be flogged. By such quaint methods the croakers and murmurers of the garrison were silenced ; and meanwhile work upon the defences of the fortress never ceased. It was at this time that, by the suggestion of Sergeant-major Ince of the Engineers, the now celebrated batteries were hewn out of the heart of the rock, and guns were mounted in them. Every battery was also

CH. XXI   HISTORY OF THE ARMY   415

provided with grates for heating shot, while a constant 1782.
fire was maintained upon the enemy's entrenchments.
In August the arrival of the Count of Artois and the Aug.
Duke of Bourbon at Crillon's headquarters showed that
great events were at hand; and on the 8th of September,
by advice of Lieutenant-governor Boyd, the British guns
discharged redhot shot upon the besiegers' batteries.
The experiment was completely successful, a portion of
their works being speedily kindled and destroyed despite
all efforts to save them. Irritated by this unexpected Sept. 9.
result, Crillon opened fire next day from one hundred
and seventy guns, while nine line-of-battle ships and
fifteen gunboats also got under way and poured shot
upon the fortress, though with little effect. For three
days longer the bombardment was maintained, and on
the 12th the combined fleets of France and Spain sailed
into the bay and showed that the supreme moment was
nearly come. On the side of the Allies the force afloat
included forty-seven ships of the line, besides ten of
the newly invented battering-ships mounting over two
hundred guns, and smaller craft innumerable; while
the force ashore numbered close on forty thousand men
with two hundred heavy guns. Within the fortress
Eliott's garrison, including every seaman, soldier, and
marine, mustered about seven thousand men with ninety-
six guns.

At seven o'clock on the morning of the 13th the Sept. 13.
floating batteries left their moorings, and, sailing in
admirable order to their stations on the western side of
the Rock, dropped anchor about a thousand yards from
the King's Bastion. No sooner were their anchors
down than the British batteries opened fire upon them.
A quarter of an hour later the batteries of the Allies on
the isthmus likewise opened, and by ten o'clock four
hundred pieces of artillery were hard at work. It was
noon before the enemy found the range accurately;
and meanwhile the British gunners, disregarding the
fire from the isthmus, had turned every possible cannon
upon the battering-ships, with no apparent effect.

1782. Fortunately, the Allied fleets for some reason took little or no part in the action, for the British, during the first six hours, did little execution. Then at length they began to load with redhot shot, and at about two o'clock in the afternoon smoke was seen to rise first from the flagship of the floating batteries, and shortly afterwards from the vessel of the second in command. Confusion was visible on board both of them, and towards evening the enemy's fire began to slacken; but still the British gunners worked on, though so exhausted that they drank the water in which they had washed their sponges, until at eight o'clock the fire from the floating batteries was almost silenced. Then the boats of the Allied fleets began to cluster round them, and were greeted by a storm of shot from the batteries on the Rock, where the artillerymen had now been relieved by sailors. A little before midnight the wreck of a launch drifted on to the shore with twelve forlorn men, the only survivors of a crew of sixty, clinging to it; and the British had at last before them some evidence of the destructiveness of their fire.

Sept. 14. Then an hour later, at one o'clock on the morning of the 14th, the whole scene was changed. The flagship of the floating batteries suddenly leaped into flame from stem to stern, lighting the British cannoniers to their work. Shortly afterwards another was kindled, and another, and yet another, until between three and four o'clock no fewer than six were burning furiously, and the whole bay shone bright as in the day. Instantly the gunboats under Captain Curtis sallied forth and drove away the boats from the distressed vessels; but learning from prisoners that many men were still left in them, Curtis bent all his energy to the work of rescue, till the explosion of two of them warned him to withdraw. The day dawned with old Eliott still watching from the King's Bastion, where he had spent the previous day striding up and down through the hottest of the fire; and then was seen in colder light the discomfiture of the enemy. By eleven o'clock five of the floating batteries had blown up, three were burned to the water's edge, 1782. and the remaining two were in flames, one kindled by Sept. 14. the Spaniards, the other by the British seamen. By noon the action was over, and the list of casualties put into Eliott's hand showed the trifling loss of eighty-three of the garrison killed and wounded. Of the enemy it was reckoned that at least two thousand perished, while over three hundred and fifty were taken prisoners. The vaunted attack by sea had ended in absolute and disastrous failure.

Still the batteries in the isthmus continued to fire without intermission, and Eliott made every preparation to resist a further attack, though the disappearance of the enemy's small craft gave hope that it might be abandoned. But the works on the isthmus were pushed steadily forward, and the Allied fleets still maintained their stations, with the evident design of reducing Gibraltar by starvation. There was, however, news that Lord Howe's fleet was on its way to relieve the fortress; and on the 9th of October the Spanish admiral Oct. 9. made signal to his fleet to ride at single anchor, so as to be ready to go out and meet it. It was an unfortunate order, for on the morrow a gale sprang up which threw Oct. 10. the ships into great confusion and drove one large vessel under the guns of the Rock, where she was captured. On the 11th Howe's fleet came into sight with a Oct. 11. number of transports under convoy, but was driven through the straits into the Mediterranean. The Allied fleets followed, but an easterly wind enabled Howe to return, when the transports, almost without exception, anchored in safety under the Rock, while the fleet held on its course homeward. The Allied fleets pursued Howe, as well they might with forty-six ships against thirty-three, but they never caught him and they never returned. By this timely supply of reinforcements and stores the Rock could be considered safe for another year; and though the works on the isthmus were still continued, large bodies of troops could be seen marching away. For some three months longer the useless

1783. cannonade was kept up, though with steadily waning
Feb. 2. strength, until on the 2nd of February 1783 a messenger came with the news that the preliminaries of peace had been signed. On the 5th a last shot of defiance was "wantonly fired" by the garrison over the enemy's
Feb. 6. works, and on the 6th the gates of Gibraltar were opened, having been closed for three years, seven months, and twelve days.

The regiments which took part in the defence from the beginning were the Royal Artillery, the Twelfth, Thirty-ninth, Marines, Fifty-sixth, Fifty-eighth, and the Manchester Volunteers,[1] together with Reden's, La Motte's, and Hardenberg's Regiments of Hanoverians. The Twelfth and Hardenberg's had stood side by side at Minden, and again fought together in the sortie of the 27th of November. In January 1780 the Seventy-first[2] and Stanton's[3] were added to the garrison, and in October 1782, subsequently to the grand attack, the Twenty-fifth and Fifty-ninth. The casualties from beginning to end of the siege were three hundred and thirty-three of all ranks killed, one hundred and thirty-eight wounded and disabled, seven hundred and seventy-three wounded and cured. There were also five hundred and thirty-six deaths from sickness, not including those from scurvy in 1779 and 1780, which may be reckoned at one hundred more. The great names among the defenders are those of Sergeant-major Ince, who designed the batteries hewn out of the rock; Lieutenant Koehler, Eliott's aide-de-camp, who invented new carriages to enable guns to be trained at extreme angles of depression; Captain Curtis of the Royal Navy; General Green, the chief engineer; Lieutenant-governor Boyd, who planned the King's Bastion and lies buried within it; and above all, Eliott, the greatest of the Governors of Gibraltar. Eliott's had been no ordinary career. Born in 1717, he had first joined the Twenty-third Fusiliers as ensign, becoming an engineer in 1737,

---

[1] Then numbered 72nd.
[2] 2nd battalion. [3] Then the 97th.

and an artilleryman in 1739, in which same year he was gazetted cornet in the Horse Grenadier Guards. He was wounded at Dettingen and was present at Fontenoy; he then raised the Fifteenth Light Dragoons in 1759 and served with them until 1761, when he went to Havana with Albemarle's expedition. So varied an experience has fallen to the lot of few British officers; and to his peculiar training must be ascribed his intimate acquaintance with every detail connected with the defence of Gibraltar. His knowledge of human nature has already been shown by his peculiar methods of discipline, but it was rather by example than by precept that he led his garrison to endure privation and suspense with cheerfulness. He was accounted the most abstemious man of his age, never touching meat nor strong liquor, but living chiefly on vegetables, puddings, and water. When, in August 1782, the Duke of Crillon politely sent him a present of vegetables, Eliott begged that the compliment might not be repeated, as it was his rule to receive nothing for his private use which his men could not share with him. Indeed, the only act of self-indulgence recorded of him is an order for the men to parade with their hair unpowdered; the explanation being, according to the gossip of the garrison, that the Governor had bought up all the hair-powder, in default of better ingredients for his favourite puddings.

To so modest and simple a nature the complimentary visit of the Duke of Crillon at the close of the siege, and his own formal investiture in the King's Bastion with the Order of the Bath, can hardly have been congenial. Far more impressive was the parade in which he read the thanks of the House of Commons to his garrison, and begged " his faithful companions to accept his own gratitude for their cheerful submission to the greatest hardships, their matchless spirit and exertions, and their heroic contempt of every danger." We catch another glimpse of him at the trial of Warren Hastings leading the peers to Westminster Hall as Lord Heathfield, the junior baron; but it is through the noble portrait by Reynolds that we retain our familiarity with the rugged homely features, full of genial humour and dauntless resolution, and with the right hand closed firmly on the key of Gibraltar.

The authorities for the siege of Minorca are in the Record Office: *Colonial Correspondence*, Minorca, 10-15. For Gibraltar see *Colonial Correspondence*, Gibraltar, 22-29; Drinkwater's *History of the Siege;* and in particular the section devoted to Heathfield by Lieutenant-colonel Adye, R.A., in the volume *From Cromwell to Wellington* (1899). There exists a further short journal of the siege, in print, of little value.

CHAPTER XXII

So far the narrative of the great struggle which grew 1775. out of the War of American Independence has not travelled outside the sphere of Europe and the North Atlantic Ocean : it remains now to follow it to the East Indies, where the French, finding England hard beset, made an attempt to recover from her the empire of the East. First, the reader must be reminded of the state wherein we left India in 1775. It will be remembered that each of the three Presidencies had committed itself by culpable blundering to a dangerous policy. Madras had made an enemy of Hyder Ali by refusing to observe the obligations to which it was bound to him by treaty, and had offended the Mahrattas by aiding the Nabob Mohammed Ali to take Tanjore. Bengal, by lending itself to the destruction of the Rohillas, had deprived itself of auxiliaries which might have been of great value against the Mahrattas. Bombay, by grasping at Salsette and Bassein, had involved itself in the intestine disputes of the same dangerous people ; and though it had met with greater success than it deserved in espousing the cause of Ragobah, it had seen the whole of its work undone by the cancelling of the treaty concluded by Colonel Keating, and by the substitution of a foolish, unstable, and impossible agreement, adverse to Ragobah, in its place. Thus, everywhere, the Presidential Governments had made enemies without securing a single friend.

To these difficulties an additional complication had been added at the end of 1774 by the passing of a new

1775. Act to regulate the government of India, whereby the Governor and Council of Bengal were entrusted with supreme power, and Madras and Bombay subjected to their control. In itself the measure was a wise one, and the appointment of Warren Hastings as the first Governor-General was the best that could have been made ; but the directors in Leadenhall Street, pursuant to their usual crooked policy, undid their good work by sending out three new councillors from England for the express purpose of thwarting Hastings. Of these three one only possessed some measure of ability, namely, Philip Francis, for whom, as also for the ephemeral scurrilities ascribed to him, the mystery of the letters of Junius has created a spurious fame. Yet this triumvirate at once took the government out of Hastings's hands, arraigned his conduct of the Rohilla War, and upset the whole administration of Bengal. It was they who, by their ill-timed interference with Bombay, overthrew the treaty with Ragobah and reversed the whole policy of the Government respecting the Mahrattas. It is no part of this history to trace the course of the dispute nor to tell the story of Hastings's ultimate triumph. Let it suffice that the contest continued with ever-increasing bitterness until Francis, the last survivor of the three mischievous councillors, finally took his departure for England in 1779.

But ill though matters stood at headquarters in Bengal, they were, if possible, worse in Madras. Disapproving the delivery of Tanjore to Mohammed Ali, the directors recalled the Governor who was responsible for that proceeding, and substituted Lord Pigot, who as Mr. Pigot had been Governor during the campaign of Coote and Lally, with instructions to reinstate the 1776. deposed Rajah in Tanjore. This order was duly April. enforced by Pigot, notwithstanding the vehement protests of Mohammed Ali, the Nabob averring in the last resort that without Tanjore he would be unable to meet the demands of his English creditors. To prove his case, a demand of a quarter of a million sterling was

formulated against him by a servant of the Company, 1776.
and the Council was bribed to countenance it. Sir
Robert Fletcher, always on the side of mutiny, fought
bitterly against Pigot, and the quarrel finally ended in
the arrest of the unfortunate Governor by order of the Aug.
majority of the Council. It was not until nearly a year
later that the directors decided that Pigot should be
restored and that the whole of the rebellious councillors
should be removed ; but by that time the unlucky
Governor was dead and the mischief had been done.
It will now be sufficiently clear that just decision
and coherent action were hardly to be looked for,
during these years of anarchy, from the Presidential
Governments.

The first of the errors of the British to bear fruit
was the Treaty of Poorundur, which had been concluded
with the Mahrattas by the folly of Francis and of his
factious colleagues in Bengal. Neither party to the
agreement was satisfied with it, consequently each watched
for an opportunity to violate or to supersede it. An
occasion presented itself early in 1777, through the 1777.
arrival at Poonah of the French adventurer St. Lubin,
who had contrived to obtain authority from the French
Court to negotiate for an alliance with the Mahrattas.
He now approached Nana Furnawese, the leader of the
faction then dominant at Poonah, to obtain the cession
of the port of Choule, about thirty miles south of
Bombay, for the purpose of introducing a French force
into the country ; and he offered two thousand five
hundred French troops and abundance of military stores,
together with a promise to raise and train ten thousand
Sepoys, in return for an offensive and defensive alliance.
St. Lubin was not wholly unsuccessful ; but at the end
of the year a party in Poonah, which preferred Ragobah
under British protection to a French force in support of
Nana Furnawese, proposed to the British resident a
scheme for the restoration of Ragobah by the aid of
British troops. The Government of Bombay eagerly
encouraged the project as a reversion to its original

1777. policy; and Warren Hastings, who by this time had made himself master in the Council of Bengal, as cordially approved it, having full information as to the intrigues of the French and the probability of a war with France. By his casting vote, therefore, it was determined that Bengal should assist Bombay both with troops and with money.

The Company's brigades of Bengal being stationed near the fortresses of Oude, from which the march to Calcutta would have been long, while the voyage from Calcutta to Bombay would have been still longer, Hastings resolved that the force should proceed to its destination overland. He reckoned, it is thought, on the moral effect which would be produced by the passage of such an army, in case the coming contest with France should be fought in Hindostan and not in the Deccan.

1778. Accordingly, six battalions of native infantry and a
May. corps of cavalry were concentrated at Calpee on the Jumna, from which point they started under command of Colonel Leslie for the march to Bombay. Leslie's orders were to push forward with all possible expedition; but none the less he allowed himself to be drawn into petty hostilities with the Rajpoot chiefs in Bundelcund, and thus in five months had proceeded no farther than Mhow, little more than half of his journey. He was
Oct. 3. already under recall when he died, and was succeeded by Colonel Goddard, who at once pressed the march with such alacrity that on the 2nd of November he passed
Nov. 2. the Nerbudda at Hosingabad. Here, however, he was detained by Hastings's order to negotiate an alliance with Moodajee Bhonsla, Rajah of Berar, the second in importance of the great Mahratta States,[1] against the dominant faction at Poonah. It was Hastings's hope

[1] The five states of the Mahratta Empire were ranged in the following order of importance in 1775 :—1. The Poonah Durbar; 2. Bhonsla (Berar and part of Orissa); 3. Guicowar (Guzerat); 4. Holkar (Mabao); 5. Scindia (Ugeir).—*Appendix to Fifth Report of the Secret Committee.* I have written the names as they are printed in the report, but I take Mabao to be Mhow and Ugeir to be Ujjein.

that by establishing this potentate as chief of all the Mahrattas, security might be obtained for the Company's possessions against any attacks of France.

1778.

This new policy of Hastings, ignoring as it did Ragobah, the favoured client of Bombay, was by no means to the taste of that Presidency, which accordingly decided to despatch its own force to accomplish its own ends, without awaiting the arrival of Goddard. So dilatory, however, were its proceedings that November was well advanced before four thousand men, one-seventh of them Europeans, could be embarked at Bombay. The command was entrusted to Colonel Egerton, "a bed-ridden commander,"[1] in which failing must be sought the one excuse for the action of the Bombay Government in appointing two field-deputies to control him. It is hardly credible that two Presidencies could have been guilty of this same form of imbecility, but such is the deplorable fact. One of these deputies, Mr. Mostyn, was, albeit a civilian, probably the ablest soldier of the three; the other was John Carnac, whom we have already known as an incompetent officer in Bengal; but since Mostyn almost immediately fell sick, Carnac, who as president enjoyed a casting vote, was virtually in command of the army.

Nov. 22.

Disembarking at Panwelly, a few miles to eastward of Bombay, the whole force, together with Ragobah and a few straggling horsemen, ascended the Ghauts. On reaching the summit Egerton divided his army into two brigades and an advanced guard, which three divisions moved forward in succession at the rate of about six furlongs daily, each taking up the post quitted by its predecessor. This very original method of warfare Egerton declared to have been forced upon him by want of provisions and of transport; but it was not very successful, since it encouraged the Mahrattas to harass the columns with an incessant fire of rockets, musketry, and cannon. The enemy was none the less on every occasion attacked and driven back, for there.

[1] Wilks.

1779. was no lack of good officers with the troops, though two of the best of them were unfortunately killed in the first fortnight. Meanwhile the Mahratta leaders, Madajee Scindia, Tookajee Holkar, and another, at their leisure collected fifty thousand men at Tullygaom, within eighteen miles of Poonah, from which position,
Jan. 9. however, they retired before the advance of the British, making only a show of resistance. Three days earlier Egerton had relinquished his command to Lieutenant-colonel Cockburn; but he still retained his seat on the council of management, and now, when within a day's march of his objective, he fell suddenly into despondency. In vain Cockburn protested that he could carry the army to Poonah, though he would not undertake to protect the baggage; Egerton would hear of nothing but retirement. Accordingly, after destroying a quantity of stores and sinking the heavy guns in a tank, the army, now reduced to twenty-six hundred men, entered upon its retreat.
Jan. 11. The movement was begun at night in the hope of gaining at least one march on the Mahrattas, but
Jan. 12. within three hours the advanced guard was fired upon, and a large portion of the baggage was captured. Then followed attacks on the rear; and when daylight came the army found itself completely surrounded. Fierce onslaughts upon the rear continued in rapid succession, but were most gallantly repelled by Captain Hartley with six companies of Sepoy grenadiers; and notwithstanding attacks and menaces along the whole length of the column, the army maintained its order in the retreat until three o'clock in the afternoon, when, on its approaching the village of Worgaom, the followers made a rush for the shelter of the houses. The whole line of march was thus thrown into confusion, and the enemy took advantage of the disorder to charge, inflicting heavy loss. Nevertheless, order was again restored, the village was placed in a state of defence, and the enemy was
Jan. 13. driven back. On the next morning the attack of the Mahrattas was renewed and again repulsed; but the

losses of the previous day amounted to three hundred and 1779.
fifty killed, wounded, and missing, and there was too
much reason to fear that many of the missing were
deserters. Further retreat was then deemed impracticable, though Hartley showed that it might be
safely effected; and finally a treaty was concluded with
Madajee Scindia, whereby the British restored to the
Mahrattas everything that had been theirs in 1773, and
bound themselves on the spot to send orders to the
Bengal army to retire. They were then permitted to
return in shame and humiliation to Bombay.

Such was the Convention of Worgaom, as this disgraceful agreement was termed, the blame for which
rests with the Government of Bombay, first, for endeavouring, with the true provincial spirit of Englishmen,
to show what Bombay could do without Bengal, and
secondly, for choosing such miserable instruments for
their purpose. Carnac, Egerton, and Cockburn were all
of them dismissed shortly afterwards from the Company's
service, although Cockburn had an honourable record
of good service to his credit. Further, the Bombay
Government with laudable firmness resolved not to ratify
the cessions granted under the Convention, and, pending
further orders from Bengal, made every possible effort
to recruit its forces, and to perfect its military preparations. The Bengal Government also behaved in a
manner becoming the great man at its head. Hastings,
on learning that the Bombay army had taken the field,
ordered Goddard at once to march to its assistance;
and when the news of the Convention came, he decided
to support the Bombay Government with cordiality and
without recrimination, though he declined to place
Goddard under its orders.

Goddard meanwhile, on receiving messages from
Bombay as to the situation, marched from Hosingabad
on the 26th of January, and, traversing the last three Jan. 26.
hundred miles of his journey in twenty days, reached
Surat on the 26th of February. On his arrival he was Feb. 26.
instructed to attempt to gain Futih Sing, the Guicowar

1779.
June 12.
of Baroda, over to the English side, while at the same time continuing negotiations with the chief family at Poonah; but meanwhile Ragobah contrived to escape from Scindia's custody, and his reception as a refugee in Goddard's camp practically put an end to all hope of a friendly arrangement with Poonah. Nana Furnawese, while still continuing correspondence with Goddard, lost no time in sending an envoy to engage Hyder Ali to alliance; and the ultimate issue of the negotiations, of which even then Goddard received vague intelligence, was a confederacy of Hyder Ali, Nizam Ali, and the Mahrattas for the expulsion of the British from India. The results of this formidable combination shall shortly be set forth; but it is singular, in view of later events, that at this juncture the Madras Government, as though no danger was to be apprehended from Hyder Ali, actually sent a battalion of Europeans and another of Sepoys to Goddard's assistance, in response to an application from Bengal. How ill these troops could be spared will very soon be seen, but the blame for despatching them lies with the blind and imbecile Council of Madras, and not with the Governor-General, who, with characteristic sagacity, was for dealing decisively with the Mahrattas while there was yet time.

1780.
Jan. 1.
Since Futih Sing Guicowar, after protracted negotiation, persistently evaded any definite agreement, Goddard on New Year's day 1780 moved northward from Surat upon Dubhoy, not far from Baroda, the reduction of which place effectually persuaded that chief to conclude an offensive and defensive alliance with the British. Advancing thence rapidly north-westward upon Ahmed-

Feb. 15
abad, Goddard carried that city by assault after five days' cannonade; when, hearing that Scindia and Holkar had crossed the Nerbudda and were marching upon Baroda with twenty thousand horse, he at once turned southward to meet them. Scindia then made a show of friendly overtures in the hope of wasting the campaigning season in negotiations; but Goddard was not to be deceived, and though he failed to gain any decisive

victory he held Scindia steadily at bay, and secured 1780. Guzerat, which had been acquired through the treaty with Futih Sing. A dangerous raid by the Mahrattas upon the narrow slip of land to southward of Bombay, called the Concan, on which both Bombay and Salsette depended for supplies, was repelled by the timely arrival May 24. and skilful operations of a detachment under Captain Hartley; and Goddard then retired to the Nerbudda to canton his troops during the rainy season.

Meanwhile Governor Hastings, in order to give as much annoyance to Scindia as possible, had entered into alliance with one of his most turbulent tributaries in the territory of Gohud, to southward of Agra. Goddard had already urged that a diversion should be made in this quarter, and Sir Eyre Coote, the Commander-in-chief in Bengal, had approved the project, though subject to the important condition that the force detailed for the service should be sufficient. In the face of his advice, however, three battalions of eight hundred men apiece were hastily improvised out of drafts that were waiting to join Goddard's army, placed under command of Captain William Popham, and sent away to take their chance. Fortunately, the choice of the commander was a happy one. Popham crossed the Jumna in February, promptly attacked and defeated a body of Feb. Mahrattas near Gohud, and then turned against the fort of Lahar, about fifty miles west of Calpee. Coote, knowing that Popham had no heavy guns with him, trembled with apprehension of disaster when he heard of this movement; but Popham successfully carried the fort by storm, with a loss of little more than one hundred men. Finally, Popham conceived and executed the feat whereby his name lives in Indian history, the surprise of Gwalior. This fortress, from its position on a lofty isolated rock of sandstone, from its sheer scarped sides, and from the height of its walls, was deemed impregnable. Yet on the night of the 3rd of August, Popham, Aug. 3. by skilful employment of rope-ladders, carried a score of Europeans and twelve hundred Sepoys first up sixteen

1780.
Aug. 3.

feet of scarped rock, then over forty yards of steep ascent, then over a wall thirty feet high, and so into the heart of the fortress. The garrison, surprised and dismayed by the sudden appearance of the British in their midst, surrendered without firing a shot; and Gwalior passed into Popham's hands without so much as an injury to any one of his men. There is no more memorable feat in our Indian military history for skill and daring.

Nevertheless, the operations, taken as a whole, were indecisive and unsatisfactory; and at the close of the rainy season the Bengal Government became more and more anxious to gain some solid advantage from this costly and exhausting war. Goddard was therefore instructed to besiege Bassein, while Hartley with one European battalion and four Sepoy battalions should cover the besieging army and collect the revenues of the Concan; such troops as remained being disposed to secure the safety of Guzerat.

Nov. 28. Accordingly on the 28th of November Goddard opened his trenches before Bassein, while Hartley, though enormously outnumbered, with consummate skill kept the Mahrattas from relieving the beleaguered garrison. Gradually, however, after six weeks of incessant skirmishing, Hartley was forced back inch by inch to Doogaur, nine miles east of Bassein, where he turned finally to bay, and after

Dec. 10-12. fierce fighting, which lasted over three consecutive days, repulsed the Mahrattas decisively with very heavy loss. On the 11th of December Bassein surrendered; and Goddard had just concentrated his force for further operations with high hope of success, when orders arrived from Bengal to conclude peace with the Mahrattas at the earliest possible moment, owing to urgent and pressing danger in the Carnatic. It is therefore necessary at this point to trace the course of events in Madras.

1778.

Aug. 7.

The Supreme Government at Calcutta had received intelligence early in 1778 that war with France was inevitable; wherefore, when the official news of declaration of hostilities reached India on the 7th August,

Hastings had already prepared his weapons to strike. 1778.
Sir Hector Munro at once advanced from Madras with
a considerable force upon Pondicherry, and on the 8th
was already within a league of the city. But in India, as
in America, the command of the sea was essential to
successful operations by land, and the war with France
in the East opened with a naval action fought on the
10th between the French and British squadrons, which, Aug. 2.
though indecisive, ended in the withdrawal of the French,
leaving Pondicherry at the mercy of Munro. The city,
however, made a very fine defence, and was not reduced
until the 18th of October, at a cost to the besiegers of Oct. 18.
eight hundred killed and wounded. The remainder of
the French settlements were gained more easily, with
the exception of Mahé on the Malabar coast, which was
not attacked until the beginning of the year 1779. Due
notice was given to Hyder Ali of the British designs
against the place; but Hyder was not disposed to
acquiesce easily in the capture of Mahé, which, after the
fall of Pondicherry, was his one certain source of military
supply from without, and the one direct point whereby
a French force could co-operate with him. He therefore 1779.
answered that all the European settlements on the
Malabar coast were under his protection, and that if Mahé
were attacked he would not only help to defend it, but
would further retaliate upon the province of Arcot.
True to his word, he sent troops to assist in the defence
of Mahé, where his colours flew alongside of the French
flag, and were hauled down with it on the surrender of
the place to the British. Hyder, however, did not at March.
once fulfil his threat of retaliation, but sent to Madras a
summary of his grievances against the British, which
was sufficient to cause great uneasiness to the Council.
It was resolved therefore to try the effect of negotiation;
and, accordingly, missions were sent to Seringapatam,
first in July 1779, and again in the spring of 1780, in
the hope of conciliating Hyder. Both alike failed completely. The second envoy was even denied admission
to Hyder's presence, and returned with an ominous

1780. April. message that the sovereign of Mysore no longer trusted in the sincerity and good faith of the British.

There could be no question as to the significance of such language, yet the Madras Government made no preparation for war. In the matter of European troops the Presidency was better furnished than usual, the first

Jan. battalion of the Seventy-first Highlanders having lately arrived, one thousand strong, from Europe, after taking

(1779. May.) part on its way in the bloodless capture of Goree. But though thus reinforced the Council made no effort to collect supplies, fortify posts, or organise an army for the field. Hyder, on the other hand, prosecuted his

1780. June. preparations with the greatest activity, making no secret of his designs; and at length, in June, he marched out of Bangalore, amid the prayers of all castes and creeds for his success, with the most powerful native army that had ever been seen in the south of India. His best infantry, thoroughly trained in the European fashion, numbered fifteen thousand men; another division, less carefully trained but regularly paid, counted twelve thousand men; and his whole force of all descriptions amounted to fifty-five thousand foot and twenty-eight thousand horse, which, added to rocket-men and others, made up a total of some ninety thousand native troops, besides a small corps of about four hundred Frenchmen. His commissariat was admirably organised; and, in a word, his troops were not a rabble but an army.

July 20. Descending into the plains through the Pass of Changama, he marked his advance by drawing wide circles of desolation around Madras and Vellore. Within these limits all villages were burned, all flocks and herds removed, and every human being was banished; but outside them Hyder acted rather as a guardian than as a destroyer towards the invaded territory. The Council of Madras sat paralysed with dismay. Black columns of smoke were everywhere in view before an order was issued for the movement of a single soldier.[1] Almost before the Government could realise that Hyder was

[1] Wilks, ii. 259.

moving, his headquarters were at Conjeveram, but forty- 1780.
two miles from Madras; five thousand horse, under his
son Kurreem Sahib, were at Porto Novo to the south;
and a third division, under Tippoo Sahib, was pushing
northward with all haste to the Pennar. The significance of these movements was plain enough. The
British forces were dispersed in all directions. Colonel
Baillie, with twenty-eight hundred men, was at Guntoor
on the Kistnah, and it was evidently against him that
Tippoo's corps was directed. Colonel Brathwaite was
at Pondicherry with fifteen hundred men, with Hyder
waiting to plunge into his flank if he should attempt to
march northward. Colonel Cosby, with two thousand
Sepoys, lay at Trichinopoly, well to south of Porto Novo,
and therefore under similar menace from Kurreem
Sahib's horse. Finally, the entire force at Madras itself
did not exceed five thousand men. The problem to be
solved was the concentration of these isolated parties
before they should be overwhelmed in detail.

Sir Hector Munro held the chief command in
Madras at this time. His orders were that Brathwaite should move northward from Pondicherry upon
Madras, by way of Chingleput; that Cosby should
strike from Trichinopoly against Hyder's communications; and that Baillie should move down from the
north by Tripetty, and join the main army at Conjeveram. Brathwaite at once moved up as ordered, and
on reaching Carangooly, a little to south of Chingleput,
with excellent judgment despatched Lieutenant Flint Aug. 11.
with one hundred Sepoys to occupy Wandewash. Flint
reached this important post in the nick of time; for the
native commandant, who was one of Mohammed Ali's
officers, had already agreed to surrender it to Hyder.
Having put this functionary in ward, Flint rallied the
native garrison upon his Sepoys, and on the approach
of Hyder's troops on the next day was able to oppose a
firm front to the enemy. He then set about the repair
of the fortifications, built carriages for the guns and
mounted them, manufactured powder, trained native

1780. gunners, and, with the assistance of only a single European, not only held the place in security for eighteen whole months, but made it a base of supply to the main army. So much must be said, in anticipation, of the work of this excellent officer, whose ability and resource at this critical time were of inestimable value.

The occupation of this commanding post was of unspeakable service to the detachments to southward of Madras; but to northward the safety of Baillie's division seemed to be seriously compromised by Munro's orders. It so happened that, owing to the divisions in the Council of Madras, it was impossible at this time for the Governor to secure a majority without the presence of the Commander-in-chief; and hence the command of the forces in the field devolved upon Lord Macleod, the Colonel of the Seventy-first. This officer very judiciously pointed out that Madras was the proper and only safe place for the junction of Baillie's detachment, and not Conjeveram, which was an open town forty miles distant, in a country everywhere occupied by the enemy. The truth was that Conjeveram had only been chosen at the suggestion of the Nabob Mohammed Ali, that curse of British generals, and not for military reasons. How Munro, with all the experience of General Joseph Smith before him, could have deferred to the wishes of this deplorable man, is beyond comprehension; but certain it is that he played directly into the Nabob's hand. Nettled by Macleod's criticism, he procured the illegal appointment of a new member to take his place in Council, and, to show that the junction of the army could and should be effected at Conjeveram, he took personal command of the forces in the field.

Meanwhile Hyder, after leaving a detachment before Wandewash, had marched with his main body to invest
Aug. 21. Arcot, and had recalled Tippoo's corps to that place, never doubting but that Baillie would be supported by
Aug. 24. Munro. Baillie for his part had arrived safely within twenty-eight miles of Munro's army at St. Thomas's Mount, and within rather less than that distance from

Madras, so that the two forces might have been united forthwith at the capital without difficulty or danger. But for no military purpose whatever—indeed, for no object that can possibly be divined, except to prove that Hector Munro was right and Lord Macleod wrong— the Commander-in-chief on the 26th of August marched westward, and in three days reached Conjeveram. On that same day Hyder Ali broke up from before Arcot, having first detached Tippoo Sahib with five thousand foot, six thousand horse, and eighteen guns to intercept Baillie. Then Munro's troubles began. He had started with eight days' provisions only, trusting with incredible folly to Mohammed Ali's commissaries for supplies. Needless to say, no stores were forthcoming; and Munro, therefore, found himself tied for the present to Conjeveram, wherein he slowly and with great difficulty began to accumulate a small stock of victuals. On the 3rd of September Hyder appeared six miles to westward of him in overwhelming force, and proceeded to entrench his camp to a strength which forbade all prospect of a successful attack. In this position his presence was an effectual check upon any movement on the part of Munro. 1780. Aug. 29. Sept. 3.

Meanwhile Baillie, on the 25th of August, had reached the river Cortelaur, then nearly dry, but liable to be swollen at any time by rain in the mountains, and committed the grave fault of encamping on the northern bank, instead of crossing the stream while he might. That very night a flood came down, and on the 1st of September Baillie, perceiving that it would not quickly subside, proposed to the Council that he should descend to the mouth of the river, and be transported thence by water to Madras. No reply seems to have been sent to this message; but on the 3rd of September Baillie was able to cross the river, and on the 6th he arrived at Parambakum, fourteen miles to northward of Conjeveram. On that same day Tippoo attacked him, but with no great spirit. The enemy's cavalry whirled round and round the British, but would not charge home nor Aug. 25. Sept. 1. Sept. 6.

1780.
Sept. 6. even advance within range of musketry, while the British guns were more destructive than Tippoo's in the duel of artillery. After an action of three hours, Tippoo withdrew, having suffered heavily from the cannonade, and reported that without reinforcements he could do no more. Baillie, who had lost about a hundred killed and wounded, wrote likewise to Munro that he could not force his way to Conjeveram, and hoped that the Commander-in-chief would join him at Parambakum.

On that same morning Hyder, in order to second Tippoo's operations, had made a demonstration against Munro's right, whereby he forced him to change front from east to northward; but though the guns of Baillie and Tippoo could be heard, and Hyder's army was now fairly interposed between Baillie and Munro, no
Sept. 7. action took place about Conjeveram. The next day found Munro equally inactive. He must have known that Baillie was in difficulties, but he had no carriage for the heavy cannon and stores which he had deposited in the pagoda at Conjeveram; and having for some reason taken no steps to put that building into a state of defence, he conceived himself unable to leave his position. On
Sept. 8. the 8th arrived Baillie's report of the action on the 6th, when it was evident that a movement of some kind must be made in his favour; and Munro then took the very perilous course of detaching the flank companies, about a thousand of the choicest troops in his army, under command of Colonel Fletcher,[1] to reinforce Baillie. The detachment marched on the same evening; and Hyder, fully informed by his spies of Munro's action, trusted to the guides, who were all of them in his pay, to lead it to destruction. Fletcher, however, being alive to his peril, changed his route in the course of the march, and, fetching a compass which led him clear
Sept. 9. of Hyder's troops, safely joined Baillie on the next day. By this reinforcement Baillie's force was increased to about three thousand seven hundred men.

[1] This officer must not be confounded with Sir Robert Fletcher.

So far all was well. Fletcher had accomplished the 1780. very difficult feat of outwitting Hyder, and Hyder was correspondingly annoyed; for there was now a chance that Baillie might brush Tippoo aside, and fall upon the main army of the Sultan before it could succeed in crushing Munro. Baillie lost no time in continuing his march on the night of the 9th, and had traversed Sept. 9. about five miles, harassed though not impeded by Tippoo's irregular troops and rocket-men, when, notwithstanding the urgent remonstrances of Fletcher, he resolved to halt until daylight. His plea, that he wished to have an opportunity of looking about him, was not altogether unreasonable, for his knowledge of the ground was very imperfect; but the delay was none the less fatal. Munro, apparently still blind to the fact that co-operation with Baillie was never more imperatively necessary, had remained motionless throughout the day; and Hyder, ascertaining from his spies that Munro had no intention of changing this sedentary attitude, sent away the bulk of his infantry and artillery in the evening to reinforce Tippoo. He himself waited for a few hours longer, but at four o'clock in the morn- Sept. 10. ing, finding that Munro's torpor was still unbroken, he too galloped off to take personal command of the attack on Baillie. The plan of action had already been concerted by messenger with Tippoo and with the French officers who served under him. Two miles from Baillie's bivouac the road by which he must advance debouched, with a sudden turn from west to south, from an avenue of trees into an open plain, with a village about twelve hundred yards ahead. This village was to be occupied by infantry to check the British in front, while batteries on each flank should sweep the road across the plain.

At daylight Baillie resumed his march; but when about half of his army had wheeled out of the avenue into the plain, it was met by a cannonade from Tippoo's guns on its left flank. For a time the British tramped on without returning a shot, until Baillie, finding the fire unbearable, halted and engaged the enemy's batteries

1780.
Sept. 10.
with his own guns. In a short time the superiority of the British gunners told with decisive effect, and Baillie ordered ten companies of Sepoys forward to storm the enemy's cannon. The Sepoys advanced with great steadiness, and Tippoo's artillerymen, without waiting to receive the attack, abandoned their guns and fled. Meanwhile a huge mass of several thousand cavalry, which had been concealed behind a wood on Baillie's right, now came down suddenly upon his right flank, but was met at forty yards' range with a fire of grape and musketry which mowed them down by scores. Too densely packed together to retire, these horsemen now galloped along the whole length of the British front, galled at every yard by the same destructive fire, until on reaching the extreme left flank they whirled round upon the rearguard, which consisted of a single battalion of Sepoys with four guns. So formidable was this last attack that, if the officer in command had not at once seized a strong position, the rearguard would have been overwhelmed; but he was now able to hold his own until a reinforcement of three companies enabled him to beat his assailants back. But, still unsubdued, Tippoo's horsemen now made a feint movement, as if to cut off the Sepoys who had advanced to the guns from the main body; and unfortunately those isolated companies, on hearing the cry of "Horse," doubled back, without spiking their captured cannon, in precipitate and disorderly retreat. In an instant the cavalry came down upon them and cut the greater part of them to pieces.[1] The enemy now returned to their deserted guns and resumed their cannonade, while Tippoo's infantry, drawing nearer, opened an irregular but galling fire, and the cavalry renewed its attack upon Baillie's right. Baillie therefore withdrew his infantry behind the bank of a watercourse, leaving his artillery to carry on their duel, which they did with such effect as to drive the

[1] This is the account given by both John and James Lindsay. *Lives of the Lindsays*, vol. iii. Wilks says that the losses of these Sepoys were slight.

enemy again from their guns; but the cavalry hovering on their flanks forbade the British to capture them for the second time.

1780.
Sept. 10.

There was now a lull in the action for about an hour, Baillie waiting in the assurance that Munro would soon come to his support. In due time a cloud of dust rose in his front, drums were heard beating the Grenadiers' March, and scarlet columns were seen moving out of the village. A great shout of joy burst from every man of Baillie's force. For a few minutes they thought that they were saved; and then the joy was turned to dismay when the new troops were seen to be not Munro's, but Hyder's. In a short time the plain was full of men, who spread out wide and then closed in until they surrounded Baillie's force completely, while fifty or sixty pieces of artillery swept the little band with a cross-fire from every direction. Yet both British and Sepoys, formed in hollow square, stood firm, and repulsed attack after attack, driving back Hyder's cavalry with a carnage that shook the nerves even of his best troops. But their own losses also were terrible. The British gunners were killed or wounded almost to a man, two British tumbrils were blown up, and Hyder's guns, no longer awed by an answering fire, crept up closer and closer, until, as it was said, the shot flew over their enemy into the ranks of their own comrades. At length the Sepoys, who like the rest of Baillie's troops were lying down in their ranks, became unsteady. A company of Europeans having been ordered to rise, in order to reinforce the rear face of the square, the whole of the Sepoys rose with them and crowded likewise in terror towards the rear. One of Hyder's officers, who had been disgraced for permitting Fletcher's column to join Baillie, now galloped into the disordered ranks at the head of a thousand horse, with all the vehemence of a desperate man; and the Sepoys, utterly demoralised, flung down their arms, tore off their uniforms, and fled in all directions. Yet the few hundred Europeans that remained still stood firm; and the enemy, for all their

1780. success, recoiled at the sight of their unbroken front.
Sept. 10. Baillie, however, seeing further resistance to be hopeless, now raised his handkerchief on the point of his sword, and asked quarter for the remnant of his army; whereupon one of the principal chiefs advanced and swore upon his sword that, if they laid down their arms, their lives should be spared. Baillie then gave the word to ground arms; but no sooner was the order obeyed than Hyder's squadrons, maddened by their losses, dashed forward to the work of massacre. Instantly the British snatched up their arms again, and the deadly fire which they had maintained all day rolled out once more with equal destruction. But the odds were now too great for them; and few of the devoted group were left standing when Hyder, deferring to the entreaties of his French officers, commanded that the slaughter should cease. Even then there remained the rearguard, which, too far isolated to know what had happened to the main body, and being moreover very strongly posted, made a desperate resistance, which was only overcome by the enemy at a frightful sacrifice of life. Of eighty-six European officers, thirty-six were killed or died of wounds, thirty-four were taken wounded, and only sixteen taken unhurt. The loss of men was in the same proportion, and but two hundred Europeans, most of them wounded, fell into the enemy's hands alive.[1] The whole of these survivors were carried off to Seringapatam, to be maltreated with the cruelty which is peculiar to the Oriental despot. There for the present we must leave them, only remarking that among the prisoners, desperately wounded, was Captain David Baird of the Seventy-first Highlanders.

It may be asked what Munro was doing throughout

[1] The troops with Baillie's detachment were as follows:—*Royal Artillery*, 4 officers, 77 men; *Madras European Infantry* (102nd Foot), 9 officers, 104 men; *Fletcher's reinforcement*, flank companies of 1/71st, and grenadiers of Madras European Infantry, 301 of all ranks. *Native Infantry*, 46 European officers, 3312 men. *Total*, 3853.

this terrible day. At daylight, on the first sound of the firing, he marched out four miles towards it; he then changed direction towards a cloud of smoke on his left; he next turned back again for ten miles to his right; and finally, on meeting fugitive Sepoys from Baillie's army, he retreated to Conjeveram. It is said that he was misled by his guides; it seems more probable that he was paralysed by the sense of his own folly and perversity; but in either case the result was the same. He had clung to Conjeveram for the sake of his stores; but after all he had but one day's supply of grain remaining. He therefore threw his heavy guns, with all other articles that were too cumbrous for removal, into the great tank at the station, and at three o'clock next morning retreated to Chingleput, where Mohammed Ali had promised to accumulate stores. Hyder's cavalry harassed him sharply during the march, and Chingleput was only reached with the loss of five hundred men killed and wounded, and the sacrifice of a quantity of ammunition and baggage. On his arrival Munro found, as might have been expected, that no stores were forthcoming; but he was cheered by the junction of the troops from Trichinopoly under Colonel Cosby, who, finding it impossible to act against Hyder's communications, had made a gallant but unsuccessful attempt to recover Chittapett, and had then turned north-east to rejoin his chief. After one day's halt Munro pursued his retreat, and on the 15th arrived safely at Marmalong, about four miles south of Madras, thus closing a disastrous campaign of twenty-one days.

The blunders had been great and flagrant, and, from a military point of view, Munro must be held solely responsible for one of the greatest calamities that has ever befallen the British arms. A degree of blame attaches to him which cannot be fastened on Burgoyne nor on Braddock, nor on Abercromby, nor even on Cornwallis. It is ill to select the wrong way with deliberation; it is worse to pursue it with infirmity of purpose; and Munro was guilty of both of these faults.

1780. The contentiousness, the corruption, even (as some suggest[1]) the treachery of the Council of Madras must doubtless be held ultimately accountable for the dispersion of the troops at the opening of the campaign, for the want of transport and supplies which crippled their movements, and for all the innumerable difficulties which hampered Munro, as they had formerly hampered Joseph Smith. But it is the function of British officers to rise superior to the blindness, vacillation, and delay which too frequently distinguish their civilian employers. For some of them the task is from its nature impossible, for others it is too hard; but neither plea can avail Munro. He had eyes to see, but would not perceive; he had ears to hear, but would not understand; and thus it was that the victor of Buxar, a good and gallant soldier, went near by sheer perversity to accomplish the ruin of British power in India.

[1] Innes Munro's *Narrative*, p. 134.

CHAPTER XXIII

THE news of Baillie's disaster was despatched by a special ship to Calcutta, where, as has been told, one of its first results was an order to Goddard to make peace, if possible, with the Mahrattas. The instructions to that General, however, bade him to cease hostilities only if the ruling powers at Poonah, to whom Governor Hastings had already made overtures, should take the initiative ; and it was hardly likely that Hyder Ali's late victory would encourage a pacific disposition on the part of the Mahrattas. Goddard, therefore, thought that a menace to Poonah itself would be a more effectual method of bringing the enemy to reason than the mere reduction of hill-fortresses. Waiting, therefore, only to reduce the island of Arnaul, in order to ensure the security of Salsette, he advanced towards the passes with a force of six hundred and forty Europeans and fifty-five hundred native troops. The Mahratta General at once fell back on Poonah, leaving a guard at the Bhore Ghaut, and busied himself with the collection of a formidable force at the capital, while at the same time detaching twelve thousand men to interrupt Goddard's communications with Bombay. On the 8th of February Goddard's advanced guard gallantly forced the pass of the Bhore Ghaut and pushed on to Khandallah, where it was presently joined by the greater part of the army, though Goddard's headquarters remained fixed at Campoly, at the foot of the hills.

At this point Goddard's menace against Poonah came to an end for want of sufficient troops ; and it

1781.
Jan. 18.

Feb.

1781. was not long before a blow was struck at his com-
March 16. munications. On the 16th of March a convoy, escorted
by two Sepoy battalions, was sharply attacked and only
with difficulty rescued ; and Goddard, perceiving that
his demonstration was a failure, accepted the opinion of
the Bombay Government that he should stand on the
defensive, and restore his Madras troops to their own
Presidency, where they were so urgently needed. But
retreat to Bombay was no such easy matter. Early in
April 1-3. April another convoy was attacked by a force of twenty-
five thousand Mahratta horse, and, though provided
with an escort, relatively speaking, of considerable
strength, was only brought into Goddard's camp by
remarkable skill and gallantry, and at a cost of over
one hundred men. A fortnight later Goddard began
his retreat, opposed and harassed incessantly by three
distinct bodies of the enemy, reckoned jointly at sixty
thousand men, and after much heavy fighting reached
April 23. Panwelly on the 23rd, having lost nearly five hundred
men in the four days' march. It is hardly surprising
that the Mahrattas should have counted this retreat of
the British as a signal success to themselves; for the
advance of Goddard into the Ghauts, his one false
stroke among so many that fell true, was in the circumstances almost disastrous.

More successful was a diversion in Malwa, on the
model of Captain Popham's, which was entrusted to
Feb. 16. Colonel Camac. This officer invaded Malwa in February,
and within a fortnight had penetrated to Seronje, fifty
leagues south of Gwalior, where he was surrounded by
the whole army of Madajee Scindia, which had marched
up to meet him from the westward. For seven successive days Camac endured the cannonade of his camp,
March 7. until at length he determined to retreat at all hazards,
and with great skill contrived to make his way to the
neighbouring town of Mahautpore, where he could
March 9. obtain supplies. There he turned to bay, while Scindia
encamped within six miles of him, ready to fall upon
him on the slightest movement. For a fortnight Camac

allowed this situation to continue, until he had lulled 1781.
Scindia into false security, when he suddenly attacked
him, killed great numbers of his men, and captured
thirteen guns. This success not only extricated the
British force from a very dangerous position, but produced a good moral effect. A few days later Colonel
Muir joined Camac with a considerable reinforcement ;
but his numbers even then were too weak to accomplish
anything decisive, and he failed in the object of stirring
up the lesser tributaries of the Mahrattas to insurrection.
Scindia, however, had made overtures for peace after his
defeat by Camac, which, being accepted by Muir, led to
the conclusion of a definite treaty in October 1781. Oct.
Meanwhile other negotiations, furthered by heavy
bribes, had enabled Hastings to detach the Eastern
Mahrattas of Berar from the confederacy against the
British ; and the despatch of a mission to Poonah in
January 1782 finally issued in a general peace with the
Mahrattas at Salbye on the 17th of May 1782. The 1782.
sacrifices made by the British were heavy, for the whole May 17.
of the territory acquired since the treaty of Poorundur
was restored, and the cause of Ragobah was finally
abandoned. Nevertheless, in the circumstances there
was no help for it, since it was vital for the Governor-
General to free his hands for the principal contest
against Hyder Ali and the French in the Carnatic.

For convenience of arrangement I have traced the 1780.
course of the Mahratta War by anticipation to its close,
in order to follow that of the struggle in the south
without interruption. The slight sketch given above
will, I hope, help the reader in some measure to estimate
the load of work and anxiety that pressed upon Hastings
from the west and the north, while he was staggering
under the terrible burden of troubles, now to be narrated, in the Carnatic. His task was indeed gigantic.
There was a formidable confederacy to be broken, a
more formidable enemy, flushed by success, to be met
and defeated in the field. The subordinate Government which was most nearly concerned was honey-

1780. combed by faction, imbecility, and corruption; the central administration was weakened and disorganised by past cabals in the Council of Calcutta, and the treasury was depleted by long war.

With the instinct of a true statesman he resolved to concentrate the whole of his strength against the most dangerous of his enemies, Hyder Ali. On the first news of Baillie's defeat, Sir Eyre Coote was called upon to take personal command of the troops in the Carnatic. Moreover, that there might be no such obstruction offered to him as had hampered Joseph Smith and Munro, the factious and incompetent Mr. Whitehill was suspended from his office of Governor of Madras, and the exclusive control of the treasury, as well as of the military operations, was committed to the Commander-in-chief. Armed with these powers, Sir Eyre Coote sailed for Madras, accompanied by such European soldiers as could be spared. These amounted to no more than two companies of artillery and a weak battalion of the Hundred-and-First; but a further reinforcement of six battalions of Sepoys, with sixteen guns, was also under orders to march down later, and to join him by the road along the coast. Simultaneously Nizam Ali was detached by wise concessions from the hostile confederacy, so that Coote should be relieved of any apprehension of danger from that quarter.

Nov. 5. Sir Eyre arrived at Madras on the 5th of November, when the rainy season afforded him a sufficient excuse for not moving the troops from their cantonments; but in truth they were bound to inactivity as much by want of equipment as by the weather. So lamentable were the defects in every department that Coote could not hope to move for two whole months, and even then with the army in no condition really to take the field. Fortunately Hyder had failed to improve his victory of the 10th of September by an immediate march on Madras, but had returned to the siege of
Nov. 3. Arcot. Having reduced the town to capitulation, he turned next to the simultaneous investment of the

British posts at Amboor, Vellore, Permacol, Chingle- 1781. put, and Wandewash, of which the last named, thanks to the gallantry and resource of Lieutenant Flint, still bade him defiance. Amboor surrendered on the 13th of January; and four days later Coote marched south- Jan. 17. ward with seven thousand four hundred men[1] and fifty-two guns. He was still very imperfectly provided with transport, owing to the capture of all draught-cattle by Hyder's ubiquitous cavalry, and he therefore relied for his supplies chiefly on a flotilla of small vessels, which followed his movements along the coast. In other words, he depended for his subsistence on the command of the sea, though the British squadron was at the time at Bombay. Coote's design was to relieve the beleaguered garrisons, and to draw Hyder Ali after him by advancing on Pondicherry, which, after the withdrawal of Brathwaite, had revolted in the Sultan's favour. Chingleput was relieved on the 19th; and on the morning of the 21st, Carangooly, which had been garrisoned by Hyder Ali, was taken by storm. Turning westward from thence, Coote marched on Wandewash, where he arrived on the 24th and found Flint not only safe but triumphant. The enemy had attempted five days before to introduce three thousand men disguised as Sepoys into the place, but had been driven back with heavy loss; and on the 22nd, the anniversary of Coote's great Jan. 22. victory in 1760, they had raised the siege.

Hyder, on learning of Coote's movements, abandoned the sieges which he had undertaken, concentrated his troops, and marched after him. But now there appeared before Madras the most formidable of all Jan. 25. enemies to Coote, namely, a French fleet, with French troops on board, under command of Count d'Orvés. Hyder instantly conceived the design of severing Coote's communications with Madras and with all the

[1] *European troops*—1/71st, 600; 101st, 350; 102nd, 250; artillery, 400. *Total Europeans*—1600. Ten battalions of Sepoys, 5000. Four regiments of native cavalry, 800. *Total, Europeans and Natives*—7400.

1781. grain-producing country by land, while the French fleet should intercept his supplies by sea, and thus of starving him into surrender. Coote, who had heard
Jan. 28. of the arrival of the fleet when about to move from Wandewash to Permacol, at once turned back towards Madras; but, being misled by false intelligence, he resumed his march to Pondicherry, in order to destroy the surf-boats and such military stores as might be of service to the French. This decision was very nearly fatal to him. Hyder, on the intelligence of Coote's first retrograde movement, had at once made a forced march on Conjeveram in order to cut him off from Madras; but he now followed him with all speed to the south, and threatened Cuddalore, which Coote was anxious either to protect or to demolish, lest it should serve as a base of operations for the troops expected
Feb. 5. from France. On reaching Pondicherry Coote found himself in a most embarrassing situation. He had been led on so far by false intelligence of provisions to be found in the town, and by good hope of reaching the fertile country about the Coleroon before Hyder. He now discovered that the reported provisions had no real existence, while Hyder was already moving parallel with him towards the south. To northward Coote could not move from want of food; to southward he could count only on three days' supply at Cuddalore, and when that was consumed it was not easy to see from whence more could be obtained. Perforce he advanced to Cuddalore, and there found that the worst had be-
Feb. 8. fallen him. Every road to southward was beset by Hyder's detachments, and not a grain of rice was to be procured. Unless the French squadron could by miracle be removed, and the sea thrown open for transport of supplies, Coote and the whole of his army were doomed men. For five days he remained in suspense, when to his unspeakable relief he saw
Feb. 13. the French squadron sail away to eastward, removed in the nick of time by the miraculous folly of its commander.

CH. XXIII   HISTORY OF THE ARMY   449

Thus by happy fortune the British army and the 1781.
British empire in India were saved; but Coote's transport had by this time been so much reduced that it was impossible for him to move. Hyder therefore occupied strongly all the posts which commanded communication with the southern province, and moved with his main army to the territory of Tanjore, to levy contributions and collect supplies. This was the country to which Coote himself had desired to transfer the theatre of war; but he was compelled to remain inactive at Cuddalore for five weary months. The whole army was dispirited and sickly, and a detachment from Goddard's force, which arrived under escort of the British fleet in May, served only to fill up the gaps which had been made by disease. Practically Coote could not move apart from the fleet, nor was there any retreat for him except on board the ships of Admiral Hughes's squadron. At length he determined to make a stroke at Chillumbrum, twenty-six miles to the south, which was one of Hyder's most important posts and depots of supplies on that side, and accordingly moved off in that direction on the 16th of June. Misled by June 16. false intelligence, he attempted to carry the fort by surprise, but was beaten back with the loss of two hundred and sixty killed and wounded, and of one gun captured. After a few days of delay, therefore, he fell back seven miles to Porto Novo, and began to concert preparations with Admiral Hughes for a regular siege of Chillumbrum. Hardly was his conference with the Admiral over, when he received information that June 24. Hyder's whole army was close at hand. That astute chief had no sooner heard of Coote's movement to the south than, by a forced march of one hundred miles in sixty hours, he had thrust his army between the British and Cuddalore, and was now busily fortifying a position three miles to northward of the British camp. Coote called a council of war, whose deliberations were not rendered the easier by the fact that no intelligence of the enemy's numbers or dispositions could be

obtained; but the situation was such that the council gave its voice unanimously for a general action.

Coote made every preparation to fight on the 30th of June; but his intention was frustrated by heavy rain, which, had it been prolonged for another day, would greatly have increased his difficulties. At five o'clock on the morning of the 1st of July he marched out of his camp, keeping his baggage, with its cumbrous train of followers, on his right, between his main body and the sea, under a guard of about one thousand men with six guns. An advance of about a mile brought him into an extensive plain crowded with the enemy's cavalry, where he at once formed the army in order of battle in two lines. The first line, commanded by Sir Hector Munro, was composed of the Seventy-first Highlanders, the Hundred-and-First and Hundred-and-Second Foot, five complete battalions of Sepoys with detached companies equal in strength to a sixth battalion, and two small bodies of native horse. These were drawn up in the usual order, the Europeans in the centre two ranks deep, the Sepoys on each flank of them three ranks deep, and the cavalry on the flanks of the Sepoys. The second line, under Brigadier James Stuart, consisted of four native battalions only, with the usual proportion of guns. The entire force in the two lines numbered in all about seven thousand five hundred men, including about five hundred native cavalry and five hundred artillerymen with forty-eight guns. In this order the army resumed its march, changing direction half-left from north to north-west, and moved on for another mile. Then the swarms of horse on the plain melted away, and revealed a semicircle of batteries and entrenchments commanding the front and left flank of Coote's line of advance. Massed in rear of it stood a vast host, which covered the plain as far as eye could reach, while large bodies of cavalry hovered about in every direction. Within thirteen hundred yards of the batteries Coote halted the army; and there for a full hour it stood motionless under the distant fire of Hyder's guns, while the General, riding forward, coolly examined every feature of the ground. Coote was fifty-five years old, and prematurely aged by hard work, sickness, and long residence in unhealthy climates; but he had not forgotten how to fight a battle.

1781.
July 1.

Careful scrutiny soon showed him the purport of Hyder's dispositions. Rather more than a mile to the north of Porto Novo, the road to Cuddalore for some three miles pursues a north-westerly course; and along a great part of those three miles Hyder's army was drawn up. Its right and centre consisted of the semicircle already described, and its right flank rested on a network of ravines and broken ground which practically forbade any attempt to turn the position from that side. An attack upon its centre, amid the ring of guns ready to sweep the British front and flanks, was out of the question. There remained the chance of turning the left of Hyder's batteries, by advancing due northward for a mile or more and then wheeling westward upon the left of his line. As a matter of fact, Hyder's arrangements seem to have been in a state of transition. It was plainly his intention to have rested his left upon the sea, and to have drawn his troops from thence in a wide arc across the road to the network of ravines on his right. One segment of that arc was complete, namely, that which ran from the ravines to the road; but on Hyder's left, although a strong redoubt was in course of construction half a mile from the sea, and required but another day to finish the work and to mount the guns, the curve was incomplete. Between this redoubt and the road, a space of about two thousand yards, ran a chain of sandhills parallel to the sea; and on these, though unentrenched, Hyder seems to have relied for the protection of his left. Coote, on the other hand, perceived at once that they would serve to conceal any movement of his own against Hyder's left flank. The one doubtful matter was whether a road practicable for guns could be found leading through this range of sandhills, when the British should make their wheel to westward; but Coote, on

1781.
July 1. seeing the half-finished redoubt, reckoned that such a road might exist, and he did not reckon in vain. At length about nine o'clock the General finished his reconnaissance, and drew out a battalion and five guns from the left of each line in order to cover his exposed flank and to form a third face in case of an attack on his rear. Then he gave the simple word, " Right turn," which brought the two lines into two parallel columns of three men abreast,[1] and the army filed off to northward, still under the distant fire of the enemy's guns.

A tramp of a mile and a-half brought both columns under cover of the sandhills; and now the second line under Stuart halted and fronted to the west, while Coote led Munro's division still farther to northward, directing Stuart to attack the heights before him as soon as his front should be clear. A few hundred yards more brought Coote to the object for which he sought, a road carefully constructed by Hyder through the sandhills for the withdrawal of his guns from the redoubt in case of defeat. The hills commanding the pass, being unoccupied, were promptly seized, and Coote's column, defiling through it, deployed in the plain beyond, with its right flank well protected by a thick hedge of screwpine. Coote had turned the enemy's entrenched position; and he now halted, waiting impatiently till Stuart should have driven the enemy from the sandhills which lay before his own front and to Munro's left rear. For until Stuart was in a position to secure Munro's left flank, farther advance was impossible.

But meanwhile Hyder on his side had not been idle. Divining the significance of Coote's manœuvres, he withdrew his artillery from his entrenchments to another chain of sandhills to his left, massed a large force of infantry below them, and moved his cavalry to the rear of the guns, so that he was able to gall Munro's column as it debouched from the pass, and to open a heavy cannonade upon it after its deployment. Simultaneously he detached a strong corps of infantry with guns to

[1] The Europeans, of course, two abreast.

force back Stuart's brigade, and then, in conjunction with a large body of cavalry, to fall upon Munro's left flank and rear. It was the execution, or rather the frustration, of these plans that led to the hardest fighting of the day. Stuart, fulfilling his orders to the letter, had delivered his attack upon the sandhills at the earliest possible moment, had carried them successfully, and had secured a good position for his guns. He now handled his men with conspicuous ability, repelling every attack of the enemy, and forcing them from every point of vantage which they attempted to seize. So hot was the struggle for the all-important ridge which covered Munro's left, that by one account a brass six-pounder was melted by the rapidity of the firing. Thus at length Stuart succeeded in establishing his division in echelon within supporting distance of Munro's, and enabled Coote to continue his advance. It was, however, but slowly that Coote could forge his way ahead in the face of a heavy cannonade; and Hyder, who, sitting cross-legged on a stool, was watching the battle from an eminence in rear of the centre, grew impatient, and ordered a general attack of his cavalry on both divisions of the British echelon. The horse of his left accordingly came down on Munro's left flank, but was shattered to fragments by the fire of Munro's musketry and of Stuart's artillery in front and flank. The horse of Hyder's right made a wider sweep round Stuart's left and fell upon his rear, but was thrown into confusion by the fire of a British schooner which had stood in close to shore to meet any such movement. Their leader was cut in two by a round shot, and the remainder, thinking that they lay under the fire of the entire British squadron, wavered and declined further attack.

It was now close on four o'clock. Munro's division was steadily making its way forward, and the Mysorean leaders urgently besought Hyder to retire. For some time he demurred, unwilling to believe that he was beaten, till a favourite servant drew the slippers on to his master's feet, and with the words, "We will beat them

1781. to-morrow; meanwhile mount your horse," helped him
July 1. into the saddle.   His whole army then retreated, the
artillery moving first, then, after a final volley, the infantry, and lastly the cavalry. Coote judged himself too weak in cavalry to pursue,[1] and bivouacked a mile to the westward of the battlefield. His losses were slight, little exceeding three hundred killed and wounded; those of the enemy were set down at not less than three thousand killed and twice that number wounded. The victory was not in the ordinary sense a great one, for Coote had no trophies to show of guns and prisoners taken nor of the enemy's army destroyed; but it was the salvation of Southern India. The odds against the British, according to the computation of sober writers, were at least ten to one, for Hyder's army was reckoned at eighty thousand men, of whom at least a third were trained and disciplined, and had even a small number of European officers to lead them. The most remarkable feature of the action is the readiness with which Coote, after an hour's survey, improvised his plan of attack. It is generally said that the battle was won by the turning of Hyder's left flank; but this, though in a sense true, makes an extremely misleading description. By manœuvring to threaten Hyder's left, Coote did indeed force him to forgo all the advantages of an entrenched position and to meet him in the open field; but Hyder had formed a new front and brought his artillery into a new position before Munro's division could deploy for attack, and in the actual combat it was rather Stuart's left and rear than Hyder's that were in danger. The manœuvres preceding the action were akin in principle to those whereby Lally was forced into the open field at Wandewash; but the adoption of the echelon as the best formation for attack against overwhelming numbers meets us here for the first time in Coote's campaigns.

[1] Innes Munro (*Narrative*, pp. 230, 231) criticises this caution in Coote as excessive; but he shows his prejudice in favour of his brother Scot, Sir Hector, so plainly that I hesitate to accept his adverse judgment of Coote.

Next to the general design of Coote's manœuvres, the handling of the British artillery is noteworthy, for the disposition of Stuart's guns enabled him at once to extend his weak brigade over an astonishingly wide front and effectively to protect Coote's left flank. The small proportion of British losses is doubtless attributable to the fact that the action was fought for the most part at long range, and that the British were disposed in line; while the slaughter in Hyder's army is ascribable to the destructive effect of the British artillery on the dense masses of the Mysoreans. It is also a fine tribute to the perfect drill and discipline of the men and to the nerve of their officers that, throughout the whole of the complicated movements during the seven hours of the engagement, they gave not a single opening to the swarms of cavalry that hovered about on the watch for the slightest sign of confusion. In short, it was a battle in which every man on the British side did well, for, as Coote wrote, "every individual of the army seemed to feel the critical situation of our national concerns."

1781. July 1.

After the action, Coote moved slowly northward to succour Wandewash, now under renewed siege by Tippoo Sahib, though never endangered, thanks to the indefatigable energy of Flint. Having relieved the post for the third time in his life, Coote marched to Pulicat, on the coast about twenty-five miles north of Madras, where he picked up a reinforcement of ten Sepoy battalions and two companies of artillery under Colonel Pearse, which had been sent down by Governor Hastings from Bengal. It is significant that Hyder should have made no effort to prevent this junction of troops; but unfortunately the gain of numerical strength to Coote was almost neutralised by his deficiency in supplies and transport. In spite of great reports of cattle collected at Madras during his absence, he found that he had not carriage for more than thirty-six hours' rations of rice for his army, a defect which crippled his movements and circumscribed his operations to a degree which he described as heart-breaking. He therefore

July 18.

1781.
Aug. 20.
turned his attention to the recovery of Tripassore, about thirty miles west of Madras, and took it after three days' cannonade, just as the advanced guard of Hyder Ali's army came into sight. Little grain, unfortunately, was found in the place, and three days were occupied in collecting rice before Coote could march northward to meet Hyder on his chosen ground at Pollilore. For the superstitious Mohammedan had now moved to the fortunate encampment from which he had defeated Baillie, and his astrologers had predicted for him certain victory.

Aug. 26.
Aug. 27.
A day's march brought Coote to Parambakum; and on the morrow, upon reaching the spot where Baillie had made his fatal halt on the day before his disaster, the advanced guard sighted Hyder's army in their front to westward, and extending also towards both flanks. Clouds of dust raised by a strong breeze rendered all distant objects imperceptible; but Coote had observed a thick grove on a slight eminence, with a watercourse encompassing two sides of it, about six hundred yards to the left of his line of march. This he at once occupied as a point of vantage. The first line, under Munro, was then directed to form in advance of this eminence, fronting to the south, with the second line in support; but Munro's division had hardly deployed for action before it found itself under enfilading fire of artillery at long range from the westward. The fact was that Hyder Ali had, as at Porto Novo, drawn up his main body on the left flank of Coote's advance, with its left resting on Pollilore and its right on another village farther to eastward, and had sent only a detachment forward under Tippoo Sahib to check the British in front. Coote, with no means of knowing this, blinded by the dust, and conscious only of Tippoo's enfilading fire upon Munro's line, now changed its position and drew it up behind a patch of jungle, over which Tippoo's guns, at great elevation, continued to throw shot, though with little effect. After considerable delay and difficulty it was ascertained that this patch of jungle was penetrable; and

the first line, now fronting to west, advanced through it, 1781. far apart from the rest of the army, found a good position Aug. 27. for its artillery, and forced Tippoo's guns to retire.

Meanwhile Hyder concentrated a heavy fire of artillery upon the position occupied by Coote at the grove, and it became necessary to move up every battalion of the second line in succession to hold and to extend it. Once matters wore a very ugly aspect, for one battalion of Sepoys, on being led forward to dislodge a party of Hyder's sharpshooters from a ruined village, fell into confusion and came back in disgraceful flight; but the service was effectually performed by another battalion, and the mishap set right. But meanwhile the enemy pressed harder and harder against this position, and to save his left flank from being turned Coote was obliged to withdraw a brigade from his first to his second line. Fortunately, as the day wore on the wind ceased, and with a better sight of all that was going forward both Munro and Coote grasped the true situation. The first line now changed position again and fronted southward towards Hyder's main body, with its right opposite to Pollilore; and its right brigade, advancing to the village, speedily drove out the enemy and opened a fire from two light guns, which raked the whole of Hyder's line. The enemy, who had already wavered, now hastened to retreat, and Coote galloped away to his left to order a general advance; but the ground was too much broken by scrub, watercourses, and paddy-fields for any rapid and effective movement, and the combat came to an end at nightfall with little advantage to either party. Coote's casualties amounted to four hundred and twenty-three, of which the killed numbered but fifty-three, though the wounded included Brigadier Stuart, who lost his left leg below the knee from a cannon-shot. Hyder Ali's loss was set down at two thousand killed and wounded, for the British artillery punished his army severely at the beginning of his retreat. But the action generally was unsatisfactory, not to say extremely hazardous, to Coote. The two divisions of his army were absolutely severed,

1781. and the troops were dangerously disordered and disunited by jungle and broken ground.

The action over, Coote returned again to Madras and resigned his command, as a protest against the folly of keeping together an army which was incapable of movement for want of transport. He was, however, induced to withdraw his resignation, possibly because Munro at this time was disabled for further service by ill-health, and some effort was made to get stores of victuals forward by means of bearers. Thus, on the 21st of September, Coote moved out from Tripassore and captured the small fort of Poloor, but was immediately called to westward by an urgent summons to relieve the British garrison besieged in Vellore. Hyder Ali was reported to be at Sholinghur, about thirty miles due west of Tripassore, holding a strong position to bar the British advance on Vellore; and Coote, since he was unable to prosecute operations continuously for a week together, decided to try the effect of another general action, while the enemy was still within reach.

Sept. 26. He marched accordingly on the evening of the 26th of September, but was delayed by heavy rain, which prevented his feeble cattle from moving. Hyder, whose camp lay considerably in advance of his chosen position, being fully informed of all that went on at Coote's headquarters, announced to his troops that there would be no movement on the following day; whereupon the greater part of his draught-cattle, with their drivers, dispersed far and wide in search of forage and provisions.

Sept. 27. Hyder hardly showed his usual prudence in making this announcement, for early in the morning of the 27th Coote rode forward with a small escort, and seeing a long ridge of rocks before him, which was occupied by the enemy, sent at once for a brigade to dislodge them. The ridge was quickly cleared, and the brigade then took up a position before it, so that its rear should be safe from any attack of Hyder's cavalry. Pursuing his reconnaissance, Coote presently descried the whole of Hyder's army encamped to the southward, the nearest part of it being within three miles of him. He at once 1781. summoned the whole of his forces to him, which in time Sept. 27. appeared, duly told off as usual into two lines, but marching in a single continuous column. In this formation the army filed away to its right, until the centre of the first line was opposite to the main body of the enemy, when the whole of the troops fronted in line to the left, the hostile army being then about two miles distant. The advance was then continued slowly, the right or first line moving forward entire, while the second line broke up into echelon of battalions with the left thrown back, with the object at once of supporting the baggage-guard in rear and of watching large bodies of cavalry which were hovering about its left flank. The manœuvre was in fact similar in principle to that which Coote had employed at Porto Novo and had striven to employ at Pollilore, namely, an offensive movement against the enemy's flank with one wing, pivoted on the other wing, which was echeloned in a strong position. In the event of a counter-attack by the enemy on the first line or offensive wing, Coote's quick eye had already marked a rock and a wooded eminence for the protection of its flanks, with a rocky ridge to cover its rear. His own army being far superior in drill and discipline to Hyder's, it was everything to him to force his enemy to change position, and to take advantage of the confusion that would ensue during the movement.

Hyder's main body was judiciously drawn up behind the crest of a long ridge, with its front covered with swampy rice-fields, his guns being posted on the summit of the ridge and in suitable positions behind the rocks that studded the plain before him. He had reckoned that it was impossible for Coote to attack him on that day, and he was in a manner surprised. His first object was to gain time for the return of his scattered teams from their foraging excursion, for it was a principle with him never to risk the loss of a gun ; and accordingly, without attempting to change position, he sent out vast bodies of cavalry, more than one of them exceeding

1781.
Sept. 27.
Coote's whole force in number, to hover about Coote's flanks and to charge on the slightest sign of disorder or confusion. As things fell out, the first mistake was made on Coote's side. The Second Brigade, on the extreme right of his first line, moved too far to the right while advancing to take up its assigned position; and Hyder, observing the gap thereby made in the line, at once opened fire at long range with the whole of his artillery, doubtless hoping to throw Coote's array into confusion while halted for the correction of the error. Coote, however, knew better than to halt, and, directing the Second Brigade to incline to its left, ordered a general advance of the whole division. The fire of Hyder's guns was ill-aimed, but so numerous was the host of the enemy that Coote's little force seemed to be moving into the midst of a huge circle of armies. Yet the advance was made in perfect order, though the necessity of breaking constantly from line into columns, in order to pass the groups of rocks that strewed the plain, caused wide gaps to appear between the battalions. Into these gaps Hyder now poured the masses of his cavalry. Nothing could better have suited the British, for the impetuous horsemen, after first suffering heavily from the grape of the battalion-guns during their advance, found that on entering the gaps they were torn to pieces by a cross-fire, the defiling columns having simply faced inwards to receive them, thus forming a blazing lane of musketry. One body only had the courage to run the gauntlet of this fire from end to end, but only to find the rear of the column doubled back at right angles in perfect readiness to receive them. The whole attack was thus routed with very heavy loss, and Hyder now gave the order for his guns to retire; but the Second Brigade gained Hyder's left flank in time to cannonade them as they withdrew, and captured one gun.

Meanwhile the echeloned battalions of the second line had been exposed to a succession of furious attacks in flank and rear from a distinct corps under Tippoo Sahib. Though hard pressed for a time, they held their own gallantly, until Tippoo, finding it vain to attempt to isolate them either from the first line in front or from the baggage in rear, drew off his troops and retreated to the main army. By midnight the whole of the British force was encamped on the ground which Hyder had occupied. After facing seventy thousand men and seventy guns for the whole day with rather more than eleven thousand, Coote had lost fewer than one hundred killed and wounded, while the losses of the enemy were reckoned to exceed five thousand. The action is interesting chiefly as a further example of the discipline of Coote's Sepoys and of the General's skill in manœuvre. *1781. Sept. 27.*

The chiefs of the district now withdrew their levies from the side of Hyder; and Coote, though he had hardly sufficient supplies to carry his army back to Tripassore, ventured to move still farther from it to a district which was represented to him as unexhausted. The intelligence proved to be false; and Hyder, enraged at the defection of the local chiefs, sent a force of six thousand men to burn their villages and devastate their crops. Knowing that such ravages would be fatal to his own sources of supply, Coote hastily formed a flying column, and after an absence of thirty-six hours, during thirty-two of which he had not left the saddle, returned to camp, having surprised Hyder's detachment and driven it away with the loss of everything. But meanwhile Vellore still cried out for relief, and Coote was obliged to risk the isolated advance of about two thousand men, in order to cover a greater extent of territory and endeavour to intercept some of Hyder's convoys. Hyder, always well informed as to Coote's movements, made a sudden spring upon this detachment, which had been carelessly posted, and forced it to abandon its baggage; but his attack was none the less beaten back, after hard fighting, with an acknowledged loss of three thousand men, while the British casualties little exceeded three hundred. So much discouraged was Hyder by this reverse that he made no attempt to *Oct. Oct. 23.*

1781. check Coote when, having at last collected a store of supplies, he advanced to throw them into Vellore.

Nov. 3. False intelligence now led Coote to advance farther to the north-west, a movement which was attended by no advantage, and which led to the loss of one of his intermediate posts, with the whole of its artillery, and of a store of grain which had been accumulated there.

Nov. 22. On the 22nd of November, therefore, he retreated, just as the north-east monsoon was breaking, and arrived at Madras with his army half starved, his little corps of native cavalry utterly ruined, and his means of transport much impaired. Never had commander fought against greater difficulties amid greater discouragements than he; and yet the Nabob Mohammed Ali scrupled not to give out that he had kept the British army abundantly supplied, and that but for Coote's unnecessary delays the repulse of Hyder might long ago have been accomplished. It is cruel to think of such a soldier as Coote forced to strike blow after blow, with the full knowledge that, having no means of mobility, he could make not one of them decisive, and all through the baseness of this despicable potentate and of his corrupt instruments in the Council of Madras. Certain it is that after a campaign marked by astonishing triumphs against numbers, the army marched into cantonments with little heart or hope for the work of the next campaign.

Meanwhile there had been other operations during this year besides those of Goddard and Coote. It is unnecessary to make more than bare mention of the insurrection at Benares during the visit of Governor Hastings, which so nearly cost him his life, since the measures for suppressing it have no significance except as a slight additional drain on the military resources of the British in India. But in the region of Tanjore there was more serious work. When Hyder quitted that province in June to meet Coote, he left a force behind him which was active in mischief both there and about Trichinopoly. Moreover, at the outbreak of war

between England and Holland he had agreed to cede 1781.
to the Dutch the British district of Nagore, and to
protect for them the settlement of Negapatam, on
condition that the garrison of that place should furnish
aid to him when required. By great exertions, therefore, the British collected a force of Sepoys for operations in that quarter under the command of Colonel
Brathwaite, who, after sundry small engagements, inflicted
a severe defeat on a strongly entrenched force of twice
his strength at Mahadapatam. It was then decided to Sept. 30.
besiege Negapatam, for which service Sir Hector Munro,
who was awaiting his passage to England, was placed at
the head of four thousand men drawn from the fleet
of Admiral Hughes and from Brathwaite's army in
Tanjore. The expedition arrived off Nagore on the
21st of October, successfully attacked the garrison Oct. 21.
when in the act of evacuating the place, and then
proceeded south against Negapatam. There a chain
of five redoubts, which covered the town on the
northern side, was at once carried by storm ; and, Oct. 19.
nine days after the trenches had been opened, the
place surrendered. The success was remarkable, inas- Nov. 12.
much as the besieged numbered a force of eight
thousand men, whereas the besiegers never exceeded
four thousand ; and though the speedy downfall of
Negapatam is ascribed, no doubt with justice, to the
extraordinary gallantry of the seamen and marines of
the fleet, yet no small share of credit must belong to
Munro. The result also was valuable, not only for the
capture of large quantities of naval and military stores,
but also for the possession of the place which had been
designed as the principal depot for the troops expected
from France, and for the consequent evacuation by
Hyder Ali of the whole of his posts in that quarter.

The breaking of the north-east monsoon forbade
the re-embarkation of the naval brigade for three whole
weeks, and so delayed the further operations which
were meditated against the Dutch. At length the fleet
sailed on the 2nd of January 1782 to Ceylon with about

1782. five hundred volunteers and Sepoys, who stormed the
Jan. 5. forts of Trincomalee on the 5th, and on the 11th took
possession of the finest harbour on the eastern coast of
the East Indies.

So closed the operations of 1781; and it is worth while to think for a moment of the great array of British officers who were standing at bay against heavy odds during that terrible year—of Clinton fencing with Washington at New York; of Cornwallis, misguided indeed but undismayed, fighting his desperate action of Guildford; of Rawdon contriving to stem the tide of invasion for a few days so as to save his garrisons; of Campbell helpless and deserted in his sickly post at Pensacola; of the commanders in the West Indies set down in the midst of treacherous populations and of a deadly climate; of Murray still defiant at Minorca; of Eliott proudly disdainful of perpetual bombardment at Gibraltar; of Goddard trying desperately but in vain to fight his way to Poonah; of Popham snatching away Gwalior by surprise; of Camac plucking himself by sheer daring from the midst of Scindia's squadrons; of Flint making mortars of wood and grenades of fuller's-earth at Wandewash; of Lang indomitable among his starving Sepoys at Vellore; lastly of Coote, shaken by age and disease, and haunted at every step by the spectre of famine, marching, manœuvring, fighting unceasingly to relieve his beleaguered comrades. With such men to defend it the Empire was not yet lost.

CHAPTER XXIV

DEPRESSED though the British were on the return of Coote to Madras at the close of 1781, their despondency was probably less deep than that of Hyder. Not only had he failed of success in his repeated encounters with Coote, but he had learned of the defection of Scindia from the confederacy against the British, and of the probability that much of the Mahratta force might be turned against himself. He determined, therefore, to abandon his scheme of conquest in Coromandel. Accordingly, before the close of the year, he began to dismantle most of his minor posts, ruined the fortifications of Arcot, sent away his forces and stores to Mysore, and compelled the whole population to migrate thither with their flocks and herds. The opening weeks of 1782 brought him little encouragement. He had reduced Vellore once again to extremity, and Coote, on marching to its relief, had been struck down with apoplexy; yet the indomitable British General, though thought to be at the point of death, had shaken off the fit and continued his march within twenty-four hours, accomplishing the relief of Vellore and a safe retreat to Madras in the face of Hyder's whole army. Even worse news came to the ruler of Mysore from the Malabar coast, where since August 1780 a small garrison at Tellicherry, only once reinforced during the spring of 1781, had maintained a very skilful and resolute defence against Hyder's far more numerous besieging force. In January 1782 a second reinforcement came to the beleaguered fortress

1781.

1782.

Jan. 5.

1782. under Major Abington, who, suddenly taking the offensive, fell upon the besiegers and drove them off with the loss of sixty guns, the whole of their equipment, and twelve hundred prisoners. With this brilliant success ended the siege of Tellicherry, the defence of which, though unrecorded in detail, is mentioned always by contemporary historians as one of the most gallant and distinguished services of the whole war.

Feb. 18. Then suddenly the wheel of fortune turned, and the successes of the British were arrested by a great disaster. Colonel Brathwaite, while encamped with sixteen hundred Sepoys and about threescore of Europeans a few miles south of the Coleroon, was surprised by an army of thirteen thousand men, including Lally's European regiments, under Tippoo Sahib. Brathwaite made a gallant attempt to retreat to Negapatam, but after twenty-six hours of desperate fighting was compelled to surrender. Every British officer present, with one exception, was killed or wounded; and Brathwaite, together with such of them as survived, was sent to share the captivity of Baillie's officers at Seringapatam. At least a third of his force made good their escape, but the blow was severe, and the more regrettable since Brathwaite had been warned of Tippoo's approach, but, with the too common carelessness of British officers, had neglected to take proper precautions for his safety. This success in itself, however, would have been insufficient to raise Hyder's hopes or to alter his plan of campaign, but for the arrival, three weeks later, of that succour from France on which he had based all his projects for the expulsion of the British.

1781. To appreciate rightly the significance of the event, it is necessary to glance at the course of the naval operations in connection with India since the departure of D'Orvés from Pondicherry in February 1781. In March of that year France and England had each despatched a squadron, together with reinforcements, to India, the former being under command of Admiral Suffren, and the latter of Commodore Johnstone, with

General Medows in command of the troops.¹ The 1781.
intermediate object of both was the possession of the
Cape of Good Hope ; and Johnstone, having the start
of his rival, was lying at his ease in the neutral port of
Porto Praya in the Cape de Verd Islands, when his
squadron was suddenly attacked by Suffren, and though April 16.
not seriously damaged was distanced in the race to the
Cape. He therefore returned to England with his
frigates, and sent the remainder of his ships, together
with the transports, to Bombay, while Suffren pursued
his way to Mauritius, where he arrived towards the Oct. 25.
end of October. Sailing from thence in January 1782, 1782.
Suffren arrived off Pulicat on the 15th of February, and
fought an indecisive action against Admiral Hughes,
with odds of twelve ships to the British nine, on the Feb. 17.
17th. Hughes then sailed to Trincomalee to refit, and
shortly afterwards Suffren landed his troops, some three March 10.
thousand men of all colours, at Porto Novo.

Two days later Hughes reappeared at Madras with March 12.
his fleet repaired, and, having been joined by two more
ships from England, sailed at the beginning of April
with reinforcements for the garrison of Trincomalee.
Suffren came out to meet him, and there followed a
second bloody but indecisive action off the coast of
Ceylon, at the close of which both fleets put into April 12.
different ports of the island for repairs. Since the
movements of the British army in the Carnatic depended
entirely on the control of the sea, Coote was obliged to
await the issue of the naval engagements before he could
formulate his plan of campaign ; and meanwhile the
French, in conjunction with Hyder, who now gladly
resumed operations on the side of Coromandel, had
moved from Porto Novo against Cuddalore. The
garrison, which consisted of about six hundred troops,
almost to a man Asiatic, surrendered without the least
attempt at resistance ; but, since the greater part of the

¹ These troops were the Seventy-second Highlanders (then
78th), Seventy-third Highlanders (then 2/42nd), Fullerton's (98th),
Humberstone's (100th).

1782. Sepoys at once took service with the French, it seems probable that French gold had done its work among them, and that the commandant had no alternative but to capitulate. This was an unpleasant mishap; but it was not the worst. Coote, whose temper had become much soured through age and ill-health, had fallen seriously at variance with Lord Macartney, the Governor of Madras, over the latter's interference with general military operations while the Commander-in-chief was absent in the field. The reduction of the Dutch settlements in the winter of 1781 had, in fact, been effected by Macartney's direction without a word of consultation with Coote, who was so much incensed that he would have resigned the command to General Medows. That officer, however, firmly declined to accept the responsibility, alleging, with great good sense, that his total ignorance and inexperience of Indian warfare unfitted him for the post. Coote therefore remained in command, though with no very good grace; for, among other results of Macartney's interference, fully a half of the reinforcements brought by Medows had been left on the Malabar coast, and only the Seventy-second Highlanders had been brought to Madras, the point where troops were then most sorely needed.

Amid the inaction and suspense due to these various causes, and above all to ignorance of the issue of the naval battle of the 12th of April, there came the news
May 11. that Hyder Ali and the French had appeared suddenly before Permacol, one of the British posts about twenty-five miles north of Pondicherry. Coote at once started to relieve it; but being delayed by heavy rain which caused much sickness among his troops, he had made little
May 16. progress before he heard that Permacol had fallen, and that the enemy was advancing upon Wandewash. Hyder and his allies, however, fell back on the intelligence of Coote's approach, for the French commander had orders to fight no general action until M. de Bussy, the veteran colleague of Dupleix, should

arrive to assume supreme command; and Coote on following them up found them entrenched about fourteen miles from Pondicherry, in a position which he dared not attack. He decided, therefore, to march upon Arnee, Hyder's depot of supplies in the district, in the hope of drawing him from his entrenchments and bringing him to a general action. Hyder at once sent a detachment under Tippoo Sahib by forced marches to reinforce the garrison, and himself followed on the following day with the remainder of his army, but without the French. Thus it came about that when preparing to encamp before Arnee on the 2nd of June, Coote found himself under a cannonade at long range from Tippoo's guns in his front, and Hyder's in his rear. There followed until sunset a succession of those manœuvres in which the General excelled; and at the close of the engagement Coote found himself in possession of the trophy which Hyder always grudged, namely, a gun and several ammunition-waggons. The losses of the British in the engagement amounted to only seventy-four men, but want of cavalry prevented any effective pursuit, so that the action of Arnee produced no result beyond the heightening of Coote's reputation in the eyes of Hyder. After a few days spent in hopeless effort to overtake the retreating enemy, during which one hundred and fifty men and three small guns were lost in an ambuscade, Coote was compelled by an alarming increase of sickness among his European troops[1] to return to Madras. 1782. May 30. June 2. June 18.

Meanwhile Suffren, after sundry minor operations, had put back to Cuddalore, whither Admiral Hughes followed him; and there ensued a third naval action July 6. which, though in itself indecisive, was so far disadvantageous to Hughes that, before he had finished his repairs in Madras, Suffren was able to sail to Ceylon. There, through the opportune arrival of reinforcements,

---

[1] The 72nd Highlanders suffered terribly. The regiment was reduced from 500 to 50 men fit for duty within three weeks of its landing at Madras. *Life of Sir T. Munro,* iii. 19.

1782. the French Admiral was enabled to strike a telling blow
Aug. 25. by an attack upon Trincomalee. The British garrison, though recently reinforced by two hundred men of the Seventy-second and Seventy-third, both regiments strange to the climate and terribly sickly, can hardly have exceeded five hundred men, whereas Suffren could land against them nearly five times that number. By the impulse of his pre-eminent energy and skill the siege
Aug. 30. was pressed with such vigour that on the 30th the
Sept. 2. garrison was compelled to capitulate. Two days later the British squadron was sighted off Trincomalee, and
Sept. 3. on the 3rd of September a fourth naval action was fought with odds against the British of fourteen ships to twelve. On this occasion Hughes inflicted greater damage than he received, but he could not oust Suffren from the possession of Trincomalee, and was compelled to abandon to his opponent his base, such as it was, on the eastern coast. He then withdrew to Madras, while Suffren after repairing damages hastened back to Cuddalore, thus checking any operations that Coote might have meditated for the recovery of the post. The breaking of the monsoon shortly afterwards forced Hughes to return to Bombay, and Suffren, not finding in Trincomalee the resources necessary for the squadron, carried his ships away to Acheen.

So far, therefore, Hyder Ali had gained comparatively little from the arrival of the French on the coast, and would have gained still less but for the admirable energy and ability of Suffren. Moreover, under the skilful direction of Colonel Nixon, the small British force in Tanjore had in July and August thrice defeated his far more numerous army with heavy loss. Simultaneously, the operations of Medows's reinforcement from Bombay on the Malabar coast gave Hyder much anxiety. This force, consisting of Colonel Humberstone's newly raised regiment [1] added to the handful of native troops which had defended Tellicherry, did not exceed a thousand men; yet, moving from Calicut as his base, Humber-

[1] Then numbered 100th.

stone in April had twice defeated a force of seven 1782. thousand Mysoreans, capturing two guns and inflicting a loss in killed, wounded, and prisoners of two thousand men. Hitherto Coote had naturally disapproved of the employment of troops, which he so sorely needed himself, in desultory operations ; but he now placed Humberstone's force definitely under the orders of the Governor of Bombay, and begged that the diversion on the western coast might be pushed home with all possible vigour. Humberstone therefore again took the field in September, this time using Panianee, forty miles south of Calicut, for his base ; but he effected little, and in November was forced to retreat rapidly before an army under Tippoo Sahib and Lally, which had been sent by Hyder from Tanjore. So hardly was he pressed that he made his escape only by passing his troops across a ford which was for an ordinary man chin-deep. Marvellous to say, he accomplished this feat without the loss of a man, and marched safely into Panianee. Nov. 20.

There Colonel Macleod of the Seventy-third, as Humberstone's senior, now took over the command, and fortified his position with all haste, for it was evident that Tippoo Sahib would press his attack. The works were still unfinished when Tippoo, acting on a plan skilfully designed by Lally, made an attempt to Nov. 29. storm Macleod's works with four distinct columns, one of them headed by Lally's own corps of Frenchmen. The assault, however, was repelled at all points with little difficulty. Macleod's dispositions were excellent, and Tippoo's troops no match in quality for his own. A single company of British did not hesitate to charge with the bayonet a column of whatever weight, without calculating numbers, and the Mysoreans retired in confusion, leaving two hundred dead on the field, while Macleod's losses did not exceed ninety killed and wounded. Tippoo then fell back for a short distance to await the arrival of his heavy guns ; but on the 12th Dec. 12. of December not a man of his host was to be seen. That morning a courier had come into camp from

1782. Seringapatam, having accomplished the journey of four hundred miles in four days. He brought the news that on the 7th of December Hyder Ali had expired.

Though the corpse of the great chief had been covertly buried and the fact of his death kept as secret as possible, yet the truth was known to the Government of Madras within forty-eight hours of the event. The opportunity presented by such an occurrence, in a country where the succession to every vacant throne is disputed, was a great one, and none the less since large reinforcements [1] had recently arrived in Madras from England, together with a squadron of five ships under Admiral Bickerton. Reinforcements for the French under Bussy were shortly expected, though, owing to the vigilance of the British cruisers in the Bay of Biscay, they had not yet arrived.[2] Every consideration of policy dictated immediate action on the part of the British army, whatever its condition might be; and Lord Macartney lost no time in urging this step upon the General. But unfortunately Coote had been compelled by increasing sickness to return to Bengal, and to resign his command for the present to Brigadier-general James Stuart. This officer, though in several actions he had approved himself a brave and skilful soldier, appears to have been of difficult, arbitrary, and insubordinate temper. He had taken an active part in the arrest of Lord Pigot, and his share in that transaction may perhaps have disinclined him to pay respect to any Governor of Madras, but in any case his behaviour was to the last degree obstructive. Professing disbelief in the report of Hyder's death, he averred that the army was ready to march at any moment if required. But in truth he wasted the time which should have been devoted to military preparations in drawing up complaints against every functionary, civil,

---

[1] 23rd (Burgoyne's) Light Dragoons; Sandford's Foot (101st); detachment of Rowley's Foot (102nd); one Hanoverian battalion.

[2] The first convoy and transports for Bussy's force had been captured by Admiral Kempenfeldt in December 1781. A second convoy was captured in April 1782.

naval, or military, from the Governor-general to Admiral Hughes, whose authority in the slightest degree infringed upon his own. Stuart was not wholly without excuse, for since Coote's departure Lord Macartney had taken upon himself to plan the design of the ensuing campaign, occasionally plaguing Stuart to submit a scheme of operations, and then eagerly producing one of his own. Having none of that true military instinct which, being an endowment of the individual and not of a profession, has so frequently revealed itself in civilians, Macartney of course fell into the usual pitfalls of the amateur, dispersion of force, neglect of such factors as lines of communication, and reliance on disloyal subjects of the enemy. Over and above these failings, he made overtures of peace to Tippoo, approaching him with the sword in one hand and the olive-branch in the other, which is the most fatal of all attitudes towards an Oriental enemy. 1782.

The result of all this friction was that Tippoo had been quietly proclaimed and his rule accepted for a full fortnight before Stuart made his first march to Tripassore in order to form a magazine for the coming campaign. From that day the General made no important movement until the 4th of February, when he marched slowly southward, and on the 13th offered battle unsuccessfully to the united forces of Tippoo and the French near Wandewash. Shortly afterwards Tippoo, hearing of further active operations, which shall presently be narrated, of the British on the Malabar coast, rased the whole of his strong places in the Carnatic except Arnee, and, leaving a division of his troops to co-operate with the French, returned to his own dominions. Stuart then devoted his time to the demolition of the fortifications of Carangooly and Wandewash, a detail of Macartney's plan which he adopted, perhaps, the more readily, since he knew it to be disapproved by Coote. Inasmuch as the diversion on the west coast had been made for the express purpose of drawing Tippoo thither from Coromandel, his retreat might well have been foreseen; 1783. Jan. 15. Feb. 13. March 1.

1782. but Stuart, always obstinate and incredulous, persisted in dismantling these posts, and then too late deplored the loss of such valuable centres of influence and of supply. In March he moved northward to throw provisions into Vellore, and then awaited the return of the British squadron from Bombay, which was essential to his first great object, namely, the recovery of Cuddalore.

Hughes did not make his appearance until April; and meanwhile Bussy, after many delays, had arrived April 10. with his reinforcements at Trincomalee, and had been transported thence by the indefatigable Suffren to Cuddalore. Having concerted his preliminary arrangements with the Admiral, Stuart on the 21st of April began his march southward, his transport-service on land being now so greatly improved that he could carry with him supplies for twenty-five days. The advent of Coote from Bengal to resume command was anxiously awaited, and on the 24th he arrived in safety at Madras. But the vessel in which he sailed had been chased for forty-eight hours by French men-of-war; and his health, though in appearance improved, was so much tried by the strain of anxiety and agitation that he rapidly sank, April 27. and within three days after landing was dead.

The loss of Sir Eyre Coote, though he was but the wreck of his former self, was at such a moment a great misfortune. Stuart's advance, with or without reason, was made at the rate of about three miles a day, and it June 7. was not until the 7th of June that he took up his position in two lines about two miles south of the fort of Cuddalore. His left rested on the Bandipollam hills to westward, and his right on an inlet from the sea. His front covered a space of about a mile and a-half, and his whole force numbered about eleven thousand men, of whom rather more than one-fifth were Europeans.[1]

[1] Innes Munro gives the numbers at 1660 Europeans, 8340 Sepoys, 1000 Native Cavalry. The force, according to Wilks, mustered in January nearly 15,000 men. The distribution of the

The troops under Bussy in Cuddalore seem to have 1783. been at least as strong as Stuart's in numbers,[1] so that proper investment of the fort was out of the question. On the night of the 7th the French moved out and June 7. began to entrench a position about a mile and a-half from Stuart's, but not quite parallel to it, since their right was thrown somewhat back. So quickly did these new works assume a formidable aspect, that on the 12th, after all stores had been landed, Stuart determined, on the advice of a council of war, to attack on the following morning. Accordingly, before daylight, Lieutenant- June 13. colonel Kelly with the Hundred-and-Second Foot and three Sepoy battalions, fetched a compass round the Bandipollam hills, and at about five o'clock surprised a battery of seven guns which was mounted upon a spur of the range. Turning the cannon on to the Mysorean regiments which occupied the extreme right of the French position, he speedily dispersed them, and then took ground a little farther to the north, from which he could see the main line of the French entrenchments in reverse. After due reconnaissance he sent back so encouraging a report that Stuart ordered the Grenadiers of the European regiments, with the Seventy-first, Seventy-second, and three and a-half Sepoy battalions in support, to turn the right of the French main position. The troops advanced as ordered at about half-past eight, but were received by so sharp a fire of grape and musketry from a redoubt, which formed a salient angle in the line, that they were recalled after suffering heavy loss. A battery was then sent up to the Bandipollam hills to play against this redoubt, and at half-past ten Sandford's regiment, two Hanoverian regiments, and three battalions

troops was as follows :—*First Line*—First Brigade, H.M. 71st (half battalion), 72nd, Sandford's (101st), Hanoverian detachment ; Second Brigade, Madras Europeans (now 102nd), 5 battalions of Sepoys ; Third Brigade, 4 battalions of Sepoys. *Second Line*— Fourth Brigade, 5 battalions of Sepoys ; Fifth Brigade, H.M. 71st (half battalion), 5 battalions of Sepoys.

[1] Munro gives it as 3000 Europeans, 3000 French Sepoys, 3000 Mysore infantry, 2000 Mysore cavalry.

1783.
June 13.
of Sepoys attempted a second attack upon the work with the bayonet. They were met by so terrible a fire that, though one company of Sandford's forced its way into the trenches, the rest of the regiment hung back, and the French sallying forth charged the fugitives with the bayonet and pursued them for a quarter of a mile. Lieutenant-colonel Stuart of the Seventy-second, who was watching for his opportunity, now brought forward the Grenadiers to a second attack on the right front and flank of the French, led them straight into the trenches, drove the enemy's right down upon their centre, and had cleared half the line of their entrenchments before he was pressed back by reinforcements of French troops in superior numbers. He had, however, been careful to occupy one of the French redoubts, and to reverse the front of its defences; and to this stronghold he now made good his retreat. Thereupon the action came to an end, as if by mutual consent, the British having made good their footing, though with the heavy loss of a thousand men killed and wounded, of whom over six hundred were Europeans. The Seventy-first in particular suffered terribly. The loss of the French, by their own account, did not exceed five hundred; but thirteen guns and the key of the position remained in the hands of the British, and during the night the French retired within the fortress of Cuddalore.

On that same evening, Suffren's squadron of fifteen sail came in sight. Hughes, who was lying at Porto Novo with eighteen ships, thereupon moved up to Cuddalore, but was prevented by baffling winds from
June 16. weighing anchor until the 16th, when he stood out to sea. Suffren promptly seized the opportunity to take
June 17. up his anchorage before Cuddalore, and hastily embarked twelve hundred troops to make good the deficiency of men among his crews. This reinforcement practically turned the scale against Hughes, of whose force no fewer
June 20. than seventeen hundred men were disabled by scurvy; and after a fifth bloody but indecisive action, wherein each side lost about five hundred men, he was obliged to

retire to Madras, leaving Suffren for the time supreme at sea. The French Admiral lost not a moment in disembarking two thousand men, since naval operations for the present were at an end; and Bussy used the advantage of superior force to make a sortie, which, however, was repulsed with the loss of three hundred killed and wounded and half as many prisoners. Among the captured was a certain Sergeant Bernadotte, whom we shall meet again as Crown Prince and King of Sweden.

1783.

June 25.

In spite of this success, the situation of the British was most perilous. Bussy, though nominally besieged, was superior in numbers, and Suffren held command of the sea. Stuart had summoned to his assistance the force in Tanjore under Colonel Fullarton; and though Lord Macartney had very injudiciously countermanded the movement, Fullarton had decided to obey the General rather than the Governor. But it was still a question whether this reinforcement could arrive in time. It seemed therefore that, as the most fortunate issue of his operations, Stuart could anticipate nothing better than a retreat, with the loss of the whole of his siege-train, if indeed he should be lucky enough to escape greater disaster. Very fortunately, however, on the 28th there arrived the news that peace had been made between England and France in Europe; and after three days a convention was concluded which delivered Stuart from all peril. Under this instrument it was agreed that four months should be allowed to the belligerents in India to accede to the pacification; but the Government of Madras, having with its usual weakness extended the term by one month, apprised Tippoo that hostilities against him would cease if he should evacuate British territory by the 2nd of December. How he utilised the latitude thus granted to him shall presently be seen: for the present it is best to bring to an end this weary war on the coast of Coromandel.

June 28.

July 2.

On the 3rd of July, Stuart, by order of the Council, made over his command to the officer next to him in seniority and returned to Madras, whence he was shortly

1783. afterwards sent home under arrest, having been dismissed the Company's service for persistent insubordination. In the distraction which reigned at Madras, it is difficult to decide how far he was to blame for the mishaps of his last campaign, though it cannot be doubted that he allowed his imperious and quarrelsome nature seriously to impair his ability as a soldier. But in the story of this last contest with the French in India, it is the name not of a soldier but of a sailor that is most memorable. Stuart was such as we have seen him to be, and Bussy was grown feeble and slow through age; but Suffren was a very fine officer. It is true that he never encountered a British Admiral of the calibre even of Barrington, much less of Howe, Hood, or Rodney, and that even so, after five severe actions, in three of which superiority of force was on his side, he never succeeded in taking a British ship. Yet by his great talent he had brought the British empire in India to greater peril than any enemy since Dupleix. It is also noteworthy that, whether the blame be chargeable to the inherent defects of the French naval service or to his own hasty temper, his success was marred chiefly by the disloyalty of his captains, or, in other words, by that too common failing among French officers, the inability to efface themselves and to unite impersonally as a band of brothers.

Suffren therefore sailed home sick at heart with a sense of failure, though comforted by the compliments of his former rivals on the sea; and the British were left free to deal with Tippoo Sahib alone.

CHAPTER XXV

IN the last chapter allusion was made to a British diversion on the Malabar coast which, at the outset of Stuart's campaign, drew Tippoo and the bulk of his forces from the Carnatic to Mysore. It will be remembered, too, that our last sight of operations on the western coast closed with the sudden withdrawal of Tippoo from before Panianee on the news of his father's death. On learning that Humberstone had been forced back to Panianee, the Bombay Government resolved at once to send thither General Matthews, the Commander-in-chief of the Presidency, with such troops as could be readily embarked, and to supplement these with further reinforcements as soon as possible. Matthews, however, on learning, during his voyage down the coast, of Tippoo's retreat, though not of its cause, decided to land at Rajaman Droog, about eighty miles south of Goa, where the estuary and river of Mirjee were reputed to afford the easiest route for an advance on Bednore. This city, together with vast treasure accumulated within its walls, had been taken by Hyder Ali in 1763, and had always been considered by him as the foundation of his subsequent greatness; so that its capture was an object on sentimental as well as solid grounds. The seizure of the port of Honawar or Onore, some fifteen miles to southward, would, as Matthews reckoned, give him command of a fertile strip of territory, and would not only secure his rear but afford him a sufficient base of supplies. Rajaman Droog was accordingly attacked, and taken with little difficulty;

1782.
Dec.

1782. and Matthews at once sent his transports to fetch Macleod's troops from Panianee. Honawar was taken shortly afterwards; and Macleod was just preparing to attack
1783. the fort of Mirjan, as the first step to an advance to Bed-
Jan. 12. nore by the passes of Bilghee, when new and important instructions, prompted by the news of Hyder's death, arrived from Bombay, bidding Matthews "abandon all operations on the coast and make an immediate push to take possession of Bednore."

These orders, which were positive and unconditional, contained every element of the folly which habitually characterises the interference of civilians with military arrangements. No movement could be made upon Bednore without preliminary operations on the coast, and Matthews had chosen the only base and line of action along which an advance could be made with security. Moreover, it was futile to plead the death of Hyder as a reason for forcing a new plan upon Matthews, for it was hardly likely that, five weeks after the event, he should not have been as fully apprised of it as the Council of Bombay. Matthews was much irritated by the interference. He remonstrated against the new scheme, disclaimed all responsibility for the consequences, and begged to be relieved of his command; yet with strange inconsistency he forbore either to await the result of his protests or to pursue his own designs, but, cancelling the whole of his previous dispositions, prepared to obey his new orders to the very letter. In plain language, he resolved to imperil the existence of his army in order to prove the self-evident proposition that the general on the spot is a better judge of military operations than a council of civilians at a distance, and this although he could perfectly well have followed his instructions in spirit by adhering to his own designs.

In this temper he landed his troops anew at Coondapoor, fifty miles south of Honawar, as the point of the coast which was nearest to Bednore, and, having carried this post with considerable difficulty, advanced without any regular means of transport and under a perpetual

harassing fire of rockets and musketry to the foot of the 1783.
hills. Here more formidable resistance awaited him.
Barring his line of advance there lay in succession a
breastwork defended by three thousand men, a strong
abatis four hundred yards in rear of the breastwork, and
three miles in rear of the abatis a fort, with flanking defences but open to the rear, which mounted fifteen guns.
Matthews, still protesting that the operations were none
of his choice and abjuring all responsibility for them,
now sent one division of his army under Macleod to
turn these defences, reserving less than one thousand
men for himself. The number, however, sufficed for his
purpose. The Seventy-third Highlanders carried the Jan. 26.
breastwork with a rush, bayoneted four hundred of the
enemy, pursued the rest to the abatis, drove them again
from that, and finally hunted them close under the walls
of the fort. Preparations were made for attacking this on
the following morning, but the enemy was found to have Jan. 27.
evacuated it during the night; and the advance was
therefore resumed. A barrier mounting eleven guns
was quickly abandoned by the enemy, and a second
battery of nine guns, about two miles farther on, was
stormed with the bayonet at little cost to the assailants.
From this second barrier to the top of the ghaut there
stretched one continuous chain of breastworks and
batteries, crowned by the fort of Hyderghur; but all
were carried in succession, at a loss to Matthews of
no more than fifty men killed and wounded. On the
following day overtures were made for the surrender
of Bednore, though Matthews was still fourteen miles
distant from it and Macleod had not yet rejoined him;
and the General entered into possession of the fort and
territory without encountering further resistance.

It was an astonishing performance, for Matthews had
neither provisions, transport, nor ammunition, but, like
Adams, lived simply on his captures from the enemy.
The General attributed his success to a special interposition of Providence in his favour, apparently without a
thought that it might be due, as it actually was, to the

1783. disloyalty of one of Tippoo Sahib's officers. He now sent a detachment to occupy Anantpoor, about thirty miles to the north-east, which under the same treacherous influence had offered to surrender; but by this time a loyal servant of Tippoo had guessed what was going forward, and had sent a small force to defend the place. Ignorant of this, the British advanced towards it under a flag of truce, when to their astonishment and indignation they were greeted by a sharp fire. Furious with rage, they immediately carried the town by assault, and not unnaturally gave no quarter to the garrison. Upon this fact was founded a false story that "four hundred beautiful women were left bleeding from the wounds of the bayonet, dead or expiring in each other's arms." This libel, with many other baseless accusations against Matthews's army, was, to the great dishonour of Edmund Burke, inserted in the *Annual Register*, and notwithstanding his subsequent apology and contradiction is possibly still accepted as true to this day.

March 9. On the 9th of March Mangalore also was surrendered to the British and occupied by a British garrison; but by this time Tippoo's army had begun slowly to make its way westward from Coromandel, and the danger of Matthews's position became apparent. The Government of Bombay now withdrew its positive instructions, and left the General a free hand; but the hapless man's brain seems to have been completely turned by his past success. He pointed out that he could not possibly spare more than sixteen hundred men for operations in the field, that the enemy was advancing in full force from the east, and that without reinforcements he could not, save by miracle, hold his own; but he made no effort to concentrate his troops, dilating proudly on the extent of territory in his possession without thought for the safety of his army within it. Meanwhile Tippoo drew

April 7. steadily nearer, and on approaching Bednore divided his force into two columns, one of which easily overpowered the garrison at Hyderghur, and thus cut off Matthews's communication with the coast, while the other, after detaching a force to mask Anantpoor, invested Bednore. The outer line of defence of the city, being too extensive to be held by the limited numbers of the British, was carried at the first assault, the garrison retreating in perfect order to the citadel. There a desperate defence was maintained until the whole of the works were in ruins and further resistance hopeless, when a capitulation was arranged, under which it was agreed that the garrison should receive safe-conduct for themselves and for their private possessions to the coast, but that all public property should be surrendered. It is probable that Tippoo had determined to violate the agreement in any case; but too true it is that he found sufficient justification for so doing in the attempt of the British officers to carry off with them the public treasure of Bednore. The entire garrison was thereupon put in irons and marched off as prisoners to distant destinations.

1783.

May 3.

Though almost the whole of Matthews's boasted conquests were thus lost at a stroke with disaster and disgrace, the fort of Mangalore still held its own under command of Major John Campbell of the Seventy-third, with a garrison of his own regiment and of Sepoys, numbering in all about two thousand men. Tippoo, on the fall of Bednore, had immediately detached a force against it, hoping that the mere news of the disaster would terrify Mangalore into surrender; and he was not a little astonished to hear that on the 6th of May this detachment had been attacked by Campbell twelve miles from the fort, and defeated with the loss of all its artillery. He now marched against Mangalore with his whole army, not doubting that the sight of his host would produce the desired effect, and invested the fort. By an unfortunate oversight Campbell maintained an outpost of two battalions on a hill a mile distant from the walls, and Tippoo, promptly perceiving the error, on the 23rd opened fire from several batteries upon this isolated post and followed up the cannonade by a general assault. Despite the efforts of their officers, the Sepoys occupying the hill broke and fled; and though Campbell

May 6.

May 20.

May 23.

1783. succeeded in saving a part of the fugitives by a sally from the main defences, yet four officers and over two hundred men were cut off. Campbell then called all outlying posts into the fort, and, much to Tippoo's disappointment, dismissed the bearer of a summons to surrender without so much as an answer. Greatly enraged by this defiance, Tippoo now opened a siege in form by three regular attacks, being aided therein by the professional talents of M. de Cossigny, a French officer, who, together with his European battalion, had accompanied him from Coromandel. The faces of the fortress were in a short time not only breached but reduced to ruins, and besiegers met besieged in almost daily conflict at close quarters; yet the assailants were invariably repelled with heavy loss, and Tippoo was no nearer than before to the recovery of Mangalore. At July 19. length, after fifty-six days of open trenches, Campbell, having received advice that succour was at hand, fired a royal salute; which theatrical action brought about very serious results. For within a few hours there came to him a letter signed by M. Peveron de Morlay, "envoy from France to the Nabob Tippoo Sultan," whereby Campbell was informed of the cessation of arms at Cuddalore, consequent on the conclusion of peace in Europe. The fact of this cessation had been known to M. de Morlay for fully ten days, but had been concealed by him, doubtless to curry favour with Tippoo; nor did this envoy of France scruple to allow his admission to the British defences under flag of truce to be made a cloak for the springing of a mine and for a fresh assault by the Mysorean troops. This contemptible trick was, however, a failure, for the attack was repulsed; and now M. de Cossigny, who unlike de Morlay was a man of honour, came forward and insisted on the withdrawal of all French troops and officers from Aug. 2. further share in the siege. Tippoo was thereupon compelled to agree to an armistice, one article of which stipulated for the supply of the garrison with victuals in instalments not exceeding ten days' stock at a time.

By systematic violation of this article, while cunningly 1783.
protracting simulated negotiations for a definite peace,
Tippoo contrived to reduce the provisions in Mangalore
to a dearth which seemed certain to ensure speedy
surrender. Then boldly throwing off the mask, he re- Oct. 9.
paired his old works, and renewed the siege. At this
point it is necessary for the present to leave Mangalore
and to return to the operations on the eastern coast.

It will be remembered that while Stuart was preparing to march on Cuddalore, Lord Macartney, instead of concentrating the whole of his force against the French, had planned diversions, or what passed for such, in other quarters. Pursuant to this false policy, two battalions of Sepoys were sent in May to the district May. lying between the Kistnah and the Pennar, in order to support a rebellious vassal of Tippoo. Landing at Ongola, between fifty and sixty leagues north of Madras, this force moved westward for some seventy miles to Cummum, and thence southward, reducing a succession of minor posts as it marched. On the 27th of August, however, the British commander issued orders for hostilities to cease until he could ascertain whether the enemy held themselves bound by the convention of Cuddalore; and, during the parley which followed, Tippoo's general seized the opportunity to make a treacherous attack upon one of the Sepoy battalions and cut it almost to pieces. With this mishap the operations in this quarter seem to have come to an end, and indeed they would hardly have been worth mention except as an example of the wastefulness of civilians in conducting a campaign.

In the district of Tanjore another diversion was more serious and in time more profitable. There Lieutenant-colonel Lang, the defender of Vellore during the contest between Coote and Hyder Ali, having with much difficulty collected supplies and transport, marched westward from Trichinopoly and laid siege to Caroor, some forty miles up the Cavery River. The fort was evacuated by the enemy on the 2nd of April; and Lang, moving south-

1783.
April 10.

May 4.

westward, stormed the fort of Avaracoorchee, and marched thence on Dindigul, which surrendered without resistance. Here he handed over the command to Colonel Fullarton, who, though he had held a commission for but three years, was, in virtue of the raising of his regiment,[1] the senior officer. Fullarton, however, pressed the operations with vigour, captured Darapooram, and was marching against Coimbatore when he received the summons, to which allusion has already been made, from Stuart to join him at Cuddalore. Then it was that, setting before himself the safety of Stuart's army as the first of all objects, he disobeyed Macartney's instructions, and moved towards Cuddalore with such speed that on the day of the cessation of hostilities he was within three days' march of the town. It must be recorded, in justice to Macartney, that he expressed approval of Fullarton's action; but this does not excuse the original folly of dividing the British forces, when every man should have been assembled to crush the French.

On receiving intelligence of the convention, Fullarton turned south again, and spent August and the first fortnight of September in punitive operations against the Polygars of Madura and Tinnevelly, who had thrown off their allegiance to Great Britain ever since the beginning of the war. By rapid and skilful movements, notwithstanding the intense heat,[2] Fullarton reduced these rebellious chiefs to submission, following them through forest and mountain to their remotest fastnesses, and having finished the work returned later

Sept. 25. in September to Dindigul. Here he found large reinforcements awaiting him from the army at Cuddalore, which raised his force to close upon fourteen thousand men, including two thousand Europeans,[3] with sixty

[1] Then numbered the 98th.
[2] He marched one hundred miles in four days, with the thermometer frequently marking 110°.
[3] 72nd Highlanders, Sandford's (101st), Rowley's (102nd), two Hanoverian battalions, Royal Artillery.

guns. It was a strange position for one who had only 1783.
become a soldier since February 1780, and whose
appointment as Colonel had been furiously assailed in
the British Parliament; yet he proved himself worthy
of the trust. He at once displayed his originality by
discarding Coote's system of marching in file, ready to
form line to either flank at a moment's notice, as too
cumbersome for rapid deployment against an enemy in
front or rear. It is characteristic, too, that he borrowed
his own substitute for Coote's formation from the land-
scape gardeners of the day, arranging his order of march
as a quincunx, with his European brigade in the centre,
one Sepoy brigade in front, a second in rear, and a third
and fourth on either flank. The whole of the brigades
moved in column, so that the centre brigade could deploy
immediately to any front, with two Sepoy brigades
always ready on its flanks, and two more at hand to
act as required. The innovation is remarkable as the
work of one who was practically a civilian and withou*
the slightest experience of India.

At Dindigul Fullarton remained for three weeks,
making every preparation for the invasion of Mysore,
which he foresaw would be necessary in consequence
of Matthews's disastrous operations. On the 16th of Oct. 16.
October, having intelligence of the renewal of the siege
of Mangalore, he began his march westward in the
hope of removing the pressure on the beleaguered
garrison. Having decided to make Palghautcherry,
about a hundred miles to westward, his advanced base,
he moved thither by way of Pulnee, reducing the minor
forts as he advanced. At Annamalee he entered the
teak-forest, through which, like Braddock on the Ohio,
he was forced to clear a path past huge fallen trees
and across deep ravines, his difficulties being multiplied
tenfold by a fortnight of incessant heavy rain. But he
made his way through all obstacles, and on the 4th of Nov. 4.
November encamped within ten miles of the fort of
Palghautcherry. He at once invested this stronghold
and began to open his trenches, pending the arrival of

1783.
Nov. 13. his heavy guns, which, being at length brought up with incredible labour, opened fire on the 13th. On the same night a lodgment in the covered way was effected by a small party under concealment of a torrent of rain; and the garrison, four thousand men strong, evacuated the fort in panic. Thus an advanced base of great strength was secured, which threatened Tippoo's dominions both to westward and to northward, and commanded a fertile district for supply of provisions. From this point Fullarton opened communication with the Bombay forces at Tellicherry, with a view to a combined advance on Seringapatam, and made his next move northward upon Coimbatore, which fell after a trifling resistance. Everything now seemed in good train for a successful march on the capital of Mysore.

But just at this moment Fullarton, to his bitter chagrin, received positive orders from Madras to restore all his conquests and to retire within British territory, since Commissioners had been appointed to negotiate a permanent peace with Tippoo Sahib. Greater imbecility than this could hardly have been manifested, in face of the repeated violations of the Convention of Cuddalore by this cruel, cowardly, treacherous potentate; and yet the Government of Bombay vied with that of Madras in weakness and folly. A force under Macleod, which
Nov. 22. had sailed to the relief of Mangalore, actually sailed back, under orders from Bombay, leaving Campbell and his gallant garrison to their fate; and this on the absurd ground that the day fixed for the expiration of the armistice was not yet come. Fullarton, seeing the danger that underlay his orders, decided that he would cease hostilities but would retain his conquests pending further instructions; but the same foolish commands were repeated to him, and he was obliged to fall back and to distribute his troops into cantonments. Hardly
1784.
Jan. 24. had he done so, when the Council of Madras awoke to its error, and directed him to reassemble his troops and to hold fast to Palghautcherry, if it had not been already abandoned. Fullarton lost no time in taking energetic

measures to repair the mischief; but meanwhile the handful of gallant men at Mangalore, now reduced to half of their original number and hardly able to stand owing to scurvy and starvation, had been forced to surrender the fortress, on the condition that they should be transported to Tellicherry. The terms were faithfully observed; but the trial had been too hard for the heroic man by whose dexterity and care provisions had been gathered in since October, and by whose unfailing courage and resource the garrison had been nerved to prolong its resistance. Major Campbell died on the 23rd of March at Tellicherry, and, to our shame be it said, there is little memory among us of the defender of Mangalore.

1784.

Jan. 30.

Of the negotiations which followed, and of the shameful indignities to which the envoys from Madras were subjected by Tippoo until he condescended to conclude a peace, this is no place to speak. Though peace was even more necessary to him than to the British, those indignities were meekly endured; and on the 11th of March a treaty was signed, whereby, amid the mutual restitution of conquests, certain places were held by both sides as security for the restoration of prisoners. The sufferings of the British captives under the brutality of Hyder's gaolers have been recorded in many pages, but it was reserved for Tippoo to make away with his prisoners wholesale by poison and assassination. Baillie had died before Hyder, but three of his best officers were murdered, as also were the unfortunate Matthews and most of the captains taken at Bednore. Yet one officer was spared who, if Tippoo could have looked into the future, would never have left his prison. Twice within the next fifteen years was David Baird to return to Seringapatam, and on the second visit he was to enter it over Tippoo's corpse.

So ended at length this weary and desolating war, which so nearly cost us the possession of India. Yet if India had been lost it would have been less by mistakes of commanders in the field than by distraction of counsel and infirmity of purpose among the civil

1784. administrations. Indeed, when the jealousy, faction, and corruption of the Councils of the various Presidencies is considered, it seems little less than miraculous that British rule should have survived in India. Nor can it be denied that soldiers also took their part in the intestine quarrels and their share in the profits of corruption, and must bear their full weight of responsibility for disaster. Most certainly also the saviour of India at this terrible time was not a soldier, but the Governor-General, Warren Hastings, whose courage was never shaken nor his resource exhausted either by disasters in the field or by disloyalty in the closet. Yet another civilian, Mr. Sullivan, the Agent at Tanjore, did most excellent service, particularly by his loyal support to the military commanders. The success of the operations in that quarter, especially when Fullarton was working with him, sufficiently proves that the difficulties of the British lay chiefly in their own dissensions.

In truth it is almost ludicrous to contrast the attitude of Hyder Ali in his prime, terrified by the mere lifting of Joseph Smith's finger, and of Hyder Ali with his powers sapped by age, hastening to Porto Novo to give battle to Coote. That Hyder was a very able soldier, sound in his designs, vigilant for his opportunity, and incredibly swift in action, is unquestionable; yet he was feared more by civilians than by soldiers. It was no fault of Coote that he could not give as good an account of him as Smith, the fact being that whenever he moved outside Madras he entered a country which, owing to Hyder's devastations, was as truly a wilderness, except in the matter of water, as the Sahara itself. Crippled for all continuous military operations by this cause and by want of transport, Coote cannot be said to have fought a campaign during this last period of his career. He fought actions for the relief and revictualling of his garrisons, and his operations are therefore little worth study apart from his tactics in the actual field of battle. There, however, he seems to have been one of the greatest masters of his own or of any other time. The man was never so dangerous as when within range of cannon-shot. If there was a weak point in an enemy's position, Coote hit it unerringly, and would contrive to draw his enemy out of his stronghold and to fight him on his own ground. His power of manœuvring masses of troops was marvellous. He could handle ten thousand men with the ease and precision of a sergeant drilling a squad in the barrack-yard; and thus, in spite of the terrible encumbrance of followers and baggage, he would advance with perfect confidence into the midst of cavalry that outnumbered him by six to one, with his infantry and artillery only. Indeed, it is to me surprising that his masterly use of the echelon for meeting the superior numbers of an enemy which chiefly employed shock-action, should have been so little studied during some of our recent campaigns. A great source of his strength was the implicit trust reposed in him by his troops, and in particular by the Sepoys, among whom he commanded positive adoration. A great historian has fortunately recorded the scene of the white-bearded Sepoy who, on entering the room of an officer in high command, saw on the wall a portrait of Coote, and, recognising the face which he had not seen for fifty years, "halted, drew himself up, lifted his hand, and with solemn reverence paid his military obeisance to the dead."

This devotion not only to Coote but to all the British officers was strikingly exemplified during the course of the war. By the end of 1781 the Governor of Madras was in such straits for money that the pay of most of the native battalions was four, five, and even twelve months in arrear; while the coin that was actually paid to them could not be exchanged for the value at which it was issued. Naturally there was much murmuring, with disturbances which occasionally rose to the height of mutiny; yet no discontent ever manifested itself in Coote's army, nor in any case was visited on the officers, to whom the Sepoys clung, despite the temptations offered by Hyder and by the French, with

1784.

1784. unshaken fidelity. It remains only to add that, whatever were the occasional failings of the Generals, the officers of the Indian Army showed themselves worthy of its most famous traditions. Men like Lang, Nixon, Camac, Popham, and Flint upheld the great reputation which had been handed down by Lawrence and Clive and Forde and Smith; and the very boys, just arrived from England, imbibed as if by instinct the spirit of the Indian service. Thus a young ensign named Allan, no more than seventeen years old, at the outbreak of the war reclaimed, by the unaided resources of his own mind, the mutinous garrisons of an outlying station to obedience and order, defended the post for six months, and, watching his time, withdrew his troops in safety by a clever retreat. The work was too hard for the poor lad, for he died a few months later of the strain;[1] and yet his career was typical of many. Trained early to responsibility, to self-reliance, and to study of their profession by isolation with a handful of Sepoys among treacherous and quarrelsome native chiefs, the British officer in India learned to meet every emergency with a skill, a coolness, and a resource which entitled him to stand alone among the officers not of the British Army only, but of the armies of the world.

[1] Wilks, ii. 260.

AUTHORITIES.—Wilks's *History of Mysore;* *Report of the Secret Committee;* Innes's *History of the Bengal European Regiment;* Wilson's *History of the Madras Army;* Innes Munro's *Operations on the Coromandel Coast;* *Lives of the Lindsays;* Gleig's *Life of Sir T. Munro;* Fullarton's *View of English Interests in India.* Colonel Malleson's haste and carelessness in this section of his *Decisive Battles of India* (Porto Novo) are such as to render his work a positive hindrance rather than a help. I need scarcely add that the masterly survey of the naval operations in Captain Mahan's *Influence of Sea-power* has been invaluable to me.

CHAPTER XXVI

THOUGH the peace concluded with Tippoo Sahib in 1784 could not from its nature be of long duration, it is necessary, before entering upon the story of his next contest with the British, to turn for a while to affairs in England. On the fall of Lord North, as has already been told, an administration was formed by Lord Rockingham with Fox and Shelburne as Secretaries of State. No great power of divination was needed to predict that these two Secretaries would speedily fall at variance, for the only bond of union between them was that both had been violent, reckless, and unpatriotic in opposition. Both, beyond doubt, were exceedingly able men, but both were also vain and ambitious, and each was contemptuous of the other. Shelburne had enjoyed the education of serving in time of peace in the Twentieth Foot under the colonelcy of Wolfe, while, apart from this useful experience, he stood far above Fox in political instruction; but he was a man who, for no assigned reason, was distrusted by every one, which in itself is sufficient proof that he was not straightforward. Fox, on the other hand, had never known discipline of any kind; he had always been a spoilt child, and was impatient of abstract study; but, shallow and unprincipled though he was, his worst enemy could not reproach him with crookedness or dissimulation.

The occasion for a quarrel between the two men was soon found. According to the vicious system under which the work of administration was at that

1782.

1782. time distributed, the business of the Colonies fell within Shelburne's province, and the treatment of Foreign Affairs within that of Fox. Hence each claimed a share in the negotiation of the treaty of peace, Fox in respect of the European belligerents, and Shelburne in respect of America; and each was determined to control the whole of the transactions himself. The result was that at one and the same time there were two rival emissaries from the English Government in Paris, a certain Mr. Oswald on behalf of Shelburne, and Mr. Thomas Grenville on behalf of Fox. Oswald, an extremely weak and incapable man, fell wholly under the influence of Benjamin Franklin, and was actually disposed to concede to him not only the independence of the revolted Colonies but the possession of Canada in addition. Grenville, on discovering what was going forward, wrote in horror and alarm to Fox; and Fox not unnaturally was much surprised and even more indignant. The whole affair was susceptible of explanation, for Oswald's mission, when he countenanced Franklin's astonishing proposals, was as yet informal, and Shelburne had as little intention of ceding Canada as Fox himself; but the misunderstanding was not one that could be easily set right. Fox made a final effort in the Cabinet to obtain sole control of the negotiations, and, failing to do so, resigned his office.

There can, I think, be no doubt but that Shelburne was to blame for the rupture. The underhand mission of Oswald betrays a restless anxiety to hold the first place, and a petty dexterity in seizing it, which may well have rendered such a Secretary of State impossible as a colleague. A minister who will overreach where he cannot overrule, can never be acceptable in a Cabinet; and we learn without surprise that no man who had served once under Shelburne would consent to do so again. Meanwhile, the breach was a great misfortune, for Fox in office was a very different man from Fox in opposition; and with a longer term of work and responsibility he might possibly have learned that a nation is greater than a party. It is, of course, a grave reproach 1782. to any man that high office alone can teach him the elements of common patriotism ; but that is the natural result of government by party. A leading share in the great affairs which were still to agitate Europe before the general cataclysm of the French Revolution, would perhaps have corrected many of Fox's worst failings, and rendered him a profitable servant to his country.

Simultaneously with the resignation of Fox came the death of Lord Rockingham, the one man who July 1. might have held the various sections of the Whig party together ; and Shelburne, succeeding him as Prime Minister, sought to strengthen his administration by taking in William Pitt, then twenty-three years of age, as Chancellor of the Exchequer. The negotiations at Paris were then pursued in earnest. England, as the King was never weary of reminding Fox, was greatly hampered by the resolution of the House of Commons, which declared the hopelessness of reducing America by arms ; but, on the other hand, Rodney's victory in the West Indies and the triumphant defence of Gibraltar had strengthened her hands enormously since the fall of North. In fact, though staggering under the terrible burden of the war, England was probably the only one of the combatants that had strength to continue it. America was at the last gasp. Washington could obtain neither recruits for his army nor money to pay such troops as were with him ; and the ill faith of Congress, in striving to evade a promise, made in 1780, to grant half-pay to his officers, went near to cause a mutiny.[1] The finances of the rebel states were in hopeless disorder. The provinces treated Congress exactly as they had treated England, refusing to pay the taxes which it imposed or to contribute the quotas which it had allotted to them. Even in December 1782 Franklin was saddled with the humiliating duty of begging from the French Government—itself on

[1] Washington, *Works*, viii. 255, 271, 284-86.

1782. the verge of bankruptcy—the money to discharge the unpaid wages of the American army.

When, however, the time for negotiation came, Mr. Jay, one of the American plenipotentiaries, maintained that "to think of gratitude to France was one of the greatest of follies"; and indeed the antagonism of the French and Americans on certain points of the treaty was so great that the Americans settled matters char-
Nov. 30. acteristically by signing, unknown to their allies, a separate treaty of their own with England. In vain the French protested against this action as a gross breach alike of faith and of gratitude: the thing was done; and with America detached from the alliance England was quite ready to face France, Spain, and Holland. The preliminary articles with France and
1783. Spain were signed on the 20th of January 1783, and
Jan. 20. those with Holland a few months later. The Americans obtained the Mississippi for their western boundary, and gained also a large part of the territory which, under the Quebec Act, had been included in Canada and Nova Scotia. France recovered Senegal and Goree in West Africa, her settlements in India, together with considerable trading privileges there, and St. Lucia in the West Indies; but she added only the island of Tobago to her former possessions. Spain retained Minorca and West Florida, and received East Florida in addition. Holland ceded to England the settlement of Negapatam. In fact, the European powers profited little, even in appearance, by their combination against England, and in reality accomplished little more than their own ruin. Holland was practically undone by the war; France committed herself irretrievably to bankruptcy; Spain assured to herself the speedy revolt and loss of her colonial empire. America alone, by great good fortune and by her peculiar methods of diplomacy, secured great and lasting profit.

The terms, from the nature of the case, could not have been other than humiliating to England; but the only real reproach to her was the abandonment of the

American loyalists to the tender mercies of the revolu- 1783. tionary party. Shelburne strove hard to gain an amnesty and restitution of confiscated property for them, but Franklin showed a particularly vindictive spirit in the matter, and the American negotiators were inexorable. It is, however, probable, looking to the anarchic state of the new republic and the weakness of its central authority, that any stipulation in favour of these unfortunate people would have remained a dead letter. A community which had shown its readiness to break faith not only with the allies who had carried it successfully through the struggle, but even with its own officers who had fought in the field, was not likely to keep it with prostrate enemies. Congress went through the form of recommending the loyalists to the favour of the various provincial legislatures; and the provincial mobs, by recourse to their usual methods, drove them from their midst. The total number of refugees is reckoned at one hundred thousand souls, very many of whom, as the Americans realised in 1812, made new homes in Canada and Nova Scotia. The British Government did its best by liberal grants to help them; and even Burke and Fox, who had contributed more than any two men to their ruin, joined cordially in voting the money of other people for their relief. But the distress was too often greater than could be alleviated by mere money, and the petitions of the brave men who fought and lost all for the King in the American Revolution make sad reading for an Englishman. Still, the loyalist emigration withdrew from America a great part of the choicest of her population, and the loss was hers alone. A few years later, Edmund Burke discovered in the flight of the French nobility a sufficient ground for condemning the new constitution in France; but it has been left to a highly gifted writer of our own time to apply the same reasoning to the expulsion of the loyalists from America.[1]

[1] Trevelyan, *American Revolution*, i. 428-35.

1783. The peace was of course unpopular in England; and Shelburne, who had already alienated most of his colleagues, was driven from office by a coalition between
Feb. 24. Fox and Lord North. It is true that throughout the American War Fox had denounced North in terms which would not have been inapplicable to Judas Iscariot, that he had threatened him with impeachment, and had expressed a hope that he and his fellow-ministers would expiate their crimes on the scaffold. It is true also that North had answered Fox with all the violence that lay in a singularly easy-going and sweet-tempered man. These considerations weighed little with them; and both statesmen seem to have thought they would weigh as little with others. But herein they were mistaken. People very justly said that if the former differences between the two men had been genuine, then the coalition was dishonest; but that if those differences had been simulated, then the men themselves were utterly unworthy of trust. None the less, the Coalition, under the nominal leader-
April 2. ship of the Duke of Portland, was forced upon the King; and, that nothing might be wanting to cover it with discredit, it received the public blessing and adherence of the Prince of Wales, who, under the very competent guidance of Fox himself, was advancing rapidly in a career of profligacy and extravagance. The King was naturally furious; and George the Third was a man whom it was not prudent to press too hard.

This disgraceful compact having been concluded, there remained nothing except to endeavour to secure for it popularity by means as disgraceful. The first military business after the conclusion of peace was of course the reduction of the establishment, which was begun in March 1783 by the wholesale disbandment of all newly raised regiments, with the exception of those serving in India. Of these last, four[1] were subsequently

[1] Fullarton's (98th), Bruce's (100th), Sandford's (101st), Rowley's (102nd).

disbanded in 1785 at the close of the war with Tippoo 1783. Sahib, and of the remainder Burgoyne's Light Dragoons were moved up to the place of Nineteenth; while Macleod's and Seaforth's Highlanders took their present numbers of Seventy-first and Seventy-second, and the second battalion of the Forty-second was shortly afterwards erected into a separate regiment with its present precedence of Seventy-third. The new peace establishment was fixed at about the same figure as in 1764, or, roughly speaking, at fifty thousand men,[1] any reduction that might have resulted from the loss of the American Colonies being prevented by the increased necessities of India. According to ancient practice, battalions and regiments were cut down, even on paper, to a ridiculously low figure; and by a mistake which common foresight would have avoided, the skeleton of the British Army was stripped even barer of flesh than usual. Under special Recruiting Acts of 1778 and 1779, great numbers of men had been enlisted for three years' service; and on the ratification of peace orders were immediately issued that all soldiers who March 6. had engaged themselves for this term were at liberty to take their discharge whether their time were expired or not. A bounty of a guinea and a-half was offered to all good men who would re-enlist, but the inducement was not of the slightest effect. To the consternation of the Government, the men with hardly an exception took their discharge and declined to re-engage, leaving very many regiments with no more than a handful of privates.[2]

[1] Great Britain 17,483
Plantations 9,421
Gibraltar 2,826
India 6,366
Artillery 3,282

Total . . . 39,378

To this must be added 12,000 men (after deduction of 3000 for colonial service) on the Irish Establishment.

[2] *Commander-in-Chief's Letter Books*, 29th March 1783. The Royal Scots, for instance, lost 500 out of 700 men.

1783. This blunder appears to have been the last act of Shelburne's Administration; but the Coalition no sooner came into office than it pressed for still further reduction of the Army. North was for breaking all regiments junior to the Sixty-fourth, though he knew that many officers had paid large premiums for exchange into all regiments senior to the Seventieth, in confidence that no corps which had survived the disbandment of 1764 would now be condemned. Happily, Conway, who under Rockingham's Government had been created Commander-in-chief, showed a strength in that office which he had never betrayed in Parliament, and combated North with great courage and resolution. His case was indeed unanswerable, for by the middle of November 1783 the Infantry of the Line in England had sunk to a strength of three thousand men; yet it was only by the most strenuous exertion that he averted the reduction of that number to a bare twenty-six hundred for the whole of Great Britain. It is abundantly evident that Fox and North, in their eagerness to secure a little passing popularity for the Coalition, were quite prepared to break faith with officers and to imperil the safety of the whole Empire.[1] Happily, the reign of this unscrupulous pair was destined to be short.

The business that claimed most urgent attention at the hands of the new Government related to the East Indies. In April 1782 the Report of the Secret Committee on Indian affairs, so often quoted in these pages, had been printed, and all the past iniquities of the Presidential Governments had been revealed. The House of Commons passed a resolution for the recall of Warren Hastings, among other officials, which, though supported in the Company by the Court of Directors, was negatived by the Court of Proprietors. Such a proceeding, however creditable in the abstract to the judgment of the Proprietors, showed clearly the need for

---

[1] *H.O. Commander-in-Chief.* North to Conway, 27th April. Conway to North, 22nd May, 13th November 1783.

immediate reform of the constitution of the Company ; 1783.
and Fox accordingly brought in a bill with that object.
Under this bill the patronage of India was assigned to
Commissioners, who were to be nominated from time to
time by Parliament, to be irremovable by the Crown, and
to be appointed in the first instance by the Government
then in office. This provision was at once represented
by the Opposition as an effort to secure the patronage
for the Whig party, with a view to corrupt influence
in the future. Whether the measure was framed with
any such intent, or whether in that case it would have
produced any such result, are questions which need not
detain us. An Opposition which cannot trace the
finger of the devil in every important measure of
Government is held to be unworthy of the name ; and
certainly such a Government as the Coalition deserved
that the worst construction should be placed upon its
acts. But, though the arguments in respect of patronage were urged with great ability and still greater
extravagance by William Pitt, the bill passed the
Commons, and would have passed the Lords but for
the interposition of the King. The method employed
by his Majesty was simple : he merely authorised
Lord Temple, the head of the family of Grenville, to
say that any peer who voted for the measure would be
considered by him as his enemy. The message had the
desired effect, and the bill was thrown out. The
Ministers, far from resigning, moved and carried in the
Commons a resolution which amounted to a vote of
censure on the Sovereign. The King retorted by Dec. 18.
directing them to return to him their seals, with a
particular injunction that they should not deliver them
in person ; and the command was obeyed. The constitutional aspect of the King's action does not concern
us here ; it must suffice that he believed the feeling
of the nation to be on his side, and that he was perfectly right.

On the following day it was announced in the House
of Commons, amid loud derision, that William Pitt

1783. had accepted the offices of First Lord of the Treasury and Chancellor of the Exchequer; and an easy triumph was expected over a minister of small experience and not yet twenty-five years of age. But Fox, though a great debater, was singularly wanting in judgment, and deficient above all in the true leader's quality of patience. He was outmanœuvred at all points by his young rival, and on the dissolution of Parliament in
1784. March 1784 his party suffered disastrous defeat at the polls. He fell from his high estate with the peculiar discredit which attaches to the failure of unscrupulous effort. He had staked character, principle, and reputation on a single throw, like the true gambler that he was,
May. and he had lost. Pitt came into office with a majority which kept him in power without intermission for the next seventeen years.

At this point, therefore, we enter upon the career of a great man who, equipped with qualities and attainments which could not but assure him fame as a minister of peace, was ordained by fate to become, at a crisis of supreme danger and difficulty, a minister of war. It has been remarked by Mr. Walter Bagehot that at Pitt's accession to power there were three subjects which pressed for the attention of a great statesman, namely, Ireland, parliamentary reform, and financial reform, and that Pitt dealt with all three of them. These are topics which lie without the scope of the present work, except in so far as financial reform touches the military departments; but it is, I think, open to consideration whether there were not a fourth subject, fully as important as the other three, which was neglected by Pitt, namely, military reform. On this question the reader shall presently find an opportunity of judging for himself; meanwhile, it will be convenient, for his better understanding of Pitt's military policy, to give first a slight sketch of our relations with foreign powers during these short years of peace.

The first troubles which called for Pitt's intervention abroad arose on the familiar ground of the Low

Countries. In 1781 the Emperor Joseph the Second, 1784. taking advantage of the war between England and Holland, had repudiated the Barrier Treaty, dismantled the barrier-fortresses, and forced the Dutch garrisons to withdraw from them. This demolition of the strong places was destined a few years later to lead to important results, though at the moment it excited little attention; and in 1784 the Emperor followed up his success by demanding the free navigation of the River Scheldt. This, however, was more than the Dutch would endure; and war seemed inevitable, until at length France, in cordial support of the United Provinces, managed to bring about a treaty which settled 1785. the dispute in their favour. At the same time, how- Nov. 8. ever, France formed a close military and commercial alliance with the Dutch, with the object not only of detaching from England one of her oldest allies, but of strengthening French power and influence in India. The Dutch East India Company being on the verge of bankruptcy, the French obligingly offered to garrison their settlements for them, and actually took measures to do so. By intrigues with the faction in the Dutch States which was opposed to the Stadtholder, the Prince of Orange, and therefore called itself the patriot party, the French rapidly pushed their project forward. The patriots, strong in the assurance of such powerful supporters at their back, set themselves for their part to carry a succession of measures for reducing the Stadtholder's authority and power to nullity. All this was a serious matter for England, for the Prince of Orange's party was steadily friendly to the English alliance, and the decay of English influence in Holland seemed to shake the base upon which England's foreign policy in Europe had rested for two centuries. The Stadtholder appealed to Frederick the Great, whose niece he had married, but the old King, who was now sinking fast towards his grave, was not disposed to move; and owing to the extreme feebleness of the Prince's character the work of organising resistance to

1785. the French party fell wholly on Sir James Harris, the British minister at the Hague.

Fortunately, the craft and audacity of Harris, aided by the spirit of the Princess of Orange, were equal to the occasion; and the death of Frederick the Great raised to the throne of Prussia a more active partisan of the Stadtholder in the Princess's brother, King Frederick William the Second. In June 1787 the French party took the false step of arresting the Princess when on her way to the Hague; she at once appealed to her brother; and in September a Prussian army of twenty thousand men, under the Duke of Brunswick, invaded Holland. From that moment the reaction in favour of the Stadtholder was rapid; and on the surrender of Amsterdam, Pitt, who had already come to a secret agreement with Prussia, declared openly that England would defend the Prince of Orange if he were attacked. English money was spent profusely for the arming of the Stadtholder's supporters; and for the first time since the days of Elizabeth the Scots Brigade of the Dutch army passed for a time into the pay of England.[1] The French were taken aback, for England's naval preparations showed that she was in earnest, but, their country being already almost in the throes of Revolution, they were powerless. Shortly afterwards there was signed the Triple Alliance between Great Britain, Prussia, and the Netherlands for maintaining the peace of Europe.

1786. Aug. 17.

1787.

Oct. 10.

1788. April.

A still more formidable complication arose out of the steady policy of encroachment pursued by the Empress Catherine of Russia towards Turkey, and from the consequent birth of what is now called the Eastern Question. Hitherto Russia and England had lived always on friendly terms, and Chatham had maintained it to be a principle of British foreign policy to eschew all dealing with the Turks. Lately, however, under the influence of Frederick the Great, Catherine had become alienated from England, and by

[1] *C.J.* 10th November 1787.

taking the lead in the Armed Neutrality, as well as by certain unfriendly acts in relation to commerce, had revealed her hostility with little disguise. On the annexation of the Crimea by Catherine in 1783-1784, Fox, during his brief control of foreign affairs, had used British influence steadily in her favour, being by conviction of like mind with Chatham ; but a new war which broke out between Turkey and Russia in 1787 created a situation which was not so simply to be dealt with. One after another the powers of Europe entered or were dragged into the quarrel. In February 1788 Austria stepped into the arena, hoping to gain something from the partition of Turkey ; in the summer Sweden unsheathed the sword on the opposite side, trusting to regain some of the provinces torn from her by Russia ; and in September Denmark, which was wholly subject to Russian influence, despatched an army to invade Sweden. The danger lest the Swedish provinces should fall entirely into the hands of Russia and Denmark, and lest Russia should gain absolute control over the Baltic, seemed so formidable that the Triple Alliance intervened to compel the Danes to evacuate Swedish territory. Thus England committed herself to a first step unfriendly to Russia, though not without good reason ; for the closing of the Baltic meant in those days the cutting off of her principal supply of naval stores.

The Empress Catherine, as was natural, bitterly resented this interference, and not the less for that Pitt, on the just plea of neutrality, had refused to allow English transports to be hired or English dockyards to be used by her, for an expedition which she had designed for the Mediterranean. The overtures of Great Britain to mediate between Russia and Turkey were firmly declined by the Russian Minister in England ; and Pitt was therefore obliged to turn his attention to composing the differences between the other belligerents. Now, however, he discovered that Prussia, far from regarding the Triple Alliance as a mere means for

1788. enforcing the peace of Europe, desired to use it as a weapon for her own aggrandisement, and was bent on renewing her old strife with Austria.

Fresh difficulties now sprang up on every side. In May 1789 Spain made an attack upon a British settlement at Nootka Sound, Vancouver Island, an act of aggression so wanton that it could only be met by peremptory demand for redress. Military preparations were hastened in England; and Holland and Prussia, being summoned to furnish the aid required of them under the Treaty of Alliance, responded with all possible loyalty. The dispute finally ended, after long
1790. negotiation, in the concession of the British claims and
Oct. 20. the vindication of British rights. But meanwhile another complication had been raised by a revolutionary movement in the Austrian Netherlands, which culminated in January 1790 in the expulsion of the Austrian garrisons and the signing of an Act of Union of the Belgian United Provinces. This new embarrassment to the House of Austria whetted the appetite of Prussia to the keenest point. She actually signed an offensive alliance with Turkey, which, however, owing to the protests of England and Holland, was not ratified; though King Frederick William spared no effort to lure his allies into the struggle. Pitt, on his side, was firm in resisting these endeavours, and in adhering to his original object of the pacification of Europe, with the result that the goodwill of Prussia, whatever it might have been worth, was further and
Feb. further alienated. Meanwhile the death of the Emperor Joseph had rendered easier the task of withdrawing Austria from the war; and by the incessant efforts of Great Britain and Holland the secondary combatants
Aug. were gradually detached, Sweden by the Peace of Warela, and Austria by the Convention of Reichenbach. It remained, therefore, only to reconcile the principals, Russia and Turkey.

The task of Great Britain and Prussia was now to induce Russia to follow the other powers in consenting

to peace on the basis of the *status quo ante bellum*. But 1790.
the Russian arms had been uniformly successful against
Turkey; the fortress of Ockzakow, long coveted by
Catherine, had been captured after a long and laborious
siege; and the Empress was by no means disposed to
restore either the fortress or the territory adjacent to
it. England herself, having acquiesced in Catherine's
annexation of the Crimea, could well regard her retention
of Ockzakow with indifference; but Prussia looked
upon the restoration of the fortress as of vital interest
to herself and to Europe. In view of Prussia's loyalty
over the affair of Nootka Sound, it was difficult for
England not to support her, and the two powers there- 1791.
fore agreed to put pressure jointly upon Russia. A
Prussian army was concentrated in Silesia to co-operate
with the Turks, while England undertook to send a
fleet to crush all resistance in the Baltic. Accordingly, March 28.
in March 1791, a royal message to Parliament announced
an augmentation of the naval forces to strengthen
the hands of England in procuring peace between
Russia and the Porte; but it was soon evident to
Pitt that the measure was unpopular in the country.
Fox urged the objections to it with great weight in
the Commons, and Pitt, realising that he had taken up
an untenable position, was fain to withdraw from it
without delay. The despatch of the fleet to the Baltic
was countermanded; and Catherine, opening direct
negotiations with the Porte, obtained by the Treaty 1792.
of Jassy the territory which she desired. The con- Jan. 9.
sequences to England, apart from the diplomatic defeat,
were the dissolution, in deed if not in name, of the
Prussian alliance, and the further estrangement of
Russia.

Thus three times within seven years England had
found herself on the verge of war; with France to
uphold British influence in Holland, with Spain over
the incident at Nootka Sound, and with Russia to
prevent the annexation of Ockzakow, to say nothing
of a renewal of the contest, presently to be narrated,

1792. with Tippoo Sahib in India. Nor must it be forgotten, though at present the barest mention of the fact must suffice, that in 1789 the deluge of revolution had fairly burst forth in France, and that in November 1790 Burke had given utterance to his forebodings that the waters might spread far in destruction and ruin, subsiding only when they had cut for themselves new channels. A foreign policy of boldness and decision in the midst of general disturbance throughout Europe can rest with stability on but one foundation, the foundation of military readiness. It is now time to turn from the foreign to the military policy of William Pitt.

First be it noted to his honour that one of his earliest cares was to increase our naval efficiency by the fortification of the dockyards at Portsmouth and Plymouth. The latter port, it will be remembered, had been exposed to most imminent danger in 1779, and had owed its deliverance rather to the enemy's timidity than to any strength of its own. A scheme of defence
1785. was accordingly prepared, under the superintendence of the Duke of Richmond, Master-general of the Ordnance; but the first attempts to obtain a grant for the work
1786. were so coldly received that in 1786 Pitt brought
Feb. 27. forward a resolution affirming, as an abstract proposition, the expediency of fortifying the dockyards. Modern readers, long accustomed to regard Pitt's proposition rather as an axiom, will doubtless expect that it met with ready and unanimous assent. Little do they know of the wisdom of their ancestors. In vain Pitt appealed to the precedents of centuries; in vain Samuel, Lord Hood, pleaded with all the weight of his great naval reputation that the function of British ships was to seek out the enemy's fleet and not to protect British ports; in vain three distinguished Captains of the Navy pushed Hood's argument yet further, urging that in case of hostilities with France England should always take the offensive, and affirming that many failures of the past war might have been averted if more ships could have been released for service at sea. The broad

question of military policy was at once whittled down to the usual issue between Government and Opposition. One or two obscure officers did indeed advance unsound and self-contradictory opinions of a professional kind in condemnation of the scheme ; but for the most part, incredible though it may appear, the arguments of the Opposition were based on constitutional grounds. The terms constitutional and unconstitutional, like the words orthodox and heterodox, possess a peculiar value in debate, since they are interpreted by no two men in the same sense, and can always serve to dignify factious prejudice with the robe of eternal principle. Such was the use to which they were turned in this discussion. Fortifications, said Pitt's opponents, must of course be manned if they were to be of service; but how could this be done without increase of the regular army, or at least without isolation of the militia within them from the rest of the community? Viewed in this light, as one gentleman observed in a phrase of immortal imbecility, "fortifications might be termed seminaries of soldiers and universities of prætorian bands." The leaders of the Opposition fell no whit behind the rank and file in childishness of utterance. Sheridan, who was nothing if not impudent, argued the question on naval and military grounds with as much assurance as though he had been an admiral. Fox declared with all the pomp of conscious insincerity that he "retained his great party-principles on all constitutional questions." North took the same side as Fox ; and Windham, not foreseeing that one day he would be Secretary-at-War at a very critical time, boldly averred that it was not worth while to spend money on fortifications. On a division the numbers were found to be equal, and, Speaker Cornwall giving his casting vote in the negative, the motion was lost.[1]

Such a beginning would have been discouraging but for the fact that the sentiments of the Opposition were dictated chiefly by personal animosity towards the Duke

[1] *Parl. Hist.* xxv. 375, xxvi. 1097 *sqq.*

1786. of Richmond, who, though formerly an associate of Fox in every kind of political mischief, was now content to hold office under Pitt and to use his powers for the benefit instead of to the injury of his country. Pitt, therefore, did not abandon the project of fortifying the naval stations, and both in 1787 and 1789 obtained money to strengthen certain of the ports in the West Indies. In connection with this work there was formed a corps of six hundred trained artificers, a measure doubly commendable in the interest alike of efficiency and economy; and by a special clause in the Mutiny Act these artificers were rightly subjected to military discipline. The reader will be surprised to hear that this also was regarded in certain quarters as unconstitutional. Sheridan and Fox held up their hands in horror at the idea of increasing the number of men subject to military law, and Fox declared that this clause "must operate to the surrender of our liberties." This canting nonsense fortunately met with the contempt which it deserved; and the clause was passed. Nevertheless, it was no small embarrassment to Pitt that so accomplished a debater and so unscrupulous a partisan was ready to make himself the champion of every vulgar prejudice against military reform.

I turn now from fortifications to the more important subject of the officers and men of the Army, whose condition, in at least one aspect, had been brought to Pitt's notice by the economical reforms of Edmund Burke. Economical questions are dry and difficult, but this matter is of such importance that it cannot be omitted; and I must, therefore, entreat the reader's patience while I lay before him the state of our military finance at Pitt's accession to power.

In the year 1781 there were printed a series of reports by a special Commission of Accounts, which had been appointed to inquire into the methods of the various departments in the public service. The office of the Paymaster-general was the first to be examined; and it was now revealed to the public that this functionary had for a great many years been to all intent the banker of the Army. It was the practice for him to submit to the Treasury an estimate of the sum required for the service of the Army; whereupon the Treasury, without testing the accuracy of his computation or ascertaining the amount of the balance that remained in his hands, simply paid the money over to him. From that moment there was no further check on it by any department; and the Paymaster was therefore at liberty to accumulate as large a balance as he could, and to utilise the interest thereon for his own profit. Upon scrutiny it was found that the average yearly balance in the hands of the Paymaster-general was £586,000, and the average monthly balance £869,000. Further, ancient usage permitted the Paymaster-general to retain his balance after quitting office until his accounts were finally passed, which, as such matters were then conducted, was a work of considerable trouble and delay. Under this system it was found that a sum of £473,000 issued to Lord Lincoln in 1719-1720 had vanished beyond all human discovery; but there was less difficulty in bringing to light abuses of more recent date. The average balance to the credit of Lord Holland,[1] who was Paymaster-general from 1757 to 1765, was £455,000; and his accounts had not been finally passed when the Commissioners made their report. Mr. Rigby, the next Paymaster-general, had for ten years kept a balance of about the same amount, so that these two gentlemen had between them enjoyed for nine years the use of £900,000 of the public money.

It may easily be guessed that with such balances at their disposal the Paymasters-general were never in a hurry to diminish them; and hence it became an object to render the passing of all accounts as troublesome and complicated as possible. There were certain claims, such as the officers' "clearings" (presently to be explained), which were always for some months in

[1] The father of Charles Fox.

1786. arrear of payment. Officers on half-pay, again, did not always apply for their allowance punctually; and the accounts of deputy-paymasters on foreign stations of course needed time for adjustment. In such cases the delay which filled the Paymaster's pocket was, so to speak, self-created; but in respect of ordinary regimental accounts, the necessary retardation was compassed by requiring the sum allotted to the pay of each regiment to be accounted for under six different heads.

The first of these divisions was named Poundage,[1] and dealt with the deduction of one shilling in the pound from the pay of the whole Army. From the fund thus amassed there were paid three several charges, namely, Return-poundage, which signified the refunding, in certain corps, of the aforesaid deduction; a contribution to Chelsea Hospital; and Exchequer-fees and salaries of the Paymaster-general and other officials.

The second division bore the title of Contribution to Chelsea Hospital.[2] It will be observed that this charge, or a part of it, had already appeared under the head of Poundage; but that was perhaps the more reason why it should appear again.

The third division was called Subsistence, signifying that fraction of every man's pay which remained after the elimination of certain stoppages. This, in the case of the private foot-soldier, amounted nominally but not actually to the sum of sixpence a day.

The fourth division was the Allowance for Widows, namely, the pay of two fictitious men to every troop and company. This fund was entrusted to an official, known as the Paymaster of Widows' Pensions, who exacted from every widow an initial fee of two guineas on her first drawing her pension, and an annual fee of six shillings in addition. His office was a sinecure, his annual balance varied from £24,000 to £65,000, and he grew fat literally on the spoil of the widow.

[1] For the origin of Poundage, see vol. i. of this *History*, pp. 310, 314, 317.
[2] One day's full pay of all ranks, *ibid.* p. 317.

The fifth division was entitled Off-reckonings; that is to say, the various stoppages for clothing and other matters which accounted for the difference between the full pay and the Subsistence of the soldier.

The sixth division was denominated Clearings, and was made up of three separate items: first, the "Arrears" of the commissioned officers, corresponding to the Off-reckonings of the private soldier; secondly, Agency, which signified a deduction of twopence in the pound on the full pay of the regiment, for the Agent's profit; and thirdly (a most characteristic item), "so much of the soldier's subsistence as had not been issued under the name of subsistence."

There was also a seventh division known as Respites, which meant the stoppage of all pay; but as it was occasional only, I trust that the reader will content himself with the six already expounded.

Such was the form in which the Pay Office required regimental accounts to be presented; and it need hardly be said that it differed in every respect from that which was adopted by the Treasury in drawing up the "Establishment" of the Army. According to the rules of that venerable department, the Establishment was distributed not under six but under five heads, namely, the full pay of all ranks by day and year, and allowances (each one of them carefully distinguished from the other) for Widows, Colonels, Captains, and Agents. These allowances being all of them clothed in the guise of pay to fictitious men,[1] led to endless confusion and, as a natural consequence, to dishonesty,

[1] The allowances to Widows consisted of the full pay of two fictitious men per company. The allowance to Colonels was made up of (*a*) the subsistence of one fictitious man for his own use, (*b*) the "gross off-reckonings" of four fictitious men. The allowance to Captains consisted of the subsistence of two fictitious men, for expenses of recruiting, which was placed by the Agent to the credit of the "non-effective fund"—the equivalent in the Infantry of the "stock-purse" in the Cavalry. (See vol. ii. of this *History*, p. 581.) The allowance to the Agent consisted of the subsistence of one fictitious man for his own use.

which was almost impossible of detection. In fact, the chaos of "subsistence," "gross off-reckonings," "net off-reckonings," "stock-purses," and "non-effective funds" in the financial departments of the military service was simply indescribable. The computation of "off-reckonings" alone was a branch so extensive as to give a title to an official in the Pay Office; and if he were truly a master of that most abstruse of sciences he must have been a very remarkable man.

It is not difficult to read between the lines, that the Commissioners really abandoned in despair the task of comprehending the methods of our military finance. The first great source of perplexity, as they pointed out, was, that in the statement called the Pay of the Forces not one person received, either by the day or the year, the sum affixed as the pay of his rank. Further, the pay of the Army was so compounded and decompounded that without very curious and minute investigation an officer could never judge whether he had or had not received his due. Nevertheless, perfect comprehension was not essential to the reform of such a system. From 1784 onwards the votes for the Army were distributed under the distinct heads of Pay, Clothing, Agency, Allowances, and Recruiting, while an Act to regulate the Paymaster's Office swept its most flagrant abuses summarily away. The change was not at first wholly popular in the Army, since it involved the unlearning of much that had been mastered only with infinite difficulty. We find the Adjutant-general himself railing at "Mr. Burke's infernal Bill" for its overthrow of the old constitution of "stock-purses" and "non-effective funds"; but an admission, almost in the same breath, that these funds had offered too great facilities for "manœuvre," sufficiently shows that Burke's reforms were accepted in a good and loyal spirit by the Army.[1]

So far nothing but praise can be given to Pitt's

[1] *Commander-in-Chief's Letter Books*, 20th March 1788.

military measures, financial or otherwise ; but it is now 1783-1793. necessary to examine the question whether his reforms went far enough. The reader, if he has had the patience even to glance his eye over the last few pages, will at least have noticed the number of obscure terms used in the preparation of military accounts. Let me now explain, if he has not already realised it, that the whole of these terms may be reduced to the one word stoppages —stoppages from the pay of the soldier. In former volumes of this history[1] I have traced the origin of these deductions, and have hinted at the serious consequences which they had already begun to produce in 1763. On an early page[2] of the present volume, also, I have written that the pay of the British soldier at the close of the Seven Years' War was too small. It is time to probe this matter more deeply, and to ascertain whether this insufficiency of pay was, or should have been, as patent to Pitt then as it is to ourselves after a century of time.

I have already stated the establishment of the Army, as fixed by North and Fox, on the conclusion of peace in 1783 ; and it is only necessary to add that it was maintained at the same figure by Pitt. For its weakness in numbers neither party can, I think, be blamed. The principle of reducing the military forces to the lowest dimensions was consecrated by long precedent, and was more than ordinarily justified by the alarming increase of the public debt during the past war. But if the propriety of keeping only the framework of an Army in time of peace be conceded, the necessity for assigning to it a sufficient magnitude, and for preserving it in soundness and order, must be conceded also. Conway had been successful in resisting the diminution of the frame projected by North's scheme

---

[1] Vol. i. pp. 316, 319 ; vol. ii. pp. 576 *sqq.*
[2] P. 41. Having unfortunately omitted to state my authorities on that page, I insert them here. *Commander-in-Chief's Letter Books*, 16th May 1768. *Secretary's Common Letter Book*, 13th April 1771.

of disbandment; but he failed to prevent the principle of reduction from being extended to details. The regiments existing in 1764 were indeed preserved, but the number of companies within them was diminished from ten to eight, which of course signified a corresponding decrease in the number of officers and non-commissioned officers ready to train recruits upon any augmentation of the establishment. Finally, as has been already told, the ranks had been left almost empty by the instant and simultaneous flight of almost every man who was entitled to his discharge.

This haste on the part of all the three-years' men to quit the service might well have suggested that something was amiss, but no member of the Government seems to have taken any heed. Circulars were sent to the Colonels bidding them bestir themselves to fill the gaps in their regiments; and recruiting parties were despatched in all directions. But search where they might, from end to end of Great Britain, they could not obtain recruits. The consequences of the dearth of troops were early felt, for smugglers and other lawless folk were not slow to take advantage of the opportunity; and in 1785 the recruiting parties, instead of discontinuing their labours after the spring, as usual, were directed to pursue them throughout the summer and autumn. The same instructions were repeated in the following year, after which they became for some time of annual recurrence; but the parties might just as well have remained quietly at the headquarters of their regiments, for they found it absolutely impossible to persuade men to enter the service. Moreover, such recruits as were secured by fair means or foul were no sooner caught than they were lost again by desertion.[1]

In 1787, Pitt's firm attitude towards France over affairs in the Netherlands necessitated some increase of

---

[1] *Commander-in-Chief's Letter Books*, 8th August 1783, 29th January 1785, 24th April 1786, 20th February 1787, 28th January 1788, 24th March 1789, 11th February 1790.

the Army; and the need was rendered the more urgent 1783-1793. by the aggression, shortly to be narrated, of Tippoo Sahib in India. It was therefore ordered that four new regiments should be raised, two of them in Scotland and two in England, at the expense of the East India Company; that the third and fourth of the battalions of the Sixtieth, which had been disbanded at the peace, should be reconstituted; and that the whole of the battalions at home should be increased from eight companies of forty-two men to eleven companies of sixty. The four regiments for India are still with us as the Seventy-fourth and Seventy-fifth Highlanders, and the Seventy-sixth and Seventy-seventh Foot;[1] but the difficulty in raising them was so great that leave was given to accept prisoners from Gloucester gaol, dismissed seamen, and even out-pensioners of Chelsea Hospital as recruits.[2] The Sixtieth, whose old title of Royal Americans was now meaningless, and who were for the present condemned to perpetual service in the West Indies, were obliged to buy their recruits on the Continent of Europe at seven guineas a head.[3] The rest of the British regiments on colonial service were directed to recruit in Ireland, since men could not be found in Britain; and by merciless drafting three weak battalions were scraped together to reinforce the colonial garrisons. But the main reliance of the Government for a military force rested on twelve thousand Hessians, who, in consideration of the usual subsidy, were to be ready on demand at any time during the next four years. Such were the military expedients of the son of Chatham.

Fortunately or unfortunately, the order for augmentation had not been issued more than six weeks before a more favourable turn of affairs enabled the

---

[1] Sir Archibald Campbell's (74th), Robert Abercromby's (75th), Musgrave's (76th), Marsh's (77th). *Secretary's Common Letter Book*, 22nd October 1787.
[2] *Ibid.* 25th and 31st October 1787.
[3] *Ibid.* 6th November 1787.

1783-1793. Government to revoke it. The battalions were again reduced to their former numbers on paper (for except on paper they had been little increased), though on the urgent representation of the General Officers[1] the establishment of companies was maintained at ten. Still the difficulty of obtaining recruits continued, and in the spring of 1788 the regiments quartered in Britain were recommended to send their recruiting officers to Ireland, in the hope that better fortune might await them there.[2] But in Ireland, though men were indeed rather more willing to enlist than in England, they were considerably more ready to desert. In fact, although the King gave early warning that he would confirm sentences of death if adjudged to deserters,[3] the amount of desertion at this period was appalling. In Ireland the average number of deserters from the infantry in every year was twelve hundred, or one-sixth of the total establishment.[4] The evil rose to such a height that in 1788 the Lord Lieutenant opened depots for deserters at Cork and Dublin, where they were tried, sentenced to perpetual service abroad, and shipped off in large batches, chiefly to the Sixtieth Regiment in the West Indies, where it was thought that there were fewest facilities for them to desert again. To judge by the numbers transported, the penalty was held in no great terror; but at any rate the ranks of the Sixtieth were kept well filled, and it is probable that the men themselves were much improved.[5] Nothing is more remarkable than the splendid record of this regiment in the field, at a period when few soldiers entered it untainted by crime.

[1] *Miscellaneous Orders*, 15th November 1787.
[2] *Commander-in-Chief's Letter Books*, 3rd April 1788.
[3] *Secretary's Common Letter Book*, 10th March, 1785.
[4] Letter of General Luttrell, 19th December 1784. *S.P. Ireland*.
[5] *H.O.S.P. Ireland*. Lord Buckingham to Lord Sydney, 23rd June 1788, 17th January 1789. Lords Justices to same, 7th November 1789. Chief Secretary Hobart to Evan Nepean, 12th March 1790. Lord Westmoreland to Sydney, 28th March 1791. The largest batch sent to the Sixtieth at any one time was 122.

CH. XXVI   HISTORY OF THE ARMY   519

For two years longer the Army was allowed to drift 1783-1793.
on, with or without recruits, and then in May 1790 the
quarrel with Spain over Nootka Sound brought about
the need for a second augmentation of about sixteen
thousand men. As in 1787, a bounty of three guineas
was offered to recruits, which, with two guineas more
allowed to recruiting officers, brought the charge of
levy-money to five guineas for every man enlisted.
The sum was once more found insufficient. "The
whole country," wrote the Adjutant-general, Sir William
Fawcett, in October, " is overrun with recruiting officers
and their crimps; and the price of men has risen to
fifteen guineas a head at least."[1] It is significant, too,
that the whole or parts of no fewer than eight battalions
were employed on Marines' duty on board the fleet,
plain evidence that seamen were as difficult to procure
as soldiers.[2] Then the danger of war passed away, and
in November the establishment was again reduced.
But within four months Pitt's intervention between
Russia and Turkey called for the despatch of forty
ships to the Baltic, and the Army was required to find
men to man them.[3] "We shall probably be called
upon for at least a thousand men for the fleet," wrote
the Adjutant-general plaintively at the end of March; 1791.
" how we can do it until the Fourteenth and Nineteenth
arrive home from Jamaica, I don't know."[4] His fears
were realised; though they were soon relieved by
Pitt's change of attitude towards Russia. It is easy
now to understand why Pitt strove so strenuously
for peace in Europe, for he neither had, nor apparently
wished to have, soldiers or seamen. Our wonder is

[1] *Commander-in-Chief's Letter Books*, 26th October 1790.
[2] *Secretary's Common Letter Book*, 25th May, 7th June, 10th
November 1790. "South Britain will shortly be left in a very
defenceless state. Three battalions of Guards are now under orders
for foreign service. Exclusive of the remainder of the Guards and
a few dragoons, the Thirty-third will really be the only regiment
left." Nepean to Hobart, 19th October 1790. *S.P. Ireland.*
[3] *Ibid.* 1st April 1791.
[4] *Commander-in-Chief's Letter Books*, 29th March 1791.

increased that his resolution in foreign affairs should so often have prevailed, for it needed only the defiance of the Empress Catherine to turn his high language to naught. He showed the true intent of his policy by a slight reduction of the military establishment in June 1792.

The root of all the evil in the Army, and, it should be added, in the Navy also, was that the pay of the men was insufficient and the stoppages excessive. It is literally true that the only alternatives open to the private soldier were to desert or to starve; and desertion, through a curious chain of causes, brought about its own increase. All deserters were necessarily escorted by road from quarter to quarter, frequently for as much as a hundred miles backwards and forwards; and these long marches necessarily wore out portions of the escorting soldiers' clothing very rapidly. The unfortunate men were obliged to replace these articles at their own expense, that is to say, by further stoppage from their pay, which prevented them from supplying themselves with pipeclay, blacking,[1] and other small matters essential to their proper appearance on parade. Unable, therefore, to present himself in the condition which, under pain of punishment, was required of him, "unable" (the words are those of the Adjutant-general) "even to satisfy the common calls of hunger, and being without hope of relief, the soldier naturally deserted in despair."[2] Long and anxious was the correspondence between the General Officers on this alarming state of affairs, but there was no Commander-in-chief to press such matters upon the attention of Ministers; while the Secretary at War, Sir George Yonge, was too much occupied with manœuvres for securing votes to attend to such matters as the pay of the Army. Nor were the privates the only sufferers. The subalterns were, in the Adjutant-general's opinion, even more to be pitied than they. In 1786, the Colonels of the regiments of

---

[1] Then called "black-ball."
[2] *Commander-in-Chief's Letter Books*, October 1790.

cavalry in Ireland presented a memorial, setting forth 1783-1793. that, owing to the rise in the price of forage, the whole pay of a subaltern of dragoons was scarcely equal to the maintenance of his servant and of his horse, and that cornetcies could hardly be kept filled in consequence. "The addition of a shilling a day to the subaltern's pay will, I fear, seem too considerable for the Government to grant," wrote the Adjutant-general in 1788; "but something must be done both for privates and subalterns."[1]

The duty of redressing these grievances obviously lay with Pitt, who was Chancellor of the Exchequer; but it seems that though willing to pay £36,000 a year as a retaining fee for Hessians abroad, he could afford nothing for starving officers and soldiers at home. In 1790 the King himself asked to be furnished with an account of the debts of the poor soldiers, being aware that the distress and oppression caused by those debts was the chief cause of the prevalent excessive desertion.[2] He had long seen and lamented the soldier's hard lot; and indeed there was no better friend than George the Third either to officers or to men who were deserving. Still the mischief remained unremedied, until in 1791 Fawcett, by a happy inspiration, called in the aid of Lord Barrington, the former Secretary at War, and with his support wrung from Pitt some relief for the private soldier. By a warrant issued in 1792 the iniquitous deduction known as poundage was abolished, more liberal regulations were issued as to stoppages for clothing, and a weekly allowance of bread was added to the pittance of pay which passed under the name of subsistence. The general result was that the soldier not only received food enough to keep him alive, but the magnificent sum of 18s. 10½d. a year, payable every two months, over and above all deductions for

---

[1] *Commander-in-Chief's Letter Books.* Fawcett to General Mackay, 29th May 1788. H.O.S.P. *Ireland.* Rutland to Sydney, 28th May 1786.

[2] *Ibid.* 13th and 30th April 1790.

food and clothing. But this concession was obtained only by sacrificing the claims of the unfortunate subalterns.[1]

A glance at the footnote, showing the improved condition of the soldier under the new warrant, will indicate better than any long explanation the hardships under which he had suffered. The salutary effect of the change was rapidly seen, for within a fortnight the Adjutant-general was able to report a decrease in desertion and new facility in obtaining recruits.[2] Fawcett might justly plume himself on his success, though,

[1] The new warrant put the foot-soldier on the following footing :—

			£	s.	d.
Pay at 6d. a day, per annum			9	2	6
Poundage (remitted)				12	2
Bread allowance at $10\tfrac{1}{2}$d. a week			2	5	$7\tfrac{1}{2}$
	Total		12	0	$3\tfrac{1}{2}$
From this deduct,					
Food at 3s. a week		£7 16 0			
Stoppages for necessaries (see below)		3 5 5			
			11	1	5
			£0	18	$10\tfrac{1}{2}$

Articles, etc., to be supplied to the soldier gratis.

1 pair of gaiters, 1 pair of breeches, repair of clothes, 1 "hair-leather" (queue?), share of watch-coats, worm and musket-tools (every five years), emery, brick-dust, oil . . £0 16 $11\tfrac{1}{2}$

List of necessaries to be provided by the foot-soldier out of his pay and allowances per year, as occasion may require.

1 pair of gaiters, 2 pair of gloves, repair of shoes, 1 pair of stockings, 2 shirts, foraging cap, knapsack (once in six years), pipeclay and whiting, clothes-brush (once in four years), 3 shoe-brushes, black-ball, worsted mitts, powder-bag and puff (once in three years), 2 combs, grease and powder for hair, washing at 4d. a week. Total . . . £3 5 5

Note.—The stoppage of 2d. a day for the rest of his clothing was continued, but this was taken as a matter of course, and hence the pay of the soldier is set down, as above, at 6d. a day, instead of 8d., which was its nominal amount. *Commander-in-Chief's Letter Books*, 4th, 7th, 19th January 1792.

[2] *Ibid.* 24th January 1792.

as we shall see all too clearly before long, it was but 1783-1793. short-lived. But what are we to think of William Pitt, whose ill-judged economy allowed the Army to sink into a condition which turned it from a safeguard into a peril to the State? " Pitt was of the school of Palmerston," an eminent living historian has written, " and he never allowed the armament of the country to sink into neglect."[1] Let Pitt receive due credit for his fortification of the West Indies and for his effort to fortify the dockyards; but the true armament of a country is trained men. He has been pronounced, in the opinion of the most competent judges, to be the greatest of our ministers of finance; and his claim to the title rests firmly on the reforms effected on his first entry into office. But surely it is a blot on any man's financial administration that the money voted for the pay of the Army should have been spent in converting soldiers into deserters, honest men into outlaws. Surely it is a grave reproach to a statesman, not less on financial than on general grounds, that with full knowledge of the condition of the private soldier (I say nothing of the seaman) he should have left him to starve from 1784 to 1791, doled him out a grudging pittance in 1792, and increased his pay, under menace of mutiny, practically threefold in 1797.

Unfortunately, it was not in respect of the regular Army only that Pitt permitted economy to interfere with efficiency. Only two-thirds of the Militia were called out for training during these years, the remaining third being exempted. This would have been a less serious matter had the principle of rotation, that is to say, of passing through the ranks every man liable to service, been observed according to the original design of the Militia Act. Attention was called to the im-

[1] Lecky, *History of England* (Cabinet ed.) vi. 66. Let me disclaim any carping spirit in this quotation. No one, I think, can appreciate the labours of a historian so thoroughly as a fellow-toiler, however humble, in the same field ; and to appreciate Mr. Lecky's work is to admire it.

portance of this principle in the House of Lords, and it was shown that, if economy were the object, it would be better and cheaper to call out a much smaller number every year and to make the men serve for three years only, but to insist that every man should take his turn at least for that period.[1] Considering that the Militia Act was the most valuable, even though not the most famous, creation of his great father, it is rather surprising that Pitt did not adopt some suggestion of this kind. But he did not; and the result was that no more than twenty thousand militia were trained during these years, and they almost to a man paid substitutes, who would otherwise have enlisted in the Army. In Ireland, indeed, he did make an effort to establish an efficient Militia;[2] for there the Volunteers still clung to their arms, and there was too much reason to fear lest those arms should pass into dangerous hands. A Militia Bill was accordingly prepared and even printed; but, owing to the jealousy of the Volunteers, it was judged inexpedient to introduce it into the Irish Parliament. The project was therefore dropped, through no fault of Pitt's, and the national defence of Ireland remained at the mercy of the Volunteers.

Another disadvantage from which the Army suffered greatly during these years was the want of a Commander-in-chief; for, apparently from motives of economy, no successor was appointed to Conway on his retirement in 1784. Thus the entire control and patronage of the Army fell to the Secretary at War, with very evil effects to its discipline. The letters of the Adjutant-general abound in complaints of his powerlessness to enforce regulations, and of the abuses which sprang up in consequence. Officers belonging to regiments in colonial garrisons reverted to the old habit of

[1] This was Lord Stanhope's suggestion. *Parl. Hist.* 16th June 1786.
[2] *H.O.S.P. Ireland.* Sydney to Rutland, 11th January 1785. The draft of this very able despatch is in Pitt's hand. Though of considerable length, and evidently written with extreme rapidity, there is not an erasure in the whole of it.

evading duty with them, not the less readily since 1783-1793. field-officers set the example; and Fawcett was obliged to appeal to the Deputy-Secretary at War to threaten them with the penalties that they had deserved. "Two of them, being members of Parliament," he wrote, sarcastically, "are in no danger of being superseded, so long as they vote on a certain side of the question."[1] Thus discipline was as usual sacrificed to the supposed exigencies of Government by party, and colonial garrisons were left without officers, just as if Minorca had never fallen, and Byng had never been shot, and Newcastle had never been driven from office by the elder Pitt.

In Ireland symptoms of even more dangerous indiscipline had shown themselves. During 1785 and 1786 there was much trouble in Munster with the lawless bands known as the Whiteboys, which were only suppressed by the employment of a large body of troops. For such work cavalry was especially in request, and, to judge by the list of regiments on the Irish Establishment, there should have been no lack of mounted troops. It was, however, found that the four regiments, then known as the First to the Fourth Horse, and since 1788 as the Fourth to the Seventh Dragoon Guards, were absolutely useless and untrustworthy. These corps were a curious survival of King William's day, being mounted on the old-fashioned black war-horse, which was already becoming rare and is now long since extinct. Since their ranks were filled with old soldiers, and both men and horses had been drilled for countless years in the execution of the same evolutions, they had probably no peers in the world for precision of movement and stateliness of appearance; but for any true military purpose they were valueless and obsolete.

This failing was easily corrected by converting them into dragoons, with the titles above mentioned, but the real evil in them was of deeper root. They had been 1788. March.

[1] *Commander-in-Chief's Letter Books.* Adjutant-general to Lewis, 24th September 1788.

1783-1793. quartered in Ireland for so long that they were popularly known as the Irish Horse, and, to use the words of the Duke of Rutland, having become virtually provincial regiments, raised among the disaffected and liable to constant seduction, they were absolutely a source of danger. The obvious remedy was that they and the rest of the cavalry in Ireland should take their turn in rotation to be quartered in Great Britain; and this step was persistently urged by the Lord Lieutenant, but without success. The Colonels, whose property they were, resisted the change, and nothing was done. "I am convinced," wrote Chief Secretary Orde, "that the day will come when repentance will be felt too late for giving way to these selfish objections."[1] Such a day did come, in respect not of the regiments immediately in question, but of another which was in precisely the same case and was quartered in Ireland at this very time. Then the Commander-in-chief swept its very name with ignominy from the list of the Army. Had there been such a Commander-in-chief in 1786 this danger and disgrace might have been avoided.

There was yet another complication which, though in its origin the work of no human hand, wrought not a little to weaken still further the enfeebled discipline of the Army, namely, the mental malady which disabled the King from October 1788 until February 1789. It is probable that the stability of the King's reason was always perilously insecure, and that more than once, in times of great anxiety and stress, it had already gone near to be overset;[2] but now it fairly collapsed, and the

---

[1] *H.O.S.P. Ireland.* Rutland to Sydney, 14th February 1784, 26th September 1786. Orde to Nepean, 10th March 1786.

[2] I may perhaps venture to suggest that George III.'s mental condition might be traced with some accuracy through careful study of his handwriting. While going through the large collection of his holograph minutes at Dropmore, without a thought of his sanity or insanity, my attention was suddenly arrested by a change, not in the substance, but in the written character of the documents; and on comparison of the dates I found that this change corresponded with the first manifestations of mental failure.

throne was to all intent left vacant. The prospect of a 1788-1793. Regency roused the dormant hopes of the Opposition, for it was tolerably certain that if the Prince of Wales should take his father's place he would dismiss Pitt's Administration and call Fox and his friends into office. There is no need here to enter into the heated debates on the Regency Bill which was brought forward by the Government; let it suffice that Fox, whose "old party principles on all constitutional questions" forbade him to sanction the fortification of the dockyards, became the champion of the divine right of princes when he saw the chance of climbing into power on the Regent's shoulders. The evil was arrested by the King's recovery; but meanwhile the Prince of Wales and his company had laid their plans for turning the patronage of the Army to their own account. There was to have been a general promotion, extending to the captains made in 1776; a vast number of colonels were to have been advanced to the rank of major-general in order to include Lord Rawdon in the list; ten aide-de-camps were to have been appointed for the Regent, with the rank of colonel; the Regent himself, and his brothers the Dukes of York and Gloucester and General Conway, were to have been created field-marshals; the Duke of York was to have been Commander-in-chief, and Fitzpatrick, Fox's dearest friend, Secretary at War. "Thank God, the King's recovery has prevented all this mischief," wrote Fawcett fervently; and though, as shall be seen in due time, the Duke of York was afterwards to approve himself a Commander-in-chief of great merit, there can be no doubt that the disappointment of these unscrupulous designs was a great deliverance for the Army. But it is not difficult for any man to understand the injury wrought upon good order and discipline by the mere broaching of such projects.[1]

In such lamentable circumstances, the energies of all thoughtful officers during this period turned them-

[1] *Commander-in-Chief's Letter Books.* Fawcett to Colonel Musgrave, 8th April 1789. *Cornwallis Correspondence,* i. 419, 425, 446.

selves chiefly into technical channels. General Luttrell, afterwards Lord Carhampton, did indeed attack the difficult question of recruiting by the formulation of an ingenious scheme of short service;[1] but with no sign of immediate result. Nor, curiously enough, was advantage taken of an extension of the Territorial System which had been effected in 1782 by the affiliation of every regiment of infantry to some county or part of a county.[2] In the matter of assimilating the troublesome variations which distinguished the British from the Irish Establishment, some progress was made,[3] but herewith the efforts of military men for administrative reform were exhausted. In fact, though the training of the Army was reckoned to be their concern, the making and organisation of it were treated as a matter for civilians to determine, from the depth of that wisdom which is supposed to flow from the strife of factions.

The question of training the soldier had, however, assumed an importance which might worthily occupy the strongest intellects of military men. The American War had wrought a revolution in tactics. The enemy encountered by the British had been indeed civilised, but untaught, undisciplined, unfettered by military traditions, and, it must be added, not guiltless of abuse of the customs of war. It is true that the Americans had formed a certain number of regular

[1] The scheme was as follows :—Enlist infantrymen for seven years (then the usual period for apprentices). Let any that will re-engage for another seven years receive half-bounty and an extra guinea a year, to be paid to them in a lump at the end of their fourteen years, so as to set them up in a trade. Let those who will re-engage for a third term of seven years receive their seven guineas then, and a pension at Chelsea or Kilmainham at the close of twenty-one years. Cavalry should be enlisted for ten years. Their pay should be increased, which could be accomplished without additional expense if the clothing of the men were more economically managed. H.O.S.P. Ireland, 501, 19th December 1784.

[2] *Commander-in-Chief's Letter Books*, 31st August 1782. These county titles of 1782, with a few alterations, lasted until the present Territorial System was adopted.

[3] Sydney to the Chief Secretary, 6th March 1788. *S.P. Ireland.*

regiments; but manœuvres and pitched battles on any considerable scale had been rare, and when they had taken place had turned invariably to the advantage of the British. At Brooklyn, Whiteplains, and Brandywine, Howe had outmanœuvred and outfought Washington, not always with superior numbers on his side; and in fact, wherever the Americans attempted to fight according to accepted rule, they had been beaten. It was wholly by irregular warfare that the Americans had got the better of the British, so far as they had got the better of them at all. Their natural shrewdness had shown them that irregular tactics were best suited to a wild and thinly populated country, and they had practised them accordingly with great success. By such tactics and no other had Burgoyne been vanquished. The methods of Flanders were impossible in the interminable forests through which he had advanced; and cunning marksmen hidden in trees had thinned his numbers, particularly in respect of officers, far more than the musketry of the American platoons. Drill and discipline could make the British soldier stand and be killed; but they could not avail him to silence the unseen rifle which, safely ensconced beyond the range of his own musket, struck down first his officers, then his sergeants, and at last himself.

The British therefore had no alternative but to learn from their enemies, to pit individual against individual, marksman against marksman, irregular fighting against irregular fighting. Tarleton, Simcoe, and Ferguson had met the Americans with their own weapons; they had suffered severe defeats it is true, for their duties compelled them to run great risks, but they had achieved also remarkable successes. The methods of their irregular corps also were to a great extent forced upon the whole of the British troops, owing partly to the deadly marksmanship of the American riflemen, but still more to the fact that almost every important action of the war was fought on heavily wooded ground. Thus the British infantry in the field in 1780 and 1781 had

1783-1793. lost in great measure, if not entirely, the solidity and precision which had distinguished it at Fontenoy and at Minden. The depth of the ranks had been reduced from three to two, the files had been opened, and all movements had been conducted loosely and irregularly, with an independence of action on the part of small units and of individuals which was wholly at variance with the received doctrines of Europe. This looseness of formation had been further encouraged by the very small part played by cavalry, as distinguished from mounted infantry, throughout the operations. It is true that Tarleton and, still more conspicuously, the American Colonel Washington had occasionally wrought great results by the charge of a mere handful of sabres. It is true also that Morgan's solid array had not only repulsed but annihilated Tarleton's thin attacking line at Cowpens, and that Clinton had ascribed the whole disaster to Tarleton's reduction of the orthodox three ranks to two. But none the less British officers returned from America with a fixed idea that the firearm was now all in all, that the shock of the bayonet was so rare as to be practically obsolete, and that the greater the frontage of fire that could be developed, the better. They were therefore disposed to abolish the third rank in the infantry altogether, since its fire, if not positively dangerous to the two front ranks, was wholly ineffective; to shorten the old musket, which had been made long on purpose for use in three ranks, and to devote the weight thus saved to enlargement of the bore; and finally, to maintain the loose ordering of files —or, in other words, a wide lateral interval between man and man—in order to give to every individual greater freedom of action.[1]

On the other hand, officers who had stayed at home during the war, and especially one of them who had frequently witnessed the Prussian manœuvres, perceived in these doctrines not a little that was dangerous. This

[1] *Miscellaneous Orders*, 1789, vol. xxxiv. p. 49. Dundas's *Principles of Military Movements*.

officer was Colonel David Dundas, at this period on the staff of headquarters in Dublin. He was a lean, dry, crabbed Scot, who as a youth had walked from Edinburgh to Woolwich in order to gain the post of lieutenant-fire-worker in the Royal Artillery; but he lacked neither brains nor diligence, and was an enthusiast in his profession. In 1785 he witnessed the last manœuvres carried out under the eye of the Great Frederick. He saw three thousand cavalry advance at the trot in column of squadrons, and deploy for attack over a front of a mile in less than three minutes. He saw the infantry also manœuvre in flexible columns, deploying in battalions and brigades with beautiful accuracy on their appointed alignment, not with intervals between files or even between companies, but shoulder to shoulder, solid and steady, three ranks deep. Cornwallis, fresh from America, was also present, and hit a blot in the proceedings, of which, in the light of subsequent events, it is curious to read.[1] But Dundas was asking himself, first, if British infantry in the new loose formation could contend successfully with these Prussian battalions and squadrons ; and secondly, whether a British officer who attempted to manœuvre a brigade or a division after the Prussian manner could be sure that any two of his battalions would execute the necessary movements on the same principle or in the same way. The answer to these questions was necessarily in the negative, for though regulations for field-movements did exist in the British Army, no man could say which of them were in force or which obsolete. Colonels had always claimed and exercised the right to employ their own peculiar systems for their own regiments,[2] and there was too much reason to fear that they

1783-1793.

[1] "Their manœuvres were such as the worst general in England would be hooted at for practising; two lines coming up within six yards of one another and firing until they had no ammunition left; nothing could be more ridiculous." *Cornwallis Correspondence*, i. 212.

[2] General Harvey, when Adjutant-general, fought hard against what he called "the d—d whims of individuals" in this respect. *Commander-in-Chief's Letter Books*, 13th February 1772.

would establish the irregularity imported from America as a regulation for themselves. Finally, the extreme weakness of British regiments in time of peace, and the impossibility of assembling battalions sufficient to train officers in the handling of large bodies of troops, made the need for uniformity of system and of principle the more urgent.

The principal officers at headquarters in London and in Dublin were heartily in accord with Dundas, and the King himself accepted the dedication of the large quarto volume wherein Dundas embodied his system in 1788. The Commander-in-chief in Ireland was charged to try the new drill experimentally with the garrison of Dublin, and the Adjutant-general made it his business to procure for it the favour of the Duke of York, then Colonel of the Coldstream, and of the Brigade of Guards. Favourable reports having been received by all parties, the new regulations were sent out to India, and in March 1792 were brought into force by general order for the whole Army.[1] With their contents I shall not trouble the reader, except to remark that the formation in three ranks was, in theory at any rate, retained, which was natural, considering that the new system was based entirely on the Prussian principles. There can be no doubt, however, that it marked a great advance on all previous efforts; and in effect this drill-book of Dundas has been the foundation of all similar books that have since been issued. Perhaps its most valuable feature was that it laid down for the first time instructions for teaching the recruit how to march, his step being regulated by pace-stick and plummet. But when it is remembered that even under such a master as Coote the only form of column known in India was that obtained by giving the line the simple words " Right turn " or " Left turn," it may be guessed that the introduction of new and less cumbrous forma-

[1] *Commander-in-Chief's Letter Books*, August 1788, 24th May, 11th November 1789, 6th April 1790, 4th February, 23rd March 1792.

tions was a great gain.[1] There was, however, so much that was rigid, formal, and unnecessary in Dundas's drill that it gained for him the nickname of "Old Pivot"; while he also made the fatal mistake of distributing the whole science of military evolution into eighteen manœuvres, which were a sad stumbling-block to slow-witted officers. "General," said Sir John Moore to him in 1804, "that book of yours has done a great deal of good, and would be of great value if it were not for those damned eighteen manœuvres." "Why—ay," answered Dundas slowly in broad Scots, "blockheads don't understand."[2] We shall see in due time that Moore sifted out all that was best both of Prussian teaching and of American experience for the training of the Light Division; meanwhile, it is sufficient to impress upon the reader that we owe our adoption of double in lieu of triple rank—a very notable matter in our military history—to the American War.

Dundas's regulations constituted by far the most important and beneficial reform that had been effected in the Army for many years, but the British officer was not negligent of other useful matters. In 1787 it was at last decided that some difference in clothing should be made for troops serving in the East and West Indies; though the change did not at once go further than the proposal to introduce white hats, "cocked and ornamented according to pattern." In 1789 Colonel Musgrave carried improvement rather further by submitting a list of a complete kit for the soldier in India,

[1] For example, under Dundas's system each company was divided into two platoons, and each platoon into two subdivisions. Taking the company at 60 men, a platoon would be 30 men (10 files) and a subdivision 15 men (5 files). Thus a battalion could be manœuvred in columns either of 20 men, or 10 men, or 5 men abreast, the last-named being sufficiently narrow to serve as a column of route. It will be seen that in 1791-1792 Cornwallis used the column of platoons (or, as he called it, half-companies) for all manœuvres in Mysore.

[2] Bunbury. *Great War with France*, p. 46. A list of the eighteen manœuvres will be found in Grose's *Military Antiquities*, ii. 191.

1783-1793. including a round white hat, a jacket instead of a coat, trousers in lieu of breeches, and, generally speaking, garments better suited than English clothing to a tropical climate. Curiously enough, Lord Cornwallis recommended that the colour of the hat should be changed to black, and ultimately it was ordained that in future every recruit for the East or West Indies should be provided with a black hat at least six inches high in the crown and four inches wide in the brim.[1] In these days of helmets such a head-dress does not sound peculiarly well-fitted for the torrid zone, but it must be remembered that at this period the cocked hat, which was worn by the whole Army excepting the Light Dragoons, had attained to its most senseless and preposterous shape. Evolved originally, of course, from the broad-leafed hat of the cavalier, the cocked hat had passed through the stage of being looped up first on one side, according to a fashion recently reintroduced, then on three sides, making the three-cornered hat of George the Second's time, and finally on the back and front only, thus affording neither shade to the eyes nor shelter to the back of the head. In fact, the unsuitability of the head-dress was such that anything with a peak or a brim was an improvement on it.[2] Another change of importance to the soldiers' health was the substitution of black gaiters for the white spatterdashes with which Hogarth's pictures have made us familiar, and which are still to be seen on the legs of the drum-majors of the Guards on great occasions. This alteration was made first in 1767, and no doubt saved many a man from rheumatism, for the white gaiters must frequently have been donned when still damp with whiting; but it was not until 1784 that the danger of the same evil was averted by an order that black

[1] *Commander-in-Chief's Letter Books*, 17th November 1787, 17th March 1789. *Miscellaneous Orders*, 1791, vol. xxxiv. *Secretary's Common Letter Book*, 1st July 1790.

[2] The Light Infantry had a cap of black leather instead of the cocked hat.

gaiters should in future be of wool and not of linen.[1] 1783-1793.
It was, however, not yet time for the abolition of long
hair, pomatum, and powder, which no doubt added
greatly to the amenity of the soldier's appearance,
but cost him much time and ate somewhat deeply
into his scanty pittance of pay. In July 1776, when
Howe and Burgoyne were fairly started on their march
to disaster, the King solemnly issued an edict that the
hair of the Infantry should be dressed in a uniform
manner "in the mode that is called clubbed";[2] and
this absurdity was destined to endure for yet some
years.

A few minor changes in equipment must also be
recorded before we take leave of the Infantry. One of
the first orders issued after the return of the Army
from America was that the manual exercise should be
performed in two and a half minutes, with one minute
more for going through the firing positions in the three
ranks. This pointed to the attainment of great speed
in loading, and therefore to greater expenditure of
ammunition.[3] Accordingly, the waist-belts of Infantry
were transferred to their right shoulders so as to carry
a second cartridge-pouch, and the number of rounds
contained in the two pouches was raised to fifty-six.
Thus originated the cross-belt of later days. The
Light Infantry also, who had hitherto carried a powder-
horn and bullet-bag, were provided with cartridges and
with a small priming-horn. The Grenadiers on their
side laid aside their swords and matches and became
more nearly assimilated to the battalion-companies.
Two more venerable weapons also disappeared at this
time. The halberd, which had been already displaced

[1] *Commander-in-Chief's Letter Books*, 15th September 1767, 21st July 1784.
[2] *Ibid.* 27th July 1776.
[3] *Ibid.* 20th March, 21st July 1784. The speed attained in loading was remarkable. Sir John Moore, when a boy of fourteen, could load and fire five times in a minute. *Life of Sir John Moore*, i. 9. Major Patrick Ferguson could do still greater wonders with a rifle, and make excellent practice.

1783-1793. by the fusil[1] in the case of sergeants of Grenadiers in 1769, was utterly abolished in 1792, and a pike substituted for it.[2] In 1786 the spontoon or half-pike ceased to be the weapon of the Infantry officer, as it had been for a full century, and was replaced by the sword.[3] Subalterns had for some time past been armed with a fusil, and the privilege of carrying the same weapon had been accorded to all the officers,[4] apparently, of the Seventh and Twenty-third Fusiliers; but it was with spontoon in hand that the great Marlborough had marched past the King at the head of the First Guards, and the disappearance of the ancient arm was emblematic of very much. Finally, it is worth noting as a minute point that in 1791 the field-officers of all regiments were required to wear epaulettes, which in many cases served to show their superior rank, thus originating a distinction, which as yet there was not, between the dress of different grades of regimental officers. Hence arose the use of two very familiar badges; for officers of Grenadiers bore a grenade embroidered on the epaulette, and those of Light Infantry a bugle-horn, which instrument had come fairly into use during the past war.[5]

---

[1] The fusil was simply a musket of less than the ordinary length and weight. The musket at this time was 3 feet 8 inches long in the barrel and weighed 14 lbs. It was very shortly afterwards altered to 3 feet 6 inches of length in the barrel, and to a weight of 12 lbs., the bore being ·550 of an inch, or (in sporting parlance) 14½.

[2] *Commander-in-Chief's Letter Books*, April 1769. *Secretary's Common Letter Book*, 9th May 1792.

[3] *Secretary's Common Letter Book*, 3rd April 1786.

[4] *Commander-in-Chief's Letter Books*, 31st July 1770.

[5] *Ibid.* 30th June 1791. The want of distinction to mark the different ranks of officers led sometimes to unpleasant consequences. At St. Lucia a captain, who was taken prisoner by the French, was treated as a private because his coat was very much the worse for wear. Colin Lindsay, who tells the story, adds, "He wore no shoulder-knot, it being often the custom of our Light Infantry officers to wear instead of them a sort of fringe called wings." He adds that in the French army there were distinctions to mark every rank of officer. Lindsay also mentions that after the action of 18th December 1778 the Light Infantry bugle-horn was employed to sound a parley instead of a drum, and that

From the Infantry I pass to the Cavalry, which 1783-1793. needed reform even more than the sister service. The experience of the American War, as I have already shown, had leaned entirely on the side of mounted infantry as against the cavalry proper; and it is therefore remarkable that the changes now effected should have been wholly in favour of cavalry and opposed to mounted infantry. The firelock or musket was taken from all dragoons and a carbine substituted for it, while the bayonet, though retained by the heavy dragoons, was discarded by light cavalry. Burgoyne and Eliott, both of them sometime colonels of light dragoons, seem to have been principally responsible for this change, for they had advocated the cause of the carbine, and even of a rifled carbine, in 1772, with the result that a weapon of accuracy up to the range of five hundred yards was produced, though not apparently adopted, in 1787. It was further ordained that all swords should in future be of one pattern and should be tested before issue; and some effort was made to reduce the saddlery and accoutrements to uniformity.[1] Finally the Light Dragoons, who represented the cavalry proper, were distinguished more decidedly from their heavy brethren by being dressed in blue, with a leather fur-combed helmet in lieu of the cocked hat;[2] and the number of their regiments was increased from six to twelve.[3] For the Cavalry, as for the Infantry, Dundas produced a new system of exercise, based upon

the French, not understanding this novelty, fired on the flag of truce; when the horn first came into use I confess that I cannot say. I suspect it to have been borrowed from the Hessian Jägers, who certainly possessed it. Probably when the first company or corps of Jägers, or, as we should say, of huntsmen and gamekeepers, was raised, they brought their hunting-horns with them and applied the calls of the chase to military purposes. Lindsay's story is in *Lives of the Lindsays*, iii. 346-48.

[1] *Commander-in-Chief's Letter Books*, 31st May 1788, 2nd August 1788; *Miscellaneous Orders*, xxxiii. p. 306, 1787.
[2] *Secretary's Common Letter Book*, 10th April 1784.
[3] The 8th, 9th, and 14th were made Light Dragoons in 1775-6; the 7th, 10th, 11th, 12th, and 13th in 1783.

1783-1793. the same principles and therefore combining the same merits and the same defects. In the mounted service, however, the old formation in three ranks had been finally abolished in 1771, and was not, as in the Infantry, restored. The besetting sin of the Cavalry seems to have been the sacrifice of sound practical training to a love of display. Officers appear to have thought it sufficient if their squadrons could execute a certain number of evolutions with rapidity, and charge at headlong speed. It seems never to have occurred to them that the rally after the charge is the true test of a well-trained cavalry. Amherst in 1779 perceived the evil, and issued a general order forbidding the "continued vehemence of the charge," which served only to break up the squadrons; and he went so far as to order that they should advance to the attack always at the trot, and break into a gallop only when within fifty yards of the supposed enemy.[1] Nevertheless, this old defect of British Cavalry continued throughout the Peninsular War, and, as is well known, was conspicuous at Waterloo. The probability is that it was due as much to bad riding as to any one cause, and that this failing in its turn was ascribable to want of facilities for the imparting of proper instruction. Two regiments, the Blues and the Queen's Bays, seem to have built for themselves riding-schools, but these were the only two to be found in the United Kingdom.[2] Nevertheless, something was at least done to direct attention to the question by Lord Pembroke, the Colonel of the Royal Dragoons, who in 1761 published a small volume for the instruction of the soldier in horsemanship. Judging by the fact that this book reached a third edition in 1778, we may reasonably infer that it had passed into general use.

A single small incident alone remains to be noticed before dismissing this review of the Cavalry. The conversion of the old regiments of horse into Dragoon

---

[1] *Commander-in-Chief's Letter Books*, 30th August 1779.
[2] *Ibid.* Harvey to Blaquiere, February 1773.

Guards has already been recorded; almost at the same time the hand of reform overtook the still more useless corps known as the Horse Guards and Horse Grenadier Guards. It was none too soon, for though the two troops of Grenadiers might have been accounted in some degree soldiers, the Horse Guards were simply a collection of London tradesmen, and, in the Duke of York's judgment, "the most unmilitary troops that ever were seen."[1] Both Horse Grenadiers and Horse Guards were now reorganised[2] into the two regiments which still stand at the head of the Army List with the title of First and Second Life Guards. In spite of their exalted position these are in reality the youngest, in one sense, of our regiments of disciplined horse. "If they keep exactly to the standard which they have settled," wrote the Duke of York, "they will be the finest bodies of men that ever were seen." The prediction has been very fully verified.

Passing next to the Artillery we find like progress as in the other branches of the service; for, though there was little change in organisation, the corps was augmented in January 1793 by the formation of two companies of Horse Artillery, the first germ of many famous batteries.[3] One great distinction of these companies, apart from the mounting of all the gunners, was that they possessed their own trained drivers, and thus set a precedent for a very useful reform which, a few years later, was to be extended to the whole of the Artillery. The Engineers also were not forgotten. Early in 1785 Colonel Barré in the House of Commons called attention to the grievances of this small but deserving body of officers; and now that the question of fortifying our naval stations had been seriously

[1] *Cornwallis Correspondence*, i. 402.
[2] *Secretary's Common Letter Book*, 14th March 1788.
[3] It is somewhat singular that the units of the Horse Artillery should have begun as companies, continued as troops, and ended as batteries.

1783-1793. brought forward, there was the more need for their relief and encouragement. The Duke of Richmond took the matter in hand, and in April 1787 the corps was reorganised as the Royal Engineers, with precedence of the Royal Artillery; while in October of the same year there was formed the body of Military Artificers which gave such a shock to the exquisite constitutional sensibility of Fox.[1] Nor was the Ordnance Office less watchful over its material than over its men. In 1787, a Mr. Walton's powder-mills at Waltham were purchased by the nation, for the manufacture of its own powder. Certain mills at Faversham had been bought for the same purpose in 1759, but apparently had been little used, since throughout the American War, as at previous periods, gunpowder was obtained from private merchants, with results that called forth bitter complaints from Admiral Barrington in 1779. Exhaustive experiments were therefore made by the Controller of the Laboratory—a certain Major Congreve, whose fame is not yet wholly extinct—and it was decided that henceforth it would be a more satisfactory as well as a cheaper arrangement for the country to make its powder for itself.[2] There was, therefore, ground for hope that British ships might no longer be sent to sea with defective ammunition, as the result of some petty political job.

Lastly, three small matters relating to Colonial Defence must arrest our attention for a moment before we return to the wars in the East Indies. In 1789 a small corps of some three hundred men, soon afterwards increased to five hundred, was enlisted for the protection of a penal settlement newly established at Port Jackson in New South Wales. Two years later a somewhat similar corps was raised for service in Upper Canada, under the command of Colonel Simcoe, retaining the green uniform faced with blue which had been made

---

[1] *Miscellaneous Orders*, 25th April 1787. *Warrant Books*, 10th October 1787.

[2] *Warrant Books*, 11th October 1787.

famous by the Queen's Rangers.[1] Yet a few months 1783-1793. later, in January 1792, a regiment of four troops of Light Dragoons was formed for permanent service in Jamaica; but, since those were the palmy days of the West Indies, the island paid for these troops herself, whence they were known as the Twentieth or Jamaica Light Dragoons.[2] Little more than a century has passed since those days, and now we see the once wealthy Jamaica fallen from her high estate and wholly dependent on the Mother Country for protection; whereas Canada and Australia return to her, in her time of need, her first assistance multiplied an hundredfold.

[1] *Secretary's Common Letter Book*, 30th September 1791.
[2] *Ibid.* 20th January 1792. This regiment was disbanded in 1819, but its honours are kept by the present Twentieth Hussars.

CHAPTER XXVII

1784. I RETURN now to the narrative of events in the East Indies. The question of Indian administration had, as we have seen, engaged the particular attention of the English Government, and had even wrecked the Coalition Ministry of Fox and North. Pitt, therefore, in 1784 introduced a new India Bill, vesting the supreme authority over the civil and military affairs of the Company in a Board of six Privy Councillors, inclusive of one Secretary of State and the Chancellor of the Exchequer, and placing the appointment of the Commander-in-chief in the hands of the Crown. To put an end to ambitious schemes of aggression, the Governor-general and Council were restrained by this Act from declaring war or entering into warlike treaties except "when hostilities should actually have commenced, or preparation should actually have been made for the commencement of hostilities against the British nation in India." This provision, though not in itself unjustified by past events, was from a military point of view simply insane; for if it had any meaning at all, it signified that an enemy must be allowed to complete his preparations before he could be attacked. Such a clause could not restrain an unscrupulous Governor-general, though it might greatly hamper a conscientious one; and the Government was careful to select a conscientious man in the person of Lord Cornwallis to unite in himself the posts of Governor-general and Commander-in-chief. He accordingly sailed for Calcutta in 1786.

The mischievous tendency of this restriction was 1786. greatly strengthened by the shameful attack delivered against Warren Hastings on his return from India at the end of 1785. The moving spirit in this persecution—for such it was in reality—was Edmund Burke, whose just indignation over past abuses in all three of the Presidencies had wrought him up to a perfect frenzy. Indeed, whenever Burke forsook calm and philosophic speculation in the closet for the turmoil of current political controversy, he became transformed from a great and profound thinker, with utterance of like nobility with his thoughts, into a mere ranter, incapable of distinguishing fact from fiction or dignified reprobation from vulgar abuse. His was one of those diseased minds, widely different in constitution and capacity, whose aberrations added incalculably to the perplexities of England during the last forty years of the eighteenth century; Chatham's was another, and King George's the third. It must be added, also, that the disorder of Burke's brain impelled him, in this instance, in an extremely unfortunate direction. There can be no doubt that he had himself been concerned with some very questionable transactions in India, and with one very scandalous job in particular, which leaves me unwillingly but decidedly sceptical as to his honesty.[1]

Be that as it may, it occurred to Burke in an evil hour to make Hastings the scapegoat for all the sins of British administration in India; and, to the shame of all parties, he carried Parliament with him. The subject is not wholly foreign to this work, for it was principally as a minister of war that Hastings had done such conspicuous service to his country, and it was in a distinguished officer that he found his ablest champion. Samuel, Lord Hood, protested manfully in the Commons against the folly and injustice of arraigning any officer upon finding some part of his conduct exceptionable. There never was a man in command in time of

[1] See Major Scott's speech of 14th May 1788 in *Parl. Hist.*, and *Cornwallis Correspondence*, i. 463 *sqq.*

1787.
Feb. 20.

war, he urged, who had not found it his duty to do as an officer what he could not reconcile to his own sense of justice or to his own feelings in his private capacity; and he gave an instance of extremely arbitrary but necessary action of his own while commanding the fleet in the West Indies. "I feel for those who come after me," he concluded; "every man trusted with foreign command in time of war must in future serve with a halter round his neck." These arguments were far too sensible to appeal to the House of Commons. As Hood had pointed out in very telling language, such charges as those against Hastings were preferred not so much from enmity to him or from any regard to justice, as in order through him to worry a minister and impede the public business of the nation. The impeachment of Hastings was resolved upon; and the management of it appears to have been left chiefly to Burke. In such violent and unpractical hands the scheme of the trial was projected upon principles that denied the elements of fair treatment to the accused, and upon a scale which was calculated to protract the proceedings through the term of at least one generation.

The scene at the opening of the impeachment is described in one of the immortal passages of our literature. Burke's speech, we are told, has seldom been surpassed for stately eloquence; certainly it has never been surpassed for irrelevance and extravagance of statement. The orator dragged in every scandal, real or imaginary, that had dishonoured British rule in India, whether Hastings had been concerned with it or not, and he wept aloud over a tale of atrocities which was absolutely and demonstrably fictitious. It would seem incredible, did we not know that Burke had on as baseless authority printed a shameful libel upon British officers in the *Annual Register*. At length he concluded his oration, to be followed by Fox with another of the same kind, and by Sheridan with a third; each of the three denouncing Hastings as though he were a condemned criminal. A stranger trio to press accusations of extortion and corrupt dealing was never brought 1788. together—Burke under such suspicion as I have indicated, Fox the ruined gambler and keeper of a farobank, and Sheridan who, while raving against the spoliation of the Princesses of Oude, was capable at any time of wheedling his washerwoman out of half a guinea. However, their vanity as orators was gratified by the hysterics of foolish women ; and the lawyers rejoiced over a case which cost the public five thousand pounds in the first week.[1] Fourteen days out of thirty-five given up to the trial in the first session of Parliament were consumed in speeches ; and since the charges filled whole printed volumes, it may be judged that very little progress was made with them.

Early in the next session the friends of Hastings drew attention to the fact that the trial had already cost £18,000 ; in reply to which Burke declared himself ashamed that so paltry a matter as expense should be even mentioned. No one would have guessed that in those same days no money could be found to save British soldiers from starvation. The trial dragged on to its second year, and in 1789 Hastings presented a petition against the shameful expense to which it subjected him, and against some utterly indefensible language used towards him by Burke. Then the House of Commons began to realise that by committing itself to the impeachment, and, above all, by entrusting the management to such men as Burke and Fox, it had placed itself in a most foolish and embarrassing position. Major Scott of the Indian Army, who was the mouthpiece of Hastings in the House, has always been condemned as an extremely injudicious advocate, and it is quite possible that he may have been a very tedious one ; but his criticism of the management and the managers was most damaging and quite unanswerable. It was, however, too much to expect of a representative assembly that it should confess itself in the wrong, even to do justice to a great public servant. The dreary travesty

[1] *Courts and Cabinets of George III.*, ii. 357.

1788-1795. of a trial was prolonged through year after year. Burke came down to Westminster Hall with more speeches, and descended to a level of vituperation so low and vulgar that on one occasion he startled even the calm, long-suffering Hastings into springing to his feet. If he had knocked Burke down and horse-whipped him, the punishment would not have been in excess of the provocation. At length, in 1795, after the majority of the charges had been dropped and the accused had been absolutely ruined by his expenses, the end came. Hastings was solemnly acquitted, and the curtain dropped on the most tedious and discreditable farce that has ever disgraced the stage of Parliament.

The storm was already bursting over the head of Hastings when Cornwallis took ship for Calcutta; wherefore it is hardly surprising that he should have opened his administration in India with an act of ill-judged timidity. At the very moment of signing the Treaty in 1784, Tippoo Sahib had openly avowed to his subjects and to his French allies that he awaited only a favourable moment to renew with them his effort to overthrow the power of the British. Meanwhile, it was tolerably certain that he would seek vengeance against Nizam Ali and the Mahrattas for their desertion of Hyder Ali's confederacy for that object; and those powers therefore resolved to protect themselves by an attack on Tippoo, feeling some confidence that the British, if called upon, would come to their assistance. This confidence rested on the unconcealed hesitation of Warren Hastings to assent to the Treaty of 1784, and on an undertaking of the Bombay Government to support the Mahrattas and the Nizam with three battalions; consequently, it was rudely shaken when Cornwallis cancelled all existing agreements, 1786. declaring that henceforward the British would engage in Sept. none but defensive wars. The announcement was uncalled for and injudicious, but it was the natural fruit of the clause in the East India Act, which virtually proclaimed aloud that Tippoo might choose his own time for attack.

The intrigues of the French to obtain possession of 1787. the Dutch settlements in the East Indies seemed to promise to Tippoo that the time for prosecuting his designs against the British was almost come; and at the beginning of 1787 he actually sent ambassadors to Paris, who were warmly received by the French Court. It was on the alarm caused by this mission that the new regiments, numbered the Seventy-fourth to the Seventy-seventh, were raised for the service of the East India Company; but the energy of Sir Archibald Campbell, the Governor of Madras, frustrated the schemes of the French in India, while the craft of Harris and the firmness of Pitt accomplished the same end in Europe. The disappearance of the danger led, however, to one curious result. While the apprehension of war was yet lively, the Company had gladly embraced an arrangement under which four King's regiments were raised for them, their own recruiting-service being to the last degree unpopular; but immediately that the aspect of affairs became peaceful they endeavoured to repudiate it, and even refused permission for these troops to be embarked for their destination. The necessity for maintaining a strong European garrison in India was so manifestly imperative, and the condition of the Company's own European troops so deplorable, that Pitt resolved to carry the matter with a high hand. A bill, known as the East India Declaratory Act, was introduced to compel the Company to defray the cost of raising, transporting, and maintaining the troops necessary to the security of India; and the measure, though combated with great vigour by the Opposition, was duly passed into law. Thus a proper garrison was assured for our East Indian possessions.

Meanwhile, Cornwallis grappled manfully and successfully with the task of purifying the administration and re-establishing the credit of the territory committed to his charge. The Company's army he described as being in a shocking state, particularly the European portion of it, though under his care the native regiments

1788. rapidly improved. It seems that the evolutions of the Bengal Sepoys consisted of "dancing about in various forms to jig-tunes," and that they had not the most distant idea of great manœuvres; while discipline was impaired by pecuniary relations between officers and natives of so questionable a nature as to call for very peremptory suppression.[1] It may easily be understood, therefore, that, quite apart from all restraints laid on him by the East India Act, Cornwallis was anxious to preserve peace for as long as possible, and that he was even prepared to interpret those restrictions with greater rigidity than was contemplated by his chief, Henry Dundas. He was alive to the danger of having war forced upon him before he could find allies; and he had a just cause of war, of which he could avail himself at any time, against Tippoo, owing to the Sultan's detention and brutal treatment of certain British subjects who should have been liberated under the Treaty of 1784. But though the Mahrattas and the Nizam pressed him, as he said, almost daily for an alliance, yet he always refused it. Moreover, to make matters worse, the British Government in London, without consulting Cornwallis, asked the French Government to intercede for the release of these prisoners, which was tantamount to a confession that they were aware of Tippoo's infraction of the Treaty, but were afraid to resent it.[2]

Meanwhile Tippoo, after gaining various advantages in the field over Nizam Ali and the Mahrattas, had been called away at the beginning of 1789 by a revolt in Malabar. The suppression of this rising he converted into a holy war for the propagation of the Mohammedan creed. Multitudes of his intended victims fled to Travancore, some by way of Tellicherry and from thence by sea, while others from farther south passed through the territory of Cochin. Greatly enraged with

[1] *Cornwallis Correspondence*, i. 235, 239, 241, 245, 258, 276, 279, 311, 317, 340, 401, 451.
[2] *Ibid.* pp. 406, 459, 496.

the Rajah of Cochin for assisting the refugees, Tippoo 1789. prepared to take vengeance on him ; but in order to reach him he had first to cross the barrier known as the lines of Travancore, which had originally been thrown up by the sovereigns of Cochin and of Travancore to cover the northern frontier of both districts. The situation thus brought about was not a little singular. The lines ran first for rather less than a mile across the slender island of Vipeen, at the mouth of the estuary of Cranganore ; and so much of them was within the boundaries of Cochin, which was tributary to Tippoo. But the settlements named Cochin, at the southern extremity of the island, and Ayacotta at its northern extremity, together with Cranganore on the mainland over against it, were all of them Dutch. On the mainland itself the lines ran for some thirty miles in a north-easterly direction ; and this portion of them belonged to Travancore, the ruler of which was the friend of the British, and had been described as such in the Treaty of 1784. Tippoo Sahib had long been anxious to achieve the conquest of Travancore, and in 1788 had even attempted it by indirect means ; but Sir Archibald Campbell had given him plainly to understand that any aggression against the Rajah should be treated as a declaration of war, and had despatched two battalions to aid in the defence of the lines. Nor did Campbell act thus without good reason, for the possession of Travancore would have enabled Tippoo to turn the left flank of the British on his next invasion of their territory in Coromandel ; and it was notorious that such an invasion was only a question of time.

For the moment Tippoo allowed the matter to rest, his preparations being not yet complete, and meanwhile he tried his utmost, both by threats and by offers of purchase, to acquire Cranganore and Ayacotta from the Dutch ; but only to find himself forestalled by the Rajah of Travancore. He therefore hastened the augmentation of his forces, and concentrated some thirty-five thousand men, ready for action, at Coimbatore. Cornwallis, who

1789. was anxiously watching these proceedings, thrice gave
Aug., Sept. strict orders to the Madras Government that an attack
Nov. on Travancore by Tippoo should be treated as a declaration of war, and that every preparation should be made for a campaign; and he was very confident that the Sultan, in the face of these precautions, would hesitate to embark in hostilities. Tippoo, however, being aware that Sir Archibald Campbell had left Madras, and that his successor, Mr. Hollond, was a corrupt and incapable civilian, conceived with only too much reason that he might venture to take liberties. He therefore marched from Coimbatore, attacked the lines of Travancore with fourteen thousand men, and to his great disgust sustained
Dec. 29. a humiliating defeat. Much disconcerted, he sent a
1790. shuffling letter of explanation to Madras; whereupon Hollond, in direct disobedience of Cornwallis's orders, instead of pushing forward military preparations with all possible energy, actually wasted several weeks in negotiation, excusing himself on the pretext of economy and of his assurance of the Sultan's amicable intentions. Cornwallis was furious. He resolved to go to Madras in person to supersede Hollond, and only abstained on hearing that General Medows, the gallant defender of St. Lucia, was on the point of arriving there from Bombay in order to assume the Government. He did not fail, however, a few months later, to put Hollond forcibly on board ship, and to send him home under arrest; and if he had hanged him on the first tree, the punishment would not have been excessive. Meanwhile the mischief was done; and Cornwallis knew it but too well. "The very criminal conduct of the late Governor," he wrote, "will prevent our making much progress before the setting in of the rains in the Mysore country, and what is worse, will probably occasion the loss and destruction of the territories of our ally the Rajah of Travancore."[1] His forebodings were just. After three months spent in bringing heavy guns to the spot, the Sultan easily forced the passage of the lines; the two British battalions,

[1] *Cornwallis Correspondence*, ii. 8.

CH. XXVII HISTORY OF THE ARMY 551

with three more[1] which had been sent under Colonel 1790.
Hartley from Bombay, retired to Ayacotta, being too
weak to take the offensive; and Tippoo ravaged
Travancore with merciless devastation. April-May.
Cornwallis, judging himself at last to be freed from
the restraints of the East India Act, lost no time in
opening negotiations with the Mahrattas of Poonah and
with Nizam Ali ; and in due time an alliance, defensive
and offensive, was concluded, under which the two June, July.
native powers undertook, in return for liberal promises,
to furnish each a contingent of ten thousand horse to
act with the British forces. Meanwhile Medows, having
arrived at Madras in the middle of February, pressed
the military preparations forward with great vigour, and
on the 24th of May took command at Trichinopoly of
fifteen thousand men.[2] The plan of campaign, of which
Cornwallis was not greatly enamoured, resembled in its
main features that contemplated by Fullarton in 1783-
1784. The principal army was to reduce Palghautcherry
and the forts of the province of Coimbatore, and having
secured this rich country as a base of supply, was to
ascend the Gujelhutty Pass and invade Mysore from
the south. A second force of three brigades, to be
composed chiefly of troops from Bengal under Colonel
Kelly, was meanwhile to penetrate into Baramahal,

[1] Seventy-fifth Highlanders and four native battalions.
[2] *Cavalry Brigade.*—Lieut.-colonel Floyd. H.M. 19th Light
Dragoons, four regiments of Madras Native Cavalry.
Artillery.—Three and a half companies Bengal Artillery, six
companies of Madras Artillery.

    RIGHT WING.—Colonel Nixon :—
First European Brigade.—Major Skelly (H.M. 74th Regiment),
H.M. 36th and 52nd.
First Native Brigade.—Three battalions of Madras Sepoys.
Second Native Brigade.—Three battalions of Madras Sepoys.

    LEFT WING.—Lieut.-colonel Stuart (H.M. 72nd Regiment):—
Second European Brigade.—H.M. 71st and 72nd Regiments, one
battalion Madras Europeans (now 102nd).
Third Native Brigade.—Three battalions of Madras Sepoys.
Fourth Native Brigade.—Three battalions of Madras Sepoys.
Colonel Musgrave in command of the whole line.

1790. alike to protect the right flank and communications of the main army, and to parry any stroke of Tippoo against the Carnatic. The objection to the plan was the great distance of the field of operations from the true base at Madras, and the length and consequent weakness of the chain of posts that connected the one with the other.

May 26. On the 26th of May, Medows began his march westward, but his transport and commissariat-service
June 15. were so defective that he consumed twenty days in traversing fifty miles to Caroor, which was abandoned by the enemy on his approach. The season was not favourable to the opening of a campaign. The south-west monsoon, after shedding torrents of rain on the western coast and on the highest range of mountains, parts with its remaining moisture on the lower hills, and rushes over the eastern plains in the form of a hot wind, a trying visitation even in temperate latitudes, but within ten degrees of the equator most distressing and deadly. More than twelve hundred sick were deposited at Caroor before a shot had been fired, and it was nearly three weeks before the army was in a
July 3. condition to move again. The forts of Avaracoorchy
July 5, 10. and Darapooram were then occupied without resistance; one brigade was left in the vicinity of the latter place for the protection of convoys, and on the 21st of July
July 21. Medows took possession, without dispute, of Coimbatore. So far an advance of one hundred and fifty miles had occupied fifty-six days, and sickness had decimated the numbers of the army. An advanced force under Colonel
July 23. Stuart was now detached for the siege of Palghautcherry, but on moving twenty miles to eastward met the full force of the rains, and finding its way barred by a succession of torrents, was compelled to return to
Aug. 5. Coimbatore. Stuart, however, was again sent out, this time about a hundred miles to the south-east, for the capture of Dindigul, while yet another detachment under Colonel Oldham marched on the 1st of August upon Erode. During these operations Tippoo had shown no sign of resistance. It had been hoped that he

would have fought a general action to save Coimbatore; 1790.
but he had retired northward to the plateau of Mysore,
leaving four thousand cavalry under Said Sahib as a
corps of observation, with orders to harass the British
communications. Colonel Floyd with the cavalry-
brigade was thereupon appointed to deal with Said
Sahib, which he did most effectually, defeating him in
a succession of brilliant little skirmishes, and, to
Tippoo's great anger, driving him across the Bahvani
River in full retreat towards the passes of the Ghauts.
Floyd, however, being not yet satisfied, obtained a reinforcement of infantry, and himself crossing the river,
captured by surprise the fort of Sattiamungalum, on
the northern bank. Then, having driven Said Sahib's Aug. 26.
whole force up the Gujelhutty Pass, he left a battalion
of Sepoys to hold Sattiamungalum, and, repassing the
river with the remainder of his force, put forth all his
energy and vigilance to bar the fords across it. For the
first time, as he wrote with just pride,[1] the superiority
of European over Native horse had, thanks to the
Nineteenth Light Dragoons, been established in India.

Screened by such protection, the work of the detachments prospered. Erode fell on the 6th of August Aug. 6.
and set the greater part of Oldham's force free to join
Floyd, while Stuart, after a short siege and one unsuccessful assault, received the surrender of Dindigul. Aug. 23.
On his return to Coimbatore he was detached once
again to capture Palghautcherry, which was essential to
ensure alike the means of communication with the
contingent from Bombay and the safety of Medows's
left flank and rear. So far all had gone reasonably
well. The chain of posts, beginning with Tanjore and
Trichinopoly, had been established for the transit of
stores to the Gujelhutty Pass, though neither Caroor,
Erode, nor Sattiamungalum could be esteemed good
defensible depots; the district of Coimbatore had been
mastered, and the flanks of the army to all appearance
secured. But meanwhile Medows's force, already much

[1] Biddulph, *The Nineteenth and their Times*, p. 71.

1790. weakened, was dangerously dispersed; for, apart from all minor detachments, it was now distributed into three divisions of about equal strength at Palghautcherry, Coimbatore, and Sattiamungalum. Moreover, Hartley's contingent from Bombay had only just begun to move on Palghautcherry, while Kelly's division from Bengal was still in course of organisation at Arnee, fifty leagues to northward, and not yet in a condition to take the field. Medows talked of ascending the Gujelhutty Pass in October, but he reckoned without Tippoo Sahib, who saw his opportunity and was not slow to seize it.

Sept. 2. Leaving Seringapatam on the 2nd of September with some forty thousand men and a large train of artillery, the Sultan reached the head of the Gujelhutty Pass on the 9th, and having parked his heavy baggage on the summit, began the descent of the defile. On the

Sept. 10. 10th his cavalry was observed by Floyd's patrols, and

Sept. 12. on the 12th the Colonel sent an express messenger to Medows at Coimbatore, reporting that the main force of the enemy was before him under Tippoo in person. No doubt he looked for orders to retire immediately, but he would have done better not to have awaited them. On that day his patrols scoured the course of the Bahvani as usual; but no sooner had they returned than a part of Tippoo's force began to pass the river at the ford of Poongar, while the main body moved some ten miles farther down the northern bank in order to overwhelm Sattiamungalum and to cross the stream below

Sept. 13. it. Early on the morning of the 13th a few squadrons of Floyd's cavalry, while on their way to reconnoitre the ford at Poongar, met a large body of the enemy's horse and charged them successfully, but were at once obliged to fall back by the advance of some seven thousand men upon their front and flanks. The officer in command of the British with great readiness took up a position amid a network of cactus-hedges, and, dismounting his men, kept the enemy at bay with the carbine, until Floyd arrived with reinforcements to extricate him, and drove back the Mysoreans with very heavy loss.

CH. XXVII HISTORY OF THE ARMY   555

Floyd then returned to his camp opposite Sattia- 1790.
mungalum, but his weary troopers were hardly out of the Sept. 13.
saddle before a second division of Tippoo's force came
up from the west upon his left flank, while the Sultan's
main army appeared on the north bank of the river and
opened fire from nineteen heavy guns upon his front.
Floyd at once changed position to check the attack on
his flank, but it was impossible for him to withdraw his
handful of twenty-eight hundred men and eleven guns
by daylight in the presence of numbers so overwhelming; and he had no alternative but to endure until
nightfall a cannonade, to which want of ammunition
forbade him to reply. The welcome darkness came at
last and the enemy retired to a distance of six miles;
but the casualties among the British had been serious.
Three of the guns had been disabled, great numbers of
the horses and cattle had been killed, and the native
drivers had most of them deserted. At midnight it
was resolved to retreat to Coimbatore; but it was first
necessary to withdraw the garrison from Sattiamungalum
in basket-boats, which operation, through the misconduct of an officer, occupied four hours. Thus the
day was already come before the column was fairly on Sept. 14.
march, leaving behind it three disabled guns.

Fortunately the Mysorean army, having been overtaken by heavy rain while retiring, had encamped in
disorder; hence some hours elapsed before Tippoo
could collect and set in motion a force of some fifteen
thousand men for the pursuit. Meanwhile Floyd was
heading southward upon Cheyoor, the more direct
road to Coimbatore by Velladi being barred by the
force that had threatened his flank on the previous
day. For twelve miles his route lay through open
ground, and he was able to march with infantry,
cavalry, and baggage in three parallel columns; but
before he could enter the enclosed country Tippoo's
cavalry and light artillery, being fresh and well equipped,
overtook his rear and captured nearly the whole of his
baggage. At about eleven o'clock he reached Oocaro,

1790.
Sept. 14.
from which point his way lay along a single road through a tangle of cactus-hedges. Here he halted to reform the column, sending the cavalry on in advance while the infantry took up the duty of rearguard; but the enemy was pressing forward so rapidly on both flanks that he could make no long stay. Three more guns were here abandoned for want of cattle to drag them; the baggage of the officers was sacrificed, and their bullocks taken to haul the five remaining cannon; and the retreat was hastily resumed amid a storm of rockets and artillery-fire, directed diagonally upon the right and left rear. Towards evening Floyd's advanced parties entered Cheyoor and were preparing to encamp, when Tippoo's main body closed with the rearguard and compelled Colonel Oldham to form the whole of the British infantry on a ridge in order of battle. Tippoo promptly directed a large body of cavalry to fetch a compass and fall upon Oldham's rear, holding his infantry ready to attack his front on the first sign of disorder. But weary, harassed, and weakened though they were by nearly forty hours of incessant marching and fighting, the Thirty-sixth and the four faithful Native battalions on their flanks were to show no disorder that day. Two deep they stood to defy the infantry in their front; two deep they faced about to meet the charging horsemen in their rear and hurled them back even at the bayonet's point; and two deep they turned about once more to confront the now wavering mass of Tippoo's battalions. At this moment a troop of the Nineteenth Light Dragoons returned from a short reconnaissance beyond Cheyoor into the village, and was hailed by the camp-followers as Medows's advanced guard. Floyd shouted the welcome falsehood to his cavalry, who hastened back with cheers to rejoin the infantry. Oldham seized the moment to advance to the attack, and the cavalry, closing in upon both flanks of Tippoo's infantry, chased them in confusion from the field.

Even so, however, Floyd's work was not yet done.

Medows was indeed in motion to join him, but, unaware 1790.
of his line of retreat, had marched to Velladi; and with
the fate of Baillie before his eyes, Floyd dared not risk
an hour's delay in effecting a junction. Before daylight, therefore, his exhausted troops were again on the Sept. 15.
march, and on the same evening he reached Velladi,
only to learn that Medows had advanced farther
northward upon Denaikankotta. Brigade-major Dallas,
an officer who had spent his days in leading squadrons
to the charge and his nights in repairing gun-carriages,
volunteered to go forward alone to recall the General;
and Medows, instantly countermarching, united his force
with Floyd's at Velladi on the following day. "My Sept. 16.
dear Colonel, yours is the feat and mine the defeat,"
was his greeting to Floyd; and the epigram was as just
in its censure of his own imprudence as in praise of his
colleague's ability and resource. A great disaster had
indeed been averted, but only at a cost of nearly six
hundred men killed, wounded, and missing, one-fourth
of whom were Europeans. Very fortunately, Tippoo
had retired behind the Bahvani on learning of Medows's
movement to Velladi. Had he followed up Floyd on
the 15th, and condemned his troops to a third day of
fighting after two days already passed without food or
rest, he could hardly have failed to annihilate them.

After two days' halt Medows returned to Coimbatore, where Stuart, having captured Palghautcherry
after a short siege, presently joined him. But the time
thus occupied in the concentration of the army left
Tippoo's hands absolutely free for some days, and he
promptly seized this opportunity for a raid upon the
British communications. On the 25th he appeared Sept. 25.
before Erode, which being indefensible was evacuated
at his approach, not without sacrifice of valuable stores.
On the 29th Medows marched with his whole force
from Coimbatore; but so well were Tippoo's movements screened, that the General actually advanced
northward for some way before he ascertained the
direction of the Sultan's army, when he wheeled hastily

1790. Sept. — to eastward to follow in its track. Tippoo thereupon moved a few miles to the south of Erode, which placed him within striking distance of Caroor, Darapooram, and Coimbatore to east, west, and south. Medows, as he knew, was bound to move to Caroor in order to pick up a convoy, and he hoped then to make a spring upon Coimbatore, where the British battering-train was stored; but that post having been opportunely reinforced by Colonel Hartley, he turned upon Darapooram, and after a few days' siege forced the weak garrison to
Oct. 8. capitulate. Meanwhile Medows, after meeting his convoy, had heard with dismay how great had been the danger of Coimbatore, and decided to return and improve its defences before venturing again to withdraw his army to a distance. Medows was, in fact, in the position of an admiral who dares not take his fleet to sea because his dockyards are unfortified. Three weeks were lost before he could move northward again from Coim-
Nov. 2. batore; and when he reached Erode, on the 2nd of November, he found a strange population streaming through it from the west. Later experience taught Medows that Tippoo invariably displaced the villagers from around his line of march lest his movements should be betrayed, but as yet the General was unable to interpret this sign. He hesitated for a week, until Floyd, pushing a strong reconnaissance to west-
Nov. 8. ward, discovered that Tippoo's whole army had crossed the Cavery some days before and was in full march to the north. His design was now manifest, namely, to fall upon the Bengal division which had been so long assembling at Arnee; and very cleverly he had veiled his movements.

This Bengal division,[1] nine thousand men strong,

[1] *First Brigade.*—H.M. 74th. Three battalions Bengal Native Infantry.
Second Brigade.—H.M. 76th. Three battalions Bengal Native Infantry.
Third Brigade.—One battalion of Madras Europeans, two battalions Madras Native Infantry, one regiment of Madras Native Cavalry.

CH. XXVII HISTORY OF THE ARMY 559

after long delay owing to the depletion of the arsenals, 1790. had at last moved from Arnee at the end of September, the command having devolved, through Colonel Kelly's death, upon Colonel Maxwell. A month's march Oct. 24. westward brought it within the boundaries of Baramahal, pursuant to the original plan of campaign; and in the first week of November Maxwell fixed his headquarters at Caveripatam. On the 9th the appearance Nov. 9. of large bodies of cavalry heralded Tippoo's approach, and on the following day the Sultan manœuvred constantly with his whole army for a favourable opening to attack. Foiled, however, at every point by Maxwell's admirable dispositions, he withdrew to southward on the evening of the 14th, for he knew that Medows was coming up on his track. In truth that General, after crossing the Cavery with great Nov. 8-10. difficulty, had hurried northward from the river at the top of his speed, and was already nearer than Tippoo had reckoned. On the 15th Medows's advanced Nov. 15. guard ascended the southern barrier of Baramahal by the pass of Tapoor, and, looking out over the plain within, observed the pitching of tents and every sign of an encamping army some six miles away. Three signal-guns were fired in the assurance that the force must be Maxwell's, when to the general surprise the tents were instantly struck, and a hasty movement of several columns westward betrayed the host to be the Sultan's. Continuing his march northward for another day, Medows on the 17th joined hands with Maxwell, and found himself at the head of the finest army thitherto sent into the field by the British in India.

For a short time Tippoo hesitated whether or not to ascend the Policode Pass into Mysore; but reflecting that British territory was preferable to his own as the seat of war, he turned southward to the pass of Tapoor for a raid upon Trichinopoly. His army had just Nov. 18. reached the northern end of the defile when the appearance of Medows's advanced guard a few miles to his left showed him that the British were marching to

1790.
Nov. 18.

this same point; but none the less he ordered his army to enter the pass, himself taking personal command of two thousand horse to protect its rear. A rapid advance of the British would almost without fail have cut off a considerable part of his force and engaged the remainder at great advantage; and this course was strenuously urged by Colonel Stuart. Medows, however, forbade him to make the attempt; and though three of Tippoo's battalions were separated from the rest and driven into the jungle, the remainder of his troops traversed the defile with little loss and continued their march to the Cavery. Thus an opportunity of striking a heavy blow at the Sultan was lost.

Tippoo, having distanced his pursuers, made no halt, but followed the north bank of the Cavery downward, giving out that he would cross the river below Caroor. Medows, toiling after him, caught sight of the rear of his columns opposite to that place, and, making sure that he was bound southward, wrote boldly of ascending the Ghauts into Mysore as the best means of bringing his enemy to action. The news of the Sultan's

Dec. 12. arrival before Trichinopoly, however, led him hurriedly eastward for the safety of that important post. Tippoo had fortunately accomplished nothing but the plunder of the island of Seringham, but he now turned northward into the heart of Coromandel, pillaging, burning, and destroying as he went. At Thiagar he halted to besiege the fort, but there Captain Flint, the hero of Wandewash, was in command; and after the repulse of two successive attacks Tippoo judged it prudent to leave so redoubtable an adversary alone. Trinomallee, some thirty-five miles farther north, having no garrison, fell an easy victim. The unhappy town was sacked, and the inhabitants treated with revolting barbarity. Permacol, which was held by a company of irregular native

1791.
Jan. 23.

infantry, was by their treachery surrendered; and from thence Tippoo turned south-east to Pondicherry, where he remained for several weeks engaged in negotiations with the French. He even dictated letters to the King

CH. XXVII HISTORY OF THE ARMY 561

of France, asking him for six thousand troops, to be 1791. transported, clothed, and maintained at his own expense, and engaging with their help to drive the British from India and to ensure the possession of their settlements to him. Poor Louis the Sixteenth was already virtually a prisoner in the Tuileries when these proposals reached him, and he had learned enough to shake his head over them. "This reminds me of the American business," he said; "which I can never think of without regret. The lesson was too severe to be forgotten."

Meanwhile the British force moved northward for some distance in Tippoo's track, and then, leaving him encamped on the hills above Pondicherry, marched to Madras, where the Governor-general had arrived to Jan. 29. take the army under his personal command. Ill though matters had gone in Coromandel, there came cheerful news from Malabar. On the 10th of December, Colonel Hartley, with three battalions and six guns, had attacked nine thousand of the enemy at Calicut, killed and wounded a thousand of them, and utterly routed the rest, while his own casualties did not exceed fifty-two. Four days later General Robert Abercromby, a brother of the more famous Sir Ralph, had appeared with a force from Bombay before Cannanore, reduced it by a vigorous attack within twenty-four hours, and followed up this stroke by the capture and unquestioned occupation of the entire province of Malabar. Thus, in spite of all mishaps, it was not wholly without encouragement that Cornwallis entered upon his first Indian campaign.

CHAPTER XXVIII

1791. THOUGH there had been no question either of cessation of hostilities or of winter-quarters, the campaign of 1790 had been effectually closed. Cornwallis, when he left Calcutta to assume command of the force in the field, had made up his mind that the whole scheme of operations must be radically changed, that Madras itself must be the actual base, that the line of communications must follow the chain of posts which long experience had shown to be efficient and defensible, and that, as a natural consequence, the invasion of Mysore must be pushed from the north-east instead of from the south. Between Madras and the foot of the Ghauts, Vellore and Amboor were the obvious places for intermediate magazines; there then remained the task of ascending one or other of the passes to the table-land of Mysore and of taking from the enemy Bangalore, some ninety miles farther on, as the next post in the line. This was likely to prove an arduous enterprise, for Bangalore was reputed the strongest fortress in Mysore; but, on the other hand, its very strength, when once it had fallen into British hands, would make it the more perfect as an advanced base from which to reach the final objective of Seringapatam.

Such was the design projected for the principal army under Cornwallis himself, carrying with it of necessity the evacuation of the posts captured by Medows in the past campaign. Palghautcherry alone, with Coimbatore as an outpost, were strongly held, for the collection of the revenues of the district and for the

support of any force acting from the side of Malabar. 1791.
Every man thus released for service in the field was
sent to join the Bombay army under Sir Robert Abercromby, which, operating from Tellicherry as its base,
was to advance upon Seringapatam by the pass of
Peripatam. This was one diversion to distract a part
of Tippoo's force from Cornwallis; and it was hoped
that the troops of the Nizam and of the Mahrattas,
which for some months had been feebly besieging
Darwar and Copul, to the north of the Toombuddra,
would also co-operate by an invasion of the Sultan's
dominions from the north. The main difficulties, as
Cornwallis well knew, would be those of transport and
supply, for when once his army was planted on the
plateau of Mysore it was certain that Tippoo would draw
about it a ring of devastation. It was moreover essential
that Seringapatam should be taken before the monsoon
should burst in June. The General therefore bent all
his energy to the collection of supplies and draught-
animals from Bengal, and for the first time employed
elephants in large numbers for purposes of transport in
a British Army. The campaign conducted according
to the new plan could not but be difficult and trying,
but, as Cornwallis had learned from sad experience in
Carolina, anything was better than an insecure line of
communications.

Throughout the month of January the principal
army was concentrated at Vellout, some eighteen miles
west of Madras, the arrival of animals from Bengal by
sea having been seriously delayed by contrary winds.
At length all was ready, and on the 5th of February Feb. 5.
Cornwallis began his march with his whole force towards
the west. He had carefully spread reports of his intention to ascend the passes near Amboor and to penetrate into Baramahal; and Tippoo no sooner heard of
his movement than he hastened back from Pondicherry
through the passes of Changamah and Policode. Cornwallis, for his part, proceeded by easy marches through Feb. 11.
the classic ground of Coote's contest with Hyder to

1791.   Vellore; from whence, after constant feints to the south-west, he wheeled suddenly northward to Chittoor,
Feb. 16. and there turning sharply to the westward ascended the
Feb. 21. Ghauts through the easy pass of Muglee. By the 21st his entire army was encamped at Palamnair, safe on the table-land, without the firing of a shot. This skilful opening of the campaign deservedly won for Cornwallis the confidence of his troops.

After three days' halt for the distribution of sixty-
Feb. 24. four elephants, which here joined the army, Cornwallis resumed his march west and south by the familiar route of Mulwagal, Colar, and Ooscotta upon Bangalore, finding at first no lack of forage and meeting with no resistance. Tippoo's long inactivity before Pondicherry, and his confidence that the British would never invade Mysore while he lay in the Carnatic, had enabled Cornwallis to steal a march on him; and in his bewilderment
Feb. 27. he showed much indecision. It was not until the British were approaching Colar that a few of the Sultan's famous light horse appeared in their front, and
March 2. not until three days later, when the invaders were within two days' march of Bangalore, that his troops were seen in real strength. Then it soon became evident that the Sultan meant to pursue his usual tactics of hanging on his enemy's skirts, destroying his baggage, laying waste the country before him, and burning or
March 5. removing all grain and forage. On the 5th of March —the day which brought the British to the walls of Bangalore—Tippoo made a demonstration in force against their left flank, which Cornwallis met by drawing up five brigades of infantry on a range of heights to confront him, and passing forward the rest of the army, with its baggage, behind the screen of this formation. After an hour's halt the line of infantry, with the two brigades which constituted its support, broke into column[1] and continued its march in the same order,

---

[1] Column of half-companies seems to have been the favourite formation of Cornwallis, when the ground permitted, which shows a great advance on the long-drawn files of Coote.

ready to form a front at any moment. This simple 1791. manœuvre, which was conducted by Cornwallis in person, inspired his officers with a profound belief in his ability;[1] and their admiration was increased when, on reaching the encampment before Bangalore, they learned that there had been no loss whatever of stores, and but five casualties among the troops during the day. Such handling of troops in compact yet flexible columns was evidently new to them.

On the morning of the 6th, Cornwallis shifted his March 6. camp to the north-east face of the town; and in the afternoon the whole of the cavalry and one brigade of infantry were moved out to the south-west to cover a reconnaissance by the engineers. This covering party was just about to retire when about a thousand of the enemy's horse suddenly appeared before it. Tippoo on this same day had made a circuitous march, concealed by the unevenness of the country, to the westward of Bangalore; and a considerable part of his army was still on its way to his chosen camping-ground when Floyd's cavalry was reported to be approaching, straight upon the flank of his line of march. Thereupon the Sultan sent out the one body of his horse which was not engaged in foraging; and this was the corps which now appeared in Floyd's front. Floyd instantly rode at them with the Nineteenth and one native regiment of cavalry in line, while the remainder of his brigade supported him in column of regiments. The Mysorean horse at once retired, and Floyd, riding after them, saw the infantry, baggage, and guns which composed the rear of Tippoo's column. He had strict orders to attempt no enterprise; but the temptation was irresistible. He led the Nineteenth straight to the attack, drove the infantry from their guns, and, without waiting to secure his trophies, pursued the fugitives into a difficult and rugged country full of rocks and ravines. The regiment to his right also charged, dislodged a body of infantry, and chased them to the same ground;

[1] See, for instance, Mackenzie's *Sketch of the War*, ii. 22.

1791.
March 6.
another of his regiments deployed to his left and attacked with the like success; and Floyd was still advancing to disperse a body of infantry which had rallied on an eminence, when he was struck in the jaw by a bullet, and fell to the ground as one dead. The men behind him swerved or went about, which threw the whole line into confusion; and very soon the whole of the Nineteenth were falling back. The native regiment on the right continued its advance and was in danger of being cut off, until Major Dallas galloped up from the rear and urged Floyd to halt. The Colonel, who had been remounted by some of his men and was recovering from the shock of his wound, thereupon caused the Nineteenth to face about; but meanwhile the enemy had rallied from their disorder. Their recaptured guns, together with the cannon in the fort, opened a cross-fire, and disaster seemed inevitable, when Major Gowdie, with excellent judgment, brought forward his brigade of infantry to cover the retreat of the cavalry. Thereupon Floyd's squadrons quickly reformed and in due time returned, without further mishap, to camp. The casualties in men did not exceed seventy-one, but over two hundred and fifty horses were lost, while the remainder of those that had taken part in the attack, having been severely pressed while in poor condition, were rendered nearly useless. It was an unlucky affair, since, but for Floyd's fall, it might have issued in brilliant success; but, as things fell out, the Commander-in-chief found one-third of his small force of cavalry disabled. "I never saw him completely angry until that evening," wrote one of his staff; and it is said that even long afterwards Cornwallis could never think of the occurrence without vexation.

Cornwallis now proceeded with the very difficult task appointed to him, namely, the capture of a strong fortress in the presence of a superior force without the aid of a covering army. He had encamped, as has been told, on the north-eastern side of the place, and there he remained, for he had not nearly troops enough

to invest it completely. Bangalore consisted, as was 1791.
usual in India, of a fort proper and a *pettah*, or fortified
town, adjoining to it. The fort proper was of oval
form, with a total perimeter of about a mile. It was
solidly built of stout masonry, with twenty-six round
towers at equal intervals from each other, and was
surrounded by a ditch; and it possessed two gates, the
Mysore or southern and the Delhi or northern gate.
Immediately to the north of it lay the town, some three
miles in circumference, which was enclosed first by an
indifferent rampart with redoubts and flèches,[1] then by
a belt of impenetrable thorn about a hundred yards in
width, and finally by a ditch, these barriers being inter-
mitted only in the space that lay immediately opposite
to the fort. Tippoo had thrown eight thousand men
into the fort, nine thousand more (of which three-
fourths were irregular troops) into the town, and had
then retired with the remainder of his force to a position
some six miles to westward. Cornwallis decided that
the town should first be carried, in the hope that its
position and the supplies hoarded within it would
facilitate the regular operations of the siege.

Accordingly, at dawn of the 7th of March, the March 7.
Thirty-sixth Foot and a battalion of Bengal Sepoys
moved off with their battalion-guns to the attack of a
gateway on the northern face of the town, four heavy
guns following them in support. A flèche which
covered the gate was speedily carried with the bayonet,
and the storming party then pushed on by a winding
way, hardly wide enough to admit half a company
abreast, across the ditch and through the belt of thorn
to the inner gate. Here the advance was checked, for
the gateway had been built up with masonry upon
which field-guns could make no impression; and the
party perforce remained halted for some time under a
galling fire until the heavy guns could be brought forward. By their shot a small opening was at length

[1] A flèche is a field-work of two faces, like an arrow's head;
a redoubt has, properly speaking, four faces.

1791.
March 7.
made; and Lieutenant Ayre, a small and slender subaltern, being hoisted up by the grenadiers, contrived to creep through it. General Medows, who was always most facetious when the fire was hottest, watched the gallant fellow disappear through the gap and then turned to the grenadiers of the Thirty-sixth with the words, "Well done. Now, whiskers! Support the little gentleman." A few more men managed to crawl after Ayre, and opened a sally-port for the entry of the rest. The garrison was then quickly beaten back under the guns of the fort, and within two hours two-thirds of the town were in possession of the British. Large stores of forage, valuable beyond estimation to Cornwallis, thus fell into his hands.

Meanwhile Tippoo, frantic with rage at the audacity of the attack, set his whole army in motion as if to turn Cornwallis's left, at the same time detaching six thousand men to reinforce the garrison, which had rallied under the cannon of the fort, and with them to retake the town. Cornwallis, divining his intention, manœuvred to foil the turning movement, but lost no time in strengthening his force within the walls. The attack of the Mysoreans upon the town was delivered with unusual spirit and resolution; but after a short exchange of volleys the Thirty-sixth and Seventy-sixth, with two Sepoy battalions, cut matters short by clearing the streets with the bayonet. Gathering impetus from success, they then drove the enemy from quarter to quarter, until they fairly swept them out of the town, with a loss of over two thousand killed and wounded. The casualties on the British side amounted to one hundred and thirty, of which no fewer than one hundred occurred among the Europeans. Among the fallen was Lieutenant-colonel Moorhouse, who was killed while bringing up the heavy guns to the first attack on the gate; his ardour being such that, though wounded in two places, he never relaxed his exertions until two more bullets laid him dead. Colonel Wilks[1]

[1] *History of Mysore,* iii. 125.

has sketched the character and career of Moorhouse in words which should not be forgotten. "He had risen from the ranks, but Nature herself had made him a gentleman; uneducated, he had made himself a man of science; a career of universal distinction had commanded universal respect, and his amiable character universal attachment." There are few soldiers who might not envy the death and the epitaph of this humble taker of the King's shilling.

1791.
March 7.

The forage captured in the town was very welcome to the army, for the draught-bullocks were already dying by hundreds, and even the cavalry dared not move outside the circle of their piquets in the face of the swarms of Mysorean horse. The singular nature of the operations became more and more unpleasantly manifest. Batteries were indeed thrown up to breach the defences of the fort; but the besiegers, as at Delhi two generations later, were themselves in a fashion besieged, for the garrison opposed to them was constantly relieved, while the whole of the enemy's field-force lay in constant menace before them. From sunset to sunrise every man of Cornwallis's troops was accoutred and every horse saddled; and on every day Tippoo's manœuvres became more threatening and more dangerous. At length, on the 21st, though the breach was still very imperfect, Cornwallis resolved to assault without further delay, trusting to a narrow causeway to carry his stormers across the ditch. At eleven o'clock, in bright moonlight, the grenadiers of his European regiments[1] advanced with scaling-ladders in perfect silence, made their way over a trench that had been cut across the causeway, and gained not only the breach but the ramparts on its flank before they encountered serious resistance. The supporting battalions then swarmed after them, the companies turning right and left alternately to clear the ramparts; and after an hour of deadly work with the bayonet all opposition was overcome, and the fort was in possession of Corn-

March 21.

[1] 36th, 52nd, 71st, 72nd, 74th, 76th, 102nd.

1791.
March 21. wallis. Tippoo, who, in spite of his adversary's secrecy, was fully aware of his plans, had given timely warning to the garrison to expect the attack, and had himself advanced to within a mile of the walls during the assault. But he came too late to avert the disaster, and after standing in silent stupor for a while, he returned to his camp. Over one thousand bodies of the enemy were actually buried after the storm, but the casualties of the British during the whole operations of the siege were less than five hundred.

Thus had Cornwallis established himself within the territory of Mysore, and secured his base for an advance upon Seringapatam. But his difficulties were still only beginning, for the captured forage was by this time consumed, the cattle were dying faster than ever, and the camp was pestilential with the stench of unburied carcases. Having repaired the defences of the fortress,
March 28. he on the 28th marched northward, with the double object of meeting a convoy of supplies from Amboor, and of forming a junction with a corps of cavalry prepared by Nizam Ali for service with his army. Tippoo likewise had moved in the same direction; but owing to the exhausted condition of his cattle Corn-
April 12. wallis was unable to pursue him. On the 12th of April the junction with the Nizam's troops was effected at Cottapilly, about eighty miles north of Bangalore, and the united force then turned south-eastward to Vencatigerry, where reinforcements of four thousand Native and seven hundred European troops, besides a quantity of stores, were awaiting its arrival. From thence Cornwallis marched again for Bangalore, with his cattle much improved by the forage obtained in the north; but
April 28. before he reached his destination he had already discovered that the Nizam's ten thousand horse were an encumbrance rather than a help. They were, in fact, a mere gang of mounted plunderers, afraid to fight or to go afield for forage, and greedy consumers of the army's supplies.

Meanwhile, with the help of European officers and

CH. XXVIII HISTORY OF THE ARMY 571

small contingents of the Company's Sepoys, the main 1791.
armies of the Nizam and of the Mahrattas had accomplished a few small captures in the north. Moreover, on the 22nd of February, Abercromby had moved
eastward from Tellicherry with nine battalions,[1] pursuing
his way through the territory of the friendly Rajah of
Coorg upon Periapatam. Owing to the ruggedness of
the country and the density of the jungle the march was
most laborious, and it was only by fixing tackles to large
trees that the guns and heavy stores were hauled through
sixty miles of forest to the summit of the Ghauts and
beyond it. Some time was spent in the collection of
stores at the head of the range, and on the 15th of May May 15.
the army descended into Mysore and encamped at
Periapatam, some forty miles west of Seringapatam,
awaiting further orders from Cornwallis.

The early days of May had, however, been far from
easy to the Commander-in-chief. His advanced base
was, it was true, firmly secured, but the season was far
spent, and his transport, despite the new resources
received at Vencatigerry, was still insufficient for a
march of one hundred miles with the prospect of a siege
at the end of it. Nevertheless, recent events in France
and the general weal of the British East Indies imperatively demanded a speedy conclusion of the war ;
and Cornwallis therefore called upon all officers to give
up all private means of transport, which they possessed
or could obtain, to the public service. The appeal was
answered in the best spirit ; but the supply was still
unequal to the need. After all possible exertions,
draught-animals could not be found sufficient to transport more than twenty days' provisions, or more than
fifteen battering-cannon over and above the fifty-two guns
that formed the field-train. In the matter of ammunition much was accomplished by offering payment to
women and boys to carry each an eighteen-pound shot ;
but the situation was none the less such that the General

[1] H.M. 73rd, 75th, 77th, 103rd (then Bombay Europeans), five
battalions of Sepoys.

1791.
could not embark without grave misgivings on his new adventure.

May 4. On the 4th of May he marched with his whole force, accompanied by the rabble of the Nizam, and hoping soon to be joined by a more efficient contingent of Mahratta horse, for which he had applied according to the terms of the treaty. He chose the eastern route by Cancanhilly and Sultanpettah, since the more direct road to Seringapatam by Chinapatam and Ramgerry was obstructed by redoubts and batteries, and occupied by Tippoo in force. Cornwallis, however, gained little by this deviation after the first march. On every subsequent day the army saw ahead of it the cloud of smoke which signified that Tippoo's light horse were burning every village and every blade of forage above ground to ashes. Hidden stores no doubt there were in plenty, but not a living human being could be found to show where they lay. Rain fell constantly, the road was rough, and the country was rugged, covered with jungle and seamed with rivulets. The exhausted cattle fell down by hundreds in their yokes, and the Mysorean horse, with just contempt for the miserable levies of the Nizam, hovered about the column ready to pounce upon any party in distress. Never had the rearguard of an army more miserable and distressing duty than on this

May 10. march. At length, on the 10th, the columns emerged at Malavelly into easier country, where they found a welcome supply of grain and abundance of pasture for the cattle. A day's halt was granted, and parties were sent forward to examine the fords of the Cavery, which, however, were found to be everywhere impassable. Anxious to

May 13. cross the river so as to effect his junction with Abercromby, Cornwallis then advanced to Arikera, about nine miles east of Seringapatam, where there was a ford of better reputation than the rest. This, however, proved also to be impassable; and Cornwallis realised that his only means of joining Abercromby was to cross by the ford of Caniambaddy, eight or nine miles west of Seringapatam, and that he would probably have to fight his way to it.

Meanwhile Tippoo also was in difficulties. He remembered that his father had always failed in general actions, and had succeeded only when striking at small detachments; but his present opponent adhered to the inconvenient practice of keeping his troops together. He would gladly have ventured a blow at Abercromby, but after the experience of Bangalore he dared not leave Seringapatam exposed to an attack by Cornwallis. He therefore decided for once to hazard a general action, in the hope at least of crippling Cornwallis sufficiently to compel his retreat; and with this view he took up a position close to the eastern end of the island of Seringapatam, with his right resting on the river and his front to the east. Cornwallis caught sight of his array from Arikera, and likewise conceived a desire for a general action; but the position of Tippoo proved to be not such as to invite attack. His right was covered by the river, and his line was extended along a rugged and apparently inaccessible ridge, strengthened by batteries and protected on the whole length of its front by a swampy ravine. Moreover, on nearer approach to the position, the ground over which the British must advance was narrowed by a rocky ridge to a width of less than a mile. A direct assault was plainly out of the question; but Cornwallis ascertained that it was possible, by a wide detour to northward, to ascend the tail of the range of hills whereon the Sultan's army was disposed. He therefore resolved by a night march to turn his left flank, and by gaining his rear before daylight to cut off the retreat of his main army to Seringapatam. Six European[1] and twelve Native battalions, together with the cavalry,[2] were therefore ordered to march at eleven o'clock that night, and the Nizam's horse to follow them at daylight.

Before the hour appointed for the march a thunderstorm of unusual violence broke over the country. The cattle, scared by the lightning and shivering under

1791.

May 14.

---

[1] H.M. 36th, 52nd, 71st, 72nd, 74th, 76th.
[2] 19th Light Dragoons and four Madras Native regiments.

torrents of rain, could hardly be made to move. Almost every corps lost its way, the guides being bewildered by the incessant contrast of dazzling light and impenetrable darkness; and Cornwallis, after advancing for some four or five miles, found himself alone with a single company and a single gun. There was no alternative but to halt until dawn, and since the design must thus be betrayed to the enemy, to pursue it with such favour as fortune might grant in the open day. With the coming of the light the march was resumed, and the British were actually descending into the ravine, which lay between them and the end of the range of hills, before the enemy took the alarm. It must have been a cruel reflection to Cornwallis that, but for the thunderstorm, he would have taken the Mysorean army completely by surprise; but weather is one of the chief elements in the fortune of war. As things fell out, Tippoo had time to make new dispositions; and it speaks not a little for his ability that he apprehended the whole situation with admirable quickness. Two or three miles to his left the range on which he lay ran out into a strong, rocky ridge, pointing perpendicularly to the advance of the British columns. If he could occupy this ridge before Cornwallis, he could hold him in check long enough to gain time to change his own position to his left, and to form a new front to the north. Without a moment's hesitation he despatched a strong body of cavalry and infantry with eight guns to seize this bulwark, and set the rest of his army in motion to take up their ground on its right, with their right flank resting on the ravine which had hitherto covered his front. The head of the British column, advancing with all haste to secure this same coveted ridge, found itself forestalled by Tippoo's detachment, and halted under the shelter of a lower cluster of rocks to form for attack.

Tippoo's line of battle now assumed somewhat of the shape of a joiner's square, the rocky ridge forming a salient angle on his left centre; and it was therefore

necessary for Cornwallis to deploy in conformity with 1791.
this disposition. Some loss was suffered from the May 15.
enemy's cannon during the process, while the Mysorean
cavalry hovered constantly about his left, watching for
an opportunity to attack, and occasionally charging even
up to the bayonets. At length, after much delay owing
to the weakness of the draught-cattle, the formation of
the line was completed, and Colonel Maxwell, on the
British right, advanced with five battalions to the attack
of the ridge. The Mysoreans, true to Hyder's traditions, at once withdrew their guns under fire of their
infantry; but Maxwell, having secured his flanks against
any attack of cavalry, pushed his men forward so
rapidly that he overtook and captured three of the
guns on the reverse slope of the ridge. The British
left then advanced against the main body on Tippoo's
right, which simply retired steadily from height to height
to cover the retreat of the guns. Maxwell made a bold
attempt to thrust himself past the enemy's left flank to
their rear, by throwing Floyd's cavalry upon the infantry
that was retiring before him; but though the squadrons
charged gallantly home and cut down numbers of the
enemy, their horses were too much exhausted to press
the attack with decisive effect. More, possibly very
much more, might have been accomplished had not the
Nizam's cavalry, through sheer perversity if not
treachery, planted itself in an unwieldy mass athwart
the line of Maxwell's advance, and blocked the way
completely for a considerable time. Thanks to these
worthless allies of Cornwallis, Tippoo's army made good
its retreat into Seringapatam with a loss of no more than
one or two thousand men, while the British casualties
reached the number of nearly five hundred, one-third of
them falling upon the Europeans. In a word, Cornwallis's bold stroke had failed, through no fault of his
own, but by the fortune of war.

He now marched round the northern and western
sides of Seringapatam to Caniambaddy; but even here
the admirable activity and vigilance of the Mysorean

1791. horse forbade any communication with Abercromby. There was neither news nor sign of the coming of the Mahrattas; and it was too evident that all hope of further operations must for the present be abandoned, since, owing to the mortality among the animals, not only the guns, but all the public carts in the army, were now
May 21. dragged along by the troops. On the 21st Cornwallis wrote the orders for Abercromby to return to Malabar, and on the 22nd the whole of the battering-train and heavy equipment of his own force was destroyed. Still not a word came from Abercromby; and the sight of a large body of Mysorean troops advancing towards Periapatam so alarmed Cornwallis for his colleague's
May 24. safety, that he took the hazardous step of passing three brigades across the Cavery to make a diversion in his favour. Abercromby, however, effected his retreat in safety, though he too was compelled to destroy some and to bury others of his heavy guns, and lost not only most of his cattle from the severity of the rains, but a large portion of his baggage. All this was unknown to
May 26. Cornwallis, who waited in painful anxiety till the 26th, when he was driven by the appalling state of his camping-ground to retreat from Caniambaddy. The air was poisoned by the corpses of animals and men, for many of the followers had actually died of hunger, and even the Sepoys were starving. Fasting, dispirited, and chilled by bleak wind and drizzling rain, the army crept away in misery to northward, the horses even of the dragoons being taken for conveyance of the sick. Only half of the first march had been accomplished when the advanced guard was startled by the appearance of two thousand horse in their front. Dispositions were at once made for meeting an attack, and firing had actually begun, when one of the horsemen cried out loudly that he was a Mahratta, and begged that the fire might cease. These squadrons were in fact the advanced guard of some forty thousand Mahratta cavalry, which with two battalions from Bombay and twenty guns had marched down from the north, but even in such over-

...elming force had failed to pierce the screen of Tippoo's 1791.
...rols and send news of their approach. Had Cornwallis known but one week earlier of their coming, he might have pursued his original design against Seringapatam; but now his siege-train was destroyed, and ...was too late. Seldom was there a more unlucky ...mander.

The retreat was therefore continued, though without ...te, and with diminished distress, for the Mahrattas ...brought with them vast quantities of supplies, which ...y sold at the profit which accrues to the monopolist.

...the 11th of July Bangalore was reached, and Corn- July 11. ...lis, having deposited his sick and his heavy stores, ...ved eastward with the army in order to open up ...communications with the Carnatic. First he ...ved to Oosoor, which was evacuated by the enemy, ...thence to the Policode Pass, where some few days ...e spent in reducing Rayacotta and other hill-forts ...ch commanded the defile. Thus not only was a ...way opened for convoys from the plains, but the ...lets into Baramahal were closed to Tippoo's raiding ...ties.

The Sultan, however, had no sooner found the ...ssure about his capital relaxed, than he had despatched ...rong force for the recapture of Coimbatore. It had ...n intended that the garrison of this post should, if ...eatened, at once evacuate it and retire to Palghautcherry; but the officer in command, Lieutenant ...almers, finding two or three serviceable guns and ...eral swivels in the place, determined to defend it. ...s whole force consisted only of six score of *Topasses*, ...mixed European and Asian blood, with a hundred ...tinous Travancoreans under a young Frenchman ...ned de la Combe; and the powder in his magazine ...of inferior quality. The besiegers, on the other ...d, when they first invested the place on the 11th of June 11. ...e, comprised two thousand regular infantry with ...ht guns, besides irregulars and cavalry. Yet Chalmers ...d this force at bay for two whole months, and even

1791.
Aug. 11.

repulsed a determined assault by the simple expedient of rolling down barrels of powder which exploded among the assailants. The number of the dead left within the limits of the ditch alone by the enemy's storming-parties after this attack exceeded the whole strength of the garrison; and the defenders, following up their victory, actually captured two guns. On that same day a weak battalion of Sepoys and some irregular infantry with six guns arrived from Palghautcherry to reinforce the post, and Chalmers lost no time in driving the besiegers across the Bahvani with the loss of most of their stores. He then returned to improve the defences of Coimbatore, never doubting but that Tippoo would renew his attack upon it, and obtained an English officer, Lieutenant Nash, to take the place of de la

Oct. 6.

Combe, who had retired to Travancore. On the 6th of October one of the Sultan's most skilful leaders arrived before the place with eight thousand regular infantry, fourteen guns and four mortars, besides a large force of irregulars and cavalry; and the siege was begun anew. Again Chalmers kept the enemy at a distance

Nov. 6.

until the 6th of November, when, both he and Nash being wounded, he consented to capitulate on condition that the garrison should withdraw to Palghautcherry. The terms were however violated, as was so common with Tippoo, and they were removed as close prisoners to Seringapatam. By his singular gallantry Chalmers had forced the Sultan to convert a mere raid into a serious operation, which cost him much trouble and loss.

Long before the second siege of Coimbatore was begun, Cornwallis had entered on the preliminary operations of a new campaign. His first object was to open a line of communications to the north-east, where the Nizam's troops were engaged in the siege of Goorumconda, in order alike to maintain touch with them and to utilise the resources of the country. With this object six battalions of Sepoys and the Hundred-and-Second

Sept. 13.

Foot were sent northward under Major Gowdie, who,

after capturing two or three minor forts without diffi- 1791. culty, sat down before the mighty stronghold of Nundydroog. This celebrated fort lies about thirty-six miles north of Bangalore, and is perched on the summit of an enormous mountain of granite, the walls being over three miles in girth, and the base of the mountain twelve miles in circumference. Two-thirds of this huge rock are absolutely inaccessible, and the only practicable face was protected by walls of immense thickness, with outworks which afforded a formidable flanking fire to cover the gateway. A second hill adjacent to it was selected by the British as the first site of a battery, but was found to be too far distant to maintain a destructive fire. It was therefore resolved to proceed by regular approaches upon the face of the mountain itself; and with incredible difficulty and labour guns were dragged up by the help of elephants. Batteries were then raised, and by the 17th of October two breaches had been made in the walls. On the 18th Oct. 18. Cornwallis moved up with his whole army in order to overawe the besieged; and it was resolved without further delay to assault.

The flank-companies of the Thirty-sixth and Oct. 19. Seventy-first were detailed to form the stormingparty, with the Hundred-and-Second in support; and when the moon rose on the early morning of the 19th, the signal was given and the assailants made a rush for the breach. Instantly the hill was illuminated with blue lights in every direction, and the garrison opened a heavy but ill-directed fire, while, far more destructive than musketry or cannon, huge stones came bounding down with frightful velocity from the summit. But the impetuosity of the troops carried them swiftly over the breaches, from which they pursued the defenders so hotly to the inner wall that they were able to force the gate and enter the internal works almost on the backs of the fugitives. These defences in turn were speedily cleared, and therewith the fighting came to an end.

1791. The loss of the storming-party was no more than two killed and twenty-eight wounded, and the whole of the operations did not cost the British more than one hundred and twenty men. Thus after three weeks of siege fell Nundydroog, a fortress of such strength that it had once defied Hyder Ali himself during three long years of blockade. So great was the moral effect of the capture that a neighbouring fort, little less formidable, was surrendered at the first summons.

A portion of the battering-train was now sent northward to the assistance of the Nizam's army before Goorumconda; but meanwhile Tippoo had directed a force to be detached to Baramahal from the troops investing Coimbatore, in order to threaten Cornwallis's communications to the south-east. Colonel Maxwell thereupon marched with the Seventy-fourth and three Sepoy battalions to repel this party, and, moving with great rapidity, attacked and almost annihilated one body of the raiders in a hill-fort. Having driven the remainder over the Ghauts, Maxwell tried to take the fort of Kistnagerry by storm, but, failing in the attempt, returned on the 30th of November to Bangalore, with his principal object accomplished. The communications to east and north being thus cleared, it now remained to reduce several strongholds to southward, interposed between Bangalore and Seringapatam. This work should, perhaps, more properly have formed part of the operations of a general advance; but Cornwallis's preparations were not yet complete; his cavalry was still in the Carnatic procuring remounts; and, above all, the arrival of the Mahratta contingent, owing to the selfish trickery of its chief, was constantly delayed. Not to waste valuable time, therefore, Cornwallis detached Colonel Stuart with the Fifty-second, Seventy-third, three Sepoy battalions, and a small battering-train for the siege of Savandroog, a hill-fortress lying rather more than twenty miles south and west of Bangalore. Simultaneously he disposed the remainder of the army so as to shield the operations 1791. from all interruption from Seringapatam.

Savandroog, the Rock of Death, so called not less for its stupendous size and strength than for the deadly climate that encompassed it, rises to a height of some nine hundred feet from a chaos of precipitous ravines, then clothed everywhere with almost impenetrable jungle. The circumference of its base is eight miles, and it was embraced on all sides by walls and fortifications. Towards the summit it is riven by a deep chasm into two distinct hills, each strengthened by its own system of works and each out of range of the other. Tippoo hailed the news of the British enterprise against it with joy, for he reckoned that half of the Europeans must perish of sickness, and the remainder be destroyed in the assault. Nevertheless, with enormous labour a road was cut through the jungle, heavy guns were dragged over rock and ravine to the foot of the mountain, and on the 17th of December two batteries Dec. 17. opened fire upon the wall of the eastern hill. So little damage was done, owing to the massive construction of the masonry, that a new battery was erected within a range of two hundred and fifty yards, which in two days effected a practicable breach. The jungle on which the garrison had counted so much for their defence now turned to the advantage of the besiegers, for without it they could hardly have dragged themselves up the precipitous steep to the attack. Moreover, they were now able under its shelter to form a lodgment within twenty yards of the breach; and on the night of the 21st it was determined to make the Dec. 21. assault.

The flank-companies of the Fifty-second and Seventy-sixth were appointed to carry the eastern hill and scour its works towards the western side, with the remainder of the Fifty-second and the Seventy-second in support. The flank-companies of the Seventy-first were ordered to disperse any hostile force in the chasm between the two hills; and parties were detached all

1791.
Dec. 21. round the base of the mountain to distract the attention of the enemy and prevent their escape. At eleven o'clock the storming-party rushed at the breach, followed by their supports, while the band of the Fifty-second played "Britons, strike home." But there was no enemy to be struck on the eastern hill, for the whole of the garrison fled in panic along a narrow path towards the west, where a few well-directed shots served to increase their confusion and impede their flight. The grenadiers of the Fifty-second and a handful of the Seventy-first pressed them so hard in pursuit that they entered the defences of the western hill with them, and carried the summit of that also. About one hundred of the defenders were killed on the western hill, and several more fell over the precipices in the haste of panic. Within less than an hour the fortress so long deemed impregnable was taken, at a cost to the British of a single wounded man.

Dec. 23.
Dec. 24. Two days later Stuart moved a few miles westward to the fort of Ootradroog, which was stormed out of hand by the impetuosity of the troops, the garrison having apparently no courage to defend the succession of walls upon which they had relied for protection. To cover their retreat, however, the runaways resorted to the device of letting loose against their pursuers a herd of wild cattle, which played their part right gallantly, plunging straight into the British ranks and tossing several men high into the air. The animals, however, could not stem the tide of the British advance, and Ootradroog was captured with no greater loss than two men wounded and about thirty badly contused by the cattle. Since the place contained large hoards of grain and an excellent supply of water, Cornwallis decided to use it for his hospital and as an advanced depot for the coming operations. Meanwhile, another detachment had stormed the fort of Ramgerry, on the direct road from Bangalore to Seringapatam, and had thereby scared another fort adjacent to it into surrender. Thus within a very short space a line of posts had been established to

the southward, not without great moral effect upon the enemy. The necessary supplies for the campaign had also been brought up by great exertions from the Carnatic ; and all was ready for the final advance upon the capital of Mysore.

1791.

CHAPTER XXIX

1791.   WHILE Cornwallis had been pushing forward his preparations on the side of Madras, Abercromby had been not less active on the side of Bombay. In November he returned to Malabar, bringing with him or receiving from Palghautcherry all the means of a good equipment,
Dec.   and in December he began his march with nine thousand men. After three weeks of incessant and most arduous labour, he brought a battering-train of fourteen heavy guns up to the head of the Ghauts; and on the 22nd of
1792.   January 1792 he made his first march from the head of
Jan. 22.   the Ghauts towards Mysore.
Jan. 25.   Three days later, Cornwallis's whole army of twenty-two thousand men united with the eighteen thousand horse which formed the Nizam's contingent, at Savandroog. Of the Mahrattas only a very small party was present, the bulk of their force having gone on a plundering expedition to the north-west, in defiance of all agreements. Their absence was the more unsatisfactory, since from the difficulty of procuring remounts only two regiments of Native Cavalry beside the Nineteenth Light Dragoons[1] were able to

---

[1] Order of Battle.
Army commanded by Earl Cornwallis, Commander-in-chief. Major-general Medows, second in command.
  RIGHT WING (from right to left).—Lieut.-col. Stuart :—
  Third Brigade.—Lieut.-col. Cockerell. Four battalions of Bengal Sepoys.
  First Brigade.—Lieut.-col. Nesbitt. H.M. 36th, 76th, 52nd.
  Fourth Brigade.—Lieut.-col. Russell. Three battalions of Bengal Sepoys.

take the field. But Cornwallis, not being disposed to 1792. wait longer for the Mahrattas, moved a few miles to the south-west against Hooliadroog, which at once surrendered. Leaving a garrison here and at an intermediate post to secure communication with Ootradroog, the Commander-in-chief on the 1st of February began Feb. 1. his advance in earnest. Every human dwelling went up in smoke and flames as his army drew near, but the invasion was not to be stemmed by such expedients; and on the 5th the troops climbed the last hill which Feb. 5.

LEFT WING.—Lieut.-col. Maxwell.
Sixth Brigade.—Major Langley. Four battalions of Coast Sepoys.
Second Brigade.—Lieut.-col. Knox. H.M. 72nd, 74th, 71st.
Fifth Brigade.—Lieut.-col. Baird. Four battalions of Coast Sepoys.

RESERVE.—Lieut.-col. Floyd.
Cavalry Brigade.—19th Light Dragoons, two regiments of Madras Native Cavalry.
Seventh Brigade.—Major Gowdie. 102nd Foot, one Sepoy battalion.

PARK OF ARTILLERY.—Colonel Duff. 46 field-guns, 4 howitzers, 36 mortars, and siege-guns. 1145 European artillery, 3077 Native artillery.
Attached to the Nizam's Contingent.—Two battalions of Coast Sepoys.

Europeans . . .	6,066
Native troops . . .	15,967
Total . .	22,033

Army of Major-general Abercromby.
First Brigade.—Colonel Balfour, H.M. 75th. Two battalions of Sepoys.
Second Brigade.—Lieut.-col. Pechè, H.M. 77th. Two battalions of Sepoys.
Third Brigade.—Major Stirling, 103rd Foot. Two battalions of Sepoys.
Reserve.—Lieut.-col. Hartley, H.M. 73rd. Grenadier battalion, one Sepoy battalion, 20 field-guns, 16 pieces of siege artillery.

Europeans . . .	3026
Native troops . . .	5932
Total . .	8958

1792.
Feb. 5.

divided them from their goal, and saw before them a view, grand beyond description, of the valley of the Cavery and the city of Seringapatam, with the army of the Sultan encamped about its walls.

About six miles to northward of the city Cornwallis halted, with inward thanksgiving. He had feared lest Tippoo should have left a sufficient garrison under a resolute leader for defence of his capital, and turned the bulk of his force against the British lines of communication. But there the whole of the Mysorean host lay beneath his eyes; and it was plain that, untaught by the bitter experience of Bangalore and Savandroog, the Sultan counted on his fortifications to ensure his triumph. Tippoo was not wholly without ground for his faith in the strength of Seringapatam. The city itself lies ensconced on a triangular island between two branches, each from two to five hundred yards wide, of the Cavery; the extreme length of the triangle being six thousand yards, and the extreme breadth twenty-five hundred yards. In the western angle stood the fort, of quadrangular form; its northern wall overlooking the river for nearly a mile along the northern front of the island, from which point batteries with flèches and bastions continued the chain of fortifications to the eastern angle. These works, together with the Cavery itself, which though fordable in many places was everywhere rocky and difficult, formed the innermost line of defence. On the north bank of the Cavery, starting from a point about a thousand yards above the island, there ran a broad belt of thorny shrubs, which trended first to northward for a mile and a-half, so as to embrace a fortified eminence called the Mosque Redoubt, and, turning thence south-eastward for some seven thousand yards, rejoined the river close to the heights where Tippoo had offered battle in May 1791. The hill nearest to the island, named Carighaut Hill, was crowned by a redoubt, which, however, was still unfinished; and this work, together with the Mosque

Redoubt, constituted practically advanced posts on the flanks of the position. In rear of them and within the belt of thorn was an interior system of seven more powerful and well-constructed redoubts, supported by the fort and by each other, which formed the main position of the Sultan's army. In all, some three hundred guns were mounted to defend this northern front. It is true that the Carighaut Redoubt was still incomplete, but Tippoo reckoned that there would be ample time to finish it, feeling confident that Cornwallis would undertake no important enterprise until he should have been joined by Abercromby. His confidence was increased when at noon of the 5th he saw the British army move away with a wide sweep to westward, and take up a strong position some two miles remoter than before from the island of Seringapatam.

1792.
Feb. 5.

Early on the morning of the 6th, English troops ascended the Carighaut Hill, evidently for the purpose of reconnoitring the defences; but still the Sultan remained unsuspicious. None the less, throughout the day Cornwallis and his staff were hard at work, and orders for an attack in three divisions were issued at sunset.

Feb. 6.

The right division, consisting of two European[1] and five Sepoy battalions under the command of General Medows, was appointed to penetrate the left flank of the enemy's encampment about a mile to south of the Mosque Redoubt, carry all the interior works, overthrow the troops of Tippoo's left wing, and establish communication with the centre division.

This centre division, under Cornwallis himself, was parted into three distinct sub-divisions. Of these, the first and foremost consisted of six flank-companies of the Fifty-second, Seventy-first, and Seventy-fourth, the battalion-companies of the Fifty-second, and one battalion of Bengal Sepoys, under Lieutenant-colonel Knox: its function was to break into the centre of the enemy's camp, mix with the fugitives, and pass over with them into the island. The second or middle sub-division,

[1] 36th and 76th.

1792.
Feb. 6. made up of the Seventy-first and two battalions of Sepoys, under Colonel Stuart, was charged to follow that of Knox as far as the rear of the camp, then to turn to the left, take Tippoo's right wing in rear and overthrow it, and try to force a way into the island. The third sub-division, composed of the battalion-companies of the Seventy-fourth and two battalions of Sepoys, formed a reserve under Cornwallis himself.

The left division was entrusted to Lieutenant-colonel Maxwell, with David Baird for his second in command. He, with the Seventy-second and four native battalions, was instructed to storm the works on Carighaut Hill, descend and turn the right of Tippoo's lines, and join hands with Stuart. The remainder of the army was left under Floyd's command to protect the camp. It was reckoned that the Sultan had fifty thousand fighting men, besides irregular levies, in and about Seringapatam: the utmost strength of the British attacking column was eight thousand seven hundred bayonets.

At six o'clock, directly after the dismissal of evening parade, the officers received their instructions, and the selected men fell in again, rejoicing greatly that they were to be unencumbered with cannon. The Nizam's officers and the Mahrattas were on the contrary horrified beyond expression, more especially when they learned that the Commander-in-chief was accompanying the centre attack in person. At half-past eight on a calm, still night the columns moved off in perfect silence, with the moon just risen to light them to their work. Maxwell's division, well knowing the ground over which it had fought in May, was the first by a few minutes to come into action. The redoubt on Carighaut Hill, in itself strong, was further protected by a double line of breastworks and was held by a strong force of infantry; but the flank-companies of the Seventy-second, with Baird at their head, speedily surmounted every obstacle and drove the enemy from the post, with trifling loss to themselves. Leaving a small force to guard the captured works, Maxwell quickly descended the hill and, though somewhat galled by the bullets of a corps concealed in the watercourse at its base, pushed on to the river Lockany, which lay athwart his front, forded it under a heavy fire from the right of Tippoo's line, and made his way successfully, according to his orders, into the Mysorean camp.

Just as the attack on Carighaut Hill had begun, Knox's party in the centre, led by a battalion-company of the Fifty-second, came upon an advanced post of cavalry and rocket-men, who, seeing that resistance was hopeless, discharged their rockets to give the alarm and instantly retired. The column continued its advance in perfect silence, but every man by a common impulse doubled the speed of his march. They reached the tortuous Lockany River and forded it, still in silence, traversed another five hundred yards and were fording the stream again, when suddenly there burst from the hedge before them a storm of musketry so close and rapid that the flashes seemed like one continuous flame. The bullets flew thickly about the water, but the column pushed on patiently and silently till the leading companies, being at length close to the hedge, fired a single volley, and with one tremendous shout dashed forward with the bayonet. The pioneers hurried to the front with their axes to clear the way; but the troops would not wait. Some crept through, some crawled under, some leaped over; all went on. Every man struck in with the bayonet at the foeman nearest to him in furious combat hand to hand; but already numbers of the enemy had turned their backs and were flying in wild confusion towards the island. The five foremost companies[1] hurried after them in hot pursuit; and Tippoo Sahib himself had only just time to mount his horse and gallop away to the fort before the leading men of the Fifty-second dashed past his tent, killed many of his attendants, and drove the rest before them to the river. Pressing hard on the heels of the fugitives,

---

[1] The flank-companies and one battalion-company of the 52nd, grenadier-companies of the 71st and 74th.

1792.
Feb. 6. they entered the water with them at a ford close to the foot of the north-eastern glacis, and found themselves fairly surrounded by enemies. The bottom was everywhere rocky and slippery, the water frequently waist-deep, and the current so rapid that a man who lost his foothold was swept away beyond recovery; but even under these strange conditions the British pursued the fight furiously. All discipline and cohesion were lost; each man relying solely on his individual strength struck out savagely all round him with the bayonet, with the butt, and even with his fists, until the water flowed thick with the corpses of the fallen.

When the opposite bank was gained, discipline reasserted itself forthwith. The five companies were reformed, Captain Monson as senior officer took command, and the whole moved off in perfect order to make their way across the island. Their route lay along the main street of the bazaar, between the foot of the glacis and the mud wall which enclosed the town; and their progress was blocked by a swarm of fugitives pouring across the street from the east to seek shelter under the ramparts. The slopes of the glacis, the covered way, and the ramparts on the one hand, and the town and bazaar on the other, were crowded with armed men, not one of whom had the courage to pull trigger; and the tiny British column, opening outwards[1] by divisions, half-right and half-left, poured on them an oblique fire which was frightfully destructive. Thus this handful of men pushed on unresisted for more than a mile, when they were met by the fire of cannon from a redoubt at the southern end of the street, and by a discharge of musketry in both flanks. This attack was at once answered by a charge with the bayonet, and in a very short time the street was cleared and the redoubt captured. Monson then occupied this work, and strove by loud cheering and beating of the Grenadiers' March to indicate his position to the

[1] The old formation for "street-firing," such as was practised at the attack of Fort St. Lazar in 1740.

remainder of the column. Failing, however, to perceive 1792.
the least sign of them, he decided for the present to Feb. 6.
hold the redoubt and give some rest to his exhausted
men.

It is now time to relate the adventures of the rest
of the centre division. The battalion-companies of the
Fifty-second and the regiment of Bengal Sepoys, which
belonged also to Knox's party, had followed the five
leading companies for some way through the enemy's
camp, until the speed of the advance was checked by
a tract of rice-fields. The rear of the column then
moved somewhat further to the right, and so lost touch
of the van. Knox himself, with the light companies of
the Seventy-first and Seventy-fourth, did indeed advance
so closely in the track of Monson's party that he reached
the ford only five minutes behind them. Crossing the
river, he came upon a few belated men of the Fifty-
second on the opposite bank, added them to his own
two companies, and turned to his left into the town,
beating the Grenadiers' March. Meanwhile the remainder of the Fifty-second, under Captain Hunter,
with three companies of Bengal Sepoys, also became
separated from the rear of the column and equally lost
touch with Knox in advance. Hence they missed the
ford under the glacis, and crossed by another rather
further down the river, opposite a garden called the
Dowlut Bagh, into which they forced their way. Here
Hunter, thinking that his companies had been the first
to cross the water, decided to halt and await the
remainder of the column; thus making a third weak
isolated party in the island of Seringapatam.

Meanwhile, the rest of this centre column had
received a temporary check. The rear companies of
the Bengal Sepoys, less fortunate than the three leading
ones with Hunter, had been assailed by a sharp fire
on their right flank when approaching the hedge, and,
their commanding officer being killed, had fallen back
in confusion. Colonel Stuart at once brought forward
the Seventy-first, which speedily forced its way through

1792.
Feb. 6.

the hedge, when the broken Sepoys rallied behind them with creditable readiness. With the Seventy-first in the van and these Sepoys added to two more native battalions in support, Stuart advanced some little way further and then wheeled to his left to break the right wing of Tippoo's army. On approaching the Sultan's Redoubt, which was the most easterly of the interior defences, he was confronted with a large body of the enemy's horse; but the Seventy-first, halting as steadily as on parade, gave them one crushing volley which sent them flying back in disorder with no heart to advance again. Stuart then prepared to storm the redoubt, but finding it to be abandoned, occupied it at once with one hundred and fifty men. He then pursued his march eastward, dispersing the Mysorean foot before him, till at the extreme edge of the encampment he came upon a line of infantry drawn up as if to oppose him. He had just given the word to fire a volley and charge with the bayonet, when in the nick of time he discovered the troops to be Maxwell's. The two divisions then united and prepared to force their passage across the river in the face of the enemy's batteries.

Meanwhile, Cornwallis had formed his reserve-battalions near the Sultan's Redoubt, and was waiting for Medows to join him from the west. But in that quarter things had gone ill. The intention had been that Medows's column should avoid the Mosque Redoubt and penetrate the bound-hedge far in rear of it; but by the fault of the guides the troops were led straight upon it. As fate ordained, the enemy in the redoubt and to right and left of it remained steady until the leading battalions of the British were close upon them, when they poured on them a heavy fire of grape and musketry. Thereupon six companies of the Thirty-sixth at once deployed to attack the enemy on the left of the redoubt, while its flank-companies, together with those of the Seventy-fourth, made a dash at the work itself. The assailants soon cleared the Mysoreans out of the covered way, but were unable to cross the ditch, until they found a pathway by which they contrived to pass, when they drove the defenders into the inner circle of the redoubt, completely cutting off their retreat. The Mysoreans, however, still resisted most gallantly, and, turning a gun upon the gorge, swept away with a storm of grape a party which attempted to attack them with the bayonet. The British then found a point of vantage from which they could shoot down any men who attempted to reload the gun; and a second charge with the bayonet finally drove this brave garrison out of the work. Four hundred of them were slain on the spot, and the whole of the fugitives were killed or taken. A party of infantry, which attempted to reinforce the redoubt during the attack, was dispersed by a single volley; and thus the right division fairly established itself on the skirts of Tippoo's camp. But the success of the British had cost them eleven officers and eighty men of the very flower of the army.

Leaving four companies of the Thirty-sixth to hold the captured redoubt, Medows reformed the column and turned eastward to join Cornwallis. A deserter offered to lead him through the camp to the river, but Medows, judging it inexpedient to risk further loss by an attack on the remaining redoubts, resolved to incline northwards so as to leave them on his right hand and, on striking the track of Cornwallis, to join him by that route. Unfortunately, just at that period the firing everywhere ceased for a time, so that there was no clue to the position of any of the British troops. The column became entangled in some rice-swamps, moved still further northward to clear them, missed the track of Cornwallis, and found itself at last at Carighaut Hill, without the slightest intelligence of the Commander-in-chief.

Such, then, was the position from two to three hours before dawn. Hunter, Knox, and Monson were posted in three small isolated parties across the middle of

1792.
Feb. 7.
the island from north to south, without knowledge of each other's presence, and therefore without communication. Maxwell and Stuart, united, were preparing to enter the island at the eastern angle. Cornwallis, with perhaps one thousand men, lay near the Sultan's Redoubt; two hundred more men were in the Mosque Redoubt; and Medows's column, comprising not much less than half the strength of the entire attacking force, was for the present out of action. Worst of all, not one of these scattered parties had the least idea where another was to be found. Unless these several units could be concentrated before daylight, there was every probability that Tippoo might overwhelm them in detail.

Fortunately, every officer realised the urgency of the danger. Firing had ceased soon after the capture of the Mosque Redoubt, for the simple reason that no commander except Stuart had sufficient troops with him to make any further movement. Knox had tried in vain to force his way with his handful of men through the town to the eastward, but had been met by repeated charges of cavalry which, though repulsed by his volleys, only made way for solid columns of infantry. In the presence of numbers so overwhelming, he thought it more prudent to desist from the attempt and look to his own defence. At this critical period, however, Stuart and Maxwell set their troops in motion, and the renewal of the firing thereupon cleared up the whole situation. Their united divisions advanced with the least possible delay to the banks of the river in order to cross to the island; but being unable to find a ford and meeting with a tremendous fire from the enemy's batteries, they were beaten back with considerable loss. At length, however, Baird discovered a ford, passed it, and effected a lodgment with a small party of men on the opposite bank. He had no sooner sent back a report of his success than the thunder of the Mysorean guns suddenly ceased. Knox, on hearing them open fire, had immediately divined the cause, and sent his men to attack them from the rear. Utterly surprised by this unexpected onslaught and terrified at the sight of the bayonets, the 1792. gunners instantly forsook the cannon and took to their Feb. 7. heels. The remainder of Maxwell's and Stuart's divisions then crossed the river unmolested, though the water was so deep that their ammunition was spoiled; and Stuart thereupon formed his whole force across the eastern end of the island, with his flanks resting on the two branches of river and his right almost touching Carighaut Hill. There Knox's detachment was safely gathered in; and shortly before daylight Monson's five companies also joined Stuart, attracted by the sound of the firing. Lastly Hunter, after striving in vain to send a messenger to Cornwallis for orders, recrossed the river from the Dowlut Bagh, dispersed an isolated force of the enemy on the northern bank, and safely reached the Commander-in-chief at the Sultan's Redoubt.

He came at an opportune moment, for his men had hardly changed their wet ammunition for dry before a large body of troops from Tippoo's centre, having rallied from their panic, fell upon Cornwallis's reserve with the greatest resolution. Happily, the thirteen companies of Europeans with the two battalions of Sepoys stood firm under the eye of the Commander-in-chief, for the attacks were renewed again and again and were not finally repulsed until near the dawn. Cornwallis then withdrew his little force to Carighaut Hill lest it should be exposed to the guns of the fort, and there at length, to his great relief, he encountered Medows. Without delay he despatched orders to Floyd to shift the camp to Carighaut Hill, and sent the Thirty-sixth and a battalion of Sepoys, with a supply of ammunition, to reinforce Stuart on the island.

The light was now strong, and Tippoo, who had ensconced himself in a detached work at the north-east angle of the fort, was able to see for himself the strength and weakness of the British dispositions. The isolated party in the Sultan's Redoubt first attracted his notice; and, confident in the knowledge that it could not be reinforced under the fire of guns of the fort, he selected

1792.
Feb. 7.

this as the first object of attack. The work itself being open to the rear, the little garrison tried hard to close the gorge with a gun-carriage, but this slender protection was quickly knocked to pieces by the cannon of the fort and by two field-pieces advanced by Tippoo for the purpose. After a heavy cannonade, a strong body of infantry moved up to the assault. Their attack was valiantly met and repulsed, though with heavy loss to the defenders, who were further greatly distressed by the fact that they had not a drop of water either for the sound or the wounded. Fortunately, two bullocks laden with ammunition had strayed into the ditch, which enabled the little party to prolong its defence; for presently two thousand horse advanced rapidly as if about to charge into the gorge, and four hundred of them, dismounting, made a gallant attempt to carry the work with the sabre. They, too, were beaten back; and finally, at two o'clock, a third attack was delivered by Tippoo's European regiment of about three hundred and fifty men. Great things were expected of these troops, but they would not face the fire of the little band of exhausted British, and retired in disorder after the loss of a few men. No further attempt was made to recapture the redoubt, and at four o'clock the survivors of the garrison were able to withdraw to the island, almost at the last gasp from hunger, thirst, and fatigue. Of six officers with this gallant little party, Captain Sibbald of the Seventy-first and Lieutenant Buchan of the Bengal Artillery were killed, and three more were wounded. Out of eighty men of the Seventy-first, fourteen gunners, and fifty Sepoys, nineteen were killed and twenty-two grievously wounded. On the next day the name of Sultan's Redoubt was changed to Sibbald's Redoubt.

This onset having failed, Tippoo at five o'clock directed two brigades against Stuart's force on the island; but these also were repulsed without difficulty and driven out of the town. The British lay on their arms all night, awaiting a second attack, but none was delivered ; and when the morning came, it was found 1792. that the enemy had evacuated not only their fortified Feb. 8. camp to the north of the Cavery, but the whole island of Seringapatam excepting the fort. Thus, after more than thirty-six hours of constant work, Cornwallis had accomplished his object and won a great and decisive victory. The casualties of the British were five hundred and thirty-five, more than half of the fallen being Europeans; and it is significant that three-fifths of the losses fell upon the centre division. The number of the Mysoreans that perished, chiefly by drowning in the river, was reckoned at four thousand, but it is said that the total number missing, owing to flight and desertion, exceeded twenty thousand. The trophies of the victors were eighty captured guns.

Writhing under his defeat, Tippoo on this same day sent Lieutenants Chalmers and Nash to Cornwallis to sue for peace, and simultaneously a party of horse to assassinate him. Both missions failed of their object. Cornwallis at once invested the fort and summoned Abercromby from Periapatam, who effected his junction with the main army on the 16th. On the 14th envoys from Tippoo had again presented themselves to negotiate a treaty ; but Cornwallis suspended operations not for a moment, and by the 19th his trenches had been opened against the north and south-western sides of the fort. On the 22nd Tippoo attempted a sortie, which was repulsed with heavy loss, and on the next day he Feb. 23. accepted Cornwallis's proposals as a basis for a treaty, sending to him his two sons as hostages. For fully another month he contrived to protract the negotiations until Cornwallis, none too soon, brought them to a peremptory close ; and on the 19th of March the March 19. definitive treaty was signed. Under its provisions the Mahrattas and the Nizam recovered a great part of the territory taken from them by Hyder, while the British received Malabar and Coorg on the west, with Dindigul and Baramahal on the east, thus securing a sure barrier on both sides against Mysore.

1792. So ended this arduous and exhausting war, whereby for the first time the power of Hyder Ali's house was seriously shaken. One further war remained yet to be fought before it should be overthrown for ever; but the narrative of these campaigns sufficiently shows how formidable was that power when wielded by a crafty and tenacious prince who would shrink from no treachery, cruelty, nor devastation to preserve it. From a military point of view the war is interesting chiefly as a study of the contest, so familiar to English officers, between the posts on a long line of communications and a singularly mobile and efficient cavalry. The Mysorean light horse was superlatively excellent for purposes of partisan warfare. They veiled the movements of their own army in a cloud of mystery; they hung about their enemy like rooks about a heron, hustling, threatening, swooping, always too far away to receive injury, always near enough to inflict it. No messenger could pass through them; no hostile foraging party could move outside the circle of its own picquets without being cut off. Let a waggon break down, or a bullock fall exhausted in the yoke, the active horsemen thronged instantly to the spot, as the vultures descend, from no man knows whence, to gorge themselves on a corpse. To operate against such an enemy in small detachments was to court disaster; and Cornwallis, with the fate of Baillie and the experience of America before him, no sooner took command than he made concentration the keynote of the campaign. He shuddered at the cost of the military preparations, and it went to his heart to depreciate the credit of the British East Indies, which he had done so much to restore; but he faced facts boldly, and a man who faces facts has gone far on the road to accomplish his purpose. He was still somewhat of an impatient general. He realised that it was better for him to move with a large and cumbrous force, despite all difficulties of transport and supply, and to advance even at a snail's pace, securing his communications as he went, rather than risk the destruction of a number of small columns in detail. But his first hasty descent upon Seringapatam in 1792. 1791 evinces somewhat of the same spirit which made him the victim of Greene in Carolina ; and though the arrival of the Mahrattas a week earlier might have brought him a triumph, yet their arrival a week later might have turned his retreat into a disaster.[1] But the temptation to close the war at a stroke was very great; and it does not necessarily follow that a man has chosen the wrong path because he fails at once to reach his goal.

For the rest, Cornwallis showed a nerve, audacity, and swiftness in action which seem to me to entitle him to high rank among commanders. The siege of Bangalore in the face of Tippoo's superior force, the storming of the town, the bold march upon Tippoo's flank before Seringapatam, the assaults on Nundydroog and Savandroog, and lastly the attack on Seringapatam itself, were all of them enterprises that called for no common degree of skill and resolution, and they were therefore the more telling in their moral effect. It is evident, too, that he was remarkably deft in the handling of large bodies of troops in the face of an enemy ; and it may be conjectured that in this respect he had learned much from General Howe during the American War. But his dash and vigour were so conspicuous, that the station in which, perhaps, he would have shone most eminently would have been in the command of a large body of cavalry in operations on a really great scale. It is noticeable that his force of mounted troops was far larger and more efficient than had yet been committed to any general in India ; for after 1784 trained native cavalry under European officers may be said at last to have become a great and important factor in the presidential armies. Floyd's unfortunate mishap before Bangalore no doubt lessened his credit not a little with the Commander-in-chief, but none the less his good service with his brigade should not be depreciated, and he should be honoured as the first of our great leaders of cavalry in India. Still, I

[1] *Life of Sir T. Munro*, i. 120.

1792. venture to think that Cornwallis in his place would have been even greater both in the training and the leading of light horse.

One supreme quality of a general Cornwallis possessed in very great measure, namely, the gift of attaching to himself all ranks of his army. Medows was so cheerful and sweet-tempered a man that it is difficult to conceive of him as resenting supersession by any officer, least of all by the Commander-in-chief; but it is noticeable that his relegation to a secondary position only made him the more zealous and unselfish in his work. With such an example before them, it is no wonder that the officers without exception vied with each other in loyal sacrifice of self. By the men also both Cornwallis and Medows were adored, and right well did they deserve it, for, apart from their constant care for the welfare of the rank and file, both of them gave up their prize-money, some £11,000 in value, to the army. Both also returned to the Company the gratuity allotted to them for their service in the field, amounting in Cornwallis's case to £41,000 and in Medows's to £10,000. They lost heavily by this sacrifice, for their expenses had been very great; but they made it cheerfully and without hesitation for the relief of India and the general weal of the Empire, being not only brave and able soldiers but true and patriotic citizens.

In the face of these facts, it will hardly be credited that one, Lord Porchester, in the House of Commons was base enough to insinuate that Cornwallis had entered upon the war from motives of avarice. Such an imputation could only be met rightly with contempt; and yet it is impossible not to feel indignation against the factious politicians who, safe under the shelter of Parliamentary privilege, discharged such shafts of calumny against an absent man. Fox was of too generous a nature to descend to the level of Lord Porchester; yet he, too, did not hesitate, though published evidence to the contrary lay before him, to stigmatise the war as wanton and unnecessary, and to charge Cornwallis with deliberate infraction of the East India Act. "The House of 1792. Commons at present," wrote General Grant, " puts me a little in mind of the American War. Tippoo has not so powerful and numerous supporters as Jonathan had ; but if the devil was to appear in the figure of an Asiatic prince and disturb the peace and quiet of the British Government, he would find some friends in this country." [1] Matters have altered little in this respect during one hundred and ten years ; but fortunately the words of folly and faction perish, whereas the deeds of duty and discipline endure.

[1] *Cornwallis Correspondence*, ii. 112, and see also pp. 124, 126, 129, 175.

AUTHORITIES.—Wilks's *History of Mysore*, Mackenzie's *Sketch of the War with Tippoo Sultan*, Dirom's *Narrative of the Campaign in India*, Wilson's *History of the Madras Army*, Ross's *Cornwallis Correspondence*. Colonel Biddulph's *XIXth and their Times* is especially valuable for its account of the cavalry, and in general offers a pleasing contrast to the ordinary class of Regimental Histories. It is a pity that there are not more of the same merit.

INDEX

Abercromby, Sir Ralph, 561
Abercromby, General Robert, successes of, in India (1790), 561; march of, to Peripatam, 571; fails to join Cornwallis in Mysore, 576; march to Mysore, 584
Aberdeen, patriotic action of, after Saratoga, 245
Abington, Major, 466
A'Court, General, 40
Adams, Samuel, 38; skill of, in organising rebellion, 44, 259
Adams, Major Thomas, succeeds to Bengal command, 68; defeats Meer Cossim at Cutwa, 70; occupies Moorshedabad, 71; victory of, at Gheria, 72; attack on Oondwa Nullah, 74; successful action there, 76-79
Agnew, General, 213
Ahmedabad, 144; Goddard takes, 428
Albany, 199, 206, 242
Allahabad, British success at, 104; British garrison in; 105, 137
Allan, Ensign, gallantry of, 492
Allen, Ethan, 153
Allentown, 253
Alumgeer II. (Mogul Emperor, 1759), 84
Amboor, besieged by Hyder Ali, 120, 447, 562
America, North, jealousy of different provinces in, 3; tie to Mother Country weakened, 7; danger of, from Indian attacks, 11
American Colonies—unwillingness of, to help in own defence, 19 *et seq.*; hostility of, to Mutiny Act, 30, 31; wrangles of, over boundaries, 32; temporary revival of loyalty in, 43; anger of, at appointment of Crown judges, 44; tea outbreak, 45; Port of Boston closed, 46; Congress issues declaration of rights, 46; coercive acts in Massachusetts a failure, 47; effect of campaign of 1776 on, 195; assisted in revolt by

foreign powers, 197; effects of peace of 1783 on, 496
Carolina, North, 274, 305, 314, 321, 343, 352, 359
Carolina, South, 274, 305, 312, 321
Connecticut, 19, 282
Delaware, 20, 21
Georgia, 273, 322, 343
Maryland, 9, 372, 390
Massachusetts, 5, 36, 44
New Hampshire, 20
New Jersey, 20, 195, 202, 392
New York, British garrison in, 7, 11; evades Mutiny Act, 31; extent of, in 1776, 181; importance of, strategically, 306, 337, 352, 378
Pennsylvania, 15, 20, 312, 328
Rhode Island, 20, 44, 48, 206, 257, 316, 329, 352, 391
Virginia, 19, 22, 32, 312, 353, 378, 390
Stamp Act—stamp duties first imposed, 25; justice of act, 26; tumult over, in Boston, 27; repeal of, 29
Trade and Navigation Acts—systematically violated, 24; outcry against, in 1764, 27; Otis's agitation against, 29; Dalrymple sent to Boston to enforce, 33; import duties repealed, 39; tea duty not removed, 43; acts reinforced, 44, 169; Chatham in favour of continuance of, 247
American Independence, War of—Boston rising against troops, 37; address of Congress to militia, 149
Operations of 1775—Smith defeated at Lexington, 150; Crown Point taken, 153; Americans entrench at Breed's Hill, 155; Bunker's Hill, 155-160; expedition to Canada, 162-165; Washington and Congress, 176
Operations of 1776—Howe evacuates Boston, 177; Carleton's success in Canada, 178; Arnold defeated at Lake Champlain, 179; Arnold

603

HISTORY OF THE ARMY

retreats in safety to Ticonderoga, 180; Clinton defeated at Charleston, 181; Brooklyn action, 183-186; escape of Washington's army, 187; Howe drives Washington behind the Crotton, 188-190; Fort Washington surrenders, 191-193; Cornwallis pursues Washington, 194; general effect of campaign, 195; American army reorganised, 197; Washington crosses the Delaware, 199, and captures Trenton, 200

Operations of 1777—Cornwallis duped by Washington, 200-202; effect of last campaign cancelled, 203; scheme for invading New York from Canada, 204-208; confusing instructions of home government to British generals, 208; winter fighting in New Jersey, 209; Howe's expedition to Philadelphia, 211; Washington defeated at Brandywine, 213-216; Philadelphia occupied by British, 217; Washington attacks camp at Germantown, 218-221; Burgoyne at Quebec, 223; march of, to Ticonderoga, 224; Fraser's action at Skenesborough, 225; Burgoyne's attempt on Bennington, 228; St. Leger's failure on the Mohawk, 229; Burgoyne's action at Bemis Heights, 232; Clinton storms Fort Clinton, 235; Burgoyne surrounded at Saratoga, 237; capitulation of, 239; minor successes of Howe, 252

Operations of 1778—Clinton evacuates Philadelphia, 253; rearguard action at Freehold, 254; French fleet in the Delaware, 255; naval action off Rhode Island, 256; expedition to Georgia, 270; Campbell's success at Savannah 272

Operations of 1779—Augustin Prevost reduces Upper Georgia, 273; Mark Prevost's action at Briar Creek, 275; his march to Charleston, 276; his withdrawal to Savannah, 277; Lincoln and d'Estaing besiege Savannah, 278; siege raised, 280; Clinton's operations, 281; Maclean's success at Penobscot, 283; Clinton evacuates Rhode Island, 285; proposed attack on New Orleans, 301; storm of Omoa, 303

Operations of 1780—plan proposed, 303-306; siege of Charleston, 307-310; Tarleton's success in South Carolina, 311; Cornwallis defeats Gates at Camden, 319; Tarleton surprises Sumter, 320; Ferguson entrapped at King's Mountain, 323; Cornwallis retreats to Winnsborough, 324; failure of French fleet at Newport, 326; Arnold's correspondence with Clinton, 329; André hanged as a spy, 331; skirmish at Blackstocks, 357

Operations of 1781—mutiny in Washington's army, 353; abortive French attempt on Chesapeake, 354; Cornwallis advances into North Carolina, 359; Tarleton defeated at Cowpens, 362; Greene meets Cornwallis at Guildford, 365-375; friction between Cornwallis and Clinton, 376; Cornwallis invades Virginia, 378; Lee takes Fort Watson, 379; Rawdon defeats Greene at Hobkirk's Hill, 380; siege of Ninety-Six, 382; action at Eutaw Springs, 384; Cornwallis marches against Lafayette, 388; Clinton hindered by Germaine, 390; arrival of de Grasse's fleet, 392; Washington marches against Cornwallis, 393; surrender of Yorktown, 395

Amherst, Jeffery, Lord, conduct of his officers, 6; his force in 1763, 12; despatches Bouquet against Indians, 15; resigns command, 19, 249, 297
Amyatt, Mr., mission of, to Meer Cossim, 65
Anantpoor, 482
André, Major John, *Journal* of, 214, 329; hanged as a spy, 331
Andros, Sir Edmund, 37
Annamalee, 487
Anse du Choc (St. Lucia), 265
Antilles, the, legislature of, on English model, 3
Aratoon, 64
Arbuthnot, Admiral, 284, 307, 326, 352, 388
Arcot, 116, 434
Arcot, Nabob of, 134
Arikera, 572
Armed Neutrality, the, 343
Arms, Armour, and Accoutrements :—
Carbine, carried by cavalry, 537
Epaulettes first worn, 536
Fusil, 535
Halberd, replaced by fusil, 535
Helmets, new pattern for dragoons, 537
Spontoon, disappearance of, 536
Sword, 536; uniform pattern insisted on, 537
Waist-belt, change in infantry, 535
Arnaul, island of, 443

INDEX 605

Arnee, 558
Arnold, Benedict, 153, 161; besieges Quebec, 162-165; skilful retreat of, from Crown Point, 180, 230; at Bemis Heights, 232; at Saratoga, 238; treachery of, 328, 352, 377, 399, 401; his military ability estimated, 404
Artillery, Royal. *See* Regiments
Ashe, General, 275
Ashley River, 308
Ashtown, 216
Assunpink River, 200
Augusta, 273, 310, 381
Austria and Eastern Question, 505
Avaracoorchee, 486, 552
Ayacotta, Dutch settlement at, 549
Ayre, Lieutenant, 568

Babul Nullah River, 139
Badara, victory of, destroys Dutch influence in India, 49
Bagehot, Walter, quoted, 502
Bahamas, the, garrison of, 11, 161; rebellion in, 260
Bahvani River, 557
Baillie, Colonel, 433; repulses Tippoo Sahib, 436; defeat and surrender of, 437-442
Baird, Colonel David, 489, 585, 588
Balcarres, Lord, 238
Balfour, Colonel, 376, 585
Bangalore, objective of operations of 1768, 123; and of those of 1791, 564, 432, 562. *See* Battles.
Baramahal, conquest of, by Hyder Ali, 111; 551
Barbados. *See* West Indies
Baroach, Nabob of, 141
Baroda, 428
Barré, Colonel, deprived of his appointment, 40, 46, 172, 300, 539
Barrington, Admiral, 264, 540
Barrington, Lord, Secretary-at-War, 40, 171, 521
Bassein, Port of, 141, 421
Basseterre (St. Kitts), 334, 407
Battenkill, 228
Battles, Combats, and Sieges:—
  Arass, 144
  Arcot, 446
  Arnee, 469
  Bangalore, 564-570
  Baugloor, 129
  Bednore, 481
  Beerpore, 60
  Bemis Heights, 232
  Bennington, 228
  Biggin's Bridge, 309
  Blackstocks, 357

Battles, Combats, and Sieges:—
  Brandywine, 213-216
  Briarcreek, 273
  Brooklyn, 181-186
  Bushy Run, 16-18
  Buxar, 95-102
  Calicut, 561
  Camden, 318
  Cannanore, 561
  Caroor, 485
  Charleston, 307-310
  Chillumbrum, 449
  Coimbatore, 577
  Cowpens, 360-363
  Cuddalore, 475
  Cutwa, 70
  Doogaur, 430
  Eutaw Springs, 384
  Fort Washington, 190-193
  Freehold, 254
  Germantown, 217-221
  Gheria, 72
  Gibraltar, 412-420
  Gohud, 429
  Guildford, 368-373
  Hobkirk's Hill, 379
  Kalpee, 104
  King's Mountain, 323
  Korah, 104
  Kutra, 138-141
  Lexington, 150
  Mahadapatam, 463
  Mahautpore, 444
  Mahé, 431
  Mangalore, 484
  Manjee, 66
  Mulwagal, 127
  Negapatam, 463
  Nundydroog, 579
  Omoa, 303
  Oondwa Nullah, 78
  Ooetradroog, 582
  Paniput, 63, 110
  Parambakum, 435
  Patna, 51, 80-83, 90
  Pollilore, 456
  Pondicherry, 431
  Porto Novo, 449
  Quebec, 162-165
  Saratoga, 237
  Sattiamungalum, 553
  Savandroog, 581
  Savannah, 272, 278
  Seringapatam, 588-597
  Skenesborough, 224
  Suan, 62
  Tanjore, 137
  Tellicherry, 466
  Travancore, 550
  Trinomalee, 117, 470

Battles, Combats, and Sieges :—
  Vigie, 265
  Worgaom, 426
  Yorktown, 395
Baugloor, 124 ; Wood's disaster at, 129
Baum, Colonel, defeated at Bennington, 227-229
Beaufort Island (Carolina), 276
Bednore, 479
Behar, passes under control of East India Company, 105
Bellamont, Lord, 245
Benares, Clive stipulates for garrison in, 105
Bengal, passes under control of East India Company, 105, 110, 42 ; Sepoys in Cornwallis's army, 567, 584
Bermuda, independent spirit of, 5 ; garrison at, 11 ; American raid on, 161 ; sympathy of, with American rebellion, 260 ; Bermuda papers, 5
Bernadotte, his service in India, 477
Bernard, Governor, 30, 44
Biddulph, Colonel, *The XIXth and their Times,* 601
Bickerton, Admiral, 472
Billingsport, 217
Birmingham, patriotic action of, after Saratoga, 245
Black River, 409
Blakeney, Major, 245
Bloomingdale, 187
Bombay, effect of Mahratta success on, 137 ; expensive policy of, 141, 421
  Council of, 142 ; responsibility of, for Mahratta War, 143 ; Convention of Worgaom, 427 ; and General Matthews, 480, 482
Bonass Nullah, Munro's cavalry ambuscaded at, 95
Boodicota, Pass of, 124
Bordenton, 195
Boston, 9 ; riot against Stamp Act, 27 ; mob law in, 34 ; bad treatment of our soldiers in, 36 ; the "Boston Massacre," 38 ; the "Tea Party," 45 ; strategic position of, 155 ; Howe evacuates, 177 ; riot between French and American seamen, 257. *See also* American Colonies.
Bouillé, Marquis de, 263
Bouquet, Colonel, campaign of 1763, 15 ; defeats Indians at Turtle Creek, 16 ; handicapped by colonies, 21 ; death, 22 ; authorities for campaign quoted, 23
Boyd, Governor, 298, 418
Braddock, General, officers of, and colonials, 6
Bradstreet, Colonel, unsuccessful expedition of, against Indians, 20

Brathwaite, Colonel, 433, 447, 463 ; defeated by Tippoo Sahib, 466
Breed's Hill, 155
Breyman, Colonel, 228, 238
Brimstone Hill (St. Kitts), 334, 407
Brooke, Captain, gallantry of, at Mulwagal, 127
Broome, *History of Bengal Army,* quoted, 108
Browne, Colonel, 382
Browne, Governor, 261
Bruère, Governor, 261
Brunswick, 194
Brunswick, Duke of, 504
Buccleugh, Duke of, 288
Buchan, Lieutenant, killed at Seringapatam, 596
Bulwant Singh (Rajah of Benares, 1765), 105
Bundelcund, Rajah of, 25
Burford (or Buford), Colonel, defeated by Tarleton, 311
Burgoyne, General John, 108, 154, 179, 205, 208 ; prepares for campaign of 1777, 223 ; action near Skenesborough, 225 ; reaches Fort Edward, 226 ; fails in attack on Bennington, 228 ; critical position, 231 ; Bemis Heights, 231-234 ; capitulates at Saratoga, 239 ; defence of his operations, 241, 404
Burke, Edmund, on smuggling, 8 ; antimilitary spirit of, 11 ; attitude on Stamp Act, 28-32 ; speech on American taxation, 46 ; speech on Nabob of Arcot's debts, 134, 148 ; opposes Militia Bill, 172, 196, 246, 248, 348 ; charges of, against Matthew's army, 482-497 ; attacks Hastings, 543 ; speech on impeachment, 544
Burlington (New Jersey), 200
Burt, Governor, 300, 334
Bussy, Mons. de. *See* de Bussy
Bute, Lord, unpopularity, 9 ; reduces army establishment, 10 ; succeeded by Grenville, 24
Byron, Admiral, 258, 266, 268

Caillaud, Colonel, commands against Shah Alum, 50-63 ; resignation of, 113
Calcutta, Council of, foolish treaty with Mahrattas, 146
Calder, Brigadier, 333
Calpee, 429
Camac, Captain, success against Sindia, 444, 492
Cambridge (Mass.), Congress meets at, 149

INDEX 607

Camden, 310
Campbell, Sir Archibald, 549
Campbell, Colonel Donald, 124
Campbell, Lord Frederick, 288
Campbell, Brigadier John, 301, 351; defence of Mangalore, 483; death, 489
Campbell, Colonel (of Maclean's regiment), expedition to Georgia, 270; victory at Savannah, 272; death, 507
Canada, work of absorbing French and Spanish in, 3; effect of Quebec Act on, 46; failure of American invasion of, 162-165; unwillingness of Canadians to serve, 223
Canara, 141
Cancanhilly, 572
Caniambaddy, 572
Cannanore, taken by Abercromby, 561
Cape Fear, 173
Cape Fear River, 313
Cape Gracias a Dios, 338
Carangooly, 433, 447, 473
Carhampton, Lord, 528
Carribean Sea, jealousy of different islands in, 3; British troops in, 6; rebellion of Caribs, 42
Carighaut Hill, 586, 595
Carleton, General Sir Guy, 153, 162; defeats Arnold in Canada, 179, 204, 223; his comment on Saratoga, 242
Carlisle, Bouquet concentrates at, 15
Carnac, Major, defeats Shah Alum at Suan, 62; second in command at Gheria, 72, 76; apathy of, 88; dismissed, 92; reinstated, 103, 425
Carolina, South, negro question in, 274. *See also* American Colonies
Caroor, 552
Carstairs, Captain, defeated at Manjee, 67
Castries Bay (St. Lucia), 264
Catawba River, 315
Catherine, Empress of Russia, 504
Catholics, repeal of disabilities of, 289, 292
Caveripatam, taken by British, 114; overpowered by Hyder Ali, 115; evacuated, 123; Maxwell's headquarters at, 559
Caveriporam, Pass of, occupied by Colonel Wood, 123
Cavery River, 559
Chad's Ford, 213
Chalmers, Lieutenant, defends Coimbatore, 577; sent to Cornwallis by Tippoo, 597
Chambly, surrender of, 162
Champion, Captain, 81, 94; action at Kutra, 138-141

Chandernagore, restored to France by Peace of Paris, 49
Changama, Hyder Ali defeated at, 116; Pass of, 432, 563
Charleston, Clinton's reverse at, 181, 314, 359, 387
Charlottetown, 316
Charlotteville, 388
Chastellux, Marquis de, 363
Chatham, William Pitt, Earl of, 4, 10; refuses to join ministry, 24; attitude on Stamp Act, 28; accepts a peerage, 29; rebukes New York, 31; illness of, 33; resignation, 39; misunderstands American question, 148; denounces employment of Indians, 244; effort made to put him in office again, 247; death, 248; Chatham correspondence, 31
Chaudière River, 162
Chesapeake River, operations on, 281, 354, 392, 407
Chester, 216
Chickahominy River, 388
Chinapatam, 572
Chittapett, 441
Chittoor Pass, 564
Choule, 423
Christie, General, 407
Chunar, capitulates to British, 104; Clive stipulates for British garrison in, 105
Clarke, Captain, 341
Clinton, General Sir Henry, 154, 158, 180; at Brooklyn, 183, 194, 211, 234; appointed to succeed Howe, 250; evacuates Philadelphia, 253; sends expedition to Georgia, 270; his want of troops, 280; policy of raids, 282; evacuates Rhode Island, 285; his position in 1779, 304; siege of Charlestown, 307-310; returns to New York, 310, 321, 325, 329, 333, 352, 355; friction of, with Cornwallis, 358, 374, 376, 387, 388; his ill-luck, 397-404
Clive, Robert, effect of his departure from India, 49-51; returns to India, 104; reorganises army and administration, 105; returns to England, 107; suicide, 108; his services to England, 108
Clothing, articles of, supplied out of soldier's pay, 522; reform in, for tropical service, 533
Cochin, Rajah of, 1789, 549
Cochrane, Captain, 51
Cockburn, Colonel, 407, 426
Cockerell, Colonel, 584
Codrington, Governor, letters of, 5, 263

Coimbatore, 486, 549; taken by Medows, 552, 562, 577
Colar, surrenders to Campbell, 124; Wood's retreat to, 129; 130, 564
Collier, Sir George, 283, 307, 376
Concord, 216
Congaree River, 312
Congress, establishes American army, 197; ill-faith of, after Saratoga, 239; 285; treatment of loyalists, 497. *See also* American Colonies
Congreve, Major, 540
Conjeveram, military station at, 119, 433
Connecticut, 282. *See also* American Colonies
Conway, General, 40, 96, 167, 515
Coondapoor, 480
Coorg, Rajah of, 571
Coote, Sir Eyre, 429; takes command in Carnatic, 446; defeats Hyder Ali at Porto Novo, 448-455; indecisive action at Parambakum, 456; march to relieve Vellore, 458, 465; success at Arnee, 469; resigns command to Stewart, 472; death, 474; his ability estimated, 490
Copul, 563
Corah, Mahratta invasion of, 137
Corbet, Major, 346
Cornwall, Speaker, 510
Cornwallis, Charles, Marquis, expedition to Cape Fear, 180; at Brooklyn, 183, 192; march on Fort Lee, 193; march on Trenton, 200; asks for reinforcements, 207; at Brandywine, 213, 284, 307, 310, 314; operations in Carolina, 314-324, 352, 354; change in character, 358, 364; meets Greene at Guildford, 368-375; abandons the Carolinas, 377; enters Virginia, 387, 389; surrenders Yorktown, 394; his strategy criticised, 396; Commander-in-Chief in India, 542; reforms Indian army, 547; forms alliance with Nizam Ali, 551; composition of his army against Tippoo, 551; takes personal command, 561; skilful passage of the Ghauts, 564; besieges Bangalore, 566-570; marches on Seringapatam, 572; first action fails, 574; obliged to retreat, 576; besieges Nundydroog, 579; campaign of 1792, 584; siege of Seringapatam, 587-596; peace signed, 597; his strategy in India estimated, 599; self-sacrifice of, 600
Coromandel, French renounce possessions in, 109, 465; pillaged by Tippoo, 560

Cortelaur River, 435
Cosby, Colonel, 433
Cottapilly, Cornwallis's junction with Nizam at, 570
Coventry, patriotic action of, after Saratoga, 245
Craig, Major, 359, 387, 404
Cranganore, estuary of, 549
Crillon, Duke of, 409, 419
Crimea, Catherine II. annexes, 505
Cromwell, Oliver, compared with Washington, 403
Cross Creek, 314, 374
Crotton River, 188-190, 392
Crow, Lieutenant, 82
Crown Point, Arnold's retreat from, 180, 205
Cruger, Colonel, 382
Cuddalore, 448; Convention of, 485
Cul de Sac Bay (St. Lucia), 264
Cummum, 485
Cunyngham, Governor, 300
Curtis, Captain, 418

Dallas, Major, 566
Dalling, Governor, 302, 339, 351
Dalrymple, Colonel, sent to Boston, 33
Dalrymple, Major, storms Omoa, 302
Dan River, 366
Danbury, 209
Darampoory, taken by Wood, 122
Darapooram, 486, 552
Darby, Admiral, 345
Dartmouth, Lord, 149, 173, 174
Darwar, 563
De Barras, 392
De Bussy, 468, 474
De Cossigny, 484
D'Estaing, Marquis, commands French fleet in America, 255; sails for Martinique, 258; arrives, 264; repulsed at Vigie, 265; takes Grenada, 268; operations in Georgia, 277-280
De Grasse, Count, 267, 349, 383; arrives at the Chesapeake, 392; 395, 407; taken prisoner, 409
De Guichen, Admiral, 327; action against Rodney, 336
De la Combe, 577
De Morlay, 484
D'Orvés, Count, 447, 466
De Rochambeau, Count, 326, 352
De Rullecourt, Baron, 346
De Ternay, Admiral, 326, 352
Deane, Silas, 196
Delancy, Captain Oliver, 154
Delancy, Mr., 204
Delaware River, 199
Delaware (Indian) settlement, Bouquet's

INDEX

expedition to, 21. *See also* American Colonies
Demerara, 349
Denmark and Armed Neutrality, 343; and Triple Alliance, 505
Despard, Lieutenant, 339
Digby, Admiral, 393
Dilworth, 214
Dindigul, taken by Wood, 122; taken by Lang, 486, 552
Dirom, Major, *Narrative of the Campaign in India*, 601
Dominica, 11
Dorchester Heights, 155
Douranee cavalry, 97, 101
Dowlut Bagh, the (Seringapatam), 591
Drake, Admiral, 349
Draper, Sir William, 411
Drill or Exercises—Irregular tactics taught by American War, 529; Dundas's system, 532; cavalry evolutions, 538
Dubhoy, 146
Duff, Colonel, 585
Dundas, Colonel David, system of exercise, 531-533
Dundas, Henry, 548
Du Pré, Governor, 134
Dupleix, 468
Dutch, the, hopes of Indian empire destroyed, 49; in British army, 86; in West Indies, 260; alliance with American Colonies, 344; in India, 468, 496; alliance with French, 503

East India Company, exports tea to American colonies, 45; position of, in 1761, 49; corruption of, 65; sovereignty of Bengal secured by, 105; instructions to Warren Hastings, 138; selfish policy of, 146; Fox's East India Bill, 501; Pitt's Bill, 542; Declaratory Act, 547
Eastern Question, beginning of, 504
Edinburgh, patriotism of, after Saratoga, 245
Edisto River, 308, 312
Egerton, Colonel, 425
Elephanta, 142
Eliott, General, 298, 345; defence of Gibraltar, 412-420
Ellis, Welbore, Secretary-at-War, 40
Ellis, Mr., treacherous seizure of Patna, 65
English Harbour (Antigua), 262
Erode, besieged by Colonel Oldham, 552
Essequibo, 349

Fawcett, General William, makes improvements in soldier's pay, 521

Ferguson, Major Patrick, 257; defeated at King's Mountain, 323, 404
Fisher, Captain, 55
Fiske, Mr., quoted, 37, 150, 212, 228, 254, 347, 405
Fitzgerald, Major, defends convoy against Hyder, 121; saves Wood's army, 130
Fitzmaurice, *Life of Shelburne* referred to, 208
Fitzpatrick, Secretary-at-War, 527
Flatbush, 183
Flatland Ford, 217
Fletcher, Colonel, 436
Fletcher, Major Sir Robert, 102, 103, 423
Flint, Lieutenant, 433, 447, 492, 560
Florida, position of foreign colonists in, 3, 297; recaptured by Spain, 352; retained by Spain at peace, 496
Floyd, Colonel, 551; success against Said Sahib, 553; skilful retreat to Velladi, 554-557; wounded near Bangalore, 566, 575, 585; a good cavalry leader, 599
Forbes, *Oriental Memoirs*, 147
Forde, Colonel, 50, 110
Fort Anna, 225
Fort Bedford, 13
Fort Clinton, 235
Fort Cumberland, 13
Fort Detroit, 12, 14, 15, 19
Fort Edward, 226
Fort Frontenac, 20
Fort Granby, 381
Fort Johnston, 308
Fort Le Bœuf, 12
Fort Lee, 187, 193
Fort Ligonier, 13
Fort Miamis, 13
Fort Montgomery, 235
Fort Motte, 381
Fort Moultrie, 180, 308
Fort Ouatanon, 14
Fort Pitt, 13
Fort Presquile, 12
Fort Royal, 409
Fort St. Joseph, 13
Fort St. Juan, 539
Fort St. Philip, siege of, 409
Fort Stanwix, 229
Fort Washington, 187, 190-193
Fort Watson, 378
Fox, Charles James, 172, 196, 246, 291, 295, 343, 348, 406, 493; resignation of, 495; 497; in the Coalition Ministry, 498, 509, 527; speech on impeachment of Hastings, 544; unfounded charges of, against Cornwallis, 600

France, French colonists in Canada, 3; loss of power in North America, 7; effect of this on colonies, 8; French in British Army, 86; treaty with American colonies, 246; in West Indies, 260; attack on Jersey, 346; share in American success, 401; attempt to recover India, 421, 466-477; peace signed, 496; fresh intrigues in India, 547
Francis, Colonel, 225
Francis, Philip, 422
Franklin, Benjamin, in favour of British troops in America, 25, 348, 494
Frazer, Brigadier Simon, action at Skenesborough, 224; at Bemis Heights, 232; wounded at Saratoga, 237; 407
Frederick the Great, unfriendliness to England, 10, 29, 197, 344, 503
Frederick William II., 504
French. *See* France
French Creek, 217
Fullarton, Colonel, 477, 486; invades Mysore, 487, 492, 551
Fullerton, Dr., heroism at Patna, 52
Futteh Sing, 146, 427
Fyzabad, Carnac's army at, 104
Fyzullah Khan (Rohilla chief), 141

Gage, General, succeeds Amherst, 19; letters to Halifax, 31, 33, 42; appointed Governor of Massachusetts, 45; fortifies Boston Neck, 48; warns Government of nature of American resistance, 149; bad generalship of, at Bunker's Hill, 155-160; recalled, 173, 223
Galloway, Joseph, 398
Garth, General, 341
Gaspee, H.M.S., affair of, 44
Gates, Major-General Horatio, 161, 232, 239; jealousy of Washington, 251, 316; defeated at Camden, 319
George II. and colonies, 4
George III., personal government of, 39, 170, 247, 249, 406, 498; and East India Bill, 501; and desertion, 518; good friend to soldiers, 521; insanity of, 526
George Prince of Wales (afterwards Regent), 498, 527
Georgetown, 314
Georgia. *See* American Colonies
Germaine, Lord George, made Secretary-at-War, 174, 181, 204, 207, 223, 242, 250, 267, 280; wrong-headed policy of, 298, 301, 305, 332, 350, 354; his disloyalty to Clinton, 377; confusing orders of, 390; responsible for American disasters, 397; resignation of, 406
Ghauts, the, 425, 564
Gibraltar, garrison of, 11; Hanoverian troops sent to, 170; Spain's wish to recover, 297; blockade of, 299, 345; siege of, 412-420
Gladwyn, Captain, Commandant at Detroit, 13; defence of Fort Detroit, 14, 15
Glasgow, patriotic action of, after Saratoga, 245
Gleig, *Life of Warren Hastings*, 147, 492
Glenn, Lieutenant, successful convoy action of, 69; killed at Gheria, 74
Gloucester, 391
Gloucester, William, Duke of, 527
Goa, 479
Goddard, Colonel, 424, 428; besieges Bassein, 430, 443
Goorumconda, 578, 580
Gordon, Duke of, 288
Gordon, Lord George, 292; Gordon riots, 296
Gordon, Brigadier Robert, 142
Goshen (Penna.), 216
Gowdie, Major, 566, 579, 585
Grafton, Duke of, 39; negotiations with Mahomet Ali, 135, 297
Granard, Lord, 245
Granby, John, Marquis of, Master of the Ordnance, 40
Grant, General James, 184, 213, 258, 264; operations in West Indies, 266-269; attacked in Parliament, 293, 404, 601
Grant-Duff, *History of the Mahrattas*, 147
Graves, Admiral, 326, 391
Gravesend Bay, 183
Grenada. *See* West Indies
Grenadines, the, 11
Greene, Nathaniel, Major-General, 155, 191, 193, 198, 215, 255, 327, 357, 365; commands at Guildford, 365-375, 378; reverse at Hobkirk's Hill, 379; attacks British at Eutaw Springs, 384, 398; estimate of his ability, 403
Grenville, Thomas, 494
Grey, General (afterwards Sir Charles Grey, K.B., and first Earl Grey), 213; destroys Wayne's camp, 217, 251, 404
Gros Islet Bay (St. Lucia), 409
Gujelhutty, strategic importance of Pass of, 123, 551
Guntoor, 433
Gurghis Khan, 64
Gurrah River, 139

INDEX 611

Haarlem Heights, 187
Hackinsack River, 193
Haldimand, General, 284
Halifax (Nova Scotia), garrison at, 11; English headquarters moved from Boston to, 177
Hall, Colonel, 366
Haly's Ford, 365
Harris, Sir James, 504
Harris, Captain (afterwards Lord Harris of Seringapatam), at Bunker's Hill, 159; in campaign of 1790, 551
Hartley, Captain, 426; repulses Mahrattas at Doogaur, 430, 551, 559, 585
Harvey, General, 41; his opinion of American War quoted, 167, 169
Hastings, Marquess of. *See* Rawdon
Hastings, Warren, 107; deal with Shuja Dowlah, 138, 419; appointed first Governor-General, 422; policy of, 424, 445, 455, 462, 490; proposed recall of, 500; persecution of, 543; impeachment and acquittal, 544-547
Havana, 7; Spanish base at, 309
Haw River, 367
Hay, Mr., mission to Meer Cossim, 65
Hay, Governor (of Barbados), 261
Hell Gate, 188
Hessians, in British army during American War, 188, 192, 199, 201, 517, 521
Hillsborough, 315, 367
Hodgson, Mr., 303
Hog Island, 141
Holkar (Mahratta chief), 142
Holland. *See* Dutch
Holland, Lord, 511
Holland, Mr., 550
Holwell, Mr., temporary Governor of India, 51
Honawar, 480
Honduras, 302, 409
Hood, Admiral Sir Samuel (afterwards Lord Hood), 349, 392, 407, 508; defends Warren Hastings, 543
Hooliadroog, surrenders to Cornwallis, 585
Horen's Hook, 187
Hosingabad, 427
Hotham, Admiral, 264
Howe, General Sir William, 154; commands left at Bunker's Hill, 156, 169, 175; action at Brooklyn, 181-186; inactivity afterwards, 188; attacks Fort Washington, 190-193; goes into winter quarters, 195; plan for 1777, 199; hampered by Germaine, 204; directed to attack Philadelphia, 208, 209; Quibbletown, 210; reaches the Chesapeake, 212; action at Brandywine, 213-216; succeeded by Clinton, 250; his work during the war, 253, 404; Cornwallis's debt to, 599
Howe, Lord, 182, 255, 307, 376
Humberstone, Colonel, 470. 479
Hunter, Captain, at Seringapatam, 591
Huger, General, 309
Hughes, Admiral, 449, 467, 473, 476
Hutchinson, Lieutenant-Governor, withdraws Boston garrison, 38
Hyder Ali, sketch of his career, 111; takes offensive against British, 114; defeated by Smith, 115-129; operations of, 1768-69, 120-131; defeated by Mahrattas in 1770, 136; desires British alliance, 136; dangerous enemy to British power in India, 147, 421, 431; invests Arcot, 434; defeats Baillie, 437-441; campaign against Coote, 447; defeated at Porto Novo, 451; action at Pollilore, 456; abandons Coromandel, 465; takes Cuddalore, 467; death, 472
Hyderghur, 481

India, power of French broken in, 3; Pondicherry restored at Peace of Paris, 49; war with Shah Alum, 49-63; war with Meer Cossim, 65-83; alliance of Meer Cossim, Shuja Dowlah, and Shah Alum, 84; Carnac's operation of 1764, 88-92; Munro's operations, 94-104; settlement of Bengal, 105; rise of Hyder Ali, 111; operations of Colonel Joseph Smith against (1768), 113-130; peace made, 131; 1774 campaign against the Rohillas, 138-141; First Mahratta War, 103-147; Second Mahratta War, 421-430; Warren Hastings first Governor-General, 422; alliance between Hyder Ali and the French, 431; war against Hyder (1780-82), 433-480; Tippoo Sahib, first war with, 480-489; Pitt's India Bill, 542; impeachment of Warren Hastings, 544; Cornwallis appointed Governor-General and Commander-in-Chief, 546
Second War against Tippoo Sahib—operations of 1790, 547-562; operations of 1791, 562-584; operations of 1792, 585-596; peace signed, 597
Indians, position after conquest of Canada, 3, 12; rising under Pontiac, 13-19; Senecas join Pontiac, 19; Iroquois remain loyal, 19; provocation of, by

Virginia and Pennsylvania, 32; employment of, during war, 223, 230
Innes, Lieutenant-Colonel, *History of Bengal European Regiment* quoted, 108, 492
Ireland, military establishment in 1763, 10; increased, 40; volunteer associations in, 294; old-fashioned cavalry in, 525
Iroquois. *See* Indians
Irving, Captain James, attack on Oondwa Nullah, 76-79; assault on Patna, 81
Isle of Man, smuggling in, 8

Jats, the, 104, 137
Jamaica. *See* West Indies
James Island, 276, 308
James River, 388
Jassy, Treaty of, 505
Jennings, Captain, 85
Jersey, French attack on, 346
John's Island, 308
Johnston, Commodore, 466
Jones, Paul, 287
Joseph II., Emperor of Germany, 503

Keating, Colonel, 143; victory at Arass, 145, 421
Keith, Governor, 261
Kelly, Colonel, 475, 551, 559
Kemble, Colonel, 340
Kennebec River, Arnold's operations at, 162
Kennett Square, British encamp at, 213
Keppel, Admiral Augustus, 287
Khandallah, 443
Kingsbridge, 187, 391
Kip's Bay, 187
Kistnagerry, blockade of, 114; strategic importance of, overrated by Madras Council, 123; holds its own against Hyder Ali, 130; besieged by Maxwell, 580
Knox, Captain, defence of Patna, 55-60; Adams's Q.M.G., 72; skill as an engineer, 75; at siege of Patna, 81; dies at Calcutta, 85
Knox, Lieutenant-Colonel, 585, 589
Knyphausen, General, 190; at Brandywine, 213-216, 253; left in New York, 307
Koehler, Lieutenant, 418
Kosciusko, entrenches Bemis Heights, 231, 357, 382
Kuddum Hoosein (Nabob of Purneah), joins Shah Alum, 57; defeated by Knox, 58
Kurreem Sahib, 433

Lafayette, Marquis de, 255, 325, 353, 388, 392
Lahar, 430
Lally Tollendal, Hyder Ali's service under, 111, 466, 471
La Martine, Lieutenant Claude, 37, 68
Lanesborough, Lord, 245
Lang, Colonel, 485, 492
Langley, Major, 585
Law (French officer), joins Shah Alum against English, 55
Lawrence, Stringer, 113
Lawson, Major-General, 370
Lee, Major-General Charles, 161, 190, 193; taken prisoner, 194, 208, 254
Lee, Colonel Henry, 357, 378, 381
Leeward Islands. *See* West Indies
Leith, Sir Alexander, 340
Leslie, Major-General, 358, 364
Leslie, Colonel, 424
Ligonier, Field-Marshal Viscount, Commander-in-Chief, ousted by Lord Granby, 40
Lincoln, Major-General, 273, 275; operations in Georgia, 277-280; defence of Charlestown, 308
Lincoln, Lord, 511
Lindsay, Sir John, 135
Liverpool, patriotic action of, after Saratoga, 245
Lockany River, 589
Long Island, 181
Louis XVI. and Tippoo Sahib, 561
Lucknow, Clive stipulates for garrison in, 105
Lynhaven Bay, 392

Macartney, Lord, 468, 472, 485
Macaulay, Lord, *Warren Hastings* quoted, 60
Macgowan's Hill, 188
Mackay, Major-General, 35
Mackenzie, Lieutenant Roderick, *Sketch of the War with Tippoo*, 601
M'Lean, Colonel Allan, 163
Maclean, Colonel Francis, 282, 307, 471
Macleod, Lord, 245, 434, 480
Macleod, Lieutenant, 372
Madajee Sindia (Mahratta chief). *See* Sindia
Madoo Rao (Peishwar of Mahrattas, 1770), 135; death, 136
Madras, position of, after Peace of Paris, 109; operations of 1767 in, 113-121, 421; Madras Sepoys in Cornwallis's army, 551
Council of—corruptness of, 112; inefficiency, 116; mismanages commissariat, 122; hampers Smith's operations, 123; rejects Hyder Ali's

INDEX 613

peace proposals, 126; makes overtures itself, 131; its stupid policy, 136, 428, 432; responsibility for disasters of 1780, 442; negotiations with Tippoo Sahib, 488
Mahan, Captain, quoted amongst authorities, 405, 492
Mahé, restored to France by Peace of Paris, 49
Mahon, Lord, *History of England* quoted, 41
Mahon, Port, 300, 410
Mahrattas, alliance with Shuja Dowlah, 104, 106; defeated at Paniput, 110; Hyder Ali and the, 112; ambitious policy, 135; effect of their successes, 137; First Mahratta War, 143-147, 421; states of, enumerated, 424; Second Mahratta War, 424-430, 443; peace made at Salbye, 445; Tippoo makes war on, 548; Poonah Mahrattas our allies, 551, 563, 576; uselessness as allies, 584; benefit by our peace with Tippoo, 597
Maitland, Colonel, 277
Malabar, conquest of, by Hyder Ali, 110; rebellion against him in, 221; revolts against Tippoo, 548; captured by Abercromby, 561
Malavelly, 572
Malitur, 144
Malleson, Colonel, 108, 133, 492
Maloor, 125
Malwa, Carnac's invasion of, 444
Manchester, patriotic action after Saratoga, 245
Mangalore, garrison of, surrenders to Hyder, 121, 482
Manhattan Island, 181
Markar, organises Meer Cossim's army, 64; defeats British at Manjee, 66; bought by Shuja Dowlah, 94; commands at Gheria, 72
Marion, Francis, 321, 356, 379
Marjoribanks, Major, 384
Marlborough, Duke of, compared with Clive, 108
Marmalong, 441
Martin, Governor, 164
Maryland. *See* American Colonies
Massachusetts. *See* American Colonies
Matthews, General, 192, 479; takes Bednore, 481; his army captured by Tippoo Sahib, 483
Mawhood, Colonel, 201
Maxwell, Colonel, 559, 575, 580; commands left in advance on Seringapatam, 585
Mediterranean, operations of 1781 in, 409

Medows, General, defence of St. Lucia, 467; in India, 550; March to Caroor, 552; imprudence of, 557; crosses River Cavery, 559; at Bangalore, 565; second in command in 1792 campaign, 584; Seringapatam, 588, 592; popularity of, with his men, 600
Meer Cossim, appointed Meer Jaffir's successor, 61; clever administration of, 64; causes of rupture with English, 65; Calcutta Council declare his deposition, 67; defeated at Oondwa Nullah, 79; murders British prisoners, 80; alliance with Shuja Dowlah, 85; death, 94
Meer Jaffir, 49; superseded by Meer Cossim, 62; reinstated, 71, 84, 87, 88; death, 105
Meer Sahib, 126
Meerun (son of Meer Jaffir), 51; his treachery hampers British, 55; killed by lightning, 61
Mercer, Major-General, 201
Mhow, 424
Middlebrook, 210
Military artificers formed, 540
Militia, depended on to secure safety of Great Britain, 11; decay of, 171; Militia Bill of 1775, 172; strengthened in 1779, 290; Pitt's policy towards, 523
Minorca, Spaniards in, 3; garrison of, 11; Hanoverian soldiers sent to, 170, 297; Eliott's defence of, 299; fall of, 411; retained by Spain at peace, 496
Mirjee River, 479
Mississippi River, Spanish take our posts on, 302; boundary of America after peace, 496
Mobile, garrison of, 11; unhealthy station, 41, 261, 341
Mogul cavalry, at Buxar, 96
Mogul Empire, 109
Mohammed Ali (Nabob of Carnatic, 1763), 109, 112, 128, 134, 135, 136, 421, 434, 464
Mohammed Taki Khan, placed in command of Meer Cossim's troops, 68
Mohawk River, St. Leger's operations on, 229-231
Mongeer, made capital of Bengal, 64; taken by British, 80
Monk's Corner (Carolina), 381
Monson, Captain, 590
Montague, Admiral, 44
Montgomery, Brigadier Richard, 161; siege of Quebec, 162-165
Montreal, fall of, 9
Montserrat, captured by French, 409

Moodajee Bhonsla (Rajah of Berar, 1778), 424
Moore, John (afterwards General Sir John), first action of, 283, 404, 533
Moorhouse, Colonel, killed at Bangalore, 568
Moorshedabad, 64
Moran, Captain, 76
Morari Rao, Hyder Ali attacks, 125
Morgan, General Daniel, 164, 237, 357; his success at Cowpens, 360
Morne Fortuné (St. Lucia), 264
Morris, Robert, 198
Morristown, 202, 210, 392
Mosque Redoubt, the (Seringapatam), 594
Mostyn, Mr., 425
Moultrie, General, 275
Muglee, Pass of, 564
Muir, Colonel, 445
Mulwagal, captured by Campbell, 127; recaptured by Hyder, 127; Wood's attack on, 128; Cornwallis at, 564
Munro, Major (Colonel) Hector, appointed to Indian command, 92; victory at Buxar, 93-102; resigns his command, 103; siege of Pondicherry, 431, 433; apathy of, 437; criticism of his campaign, 441, 450, 463
Munro, Innes, 454, 492
Murray, Lord James, 290
Murray, General James, 299, 345, 410
Musgrave, Colonel, 219, 533, 551
Mutiny Act, 30; opposition to, in Irish Parliament, 295
Myhie River, 144
Mysore, power of, under Hyder, 111, 479; invaded by Fullarton, 487; invaded again in 1790, 551; Cornwallis's plan for invasion, 562; excellence of Mysorean cavalry, 598. *And see* Hyder Ali, Tippoo Sahib

Nagore, 463
Nana Furnawese (Mahratta leader, 1777), 423, 428
Narain Rao (Peishwar of Mahrattas), murdered, 142
Narragansett Bay, 326
Nash, Lieutenant, 578, 597
Navigation Acts, 7. *See* American Colonies
Navy, the Royal, establishment reduced, 1774, 170
Negapatam, 466; ceded to English by Dutch, 496
Nelson, Horatio, Captain, 304, 339
Neriad, 144
Nesbitt, Colonel, 585

Nevis, island of, 5, 409
New England, independent spirit of provinces in, 5; needs aid of Imperial troops, 6. *And see* American Colonies, Connecticut, Massachusetts, New Hampshire, Rhode Island.
New Jersey. *See* American Colonies
New Orleans, a Spanish possession, 7, 25
New Rochelle, 189
New York, British garrison at, 7, 11; evades Mutiny Act, 31; extent of, in 1776, 181; importance of British remaining in, 306
Newport (Rhode Island), 326
Newark (New Jersey), 195
Niagara, 12
Nicaragua, Polson's expedition to, 303, 339
Nicholl, Lieutenant, 89, 99
Nicholson, Governor (of Maryland), 9
Ninety-Six, 310, 382
Nixon, Colonel, 470, 492, 551
Nizam Ali (Viceroy of Deccan), 109, 112, 114; treaty with Madras Council, 120; defeated by Mahrattas, 135, 428, 446, 546; alliance with English, 551, 563, 570; worthlessness of his cavalry, 575, 578, 597
Nook's Hill, 177
North, Lord, succeeds Grafton, 39, 246, 406, 493; in Coalition Ministry, 498
North America. *See* American Colonies
Nottoway River, 387
O'Hara, Brigadier Charles, 374, 404
O'Hara, Lieutenant, 374
Ockzakow, 507
Old Point Comfort, 390
Oldham, Colonel, 552
Ongola, 485
Oocaro, 555
Oondwa Nullah, Meer Cossim entrenches at, 74; storm of, 76-79
Ooscotta, 124, 564
Oosore, captured by British, 125; besieged by Hyder, 129; Cornwallis at, 577
Orange, Prince of, 504
Orde, Chief Secretary, 526
Ordnance, Office of, 540
Orissa, passes under East India Company, 105
Oswald, Mr., 494
Otis, James, attack on commercial code, 9; agitates against Trade Acts, 29
Oude, Nabob of, 50
Oughton, General, 292

Pacolet River, 356

INDEX 615

Paine, Thomas, 247
Palamnair, Cornwallis encamps at, 564
Palghautcherry, 487, 551; captured by Colonel Stewart, 557, 562, 579
Palliser, Admiral, 287
Panianee, 471, 479
Panwelly, 425
Parker, Sir Hyde, 335
Parker, Admiral Sir Peter, 180, 195, 302, 350
Parliament and the Army, Act for forcing colonies to support troops, 31; petty spite against officers, 107; unpatriotic conduct of Opposition after Saratoga, 246; Wilkes' Bill against new regiments, 248, 288; unfitness of Commons to criticise operations, 293
Parliament and the Navy, 287
Patna, attacked by Shah Alum, 50; besieged by Adams, 80
Paulus Hook, 282
Pay, of private soldier, 42; desertion in India due to arrears, 61; bad faith of Calcutta Council over, 87; the "batta" in India, 106; bounties, 179, 499; of native troops, 491; Paymaster-General's accounts, 511; divisions of, 512; system of allowances, 513; insufficiency of, 520; improved by General Fawcett, 520
Pearse, Colonel, 455
Peché, Colonel, 585
Peedee River, 313
Peekskill, 209
Pell's Point, Howe lands at, 188
Pemble, Major, 95
Pembroke, Henry, Earl of, *Manual of Horsemanship*, 548
Pennsylvania. *See* American Colonies
Penobscot, 282
Pensacola, garrison of, 11; unhealthy station, 41, 250; strategic position of, 261, 302, 341
Percy, Lord, 151; at Brooklyn, 183, 188, 192
Peripatam, 571, 576
Permacol, 447, 468
Philadelphia, 199
Phillips, General, 224, 231, 352, 377; death, 387
Phips, Sir William, 35
Pierson, Major, 346
Pigeon Island (St. Lucia), 409
Pigott, Mr., 255, 422
Pitcairn, Major, 155
Pitt, William (elder). *See* Chatham
Pitt, William (younger), Chancellor of Exchequer, 495; speech on East India Bill, 501; First Load of the Treasury, 502; pacific policy of, 506; military policy of, 508, 515, 523; India Bill, 542
Policode Pass, 559, 563, 577
Pollilore, 456
Poloor, 458
Polson, Captain, 338
Polygars, 486
Pondicherry, restored to France by Peace of Paris, 49, 109; occupied by Tippoo Sahib, 560
Pontiac (Ottawa chief), plans confederation of Indian tribes, 12; success against British, 14
Poonah, conference of, 135; British resident sent to, 141, 443
Poorundur, Treaty of, 423
Popham, Captain William, surprise of Gwalior, 429, 444, 492
Porchester, Lord, unfounded attack on Cornwallis, 600
Port Castries (St. Lucia), 336
Port Jackson, 540
Port Royal (Jamaica), 262
Porto Novo, 433, 467
Porto Praya, 467
Porteous Riots, 296
Portland, Duke of, 498
Portsmouth, 391
Portugal, attempt to regain Indian possessions, 142
Pownall, Governor, 30, 223, 246
Prescott, General, 333, 407
Preston, Captain, imprisoned by Boston magistrates, 38
Prevost, General Augustin, 270, 273
Prevost, Colonel Mark, 273; success at Briar Creek, 275
Princetown, 194, 201
Pulicat, 455
Pulnee, 487
Putnam, Major-General, 182, 235

Quebec, 7, 11; besieged by Americans, 162-165
Quebec Act, opposition to, 46, 496

Ragobah *or* Rugonath Rao (Peishwar of Mahrattas), 142; at Arass, 144, 421, 428
Rahl, Colonel, 189, 199, 200
Ramgerry, 572; stormed by British, 582
Ramnarain, Rajah, native governor of Patna, 51
Rariton River, 253
Rawdon, Lord, Bunker's Hill, 159, 270, 307, 315, 324, 352, 356, 374; success at Hobkirk's Hill, 379; relieves Ninety-Six, 383, 404, 527

Rayacotta, 577
Recruits, difficulty of obtaining, 40, 516; recruiting in America, 1771, 43; George III. and recruiting, 170; enforcement of Vagabond Act, 173; Washington's source of, 401; Recruiting Act, 1778, 499; in Ireland, 518
Regency Bill, 527
Regiments :—

   Cavalry—
First Life Guards, 539
Second Life Guards, 539
Fourth Dragoon Guards, 525
Fifth Dragoon Guards, 525
Sixth Dragoon Guards (Carabineers), 525
Seventh Dragoon Guards, 525
Sixteenth Light Dragoons (now Lancers), 173, 182, 192, 213, 253
Seventeenth Light Dragoons (now Lancers), 154, 177, 182, 236, 253, 310, 362
Eighteenth Light Dragoons (now Hussars), 10
Nineteenth Light Dragoons (now Hussars), 551, 565, 584, 585
Twentieth Light Dragoons (now Hussars), 541
Royal Artillery, in India, 105, 177, 213, 264, 418 (Gibraltar), 447, 486; reorganised, 539

   Foot Guards—193, 213, 359, 369, 387

   Infantry—
Third Foot (Buffs), 382
Fourth Foot, 159 (Bunker's Hill), 182 (Brooklyn), 192, 209, 213, 264
Fifth Foot, 156 (Bunker's Hill), 182 (Brooklyn), 213, 264
Sixth Foot, 42
Seventh Foot (Fusiliers), 153, 236, 307, 359
Ninth Foot, 173, 225, 232
Tenth Foot, 159 (Bunker's Hill), 182 (Brooklyn), 192, 213
Twelfth Foot, 418 (Gibraltar)
Fourteenth Foot, 33, 42, 519
Fifteenth Foot, 173, 180, 182 (Brooklyn), 192, 209, 213, 264
Sixteenth Foot, 301, 359
Seventeenth Foot, 173, 182 (Brooklyn), 201, 213, 311, 387
Eighteenth Foot (Royal Irish), 159 (Bunker's Hill)
Nineteenth Foot, 382, 519
Twentieth Foot, 173, 232
Twenty-First (Scots Fusiliers), 232

Regiments :—
   Infantry—
Twenty-Second Foot, 159 (Bunker's Hill), 182 (Brooklyn)
Twenty-Third (Royal Welsh Fusiliers), 159, 182 (Brooklyn), 192, 209, 213, 256, 307, 317, 359, 369, 387
Twenty-Fourth Foot, 173, 232
Twenty-Fifth Foot, 418 (Gibraltar)
Twenty-Sixth Foot (Cameronians), 153, 236
Twenty-Seventh Foot (Enniskillens), 173, 182 (Brooklyn), 192, 209, 213, 264
Twenty-Eighth Foot, 173, 180, 182 (Brooklyn), 192, 213, 264
Twenty-Ninth Foot, 33
Thirtieth Foot, 382
Thirty-First Foot, 42
Thirty-Second Foot, 42
Thirty-Third Foot, 213, 307, 317, 359, 369, 387, 519
Thirty-Fourth Foot, 173
Thirty-Fifth Foot, 159 (Bunker's Hill), 182 (Brooklyn), 264
Thirty-Sixth Foot, 159 (Bunker's Hill), 551, 567, 568, 569, 579, 584, 595
Thirty-Seventh Foot, 173, 180, 182 (Brooklyn), 213
Thirty-Eighth Foot, 156 (Bunker's Hill), 182 (Brooklyn), 192
Thirty-Ninth Foot, 418 (Gibraltar)
Fortieth Foot, 182 (Brooklyn), 201, 213, 264
Forty-Second Highlanders (Black Watch), 15, 21, 159, 192, 307, 499
Forty-Third Foot, 156 (Bunker's Hill), 182, 387
Forty-Fourth Foot, 182, 209, 213
Forty-Fifth Foot, 182, 291
Forty-Sixth Foot, 173, 180, 182, 213
Forty-Seventh Foot, 159
Forty-Eighth Foot, 263
Forty-Ninth Foot, 182, 213, 264
Fiftieth Foot, 42
Fifty-Second Foot, 156, 182, 192, 551, 569, 580, 584, 589, 591
Fifty-Third Foot, 173, 234
Fifty-Fourth Foot, 173, 180, 182
Fifty-Fifth Foot, 14, 182, 201, 213, 264
Fifty-Sixth Foot, 418 (Gibraltar)
Fifty-Seventh Foot, 180, 182
Fifty-Eighth Foot, 418 (Gibraltar)
Fifty-Ninth Foot, 159, 418
Sixtieth Foot, 13, 15, 21, 171, 267, 301, 338, 517
Sixty-Second Foot, 175, 232

INDEX 617

Regiments :—
  Infantry—
  Sixty-Third Foot, 159 (Bunker's Hill), 182, 236, 307, 356, 384
  Sixty-Fourth Foot, 35, 182, 209, 213, 307, 384, 500
  Sixty-Fifth Foot, 35, 159
  Sixty-Eighth Foot, 42
  Seventieth Foot, 10, 42
  Seventy-First Highlanders, 245, 418, 447, 475, 499, 551, 569, 579, 581, 585, 589
  Seventy-Second Highlanders, 245, 467, 486, 499, 551, 569, 581, 585
  Seventy-Third Highlanders, 467, 481, 571, 580, 585, 589
  Seventy-Fourth Highlanders, 517, 547, 551, 569, 585
  Seventy-Fifth Highlanders, 517, 547, 571, 585
  Seventy-Sixth Foot, 517, 547, 568, 569, 580, 584
  Seventy-Seventh Foot, 517, 571, 585
  Hundred and First Foot, 50, 73 (Gheria), 85, 93, 140 (Kutra), 447, 475
  Hundred and Second Foot, 113, 447, 475, 569, 579, 585
  Hundred and Third Foot, 89, 93, 571, 585

  Regiments since Disbanded—
  19th (Manners's Horse), 289
  20th (Philipson's Horse), 289
  21st (Douglas's Horse), 289
  22nd (Holroyd's Light Dragoons), 290
  71st (Fraser's Highlanders), 173, 182, 291, 317, 359, 369, 387
  72nd (Manchester Volunteers), 418
  74th (Campbell's), 246, 282
  75th (Picton's), 246
  76th (Macdonnell's), 246
  77th (Murray's Athol Highlanders), 246
  79th (Liverpool Regiment), 246, 338
  80th (Edinburgh Regiment), 246
  81st (William Gordon's), 246
  82nd (Francis Maclean), 246
  83rd (Glasgow Regiment), 246
  84th (Royal Highland Emigrants, Allan Maclean's), 163
  84th (Coote's, 1763), 68
  85th (Lord Harrington's Foot), 290, 341
  86th (Duke of Rutland's Foot), 290, 336, 349
  87th (Lord Winchilsea's Foot), 290, 336

Regiments :—
  Regiments since Disbanded—
  88th (Keating's Foot), 290
  89th (Munro's Foot, 1764), 92
  89th (Cary's Foot, 1779), 92, 290
  90th (Morgan's Foot, 1764), 92
  90th (Tottenham's, 1779), 336
  91st (Acland's Foot), 290, 336
  92nd (James Stewart's Foot), 290, 341
  93rd (M'Cormick's Foot), 290
  94th (Dundas's Foot), 290
  95th (Reid's Foot), 290
  96th (White's Foot), 290
  97th (Stanton's Foot), 290, 418
  98th (Fullarton's), 293, 498
  99th (Rainsforth's Foot), 293
  100th (Humberstone's), 293
  100th (Bruce's), 498
  101st (Sandford's Foot), 486, 498
  102nd (Rowley's), 344, 486, 498
  104th (Douglas's), 344

  Regiments not numbered but known by Colonels' Names—
  Cunnyngham's (Foot), 344
  Dalrymple's (Foot), 338
  Egerton's (Fencibles), 290
  Fauconberg's (Fencibles), 290
  Gorham's Rangers, 14
  Lister's (Dragoons), 290
  Maunsell's (Foot), 344
  Montgomery's (Highlanders), 15
  North's (Fencibles), 290
  Ross's (Foot), 344

Royal Engineers, 539

Royal Marines, 93, 159 (Bunker's Hill)
Reichenbach, Convention of, 506
Reinhard. *See* Sumroo
Reynolds, Sir Joshua, portrait of Heathfield, 420
Rhode Island. *See* American Colonies
Richmond, Duke of, 244; unpatriotic conduct of, 291, 297, 298, 508, 540
Richmond (Virginia), 388
Riedesel, General, 225, 231
Rigby, Mr., 511
Roanoke River, 387
Robertson, Captain, 380
Robertson, William (historian), 148
Rochford, Lord, 298
Rockingham, Marquis of, administration of, 28; fall of, 29; comes into office again, 406; 1782 administration, 493, 495
Rodney, George, Admiral (Lord Rodney), 269; defeats Spanish at Gibraltar,

299, 304, 329, 336, 337; captures St. Eustatius, 347; recalled, 406; action of the Saints, 409, 495
Rogers, Major, famous ranger, 11
Rohillas, the, 97, 104; enmity of Mahrattas to, 137; British campaign against, 138, 421
Ross, Captain, 358
Ross, Charles, *Cornwallis Correspondence*, 601
Ross, Lord, 245
Russell, Colonel, 384
Russell, Governor, 261
Russia, 343; England's policy towards, 504
Rutledge, Mr., 277
Ryswick, Peace of, 9

Said Sahib, 553; routed by Floyd, 353
Saint Augustine, 250
Saint Clair, General, 224
St. George's Key, 302
St. John, siege of, 162-277
St. Leger, Colonel, 205, 224; captures Fort Stanwix, 229; obliged to retreat, 230
St. Lubin, Chevalier, appointed military adviser to Smith, 124, 423
St. Lucia. *See* West Indies
St. Nicholas, 262
St. Vincent. *See* West Indies
Salabat Jung (Viceroy of Deccan, 1763); deposed, 109
Salisbury, 316
Salsette, Island of, 141
Saluda River, 313
Sandusky, 14
Sandwich, Lord, 148, 170, 287
Sandy Hook, 181
Santee River, 310
Sault St. Mary, evacuated by British, 14
Savannah River, 312
Schloesser, letter to Bouquet quoted, 13
Schuyler, General, 226
Schuylkill River, Washington's passage of, 217
Scott, Major, 543; defends Hastings, 545
Senecas. *See* Indians
Sepoys, mutiny of, in 1764, 87, 93; at Buxar, 98; repulse Hyder's troops at Caveripatam, 115, 144. *See also* India
Serah, 111
Seven Years' War, pride of colonists in British arms in, 4
Seringapatam, 440, 489, 556, 562; Cornwallis marches on, 572; first attack on, fails, 575; second advance on, 585; strategic position of, 586

Seringham, 560
Seronje, 444
Shah Alum, claim to Bengal, 49; success at Patna, 51; defeated at Suan, 62, 85; rejoins British after Buxar, 102; joins Mahrattas, 138
Sheikh Zadas, the, 97
Shelburne, Lord, 293, 406, 493; becomes Prime Minister, 495; resignation of, 498
Sheridan, Richard, 509; speech on Warren Hastings, 544
Shitab Roy, 56; gallantry at Beerpore, 60
Sholingur, 458
Shujah Dowlah (Nabob of Oude), protects Meer Cossim, 84; bold attack on British, 89; defeated at Patna, 90; retreats to Buxar, 92; defeated there, 95-102; anxiety for peace, 103; surrenders, 104; designs on Rohilcund, 138; treachery at Kutra, 139
Sibbald, Captain, killed at Seringapatam, 596
Simcoe, Major, 257, 307, 404
Singarapettah Pass, 115; convoy action at, 120
Sindiah, 138, 143, 425, 444, 465
Skelly, Major, 551
Skinner, Mr., 204
Smith, Colonel Joseph, Commander-in-Chief in Madras, 113; hampered by Council, 114, 119; success at Trinomalee, 117, 119; operations of 1768, 120-128; recalled to Madras, 129; resumes command, 131; estimate of his ability, 132; takes Tanjore, 137
Smith, Colonel, 150
Sooty, Meer Cossim at, 72
Sorel, 179
Spain, Spanish colonists, 3; decay of naval power, 7; attack on Falkland Islands, 41; helps American colonies, 197; war with England, 289; blockade of Gibraltar, 299; fighting in America, 301-304; takes Minorca, 411; fresh efforts against Gibraltar, 412-420; peace with England, 496; attack on Nootka Sound, 605
Speedy, Sergeant, 80, *note*
Stamp Act. *See* American Colonies
Stanhope, Lord, 524
Staten Island, Howe concentrates at, 181
Steuben, Baron, 358
Stevens, General, 370
Stibbert, Major, 95
Stillwater, 226

INDEX 619

Stirling, Colonel, 192
Stirling, Earl of (American general), 183
Stirling, Major, 525
Stony Point, 282
Stewart, Brigadier-General James, 383, 452; succeeds to Coote's command, 472; action at Cuddalore, 475; dismissed, 477
Stewart, Colonel, 476, 551; takes Palghautcherry, 557, 560; besieges Savandroog, 581, and Ootradroog, 582; commands right in advance on Seringapatam, 584, 591 *et seq.*
Suffren, Admiral, 466, 470, 476
Sugar Hill, 224
Sullivan, General, 183, 213, 255
Sullivan's Island, 308
Sultanpettah, 572
Sultan's Redoubt, the (Seringapatam), 592
Sumroo (Reinhard), forms Meer Cossim's army, 64; commands at Gheria, 72, 90; bought by Shuja Dowlah, 94; commands at Buxar, 97-102; deserts Shuja Dowlah, 104
Sumter, Colonel Thomas, 315; escapes from Tarleton, 320, 356, 381
Surat, 141
Sweden and Armed Neutrality, 343; and Triple Alliance, 505

Tanjore, operations of 1783 in, 485; Rajah of, 136, 422, 462
Tannah, taken by British, 1774, 143
Tapoor, Pass of, 559
Tarleton, Major Banastre, 257, 307; success at Biggin's Bridge, 309; at Camden, 318; surprises Sumter, 320, 356; action at Blackstocks, 357; defeated at Cowpens, 360, 404, 530
Taws, Captain, 279
Tellicherry, Abercromby's base in 1791, 563
Temple, Lord, 502
Territorial System, beginning of, 291
Thiagar, 560
Throg's Neck, 188
Ticonderoga, 153, 161, 180, 206, 243
Tiger River, 356
Tingricottah, besieged by Wood, 122
Tippoo Sahib, 119, 433; repulsed by Baillie, 435, 455, 466, 469, 471; proclaimed Hyder's successor, 473, 482; retakes Bednore, 483; makes peace 1784, 489, 508, 546; recommences hostilities, 547; defeated at Travancore, 550; descends the Gujelhutty Pass, 554; pursues British under Floyd, 555; clever manœuvres, 557; escapes from Medows, 560; proposal to Louis XVI., 561; leaves Pondicherry, 564; fails to raise siege of Bangalore, 568; foils Cornwallis's attack near Seringapatam, 573; retakes Coimbatore, 578; awaits Cornwallis's second advance, 586; defence of city, 589; failure of attack on Sultan's redoubt, 596; sues for peace, 597
Tobago. *See* West Indies
Tomson, General, 179
Tookagee Holkar, 426
Townshend, Charles, fatal result of American policy, 33
Trade and Navigation Acts, nature of, 7. *See also* American Colonies
Travancore, Rajah of, 550
Trenton, 194
Trevelyan, Sir G. O., *American Revolution* quoted, 497
Trichinopoly, 119, 433, 485, 551, 560
Trincomalee, 464, 467
Trinomalee, 115; sacked by Tippoo, 560
Tripassore, taken by Coote, 456, 473
Tripatore, taken by British in 1767, 114; useless as military station, 119
Triple Alliance, 504
Turkey, Russian aggression in, 507
Turtle Bay, 187
Tybee, 308

Valley Forge, 251
Vaniambaddy, taken by British, 114; defects as military station, 119
Vansittart, succeeds Clive in Bengal, 50, 61
Vaughan, General, 213, 334, 346, 404
Velladi, Floyd's junction with Medows at, 557
Vellore, 116, 119, 447, 465, 562
Vellout, 563
Vencatigerry, Pass of, captured by English, 524; brave defence of, against Hyder Ali, 130, 570
Vipeen, island of, 549
Virginia. *See* American Colonies
Volunteers, Middlesex, 1779, 290; Tower Hamlets, 290; Board of Works, 290
Von Donop, Count, 199, 221
Von Heister, General, 184
Von Kalb, Baron, 319
Von Steuben, Baron, 252

Waldecker, in British army, 301
Wandewash, English military station at, 119, 433, 447, 455, 473

Wayne, General, defeated by Grey, 217
War Office, officers punished for political indiscipline, 40; disbands regiments, 499; no commander-in-chief appointed after 1784, 524
Warela, Peace of, 506
Warwick, patriotic action of, after Saratoga, 245
Washington, George, chosen commander of rebel army, 161; difficulties of, 175; defeated at Brooklyn, 182-185; clever retreat to New York, 186; driven behind the Crotton, 188-190; defeated at Fort Washington, 191-193; retreats to Pennsylvania, 194; induces Congress to establish army, 197; crosses the Delaware, 199; takes Trenton, 200; brilliant movements of, 202; state of his army in 1777, 209, 251; refuses battle at Quibbletown, 210; puzzled by Howe's movements, 211; defeated at Brandywine, 213-216; attacks British camp at Germantown, 217-221; action at Freehold, 254; embarrassed by French officers, 257; policy of raids, 282; hindered by Congress, 285; his depression in 1780, 325-327; action in André's case discussed, 330, 353; letter from, intercepted by Clinton, 388; takes post at White Plains, 391; marches on Virginia, 393, 398; estimate of his ability, 402; compared with Cromwell, 403, 495
Washington, William, 357, 371, 384, 530
Wateree River, 313
Watson, Commodore, 142
Webster, Colonel, 318, 365, 374, 404
Wedderburn, General David, 141
Wemyss, Colonel, 288
Wemyss, Major, 256
West Indies, French and Spanish colonists in, 3; not able to undertake own defence, 6; strength of tie to Mother Country, 7; smuggling in, 8; danger of negro insurrection, 11; rebellion of Caribs, 42; effect of American War on, 259
Windward Group—
 Antigua, 262, 333, 407
 Barbados, 4, 8, 259, 262, 335, 347, 407
 Dominica, 11, 262, 300
 Grenada, 11, 262, 300
 Guadeloupe, 262
 Martinique, 262, 300, 336, 349, 407
 St. Cruz, 260

West Indies :—
Windward Group—
 St. Eustatius, 260, 343, 347, 407
 St. Kitts, 260, 300, 333, 407
 St. Lucia, 250, 262; captured by English, 265, 333, 337, 349
 St. Vincent, 11, 41; surrenders to French, 267, 300, 346
 Tobago, 11, 261, 300, 349, 497
Leeward Group—
 Cuba, 262
 Haiti, *also called* St. Domingo *and* Hispaniola, 262
 Jamaica, 11; disloyalty in, 259, 297, 335, 341, 350, 541
 Porto Rico, 335
Strategic consideration of, 261, 300, 334
Operations of 1778—(Windward Sphere) French capture Dominica, 263; Grant and Barrington seize St. Lucia, 263; Admiral Hotham arrives at Barbados, 264; d'Estaing arrives at Martinique, 264
Operations of 1779—(Windward Sphere) repulse of the French from St. Lucia, 264, 266; Byron's fleet arrives at St. Lucia, 266; St. Vincent surrenders to French, 267; French take Grenada, 268; Grant sails for England, 269; Vaughan appointed Commander-in-Chief, 334
Operations of 1780—(Windward Sphere) Rodney engages de Guichen, 336; hurricane, 338; *(Leeward Sphere)* siege of St. Juan, 339; Spanish take Mobile, 341
Operations of 1781—(Windward Sphere) capture of St. Eustatius, 347; de Grasse attacks Tobago, 349; Rodney returns to England, 350; French take St. Eustatius, 407; *(Leeward Sphere)* Spanish attack Pensacola, 351
Operations of 1782—(Windward Sphere) fall of St. Kitts, 408; Rodney's action at the Saints, 409; *(Leeward Sphere)* Spanish take Bahamas, 409
White Plains, 391
Whitehill, Mr. (Governor of Madras), 446
Wilkes, John, 40, 248, 296
Wilks, Colonel Mark (historian of Mysore), quoted, 132, 135, 492, 568, 601
William III. and colonial troops, 31
Williamsbury, 388
Wilmington, 212, 359, 387
Wilson, *History of Madras Army*, 133, 492, 601

INDEX

Windham, William, 509
Winnsborough, 324
Wolfe, James, 493
Wood, Colonel, 115; his operations in Baramahal, 122; responsible for Smith's failure at Boodicota, 125; resigns command, 126; reinstated, 127; narrow escape at Mulwagal, 128; defeated at Arlier, 129; recalled under arrest, 130
Wood Creek, 226

Yadkin River, 365
York, Frederick Duke of, 527, 532, 559
Yorktown, 388, 391; surrender of, 394

END OF VOL. III

Lightning Source UK Ltd.
Milton Keynes UK
UKHW022151090223
416748UK00012B/110